WHAT THE BIBLE IS ALL ABOUT®

HENRIETTA MEARS

Picture acknowledgments

Photographs
All photographs by Tim Dowley and
Peter Wyart, trading as Three's
Company, except as listed below:
Bible Scene Tours: p. 331
Billy Graham Evangelistic
Organisation: p. 9
Church's Ministry to the Jews: p. 373
Greek Tourist Board: p. 298
Jordanair: p. 151
Clifford Shirley: p. 165
Jamie Simson: pp. 25, 30, 83, 153, 175,
281, 323, 339, 341, 361

Illustrations
Alan Parry: pp. 5, 41
Richard Scott: pp. 43, 147

WHAT THE
BIBLE
IS ALL ABOUT®

Henrietta Mears

Regal
FROM GOSPEL LIGHT

Published by Regal Books
A Division of Gospel Light
Ventura, California, U.S.A.

This edition © 1999 Angus Hudson Ltd/
Tim Dowley & Peter Wyart
trading as Three's Company

Cover Design by Kevin Keller
Book Design by Peter Wyart, Three's Company
Edited by Bayard Taylor and Virginia Woodard
Abridged by Robert Backhouse

What the Bible Is All About® is a registered trademark of Gospel Light. Any use of this name is prohibited without the express written consent of Gospel Light.

Library of Congress Cataloging-in-Publication Data
Mears, Henrietta C. (Henrietta Cornelia), 1890-
   What the Bible is all about/ Henrietta Mears.
         p. cm.
   ISBN 0-8307-2431-1
   1. Bible—Criticism, interpretation, etc. I. Title.
BS511.2.M42 1999
220.6'1—dc21
                                        99-14830
                                            CIP

Rights for publishing this book in other languages are contracted by Gospel Literature International (GLINT). GLINT also provides technical help for the adaptation, translation and publishing of Bible study resources and books in scores of languages worldwide. For further information, contact GLINT, P.O. Box 4060, Ontario, CA 91761-1003, U.S.A. You may also send e-mail to Glintint@aol.com, or visit their web site at www.glint.org.

Worldwide coedition organized and produced by
Angus Hudson Ltd,
Concorde House, Grenville Place,
Mill Hill, London NW7 3SA, England
Tel: +44 181 959 3668
Fax +44 181 959 3678

Printed in Singapore

Contents

Books of the Major Prophets

Books of the Minor Prophets

Part Two: The New Testament

The Gospels

History

Letters of Paul

Foreword

Dr. Billy Graham

Millions of people today are searching for a reliable voice of authority. The Word of God is the only real authority we have. His Word sheds light on human nature, world problems and human suffering. But beyond that, it clearly reveals the way to God.

The message of the Bible is the message of Jesus Christ who said, "I am the way, the truth, and the life" (*John 14:6, KJV*). It is the story of salvation; the story of your redemption and mine through Christ; the story of life, of peace, of eternity.

Our faith is not dependent upon human knowledge and scientific advance, but upon the unmistakable message of the Word of God.

The Bible has a great tradition and a magnificent heritage. It contains 66 books written over a period of several hundred years by many different men. Yet the message, divinely inspired by the Holy Spirit, is clear throughout. The 66 books become one.

The Bible is old; yet it is ever new. It is the most modern book in the world today. There is a false notion that a book as ancient as the Bible cannot speak to modern needs. People some-

Dr. Billy Graham

how think that in an age of scientific achievement, when knowledge has increased more in the past 25 years than in all preceding centuries put together, this ancient Book is out-of-date. But to all who read and love the Bible, it is relevant for our generation.

It is in the Holy Scriptures that we find the answers to life's ultimate questions: Where did I come from? Why am I here? Where am I going? What is the purpose of my existence?

One of the greatest needs in the Church today is to come back to the Scriptures as the basis of authority, and to study them prayerfully in dependence on the Holy Spirit. When we read God's Word, we fill our hearts with His words, and God is speaking to us.

William Lyon Phelps, called the most beloved professor in America, and one-time president of Yale University, made the oft-quoted statement, "I thoroughly believe in a university education for both men and women; but I believe a knowledge of the Bible without a college course is more valuable than a college course without the Bible."

One of the greatest tragedies today is that, although the Bible is an available, open book, it is a closed book to millions—either because they leave it unread or because they read it without applying its teachings to themselves. No greater tragedy can befall a person or a nation than that of paying lip service to a Bible left unread or to a way of life not followed.

The Bible, the greatest document available for the human race, needs to be opened, read and believed. One survey indicated that only 12 percent of the people who said they believe the Bible actually read it every day; 34 percent read it only once a week, and 42 percent read it only once in a great while.

This book, *What the Bible Is All About*, will help make the reading and study of God's Word interesting, challenging and useful. We commend it to you.

Preface

William T. Greig Jr. *Chairman, Gospel Light*

In the early 1950s my wife, Doris, and I were invited to teach the high school class in a small Baptist church in a suburb of Minneapolis, Minnesota. We were newly married and accepted the challenge with some trepidation. We agreed we would do better if we divided the group. I would teach the boys and Doris would teach the girls.

Doris and I both wanted to understand the Bible better. Doris had become a believer in a Billy Graham meeting at a Youth for Christ conference about two years earlier. I was fortunate to have been brought up in a Christian home and had been taught the Word by my parents since childhood. Yet we each hungered to know more of the Word. We also were aware that the kids in Sunday School knew precious little of Bible truth. So we decided to tackle the daunting task of teaching each of our classes through the entire Bible—all sixty-six books—in one year, fifty-two weeks. We secured a high school course then published by Gospel Light called the *Scripture Panorama Series.*

This classic course was authored by Dr. Henrietta C. Mears, founder of Gospel Light. She believed firmly that no young person in her Sunday School should be able to say what a young college man had told her many years before: "If I had to pass a test in the Bible, I would absolutely flunk!" So she wrote this "crash" course for people who knew little if anything about the Bible, but who wanted to know

enough to understand the essential message of each of the books as they studied or read devotionally. The central theme of the entire Word of God is His dealings with His people and His provision of salvation through faith in Jesus Christ the Messiah—promised throughout the Old Testament and revealed fully in the New Testament.

Doris and I learned much that year, and so did our classes. It was intense, but rewarding. Nothing of great value is ever accomplished without consistent effort invested on our part. You only get out what you put in. So it was with this course. It was a spiritual growing experience for all, and it helped us both to grow in grace and in our relationship to Jesus Christ and to each other, not to mention our class members.

In the mid-1950s I was challenged by Richard Woike, president of the Christian Business Men's Committee, to read through the Bible every year. He would buy a new Bible each year on his birthday and read through it from Genesis through Revelation in one year. I liked the idea, but got bogged down in Leviticus and Numbers, as many do. So I developed my own plan, which I found particularly rewarding. I began in Genesis, Job and Matthew and read a page or two of each section every day. This took me through the entire Bible in one year. It was rewarding, particularly having this book *What the Bible Is All About* at my side, to answer hard questions and give me perspective about each book.

I decided I wanted more time each day for personal reflection and cross-referencing, so I developed a two-year plan, which also allowed me time to adopt Richard Woike's other discipline: He wrote in the head margin of every page the key message he learned from that page. This Bible reading plan is adapted in the form of bookmarks, included with this volume. You will find them at the back of the book. Keeping a copy of *What the Bible Is All About* on hand as you read through the Bible will give you an unforgettable experience. You will grow both in your knowledge of the Word of God and also in your relationship to the Living Word, the Lord Jesus Christ.

In the early 1960s, a friend in the Billy Graham Association (BGA) headquarters in Minneapolis inquired about creating a book out of the *Scripture Panorama Series* teacher's books. Working together we jointly published *What the Bible Is All About*. Dr. Graham, who had a close relationship with Henrietta Mears going back to the late 1940s, wrote the foreword. A copy was given by the BGA to each person who responded to Dr. Graham's invitations in crusades, on TV or on radio. Millions of copies were given away through the years.

Dr. Mears believed firmly that the Bible is the authority of the teacher so the teacher should teach directly from an open Bible, though some of us need outlines and personal notes to be more effective. Teachers and class members alike will grow deeper in their knowledge of the truth and their personal relationship to Jesus Christ, the Living Word, as they are taught spiritual truth directly from the Bible by the Holy Spirit. Jesus promised that His Holy Spirit would lead us into all truth (*John 17:1*).

George Barna tells us that at the close of the twentieth century the vast majority of people, including many Christians, do not believe in absolute truth. According to Barna, 71 percent of all adults say there is no such thing as absolute truth. This is divided into groups: 78 percent among baby busters; 68 percent among born-again Christians; 71 percent among those who attend a mainline Protestant church; 75 percent among those who attend a Catholic church. This book can be used by the Holy Spirit to open His Word to us and teach us God's absolute truth, Jesus Christ.

How to Use This Book

The purpose of this book is to familiarize the reader with the Bible through a general overview. This book contains 48 chapters, spanning from Genesis to Revelation. These chapters can be studied one chapter a week for the year. At the beginning of each chapter is listed a Selected Bible Reading section, suggesting a Scripture reading for each day of the week related to the chapter.

"A Glossary of Bible Words" in the appendix explains unfamiliar words that may be new to the reader, including a pronunciation guide for many of the words.

1. UNDERSTANDING

the Bible

The Bible portrays Jesus Christ, the Savior of the World

"Behind and beneath the Bible, above and beyond the Bible, is the God of the Bible."

The Bible is God's written revelation of His will to humanity.

Its central theme is salvation through Jesus Christ.

The Bible contains 66 books, written by 40 authors, covering a period of approximately 1,600 years.

The Old Testament was written mostly in Hebrew (a few short passages in Aramaic). About 100 years (or more) before the Christian Era the entire Old Testament was translated into the Greek language. Remember, our English Bible is a translation from these original languages.

The word "Bible" comes from the Greek word *biblos*, meaning "book."

The word "testament" means "covenant," or agreement. The Old Testament is the covenant God made with people about their salvation before Christ came. The New Testament is the agreement God made with people about their salvation after Christ came.

In the Old Testament we find the covenant of law. In the New Testament we find the covenant of grace that came through Jesus Christ. One led into the other (*Galatians 3:17-25*).

The Old commences what the New completes.

The Old gathers around Mount Sinai—

The New around Mount Calvary.

The Old is associated with Moses— The New with Christ (*John 1:17*).

The authors were kings and princes, poets and philosophers, prophets and statesmen. Some were learned in all the arts of the times and others were unschooled fishermen. Other books soon are out-of-date, but this Book spans the centuries.

Most books must be adapted to age, but old and young alike love this Book.

Most books are provincial and only interest the people in whose language it was written, but not this Book. No

Selected Bible Readings

Sunday:	God-Given *(2 Timothy 3:10-17)*
Monday:	Should Be Treasured *(Deuteronomy 11:1-9; Joshua 1:8,9)*
Tuesday:	Should Be Kept *(Psalm 119:9-18)*
Wednesday:	A Lamp *(Psalm 119:105-117)*
Thursday:	Food *(Isaiah 55:1-11; Matthew 4:4)*
Friday:	Fulfilled *(Luke 24:36-45)*
Saturday:	Complete *(Revelation 22:8-21)*

one ever stops to think it was written in what are now dead languages.

The Old Testament begins with God (*Genesis 1:1*).

The New Testament begins with Christ (*Matthew 1:1*).

From Adam to Abraham we have the history of the human race.

From Abraham to Christ we have the history of the chosen race.

From Christ on we have the history of the Church.

"Most people's knowledge of history is like a string of graduated pearls without the string," said a historian. This statement seems to be especially true of Bible history. Many people know the Bible characters and the principal events, but they are hopelessly lost when they are called upon to connect the stories in order. Anyone who has experienced the thrill of learning to place the individual characters in their right setting as to place and time can realize the difference it makes in the enjoyment of God's Word.

Pick up the "pearls" in the Scriptures and string them into order from Genesis to Revelation so that you can "think through" the Bible story.

Interesting Facts

Old Testament Books
Law—five
Historical—twelve
Poetical—five
Prophetical—seventeen
(Major, five; Minor, twelve)

New Testament Books
The New Testament was written to reveal to us the character and teaching of Jesus Christ, the mediator of the New Covenant, by at least eight men, four of whom—Matthew, John, Peter

and Paul—were apostles; two—Mark and Luke—were companions of the apostles; and two—James and Jude—were brothers of Jesus. The books were written at various times during the second half of the first century.

The books in the New Testament may be grouped thus:
Gospels—four
History—one
Prophecy—one
Epistles—twenty-one
(Pauline, thirteen; General, eight)
God, humanity, sin, redemption, justification, sanctification, glorification: In two words—grace, glory. In one word—Jesus.

Christ quotes from twenty-two Old Testament books: in Matthew, nineteen times; in Mark, fifteen times; in Luke, twenty-five; in John, eleven.

The book of Hebrews quotes the Old Testament (quotations or allusions) eighty-five times.

Revelation quotes the Old Testament 245 times.

How to Study the Bible

Remember that in God's Word the foundation of Christianity is laid in the revelation of the one and only true God. God chose a people (the children of Israel) to show forth this truth and to preserve a record of Himself.

1. Look for purpose—God's plan for salvation.

The Bible tells us of the origin of sin and how this curse separated us all from God. We discover how utterly impossible it was for the law to bring to us the salvation we need, for by the deeds of the law could no flesh be justified, for "all have sinned" (*Romans 3:20-23*). Then we find the promise of a Savior, One who was to come "to seek and to save what was lost" and "give his life as a ransom for many"

Old Testament—*Principal Places*

The twelve principal places around which the history of the Old Testament is written are:

1. Eden (Genesis 1—3)

2. Ararat (Genesis 8:4)

3. Babel (Genesis 11:1-11)

4. Ur of the Chaldees (Genesis 11:28—12:3)

5. Canaan (with Abraham) (Genesis 12:4-7)

6. Egypt (with Joseph) (Genesis 37—45, esp. 41:41)

7. Sinai (Exodus 19:16—20:21)

8. Wilderness (Numbers 14:26-35)

9. Canaan (with Joshua) (Joshua 1:1-9)

10. Assyria (captivity of Israel) (2 Kings 18:9-12)

11. Babylon (captivity of Judah) (2 Kings 24:11-16)

12. Canaan (Palestine—return of the exiles) (Ezra 1:1—2:70).

As you build the story of the Bible around these places you see the whole history in chronological order.

Still another way to think through the Bible is by following the great facts in order.

Old Testament—*Principal Facts*

1. Creation (Genesis 1:1—2:3)

2. Fall of man (Genesis 3)

3. Flood (Genesis 6—9)

4. Babel (Genesis 11:1-9)

5. Call of Abraham (Genesis 11:10—12:3)

6. Descent into Egypt (Genesis 46—47)

7. Exodus (Exodus 7—12)

8. Passover (Exodus 12)

9. Giving of the Law (Exodus 19—24)

10. Wilderness wanderings (Numbers 13—14)

11. Conquest of the Promised Land (Joshua 11)

12. Dark ages of the chosen people (Judges)

13. Anointing of Saul as king (1 Samuel 9:27—10:1)

14. Golden age of Israelites under David and Solomon—united kingdom (2 Samuel 5:4-5; 1 Kings 10:6-8)

15. The divided kingdom—Israel and Judah (1 Kings 12:26-33)

16. The Captivity (2 Kings 17; 25)

17. The Return (Ezra).

(*Luke 19:10; Matthew 20:28*). We see all through the ages one purpose is evident, that of preparing a way for the coming of the Redeemer of the world.

2. Ask the Holy Spirit to guide you.

There is no royal road to learning and certainly there is no royal road to knowledge of the Bible. The Spirit of God will lead us into all truth, to be sure, but God's command is that we do our best to be approved, workmen unashamed (*2 Timothy 2:15*).

3. Read attentively.

Give to the Bible attention with intention, and intention will necessitate attention. We must come to it with a

New Testament—*Principal Facts*

1. Early life of Christ (Matthew 1:18—2:23; Luke 1—2)

2. Ministry of Christ (Gospels of Matthew, Mark, Luke and John)

3. Church in Jerusalem (Acts 1—2)

4. Church extending to the Gentiles (Acts 10—11, 13—20)

5. Church in all the world (Romans 10—11,15; Ephesians 2:22-23).

Principal Periods

I. Period of the patriarchs to Moses—Genesis

    A. The godly line—leading events

        1. Creation

        2. Fall

        3. Flood

        4. Dispersion

    B. The chosen family—leading events

        1. Call of Abraham

        2. The descent into Egypt—bondage

II. Period of great leaders: Moses to Saul—Exodus to Samuel

    A. Exodus from Egypt

    B. Wandering in wilderness

    C. Conquest of Canaan

    D. Rule of the Judges

III. Period of the kings: Saul to the captivities—Samuel, Kings, Chronicles, the prophetical books

    A. The united kingdom

        1. Saul

        2. David

        3. Solomon

    B. The divided kingdom

        1. Judah

        2. Israel

IV. Period of foreign rulers: Captivities to Christ—Ezra, Nehemiah, Esther, Prophecies of Daniel and Ezekiel

    A. Captivity of Israel

    B. Captivity of Judah

V. Christ—the Gospels

VI. The Church—Acts and the Epistles

    A. In Jerusalem

    B. Extending to the Gentiles

    C. In all the world

purpose and have a clearly defined object.

Many say, "The Bible is so great. I don't know where to begin and don't know how to go on." This is often said quite earnestly and sincerely. It is true that unless we have some method, we shall assuredly lose the very best results, even though we may spend much time with the Book.

4. Make a reading plan (or use one of the reading plans provided at the back of this book).

Do you want to read through the Bible? Leave 80 hours for it. Schedule that time. How much time can you give each day? How many days a week? This is a highly practical proposition and should be seized by the very busiest. The Bible reveals the will of God so as to lead us into it. Each book has a direct teaching. Find out what it is and conform to it. This is our purpose. We are going to consider a book of the Bible in each chapter of this book.

Now the Bible, although it is a library of books, is also "the Book." It is a story, a grand story that moves on from commencement to finish. Here surely is something that is phenomenal in literature.

Remember, the books of the Bible were given to us by 40 different authors over a period of about 1,600 years. All these are brought together and bound and are called "the Book." We can begin at Genesis and read on through to the end. It is not jarring. We can pass from one style of literature to another as easily as though we were reading a story written by one hand and produced by one life, and in-deed we have here a story produced by one Mind (*2 Peter 1:21*) though not written by one hand.

5. Appreciate the Bible's uniqueness.

Although divine, it is human. The thought is divine, the revelation is divine, the expression of the communication is human. "But men [human element] spoke from God as they were carried along by the Holy Spirit [divine element]" (*2 Peter 1:21*).

So we have here a book unlike all others. The Book, a divine revelation, a progressive revelation, a revelation of God to humanity communicated through men, moves on smoothly from its beginnings to its great end. Way back in Genesis, we have the beginnings; in Revelation we have endings; and from Exodus to Jude we see how God carried out His purpose. We can't dispense with any part of it.

Bible history takes us back into the unknown past of eternity and its prophecies take us into the otherwise unknown future.

The Old Testament is the foundation; the New Testament is the superstructure. As Augustine said:

The New is in the Old contained,
The Old is in the New explained.
The New is in the Old latent,
The Old is in the New patent.
The Old Testament and New Testament constitute a divine library, one sublime unity, origins in past to issues in future, processes between, connecting two eternities.

One Book, One History, One Story
The Bible is one book, one history, one story, His story. Behind 10,000 events stands God, the builder of history, the maker of the ages. Eternity bounds the one side, eternity bounds the other side, and time is in between: Genesis—origins, Revelation—endings, and all the way between, God is working things out. You can go down into the minutest detail everywhere and see that there is one great purpose moving through the ages: the eternal design of the almighty God to redeem a wrecked and ruined world.

The Bible is one book, and you cannot take it in texts and expect to comprehend the magnificence of divine revelation. You must see it in its completeness. God has taken pains to give a progressive revelation and we should take pains to read it from beginning to end.

Another way we can study the Bible is by groups—law, history, poetry, major and minor prophets, Gospels, Acts, Epistles and Revelation. Here again we find great unity for "'it is written about me in the scroll—I have come to do your will, O God,'" says Christ (*Hebrews 10:7*). Everything points to the King!

Each book has a message, and we should endeavor to discover what that message is. Read until you discover the message of the book. For instance, in

John it is easy to discover the purpose. It is stated in John 20:31. It is not always given clearly, but the truth may be found. Believe that every book is about something and read and reread until you find out what that something is.

First we read the Book, not read books about the Book, nor turn to the comments. They will come in good time, perhaps, but give the Book a chance to speak for itself and to make its own impression; to bear its own testimony. As Johnny Cash is credited with saying: "The Bible sure does throw a lot of light on the commentaries."

Let the Spirit of God Himself teach you. We all have a right to read it for ourselves. "No prophecy of Scripture came about by the prophet's own interpretation" (2 Peter 1:20). Read it seeking for illumination. It is a revelation and He will flash light upon the page as you come humbly.

The Bible is a whole and we can't tamper with it. For example, to add anything to the book of Revelation or to take anything from it would mar its absolute perfection (*Revelation 22:18-19*). The canon of Scripture is closed. Other works throw valuable light upon it, but this stands unique, alone, and complete, and these parts all partake of the perfection of the whole.

Read a Book a Week
So we come to these books as complete in themselves, yet bearing in mind their vital relation to what precedes and what succeeds. We should read them one at a time. Read a book in a week.

Don't give yourself time to lose the impression made by the first reading before you get to the second and don't suppose that you can grasp the content and intent of any book at a single reading.

The Garden Tomb, Jerusalem. Jesus rose from the dead. He is not merely a historical character, but a living Person.

Christ, the Living Word

The Old Testament is an account of a nation (the Jewish nation). The New Testament is an account of a Man (the Son of man). The nation was founded and nurtured of God in order to bring the Man into the world (*Genesis 12:1-3*).

God Himself became a man so that we might know what to think of when we think of God (*John 1:14; 14:9*). His appearance on the earth is the central event of all history. The Old Testament sets the stage for it. The New Testament describes it.

As a man Christ lived the most perfect life ever known. He was kind, tender, gentle, patient and sympathetic. He loved people. He worked marvelous miracles to feed the hungry. Multitudes—weary, pain ridden and heartsick—came to Him, and He gave them rest (*Matthew 11:28-30*). It is said that if all the deeds of kindness that He did were written, the world could not contain the books (*John 21:25*).

Then He died—to take away the sin of the world, and to become the Savior of men.

Then He rose from the dead. He is alive today. He is not merely a historical character, but a living Person—the most important fact of history and the most vital force in the world today. And He promises eternal life to all who come to Him.

The whole Bible is built around the story of Christ and His promise of life everlasting to all. It was written only that we might believe and understand, know and love, and follow HIM.

Assume that the Bible is just what it appears to be. Accept the books as we have them in our Bible as units; study them to know their contents. You will find a unity of thought indicates that one Mind inspired the writing of the whole series of books; that it bears on its face the stamp of its Author; that it is in every sense the WORD OF GOD.

Part One
The Old Testament

Books of Law
of the Old Testament

Genesis • Exodus • Leviticus Numbers • Deuteronomy

2. UNDERSTANDING

Genesis

Genesis Portrays Jesus Christ, Our Creator God

Genesis is the seed plot of the Word of God. The title Genesis, which is Greek, means "origin," and the first word in the Hebrew of Genesis is translated "in the beginning"—words that indicate both the scope and the limits of the book. It tells us the beginning of everything except God. Another thing to notice is that it tells only of beginnings. There is no finality here. Upon its truths all the future revelation of God to people is built up.

Satan appears to have special enmity for the book of Genesis. No wonder the adversary has bent his attacks upon it. It exposes him as the enemy of God and the deceiver of the human race; it foretells his destruction; it depicts his doom (*Genesis 3*).

Without Genesis our knowledge of a creating God would be pitifully limited; we would be woefully ignorant of the beginnings of our universe.

Genesis is the book of beginnings:

1. the beginning of the world (*1:1-25*)
2. the beginning of the human race (*1:26—2:25*)
3. the beginning of sin in the world (*3:1-7*)
4. the beginning of the promise of redemption (*3:8-24*)
5. the beginning of family life (*4:1-15*)
6. the beginning of civilization (*4:16—9:29*)
7. the beginning of the nations of the world (*10,11*)
8. the beginning of the Hebrew people (*12—50*).

Adam began with God and fell through disobedience (*3:1-24*).

Abel began with God by the blood of sacrifice (*4:4*).

Noah began with God by way of the ark (*6:8,14,22*).

Abraham began with God when he

Selected Bible Readings

Sunday: Creation
(*Genesis 1:1-5; 26-31; 2:7-22*)

Monday: The Fall
(*Genesis 3:1-24*)

Tuesday: The Flood
(*Genesis 6:1-7; 7:7-24; 8:6-11; 18-22; 9:1-16*)

Wednesday: Beginning of Languages
(*Genesis 11:1-9*)

Thursday: The Abrahamic Call and Covenant
(*Genesis 12:1-9; 13:14-18; 15:1-21; 17:4-8; 22:15-20; 26:1-5; 28:10-15*)

Friday: Story of Joseph
(*Genesis 37:1-36; 42*)

Saturday: Jacob's Final Blessing
(*Genesis 49*)

built altars (12:8).

These all made new beginnings for the race.

Genesis is the record of the beginnings of all these things. No wonder that when people, because of spiritual blindness (*Ephesians 4:18*), reject God's revelation in this peerless record of beginnings, they worship chance as the creator, beasts as their ancestors and fallen humanity as the flower of natural evolution!

Genesis begins with "God" but ends "in a coffin." This book is a history of human failure. But we find that God meets every failure. He is a glorious Savior. We find that "where sin increased, grace increased all the more" (*Romans 5:20*).

Genesis gives us at least 2,000 years of record. It is not entirely history; it is a spiritual interpretation of history. In two chapters God flashes on the wall an account of the creation of the world and of humanity. From there on we see the story of redemption. God is bringing lost people back to Himself.

Its authorship by Moses, its scientific accuracy and its literal testimony to human sin as deliberate disobedience to God have all been bitterly assailed. The Word of God, however, definitely declares Genesis to be one of the living oracles delivered to Moses. To its infallible truth and its testimony to the Messiah, our Lord Jesus set His seal (*John 5:46-47*).

Many origins are recorded in the first eleven chapters: natural universe, human life, sin, death, redemption, civilization, nations and languages.

The remainder of the book from Genesis 12 delves into the beginnings of the Hebrew people, first in its founding through Abraham, then in its subsequent development and history through the great figures of Isaac, Jacob and Joseph. This great Hebrew

Marshlands near the site of Ur, Mesopotamia, the city Abraham left to go to Haran.

nation was founded with a definite purpose that through it the whole world should be blessed.

God promised Abraham, a believer in Him, that his descendants:

1. Should inherit the land of Canaan (*Genesis 12:1-3*)
2. Should become a great nation
3. Through them all nations should be blessed.

God repeated these promises to Isaac and Jacob (*Genesis 26:1-5; 28:13-15*).

Seven great names and messages are:

1. Bow with Abel at the cross of the slain lamb.
2. Catch step with Enoch and walk with God.
3. Believe God and launch out with Noah on God's waters.
4. Go forth with Abraham in faith.
5. Dig wells with Isaac and get down to divine resources.
6. Climb ladders with Jacob and see God.
7. Be true like Joseph and live with God.

Genesis answers the great questions of the soul:

1. The eternity of God.
2. Where did we come from?
3. Whence came sin?
4. How can sinful people get back

to God (Abel's sacrifice)?

5. How can we please God (Abraham's faith)?

6. How can we have power with God and people (Jacob's surrender)?

Three words also might give us the outline of Genesis:

1. Generation—"In the beginning God" (1:1)
2. Degeneration—"Now the serpent" (3:1)
3. Regeneration—"Now the Lord" (12:1, *KJV*).

Genesis is the record of human failure, first in an ideal environment (Eden), then under the rule of conscience (from the Fall to the deluge) and finally under patriarchal rule (Noah to Joseph). In every case of human failure, however, God met human need with marvelous promises of sovereign grace. It is therefore fitting that the Bible's first book should show us the failure of humanity under every condition met by the salvation of God.

Hints of the Messiah:

Remember, Jesus Christ is the center of the Bible. He is somewhere on every page. In Genesis we see Him in type (the foreshadowing of Christian meanings in Old Testament people and events) and prophecy (supernatural knowledge given by God to holy people to reveal truth and to foretell events) in:

1. Seed of woman (*3:15*)
2. The entrance into the ark of safety (*7:1,7*)
3. The offering up of Isaac (*22:1-24*)
4. Jacob's ladder (*28:12*)
5. Judah's scepter (*49:10*)
6. Joseph lifted from pit to throne (*37:28; 41:41-44*).

The patriarchal period

The period of the patriarchs is the groundwork and basis of all history. It covers the time from Adam to Moses. In consequence of the failures on the part of people during this early period, God called out an individual. He put aside the nations and called a man, Abraham, who was to become the father of the Hebrew nation. We enter into this period in Genesis 12.

God called out Abraham and made a covenant with him, known as the Abrahamic Covenant. Be familiar with this covenant (*Genesis 12:1-3*). God repeated that covenant to Abraham's son, Isaac, and again to his grandson, Jacob (*Genesis 26:1-5; 28:13-15*). He repeated it to no one else.

These three, therefore, are the covenant fathers, and that is why you read in Scripture "I am the God of your fathers, the God of Abraham, Isaac and Jacob" (*Acts 7:32*). He never adds anyone else. God gave His covenant to these three and it is for them to communicate it to others. What is the covenant? Read Genesis 12:1-3; 26:1-5; 28:13-15.

From family to nation

A very large portion of the story of Genesis is devoted to Joseph (*Genesis 37—48*). Why? Because Joseph is the link between the family and the nation. Up till the time of Joseph it is a family, the family of Abraham, Isaac and Jacob. Some seventy souls are found at the end of the book of Genesis, constituting the family of Jacob. But still it is a family with which God is dealing. Read about this family and the blessings Jacob gave to each of his sons in Genesis 49.

The moment we turn over the page and step into Exodus it is a nation, not a family. During the long period from the end of Genesis to the opening of Exodus this nation has developed. Joseph is the link between the family and the nation.

Joseph is a character presented without fault—not that he had no faults, but his faults are not recorded. He was a man of flesh and blood like us. God honored him, for there are at least 130 parallels between the life of Joseph and the life of Jesus. He is therefore the messianic patriarch, the patriarch who reflected the Christ Himself.

The Author of Genesis

The age-long Hebrew and Christian position is that Moses, guided by the Spirit of God, wrote Genesis. The book closes approximately three hundred years before Moses was born. Moses could have received his information only by direct revelation from God or from historical records to which he had access that had been handed down from his forefathers. See what Jesus said about Moses (*Luke 24:27; John 7:19*).

Moses did make use of writing (*Exodus 34:27; Numbers 17:2; Deuteronomy 6:9; 24:1,3; Joshua 8:32*). No doubt the creation story was written long before, maybe by Abraham or Noah, or Enoch, the grandson of Adam (*Genesis 4:17*). Who knows? Abraham lived in a society of culture, books and libraries. He no doubt made careful and accurate copies of all that happened to him and of the promises God had made to him. He put it down on clay tablets in the cuneiform writing (the alphabet of the Babylonians) to be handed down in the annals of the nation he was founding.

Creation *Genesis 1—2*

As the book begins we see these words untarnished by the ages, "In the beginning God created the heavens and the earth." In these few simple words we have the Bible declaration of the origin of this material universe. God called all things into being by the word of His power. He spoke and worlds were framed (*Hebrews 11:3*). Interpretations

of the method of God may vary but the truth of the fact remains.

God's creative work was progressive:

1. The world of matter—1:3-19
2. The system of life—1:20-25
3. Humanity, the crown of Creation—1:26-27.

Who was the God mentioned so many times in the first thirty-one verses of Genesis? Read John 1:1 and Hebrews 1:1. Here we see that the One who redeemed us by His precious blood, our Savior, was the Creator of this universe. Someone has said that God the Father is the architect; God the Son, the builder and God the Holy Spirit, the beautifier of the universe. We find the Holy Spirit in Genesis 1:2.

In chapter 1 we have the account of Creation in outline, in chapter 2 part of the same in detail. The detail concerns the creation of humanity, for the Bible is the history of the redemption of humanity.

Know this, God created people in His own image to have fellowship with Himself. But we have cut ourselves off from God by sin. Only when sin is removed can we have fellowship again. This is why Jesus Christ came to this earth: that he might bear "our sins in his body on the tree" (*1 Peter 2:24*).

God called all things into being by the word of His power; He spoke and worlds were framed.

The Fall *Genesis 3—4*

Adam and Eve were created in a state of innocence but with the power of choice. They were tested under the most favorable circumstances. They were endowed with clear minds and pure hearts, with the ability to do right. God gave them His own presence and fellowship (*Genesis 3:8*).

Satan, the author of sin, acting through a serpent, tempted Adam and Eve to doubt God's Word. They yielded to the temptation and failed in the test. Here sin entered the world. Satan still influences people to disobey God. The results of Adam's and Eve's sin are enumerated in Genesis 3. They were separated from God, the ground was cursed and sorrow filled their hearts.

In mercy, God promised One who would redeem us from sin (*Genesis 3:15*). The offspring of the woman (the virgin-born Jesus) would come to destroy the works of the devil (*1 John 3:8*).

Immediately after the Fall, people began to offer sacrifices unto the Lord. No doubt these sacrifices were ordered of God. They were for the purpose of keeping before people the fact of their fall and of the coming sacrifice. It would be by the shedding of Jesus' blood that people were to be redeemed from sin and death (*Hebrews 9:22*).

Two of Adam's sons, Cain and Abel, brought their sacrifices unto the Lord. Read Genesis 4:3,4. Abel's offering was accepted while Cain's was rejected. From our knowledge of the Word, it is quite evident that it was not accepted because any sacrifice brought to the Lord must be brought with proper motivation and through faith and obedience. Cain became angry with his brother Abel and in his wrath killed him.

MEDITERRANEAN SEA

EGYPT

Nile R.

The first writing began when God put a "mark" or "sign" on Cain (*Genesis 4:15*). That mark stood for an idea and the people knew what it stood for.

Long before God gave the law to Moses (*Exodus 20*), we find several very definite ordinances given in the book of Genesis. At the very beginning God instituted the Sabbath (*Genesis 2:1-3*) and marriage (*Genesis 2:24*).

The law of the tithe was evidently observed. Read about Abraham's tithe in Genesis 14:20, and read Jacob's

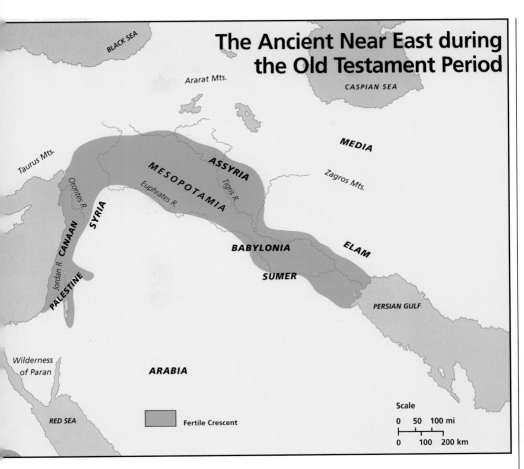

The Ancient Near East during the Old Testament Period

BLACK SEA

Ararat Mts.

CASPIAN SEA

Taurus Mts.

MEDIA

ASSYRIA

MESOPOTAMIA

Zagros Mts.

Orontes R.

Euphrates R.

Tigris R.

SYRIA

CANAAN

Jordan R.

PALESTINE

BABYLONIA

ELAM

SUMER

PERSIAN GULF

Wilderness of Paran

ARABIA

RED SEA

Fertile Crescent

Scale

0	50	100 mi

0	100	200 km

words in Genesis 28:22. God has evidently made people realize from the very beginning that they were only stewards of all they had.

This civilization before the flood is called the "antediluvian civilization." It perished in the judgment of the flood. It was the civilization started by Cain. It ended in destruction.

The Bible teaches and the archaeologist confirms that the people of the world before the flood were not mere savages. They had attained a considerable degree of civilization.

Turn to Genesis 4:16-22 and see what is mentioned of early civilization in the Scriptures.

1. Herdsmen: see 4:20
2. Musicians: see 4:21
3. Artificers and manufacturers: see 4:22
4. Builders: see 4:17

The civilization founded by Cain may have been equal to that of Greece or Rome, but God's judgment was upon it. Why? (6:5-7).

The Flood *Genesis 5—9*

The account of the flood in the Bible is very plain and straightforward. The story is not told because it is startling or interesting, but because it is an incident in the history of redemption that the Bible relates. Evil had grown rampant. It threatened to destroy everything that was good. Only one righteous man remained, Noah. God sent the flood to restore good upon the earth.

Adam and Eve had yielded to an outward temptation, but now people had yielded to temptation which was within. See Genesis 6:5. God was going to separate the righteous from the wicked. He was taking the first step toward a chosen nation.

After the Fall, God gave the world a new beginning, but soon the wickedness of people increased until there remained but one righteous man, Noah.

God had been long-suffering in His patience with people. The Holy Spirit had been in conflict with people. Noah had warned them for 120 years while he was building the ark. Even after Noah and his wife and his three sons and their wives—taking with them two of every unclean animal and fourteen of every clean animal—had entered into the ark of safety, there was a respite of seven days before the flood came; but God's mercies were refused and so people had to perish (*Genesis 6—7*). Noah was saved from the flood by the ark (a perfect type or Old Testament picture example of Christ, our Ark of safety). When he came out, the first thing he did was to erect an altar and worship God (*Genesis 8:20*).

Out of the fearful judgment of the earth by the flood, God saved eight people. He gave the purified earth to these people with ample power to govern it (*Genesis 9:1-6*). The most solemn responsibility God gave to humans is the taking of a life for a life (*Genesis 9:6*). God established capital punishment for homicide.

Archaeological discovery in Mesopotamia bears evidence of the flood, both in the cuneiform writings and in the actual flood deposits. The cuneiform libraries seem to have given us ample accounts of, and references to, this catastrophe. A clay prism has also been found on which are inscribed the names of the ten kings who reigned before the flood.

Babel *Genesis 10—11*

After the flood the world was given a new start. But instead of spreading out and repeopling the earth as God had commanded, they built the great tower of Babel in defiance of God. In judgment God sent a confusion of tongues and scattered them abroad.

The human race was then divided into nations speaking different languages, according to Noah's three sons, Shem, Ham and Japheth. Shem's sons settled in Arabia and to the east; Ham's sons settled in Africa; Japheth's sons settled in Europe.

As we read the story in Genesis 11:1-9, the narrative seems to imply that the people were at cross purposes with God. As a result there was this confusion of tongues and dispersion abroad. A difference in language tends to separate people in more ways than one and to check progress in commerce, in arts and in civilization.

The main body of Noah's descendants seems to have migrated from Armenia, where Noah's family left the ark, back toward the plain of Babylonia where they built the tower.

The Call of Abraham
Genesis 12—38

In spite of the wickedness of the human heart, God wanted to show His grace. He wanted a chosen people:
1. To whom He might entrust the Holy Scriptures
2. To be His witness to the other nations
3. Through whom the promised Messiah could come.

He called a man named Abram to leave his home in idolatrous Ur of the Chaldees to go to an unknown land where God would make him the father of a mighty nation (*Genesis 12:1-3; Hebrews 11:8-19*). This begins the history of God's chosen people, Israel.

Wherever Abraham went, he erected an altar to God. God signally honored him by revealing Himself to him. He was called "God's friend" (*James 2:23*). God made a covenant with him that he should be the father of a great nation and that through him the nations of the earth would be blessed (*Genesis 12:1-3*). His family became God's special charge. God dealt with them as with no other people. The Jews are always spoken of as God's chosen people.

Through Isaac, Abraham's son, the promises of God were passed down to Jacob, who, despite his many faults, valued God's covenant blessing. He was enthusiastic about God's plan of founding a nation by which the whole world would be blessed. Jacob in his wanderings suffered for his sin, and through chastening came out a great man. His name was changed to Israel, a prince with God (*Genesis 32:28*). This is the name by which God's chosen people were called—Israelites. His twelve sons became the heads of the twelve tribes of Israel. Read Genesis 49.

Descent into Egypt
Genesis 39—50

Isaac and Rebecca made the mistake of playing favorites with their two sons. Isaac favored the hunter Esau. Rebecca favored the quiet Jacob. Jacob did the same thing in the treatment of Joseph, which aroused jealousy in the other sons. Joseph is one of the outstanding noble characters of the Old Testament. It was through Joseph that Jacob's family was transplanted into Egypt. Joseph's life is one of the most perfect illustrations in the Bible of God's overruling providence. He was sold as a slave at seventeen. At thirty he became ruler in Egypt; ten years later his father, Jacob, entered Egypt.

After Isaac's death and after Joseph had been sold into Egypt, Jacob and his sons and their children, numbering seventy in all, went down into that land because of a famine. Here they were exalted by the Pharaoh who was reigning at that time. When he learned that they were shepherds, he permitted them to settle in the land of Goshen where they grew in number, wealth and influence.

God knew it was necessary that the Israelites leave Canaan until they had developed national strength so they would take possession of the land of Canaan. God wanted to safeguard them against mingling and intermarrying with the idolatrous peoples then in the land.

Read Jacob's dying words to his twelve sons (*Genesis 49*). We see here again the promise to Judah of a descendant who is to be the coming ruler. Remember, Christ is called the Lion of the tribe of Judah (*Revelation 5:5*).

The book of Genesis ends in failure. The last words are in a coffin in Egypt. Death only marks the pathway of sin; the wages of sin is death (*Romans 6:23*). The people needed a Savior!

Eight names are mentioned in Genesis that we should remember in order: God, Adam, Satan, Noah, Abraham, Isaac, Jacob and Joseph.

Six places are of supreme importance in connection with the history of Genesis—Eden, Ararat, Babel, Ur of the Chaldees, Canaan (Promised Land) and Egypt.

3. UNDERSTANDING

Exodus

Exodus Portrays Jesus Christ, Our Passover Lamb

Exodus follows Genesis in much the same relation as the New Testament stands to the Old Testament. Genesis tells of humanity's failure under every test and in every condition; Exodus is the thrilling epic of God hastening to the rescue. It tells of the redeeming work of a sovereign God.

Exodus is preeminently the book of redemption in the Old Testament. It begins in the darkness and gloom, yet ends in glory; it commences by telling how God came down in grace to deliver an enslaved people, and ends by declaring how God came down in glory to dwell in the midst of a redeemed people.

Exodus, which is Greek, means "way out." Without Genesis the book of Exodus has no meaning. It begins with the Hebrew word *we*, which means "And" or "Now" *(KJV)*. The story is just continuing. This book, like many other books of the Old Testament, begins with the word "And." This seems to point to the fact that each author was not just recording his own story but only his part in a great drama that began in the events of the past and looked forward to that which would come. Take the five books of Moses—Genesis, Exodus, Leviticus, Numbers and Deuteronomy. Each book is about something and those five things are vitally related to one another.

The Great Hero, Moses
The book gives us the story of Moses, the great hero of God. D. L. Moody (Dwight Lyman Moody, 1832-1899, American evangelist) said that Moses spent

> Forty years thinking he was somebody
> Forty years learning he was nobody
> Forty years discovering what God can do with a nobody. See Hebrews 11:23-29.

The Law
The last half of the book *(chaps. 19—40)* teaches us that the redeemed must do the will of their Redeemer,

Selected Bible Readings

Sunday:	Bondage *(Exodus 1:1-22)*
Monday:	The Call of Moses *(Exodus 3—4)*
Tuesday:	The Plagues *(Exodus 7:20—11:10)*
Wednesday:	The Passover *(Exodus 12:1-51)*
Thursday:	The Law *(Exodus 20:1-26)*
Friday:	The Worship *(Exodus 25:1-9; 28:1-14,30-43)*
Saturday:	Moses' Commission Renewed *(Exodus 33:12—34:17)*

consecrating themselves to His service, and submitting to His control. Therefore, the moral law is given, followed by the ceremonial law which was in part provision for the violator of the moral law.

The Tabernacle

God gave the Tabernacle as a detailed picture of the Redeemer to come, in His many offices, and as a dwelling place for His visible glory on earth. Its wonderful typology is rich in Christian truth.

The Bondage *Exodus 1:1-22*

As this book opens, three-and-a-half centuries have passed since the closing scene of Genesis. The book of Genesis is a family history. The book of Exodus is a national history. We have no account of what happened during this long period of silence. The patriarch, Abraham, died when Jacob, his grandson, was fifteen years old. Jacob's favorite son Joseph had been sold as a slave into Egypt and had risen to great power and influence. The sons of Jacob had gained great favor because of their brother Joseph. Only seventy people went down into Egypt, but before they left Egypt the people had grown into a nation of 3,000,000.

When Joseph died and a new dynasty came to the throne in Egypt, the wealth and great numbers of the children of Israel made them objects of suspicion in the eyes of the Egyptians. The pharaohs, wishing to break with them, reduced them to a slavery of the worst sort. This was hard for a people who had lived free, having had every favor upon them. They remembered the promises God had given to Abraham and his descendants, and it made this bondage doubly hard to understand (*Genesis 12:1-3ff.*).

The story told in the books of Exodus, Leviticus, Numbers and Deuteronomy shows that God did not forget the promise He had made to Abraham—"I will make you into a great nation" (*Genesis 12:2*).

The family records of Abraham, Isaac and Jacob no doubt had been carried into Egypt, and there became part of Israel's national annals. Through the long years of bondage, they clung to the promise that one day Canaan would be their home.

We will see God coming down to deliver the people from Egypt (*Exodus 3:7,8*). Now the individuals and families had been organized into a nation. God was going to give them laws with which to govern themselves. He was going to take them back to the land He had promised them.

The Exodus *Exodus 3—4*

Think of the preparation that had to be made for moving so great a host, see Exodus 12:37-38.

No doubt it was a well-organized expedition. Moses had appealed to Pharaoh again and again to let the children of Israel go (*Exodus 5:1; 7:16*). The plagues and the negotiations Moses had to make with Pharaoh must have lasted for nearly a year. This gave the children of Israel more time to gather their things. The plagues taught the children of Israel some great things, besides forcing Pharaoh to let the children of Israel go.

In the construction of any great edifice, a blueprint has to be drawn and a pattern made. Our salvation was designed by God before the foundation of the world (*Ephesians 1:4*). We find the pattern in the book of Exodus. Exodus is the historical picture of divine grace in the redemption of humanity by God to Himself by Jesus Christ, who is at once our great Apostle (Moses) and High Priest (Aaron) (*Hebrews 3:1*).

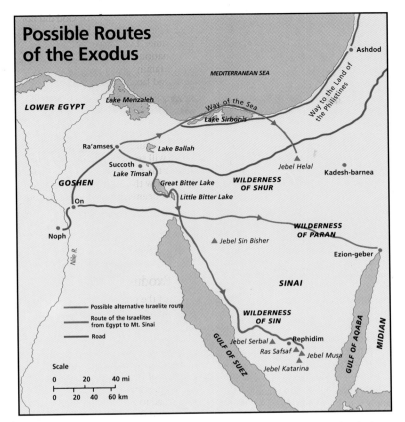

Possible Routes of the Exodus

MEDITERRANEAN SEA

Ashdod

LOWER EGYPT

Lake Menzaleh

Way of the Sea

Way to the Land of the Philistines

Lake Sirbonis

Ra'amses

Lake Ballah

GOSHEN

Succoth
Lake Timsah

Great Bitter Lake

Little Bitter Lake

Jebel Helal

Kadesh-barnea

WILDERNESS OF SHUR

On

Noph

Nile R.

Jebel Sin Bisher

WILDERNESS OF PARAN

Ezion-geber

SINAI

— Possible alternative Israelite route
— Route of the Israelites from Egypt to Mt. Sinai
— Road

WILDERNESS OF SIN

Jebel Serbal
Ras Safsaf
Jebel Katarina

Rephidim
Jebel Musa

GULF OF SUEZ

GULF OF AQABA

MIDIAN

Scale

0   20   40 mi

0   20   40   60 km

The story of Exodus is repeated in every soul that seeks deliverance from the enmeshing and enervating influence of the world. From this point of view, the book is human, from the first verse to the last. The things that happened were by way of example, and they were written for our admonition (*1 Corinthians 10:6-11*). We study Exodus in order to see God's way of delivering sinful people, and His gracious purposes in thus rescuing them.

The Passover *Exodus 12—19*

Exodus 12 gives us the thrilling story of the Passover, the clearest Old Testament picture of our individual salvation through faith in the shed blood of our Lord Jesus Christ. In this chapter is the basis for calling Christ the "Lamb of God, Christ our Passover," and the many tender references to His crucifixion as the death of our own Passover Lamb.

"For Christ, our Passover lamb, has been sacrificed" (*1 Corinthians 5:7*).

As the Passover chapter is the heart of the book, so is the whole book a pattern of our salvation.

The Passover is the prominent feature of Exodus (*chap. 12*). Perhaps the children of Israel did not know the significance of this feast the night before they left Egypt, but they believed God and obeyed.

God had sent nine plagues on Egypt in order to make Pharaoh willing to let His people go. Almost a year had passed and with each plague there was a hardening of Pharaoh's heart. Finally God said that the firstborn in all Egypt should die. This tenth plague would have fallen on the Israelites, too, had they not killed the paschal lamb and been protected by its blood of redemption (*Exodus 12:12,13*).

Every person should study the divine order of the Passover as it is given in Exodus 12.

1. "Take a lamb" (*Exodus 12:3*): see also Hebrews 9:28; Isaiah 53:6; John 19:14; 1 Corinthians 5:7. It was not the spotlessness of the living lamb that saved them (*Hebrews 9:22; 1 John 1:7; Revelation 1:5*). It was not Christ's sinless life that saves us, but His death on the cross.

2. "Strike the lintel and the two side posts with the blood" (*Exodus 12:22, KJV*). It is not enough for the lamb to be slain. The blood was sufficient but not efficient unless applied.

Every Israelite head of family had to apply it to his own household; notice over the doorway, not under. What have you done with the blood, the blood of our Passover Lamb who died on Mount Calvary? (Luke 23:33 [*Calvaria* is Latin for "skull"]; see also *John 1:12*).

The hyssop—a common weed obtainable by everyone—is typical of faith. The blood on the lintel is that which saved; not what they thought about it, but what they did with it counted. "When I see the blood, I will pass over you" (*Exodus 12:13*).

Not blood in the basin but blood applied saves a soul. Not all the blood shed on Calvary's cross can save a soul from death unless it is applied, then—"When I see the blood, I will pass over you."

Not feelings, not personal worthiness, but one thing saved them—"the blood" (*Hebrews 9:22*).

3. "Eat the lambs" (*Exodus 12:7*). After the blood was shed and applied to the doorframe, then there was direction for nourishment. So with us: salvation first, then feeding—fellowship, worship, walk and service.

Feeding did not save them, but blood first; then nourishment was possible (*John 6:54-58*). "My flesh is real food."

4. "Remove the yeast" (*Exodus 12:15*). "Search me, O God, and...see if there is any offensive way in me" (*Psalm 139:23-24*). Yeast (or "leaven," *KJV*) is often a type of sin: "Be on your guard against the yeast of the Pharisees and Sadducees" (*Matthew 16:6*); "Get rid of the old yeast" (*1 Corinthians 5:7*).

Leaven of unrighteousness must be removed from our lives if we are to eat with God.

5. "Eat the meat...with bitter herbs" (*Exodus 12:8*). Christ tasted the bitter cup for us and some bitterness we, too, must suffer. "No discipline seems pleasant at the time, but painful" (*Hebrews 12:11*).

The lamb was to be feasted upon not raw, not unbaked, but as a suffering lamb which had passed through fire. It was to be eaten in haste with nothing remaining. Not a bone was to be broken! Christ's body was broken, but not His bones (*Psalm 34:20; John 19:36*).

6. "Be dressed and ready to travel" (*Exodus 12:11, CEV*). They ate the food standing, fully dressed, ready to go. All provision was made for the journey. What a contrast that night! Peaceful feasting in the houses of Israel; awful mourning in the houses of Egypt!

We have read here of the Passover. Now comes the Passage. The Passover sealed them. The Passage of the Red

Sea steeled them. They left Egypt under the blood, a marked people. They passed through the Red Sea a directed, determined people. God led them out and shut the door behind them!

"When I came out of Egypt" (*Exodus 13:8*). When did you come out? (Remember, Egypt represents allegiance to the world.)

The Giving of the Law
Exodus 20—24

In Exodus 20—24 we see the law given, broken and restored. Up till this time in Israel's history all has been grace and mercy. God had heard the cry of their bondage and answered them. God selected a leader and trained him. God defeated their enemies. God fed them and yet they rebelled. Now a new order of things is brought about at Sinai.

The law demands nothing short of perfection. The psalmist says, "The law of the Lord is perfect" (*Psalm 19:7*; read *verses 8-11*). Only one Man since it was given has been able to keep it perfectly. Christ not only kept the law, but He also paid the complete penalty for the broken law. Christ suffered that we might be spared (see *Hebrews 9:13-15; 10:1-22; 1 Peter 1:18-20*).

If we could not keep the law, why was it given? That we might know our exceeding sinfulness. The law did not make us sin, but it showed us that we are sinners. (Read *Galatians 4:4,5; Romans 8:1-4; 3:19-28.*)

The law is God's mirror to show us our exceeding sinfulness. "So then, the law is holy, and the commandment is holy, righteous and good" (*Romans 7:12*).

Two mountain peaks stand in contrast to each other in God's Word.

1. Mount Sinai, with all of its horror thundered forth the law (*Exodus 19*).

2. Opposite this God places Calvary.

The view from Mount Moses, traditionally identified with Mount Sinai, where Moses was given the Law.

Calvary took away all the fire and thunder and made possible a meeting place between God and the sinner.

We each have a choice about how we shall approach God, either by law or by blood (*Hebrews 12:18-29*).

No provision was made in the law for failure. It is all or nothing—the whole law or a broken thing. One flaw in a character mars the perfection God requires under the law.

Laws may be divided into two parts:

1. Laws regarding our attitude toward God.

2. Laws regarding our attitude toward our fellow humans.

We are told that God spoke all these words (*Exodus 20:1*). God gave the whole testimony and the people assumed the whole responsibility of keeping it. Read what the people said in Exodus 19:8. Why did Israel accept the law rather than cry for mercy? Human pride always makes us think that we can please God by ourselves. Before Israel even received the law or started to keep it, they were dancing around the golden calf, and worshiping a god they had made (*Exodus 32:1-10,18*).

The Building of the Tabernacle *Exodus 25—40*

Exodus 25—40 gives us one of the richest veins in inspiration's exhaustless mines. We must use our imagination and reason as we enter the holy precincts and gaze upon the significant furniture. God told Moses He wished a sanctuary or holy dwelling place that should point to Christ and tell of His person and work.

The Outer Court:

Herein we see the altar on which the burnt offerings were sacrificed. Remember, Christ is our sin-offering (*27:1-8*).

The bronze basin was there for the cleansing of the priests before they could enter into the holy place to render their service (*30:18*).

The Holy Place:

Herein was the golden lampstand (*25:31-40*), typifying Christ, the Light of the world; and the Bread of the Presence (*25:23-30*), for Christ is the Bread of life; and the golden altar of incense (*30:1-10*), symbolizing Christ's intercession for us.

Holy of Holies:

Now if we draw back the beautiful veil (which typifies the body of Christ), we will see the Ark of the Covenant, the symbol of God's presence. Into this holy of holies, the high priest came only once a year to sprinkle the blood of atonement. The book of Hebrews tells us that Christ is not only our High Priest, but that He was also our atonement, and so we can go into the holy of holies (the presence of God) at any time with boldness.

The Tabernacle itself:

The Tabernacle, having the cloud of glory over it, taught the people that God was dwelling in their midst (*25:8*).

The Tabernacle was the common center and rallying point that could be moved from time to time.

4. UNDERSTANDING

Leviticus

Leviticus Portrays Jesus Christ, Our Sacrifice for Sin

"Get right," say the offerings. There are five of them: burnt offering, grain offering, fellowship offering, sin offering and guilt offering.

"Keep right," say the feasts. There are eight of them: Sabbath, Passover, Pentecost, Trumpets, Atonement, Tabernacles, the Sabbath year and Jubilee.

Leviticus is called the Book of Atonement (*Leviticus 16:30-34*).

God says, "Be holy, because I am holy" (*Leviticus 11:44-45; 19:2; 20:7,26*).

The book of Leviticus is God's picture book for the children of Israel to help them in their religious training. Every picture pointed forward to the work of Jesus Christ.

The title of Leviticus suggests the subject matter of the book—the Levites and the priests and their service in the Tabernacle. It is also called the Book of Laws.

We remember in the book of Exodus how God gave Moses the exact instructions about how to build the Tabernacle and about the institution of the priesthood to carry on the service in this holy place.

Like Exodus, Leviticus begins with the Hebrew word *we* ("and"). As this book opens, the children of Israel are still at Mount Sinai. God is continuing to give His instructions for orderly worship in the Tabernacle.

In Genesis, we see humanity ruined.
In Exodus, humanity redeemed.
In Leviticus, humanity worshiping.

Leviticus is a timely book for it insists on keeping the body holy as well as the soul. It teaches that the redeemed ones must be holy because their Redeemer is holy. It gives us not only the key for our spiritual life and its holy walk, but it also surprises us with real lessons in hygiene and sanitation for the care of the body. The Jewish people are wonderful evidence of the result of this latter in their long and vigorous lives.

It is a divine book. The opening verse affords us the clue to the whole, "The Lord called to Moses and spoke to him from the Tent of Meeting." Leviticus is God speaking to us through the Tabernacle and its meaning.

It is a personal book. The second verse intimates this: "When any of you brings an offering to the Lord." Notice, He expects each person to bring his or her own gift. The way is

Selected Bible Readings

Sunday:	Burnt Offering (*Leviticus 1*)
Monday:	The Priests (*Leviticus 8*)
Tuesday:	Pure Food Laws (*Leviticus 11*)
Wednesday:	The Day of Atonement (*Leviticus 16*)
Thursday:	The Feasts of Jehovah (*Leviticus 23*)
Friday:	God's Pledge (*Leviticus 26*)
Saturday:	Dedication (*Leviticus 27*)

often as important as the gift. Have you an offering for the Lord? Then this book will appeal to you.

Sacrifice and Separation
Leviticus 1:1—6:7

One of the most important questions in life is "How may an unholy people approach a holy God?"

At the very beginning of the book we see God making provision for His people to approach Him in worship. This book shows redeemed Israel that the way to God is by sacrifice and the walk with God by separation.

Isn't it strange that deep down in every heart there is a sense of guilt and the feeling of a need of doing something to secure pardon or gain the favor of the one wronged? Pagans bring their sacrifice to the altar of their gods, for they realize that they cannot do anything about their sin themselves. They must make atonement for it.

Pagans cannot see beyond their sacrifices. When we look at the sacrifices in this book, we find that they are only types, or symbolic representations that point to the Perfect Sacrifice for sin which was to be made on Calvary.

All the sacrifices in this book point to "the Lamb of God, who takes away the sin of the world" (*John 1:29*).

Sin may be forgiven, but it must receive its penalty. "The wages of sin is death" (*Romans 6:23*). Sin keeps us from drawing near to God. He is "too pure to look on evil" (*Habakkuk 1:13*).

There can be no fellowship between God and the sinner until sin has been dealt with; the only way is sacrifice. "Without the shedding of blood there is no forgiveness" (*Hebrews 9:22*).

Five offerings are described in Leviticus. God wants us to understand the awful reality of sin, so He asks for a sacrifice each day.

Here is a list of the offerings, with a keyword to identify them. Learn this simple outline to fix in mind the first six chapters of Leviticus.

1. Burnt Offering: "Surrender" of Christ for the world—Leviticus 1
2. Grain Offering: "Service" of Christ in life—Leviticus 2
3. Fellowship Offering: "Serenity" of Christ in life—Leviticus 3
4. Sin Offering: "Substitute" of Christ for sin—Leviticus 4—5:13
5. Guilt Offering: "Satisfaction" by Christ for demands of God—Leviticus 5:14—6:7.

The Burnt Offering—Leviticus 1:
The offerings start with the burnt offering and end with the guilt offering.

The burnt offering is a type of Christ offering Himself without spot to God. There were daily burnt offerings. Christ offered Himself in the sinner's place (*Leviticus 1:4*).

This was an offering of Dedication. Why first? Because sacrifice comes first. No one begins with God until all has been yielded to God. (See *Leviticus 1:3.*) This was the most common sacrifice in the ancient Temple.

Dedication is our part.

Consecration is God's part.

We dedicate ourselves to God.

He consecrates us—to His service.

We sing, "Take my life and let it be consecrated, Lord, to Thee." (This is a burnt offering.)

The Grain Offering—Leviticus 2:
This is the sacrifice of daily devotion.

As the burnt offering typifies Christ in death, so the grain offering typifies Christ in life.

The fine flour speaks of the character of Christ—His perfection in thought, in word, in action.

Let us feed on the perfect grain offering.

An artist's impression of a sacrifice being offered in front of the Tabernacle.

We must come to Him first with our whole burnt offering. Then we keep coming with our continual grain offering. It is our very best, our gift of life. Notice, the slain offering must come first.

The Fellowship Offering—
Leviticus 3:

Christ is our peace (*Ephesians 2:14*). He has reconciled all things to Himself "by making peace through his blood, shed on the cross" (*Colossians 1:20*).

This offering represents fellowship and communion with God. It is an offering of thanksgiving.

The Sin Offering—Leviticus 4—5:

This shows us Christ on the cross in the sinner's place.

In this offering we see an acknowledgment of sin, "When anyone sins . . . he must bring" (*4:2-3*). This offering is for expiation. In the other offerings the offerer comes as a worshiper, but here as a convicted sinner. God holds us accountable for our sin. We are like criminals who have been tried, found guilty and sentenced to death.

Though placed last, the sin and guilt offerings are included in all that goes before. The only reason burnt offerings, grain offerings or fellowship offerings can be made is that the blood of pardon has been shed. God has accepted the one offering of His Son, which every lesser offering typified (symbolically represented).

In non-Christian religions, worshipers bring sacrifices to their god; Christians accept the sacrifice from their God.

The Guilt Offering—
Leviticus 5:14—6:7:

Christ has even taken care of our sin against others.

The blood of the guilt offering cleanses the conscience and sends the trespasser back to the one he or she has wronged, not only with the principal but with the fifth part added (*6:5*). The injurer is forgiven and the injured becomes an actual gainer.

It is a grave error to suppose that you are safe and right if you live up to your own conscience. God has scales. We can never comprehend His holiness.

None of these sacrifices forgave sin. They only pointed forward to the true Sacrifice, God's very own Son (*Hebrews 10*).

Notice that bullocks, oxen, goats, sheep, turtle doves and pigeons were mentioned for sacrifice. The offering was determined by the ability of the one who brought it.

What we bring is our sin; what Christ brings is the offering and the atonement for sin.

The Priest *Leviticus 8—10*

We have been studying the great subject of sacrifice, but no one could bring his or her own sacrifice to God. Each one had to bring it to the priest and he in turn would offer it to God.

God chose one tribe out of the twelve to care for the Tabernacle. This was the tribe of Levi. One family of Levites, Aaron's, should be the priests. The priests had charge of the sacrifices and were supported by the tithes of the people.

The priest offered the prayers and praises and sacrifices of the people to God in their behalf. He stood for them and pleaded their cause.

The burdened Israelites who desired to approach God brought their animals to the court of the Tabernacle. At the altar of burnt offerings they laid their hands on an animal's head to express penitence and consecration. The animal was killed and its blood sprinkled on the altar.

The priest representing the worshiper then came to the laver, in which he washed his hands, thus indicating the clean life that should follow the forgiveness of sins. He entered the holy place, passed by the sacred furnishings, the lampstand, the table of bread, and came to the altar of incenses, where prayer was offered.

One day in the year the high priest passed beyond the veil that separated the holy and the most holy place and stood before the mercy seat, with the blood of the atonement, to intercede for the people.

The priest could not consecrate himself. Moses acted for God in this service. Each priest presented his body a living sacrifice for service, just as Paul wants us to do in Romans 12:1-2.

The priests had charge of the sacrifices. The Levites were their assistants. They took care of the Tabernacle, formed choirs, were guides and instructors in the later Temple.

Notice the opening of Leviticus 10. At the very beginning of the history of the work of the priesthood evidences of failure could be noticed. Nadab and Abihu, two sons of Aaron, offered "strange fire" *(KJV)* before the Lord "contrary to his command. So fire came out from the presence of the Lord and consumed them."

We read in Leviticus 10:3 that Aaron held his peace. He was their father, but he dared not question God. We talk too much before God. We must learn to walk softly in the divine Presence. The other priests were solemnly charged to show no signs of mourning and to abide at their posts.

The priests were the ministers of the sacrifices we have just been studying. Each was a picture of the great sacrifice of Christ for the sin of the world.

Animal sacrifices are no longer necessary because all sacrifices were fulfilled in Christ. Therefore priests are no longer necessary. Christ Himself is the great High Priest for humanity (*Hebrews 2:17; 4:15*). He is the only Mediator between God and humanity.

The Tabernacle

No one else can come between God and humanity.

Christ is our High Priest and He is at the right hand of the Father today making intercession for us. We approach God by Him and Him alone (*Hebrews 10:12; 7:25; John 14:6*).

When we see Christ as Sacrifice, we see beauty and completeness.

When we see Christ as Priest, we see His divine perfection. See Hebrews 4:15.

As Sacrifice He establishes the relationship of His people with God.

As Priest He maintains that position.

We read of this perfect and eternal priesthood in the book of Hebrews. Heaven, not earth, is the sphere of Christ's priestly ministry. He never appeared in the Temple on earth to offer sacrifice. He went there to preach and teach but not to sacrifice. Except in the sense that all believers are priests (*1 Peter 2:5*), there is no such thing as a priest on earth. The believer is a spiritual priest. It is not necessary that any child of God go before any person on earth to obtain entrance into the presence of God. Every Christian has the right to enter because he or she knows Jesus Christ. The Lord said, "I am the way" (*John 14:6*). "Let us then approach the throne of grace with confidence, so that we may receive mercy and find grace to help us in our time of need" (*Hebrews 4:16*).

Eight Feasts *Leviticus 23; 25*

As the first part of the book has to do with offerings and the offerers, so the last part of the book deals with feasts and feasters.

Five great festivals are mentioned in Leviticus 23.

The sacrifices spoke of the blood that saved.

The feasts spoke of the food that sustains.

Both are of God.

The sacrifices correspond to the cup of the Lord's Supper that reminds us of Christ's death on the cross whereby we are redeemed. The bread of the Communion witnesses to His life of which we are partakers.

The Feast of the Sabbath—23:1-3:

The Sabbath was given the foremost place. It was a perpetually recurring feast to be obeyed through the whole year on every seventh day. It was a day of worship and rest, celebrating the finished work of God in creation (*Genesis 2:2-3*). Christians celebrate the first day of the week, the day our Lord arose from the grave (*Luke 24:1; Acts 20:7; 1 Corinthians 16:2*). Thus we celebrate the finished work of redemption.

The Feasts of the Passover—23:4-5 and Unleavened Bread—23:6-8:

The Passover spoke of redemption and was celebrated every spring at our Easter time. It was the Fourth of July for the children of Israel. They did not celebrate it by fireworks and parades but by a great service of worship to God. All the Israelites who could, made their way to Jerusalem.

Passover lasted one day, but the Feast of Unleavened Bread that immediately followed lasted seven days. With these the year commenced.

The Jewish people were still celebrating this feast when our Lord was on this earth. Read in the Word the times that He went to the Passover feast (*Luke 2:41-52; Matthew 26:19; John 13*).

The Feasts of First Fruits—23:9-14 and Pentecost—23:15-22:

The Israelites observed first fruits during the Feast of Unleavened Bread. This feast of the first fruits typified Christ's resurrection and ours (*1 Corinthians 15:20*). Fifty days later Passover was observed. Fifty days after Christ's resurrection, the Holy Spirit descended upon the disciples and the Church was born. Pentecost was the birthday of the Church. The death and resurrection of Christ had to be accomplished before the descent of the Holy Spirit.

The Feast of Trumpets—23:23-25:

This has become the New Year's Day (Rosh Hashanah) of the Jewish people. The children of Israel celebrated it in the fall, in September or October. This feast points forward to the future gathering of the dispersed people of Israel (*Zechariah 14:16*).

Day of Atonement—23:26-32:

The Day of Atonement followed the Feast of Trumpets by ten days. This was the most solemn day of the year of God's chosen people. On this day the sins of the nation were confessed. Confession is always the first step toward righteousness. It reveals a right attitude toward sin. It leads to a desire for forgiveness. God says, "If we confess our sins, he is faithful and just and will forgive us our sins and purify us from all unrighteousness" (*1 John 1:9*).

On this day Jehovah's (Jehovah is a form of the divine name, more properly, "Yahweh") relationship to His people was established—all the nation's sins, failures and weaknesses of the people were atoned for. The blood was shed and the sins of the people were covered so that God could take up His abode in the midst of His people in spite of their uncleanness.

We learn in Leviticus 16 that God was hidden behind a veil in the Tabernacle and the priests and the people were to remain at a distance. Read Leviticus 16:2. The way was not yet made open to approach God. Now "we may approach God with freedom and confidence" (*Ephesians 3:12*). We can run into God's presence at any time for Christ has made the way possible for us. In the book of Leviticus, God was shut in from humanity and humanity was shut out from God.

The Day of Atonement was the only day in the year when the high priest was permitted to enter the holy of holies. He went in with an offering for the atonement of the sin of the people. Atonement means "cover." This offering "covered" the sins of the people until the great sacrifice on Calvary was made. None of these offerings "took away" those sins. Read Hebrews 10:1-2,11-12.

The Feast of Tabernacles—23:33-36:

This was the last required feast of the year. Also called the Feast of Booths or Ingathering, it commemorated the time when the children of Israel lived in tents during their wilderness journey. It was celebrated in the fall of the year and lasted an entire week. The people lived in booths out-of-doors and heard the reading of the Law.

The Feast of Tabernacles reminded them of their dependence upon Jehovah and the blessings that would come if they would be obedient to His will.

The Sabbatical Year—25:1-7:

This was the year of meditation and devotion. It was a year-long Sabbath. The purpose and character of the Sabbath was magnified. This God did every seven years.

God wanted to impress upon them that the very land was holy unto Him. This is why Palestine is called the Holy Land. There was quiet over the whole land during these days. Every day was like the Sabbath, and the minds of the people were kept on the things of the Lord. The law was read.

The Year of Jubilee—25:8-55:

This was celebrated every fiftieth year. It was inaugurated on the Day of Atonement with the blowing of trumpets. As in the sabbatic year, the land was not cultivated. All slaves of Israelite blood were freed. The blowing of the trumpets that ushered in the year released every bondperson. Jewish historians tell us that the Year of Jubilee was observed at the time of the fall of Judah in 586 B.C. References are made to it in Isaiah 5:7-10; 61:1-2; Ezekiel 7:12-13; 46:16-18.

Another outstanding event was the restoration to the original owner of all land that had in any way been taken away. That is, it was returned to the family to whom it had been assigned in the original distribution. What a wise provision it was from an economic standpoint. But God no doubt had a more far-reaching plan bearing upon the coming of the Messiah. Every tribal and family register must be carefully kept so that the rights of all would be protected. This would apply especially to Judah, the tribe from which the Messiah was to come. From these registers our Lord's natural descent could be exactly traced.

This book is for a redeemed people, showing how God is to be approached and worshiped. The book of Exodus is the book of redemption, but the book of Leviticus tells how the redeemed ones can worship God.

Only through the blood of Christ can we have access to God.

God demands a holiness that Christ alone can give, for we are sharers in his holiness (*Hebrews 12:10*).

In Genesis we see humanity ruined.
In Exodus, humanity redeemed.
In Leviticus, humanity worshiping.

Seven is a significant number in Leviticus:

Every seventh day was the Sabbath.
Every seventh year was a sabbatic year.
Every seven times seven years was followed by a year of Jubilee.
Pentecost was seven weeks after Passover.
In the seventh month were the feasts of trumpets, tabernacles and atonement.
Pentecost lasted seven days.
Passover lasted seven days.
This book, like Revelation, is built around a series of seven.

5. UNDERSTANDING

Numbers

Numbers Portrays Jesus Christ, Our "Lifted-up One"

The children of Israel were saved to serve. So is every child of God today.

Beware of unbelief! The apostle Paul says to us, "You were running a good race. Who cut in on you and kept you from obeying the truth?" (*Galatians 5:7*). Unbelief hinders blessing. God tells why we cannot enter into His blessings (*Hebrews 3:19*).

This book might be called the Wilderness Wandering from Sinai to the border of Canaan, the land of promise, covering about forty years.

Numbers is also called the Book of the March and the Roll Call (*Numbers 33:1-2*).

It might, too, be called the Book of Murmurings because from beginning to end it is filled with the spirit of rebellion against God. Read what God says about this in Psalm 95:10.

Numbers is indeed the book of the wilderness, recording the pitiable failure of Israel at Kadesh-barnea, and the consequent wanderings and experiences of the people in the wilderness. It records the pilgrimage, warfare, service and failure of the second generation of the nation after the Exodus from Egypt. This, however, is not all the message of Numbers. The first ten chapters give us the divine legislation; chapters 11—20 tell the story of the nation's failure; but the closing chapters of the book record Israel's return to Jehovah's favor and final victory, even in the wilderness.

While the annals of many powerful nations of that same time are lost to the world, those of a comparative handful of people are preserved. The reason for this is that the Messiah who would redeem the world was to come from this people. In 1 Corinthians 10, we learn that the things that happened to them were "examples" unto us. In other words, their whole history was an "object lesson" to us, illustrating God's dealing with us today. The key thought is discipline.

If you know five names, you will master the story of the book of Numbers.

Moses, the great leader.

Aaron, the high priest, Moses' brother.

Miriam, who was Moses' and Aaron's sister.

Joshua and Caleb, the two spies who dared to believe God, the only men of their generation who lived to enter Canaan.

The geography of the book takes us:
1. From Sinai to Kadesh
2. From Kadesh around back to Kadesh
3. From Kadesh straight to the border of Canaan.

The children of Israel learned:

1. That they must trust God, not people, in the day of crisis (*Psalm 37:5*). Read Numbers 13:26—14:25.

2. That God would supply all their need according to His riches (*Philippians 4:19*).

He gave them food—Numbers 11:6-9

He gave them meat—Numbers 11:31-33
He gave them water—Numbers 20:8
He gave them leaders—Numbers 1:1,3
He gave them a promised land—
Numbers 14:7-8.

3. That they must worship God according to His instructions.

It was God's plan that the children of Israel should go straight into the land He had promised them, the land of Canaan, but the people would not. God said that all those at Kadesh over twenty years old, except Joshua and Caleb, would have to die. A new generation arose during the forty years of wandering, but at the end the nation was about as strong in numbers as the day they left Egypt. (Read *Numbers 26*.)

Preparation for the Journey
Numbers 1—12

As the book opens we see the children of Israel in the wilderness of Sinai. The law had been given, the Tabernacle had been built and the priests had been assigned to their service. Now God was going to prepare the nation for its work. The teachings of this book are very applicable to the Christian life.

Selected Bible Readings

Sunday:	The Guiding Cloud (*Numbers 9:15-23*)
Monday:	The Report of the Spies (*Numbers 13:16-33*)
Tuesday:	Israel's Unbelief (*Numbers 14:1-45*)
Wednesday:	Water from the Rock (*Numbers 20:1-13*)
Thursday:	The Brazen Serpent (*Numbers 21:1-9*)
Friday:	Balaam's Feast (*Numbers 22:1-41*)
Saturday:	The Cities of Refuge (*Numbers 35:6-34*)

Order is heaven's first law. We see God numbering and arranging the tribes (*chaps. 1 and 2*), choosing and assigning duties to the priests and Levites (*chaps. 3 and 4*). God is the author of order.

The thought of God numbering His people and gathering them about Himself is most precious to our hearts. He dwelt in the camp. Think of 600,000 men, twenty years old and upward, and about 3,000,000 men, women and children in this great camp! But the most glorious thing was that God was in their midst.

In the first chapter, Moses is commanded to take a census. The Lord knows all by name that are His

Part of the wilderness. As the book of Numbers opens we see the children of Israel in the wilderness of Sinai.

47

(*2 Timothy 2:19; Philippians 4:3*).

For Christians, too, there is a census, for Christ numbers His jewels and knows them who are His. "A scroll of remembrance was written in his presence concerning those who feared the Lord and honored his name" (*Malachi 3:16*).

Here were about three million people on a sterile desert, very little grass, very little water, no visible means of support. How were they to be fed? God was there!

God gave His children a cloud to guide them by day and a pillar of fire by night. It is interesting to see how they were guided a step at a time. They did not know when they were to go and when to stop, but the Ark of the Covenant (signifying God's presence) went on before, the pillar of cloud always leading (*Numbers 10:33*).

Sin crept into this well-ordered camp life. The people began to murmur against God. God sent judgment of fire (*Numbers 11:1-3*). Then they complained about their food (*11:4*). It seemed monotonous. They longed for the garlic and onions of Egypt and they wanted fish. As a result of their complaining, God sent them quails for thirty days. They made gluttons of themselves (see *Numbers 11:33*). Many became ill and died.

Then we read of the sin of Aaron, the high priest, and Miriam, the sister of Moses. God had chosen Moses to be the leader of this great people and Aaron and Miriam were only his assistants. Jealousy crept into their hearts. They wanted more honor. Read of Miriam's terrible punishment. She was smitten with leprosy for seven days (*Numbers 12:1-16*).

We find the invitation of God's marching host to the people round about them, "Come with us and we will treat you well, for the Lord has promised good things to Israel"

(*Numbers 10:29*). Can we say this, do we say it, to those about us?

The Ark of the Covenant is the Word of God in the midst.

The sound of the silver trumpet is the witness of a faithful prophet.

The pillar of fire and of cloud is the comfort and guidance of the Holy Spirit.

The Tabernacle and its ordinances are for the worship of God in the sanctuary.

Christ "the Apostle and High Priest" of our profession gives significance to it all.

We are just humans making many mistakes and capable of wandering far. God has given us these heavenly attendants and guides.

Wilderness Wanderings
Numbers 13—20

After one year at Mount Sinai, the Israelites journeyed to Kadesh. This is at the southern border of the Promised Land. Afraid to enter, they turned back and wandered in the wilderness to the south and east till that generation died. They did not travel all the time but remained in some places with their flocks and herds grazing on the surrounding hills. When the cloud lifted, they marched. They finally approached Canaan from east of the Dead Sea.

Think of the lost years from Kadesh back to Kadesh because people would not believe God. After two years in the wilderness, the children of Israel could have gone into the land of promise immediately had it not been for the sin of unbelief.

When the spies came back and told them about the giants in the land and the high-walled cities, their hearts failed them. They would not listen to Joshua and Caleb who agreed with all that was told, but added, "We should go up and take possession of the land, for we can certainly do it" (*Numbers 13:30*). But the people would not trust God. They said, "We should choose a leader and go back to Egypt" (*Numbers 14:4*).

When they refused to enter Canaan, the door was closed to them. It meant wandering in the wilderness for forty years. God said that He would not allow any of those who were over twenty years old to enter Canaan, except Joshua and Caleb.

God took the children of Israel out of Egypt so that He could take them into Canaan, the land of promise. God did not want the children of Israel just to come out of Egypt. He wanted to have them come in to the Promised Land. This they could have done in comparatively a few days; not more than two or three weeks. Remember the spies made the trip and returned within forty days. Their fear disqualified them to take over the land of promise.

One of the reports of the spies was that there were giants in the land and that the Israelites were as grasshoppers in their sight (*Numbers 13:33*).

This record tells the story of many a Christian life and in part the story of every life. Giants of selfishness and greed, far outranking the Anakim (a people the Israelites feared because they were "strong, numerous and tall" [*Deuteronomy 2:21*]), oppose our advance! But when the returns are all in, the fact remains that there is One with us stronger than they!

Like the ten, we can put difficulties between us and God and say we are not able; or like the two, we can put God between the difficulties and ourselves and say we are able!

We start out with high hope in the enthusiasm of our first love. Yonder lies the land of possibilities and achievement. Then the giants appear—giants of

Plan of the Wilderness Tabernacle

50 cubits

100 cubits

Ark of the covenant

The Most Holy Place

Veil

Altar of incense

Table of the presence

Seven-branch lampstand

The Holy Place

Bronze sea

Altar of burnt offering

Entrance

opposition from without; giants of fear from within. Our faith fails. We forget God. We compare our difficulties with our own strength rather than committing them to the great arm of God.

How the Tribes Encamped around the Tabernacle

NAPHTALI   ASHER   DAN

EPHRAIM

THE TABERNACLE

JUDAH

MANASSEH

ISSACHAR

BENJAMIN

ZEBULUN

GAD   SIMEON   REUBEN

Numbers 33 is the pitiful logbook of this journey: "They left Hazeroth and camped at Rithmah. They left Rithmah and camped at Rimmon Perez. They left Rimmon Perez and camped at Libnah" etc., to the end of this dismal chapter! An endless circle of aimless wandering with no success. When we doubt God we find this to be our experience, too. We wander around but never accomplish anything.

Before this scene ends we find Israel murmuring again, this time because of the shortage of water. Moses and Aaron again went to God. God told Moses to take his rod and speak to the rock before the people, and the rock would give forth water.

Moses' patience was at an end. The people had complained about everything. In a fit of anger he called the people rebels and instead of speaking to the rock he struck it. The water gushed out. Even though Moses disobeyed, God was faithful and kept His promise.

Is it not sad that even children of God fail under testing? Moses' error was great, yet it showed him to be just like us. Moses put himself up as God— "Listen, you rebels, must we bring you water out of this rock?" (*Numbers 20:10*). This dishonored Jehovah God. Because Moses smote the rock a sec-

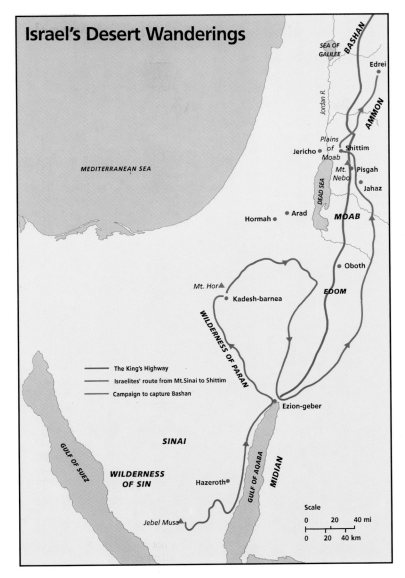

Israel's Desert Wanderings

MEDITERRANEAN SEA

SEA OF GALILEE

BASHAN

Edrei

Jordan R.

AMMON

Plains of Moab

Jericho

Shittim

Mt. Nebo

Pisgah

Jahaz

DEAD SEA

MOAB

Hormah

Arad

Oboth

Mt. Hor

EDOM

Kadesh-barnea

WILDERNESS OF PARAN

——— The King's Highway

——— Israelites' route from Mt.Sinai to Shittim

——— Campaign to capture Bashan

Ezion-geber

SINAI

GULF OF SUEZ

WILDERNESS OF SIN

Hazeroth

GULF OF AQABA

MIDIAN

Jebel Musa

Scale

| 0 | 20 | 40 mi |
| 0 | 20 | 40 km |

ond time (see first time, *Exodus 17:5,6*) instead of speaking to it, he was not permitted to enter the Promised Land. Christ, like the rock, was to be smitten once for our sins (*1 Corinthians 10:4*).

He need not be smitten again.

One of the important things we have not covered is an incident in Numbers 17.

Aaron's priesthood had been questioned, so God Himself was to confirm it. Moses gathered twelve staffs, one from the leader of each tribe, and placed them overnight in the Tent of Meeting. God put life into Aaron's alone, causing it to sprout and bud. So we find that all the authors of the religions of the world have died—even Christ died—but only Christ was raised from the dead and exalted to be our High Priest (*Hebrews 4:14; 5:4-10*).

On to Canaan
Numbers 20—36

As this scene opens, we discover that all the Israelites who left Egypt had died except Moses, Aaron, Joshua, Caleb, Miriam and the children who were under twenty years of age when the spies entered the land. While they camped in Kadesh, Miriam, Moses' sister, died (*20:1*) and Aaron, his brother, now over 100 years old, also died (*20:28*).

Israel was to move on again. They started from Kadesh-barnea, this time with faces set resolutely toward the land of promise. The way was difficult, much harder than before, but faith had been renewed, discipline had done its work and the arm of God went forth conquering and to conquer.

Learn here the lesson of God's second best. He offers the perfect way and we refuse it. It is gone forever. Every male over twenty years of age who refused to go into the land of promise the first time (except Joshua and Caleb who believed God) died in the wilderness.

But God is kind, and He sets before us another way, a second best; it may even be a third, for His mercy is wonderful.

Israel was complaining again, although over and over again God had proven to them that His way is best. They battled with the Canaanites and became discouraged. Then they grumbled because they had to march around the land of Edom instead of through it. They growled again against God and against Moses because they loathed the manna (*Numbers 21:5*). They never were content.

This time God sent venomous snakes among the people, which caused suffering and death. After they confessed their sin, Moses prayed for the deliverance of his people. God did not take away the venomous snakes, but told Moses to make a bronze snake and fasten it to a pole so that all could see it. As soon as they looked, they would live. (See *Numbers 21:6-9.*)

The Bible reveals that the whole human family has felt the ancient Serpent's sting of sin, which means death (*1 Corinthians 15:56; Hebrews 2:14-15*). The only way people can live is by looking to the One who took upon Himself the likeness of a human and was lifted up on the cross to take the sting of death upon Himself (*Philippians 2:7-8*). If we look on Him, our Savior, we shall live (*John 3:14-15*).

6. UNDERSTANDING

Deuteronomy

Deuteronomy Portrays Jesus Christ, Our True Prophet

"Observe to do" is the word of Moses to the people. He wanted them to be "doers of the word, and not hearers only" (*James 1:22, KJV*).

This book shows the blessings of obedience and the curse of disobedience.

Everything depends on obedience—life itself, possession of the Promised Land, victory over foes, prosperity and happiness. We find this book teaching the inflexibility of the law. "Thou shalt" and "thou shalt not" *(KJV)* occur over and over again—"the blessing if you obey" and "the curse if you disobey" (*Deuteronomy 11:26-28*).

The book of Deuteronomy is a collection of the orations and songs of Moses he gave as his farewell to the children of Israel. These noble orations were given as he stood on the great divide between his earthly and heavenly life. He was looking from the top of Mount Pisgah over a century crammed full of epoch-creating events. Then he turned his gaze upon the future of the people he was about to leave.

The book contains a most interesting and instructive summary of the wilderness history of Israel, and in the last chapter we find an account of Moses himself. Carefully compare Moses' review of the events with the account itself given in Exodus and Numbers. It will be found that Deuteronomy gives the divine rather than the human view. Compare Deuteronomy 1 with Numbers 13,14.

Deuteronomy is a book of remembrance. The name "Deuteronomy" means "second law," which indicates that the law is repeated. Moses did this to remind the people what God had done for them and what they were to do to serve Him when they reached the Promised Land. It omits the things that relate to the priests and Levites and includes the things that the people should know.

This book is the last of the five books of Moses. These five books are often called the "Pentateuch,"

Selected Bible Readings

Sunday:	Forward March (*Deuteronomy 1:6-46*)
Monday:	Instructions (*Deuteronomy 5:1-33; 6:4-18*)
Tuesday:	The Messiah, Prophet (*Deuteronomy 18:15-22*)
Wednesday:	God's Covenant (*Deuteronomy 30:1-20*)
Thursday:	The Song of Moses (*Deuteronomy 32:1-44*)
Friday:	God's Blessings (*Deuteronomy 33:1-29*)
Saturday:	The Death of Moses (*Deuteronomy 34:1-12*)

meaning five books.

Genesis tells of the beginnings of the chosen nation Israel.

Exodus relates the organization of the people into a nation and the giving of the law.

Leviticus tells the way this people were to worship God.

Numbers gives a story of the wanderings of this people.

Deuteronomy relates the final preparation for entering the Promised Land.

Deuteronomy covers only about two months, including the thirty days of mourning for Moses.

Moses delivered his counsels probably within a period of seven days and about a month before the passage of the Jordan River (*Deuteronomy 1:1-3*).

Moses was the writer but not the author of the Pentateuch. More than five hundred times in these first five books we find expressions such as these: "The Lord spake"; "God said." Who is the divine Author of the Bible? (See *2 Peter 1:20-21*.)

The Christian heart always quickens its beat when it comes to Deuteronomy, for this book was a favorite with our Savior. From this book He quoted in His temptation in the wilderness with His adversary the devil. The following passages were His weapons with which He repelled the tempter: Matthew 4:1-11; Luke 4:1-13; Deuteronomy 8:3; 6:16; 6:13; and 10:20. Thus this book of Deuteronomy, God's book about obedience, Moses' last charge to his people, seems to have about it the peculiar blessing and protection of Christ Himself.

Jesus often quoted from Deuteronomy. In fact, it is almost invariably from this book that He quotes. He took Deuteronomy as His code of conduct (*Luke 4:4,8,12*). He answered the devil in the hour of temptation from its writings.

If you want a taste of heaven on earth, become familiar with Deuteronomy.

Moses' First Address: "Looking Back"
Deuteronomy 1—4

As the book opens we see the children of Israel on the border of the land of Canaan, in a place where eleven days' journey, some forty years before, could have brought them. Yet it had taken them forty years. How slowly they covered the ground! What windings and turnings! How often we have to go over the same ground again and again!

Several hundred years before, God had promised to Abraham and his "seed" (Hebrew: *zerah*, offspring, descendant[s]) a rich and wondrous land upon whose borders they were standing (*Genesis 17:8, KJV*). Now they were ready to enter in after all the years of anticipation and hope. The closing chapters of Numbers found them camped by the Jordan, waiting to go over into the good promised land itself.

In Deuteronomy God is putting before the children of Israel the conditions of their entering and holding the land. We see all these conditions summed up in one great word: Obedience.

The children of Israel entered the Promised Land under the conditions of the law.

The book of Deuteronomy is one long plea for hearty obedience to God based on two grand motives of love and fear. "And now, O Israel, what does the Lord your God ask of you but to fear the Lord your God, to walk in all his ways, to love him, to serve the Lord your God with all your heart and with all your soul" (*Deuteronomy 10:12*).

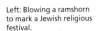

Moses' work was done. He had spent the last forty years of his life in delivering his people from the bondage of Egypt. He trained them, gave them forms of government, laws, religious institutions and molded them into a nation.

The children of Israel were now at the end of their journey, in the plain east of the Jordan, overlooking the land they had come so far to possess. It lay before them in the glories of the springtime. But the impassable Jordan river rolled between, and walled cities rose up in seemingly impregnable strength.

Moses' Second Address: "Looking Up"
Deuteronomy 5—26

In Deuteronomy 12:1 we see the key to this section. "These are the decrees and laws you must be careful to follow in the land." Israel was going into a new land and everything would depend on their constant and intelligent obedience to God who was giving them the land. God wanted to teach Israel the love that is the real fulfilling of the law (Romans 13:8-10; Matthew 22:37-40).

Moses now sets forth the law simply and clearly so that it would take a living hold of the people. God says, "You are My people; I love you. I have chosen you; I am in the midst of you. I will protect you. I am only asking you to obey Me for your good" (paraphrased from several passages). He repeatedly reminds them that they are "a people holy to the Lord" (7:6; 14:2,21; 26:19). Because God's people are His, He wants them to walk in the world in the way that befits them, separating themselves from evil (chap. 14). They should show charity toward their fellow humans (chap. 15). They must

In the first four books of the Pentateuch, God is choosing Israel. Now He is letting Israel choose Him.

Besides Moses, only Caleb and Joshua were left from the generation that had come out of Egypt. All the others were dead. The younger generation who now lived had suffered hardships in the wilderness wanderings and were ready and anxious for conquest! But Moses must rehearse the law to them. He knows his work is finished, for God has told him another will lead them into Canaan (Numbers 20:12).

Moses was now one hundred and twenty years old. We see him giving his farewell address to the people whom he had led these past forty years.

Moses gives the children of Israel a look back. He recalls the history of Israel and reviews their wanderings. He reminds them of God's faithfulness and urges them to be grateful and obedient. He likens God's care of them to a loving father who cherishes his little ones lest they should be lost in the wilderness or be injured by the heat of the sun.

gather together to worship (*chap. 16*). (See *Hebrews 10:25*.)

Today people are careless about church going and worship. This speaks of spiritual decay. God demands discipline. (See *Deuteronomy 17*.)

In Deuteronomy 18, God tells of the great Prophet, the Lord Jesus Christ. He alone knows the future. In this day, many are turning to enchanters, soothsayers, fortune-tellers, mediums, consulters with familiar spirits and the black art of sorcery. Spiritualism is rampant today! If you want to know what God thinks about the modern seance, look up Isaiah 8:19,20; Leviticus 19:31; 20:6; and study the dark story in 1 Samuel 28 in the light of 1 Chronicles 10:13.

If we read Deuteronomy 21:22-23 and compare it with John 19:31, we see why Christ was accursed as He hung between heaven and earth on the cross. In Galatians 3:10-13 we read that He is cursed because He was bearing our sin (*2 Corinthians 5:21*). What effect did this have upon Paul (*2 Corinthians 5:14-15*)?

Moses' Third Address: "Looking Out"
Deuteronomy 27—33

We see Moses giving the people some solemn warnings. He first spoke of the blessings the children of Israel could enjoy if they would be obedient. He then told them the results of disobedience.

Deuteronomy 28 is a most remarkable chapter. It traces what Israel might have been through obedience (*1-14*) and is yet to be in the millennial age to come (see *Isaiah 60—62; Zechariah 14:8-21; Jeremiah 31:1-9; Deuteronomy 30:1-10; Romans 11:25-31*).

Moses spoke to Joshua, his personal attendant throughout the wilderness wandering. He was one of the spies who dared to believe God. He was now eighty years old and Moses committed to him the leadership of this great people! Read his words in Deuteronomy 31:7,8.

The charge that Moses gave to the people and to Joshua was built on one great fact, "The Lord is with you; be strong." If God is present, fear is baseless!

This grand old man, one hundred and twenty years of age, stood a witness to the grace of God. He sang a song for Israel (*chap. 32*).

In Deuteronomy 34, after the song and final words of blessing, Moses went up to Mount Nebo's heights (sometimes called Mount Pisgah) and there God showed him the Promised Land toward which his face had so long been set. We know he died there and the Lord buried him. No one knows where.

Whether Moses himself wrote Deuteronomy 34 by revelation or whether Joshua added it later is immaterial.

The horde of slaves made into a nation by Moses wept for him thirty days. Had it not been for their perversity they might still have had him with them.

Books of History
of the Old Testament

*Joshua • Judges • Ruth
1 Samuel • 2 Samuel • 1 Kings • 2 Kings
1 Chronicles • 2 Chronicles
Ezra • Nehemiah • Esther*

7. UNDERSTANDING

 Joshua

Joshua Portrays Jesus Christ, Captain of Our Salvation

"Take possession of the land the Lord your God is giving you for your own" (*Joshua 1:11*). It is God's to give! It is ours to possess!

When we open the book of Joshua, we are beginning the second division of the Old Testament, the books of History. No book has more encouragement and wisdom for the soldier of the cross than this book of Joshua. It is full of spiritual truth.

Joshua is the book of conquest or the battlefield of the Canaan heritage. This book relates the settlement of the children of Israel in Canaan, proving God's faithfulness in keeping His promise with Abraham. What was the promise (*Genesis 12:1-3*)?

This book bears the name of Joshua, the hero of this great conquest. The name "Joshua" was originally *Hoshea*, meaning salvation, or *Jehoshua*, the Lord's salvation. Joshua is called the servant of Jehovah, one by whom God issued His orders and by whom He accomplished His purposes—God's prime minister.

The chosen people were led out of bondage by Moses, and led into the Promised Land by Joshua. In this book, Israel not only overcomes the enemy, but also occupies the land God promised them.

The nation that was led out by Moses was led in by Joshua!

Moses was dead, but the march must continue! God's voice was still speaking to Joshua. Yes, God's voice is still speaking today and if we listen we will hear Him speak to us.

God had been preparing Joshua for years. He was born in slavery in Egypt, but God led him out and made him a colaborer of Moses. He was always a valiant captain. He was the one that was almost stoned to death because he urged the children of Israel to advance into Canaan forty years earlier (*Numbers 14:6-10*).

Remember as we study this book of Joshua that God gives—people take. This book focuses on overcoming the enemy and occupying the land. God says, "Take it all."

This book seems to fall into two great parts:

1. Conquest of the Promised Land: chapters 1—12.
2. Occupation of the Promised Land: chapters 13—24.

Mobilization of the Army
Joshua 1—2

Open your Bible to the text, Joshua 1—2. We find the children of Israel right on the border of the land of promise, near the banks of the Jordan. The boundaries of the Promised Land, as given in Joshua 1:4 are: wilderness on the south, the Lebanon mountains on the north, Euphrates River on the east, and the Mediterranean on the west.

Joshua is the leader of the children of Israel now! We hear God say, "Moses my servant is dead. Now then,

Selected Bible Readings

Sunday: Joshua's Commission (*Joshua 1—2*)

Monday: Crossing the Jordan (*Joshua 3*)

Tuesday: The Fall of Jericho (*Joshua 6*)

Wednesday: The Sin of Achan (*Joshua 7*)

Thursday: Occupation of the Land (*Joshua 11*)

Friday: Caleb's Possession (*Joshua 14*)

Saturday: Joshua's Farewell (*Joshua 24*)

you and all these people, get ready to cross the Jordan River" (*Joshua 1:2*). Joshua stands with bowed head and a lonely heart, for his wise counselor and friend has gone. But God said to him, "I will never leave you nor forsake you. . . . Be strong and courageous. Do not be terrified; do not be discouraged, for the Lord your God will be with you wherever you go" (*Joshua 1:5,9*).

To the Christian, Moses represents the law. Joshua represents Christ. Christ alone can lead us into the inheritance that is ours. Paul says, "not by works, so that no one can boast" (*Ephesians 2:9*).

We see an anxious crowd of people all waiting to enter the land they had so long been promised. Can you picture the row upon row of tents and all the people wondering when Joshua would say, "Go"? Joshua sent men through the camp to tell them that in three days they would cross the

Jordan, and to be prepared for the journey (*Joshua 1:10-11*).

God called Joshua to lead the children of Israel into the Promised Land. We have the words that must have come to him in answer to a prayer for help in his great undertaking. "As I was with Moses, so I will be with you; I will never leave you nor forsake you" (*Joshua 1:5*). These words are just as true for us.

God says some very important things in this passage:

1. Set your foot down. "I will give you every place where you set your foot, as I promised Moses" (*Joshua 1:3*).

2. Take it all. "Your territory will extend from the desert to Lebanon, and from the great river, the Euphrates—all the Hittite country—to the Great Sea on the west" (*Joshua 1:4*).

Not until Solomon's day, some five hundred years later, was this fully realized (*2 Chronicles 9:26*), but it was coming all the time.

3. Be on the move. "Moses my servant is dead. Now then, you and all these people, get ready to cross the Jordan River" (*Joshua 1:2*).

4. Take the sword. "Do not let this Book of the Law depart from your mouth" (*Joshua 1:8*).

5. Go in for a full life. "Three days from now you will cross the Jordan here to go in and take possession of the land the Lord your God is giving you for your own" (*Joshua 1:11*).

Joshua called the officers together and gave them detailed directions. Hear these men speak. "Whatever you have commanded us we will do, and wherever you send us we will go" (*Joshua 1:16*). They were ready for any service.

Joshua sends two scouts to bring a report of the land. Read the story of Rahab and the spies in Joshua 2.

Joshua asked them especially to find

out the strength of Jericho for this was the first stronghold they would have to attack after crossing the river. The spies aroused suspicion but were saved from death by Rahab who hid them under flax that was spread on the roof of her house. The spies learned from Rahab that all the city was in terror of the Israelites, and they promised they would spare her and her household when the city was taken. Rahab let them down by a rope through the window of her house which was part of the city wall, and they returned to tell Joshua the good news that "all the people are melting in fear because of us" (*Joshua 2:24*).

Rahab hung a scarlet cord out of her window so that her house might be marked and spared when the city was destroyed. We find this woman's name in the genealogy of Jesus (*Matthew 1:5*).

The Canaanites, the people of the land, were the descendants of Canaan, the son of Ham. They were a wicked and idolatrous people. God had warned them in the destruction of Sodom and Gomorrah (*Genesis 19:24-25*), but they had not changed a bit. Now God was going to destroy their power and give their land to the Israelites.

Forward March *Joshua 3—5*

Read Joshua 3—5. Encouraged by the report the spies had brought, the Israelites moved from their encampment at Shittim, six miles from the Jordan, to a spot near the swollen stream. At dawn the officers passed through the camp and ordered all to watch the Ark and follow it at a distance of two thousand cubits (about a thousand yards), "then you will know which way to go, since you have never been this way before." (*Joshua 3:4*). The great leader, Joshua, instructed the

people to sanctify themselves, for on the morrow the Lord would do wonders among them (*Joshua 3:5*).

The children of Israel had followed the cloud in the wilderness. Now they would follow the Ark of the Covenant, which represented the presence of Jehovah.

The long journey in the desert was over, and the mystery of an unknown country and an unknown life lay before them.

At the beginning of the Exodus from Egypt there was a crossing of the Red Sea. Now at the close of Exodus, there is a crossing of the Jordan river. Both were most memorable events in the history of the children of Israel. Only Caleb and Joshua remained of their generation. Why?

It was the time of the overflow of the Jordan, and the people of Jericho must have thought it impossible for the Israelites to cross or they would have been there to oppose them. The way to cross the Jordan was to cross it. Joshua told the priests to take up the Ark and step into the Jordan, when the river was overflowing all its banks. When the soles of their feet touched the waters of the Jordan, they stood on dry ground. And all Israel passed over on dry ground (*Joshua 3:9-17*). With men this is impossible, but with God all things are possible.

What was the Ark? The symbol of the divine Presence. And Christ is the reality of the divine Presence. He says, "Surely I am with you always" (*Matthew 28:20*).

He goes before us and says, "Follow me," and He sends His Holy Spirit to whisper in our ear and say, "This is the way, walk ye in it." The living Ark of the Covenant is still our guide. He will guide us in the little as well as the great things of life. Yes, "If the Lord delights in a man's way, he makes his steps firm" (*Psalm 37:23*).

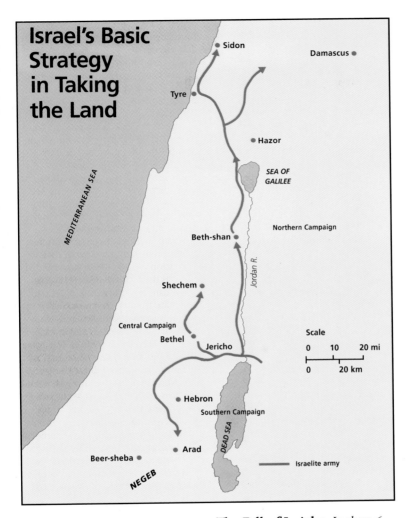

Israel's Basic Strategy in Taking the Land

Sidon

Damascus

Tyre

Hazor

SEA OF GALILEE

Northern Campaign

Beth-shan

Jordan R.

Shechem

Central Campaign

Bethel

Jericho

MEDITERRANEAN SEA

Scale

0   10   20 mi

0   20 km

Hebron

Southern Campaign

DEAD SEA

Beer-sheba

Arad

NEGEB

——— Israelite army

The Bible tells us of the crossing of the river. From the riverbed, "right where the priests stood," the stones were taken and piled up on the other shore as a lasting memorial of the wonders God did for them (*Joshua 4:3*). No formal prayer is recorded, but memorial stones are set up. The people wanted to perpetuate the memory of their great Deliverer.

The Fall of Jericho *Joshua 6*

Jericho was not far from the Jordan and about a short twenty-minute walk from the encampment of Gilgal.

The walls of Jericho had to come down so that the Israelites might proceed to conquer the Promised Land, for Jericho was the key to southern Canaan. How could this be brought about? The Israelites were confident their Leader

The Central Campaign

▲ Mt. Ebal

● Shechem

Mt. Gerizim ▲

Scale

0 ————— 5 mi

0 ——— 5 km

● Adam

Jordan R.

Bethel ●

Ai ●

● Gilgal

● Jericho

Shittim ●

PLAINS OF MOAB

—————— Israelite army

●●●●● Battle

DEAD SEA

this was Jehovah's plan of conquest. God put an invisible band around the foundation of that city wall and tightened it, and when God does that to the foundation of any structure, national or personal—beware!

It is not hard work that is needed; it is the lack of vision that makes us fail (*Proverbs 29:18*). It is easy to blow a trumpet; a little thing to walk around a wall. The hard thing is to see the good in it. Say, "Lord, one step is enough for me."

Campaign at Ai *Joshua 7—8*

The capture of Jericho gave the Israelites a chance to enter central Canaan. The next place strategically important was Ai, which commanded the entrance into the valley leading into western Canaan.

As he had done in the case of Jericho, Joshua sent spies to Ai to learn the situation. Made overconfident by their recent success, they gave poor counsel on their return, saying, "Not all the people will have to go up against Ai. Send two or three thousand men to take it and do not weary all the people, for only a few men are there" (*Joshua 7:3*). The small force was sent up the steep ascent, but when the garrison at Ai sallied forth and attacked them, the Israelites fled without striking a blow. In the disaster all saw the withdrawal of God's guiding hand. They soon learned that they could not trust in their own strength alone. "'Not by might nor by power, but by my Spirit,' says the Lord Almighty" (*Zechariah 4:6*).

One man's sin caused Israel's defeat. (Israel had become a nation and no one could act alone.) Achan had hidden the wedge of gold. Read the story in Joshua 7. Beware of the wedge of gold (*Joshua 7:13*)! Achan alone was guilty, yet we read: "Israel has sinned;

knew what they did not, and that they would soon enter the city. What was their task? Read Joshua 6.

The procession of priests, Ark, men and trumpets that marched around the city daily were the only visible means for its capture. How futile must such a march have seemed to the people of Jericho, yes, and to the Israelites themselves. But God knew what He would do.

The fall of Jericho before the blast of Joshua's rams' horns was a miracle so stupendous that the rationalist can but discredit it. The Israelites believed they were following God's plan. The seven trumpets, leading a procession seven days, and seven times on the seventh day, showed the Israelites that

The ruins of Jericho today. Jericho was the first city in Canaan to fall to Joshua and the Israelites.

they have violated my covenant, which I commanded them to keep. They have taken some of the devoted things; they have stolen, they have lied, they have put them with their own possessions" (*Joshua 7:11*).

No one can sin in total isolation. None of us live exclusively for ourselves. One stricken with chicken pox can infect an entire schoolroom.

Every sin you commit will hunt you down, find you out and make you pay.

Central Campaign *Joshua 10*

The Israelites went out a second time to Ai. This time they were victors. The taking of Ai shows real military strategy. In working for the Lord there must always be a recognition of the value of the best in human reason, but strategy without obedience is worth nothing. Dwight L. Moody said, "Work as if everything depended upon you, and pray as if everything depended upon God."

The fame of Israel began to spread far and wide. The kings of Canaan formed a league against the oncoming hosts. But we read of the treaty with the Gibeonites who played a trick on the Israelites. As a result Joshua condemned the Gibeonites to become the "woodcutters and water carriers for the entire community" (*Joshua 9:21*).

Then Joshua routed the allied army. Read about the hail storm and the prolonged daylight God sent to help His warrior (*Joshua 10:10,11,13*).

"O sun, stand still over Gibeon" (*Joshua 10:12*). Ordinary things come to a standstill when God's work is on.

Northern Campaign
Joshua 11

After all of central and southern Canaan was in Israel's possession, a new confederacy had to be faced and conquered. The northern kings had joined together and tried to break the power of the conquering Israelites. But in divine strength Joshua routed them all. This did not all happen at once. Scripture says that it took a "long time." At last the land rested from war (*Joshua 11:23*).

Jerusalem is so named here for the first time in the Bible. It is a city with a great past history and a bright future history. Here Christ will reign when He comes again in power and great glory (*Luke 21:27*).

We see God judging these wicked people, the Canaanites. At that period Canaan had already behind it a long civilized past. The country was filled with schools and libraries, with richly furnished palaces, and workshops of artisans. The cities on the coast had their fleets, partly of merchantmen, partly of warships, and an active trade was carried on with all parts of the known world.

Division of the Land
(*Joshua 13—24*)

Joshua was an old man now, about ninety years of age, and he realized that the conquest of the land was by no means complete. There yet remained "very large areas of land to be taken over" (*Joshua 13:1*). In order that the children of Israel might do this, he divided it among them.

"This is Judah's; this is Asher's; this is Simeon's; and this is Benjamin's," we hear the people saying as the scene opens. They said this even while the Amorites, the Jebusites, and the Hittites were in open possession of the Promised Land (*Joshua 13*). The di-

vision made of the land was the announcement by faith of certain things that under God's guidance they proposed to accomplish. A long struggle followed.

Although all this land was allotted to the various tribes, all of it was not conquered until the time of David. All that was subdued at the time of Joshua was the mountainous land; the cities and the plains were hardly touched.

The strong did not take the best part of the land because they were strong, leaving the fragments for the weak. Neither did the rich purchase the choicest spots, leaving the poor the more undesirable sites. They tried to determine God's will in the matter. God cares about distribution of goods.

God is concerned in a more equal division of His blessings in this world when He rules that "every man will sit under his own vine and under his own fig tree" (*Micah 4:4*).

When the assignment was made by lot no one could be jealous. They met before the Ark of Jehovah, the symbol of His presence.

"Moses . . . had not granted the Levites an inheritance among the rest" (*Joshua 14:3*). You remember that this

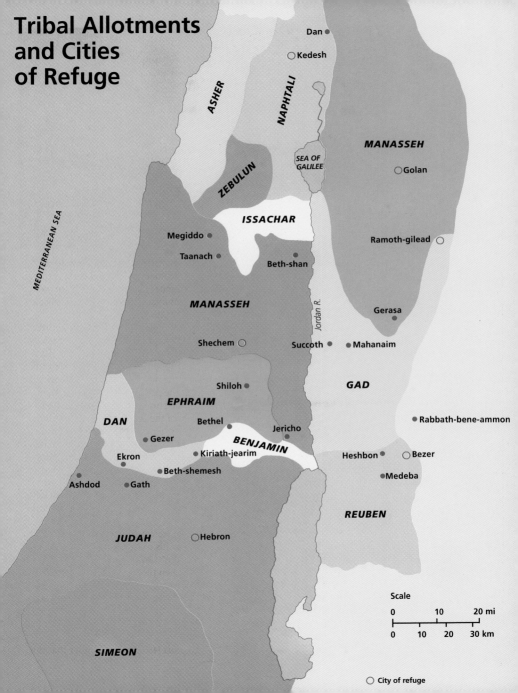

Tribal Allotments and Cities of Refuge

ASHER

NAPHTALI

Dan •

○ Kedesh

MANASSEH

SEA OF GALILEE

○ Golan

ZEBULUN

MEDITERRANEAN SEA

ISSACHAR

Megiddo •

Ramoth-gilead ○

Taanach •

Beth-shan •

Jordan R.

MANASSEH

Gerasa •

Shechem ○

Succoth • • Mahanaim

Shiloh •

GAD

EPHRAIM

DAN

Bethel •

Jericho •

• Rabbath-bene-ammon

• Gezer

BENJAMIN

Ekron •

• Kiriath-jearim

Heshbon • ○ Bezer

Beth-shemesh •

Ashdod • • Gath

• Medeba

REUBEN

JUDAH

○ Hebron

Scale

0   10   20 mi

0   10   20   30 km

SIMEON

○ City of refuge

The Cave of Machpelah, Hebron, traditional burial place of Abraham and his family. Hebron was one of the special "cities of refuge".

tribe was set apart for the sacred service of the priesthood, therefore the Levites received no land.

The Priesthood *Joshua 14*

Caleb now was eighty-five years old! Joshua and he were alone among the spies because they had dared to trust God! Caleb asked his friend Joshua for the high and walled cities! He added, "the Lord helping me, I will drive them out just as he said" (*Joshua 14:12*). He valued his inheritance because of the hard work it offered and the opportunity it gave him for conquering it! Joshua's recognition of his friend, and of his right to a choice possession was quick and generous. He granted him the mountain and blessed his aged friend.

Caleb was old but he gloried in the hardness of the task. Horace Mann (American early champion of state-sponsored public schools) said, "Difficulties are things which show what men are."

The Lord has never promised His children that they will have an easy time serving Him. In fact, Christ said, "In this world you will have trouble" (*John 16:33*). The promise is not for ease; the promise is for victory. Christ says, "I have overcome the world." We grow in adversity, for we learn to trust the Lord more. Paul said to Timothy, "Endure hardship with us like a good soldier of Christ Jesus" (*2 Timothy 2:3*).

Caleb said, "I, however, followed the Lord my God wholeheartedly" (*Joshua 14:8*).

We might call attention to the fact that the cities of refuge that God planned, spoken of in Numbers 35:6-34 and Deuteronomy 4:41-43 and 19:4-13, are now established (*Joshua 20:1-9*).

Joshua's Farewell *Joshua 24*

Joshua had become an old man. He knew that he could not live much longer. He wanted to give the people some last words of admonition.

He called first the leaders and then all the people together and urged them to remember the power and faithfulness of God and admonished them to be faithful to Him. "Now fear the Lord and serve him with all faithfulness" (*Joshua 24:14*). He warned them against apostasy. He said, "then choose for yourselves this day whom you will serve, whether the gods your forefathers served beyond the River, or the gods of the Amorites, in whose land you are living. But as for me and my household, we will serve the Lord" (*Joshua 24:15*).

It is a good thing to have people make an open confession and commit themselves to a solemn promise. These older men who had made an open confession were true to their promises.

The people said that day, "Far be it from us to forsake the Lord to serve other gods! . . . We too will serve the Lord" (*Joshua 24:16-18*).

At 110 years of age the grand old man, Joshua, died. The book closes with death. We see three graves. Joshua's, the great leader of Israel; Eleazer's, the priest; and Joseph's, whose bones the children of Israel had carried with them from Egypt and which were now buried in the land of promise.

Here is a great tribute to a great leader, "Israel served the Lord throughout the lifetime of Joshua" (*Joshua 24:31*).

Canaan, or the Promised Land, was 180 miles long and approximately 40 miles wide. The boundaries were the wilderness on the south, the Lebanon ranges on the north, the Euphrates on the east and the Mediterranean on the west.

It was in the center of mighty civilizations that made ancient history:
Egypt—300 miles to the south
Nineveh—700 miles northeast
Babylon—700 miles east
Persia—1,000 miles east
Greece—800 miles northwest
Rome—1,500 miles northwest.

Do not pray for an easy task. Pray to be stronger!

The greatness of your power is the measure of your surrender. It is not a question of who you are or of what you are, but whether God controls you.

"I . . . followed the Lord my God wholeheartedly" (Caleb).

Be sure—be sure—be sure your sin will find you out.

God commands a complete out-and-out for him.

Facts do not change; feelings do.

It is not enough to light a fire; you must put fuel on it.

8. UNDERSTANDING
Judges and Ruth

Jesus Christ, Our Deliverer Judge; Our Kinsman-Redeemer

Someone has called the book of Judges the account of the Dark Ages of the Israelite people. The people forsook God (*Judges 2:13*) and God forsook the people (*Judges 2:23*).

Ingersoll (Robert Green Ingersoll, 1833-1899, American orator known as the Great Agnostic) spoke much of "the liberty of man, woman and child." His was a godless liberty. The modern equivalent is "doing our own thing." You see this in the book of Judges.

Judges covers the period after the death of their great leader, Joshua, to the ascension of Saul to the throne of Israel. During this time, the people were ruled by judges whom God raised up to deliver His oppressed people. We read, "In those days Israel had no king" (*Judges 17:6*). It covers the history of the first 350 years in the land of promise. It gives us a record of great exploits.

It was a new hour in the history of Israel. Remember, Israel had come from a long era of bondage in Egypt to a period of forty years when she lived in tents and wandered in the wilderness. Now the march was over. The nomads were to become settlers in a land of their own. The change was not as easy for them as they expected it to be. The book of Judges is in a way another book of beginnings where we see a new nation adjusting her national life. It is filled with struggle and disasters, but also with the moral courage of a select few.

There is a decided monotony in the description of each successive stage of sin in Israel, but there is an equally remarkable variety in the instruments and methods of deliverance God used. There is something different in the story of each judge.

There are fourteen judges—Othniel, Ehud, Shamgar, Deborah, Gideon, Tola, Jair, Jephthah, Ibzan, Elon, Abdon, Samson, Eli and Samuel. (Abimelech, a petty ruler, was not called of God to judge.)

There were three types of judges:

1. The warrior-judges as Gideon and

Selected Bible Readings

Sunday: Only Partial Victories (*Judges 1—2:5*)

Monday: Institution of the Judges (*Judges 2:16—3:11*)

Tuesday: Deborah and Barak (*Judges 4:4—5:31*)

Wednesday: Gideon, the Farmer (*Judges 6:1-16; 7:16-25*)

Thursday: Jephthah's Terrible Vow (*Judges 11:12-40*)

Friday: Samson, the Strong Man (*Judges 15 and 16*)

Saturday: The Story of Ruth (*Book of Ruth*)

Samson
2. Priest-judges as Eli
3. Prophet-judges as Deborah and
   Samuel.

The chief judges were Deborah,
Gideon, Samson and Samuel.

Just how long these judges ruled we
do not know, but it is believed about
350 years. The judges were not just one
governor after another. They were
probably raised up as deliverers on
different occasions in different parts
of the land, and there could have been
overlapping of the time of their rule.

A phrase runs through the last five
chapters of the book—"Everyone did
as he saw fit" (*Judges 17:6*; "Every man
did that which was right in his own
eyes," *KJV*). Mark this phrase every
time you find it. We find the people
falling away from Jehovah and worshiping the gods of the nations round
about them (*Judges 2:13*). They forgot
that God had chosen them for a purpose—to tell the world the truth that
there is but one true God. In punishment for their sins God would deliver
them into the hand of that nation.
Then under the oppression of these
new enemies they would cry to God
for mercy and He would hear them
and send a judge to deliver them. And
so the book is full of rebellion, punishment, misery and deliverance. It
has a minor key throughout.

The book begins with compromise
and ends with confusion. This is what
happens in every unsurrendered life!

After reading Judges you may think
that the whole of these three or four
hundred years was spent in rebellion
and sin. But if you read it carefully,
you will see that only about one hundred out of these possibly 350 years
were spent in disloyalty to God.

One thing we learn in the book of
Judges is that a people who spend
much of their time in disobedience to
God make little progress during their

lifetime. The book of Numbers recounts the forty years of wandering in
the wilderness, but this book repeats
again and again a record of departure
from God.

This book is in sharpest contrast to
Joshua.

In Joshua	In Judges
Joy	Sobs
Heavenly vision	Earthly in emphasis
Victory	Defeat
Progress	Declension
Faith	Unbelief
Freedom	Servitude

Here is an outline for Judges that is
easy to remember. "Seven apostasies,
seven servitudes to seven idolatrous
and cruel nations, seven deliverances!"

We read of humans' constant failure
and God's constant mercy.

Study carefully the following:

1. The wickedness of the human
heart (*Judges 2:11-13,17,19; 8:33-35; 10:6;
13:1*).

2. God's delight in using the weak
things (*1 Corinthians 1:26-29*). Note the
stories of: Ehud, an assassin with a
homemade dagger (*Judges 3*);
Deborah, a woman (*Judges 4*; see also
Judges 9:53); Gideon, from an obscure
family in the smallest tribe (*Judges 6*);
Shamgar, a rustic with an ox goad
(*Judges 3:31*); Gideon's little pitcher-
armed band (*Judges 7*); the jaw bone
used by Samson (*Judges 15:14-19*).

3. The Holy Spirit in Judges.
Othniel—"The Spirit of the Lord came
upon him" (*Judges 3:10*). Gideon—
"The Spirit of the Lord clothed himself
with Gideon" (see note on *Judges 6:34,
NASB*). Jephthah—"The Spirit of the
Lord came upon Jephthah" (*Judges
11:29*). Samson—"The Spirit of the Lord
began to stir him" (*Judges 13:25*; see
also *14:6; 15:14*, etc.).

Over the book of Judges as a guide
to its spiritual interpretation might be
written Zechariah's great word

(*Zechariah 4:6*)—"'Not by might nor by power, but by my Spirit,' says the Lord Almighty."

Human pride would love to believe that humanity's trend is upward. But God's Word shows us that the natural course is downward.

Israel's Failure *Judges 1:1—3:4*

Joshua had died (*Judges 1:1*). Much of the Promised Land must be conquered. The first act of the children of Israel was to seek God's will about how they should commence the final conquest. They began well. They consulted God.

God appointed Judah, the kingly tribe (*Judges 1:2*). The work began in earnest but it ended in weakness. The people did not obey God.

Israel's troubles were due directly to her disobedience to God. They did not exterminate the enemies in the land, but rather worshiped the idols of the peoples and became corrupted in their morals.

The children of Israel went into the land and settled where they wanted and began to raise enough for their living. Soon enemies without would come along, catch the tribe off guard, and take people captive. Their enemies were also traitors within. God had told His people to do away with them.

Chapter 1 is a failure chapter. They did not drive out the enemy as God had commanded. "But Manasseh did not drive out the people of Beth Shan or Taanach or Dor . . . Nor did Ephraim . . . Nor did Zebulun . . . Nor did Asher . . . Neither did Naphtali . . . The Amorites confined the Danites . . ." (*Judges 1:27-36*), six nonfulfillments in succession.

Since chapter 1 records a series of disobediences, of course chapter 2 is a chapter of defeat and failure. God gave them up to their own will. God said, "'You shall not make a covenant with the people of this land, but you shall break down their altars.' Yet you have disobeyed me. Why have you done this? Now therefore I tell you that I will not drive them out before you; they will be thorns in your sides and their gods will be a snare to you" (*Judges 2:2-3*). The children of Israel brought on their own judgment upon themselves and became their own executioners. Several times Israel was on the verge of being exterminated, but thankfully God intervened. Sometimes we wonder why God didn't remove all the enemies from the Promised Land before He let the children of Israel go in. But God had a definite reason (*Judges 3:1-4*).

God uses the results of our lack of faith in Him to prove to us our sin and weakness. He does not forget His covenant, but He allows our very weakness, our guilty weakness, to drive us back to Him.

God wanted the chosen people to realize that they were a holy people. They must not mix with the wicked nations about them. They must continually separate themselves. God knew that separation makes a people strong. Christians today must remember that they cannot mix with the world. They must keep close to God and war against sin and unrighteousness. God wants us to be good warriors. Read Ephesians 6:10-18 and see the armor He provides.

And so we see that an uncritical toleration toward a people so utterly corrupt resulted in the undoing of God's chosen people. See the result of this disobedience, Judges 2:20-22.

The Judges *Judges 3:5—16:31*

Here we have a picture of seven failures, seven servitudes and seven deliverances. The Israelites intermarried with the surrounding idolatrous peoples, worshiped at their shrines and practiced their values.

First Oppression, Judges 3:7-11:
    Sin—Idolatry
    Punishment—Eight years
    Deliverer and Judge—Othniel

Second Oppression, Judges 3:12-31:
    Sin—Immorality and idolatry
    Punishment—Eighteen years
    Deliverer and Judge—Ehud and Shamgar

Third Oppression, Judges 4—5:
    Sin—Departed from God
    Punishment—Twenty years
    Deliverer and Judge—Deborah and Barak

Fourth Oppression, Judges 6—8:32:
    Sin—Departed from God
    Punishment—Midianites for seven years
    Deliverer and Judge—Gideon

Fifth Oppression, Judges 8:33—10:5:
    Sin—Departed from God
    Punishment—Civil war, etc.
    Deliverer and Judge—Tola and Jair

Sixth Oppression, Judges 10:6—12:15:
    Sin—Idolatry increased
    Punishment—Philistines and Ammonites, eighteen years
    Deliverer and Judge—Jephthah (and successors)

Seventh Oppression, Judges 13—16:
    Sin—Departed from God
    Punishment—Philistines, forty years
    Deliverer and Judge—Samson

Joshua had no successor. After his death, each tribe acted independently. There was no capital and no fixed government.

There was no unity of action, except in the time of danger when the tribes combined for their own good. When the people sinned against God, their enemies defeated them and ruled them. When in their distress they sought the Lord, He sent great leaders called judges who delivered them.

But this scene is not only filled with servitude; it also records deliverances, for God was always near His people, and when they cried, He answered. God is always brooding over His disobedient children. He promises us that He will never leave us nor forsake us (*Hebrews 13:5*). We see defeat on our part but deliverance on God's part. "Where sin increased, grace increased all the more" (*Romans 5:20*).

We see His dealings with His own rebellious people whom He has crowned with His best blessings and upon whom He has lavished His tender love. We find the patience of God and His constant readiness to respond to the least sign of penitence in His people (*Judges 3:9,15; 4:3-7; 6:6-12; 10:15-16*).

He repeated His mercy again and again although it was never appreciated. If you think on these things it will draw you nearer to this God of mercy and love and grace. Look up, repent and trust God.

We have found that God fulfilled His purpose for Israel by leaving around them in Canaan a circle of strong tribes unlike each other. It is said, "These are the nations the Lord left to test all those Israelites who had not experienced any of the wars in Canaan. . . They were left to test the Israelites to see whether they would obey the Lord's commands, which he had given their forefathers through Moses" (*Judges 3:1,4*).

One of the best-known nations whom the Lord used to test Israel was the Philistines, who had settled on the coastal plain. In wealth and civilization they no doubt presented a real contrast to the Israelites, and their equipment gave them great advantage in war. Even in the period of the judges there were imposing temples in the Philistine cities. The Israelites feared the Philistines and did not mix freely with them. They only met in war.

First Apostasy *Judges 3:7-11*

We find the Israelites settling among the Syrian nations. They seemed too ready to live at peace with these other nations and to yield not a little for the sake of peace. (Read the few verses *3:5-8* to see what they did.) They intermarried to make their position safer. They traded with the Amorites, Hivites and Perizzites. They determined on boundary lines to make things run smoothly. Next they accepted their neighbors' religion (*Judges 3:7*) and then their bad customs. But soon the Mesopotamians began to oppress them (*Judges 3:8*). The Israelites then realized that they had a God from whom they had departed. Israel was a prodigal people. They had left the God whose presence before had assured them victory. For eight years they were under the oppression of these northern nations. Year by year conditions grew worse.

It was from the far south that God sent help in answer to their pitiful cry (*Judges 3:9*). The deliverer was Othniel, who was Caleb's nephew. No doubt he had had frequent skirmishes with the Arab marauders from the wilderness. "The Spirit of the Lord came upon him, so that he became Israel's judge and went to war" (*Judges 3:10*). First he prayed, then went out to battle.

Othniel's first concern was to put away the idolatry of Israel and teach them the law of the Lord and remind them of their calling as a nation. Soon success and victory was theirs (*Judges 3:10-11*).

Othniel, the first of the judges, was one of the best. He pointed Israel to a higher level of reverence for God and

His plans. Forty years of rest followed.

No one can do real service for his or her country who does not fear God and love righteousness more than country.

Second Apostasy
Judges 3:12-31

God used different kinds of personalities to deliver His people. Israel's second judge, Ehud, is in marked contrast to Othniel, the judge without reproach.

The long peace the country enjoyed after the Mesopotamian army had been driven out let the people fall into prosperity and to lapse again into spiritual weakness (*Judges 3:12*). This time the Moabites led the attack. The punishment lasted for eighteen years. Again the people cried to God, and Ehud, with whom Shamgar's name is associated, was the deliverer (*Judges 3:15*). This Benjamite chose his own method of action and assassinated the Moabite king. His crime is one that stinks in our nostrils. But eighty years of rest for Israel followed (*Judges 3:30*).

Shamgar, the man of the ox goad, follows in line (*Judges 3:31*).

Third Apostasy
Judges 4—5

Now a prophetess arises in Israel (*Judges 4:4*). She was one of those rare women whose heart burns with enthusiasm when people's hearts are despondent. Many a queen, like England's Elizabeth II, has reigned with honor and wisdom, and often a woman's voice has struck a deep note that has roused nations.

Israel had been oppressed for twenty years (*Judges 4:3*). The oppression was terrible under Sisera. Again they cried and God heard. This time the story of deliverance is filled with romance and song. Deborah, the daughter of the people, had gained the confidence of the people to such a degree that they had appointed her as judge.

Deborah called Barak to help her. Together they delivered Israel from their oppression. The land had been so filled with Canaanite spoilers that the highways could not be used. War was everywhere, and the Israelites were defenseless and crushed; but God delivered them.

After Jabin, king of Canaan, was defeated and his nine hundred chariots turned into plowshares, we might expect that Israel would at last make a real start to accomplish her true career. The tribes have had their third lesson and should know by now the danger of leaving God. Without God they were as weak as babes. Will they not now bend themselves to Him? Not yet. Not for more than forty years. The true reformer had not yet come. Deborah's work was not in vain. She was destroying the pagan altars and improving the land. Everywhere they were plowing new ground, building houses and repairing roads. But they were falling into the old habit of friendly association with the Canaanites.

Following deliverance from this servitude the land rested for forty years.

Fourth Apostasy
Judges 6—8:32

But a fourth apostasy came (*Judges 6:1*). This time the deliverer was Gideon, a humble farmer. The Midianites had held the Israelites under bondage for seven years. So terrible was it that the people hid themselves in caves and dens and were hunted in the mountains (*Judges 6:2*). Again they cried unto the Lord. Gideon was called to act as deliverer. He broke down the altar of Baal and restored the worship of God. The story of the conflict is one of the most fascinating in history. Everyone knows the story of Gideon and his band of 300 with their pitchers and horns. Refresh yourself with this story (*Judges 7:7-24*).

After the great victory over the Midianites, the Israelites sought to make Gideon king. He refused.

Gaza

Gideon was not perfect. We find in the record some things that he should not have done, but he did have faith in Jehovah that God could honor, and He gave his name a place in the Hall of Faith in Hebrews 11.

Fifth Apostasy
Judges 8:33—10:5

A fifth time, we see the people falling into the sin of idolatry by worshiping the Baalim almost immediately upon the death of Gideon. The record is: "No sooner had Gideon died than the Israelites again prostituted themselves to the Baals" (*Judges 8:33*). How often the personal influence of the hero is everything while he is alive, but confusion follows on his death.

Gideon was one of the most successful judges to maintain order, and the country was in quietness forty years. But no sooner was Gideon's funeral over than discord began. There was no rightful ruler to follow. Gideon left many sons, but not one of them could take his place. Abimelech, a son of Gideon, unprincipled and brutal, secured the allegiance of the men at Shechem and usurped the position of king. He ruled three years in tyranny. He was slain by a woman and a period of forty-five years of quietness followed under the judgeship of Tola and Jair.

Those who are busy are those who have moved the world upward!

Sixth Apostasy
Judges 10:6—12:15

In the sixth apostasy we find the people almost entirely given over to idolatry. Their condition was appalling. God sent judgment this time from the Philistines for eighteen years. At last, sorely distressed, they cried to God. For the first time it is recorded that He refused to hear them and reminded them of how repeatedly He had delivered them (*Judges 10:13*). The true attitude of Jehovah toward them is found in this statement—"And he could bear Israel's misery no longer" (*Judges 10:16*).

Deliverance came through Jephthah. Jephthah's history is full of interest. He was a man of heroic daring and impetuous foolishness. Read the story of his vows and victories, especially the vow he made concerning his only child (*Judges 11:30-40*). After his great victory, Jephthah judged Israel only six years.

Seventh Apostasy
Judges 13—16

The seventh apostasy opens with the words, "Again the Israelites did evil in the eyes of the Lord" (*Judges 13:1*). This time they were disciplined by the Philistines under whose awful oppression they lived for forty years. Here we read the story of Samson. It is a story filled with opportunity and failure. This man was appointed of God before birth, to deliver Israel from the Philistines (*Judges 13:5*).

In those days, everything was dependent upon physical strength. That was what made a leader great. In this case, God used it to begin the deliverance from the Philistines. Everything should have been in Samson's favor, but he entered into an unholy alliance, which meant his downfall. The final fall occurred at Gaza (*Judges 16*). Nothing is more pathetic than Samson, blind and bound, grinding in the house of the Philistines, when he ought to have been delivering his nation from them (*Judges 16:20,21*).

The story ends with Samson and is taken up in 1 Samuel. The remaining chapters, and the book of Ruth, have their chronological place in this period.

The Appendix
Judges 17—21

These last chapters give us a picture of anarchy and confusion. Israel had forsaken God and now we see the depths into which they have sunk. Read Judges 17:6 and you will find the reason for it all.

First, we find confusion in the religious life of the nation (*Judges 17,18*).

Second, we find confusion in the moral life of the nation (*Judges 19*).

Third, we find confusion in the political life (*Judges 21*).

These events no doubt took place soon after Joshua's death. It gives us a picture of the internal condition of the chosen people. The story of the backsliding of individuals is followed by the backsliding of the nation.

The last chapter proves that the children of Israel had lost the way to God's house, so low had they sunk. We find faithlessness, failure and forfeiture! But God loves His own.

Understanding Ruth

This delightful story should be read in connection with the first chapters of Judges, as no doubt it gives us an idea of the domestic life of Israel at that period of anarchy. Samuel may have been the author of this book, but no one knows where or when it was written. This book, written on a separate scroll, was read at Pentecost, the harvest festival.

Ruth was the great-grandmother of David. This book establishes the lineage of David, the ancestor of Christ. It tells of the beginning of the Messianic family within the Messianic

Bethlehem viewed from nearby fields. Ruth came to Bethlehem with her mother-in-law Naomi, and married Boaz here.

nation into which, over a thousand years later, the Messiah was to be born.

There are some interesting things to notice in this book. Ruth was a Moabitess. These people were descendants of Lot. They were pagans, worshiping many gods and goddesses. God, in establishing the family that was to produce the world's Savior, chose a beautiful pagan girl, led her to Bethlehem where she met Boaz, her "kinsman redeemer," a relative of Naomi, who first made her a family member and then made her his bride. This is God's grace. He adopts the Gentiles into Christ's family. Of course we know that although Ruth was born a pagan, through her first husband, or through Naomi, she learned of the true God.

Boaz was the son of Rahab, the harlot found in Jericho. See Matthew 1:5. So we see that David's great-grandmother was a Moabitess and his great-grandfather was half Canaanite. This is found in the bloodline of the Messiah.

9. UNDERSTANDING
First Samuel

First Samuel Portrays Jesus Christ, Our King

We enter now our study of the king books. Let us look at the six before us:

- 1 Samuel—The people's choice—Saul
- 2 Samuel—God's choice—David
- 1 Kings—Solomon and Israel
- 2 Kings—Israel's kings
- 1 Chronicles—Solomon and the Temple
- 2 Chronicles—The kings and the Temple.

Royal history begins with the book of Samuel. The long period of the rule of the judges ends with Samuel. When Samuel came into power the people were in an awful state. They had practically rejected God, and we hear them clamoring for an earthly king (*1 Samuel 8:4-7*). This book begins the five-hundred-year period of the kings of Israel (approximately 1050-586 B.C.).

The events recorded in 1 Samuel cover a period of about 115 years from the childhood of Samuel through the turbulent times of Saul to the beginning of the reign of the king whom God chose—David. In the personal lives of these three men this book gives us an exceedingly graphic picture of these times. Samuel was the last of the judges; Saul was the first of the kings. The record brings us up to the time when David is ready permanently to establish the monarchy and God is ready permanently to establish David's throne (*Psalm 89*).

The book may be divided under the names of three of its chief characters—

Samuel (*1—7*); Saul (*8—15*); and David (*16—31*). The history of this book is presented to us in the attractive cloak of biography. Everyone likes a true story.

We all have known and loved the stories recorded in 1 Samuel from the time we were little children. Who does not know the story of the boy Samuel (*chap. 3*), and David and Goliath (*chap. 17*), and the friendship of David and Jonathan (*chap. 18*)?

This book, of course, is named for its most prominent figure, Samuel. Probably he wrote the greater part of it through chapter 24. Nathan and Gad finished it (*1 Chronicles 29:29; 1 Samuel 10:25*).

Samuel, the King Maker
1 Samuel 1—7

Samuel—"name of God" is the meaning of his name. This book opens with the record of Hannah, Samuel's mother, praying for a son whom God could use. Samuel, the last of the judges, was God's answer to this prayer. "But Samuel was ministering before the Lord—a boy wearing a linen ephod" (*1 Samuel 2:18*).

Throughout Samuel's long and useful life he was God's man. He was preeminently a man of prayer. This first book that bears his name is a marvelous study in the place and power of prayer, illustrated from life. He was a child of prayer (*1 Samuel 3:1-19*); he brought vic-

Selected Bible Readings

Sunday:	Samuel, "Name of God" (1 Samuel 1—3)
Monday:	Samuel, the Prophet (1 Samuel 4—7)
Tuesday:	Saul, the King (1 Samuel 8—12)
Wednesday:	Saul, the Self-Willed (1 Samuel 13—15)
Thursday:	David Anointed (1 Samuel 16—18)
Friday:	David's Adventures (1 Samuel 19—20; 22;24)
Saturday:	Death of Samuel and Saul (1 Samuel 25—26; 31)

Israel had been sinning for a long time. At length the catastrophe came in the disaster recorded at this time (1 Samuel 4).

During the next invasion of their enemies—the Philistines—Israel was defeated, the Ark was taken and Eli's sons were killed. When Eli heard all this, the old man, now ninety-eight years of age, died of the shock (1 Samuel 4).

Read the history of the Philistines' possession of the Ark.

This mention of the Philistines is the first since Judges 13—16. The bondage lasted forty years (Judges 13:1), and seems to have come to a close in the days of Samuel (1 Samuel 7:13-14), about his twentieth year as judge (1 Samuel 7:21). The battle with this enemy probably was fought about four miles northwest of Jerusalem.

The Philistines were Israel's powerful enemies living to the southwest on the coast. Perhaps this renewed action on their part was due to the death of Samson. The battle soon went against Israel. They wondered why God had deserted them. While warring against God they asked God to war for them. Read the account of the revival at Mizpeh (1 Samuel 7). We cannot win while we war against God!

After Israel's first defeat by the Philistines, did they do right by looking to the Ark of God for protection (1 Samuel 4:3-7,10)?

The Ark of God was a very poor substitute for the God of the Ark. Many people think when they wear religious symbols or perform religious rituals or give money to charitable causes that they will be safe. They think that these things are a charm, or talisman, to bring them victory. Can you give some illustrations of this?

"Man's extremity is God's opportunity!" Although at the time the loss was terrible, yet God overruled for good. Through Samuel God provided

tory to his people through prayer (7:5-10); when the nation wanted a king, Samuel prayed unto the Lord (8:6); intercessory prayer was the keynote of his life (12:19-23).

In the dark and turbulent times of Israel we hear the prayer of faith from the lips of a simple trusting woman, Hannah. She asked God for a son whom she could dedicate to Him for service (1 Samuel 1:9-19).

When Samuel was born, Hannah brought him to the Tabernacle at Shiloh. Although the corruption of the priesthood was appalling, Samuel was protected and grew as a boy in the fear of the Lord (1 Samuel 1:24-28; 2:12-26; 3:1-21).

Eli was both judge and priest at this time. He had ruled for forty years. He was an indulgent father and as a result his two sons, Hophni and Phinehas, also priests, were allowed to act in a most disgraceful manner. As a result there was moral corruption and God warned Eli of the downfall of his house.

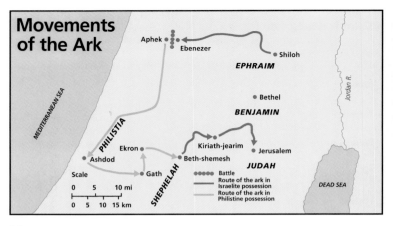

Movements of the Ark

Aphek • •
Ebenezer
Shiloh
EPHRAIM

Bethel

BENJAMIN

Kiriath-jearim
Jerusalem
Beth-shemesh
Ekron •
Ashdod
Gath
JUDAH
PHILISTIA
SHEPHELAH
MEDITERRANEAN SEA
Jordan R.
DEAD SEA

Scale
0   5   10 mi
0   5   10   15 km

●●●● Battle
—— Route of the ark in Israelite possession
—— Route of the ark in Philistine possession

(*1*) deliverance from the Philistines, (*2*) preparation for the kingdom, (*3*) a permanent sanctuary instead of a tabernacle at Shiloh and (*4*) a better priesthood.

Samuel was the last of the judges, the first of the prophets and the founder of the monarchy. Besides this, he started a school of the prophets, a kind of seminary. The record of this great man's life is beyond reproach. It is hard to find a single mistake that Samuel made.

"The Lord continued to appear at Shiloh" (*1 Samuel 3:21*). God revisited Shiloh! For Shiloh had been left. Read Judges 21:19-21. The place of worship had been turned into a place of feasting and dancing. Shiloh was the location of the house of God from the days of Joshua to Samuel. David moved it to Jerusalem. The Ark was removed by the Philistines in Samuel's childhood and from then on Shiloh ceased to be of great importance (*1 Samuel 4:3,11*).

What brought about this timely revival? Three things:

1. A praying mother, chapter 1
2. A chastened people, chapter 2
3. A faithful prophet, chapter 3.

We need a praying band of Christians, a people brought to a sense

of their need, and a consecrated preacher to bring about revival. Under the Philistine rule, Israel had no definite center of worship. Samuel grew into manhood and assumed the leadership for which he had been born. The first hopeful sign after Israel's long rebellion and defeat was that they had a sense of need. They began to want God. They "lamented after Jehovah." The Jews are going to do this again some day (*Zechariah 12:10-11*) when Christ "the one they have pierced" returns to this earth and reveals Himself to His own people.

"Well," said Samuel, "if you really mean business, you've got to show me. Do something. Prove it. How? Put away your strange gods" (author's paraphrase of *1 Samuel 7:3*). "Put away" might be translated "cut it out." If you mean business, God will mean business. Religion is not just a matter of emotion but also of the will.

The people began to lament and Samuel took advantage of this and called on them to return to their God and put away their idols. Samuel erected an altar and called it Ebenezer (*1 Samuel 7:12*). Ebenezer means "stone of help." Christ our victory is called "the stone" in both the Old Testament and the New (*Psalm 118:22; Matthew 21:42;* see also *Daniel 2:35*).

In just a brief paragraph we find the actual story of Samuel's judgeship. His home was at Ramah. From here he was a circuit rider covering his territory once a year to Bethel, Gilgal and Mizpeh, and overseeing and administering the affairs of the people (*1 Samuel 7:15-17*). We find missionaries doing this today. They choose some place as home center and then move out through the surrounding country.

Samuel established a school for the prophets at his home in Ramah. This was the beginning of the "order" of the prophets, or seers. When the Ark was taken, the priests were scattered. This is when Samuel retired to his home in Ramah. Through Samuel, God introduced a new way of dealing with Israel. He called prophets through whom He would speak. Through Samuel prophecy became a definite part of the life of Israel. Samuel gathered groups about him called "sons of the prophets." They were found in Shiloh, Gilgal, Bethel, Samaria and Ramah. (See *Acts 3:24*.)

Samuel's greatest ministry was the organization of the kingdom. The independent tribes were now going to be formed into a nation. In order to survive among other strong nations, Israel must become powerful. They had refused to take God seriously and obey Him as He had commanded them, so He permitted Samuel to find a king for them. The people wanted to be "like all the nations." God wanted them to be unlike the other nations. In Deuteronomy 17:14-20, God had prophesied that Israel should have a king, but He did not want them to become independent of Him.

Saul, the King Chosen
1 Samuel 8—15

God never intended Israel to have any king but Himself. He would send them great leaders and these in turn would receive their orders directly from Him. But Israel in her falling away had become restless. They wanted a king like the other surrounding nations. We find God granting their request. Here is a

Donkeys grazing near Samaria. Saul's search for his father's straying donkeys led him to the prophet Samuel, and to the discovery that God had selected him as Israel's king.

great lesson. We either can have God's best or His second best, His directive will or His permissive will.

Saul, their first king, was a failure. He was handsome to look at, he was tall and of a noble mien. He started out splendidly. He proved to be an able military leader. He defeated the enemies about him—the Philistines, the Amalekites and the Ammonites.

Saul was humble at first, but we find him becoming proud and disobedient to God. No man had a greater opportunity than Saul and no man ever was a greater failure. His jealousy of David bordered on insanity.

Inasmuch as Saul was granted to Israel as king in response to Israel's sinful demand for a king, contrary to God's will, did Saul ever really have a chance to "make good" in God's sight? Could he possibly have succeeded under such circumstances? Was he not condemned by God to failure even before he started as king?

We find the answer clearly in God's Word. In 1 Samuel 12:12-15, the prophet of God tells Israel that, although they had demanded their king in defiance of God (*v. 12*), if both they and their king would fear Jehovah and serve Him, all would be well. Note what follows this word of Samuel (*vv. 16-18*). Then we see the fact that Israel confesses her sin in asking for a king (*v. 19*), and Samuel reassures Israel, promising blessing if they serve God.

The only reason any soul is ever rejected by God is that that soul has first rejected God. God takes the initiative in love. "We love because he first loved us" (*1 John 4:19*). People take the initiative in sin (*1 Samuel 15:23*).

Note four things in Saul's ordination. It was a:

1. Divine ordination (*1 Samuel 9:3-20*). He went out with a bridle and came back with a scepter.

2. Prophetic ordination (*1 Samuel 10:1*). Samuel was his tutor and friend. What an advantage, but it was thrown away. How often we do this today!

3. Spiritual ordination. "The Spirit of God came upon him" (*1 Samuel 10:10*). He grieved this Spirit; then he quenched Him. If the Holy Spirit is to remain, He must be loved and obeyed.

4. Popular ordination. "Then the people shouted, 'Long live the king!'" (*1 Samuel 10:24*).

Saul failed God in several ways:

1. Saul's presumption at God's altar (*1 Samuel 13:11-13*)

2. Cruelty to his son Jonathan (*1 Samuel 14:44*)

3. Disobedience in the matter of Amalek (*1 Samuel 15:23*)

4. His jealousy and hatred of David (*1 Samuel 18:29*)

5. His sinful appeal to the witch of Endor (*1 Samuel 28:7*).

Saul waged six campaigns:

1. Against the Ammonites: Beginning of reign; against insurmountable obstacles; army mobilized with great haste; Ammonites completely ruined; Saul's prestige as king strengthened.

2. Against the Philistines: Saul's sin in assuming function of priest; God rejected Saul; bravery of Jonathan and single companion created panic among Philistines; enemy routed.

3. Against the Amalekites: Saul drove enemy into desert; marred success by disobedience; seized valuable property; lied to Samuel; prophet repeated that God had rejected him.

4. Against the Philistines: Saul in constant warfare with Philistines; boy David appeared after his anointing; met Goliath, giant of Philistines; slew him; panic caused; David won distinction.

5. Against David: Blind jealousy drove Saul to seek David's life; David

became an outcast; David repeatedly delivered; Saul, David's enemy till his death; David's immortal friendship with Saul's son Jonathan.

6. Against the Philistines: Battlefield plains of Esdraelon; when dark Saul made his visit to the witch of Endor; Samuel called up; defeat and death announced; Israel completely defeated; Saul and three sons slain.

All through the years, Samuel mourned for Saul. When Saul failed, Samuel was faithful in warning him, then in loneliness he mourned over him. Multiplied verses tell the story. (See *1 Samuel 15:35*.)

In a battle with the Philistines, Saul and his three sons met death. Here a life so full of promise ended in defeat and failure. Saul had not obeyed God absolutely.

God is showing in this book that He must be all in all; that His children have no blessing apart from Him.

David, the King Proven
1 Samuel 16—31

As the third division of the book opens we see Samuel mourning for Saul. God rebukes him and tells him to arise and anoint the new king (*1 Samuel 16:1*).

David, "the apple of God's eye," was one of the greatest characters of all times. He made great contributions to the history of Israel both spiritually and nationally.

In this book we see David as a shepherd lad, a minstrel, an armor bearer, a captain, the king's son-in-law, a writer of psalms and a fugitive. He was anointed three times and was to be the founder of the royal line of which the King of kings came.

David, Jesse's son and the great-grandson of Ruth and Boaz, was born in Bethlehem. He was the youngest of eight sons. When David was only eigh-

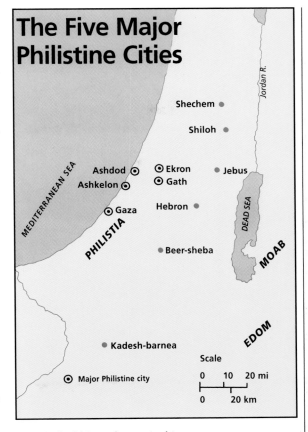

The Five Major Philistine Cities

Jordan R.

MEDITERRANEAN SEA

Shechem ●

Shiloh ●

Ashdod ⊙   ⊙ Ekron   ● Jebus
Ashkelon ⊙   ⊙ Gath

⊙ Gaza   Hebron ●

DEAD SEA

PHILISTIA

MOAB

● Beer-sheba

EDOM

● Kadesh-barnea   Scale

⊙ Major Philistine city

0   10   20 mi

0   20 km

teen, God told Samuel to anoint him king to succeed Saul. As a boy he tended his father's sheep, and we read of his brave deeds in defending them from wild beasts.

As a harpist, David's fame reached the king. Saul's melancholy caused David to be called into the court to play. One of the most charming stories of real love in friendship is found between David and Jonathan, Saul's son.

When David was promoted to a high command in the army, his great success roused the jealousy of Saul who determined to kill him. He made five attacks on David's life (*1 Samuel 19:10,15,20-*

21,23-24). But God preserved David. "If God is for us, who can be against us?" (*Romans 8:31*). David was delivered from all these dangers. Read David's words in Psalm 59. Read Psalm 37.

These were trying days for the young man David who had been appointed to the kingly office. It was natural that he should go to Samuel for protection. All this was training for the one whom God was preparing for the throne. He not only learned how to handle men, but also how to handle himself. He became independent and courageous. He learned, too, in those trying days, to trust God, not men. He always awaited God's time.

He was an outcast for no wrong that he had done but because of the insane jealousy of Saul. David grew under his trials and afflictions. Instead of letting Saul's hatred harden his heart, he returned love for hate.

He learned to be a warrior during those days, too. He was to become the head of a great nation, and God was training him for active service.

Finally David took refuge in flight. During this time Samuel died. Twice was Saul's life in David's hand but both times he spared Saul. Feeling that he should perish one day by the hand of Saul, he took refuge among the Philistines. Psalm 56 was written then. After Saul and his sons were killed by the Philistines David's exile ended.

The closing chapter of our book is draped in black. It gives the closing picture of one of the most disastrous failures. Saul died on the field of battle by his own hand. Advantages and opportunities in youth never guarantee success in manhood. One must keep true to God. Saul's undoing was not so much disobedience, as half-hearted obedience (*1 Samuel 15*). He was a victim of human pride and jealousy.

10. UNDERSTANDING Second Samuel

Second Samuel Portrays Jesus Christ, Our King

We must not only crown Christ as King of our lives, but we must also set Him on His rightful throne.

The book of 1 Samuel records the failure of the people's king, Saul. Second Samuel describes the enthronement of God's king, David, and the establishment of the "House of David" through which the Messiah, Jesus Christ, should later come. When Christ comes again, He will sit upon the throne of David (*Isaiah 9:7; Luke 1:32*).

The book of 2 Samuel is occupied with the story of David as king (*2 Samuel 5:3*). It does not tell the whole story, for it begins with 1 Samuel and runs into 1 Kings. First Chronicles deals with it from another standpoint.

The children of Israel had clamored for a king. God first gave them one after their own heart, Saul. Then He gave them one after His own heart, David.

This is the substance of 2 Samuel:

1. David was made king over Judah, 2 Samuel 1—4
2. David was made king over all Israel, 2 Samuel 5—24.

Notice the blessedness of the life that recognizes the "Lord's anointed," and puts the true King on the throne of the heart. Such a life is sheltered. "Thou wast he that leddest out and broughtest in Israel" (*2 Samuel 5:2*).

Such a life is nurtured. "You will shepherd my people Israel" (*2 Samuel 5:2; see also Psalm 23:1-2*).

Such a life is victorious, with Christ's own victory. "and you will become their ruler" (*2 Samuel 5:2*).

Night falls over the ruins of Bethshan, where Saul's body was displayed after his defeat by the Philistines. Mount Gilboa, site of the battle, rises behind.

Jesus says, "Follow me." If we obey, it means He will shield us and shepherd us and make our victory sure!

If we read 2 Samuel 7:18-22; 8:14-15, we find David at his very best, when he was at the height of his prosperity. It shows what he had become and what he might have continued to be if only he had remained faithful to God.

David was a man after God's own heart—not because of boasted perfection, but because of confessed imperfections. He hid himself in God. Read what God tells us to do when we sin, 1 John 1:9.

The story of David the shepherd is found in 1 Samuel 16 and 17; then we see him as a prince in the court, 1 Samuel 18—20; and finally an exile in chapters 21—31.

No one found anywhere in God's Word is so versatile. He is David, the shepherd boy, the court musician, the soldier, the true friend, the outcast captain, the king, the great general, the loving father, the poet, the sinner, the brokenhearted old man, but always the lover of God. We find him as a sort of Robin Hood of the Bible. We love the stories of his daring courage, his encounter with lions and bears and the giant. He was a man of wonderful personal power and charm. Can you find, as you read this book, the record that portrays the following qualities that stand out so clearly?

1. Faithfulness   5. Bigheartedness
2. Modesty   6. Trustfulness
3. Patience   7. Penitence
4. Courage

It would be well to compare Saul and David and roughly measure their stature one against the other. Both were kings of Israel. Both reigned about the same length of time, forty years. Both had the loyal support of the people, and both had the promise of God's power to back them. Yet Saul was a failure and David was a success. Saul's name is a blot on Israel's history, and David's name is honored today both by Jew and Gentile.

What is the reason for the differences? It is well for us to find out, for these same factors may work in your life and mine, and we may deliberately choose the forces that shall carry us on either course.

Saul had a brilliant start and for a while made good. But with success came pride. (Read *Proverbs 16:18.*) Thirty-five years of his reign were spent in insecurity and failure. He had lost hold upon God. He finally died a suicide in a lost battle and left his kingdom at war with its neighbors and divided in its loyalty (*1 Samuel 31*).

The immediate link between the last chapter and this ought to be reviewed. After David had spared Saul (*1 Samuel 26*), he realized that his life was in danger, but he made the great

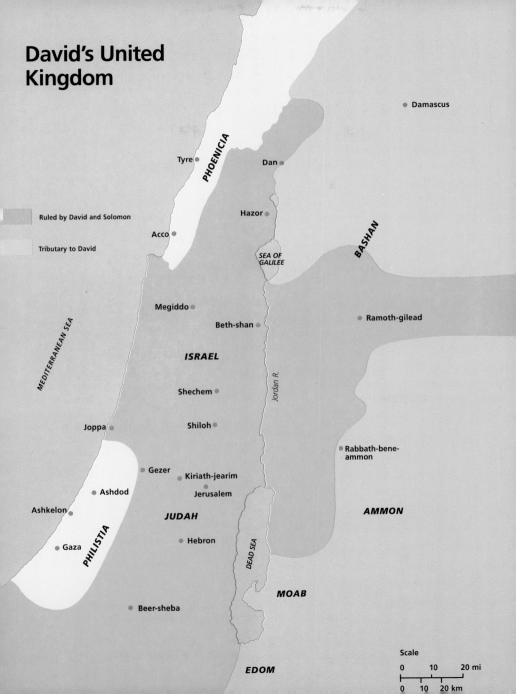

David's United Kingdom

Ruled by David and Solomon

Tributary to David

Damascus

PHOENICIA

Tyre

Dan

Hazor

BASHAN

Acco

SEA OF
GALILEE

MEDITERRANEAN SEA

Megiddo

Beth-shan

Ramoth-gilead

ISRAEL

Shechem

Jordan R.

Shiloh

Joppa

Rabbath-bene-
ammon

Gezer

Kiriath-jearim

Jerusalem

Ashdod

AMMON

Ashkelon

JUDAH

PHILISTIA

Gaza

Hebron

DEAD SEA

Beer-sheba

MOAB

EDOM

Scale

0   10   20 mi

0   10   20 km

Hebron

mistake of associating himself with the Philistines instead of quietly trusting God (*1 Samuel 27*). Meanwhile, the closing scenes and final tragedy of Saul's life took place (*1 Samuel 28—31*). David's lament about Saul's death showed his attitude. Everything was clear now for David to fulfill the divine purpose and become king of Israel.

Now 2 Samuel draws our attention. Really there is no division between the first and second books. Originally, the two books were one, covering the period from the beginning of Samuel's life to the end of David's. But 2 Samuel is occupied wholly with David.

There is no parallel account to that in 2 Samuel 2 of David's succession to the kingdom of Judah, but 1 Chronicles 11 and 12 give a vivid picture of the men of Israel as they came to make David king over the whole land. Saul was the people's choice; David was God's choice.

After the results of Gilboa when both Saul the king and Jonathan his beloved friend lay dead, David naturally desired to know what was to be the next step. So David sought guidance of God (*2 Samuel 2:1*). David did not ask about being a king, but only about the place where he should go. The nation of Israel needed a leader and the divine answer was that he should go up to the city of Hebron (*v. 3*).

Hebron was one of the most ancient cities (*Numbers 13:22*). It was in existence in Abraham's day. When Canaan was conquered it became the possession of Caleb and was one of the cities of refuge (*Joshua 14:13-15; 21:11-13*). This was David's capital for the first seven years of his reign. This made it still more important. It was fifteen miles south of Jerusalem, in the center of Judah, and a strong place. It was especially suitable as a capital of the new

kingdom, with the Philistines on the one side and the followers of Saul on the other.

David seemed every inch a king when he spared the life of Saul. He was willing to wait for God to tell him that he would surely prevail (*1 Samuel 26*). He was on the heights. David's training seemed complete.

The devil would rather throw a man when he is on the heights; he falls farther and harder. He threw David. For David now passed into one of the worst periods of his life and stayed there for almost a year and a half (*1 Samuel 27:1*). David fell from a mountain peak of spiritual victory and privilege to a black valley of defeat and he deliberately chose to stay there, weak and discouraged, for a long time.

David's faith had collapsed. Without God's counsel he left the country of God's people, went to live in the land of the enemy, hopelessly certain of dying at Saul's hand unless he would escape. He joined Achish, king of Gath, who gave him Ziklag in which to live (*1 Samuel 27:1-7*).

David lied to Achish to win his favor, saying that he had raided the people of Judah when he had not. David met calamity. At last he flung himself upon God. "But David found strength in the Lord his God" (*1 Samuel 30:6*). He asked God what to do. God answered and under His guidance David had a real victory (*1 Samuel 30*).

Notice what happened at almost exactly the same time in the lives of Saul and David. Saul, an unrepentant sinner, went down to death, dragging his family and his country with him (*1 Samuel 31:3-7*). David, a repentant sinner, is given a glorious victory over the enemy and many are saved with him (*1 Samuel 30:17-20*). We are all sinners of one kind or another. Which ending do we want for our lives?

Read David's sorrowful lament over

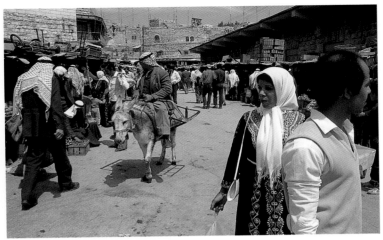
A busy scene in Hebron market. David obeyed God and returned to Hebron, where the men of Judah made him their king.

Saul and Jonathan, 2 Samuel 1:17-27.
How did Saul meet his death?
(1 Samuel 31:4).
Why is suicide wrong?
Can it ever be justified?
What motive prompts suicide?
Who fell in the same battle with Saul? (1 Samuel 31:2).
What was David's attitude when he heard of their deaths?
Might one not expect him to have been glad for Saul's death?
Still in Ziklag in the enemy's country, David asked God just what he should do, but not whether he was to be king (2 Samuel 2:1). He obeyed God and returned to Hebron where the men of Judah made him their king. Study the facts of 2 Samuel 2:8 to 4:12. Amid fighting and civil war and intrigue, David does not lift a finger to secure the kingdom of Israel. The opposition steadily weakens itself and his cause steadily grows stronger. Seven and one-half years after ascending Judah's throne, David was made king of Israel.

Why are we assured of David's success when he is made king? Saul chose the way of self; David chose God's

way. Because of this, God calls him "a man after his own heart" (compare with 1 Samuel 13:14). Notice after Saul's death David made no effort to seize the kingdom by force. After Judah claimed him as king, it was seven and one-half years before Israel crowned him. David knew that it was God's plan that he should be king of Israel, but he was willing to wait.

Some people grow under responsibility; others swell. We learn from Saul's failure that the surrendered life is the only secure and truly successful life.

David's Rise—Supremacy and Rule
2 Samuel 1—10

As this book opens, we find David just returning to Ziklag after his great victory over the Amalekites. He had come back weary in body, but refreshed in spirit because of his great success. No doubt he was wondering what had been the outcome of that great battle at Mount Gilboa. His dearest friend, Jonathan, and King Saul, were in that battle.

David was not kept in suspense long. An Amalekite from the camp of Israel came running that great distance to tell David of the disaster. Because he claimed to have killed Saul, the Lord's anointed, David dealt severely with him. (Read *2 Samuel 1:1-16.*)

David's generous heart not only forgot all that Saul had done, but remembered all that was favorable in Saul's character. Recall some of the things Saul had done against David.

How beautiful is this spirit of forgiveness! See that spirit when men nailed Christ to the cross (*Luke 23:34*) and when men stoned the martyr Stephen to death (*Acts 7:60*). David wrote a song for this occasion called "The Song of the Bow." It is filled with extreme tenderness when it speaks of his beloved friend (*2 Samuel 1:19-27*).

The death of Saul did not end David's troubles. He had formed an alliance with Achish. He had gone as near to the position of a traitor to his country as he could without actually fighting against it.

His own tribe, Judah, was by far the friendliest. They knew better how cruelly Saul had hunted him down. This is why he had thrown himself into the hands of Achish.

David inquired of God where he should set up his kingdom, and God told him in Hebron. No sooner had David gone up to the city, than the men of Judah came and anointed him king over the house of Judah. Although it was not all that God had promised David, it was a large installment, for Judah was the royal tribe.

David's start was slow and discouraging. But David had faith in God. He was patient and was willing to wait for God to lead. He was humble before God and the people. He was humble in his success, and when he sinned he genuinely repented. David's was a great career. He used every talent God gave him for the glory of his Creator and built up the people of God's choice. He brought Israel to the height of her glory, extending her boundaries from the Mediterranean to the Euphrates by conquest of battle. He left a rich heritage to his race—a heritage that included power, wealth, honor and songs and psalms. But above all, he left an example of loyalty to God.

The men of Judah who came to meet David were probably the elders of his own tribe. They came to elect him as king, and although he had been anointed privately by Samuel to indicate that God had chosen him, it was natural and necessary to repeat the anointing in public as the outward and visible inauguration of his reign.

Remember Saul was anointed privately, too (*1 Samuel 10:1*). Anointing with oil meant a divine appointment. Saul was set apart for service as a king. He was given the right to rule the people.

However, David's kingship was not acknowledged by all of the people. Abner, the captain of Saul's army, at once took steps to appoint Saul's son to take his place.

The earnest efforts of David to ward off strife and bring the people together in recognizing him as king were all in vain. The spirit of Saul, which was so antagonistic to David, was perpetuated in Abner who was determined to center the kingdom of Israel around the house of Saul, not of David (*2 Samuel 2:8-10*).

The people did not consult Jehovah (a form of the divine name, more properly, Yahweh), but merely tried to stem the popular tide in David's direction.

Civil war followed, but finally everything turned to David and he was made king of all Israel. The monarchy in Israel was never an absolute autocracy (*1 Samuel 10:25; 1 Kings 12:3*).

In the prime of his life, thirty years of age, David entered upon his complete inheritance. This was the task God intended him to do. He reigned forty years in all, including seven and one-half years in Hebron over Judah and thirty-three years in Jerusalem over the whole land. The fortress of Jerusalem was still in the hands of the Jebusites but was captured early in David's reign (2 Samuel 5:6-10).

One of the great results of David's kingship was the unity of the whole nation under him as leader. He brought the various conflicting elements into one group. We find a united people under a young leader united to God. The Israelites needed only to have kept on following David's leading down the years to have gone on from greatness to greatness. They had only to follow David's greater Son to have gone on from glory to glory!

David trusted God with all his heart and leaned not on his own understanding. He acknowledged God in all his ways and God did direct his path (Proverbs 3:5-6).

"The war between the house of Saul and the house of David lasted a long time. David grew stronger and stronger, while the house of Saul grew weaker and weaker" (2 Samuel 3:1). The cause of its weakness was that God was against it.

After seven and one-half years of opposition, David finally won the heart of all Israel by his justice and great spirit. He was left now without a rival. Representatives of all the tribes came to Hebron to anoint him king of the whole nation (2 Samuel 5).

From the anointing of David as king at Hebron, we go with him to the field of battle.

The first thing that engaged David was the capture of Jerusalem, the stronghold of Zion. Since the days of Joshua, Jerusalem alone had defied the

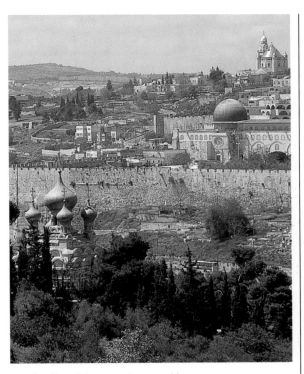

Mount Zion, Jerusalem, today. David established the nation's capital in Jerusalem.

attack of Israel. It was an impregnable fortress. David thought it was best suited to be his nation's capital. This became the residence of David and the capital of his kingdom.

What is the city of greatest importance as far as God is concerned? The record of how it came for the first time completely into the possession of God's people is given in 2 Samuel 5:6-9; 1 Chronicles 11:4-8.

After David had established the capital at Jerusalem, he wished to bring the Ark of God into the new ruling center. He realized the people's need of God. But we are not told that he consulted God. A real tragedy followed. What was it? (See 2 Samuel 6:1-19.) What do you know of God's directions for carrying the Ark?

It is not what we think, but what God

says that is important. Uzzah's human opinion was that it was all right to take hold of the Ark to keep it from falling. He was sincere, but it was directly contrary to what God said. Uzzah died. We can always know what God has said if we are willing to pay the price of knowing by studying His Word and trusting what He says (*John 7:17*).

What was the greatest thing David did for his people?

He captured Jerusalem, built it bigger and stronger, conquered the Philistines and unified the people. But all this would be of little use without putting God at the center. This is really what gave the nation unity and power. Neither a nation nor an individual can be great without Christ in its heart.

All the events in David's reign that followed the capture of Jerusalem may be summed up in these words, "And David became more and more powerful, because the Lord Almighty was with him" (*1 Chronicles 11:9*). God had been getting David ready for this reign. Training is difficult. It is good to bear the yoke in youth. Many a great person can testify to this.

The first concern of David when he settled in Jerusalem was bringing up the Ark of the testimony. His attempt to place the Ark in Mount Zion failed through want of due reverence on the part of those carrying it, but after three months it was duly placed in the Tabernacle. (Read the story in *2 Samuel 6*.)

David was an active man. He was fond of work. His wars with outside nations had ceased. Now he sought to find what he could do to improve and beautify his kingdom. He compared the elegance of his own palace with the Tabernacle where Jehovah dwelt. He thought this difference ought not to be. He called Nathan the prophet and consulted him about building a temple for Jehovah. At first it seemed as though God would let him do this, but God had a different purpose for David. Read what God told Nathan to tell David (*2 Samuel 7:4-17*).

David's spirit is again revealed in his submission to God's plan for him. God allowed him to gather materials for his son to use to build the temple.

Don't pass over the sweet story of David's treatment of crippled young Mephibosheth when he found Mephibosheth was his best friend's son (*2 Samuel 9*).

David was powerful in every art of war, although his heart was inclined to peace. Chapter 10 recounts some perilous undertakings. This story gives the closing account of David's rise to power and prepares for the terrible story of his fall.

Under David's rule, Israel reached its high-water mark. It has been called Israel's golden age. No idol worship and no worldly functions occurred when "the sweet singer of Israel," the "shepherd boy of Bethlehem," commanded the ship of state. His merchant caravans crossed the deserts and his routes went from the Nile to the Tigris and Euphrates, and Israel prospered in those days. When Israel was right with God, she was invincible against all odds.

David's Fall *2 Samuel 11—20*

We wish the life of David could have ended before chapter 11 was written. The golden era has passed away and what is left is a checkered tale of sin and punishment. In all of God's Word no chapter is more tragic or more full of warning for the child of God. It tells the story of David's fall. His sins of adultery and virtual murder were a terrible blot on David's life. He became a broken man. God forgave him but the Word says, "The sword will never depart from your house" (*2 Samuel 12:10*). He reaped just what he had sown. We see the harvest in his own house and in the nation.

Look over the steps in David's fall. You will find the steps downward in rapid succession.

First, he was idle (*2 Samuel 11:1-2*). It was the time for a king to go to war, but he was not there. He remained in Jerusalem in the place of temptation. At evening time he arose from his bed and walked on the roof of his house. He was in that idle, listless mood that opens one to temptation. He saw the beautiful Bathsheba and he wanted her. His first sin was in the fact that he saw. Don't look on evil. Ask God to keep your eyes. Refuse the admission of sin into your mind. If David had nipped the temptation in the bud he would have saved himself a world of agony and awful sin. Instead of driving it out of his mind, he cherished it.

Next, "David sent someone to find out about her" (*2 Samuel 11:3*). He makes inquiry about this woman and then he took her (*v. 4*). He brings her to his house. He forgets what is due to the faithful soldier whose wife she is.

But the next step is far worse—his sin against Uriah, one of the bravest of his soldiers. He must get rid of him. He makes Joab his confidant in sin, his partner in murder.

This sin was the more terrible because it was committed by the head of the nation. This man had been signally favored by God. He was no longer a young man. He had passed through many experiences. Then, too, the excellent service of Uriah entitled him to rewards, not death.

Why do you suppose this tragic story is given in the Bible? It bears the character of a beacon, warning the mariner against some of the most perilous rocks that are to be found in the sea of life. Never neglect watching and praying.

The Kidron valley, Jerusalem. David fled across this valley when his son Absalom attempted to take his kingdom.

A year later the prophet Nathan visited David and charged him with his sin. We can imagine the anguish of David's heart that year. We read of David's sincere repentance (*Psalm 51*). God told David that his child should die because of his sin. See how David accepted this punishment (*2 Samuel 12:13-32*). When the child died, David arose and worshiped God.

"A living sorrow is worse than a dead one," says a proverb. The death of his child was a grievous sorrow to David, but the living sorrow he endured through his beloved son Absalom we cannot imagine. The rebellion of this young man is full of tragedy. Absalom was a handsome young man, but he was treacherous. He weaned away his father's subjects by treachery. He sat at the city gate and told the farmers what he would do if he were their ruler. When men bowed in honor, he kissed their hands. He drove a beautiful chariot drawn by prancing horses. He became a favorite.

Through a spy system, he stole the kingdom from his father. When David left Jerusalem, Absalom gathered his army in Hebron and marched triumphantly into the city. Finally David prepared for battle with Absalom. During the fray, Absalom was caught by his long hair in the trees of the forest.

Absalom was heartless and cruel. David suffered alike in the day of Absalom's victory and in the dark hour of his defeat and slaying. Read his lament over Absalom when he heard the news of his death (*2 Samuel 18:19—19:4*).

David's Last Days
2 Samuel 20—24

After the rebellion was crushed, King David returned to his kingdom. New officers were installed and reconstruction began on every hand. We see David's sin in numbering the people, because God had not told him to. The land was punished with a three-day pestilence.

He gathered great provisions for building the Temple and directed his son Solomon to build it. David was only seventy years old when he died.

David was a mighty king and warrior. He ranked with Abraham, Moses and Paul. His great spirit is revealed to us in the psalms that he wrote. But he sinned. The story does not end here, because he repented. Read the great confession in Psalm 51.

David took a chaotic nation and established a dynasty that was to last to the time of the captivity, a period of more than 450 years. There never was a greater warrior or statesman than David. He made Israel the dominant power of western Asia.

The last verses of 2 Samuel 24:18-25 tell of King David's buying Araunah's threshing floor. He erected an altar there. This has special significance, for on this site the great Temple of Solomon was later built. On this sacred spot today stands the Dome of the Rock, one of the most important Islamic mosques in the world. It is a most galling thing to the Jews to have this sacred ground in the hands of the Muslims.

Do not pray for an easy task. Pray to be stronger! The greatness of your spiritual power is the measure of your surrender. It is not a question of who you are, or of what you are, but whether God controls you.

11. UNDERSTANDING

Kings and Chronicles

Kings and Chronicles Portray Jesus Christ as King

If we reject God, He will reject us. If we obey God, He will bless us. "In those days the Lord began to reduce the size of Israel" (*2 Kings 10:32*).

In the original Hebrew in which these books were written, 1 and 2 Kings formed one book, 1 and 2 Samuel another, and 1 and 2 Chronicles a third. When they were translated into the Greek language, they were divided by the translators because the Greek required one third more space than the Hebrew and the scrolls on which they were written were limited in length.

The book of Kings was written while the first Temple was standing. First and 2 Kings are just a continuation of the books of Samuel. As their name suggests, they record the events of the reign of Solomon and then of the succeeding kings of Judah and Israel. They cover a period of 400 years and tell the story of the growth and then decay of the kingdom. We see the kingdom divided. We see both Israel and Judah led into captivity. The Southern Kingdom (Judah) had twenty kings, and the Northern Kingdom (Israel) had nineteen kings.

These are two of the most important books of history in the world. Every day expeditions are digging up the records of history about which nothing has been written outside the books of the Kings. At first they may seem dry to you, but the lives of the kings, and the stories in these books prove that:

1. "God does not show favoritism" (*Acts 10:34*; "is no respecter of persons," *KJV*).
2. When our all is on the altar, God never keeps us waiting for the fire (*1 Kings 18:38*). What is the spiritual meaning of this?
3. The final captivity was because of disobedience to God. It was prophesied before (*Deuteronomy 28:49*). What has God said about the individual who forgets Him?

Kings begin with King David and end with the king of Babylon.

Kings open with the building of the Temple and end with the burning of the Temple.

Kings open with David's first suc-

Selected Bible Readings

Sunday:	Building and Dedicating the Temple (*1 Kings 6:1-14; 8:22-53*)
Monday:	Solomon's Glorious Reign (*1 Kings 10:1-29*)
Tuesday:	The Kingdom Divided (*1 Kings 12:1-33*)
Wednesday:	The Prophet Elijah (*1 Kings 17:1—18:46*)
Thursday:	Elijah and Elisha (*2 Kings 2:1-22*)
Friday:	The Captivity of Israel (The Northern Kingdom) (*2 Kings 17:7-23*)
Saturday:	The Captivity of Judah (The Southern Kingdom) (*2 Kings 25:1-21*)

cessor to the throne of his kingdom, Solomon, and end with David's last successor, Jehoiachin, released from captivity by the king of Babylon.

Remember these books of Kings cover practically the whole rule of the kings over God's chosen people. During Solomon's reign, the kingdom reached the height of its grandeur. With the death of Solomon, the kingship really ceased to be the medium through which God governed His people. The period of the prophets is introduced at this time by the great Elijah. First Kings ends with the story of this prophet. Second Kings centers around Elisha. The decline of the kingdoms is given until we see both Israel and Judah led into captivity.

The Splendid Reign of Solomon *1 Kings 1—10*

As the scene opens, we find that "King David was old and well advanced in years." He was prematurely aged for he was only seventy. His son Solomon was but nineteen. Because of David's feebleness we find a rebellion started against him. Adonijah's attempt to get his father's throne was natural because he was the oldest surviving son (*2 Samuel 3:4*). This rebellion called for prompt action, which Nathan the prophet took. David saw that Solomon was the most fit to succeed him. Solomon was God's choice (*1 Chronicles 22:9; 1 Kings 2:15*). It was clear that the choice of Solomon was popular (*1 Kings 1:39-40*). Adonijah soon saw that opposition was useless. Because of this rebellion, Solomon was crowned before David's death (*1 Kings 1:30,39,53*).

Solomon received his religious training from Nathan the prophet. This wise prophet loved Solomon and gave him the name Jedidiah, "the Lord's darling" (*2 Samuel 12:25*). Solomon's reign

began in a blaze of glory. It was splendor without surrender. And as with Saul, Solomon's life ended in an anticlimax.

"His heart was not fully devoted to the Lord his God, as the heart of David his father had been" (*1 Kings 11:4*). Remember, God wants our hearts!

Yet Solomon was a magnificent king; his throne was the grandest the world had ever seen and his life was filled with happenings of marvelous significance. His kingdom of 60,000 square miles was ten times as great as that which his father had inherited.

Solomon did not display spiritual wisdom. The book of Ecclesiastes, with its note of despair, is a confession of it. He did not have a heart at peace with God.

After David's final words of admonition to his son to be absolutely loyal to Jehovah, the king died, having reigned for forty years.

God appeared to Solomon in a dream early in his reign and asked him to make a choice of anything that he might wish. The young king's wise choice revealed his feeling of inability to do all that was put upon him. What was his request of the Lord? God gave him the wisdom for which he asked. What is God's promise to us (*James 1:5*)? "Ask for whatever you want me to give you" (*1 Kings 3:5*). This is the high privilege of each one of us. Each of our lives tell what we have asked for. What is your choice?

The youth had not been swept off his feet by his father's praise when David twice called him a wise man (*1 Kings 2:6-9*). Solomon asked for a "discerning heart." Have we a heart that listens to the Spirit's voice?

Solomon was the wisest man the world ever saw until the coming of Him who could say of Himself, "and now one greater than Solomon is here" (*Matthew 12:42*). All the earth acknowl-

Solomon Was a Great and Good Man

1. His rearing was under the religious and wise Nathan.

2. His kingship was clear. All the city rang with the glad cry, "Solomon has taken his seat on the royal throne" (1 Kings 1:46).

3. His charge from his father was full of promise (1 Kings 2:1-9).

4. His choice of wisdom from God was a divine choice (1 Kings 3).

5. His cabinet was greater than any king of Israel ever had (1 Kings 4).

6. His lifework was building the Temple. Several million dollars was expended in erecting it. Its service of dedication has gone down on record because of its sublimity.

7. The kingdom he established realized at last, after 400 years, the broad dimensions outlined to Joshua (Joshua 1:4).

8. The wealth and glory of Solomon's reign fairly took the breath of the Queen of Sheba. "There was no more spirit [breath] in her" (1 Kings 10:5, KJV).

9. His beauty of person is hinted in Psalm 45.

10. His ardent affection is seen in the song that bears his name (Song of Solomon).

Solomon was a great and glorious king, but we soon find the note of decline.

Solomon the Weak and Erring One

1. Unlike his father, David, Solomon dealt cruelly with his brother Adonijah (1 Kings 2:24-25).

2. Like Saul, his heart was lifted up in pride (1 Kings 10:18-29).

3. Led by his heathen wives, he fell into idolatry (1 Kings 11). "Do not be yoked together with unbelievers" (2 Corinthians 6:14).

---

edged Solomon, but when the greater than Solomon came His own received Him not (*John 1:11*). That is tragedy. But have you received Him?

First Solomon organized his leaders. He gathered around him a wise company of officers of state, each having his own department for which he was responsible. This led to days of tremendous prosperity in the kingdom.

The greatest undertaking of Solomon's reign was building the Temple. This was what his father, David, had longed to do. The immense foundation of great hewn stones upon which Solomon's Temple was built remains till this day under the Dome of the Rock. One stone alone is thirty-eight feet, nine inches long. The huge stones, the fragrant cedar wood and copper-covered dome gave it unusual splendor.

The Temple site was a historic spot. On Mount Moriah, Abraham offered up Isaac (*Genesis 22:2*). We saw how David secured Araunah's threshing floor and here today the Dome of the Rock stands, the sacred spot of the Muslims.

The Israelites used to have to make pilgrimages to the Temple to meet God. But now we know a wonderful truth that our bodies are the temples of God (*1 Corinthians 3:16; 6:19*). Is your body a real temple? God wishes to live in you, but He cannot if you are defiled with sin.

Three earthly temples are mentioned in Scripture. The first is Solomon's, which was destroyed by the Babylonians about 587 B.C. (*2 Kings 25:8-9*). The second was Zerubbabel's (*Ezra 5:2; 6:15-18*). This was not compa-

Plan of Solomon's Temple

Altar of incense

Ark of the covenant

10 cubits

Jachin

Bronze altar

20 cubits

Vestibule

20 x 20 cubits

Boaz

Sea of cast bronze

Inner Sanctuary, The Most Holy Place

Sanctuary, The Holy Place

rable in elegance to Solomon's. The third was Herod's Temple, an expansion of Zerubbabel's, erected on a grander scale in 20 B.C. and completed in A.D. 64. This temple was destroyed by Titus in A.D. 70. The Dome of the Rock now stands on this site.

The Glory of Solomon's Reign
Read 1 Kings 9:1-28 and 10:14-29 to find the possible, not to say the probable, dangers to Solomon in all this wonderful glory. Note his high position, his great wisdom, his countless riches. It is hard not to forget God in the hour of such prosperity. We think only of our possessions. It was this very glory that led to Solomon's downfall.

Because of Solomon's backsliding, God raised up enemies to vex him. In the book of Ecclesiastes, Solomon describes the futility of his life at this time.

The Queen of Sheba witnessed Solomon's reign at its zenith and saw the fulfillment of David's prayer for his son, offered about a year before his death.

Solomon's reputation probably had

spread through the voyages of his navy (*1 Kings 9:21-28*). The fame of Solomon was associated with Jehovah. His fame concerning the name of the Lord was the thing that interested her Majesty, the Queen of Sheba. She was impressed by (1) Solomon himself, with his wisdom and wealth, 1 Kings 10:1,7; (2) his servants, verse 8; and (3) his God, verse 9.

The Kingdom Torn Asunder
1 Kings 11—16

Solomon reigned forty years, the second great period of the complete kingdom (*1 Kings 11*). At first all went well, but later there was serious trouble. Note that Saul, David and Solomon each reigned forty years (*Acts 13:21; 2 Samuel 5:4; 1 Kings 11:42*).

Taxes under Solomon's reign had weighed the people down. Luxury and idolatry had broken down their morale. The kingdom now was to be divided. A rise to such prosperity and power as Solomon enjoyed had its dangers. It cost money and meant increased taxation, which grew into bur-

The Divided Kingdom

SIDON

PHOENICIA

Tyre

Dan

SYRIA (ARAM)

Hazor

SEA OF GALILEE

MEDITERRANEAN SEA

Megiddo

I S R A E L

Samaria

Shechem

Jordan R.

AMMON

Shiloh

Bethel

Jericho

Jerusalem

Bethlehem

Ashkelon

PHILISTIA

Hebron

DEAD SEA

J U D A H

MOAB

Beer-sheba

Mt Carmel

dens that were unbearable and that bred the seeds of unrest and revolution.

Solomon set up a great establishment in Jerusalem. He built his famous Temple, bringing in foreign workmen and materials to do it, and then he built himself a palace that dazzled his own subjects and his foreign visitors.

During this time there was much corruption, and under all these burdens the people grew restless and rebellious.

Consider the events leading up to the division. For years there had been jealousy between the Northern Kingdom (Israel) and the Southern Kingdom (Judah). The cause for the jealousy went back 300 years and was a result mainly of the jealousy between the tribes of Ephraim and Judah. Note the blessings Jacob gave to Ephraim (*Genesis 48:17-22; 49:22-26*). And from the time of Joshua, who was of that tribe, Ephraim took a leading place. The transfer of authority to Judah came under David, who was of the tribe of Judah. All this tribal jealousy was intensified by the hardships felt by the people through Solomon's high-handed actions. His demands created oppression and his unfaithfulness to God demanded judgment (*1 Kings 11:26-43; 12:4*).

When Solomon's son, Rehoboam, threatened to levy heavier burdens upon the people, his unwise headstrong action added fuel to a fire that had been gathering and burning for nearly 300 years, from the time of the judges.

The revolt of the ten tribes immediately followed (*1 Kings 12:16*), though the two tribes of Judah and Benjamin remained loyal (*1 Kings 12:17*). This tension led to the appointment of Jeroboam as king of the northern section (*v. 20*).

The Secret of Decline

A new name of great importance appears in the pages of this story: Jeroboam. This young man of low origin had risen to notice because of faithful service and deeds done. The prophet Ahijah made a startling revelation to Jeroboam. Using a Middle-Eastern symbolic gesture, he took off his new coat and tore it into twelve strips and then he said to Jeroboam, "Take ten pieces for yourself, for this is what the Lord, the God of Israel, says: 'See, I am going to tear the kingdom out of Solomon's hand and give you ten tribes'" (*1 Kings 11:31*).

The kingdom was divided. The judgment was upon Solomon for his long years of luxury and pride and power.

Sin Brings Division

Though they didn't know it, the people were carrying out the divine purpose (*1 Kings 12:15; 11:29-33*). God could not overlook the disobedience of Solomon to His clearest commands.

The kingdom of God's chosen people was divided. It has been divided for almost 3,000 years. It was divided through sin. We see this kingdom go to pieces and finally into captivity (*2 Kings 17 and 25*). It is part of the gospel, the good news, that those two great sections of divided Israel are going to be united again on this earth at Christ's return in glory. (Read the wonderful passages in *Isaiah 11:10-13; Ezekiel 37:15-28*.)

The Ministry of Elijah
1 Kings 17—22; 2 Kings 1:1—2:2

Elijah was a bolt of fire God let loose upon wicked Ahab and idolatrous Israel. He flashed across the page of history as sudden and terrible as a flash of lightning. Elijah, the Tishbite, who was of the inhabitants of Gilead, is the brief description by which he was introduced. His name Elijah means "Jehovah is my God." It fit him perfectly. He was the most outstanding of the prophets. Follow his sudden appearance, his undaunted courage, his zeal, the heights of his triumph on Mount Carmel, the depths of his despondence, the glorious rapture into heaven in the whirlwind, his reappearance on the Mount of Transfiguration (see *Matthew 17:1-8*).

He was a striking character from the highlands of Gilead. His long thick hair hung over a cloak of sheepskin. Jehovah sent him to do away with the awful worship of Baal during the reign of Ahab who had married the wicked foreign princess, Jezebel. Suddenly emerging from the desert and standing before the corrupt king in the splendor of his court, the stern prophet boldly said, "As the Lord, the God of Israel, lives, whom I serve, there will be neither dew nor rain in the next few years except at my word" (*1 Kings 17:1*). He was given power to shut up the heavens so there would be no rain for three and a half years. He called down fire from heaven before the prophets of Baal at Mount Carmel. He was the evangelist of his day, thundering out warnings to this idolatrous people. The events in this great career will intrigue you. Read them carefully.

The Ministry of Elisha
2 Kings 1—9

Elisha succeeded Elijah. He was beneficent in contrast to the fiery Elijah. Elijah trained Elisha as his successor. Elisha's ministry lasted fifty years. Most of his miracles were deeds of kindness and mercy. Elisha had a great influence upon the kings of the day, and although he did not approve of what they did, he was always coming to their rescue.

Baal worship was introduced by the

Statue of the prophet Elijah on Mount Carmel.

wicked Jezebel, and after thirty years was exterminated by Elijah, Elisha and Jehu.

The Corruption of Israel
2 Kings 1—17

Jeroboam, the ruler of the Northern Kingdom, Israel, made Shechem his capital. It seemed the natural place because it was in the center of the land.

It was the custom, according to the law, to go up to Jerusalem regularly to worship (*Deuteronomy 12:11,14; 16:6,15-16; 1 Samuel 1:3,7*). Jeroboam was afraid to have his ten tribes journey to Jerusalem, the capital of Rehoboam's kingdom, to worship God; so he made two golden calves and placed them in convenient spots—Bethel (*Genesis 28:11-19*) in the south, and Dan (*Judges 18:29-30*) in the northern end of the kingdom, so the people would not have to go to Jerusalem.

More than twenty times he is described as "Jeroboam, the son of Nebat, who caused Israel to sin." Beware of man-made religion. We must worship where and how God tells us!

Assyrians deport prisoners of war: a relief from Nineveh. The Assyrians were great and cruel warriors.

God says, "Let us not give up meeting together, as some are in the habit of doing" (*Hebrews 10:25*). God knows we need fellowship in worship to keep the spiritual coals alive.

After 200 years, the people were carried into captivity by the king of Assyria in 722 B.C. (*2 Kings 17*). Many of God's prophets had warned Israel of captivity, but they would not turn from their idolatry to Jehovah.

The Assyrians were great and cruel warriors. They built their kingdom on their pillage from other countries. Their practices were horrible. They skinned men alive and then made mounds of the skulls of men to instill fear! For 300 years Assyria was a world empire.

The Captivity of Judah
2 Kings 13—25

The Southern Kingdom tried to conquer the Northern Kingdom. For eighty years there was continuous war between them. But these wars failed. Then there was a period of eighty years of peace between these two kingdoms following the marriage of

the son of Jehoshaphat (southern king) to the daughter of Ahab (northern king). Finally there was a period of fifty years when the kingdoms intermittently warred with each other until the captivity.

In the Southern Kingdom, there was only one dynasty (Davidic) from King Rehoboam to Zedekiah. The great prophets of that day were Nathan, Isaiah, Micah, Jeremiah, Joel and Zephaniah.

About 136 years after the Northern Kingdom had been taken into captivity by Assyria, the Southern Kingdom was taken captive by Nebuchadnezzar, king of Babylon. Jerusalem was destroyed, the Temple burned and the princes led away. The people had forgotten God and refused to listen to the warnings of the prophets. God wanted His people to learn the lesson of obedience and dependence upon Him.

In 1 Kings we see the kingdom of Israel, filled with pride and arrogance, falling apart. In 2 Kings, sinning yet more, Israel goes into captivity. Surely the way of the transgressor is hard. The history of the Jews is a record of God's dealings with disobedient children. In all His punishment, He is kind and merciful for He loves them still.

The secret of the downfall of the Jewish people is found in 2 Kings 3:2: "He did evil in the eyes of the Lord." Be loyal and true to God. It does not pay to do evil.

The moving figures and powerful factors of those days were the prophets Elijah and Elisha. Elijah was the strength of Israel. Jezebel and Ahab had frightened the people into submission. But Elijah stood. Read 1 Kings 17:1, where he said, "As the Lord God of Israel liveth, before whom I stand" *(KJV)*. And there he stood for God, like a rock, in face of all the weakness of Israel.

Elijah was the champion of the Most High. He was the pastor-evangelist of Israel's day.

There is a great difference between the fall of Israel and Judah. Israel was scattered throughout the nations for an indefinite period, but God specified the length of Judah's captivity to seventy years. Judah was to return to Jerusalem, which she did later. The Messiah was to come out of Judah and God was preparing the way for Him to come to Palestine and not to Babylon or Assyria.

God was using even the rulers of foreign nations to work out His plan. Cyrus, king of Persia, for example, was going to issue a decree that would allow the Jews to return to their homeland, Palestine.

Understanding
First Chronicles

The History of Judah

Through such books as the Chronicles we get the history of the Jewish nation. Through this nation our Lord came to earth. God chose this people for the fulfillment of His great promises and purposes. He is still their God (Romans 11:1) and He has His purposes yet to be fulfilled in them. In the light of this truth, books such as the Chronicles take on new meaning and power.

Understanding
Second Chronicles

A Book of Revivals!

Great revivals under:

1. Asa—2 Chronicles 15

2. Jehoshaphat—2 Chronicles 20

3. Joash—2 Chronicles 23—24

4. Hezekiah—2 Chronicles 29—31

5. Josiah—2 Chronicles 35.

Jesus Christ is portrayed as King in the books of Kings and Chronicles.

12. UNDERSTANDING

Ezra and Nehemiah

Ezra and Nehemiah Portray Jesus Christ, Our Restorer

Understanding Ezra

Again we find that Ezra and Nehemiah were one book in the Hebrew Bible, as were the two books of Samuel and Kings. These books tell the story of the return of God's chosen people after the exile. They give the record of one of the most important events in Jewish history—the return from exile in Babylon.

The time covered by these two books is about 100 years.
Both books begin at Persia and end at Jerusalem.
Both center around the man of God who wrote them.
Both stories begin with a Persian king's decree.
Both tell of building as their chief theme.
Both books contain a long prayer of humiliation and confession in the ninth chapter.
Both end with the purification of the people.
Ezra 7:10—Ezra's keynote
Nehemiah 6:3—Nehemiah's keynote
The books of Ezra and Nehemiah tell the story of how God remembered and how He brought back His people from exile.

During the captivity, the prophets Jeremiah and Ezekiel told the Jews of their restoration and predicted that they would return to their own land and rebuild Jerusalem. Jeremiah, the prophet, told them this would happen at the end of seventy years. See Jeremiah 29:10.

Rebuilding the national life of the Jewish people covered 100 years.

Two periods of time are very important.

1. Twenty years (537-517 B.C.) from the first year of Cyrus to the sixth year of Darius when the people under Zerubbabel, the governor, and Joshua, the priest, rebuilt the Temple. For this period, read Ezra 1—6; Zechariah and Haggai; the genealogies of 1 Chronicles 1:1—9:44; the last two verses of 2

Selected Bible Readings

Sunday:	Jews Return to Jerusalem (*Ezra 1—3*)
Monday:	Discouragement and Joy (*Ezra 4—6*)
Tuesday:	Ezra's Expedition (*Ezra 7—10*)
Wednesday:	Nehemiah Rebuilds the Wall (*Nehemiah 1—3*)
Thursday:	Overcoming Opposition (*Nehemiah 4—6*)
Friday:	Nehemiah Rebuilds the Morals (*Nehemiah 7—9*)
Saturday:	Reforming Through Religion (*Nehemiah 11—13*)

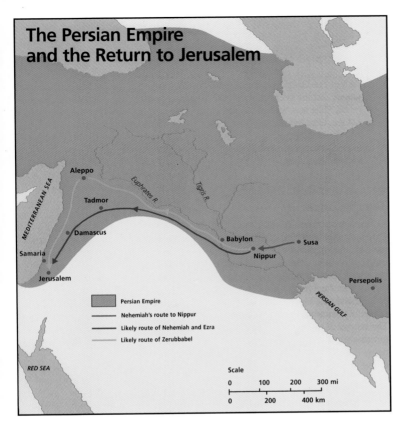

The Persian Empire and the Return to Jerusalem

MEDITERRANEAN SEA

Aleppo

Euphrates R.

Tigris R.

Tadmor

Damascus

Babylon

Susa

Samaria

Nippur

Jerusalem

Persepolis

PERSIAN GULF

Persian Empire

Nehemiah's route to Nippur

Likely route of Nehemiah and Ezra

Likely route of Zerubbabel

RED SEA

Scale

0   100   200   300 mi

0   200   400 km

Chronicles; Psalms 126; 137; and the reference to Cyrus in Isaiah 44:23 to 45:8.

2. Twenty-five years (458-433 B.C.) when Nehemiah, the governor, and Ezra, the priest, rebuilt the wall of Jerusalem and restored the city. Malachi was the prophet of this day.

Ezra gives the record of both of these periods.

Nehemiah tells of the second period, building the walls.

The book of Ezra has both a backward and a forward look.

The backward look: We find a second exodus for captive Israel. The first exodus was out of Egypt. This second exodus was from Babylon. This time

Ezra is leader in the place of Moses. Both of these great leaders dealt with Israel in a strong and merciful way.

The forward look: They came in timid, struggling relays back to Jerusalem. But God gave them a foothold. It was His city and it is His city still.

The ten northern tribes (the Northern Kingdom) were taken captive first by Assyria (*2 Kings 17*), then the two southern tribes (Benjamin and Judah, the Southern Kingdom) by Babylon (*2 Kings 25*). They were restored to their own land under the Persian empire. The Babylonians had been conquered by the Medes and

Persians. The ten northern tribes who were carried away to Assyria never returned.

In 537 B.C. the first Jews returned to Jerusalem from Babylon.

In 516 B.C. the Temple was restored.

In 479 B.C. Esther became queen of Persia. (She was wife of Xerxes.)

In 458 B.C. Ezra led second expedition from Babylon.

In 445 B.C. Nehemiah rebuilt the wall of Jerusalem.

Return and Rebuilding of the Temple *Ezra 1—6*

As the book opens (*Ezra 1:1-6*), we find Cyrus, king of Persia, making a proclamation throughout his kingdom permitting the Jews who were captives in his kingdom to return to Jerusalem.

Two hundred years before, God had prophesied that He would do this. He named Cyrus as the one He would use. The record of this remarkable prophecy, which calls a king by his name 200 years before his time, is found in Isaiah 44:28; 45:1-4.

At Cyrus's first call (537 B.C.), (*Ezra 1:1-4*) no more than 50,000 Jews availed themselves of the opportunity of returning to Jerusalem under Zerubbabel. Notice from this time the Israelites are called Jews because most of them were of the tribe of Judah and the name Jews comes from Judah.

Cyrus gave back to Zerubbabel the golden vessels Nebuchadnezzar had taken from the Temple in Jerusalem (*Ezra 1:5-11*). They started back over 700 miles of barren desert from Babylon to Jerusalem.

At the time of the captivity seventy years before, only the higher classes were taken into Babylon. The rest were left in their own land to suffer (*Jeremiah 24:5-8; 44:15*). Now everyone did not return; only the earnest and pious Jews went back.

Everything is taken care of when God is in charge. Not only money for rebuilding the Temple in Jerusalem, but also traveling expenses and all other needs were provided by God at Cyrus's direction (*Ezra 1:4,6*). Someone has said that God used Babylon as the safety deposit vault for the silver and gold vessels of the Temple.

The names of those who returned are given in chapter 2. They laid the foundation of the Temple the first thing upon returning. It was a time of great rejoicing. It is interesting to notice that before they built homes for themselves they first thought of a house for the Lord. They did not build the Temple first, but the altar (*Ezra 3:2*).

The altar was the center of the Jew's religion, the Cross the center of the Christian faith.

Read about the hindrances to the work (*Ezra 4:1-22*). Hindrances to all real work for God are to be expected. The Church must not have the help of the world.

The opposition disheartened them. They needed Haggai's message. Refer to the book of Haggai. Haggai and Zechariah, the prophets, encouraged the people from within the ranks (*Ezra 4:23—5:17*), and within four years the Temple was complete and dedicated (*Ezra 6*).

Zerubbabel's Temple was very plain and simple. It was not the sumptuous edifice that Solomon's was. In fact, it was in such contrast to the elegance of the first Temple that the old men who had seen Solomon's Temple wept aloud. But it was God's house and so the people thanked God and took courage.

Return and Reformation Under Ezra *Ezra 7—10*

Ezra appears in person in the seventh

chapter (458 B.C.). At least sixty years after the Jews had first returned to Jerusalem, he led a second expedition from Babylon to reinforce the struggling colonists in Palestine. Ezra received a commission from Artaxerxes the king (*Ezra 7:11—8:14*) who half-blindly aided in accomplishing God's plans for His people. Read Ezra *7:25* and find how impressed the king was with Ezra's love of God's Word.

This contingent under Ezra consisted of 1,700 Jews. It took them four months to make the journey, and it was financed by King Artaxerxes (*Ezra 7:12-26*). Thirteen years later this same king authorized Nehemiah to build the walls of Jerusalem (*Nehemiah 2*). Cyrus, Darius and Artaxerxes, the three Persian kings, were very friendly to the Jews.

Ezra the Scribe
Of Ezra it is said he "had devoted himself to the study and observance of the Law of the Lord, and to teaching its decrees and laws in Israel" (*Ezra 7:10*). His name means "help." He belongs to the great triumvirate of the Old Testament law (*Moses, Samuel, Ezra*). He wrote and worked to keep the record intact and to hold Israel, God's chosen people, to her divinely appointed mission. We are indebted to Ezra for the literary and ecclesiastical renaissance of that day.

Ezra instituted the synagogue worship that is the parent of our own form of worship, and assisted by the great synagogue of which he was president, settled the canon of Old Testament Scripture. Under Ezra we see the great revival of Bible study.

When Ezra returned to Jerusalem, he found things even worse than he had expected. Although the people had not returned to idolatry, they had intermarried with the people of the land and had done everything the pagans had taught them (*Ezra 9:1-4*). The princes and rulers were the worst offenders. Ezra rent his garments and literally pulled out his hair in grief! Read Ezra's touching prayer and confession (*9:5-15*).

As Ezra was praying and weeping before God, a great congregation assembled. What happened? (Read *Ezra 10:1-44*.) The people who had gathered about him through the long hours of the day came to a consciousness of the greatness of their sin as they saw how it affected Ezra. Finally one of their number spoke and acknowledged the sin. At once Ezra led them into a sacred covenant with God. Read what God says about confession of sin (*1 John 1:9*).

Nehemiah's Prayer
Now turn to Nehemiah 9 and you will find the prayer of Nehemiah. Prayer is the most important privilege of a Christian. Nehemiah's prayer began where Ezra's ended—with utter surrender to God. (Compare *Nehemiah 9:1-2* with *Ezra 9:15; 10:1.*)

See the results of this restoration of God's people to their land again:

First, through the rebuilding of the Temple, God opened the door of fellowship with Himself. Through the seventy years of suffering, they were ready to return and build and wait until He, the true Servant, should come.

Second, He renewed His promise of a coming Redeemer. It was prophesied that the Redeemer would be associated with Palestine.

Third, to make ready for the "fulness of the time" when Christ should come, as spoken of by Paul in Galatians 4:4 *(KJV)*.

Understanding Nehemiah

Repairing the City's Wall
(Nehemiah 1—7)
Nehemiah was the cupbearer at the court of King Artaxerxes. This was a position of high honor. But in this position of familiarity with the king, he had not forgotten his people. The news brought to him about Jerusalem made him very sad. This sadness could not be wholly hidden and the king detected it. The Jews had been back home for almost a hundred years, but had made no attempt to build Jerusalem beyond the restoration of the Temple, because their enemies made it almost impossible.

Nehemiah was loyal enough to his people to leave the luxury of a king's court and go back to rebuild Jerusalem, the capital of his homeland.

When Nehemiah reached Jerusalem in 445 B.C., Ezra had been there for thirteen years. Ezra was a priest and had been teaching the people the Word of God. But Nehemiah was a civil governor. After he had been there only three days, he went up and viewed the walls at night. When he saw their dilapidated condition, he encouraged the people to begin building immediately. The work was accomplished in fifty-two days by assigning a portion of the wall to each family. Their attitude was expressed in the sentence, "The people worked with all their heart" (*Nehemiah 4:6*).

First the Samaritans, the enemies of the Jews, derided them. They hindered their work so that the Jews had to keep watch night and day. Their derision turned to anger and Nehemiah divided the men into two groups, one keeping watch while the other worked.

Then opposition rose within the ranks. Some of the Jews became tired and complained that there was so much rubbish that the walls could not be built. Then, the complaint arose that the rich were demanding usury that the poor were unable to pay.

Again the enemies tried by craft to bring Nehemiah away from his building, but Nehemiah only prayed and again he foiled his enemy. The Persian kings were ever the friends of the Jews.

Nehemiah gave the city of Jerusalem into the charge of his brother Hanani (*Nehemiah 7:1-4*). When he took a census (*7:5-73*), the whole number was 42,360 besides 7,337 servants and 245 singing men and women.

Repairing the People's Morals
(Nehemiah 8—13)
All the people gathered in the street before the water gate in the city of Jerusalem and requested Ezra the scribe to bring out the book of the Law of Moses. He stood upon a pulpit of wood and read and explained the Law to the people (*Nehemiah 8:1-13*). This public reading brought true repentance to the people and a great revival broke out.

The Jews had intermarried with the idolatrous neighbors and this was the reason for their sin. Intermarriage of Christians with those who do not believe is a dangerous thing today. Paul says, "Do not be yoked together with unbelievers" (*2 Corinthians 6:14*).

Nehemiah was a man of prayer. We do not find a blot on his character. He was fearless and courageous.

The important thing in the study of the Bible is to find how Jesus Christ is portrayed in each book.

THE BIBLE portrays Jesus Christ as the Savior of the World.
GENESIS portrays Jesus Christ as our Creator-God.
EXODUS portrays Jesus Christ as our Passover Lamb.
LEVITICUS portrays Jesus Christ as our Sacrifice for Sin.
NUMBERS portrays Jesus Christ as our "Lifted-Up One."
DEUTERONOMY portrays Jesus Christ as our true Prophet.
JOSHUA portrays Jesus Christ as Captain of our salvation.
JUDGES portrays Jesus Christ as our Deliverer-Judge.
RUTH portrays Jesus Christ as our Kinsman-Redeemer.
FIRST AND SECOND SAMUEL portray Jesus Christ as our King.
KINGS AND CHRONICLES portray Jesus Christ as our King.
EZRA AND NEHEMIAH portray Jesus Christ as our Restorer.

TIME LINE—
GENESIS TO NEHEMIAH

—to 2000 B.C.	**GENESIS 1—11**
	Period: The world before Abram (Creation—Sin—Flood—Babel)
	People: Adam—Eve—Cain—Seth—Noah—Shem—Ham—Japheth
2000-1700 B.C.	**GENESIS 12—50**
	Period: Age of the patriarchs (Call of Abraham—Migration to Egypt—Growth of Israel)
	People: Abraham—Isaac—Jacob—Joseph
1700-1450 B.C.	**EXODUS—DEUTERONOMY**
	Period: Oppression in Egypt (The Exodus—The Law—Worship—Wilderness)
	People: Moses—Miriam—Aaron—Joshua
1450-1100 B.C.	**JOSHUA—1 SAMUEL 7**
	Period: Conquest of Canaan and time of the Judges (Invasion of Canaan—Bondage and deliverance)
	People: Joshua—Caleb—Othniel—Ehud—Shamgar—Deborah—Barak—Gideon—Jephthah—Samson—Eli—Samuel
1100-600 B.C.	**1 SAMUEL 8—2 CHRONICLES**
	Period: Monarchy—united, divided, declining (Kingdom established—Temple built—Kingdom divided—Destruction of Samaria—Discovery of the Law—Destruction of Jerusalem)
	People: Saul—David—Solomon—Jeroboam—Rehoboam—Ahab—Asa—Jehu—Elijah—Elisha—Jehoshaphat—Joab—Amaziah—Jeroboam II—Hoshea—Uzziah—Jotham—Ahaz—Hezekiah—Manasseh—Josiah—Jehoiakim—Zedekiah
500-400 B.C.	**EZRA—NEHEMIAH**
	Period: Return from the Exile (Decree of Cyrus—Close of Old Testament History)
	People: Zerubbabel—Ezra—Nehemiah

13. UNDERSTANDING
Esther

Esther Portrays Jesus Christ, Our Advocate

You have heard of the great Xerxes, king of Persia, the Ahasuerus of the book of Esther, of his famous expedition against Greece, and how the Greeks defeated his tremendous fleet at the battle of Salamis in 480 B.C. Historians tell us that this was one of the world's most important battles. From parallel passages in Herodotus, we find that the feast described in the first chapter of Esther was the occasion for planning the campaign against Greece (third year of his reign). Esther replaced Vashti in the seventh year of his reign (*Esther 2:16*) when Xerxes was seeking comfort after his disastrous defeat.

In the midst of this famous chapter in world history occurs the beautiful and charming Bible story of Esther. Although God's name is not mentioned in the book of Esther, every page is full of God, who hides Himself behind every word.

This book opens with a feast of the world's prince—Ahasuerus; it closes with the feast of God's prince—Mordecai. For a while Haman is exalted; at last, Mordecai. As you read this story, note the upsets in human history and the final triumph of God's chosen people.

Esther is like Joseph and David. God had each one hidden away for His purpose. When the day came, He brought them to the front to work out His plan. God hid Joseph away in a dungeon in Egypt, but when He was ready, He placed him in the position of prime minister of that country. God always has someone in reserve to fulfill His purposes.

Esther stands out as God's chosen one. She is a sweet and winsome person. She has come to the kingdom for just "such a time as this" (*Esther 4:14*). We see her taking her life in her hand. As she goes in for her people's sake unto the king, she says, "and if I perish, I perish" (*Esther 4:16*).

Two beautiful girls join hands in behalf of God's people. They are Ruth and Esther. Ruth becomes the ancestress of the Deliverer of Israel and Esther saves the people so that the Deliverer might come. God carefully protected this nation through the centuries for the purpose of blessing the whole world. They could not be wiped out before they brought the Savior into the world. This was not according to God's plans. Therefore God kept this nation according to His promise to Abraham.

In what period this story was written and who was its author are unknown. In point of time, it is placed between chapters six and seven of the book of Ezra.

The book of Esther is named for a Jewish orphan who became a Persian queen. This book and Ruth are the only books in the Bible that bear the names of women. The name "Esther" means "star."

Someone has said that all the events

of this book center around three feasts:

1. Feast of King Ahasuerus (Esther 1—2)
2. Feast of Esther (*Esther 7*)
3. Feast of Purim (*Esther 9*).

Rejection of Vashti *Esther 1*

The great feast to which Vashti refused to come, as has been learned from the inscriptions, was held to consider the expedition against Greece, for which Xerxes spent four years in preparation. King Ahasuerus of the story was Xerxes, the famous Persian monarch (485-465 B.C.).

As this book opens, the king was entertaining all the nobles and princes of his kingdom in the royal palace at Shushan. The banquet was planned on a colossal scale. It lasted 180 days (*Esther 1:4*). The men were feasting in the gorgeous palace gardens and the women were entertained by the beautiful Queen Vashti in her private apartment.

When the king and princes were in the midst of their drunken revelry, the king called for Vashti so that he could show off her beauty. Of course, no Persian woman would permit this. It was an affront to her womanhood. Vashti refused. This made the king a laughingstock. To defend himself, he deposed the queen. (See *Esther 1:12-22.*)

Selected Bible Readings

Sunday:	Rejection of Vashti (*Esther 1*)
Monday:	Crowning of Esther (*Esther 2*)
Tuesday:	Plotting of Haman (*Esther 3—4*)
Wednesday:	Venture of Esther (*Esther 5*)
Thursday:	Mordecai Exalted (*Esther 6*)
Friday:	Esther's Feast (*Esther 7—8*)
Saturday:	Deliverance of the Jews (*Esther 9—10*)

Crowning of Esther
Esther 2

The minute Ahasuerus saw Esther, he made her his queen. The little Jewish orphan girl, raised by her cousin Mordecai, was lifted to the Persian throne. According to the Roman historian, Herodotus (485-425 B.C.), at this time the Persian Empire comprised more than half the then-known world.

Between chapters 1 and 2, Ahasuerus made his historic attack on Greece with an army of five million men, suffering a terrible defeat in the famous battles of Thermopylae and Salamis (480 B.C.).

Two years later, Xerxes (Ahasuerus) married Esther. She was his queen for thirteen years. Esther, no doubt, lived for many years into the reign of her stepson, Artaxerxes. Under this king, Nehemiah rebuilt Jerusalem. Esther's marriage to Xerxes gave the Jews prestige at this court and made it possible for Nehemiah to rebuild Jerusalem. (See *Nehemiah 2:1-8.*)

The second chapter describes the scene in the great palace of Xerxes at Persepolis. Richly colored awnings were stretched across from marble pillars to silver rods, shading the exalted guests as they reclined on gold and silver seats while they feasted gluttonously and drank heavily day after day (*Esther 1:5-8*).

Note: Here, parenthetically, occurs the story of Mordecai's saving the king's life. This account figures prominently later in the book (*Esther 2:21-23*).

Plotting of Haman
Esther 3—4

We see a form casting a shadow across the picture. This scene is one of sorrow and mourning. In Esther 3—5 we read of the ascendancy of a man by the name of Haman. He was a wicked man whose day of triumph was short and whose joy endured but for a moment. (See *Job 20:4-5.*) We see him becoming the chief minister of the king.

Haman was the Judas of Israel. He was a wicked monster in the life of God's chosen people.

When Haman appears in the book of Esther, he had just been exalted to the highest position under the king of Persia (*Esther 3:1*). The high honor turned his head. He swelled with vanity and was bitterly humiliated when Mordecai, who was sitting at the gate, did not do homage to him as to the king (*Esther 3:2*).

Inflated with pride, he could not endure the indifference of any subject. The little fault of Mordecai was magnified into a capital offense. Mordecai, a Jew, could not give divine honor to a man! Haman became so enraged that he wanted to have a wholesale massacre of all the Jews in the kingdom (*Esther 3:6*). To determine the day his enemies should be destroyed, he cast lots, which fell on the thirteenth day of March, just ten months away (*Esther 3:7*). Haman tried to prove to the king that all the Jews were disloyal subjects. He offered to pay the king a bribe of millions of dollars (*Esther 3:9*). The king signed a royal decree that meant that every Jewish man, woman and child should be killed and all their property should be taken. Compare this treatment with that used by the Nazi regime.

Imagine the fasting and praying and the weeping in sackcloth that took place among the Jews (*Esther 4:1-3*).

Queen Esther saw it all and inquired of Mordecai what it meant. He gave her a copy of the king's decree that told the sad story. Then he added, "And who knows but that you have come to royal position for such a time as this?" (*Esther 4:14*).

enter unsummoned in the presence of the king. Who could tell what this fickle monarch would do? Think what he had done to Vashti!

When she had been received by the king, she used her resources. She knew the king's weakness for good living so she invited him to a banquet. Read what happened that night when the king could not sleep (*Esther 6:1-11*). How was Haman trapped (*Esther 6:6*)? At the second banquet Esther pleaded for her own life. She had Haman on the spot.

The king granted Esther's wish. Haman was hung on the very scaffold he had prepared for Mordecai, and Mordecai was elevated to the place of honor next to the king.

As you study God's Word, you will find that through the ages Satan has ever tried to destroy, first, God's people, the Jews, then the Church, and even Christ Himself. But God has thwarted his plans. Even "the gates of hell shall not prevail" *(KJV)* against His Church (see *Matthew 16:18*). God will triumph! Christ has won the victory!

Deliverance of the Jews
Esther 6—10

The book of Esther closes with the account of establishing the Feast of Purim and lifting Mordecai to the place made vacant by Haman (*Esther 10:3*). The Jewish porter became the second man, just under the king of Persia. The Feast of Purim was to be celebrated annually. It is always inspired by the dramatic story of Esther.

The Feast of Purim, celebrated even today, sets the seal upon the accuracy of the story. The feast does not celebrate the downfall of Haman so much as the deliverance of the people.

This feast celebrates a deliverance of the Jewish people from a fearful danger. It was a Thanksgiving Day for

It would do well for all of us to pause and ask ourselves this same question. Why has God allowed me to live at this particular hour? To do what is right may mean that we must jeopardize our lives. Then we must face the issue and answer with this young queen, "And if I perish, I perish."

Venture of Esther *Esther 5*

Queen Esther answers the challenge of Mordecai. She chose a course at terrible danger to herself for the sake of her oppressed people, the Jews. Once she accepted her dreaded task, she proceeded to carry it out with courage. It was a daring act for her to the chosen people. Although they had forsaken God, He had spared them. Deliverance seems to be the keynote of Jewish history.

This book of Esther is an important link in a chain of events that tell of reestablishing the Hebrew nation in their own land in preparation of the coming of the Messiah into the world. The Jewish people had escaped extermination. It was God's purpose that they should be preserved to bring forth the Savior of the world.

Character Study of Esther

Esther is a sweet and attractive character:

Beautiful and modest—Esther 2:15

Winsome—Esther 2:9-17; 5:1-3

Obedient—Esther 2:10

Humble—Esther 4:16

Courageous—Esther 7:6

Loyal and constant—Esther 2:22; 8:1-2; 7:3-4.

Books of Poetry

of the Old Testament

Job • Psalms • Proverbs
Ecclesiastes • Song of Songs

14. UNDERSTANDING

Job

Job Portrays Jesus Christ, My Redeemer

We have finished reading the historical books of the Old Testament—Joshua through Esther. Now we open the books of poetry—Job, Psalms, Proverbs, Ecclesiastes and Song of Solomon. These books tell of the experiences of the heart.

Job's key word is "tested." "But he knows the way that I take; when he has tested me, I shall come forth as gold" (*Job 23:10*).

Trials and suffering are for our education and training. The athlete is not put under strict discipline for punishment, but merely to make him ready for the race. Christ is ever preparing us for the race that is set before us (*Hebrews 12:1-2*).

Job is no doubt one of the most wonderful poems ever written. Tennyson (Alfred Tennyson, also known as Lord Tennyson, 1809-92,

English poet) called it "the greatest poem, whether of ancient or modern literature." The scene in this amazing book takes place in the patriarchal days. For all we know this book may be one of the most ancient pieces of finished literature in existence. It is one of the oldest, if not the oldest, books in the Bible. The Word of God settles the fact that Job was a real person. God speaks through the prophet Ezekiel and says, "even if these three men—Noah, Daniel and Job—were in it, they could save only themselves by their righteousness" (*Ezekiel 14:14*; see also *14:20*). If you doubt Job's existence, you will have to refute Noah and Daniel.

It is fitting that the oldest book should deal with the oldest problems. Among these is, "Why do godly people suffer?" This is the theme of the book. People have always asked why God permits good people to suffer. Haven't you wondered yourself why some good person has to die of an awful disease or has to be confined to a bed of pain? The drama of Job offers a solution to these problems. We believe it gives God's answer.

It is easy to become confused about this problem of suffering. Remember, the disciples of Christ thought that suffering was the result of sin in a life (*John 9:2*). The book of Job gives an entirely different reason for the suffering of Job. In this case, Job was being honored by God. It was the truth that

Job may be one of the most ancient pieces of finished literature in existence. It is certainly one of the oldest, if not the oldest, books in the Bible.

God could trust Job to remain faithful to God in spite of everything. How wonderful it would be if you and I learned to thank God in all that happens to us.

This book should first be read as a narrative. The story of Job is a simple one. It opens with a scene in heaven and then tells of Job's fall from prosperity to poverty. This is followed by the great discussion between Job and his four friends: Eliphaz, the religious dogmatist, much like an ancient Pharisee; Bildad, who sought to comfort Job with worn-out platitudes; and Zophar, who thought he had a corner on all religious wisdom. Then comes Elihu, the impetuous youth. Finally, the climax is reached when God speaks. Job answers, at last in a humble spirit, and the problem is solved. This is the story of the book.

Next, we should study the problem of the book. It may be stated, "Why do the righteous suffer?" We find:

1. The shallow view of Satan—that the children of God love and serve Him because it pays in riches and honor (*Job 1:1—2:8*). Satan said that Job's godliness was selfishness, that he served God for profit, that when prosperity ended he would be no more godly. He received permission to test Job (*Job 2:6*). Satan added, "Who wouldn't serve God for a handsome income of so many thousand a year? Watch him when his prosperity ends."

2. The scarcely less false view of Eliphaz, Bildad and Zophar (who agreed for the most part) that the unrighteous suffer because of their sins and the righteous are rewarded. Hence they reasoned that Job must have sinned, and this suffering was his punishment. Job was a great sufferer; therefore he must have been a great sinner. They said, "Who, being innocent, has ever perished?" (*Job 4:7*). But Job knew that his heart was true to God, and he could not accept the accusation of his friends. He showed them that their conclusion was false and that the wicked often prospered in the world (*Job 24:6*).

3. Elihu had a far more just answer of the problem, but his eloquent discourse was marred by conceit. He defended God and saw in affliction the chastisement of a loving Father. But this did not explain the reason of suffering to Job. Elihu argued that suffering was God's discipline to bring His sons back into fellowship with Himself. He believed that suffering was sent to keep us from sinning.

4. Jehovah explained to Job (by revealing Himself to him) that when men see God something always happens. The godly are allowed to suffer that they may see themselves first. Read Isaiah 6:1-5; Genesis 17:1-3; Daniel 10:4-8. When we come to the end of ourselves, God can lift us up. Job was a good man, but self-righteous. Read Job 29:1-25 and you will find the personal pronouns "I," "my" and "me" fifty-two times. It reminds one of Romans 7.

God has a wise purpose in all of our suffering. God wants to show His manifold wisdom (*Ephesians 3:10*). He wants the trial of our faith to work patience. He wants to bring out the gold as by fire. He wants to reveal real character. Furthermore, we have an unseen cloud of witnesses gathered in the great stadium of heaven to watch us in the conflict (*Hebrews 12:1-2*).

How little did Job realize that so much hung on his steadfastness and trust in God when he said, "Though he slay me, yet will I hope in him" (*Job 13:15*). I wonder if we realize today the issues that hang upon our faithfulness to God. If God could only find more of us who would trust Him, how much we might encourage others to trust!

The problem of suffering has had much light thrown upon it from the New Testament—especially from the cross of Christ. Here we see the world's most righteous Man, the world's greatest Sufferer. We know now that the righteous suffer with the wicked today because of sin that fills the world with misery. We know there are natural consequences of sin, for the godly as well as the sinner. Chastening is sometimes for training and correction. There is a suffering Christians must endure for Christ's sake and the gospel's.

The book of Job is a commentary on 1 Corinthians 11:31-32; Hebrews 12:7-11; Luke 22:31-32; 1 Corinthians 5:5. The chief subject of the book of Job is the riddle of all times: Why do the righteous suffer? But it deals with a wide scope of knowledge—the power of Satan, telling of his might and the limit of his authority; the fact of the Resurrection; and why a person should serve God.

The book of Job tells us much about human suffering. Job's friends, as thousands do today, made the mistake of thinking that all suffering was God's way of punishing sin. They asked, "Who, being innocent, has ever perished?" (*Job 4:7*).

God allowed Stephen to be stoned (*Acts 7:59*) and Paul to have a thorn in his flesh to buffet him (*2 Corinthians*). Even Jesus knew suffering.

Job's friends concluded that Job must have sinned greatly to account for such exceptional suffering. Let us find out what God proved.

What was Job's attitude toward God? He first had access to God through the blood of the sacrifice (*Job 1:5*). Then he walked with God in integrity of heart and life.

Job had a conscience right toward God. He knew his heart was true and so he could accept the accusations of his friends. He finally could show them that their conclusion was wrong and that the wicked often prosper in this world (*Job 24:6*).

God trusted Job; therefore He assigned to him this great problem of suffering.

When Job was prosperous and upright and benevolent, he was in danger of becoming self-confident, and could easily forget that he only held his power and place in this world as a steward of God.

God dealt with Job:

1. He was broken (*Job 16:12,14; 17:11*).
2. He was melted (*Job 23:10*).
3. He was softened so he could say, "The hand of God hath touched me" (*Job 19:21, KJV*). "God maketh my heart soft" (*Job 23:16, KJV*).

Job never really saw himself until he saw God. This is true of every life. See how it affected Isaiah when he, as a young man, saw God (*Isaiah 6:1-9*).

Job was all ready to reason with God, as many do today, about His dealings with him. He could not understand Him. A vision of God Himself completed the work in Job and brought him to the dust.

Job was a wealthy and happy man until disaster struck and he lost almost everything.

Listen to God speak of Job: "Will the one who contends with the Almighty correct him?" (*Job 40:2*). Think of trying to correct the God of this universe! The wisdom of people is only foolishness with God. Hear Job's answer, "I am unworthy—how can I reply to you? I put my hand over my mouth" (*Job 40:4*).

God kept dealing with Job till he came to the very end of himself! Hear him speak again, read Job 42:3-6.

We find Job a chastened, softened servant. God turned the tide and his prosperity was given back to him doubled—twice as many sheep and oxen, asses and camels! He rejoiced again in his sons and daughters, just the same number as before.

Job no longer asked a question but made a statement. See Job 19:25-26.

Job's vision of a future life, that had been uncertain before, was clear now. We had heard him asking a question multitudes have asked, "If a man dies, will he live again?" (*Job 14:14*). Paul answered this question in the great resurrection chapter of the Bible, 1 Corinthians 15. Jesus answered it in His

statement, "He who believes in me will live, even though he dies" (*John 11:25*).

What a wonderful vision of the future life we have in these words! What a prophecy of the coming of the Savior!

Job was "blameless and upright, a man who fears God and shuns evil" (*Job 1:8*).

1. He was "blameless"—complete, all-round.
2. He was "upright"—Hebrew word means "straight."
3. He "feared God"—this is the beginning of wisdom.
4. He "shunned evil"—this is his moral conduct.

Job was right with man and with God, and remember it was God who said this. God added, "There is no one on earth like him" (*Job 1:8*). What an honor God gave to Job to use these words to describe him!

As the book opens, we see Job surrounded by wealth, family, position and friends. Watch this man stripped of his wealth and reduced to poverty! His children are taken! Health is gone! Then he loses the confidence of his wife! Finally his friends go!

Satan and the Saint
Job 1:6—2:10

In Job 1:6, the "sons of God" (Hebrew: *bene ha-elohim*) presented themselves before the Lord. These "sons of God" were angelic beings, the messengers of God. The mystery is that Satan was among them. He was angelic, but he had fallen. There was no hint that he was out of place or that he had forced himself into the audience chamber.

In contrast to the Almighty, we have the figure of the adversary, or Satan. Let us stop and study this person for a while. Satan as the adversary is depicted with great clearness, representing a real being, not an imaginary one. We cannot help but contrast the Satan of the book of Job with the grotesque, gigantic, awful figure depicted by the poets. The Bible tells us that Satan comes as "an angel of light" to deceive and to tempt (*2 Corinthians 11:14*).

Satan has great power, but there are limits to his might. Satan is mighty, but God is Almighty! Satan can break through only where God allows (*Job 1:10*). What a comfort it is to know that no calamity can come to us that the Father does not allow. He who has "shut up the sea behind doors" and said, "This far you may come and no farther; here is where your proud waves halt" (*Job 38:8,11*), will never let us be tempted beyond what we can bear (*1 Corinthians 10:13*).

Remember, Satan is so held by the Almighty that he can only strike where he is given permission (*Job 1:12*).

1. Job tore his robe (*Job 1:20*). It is worthwhile for us to learn that we are meant to feel grief. Sorrow has its use in our lives. We are told "do not make light of the Lord's discipline" but be "trained by it" (*Hebrews 12:5,11*).

"Jesus wept" (*John 11:35*)! Christ does not destroy our natural emotions. Jesus told the women of Jerusalem to weep for themselves and for their children (*Luke 23:28*).

2. Job recognized that loss and sorrow are the laws of life. We have to learn that all possessions are transient. We are losing something every moment. We cannot stop and weep about everything that is taken from us. We have to learn a hard lesson—that we can live on in spite of all our losses. Begin to learn while you are young that nothing is necessary but Christ.

Only pure gold can stand the fire. All dross is burned up. God, the great metallurgist of heaven, puts us in the fire, but He watches and tries us Himself. He trusts no other. When the fire has burned long enough to destroy the impurities, He pulls us out.

God speaks to Satan, "Where have you come from?" What a tragedy in the answer! "From roaming through the earth and going back and forth in it" (*Job 1:7*). Remember, this reveals the "endless restlessness of evil." "Be self-controlled and alert. Your enemy the devil prowls around like a roaring lion looking for someone to devour" (*1 Peter 5:8*).

God speaks again, "Have you considered my servant Job?" (*Job 1:8*).

Satan said, "But stretch out your hand and strike everything he has, and he will surely curse you to your face" (*Job 1:11*). Satan's charge against Job was that a man only serves God for what he can get out of it. Really Job is not so much on trial here as God. It is less a question of Job's loyalty than it is one of God's power. Is God able "to guard what I have entrusted to him for that day" (*2 Timothy 1:12*)?

So God says, "All right, try it out! Take everything away from Job and see what happens!" (Author's paraphrase.)

Do you see that the real conflict here was between God and Satan? God was proving the truth about His statement of Job's integrity in following Him.

When the trials came, Job did not understand the meaning of all his suffering. He knew it was not because he had sinned, as his friends said. He wondered what God was doing. We will not always understand what God is working out on the battleground of our hearts. But know this: there is a reason and value to everything God allows and that "in all things God works for the good of those who love him, who have been called according to his purpose" (*Romans 8:28*).

Job proved that Satan's statement concerning God's children was a lie, that is, that they only serve Him for what they can get out of it.

When the Word is being sown, the fowls of the air come to pluck it away (see *Matthew 13:3-23*).

Remember, you can never walk before God and try to lead a godly life without Satan coming in to walk with you—accusing you, finding fault and vexing you.

What Kind of a Man Was Job?
He was a "perfect" (blameless) man (*Job 1:1*).
He was a prosperous man (*Job 1:2-4*).
He was a praying man (*Job 1:5*).
He was a popular man (*Job 29:21,25*).
He was a proven man (*Job 42:10,12*).

Job and His Friends
Job 2:11—37:24

Get acquainted with Job's friends. Let us introduce you to them. First there is courtly Eliphaz, then argumentative Bildad, and blunt Zophar, and the youthful Elihu.

There are things we can say in favor of these men, although their words of "comfort" were anything but that. The first is that they came at all. They were friends who stuck through adversity.

You notice they kept still for seven days. This is good! They seemed to be trying to find out the reason for all of Job's troubles before they spoke. Someone has said that instead of talking about Job, they came and talked with him.

They all had a reason; they wished to tell Job why they thought he was suffering as he did. They all agreed he must have sinned miserably to have caused this suffering.

Eliphaz backs his argument by a dream (*Job 4:1—5:27*); Bildad, by some old proverbs (*Job 8*); Zophar, by experience and reason (*Job 11*). Elihu came nearest the truth when he argued that suffering was God's discipline to bring the soul back into fellowship with God; but it was not the whole truth.

God called Job "perfect and upright." His friends were wrong in charging him with sin as the only possible cause of his calamities.

Wretched Comforters
The chief question returns: Why does God permit the righteous to suffer? Job cries out from the ashes, "I cannot understand it. It doesn't seem right."

Job's wife, looking on discouraged, says, "Something is wrong. Your religion is a failure. Curse God and die" (author's paraphrase of *Job 2:9*). This means nothing other than, "say goodbye to God." It is the voice of despair.

Eliphaz adds, shaking his head, "God never makes a mistake. What have you done to bring this on yourself?"

Bildad says, "God is just. Confess your sin."

Zophar next speaks, "God is all-wise. He knows man."

Elihu, God's man, says the wisest thing, "God is good; look up, and trust Him, for He is God."

The Righteous Comforter
Jehovah now is heard from the whirlwind: "Brace yourself like a man; I will

question you, and you shall answer me" (*Job 40:7*).

Now Job speaks himself: "I know that you can do all things; no plan of yours can be thwarted" (*Job 42:2*). Then comes the great confession, "My ears had heard of you but now my eyes have seen you. Therefore I despise myself and repent in dust and ashes" (*Job 42:5-6*).

This is the victory of submissive faith. When we bow to God's will, we find God's way.

The philosophy of Job's friends was wrong. Job was glad to see them and he could pour out his troubles to them, but they did not understand him.

Jehovah and Job *Job 38—42*

The scene begins with God gloriously revealing Himself. In a series of approximately sixty questions, God is saying, in effect, "Who can do all these things but Myself?" God is thus revealed to Job, and Job to himself.

As so often is true with us, when Job came into the presence of God, he forgot the speech he thought he would make (*Job 40:4-5*)! There was no arguing with God. Finally, Job went flat down on his face, repenting in "dust and ashes" (*Job 42:6*). This is the only place to learn God's lessons—on your face, with your mouth shut!

Jehovah explains to Job (by revealing Himself to him) that when men see God something always happens. The godly are allowed to suffer that they

may see themselves. Read Isaiah 6:1-5. When Isaiah saw himself as he really was, he fell on his face undone and cried out, "I am a man of unclean lips."

In Job 42 we find:

1. A Consciousness of God (*v. 5*)
2. A Collapse of Job (*v. 6*)
3. A Commission to serve (*v. 7*).

As you read the chapter, you see that Job enjoyed a double portion of prosperity from the hand of God. God allows His children to suffer in order to reveal character, to set forth an object lesson and to bring to light some hidden sin. In Job's case, that hidden sin was self-righteousness.

Job found God in his trouble. Many know God as a Creator and believe in His greatness, but they do not really know God. The more we understand His ways the more we will love Him and put our trust in Him.

Job is rich:

1. In philosophy: Ancient as the book is, it is filled with a divine record of human philosophy, and blind gropings of human wisdom. Human reason has never been able to go beyond Job's friends in explaining the great mysteries of human experience on natural grounds. (See *1 Corinthians 2:14* and *Colossians 2:8*.)

2. In gems of spiritual truth: Be sure to read the following references: Job 1:21; 5:17; 13:15; 14:14; 16:21; 19:23-27; 23:10; 26:7-14; 28:12-28; 42:1-6. These are some of the most frequently quoted and best-loved passages in the Bible.

15. UNDERSTANDING
Psalms

The Psalms Portray Jesus Christ, Our All in All

"Come, let us sing for joy to the Lord; let us shout aloud to the Rock of our salvation" (*Psalm 95:1*). Here we take this view of the Psalms in panorama. The sights that catch and hold our attention are so numerous that they defy exhaustive treatment in one short chapter.

"Ascribe to the Lord the glory due to his name; worship the Lord in the splendor of his holiness" (*Psalm 29:2*). This is the key verse to the book of Psalms. The door into the temple of praise and prayer is open. Go in with the psalmist to rest and pray. It is a real privilege to go apart during the rush of earthly things.

No doubt Psalms is the best-loved book in the Old Testament. Someone has called it the solid gold of Christian experience. Slip in wherever you will and you will find a treasure. Every psalm is a direct expression of the soul's consciousness of God. With which psalms are you familiar? Pause a moment to think.

The Hebrew title of this book is "Praise," or the "Book of Praises," which indicates that the main contents of the book are praise, prayer and worship. The name "Psalms" comes from the Greek. We find that the early Christian fathers called it the "Psalter."

The Psalms is the national hymn-book of Israel. It contains 150 poems to be set to music for worship.

Worship is the central idea. The Psalms magnify and praise the Lord, exalt His attributes, His names, His Word and His goodness. Every human experience is related to Him.

We see the life of the believer pictured in all its experiences of joy and sorrow, victory and failure.

The Psalms are full of Christ. They describe the whole program of His suffering and death. Let us look and see!

We have Christ's own warrant for looking for Him in the Psalms. He said, "Everything must be fulfilled that is written about me in the Law of

Selected Bible Readings

Sunday:	Psalms of Law (*Psalms 1; 19*)
Monday:	Psalms of Creation (*Psalms 29; 104*)
Tuesday:	Psalms of Judgment (*Psalms 52; 53*)
Wednesday:	Psalms of Christ (*Psalms 22; 40; 41*)
Thursday:	Psalms of Life (*Psalms 3; 31*)
Friday:	Psalms of the Heart (*Psalms 37; 42*)
Saturday:	Psalms of God (*Psalms 90; 139*)

Moses, the Prophets and the Psalms" (*Luke 24:44*).

His prophetic office is found in Psalm 22:22.

His priestly office in Psalms 40:6,8; 22; 49; 110.

His kingly office in Psalms 2; 21; 45; 72.

His sufferings in Psalms 22 and 69.

His resurrection in Psalm 16.

Another extremely useful classification of the Psalms may be made according to the subjects of the individual psalms:

Instruction 1; 19; 39

Praise 8; 29; 93; 100

Thanksgiving 30; 65; 103; 107; 116

Penitence 6; 32; 38; 51; 102; 130; 143

Trust 3; 27; 31; 46; 56; 62; 86

Distress 4; 13; 55; 64; 88

Aspiration 42; 63; 80; 84; 137

History 78; 105; 106

Prophecy (Psalms of the Messiah) 2; 16; 22; 24; 40; 45; 68; 69; 72; 97; 110; 118.

We speak of the Psalms as the Psalms of David. He has been considered the principal writer. He gives the keynote and his voice rises highest in the sacred choir. But there were other authors besides him. Seventy-three of the 150 psalms are assigned to him; fifty are anonymous. Psalm 90 is written by Moses. Two are written by

Solomon—Psalms 72 and 127. Besides these, Asaph, David's choir leader, the sons of Korah, a family of official musicians, and Jeduthun wrote some. But let us not be too engrossed in finding who penned them. Let us rather read and enjoy these grand expressions of praise. They are of God for you. Sing them and make them your own. Catch David's note and spirit. He wrote marching songs, prayer songs, rally songs, hilltop songs, confession songs. Sing as you march. Keep step with David and David's Lord all the way.

Many quotations from this book are found in the New Testament. At least twenty of these directly refer to Christ and His life and death.

Man *Psalms 1—41*

1. Man blessed (*Psalm 1*)
2. Man fallen from his high position and at enmity with God (*Psalms 2; 14*)
3. Man restored by his blessed Redeemer, the Man Christ Jesus (*Psalms 16—41*).

In this section we have a collection by David of the psalms that tell of the state of man—his blessedness, fall and recovery. Psalm 1 tells us of the road to success. Everyone wants to prosper. No one wishes to fail. The psalmist says that everyone may prosper. Think of it! It will be well for every young person to master the rules for success laid down here.

Things Not to Do

1. Refuse to walk in the counsel of the ungodly; do not take their advice or follow the pattern of their lives.

2. Refuse to stand in the way of sinners. Standing is even a lower step. When you stand in sin, it shows that you have been brought under the spell of evil.

3. Refuse to sit—to take the scorner's seat is to take the most despicable place possible. The scorner sits idly watching the struggles of others and cares not that many are losing the fight. You ask the scorner, "Isn't there great need in this world?" "I suppose," the scorner answers, but just sits and plays the cynic. The scorner is sure "that every minister, missionary or Christian worker is either a fool or a hypocrite."

Things to Do
1. Read the Bible.
2. Delight in it.
3. Meditate upon it.

The more you read the Word, the more you want to. As one great Christian leader has said, "The gospel feeds you, then it makes you hungry." It never grows stale. You cannot read it too often or too much.

Things That Result
When the Christian has followed the don'ts and do's, what is the result? Three things (*Psalm 1*):

"Planted"—"He is like a tree planted by streams of water"—the settled and steadfast life in a luxuriant soil;

"Purposive"—"which yields its fruit in season"—the productive life;

"Prosperous"—"and whose leaf does not wither"—the abiding, happy life.

Other psalms in this group that show the final blessings of man because of the glorious work of the Man Christ Jesus are Psalms 22; 23; 24.

Psalm 22 tells of the Good Shepherd giving His life for His sheep. We see the cross and hear the cries of our dying Savior. As you read this psalm, you will recognize the facts.

Psalm 23 tells of the great Shepherd keeping His sheep. We read, "The Lord is my shepherd, I shall not be in want." He promises to guide and provide and keep me.

Psalm 24 tells of the chief Shepherd in His glory rewarding His sheep. He is my King and He is coming to reign in power and great glory.

Psalm 22 gives a picture of Calvary. We see the crucifixion portrayed here more clearly than in any other part of the Old Testament. The psalm opens with the cry of our Lord in the darkest hour of His life: "My God, my God, why have you forsaken me?" It closes with, "for he has done it." The original Hebrew means, "It is finished"—the last cry of the Savior (*John 19:30*).

Psalm 22:6 says, "But I am a worm and not a man, scorned by men and despised by the people." This tells us of the offense of the Cross!

Read and compare these verses:

Psalm 22:1	Matthew 27:46
Psalm 22:6-7	Luke 23:35-36
Psalm 22:6-8	Matthew 27:39,41,43
Psalm 22:12-13	Matthew 27:36,44
Psalm 22:28	1 Corinthians 15:23-24

"I am poured out like water, and all my bones are out of joint. My heart has turned to wax; it has melted away within me" (*Psalm 22:14*). This depicts excessive perspiration because of physical torture. It also means the breaking of Jesus' heart.

He tells us why His heart was broken. "Scorn has broken my heart" (*Psalm 69:20*). In John 19:34-35, we read that "one of the soldiers pierced Jesus' side with a spear, bringing a sudden flow of blood and water. The man who saw it has given testimony, and his testimony is true. He knows that he tells the truth, and he testifies so that you also may believe."

Jesus died of a broken heart. He bore the reproach and shame for others. Bearing our sins hid Him from His Father's face; this is what broke His heart. Death by a broken heart is very rare. It is caused by intense agony of suffering.

"My tongue sticks to the roof of my mouth" (*Psalm 22:15*). This verse describes intense thirst. The account in the New Testament said, "Knowing that all was now completed, and so that the Scripture would be fulfilled, Jesus said, 'I am thirsty.'" Yes, Psalm 69:21 says, "They put gall in my food and gave me vinegar for my thirst." Read John 19:28-29.

"They have pierced my hands and my feet" (*Psalm 22:16*). Crucifixion! The Roman method of death by crucifixion is described here. The Jewish law did not know of this method. These words give the description of death by crucifixion—hands and feet nailed to the cross—bones of hands, arms, shoulders out of joint as a result of hanging from the cross, straining bone and muscle.

"They divide my garments among them and cast lots for my clothing" (*Psalm 22:18*). Even the act of the soldiers is described here. See Matthew 27:35.

Israel *Psalms 42—72*

1. Her Ruin (*Psalms 42—49*)
2. Her Redeemer (*Psalms 50—60*)
3. Her Redemption (*Psalms 61—72*).

Here in this section we find additional psalms compiled for use in the Temple. It opens with "a cry" from the depth of oppression—Psalms 42—49. It ends with the King reigning over the redeemed nation. "He will rule from sea to sea and from the River to the ends of the earth" (*Psalm 72:8*). Read this glorious Psalm.

Several psalms speak of penitence, but the chief is Psalm 51. It is a psalm of David. If you turn to 2 Samuel 11 and 12, you will find the story of David's sin. When you read this, notice three things David said. When Nathan the prophet was telling David the story of the despicable fellow who took the only lamb belonging to the poor man, we hear him say to David: "You are the man!" David did not try to dodge the issue but said, "I have sinned against the Lord." Then Nathan reassured him, saying, "The Lord has taken away your sin" (2 Samuel 12:7,13).

We think it strange when we read that David was "a man after his [God's] own heart." When we compare what other kings would have done under the same circumstances, we are not so surprised. But David confessed and said, "I have sinned against the Lord" (2 Samuel 12:13). That is what sin is—breaking God's law.

Notice in Psalm 51:4 these words, "Against you, you only, have I sinned and done what is evil in your sight." This psalm is a prayer of contrition and confession. David cries for mercy from a God whom he knows is merciful and full of loving kindness.

We learn from this psalm that we must confess our sin to God (1 John 1:9) and that God is just to forgive. Whenever we are sincere in our confession to God, He will cleanse our sin.

The Sanctuary *Psalms 73—89*

In the psalms of this third section we see the sanctuary mentioned or referred to in almost every one.

We see God's counsels in relation to the sanctuary. The sanctuary is seen from its ruin to its restoration in the fullness of blessing.

The Earth *Psalms 90—106*

Blessing needed (*Psalms 90—94*)
Blessing anticipated (*Psalms 95—100*)
Blessing enjoyed (*Psalms 101—106*).

The first of this group of psalms was written during the wanderings in the wilderness. The psalms are not arranged in chronological order.

Read the opening verses of Psalms 90 and 91 together. "Lord, you have

been our dwelling place throughout all generations . . . He who dwells in the shelter of the Most High will rest in the shadow of the Almighty." If God is our dwelling place on this earth, we shall live in confidence, sheltered by the Almighty. Christ says, "If you remain in me and my words remain in you, ask whatever you wish, and it will be given you" (John 15:7). The secret of a godly life is remaining or "abiding" (KJV) in the Almighty. When the devil tempted Him (using *Psalm 91:12*), the Lord answered by quoting from Deuteronomy 6:16 (see *Matthew 4:7*). Christ was victorious because He lived in the "dwelling place" described by these two psalms. We are told that there is a point of perfect calm at the center of a cyclone. There may be raging storms, snares, pestilences, terror by night, darkness and destruction, but when the soul is abiding under the shadow of the Almighty, it is safe.

If you wish to praise the Lord for His goodness, read Psalm 103. It is full of worship, adoration, praise and thanksgiving. This is great exercise for the soul.

The Word of God
Psalms 107—150

All the teaching in the Psalms is grouped around the Word of God. This section opens with Psalm 107, which gives the key: "He sent forth his word and healed them" (v. 20).

Psalm 119 is the great psalm of the whole book. It extols the Word of God, which is the great revelation of the heart and mind of the Lord. This book is "more desirable than gold, yes, than much fine gold; sweeter also than honey and the drippings of the honeycomb" (*Psalm 19:10, NASB*). Almost every verse speaks of God's Word or law or precepts or statutes.

Value God's Word:

1. It blesses little children—Matthew 19:14.
2. It strengthens young men—1 John 2:14.
3. It sanctifies and cleanses all who read it—Ephesians 5:26.
4. It protects the widows—Exodus 22:22-23.
5. It honors the aged—Leviticus 19:32.
6. It offers eternal life to everyone—John 3:36.

Praise is the highest duty that any creature can discharge. Man's chief end is to glorify God. There is no heaven either here or in the world to come for people who do not praise God. If you do not enter into the spirit and worship of heaven, the spirit and joy of heaven cannot enter you!

The Psalms begin with the word "blessed." This word is multiplied in this book. The book seems to be built around this first word. There is not one "woe" in the entire book of Psalms.

How can we make the Psalms our own in experience?

Why do you like the Psalms?

What Psalms can you quote?

Probably no other book has so largely influenced the turning points in people's lives, given expression to their deepest experiences and woven itself into every fiber of their character as the book of Psalms.

16. UNDERSTANDING

Proverbs, Ecclesiastes, Song of Songs

Jesus Christ, Our Wisdom; the End of All Living; the Lover of Our Souls

Understanding Proverbs

"Blessed is the man who finds wisdom, the man who gains understanding" (*Proverbs 3:13*).

The books classed as poetical are Job, Psalms, Proverbs, Ecclesiastes and Song of Solomon. These are not "poetical" in the sense that they are fanciful or unreal, but in form only. There is no meter or rhyme, but rather a thought rhyme expressed in parallelism—repeating the same thought in different words.

> In Psalms we find Christians on their knees.
> In Proverbs we find Christians on their feet.
> The Psalms are for the Christian's devotions.
> The Proverbs are for the Christian's walk.
> The Psalms are for the closet of prayer.
> The Proverbs are for the business place, home and playground.

We find in Proverbs that godliness is practical. Every relationship in life is mentioned. We find our duty to God, to our neighbors, the duty of parents and children, our obligations as citizens.

The Jewish people likened Proverbs to the outer court of the Temple; Ecclesiastes to the holy place; the Song of Solomon to the holy of holies. Remember that the altar of burnt offering and the laver of cleansing were in the outer court. If we come to the book of Proverbs with a cleansed and surrendered heart and mind, we will get most out of the book.

The book of Proverbs takes us out in the court of the congregation where the people are. Here they live their daily lives, and jostle each other in the highways of life. This is a book for everyday instruction. It deals with the practical affairs of life. The author, Solomon, wrote more wisely than he lived. The wise give heed to the commands of God and obey them. The foolish ignore God's will. This book divides people into two classes—wise and foolish.

Notice how the book opens—"The proverbs of Solomon." Solomon was a great king, famous for his wisdom and riches. He wrote 3,000 proverbs, 1,005 scientist of no mean ability. He was an architect of a Temple that was one of the wonders of the world, and then, too, he was a king.

That Solomon was the author of this book implies no more than that he took the lead in gathering these sayings already current among the people, given by the Holy Spirit through the centuries, and put them into the orderly arrangement we have today. See what Solomon said about this in Ecclesiastes 12:9, where it is recorded—"He pondered and searched out and set in order many proverbs."

Someone has said that they were a collection of maxims, woven into a didactic poem around a general topic, wisdom.

Several names are given in the book regarding authorship:

Solomon—Proverbs 1:1; 25:1
The wise—Proverbs 22:17
Men of Hezekiah—Proverbs 25:1
Agur—Proverbs 30:1
King Lemuel and his mother—
    Proverbs 31:1.

This book is filled with words of

songs (*1 Kings 4:31-32*). Solomon was peculiarly qualified to write this book. God had given Solomon "wisdom and very great insight, and a breadth of understanding as measureless as the sand on the seashore" (*1 Kings 4:29*). Solomon was a philosopher; he was a

A scene in Bethlehem market. Proverbs is a book of everyday instruction; it deals with the practical affairs of life.

wisdom. There is one terse saying after another.

Proverbs is divided into three sections:

1. Counsel for young men—Proverbs 1—10
2. Counsel for all men—Proverbs 11—20
3. Counsel for kings and rulers—Proverbs 21—31.

The book closes with one of the most beautiful chapters in the Word (*Proverbs 31*). This is a chapter about women's rights. "Give her the reward she has earned, and let her works bring her praise at the city gate" (*v. 31*). Wherever Christ goes, womanhood is lifted up. In non-Christian countries, where Christ is not known, woman is rarely more than a chattel or slave. In Christian lands, woman is equal to man.

This book presents a system of conduct and life. You cannot find any agnosticism here. The existence of God is assumed. Be wise and find God's way for your life! This book is to provide rules for the righteous life.

The real power and beauty in this book lie hidden in the true meaning of the word "wisdom." It is evident that this word means more than an excellent attribute. It is found that the wisdom of Proverbs is embodied in the Incarnate Word of the New Testament. Christ found Himself in this book (*Luke 24:27*).

Wisdom is represented as dwelling with God from all eternity. "I was appointed from eternity, from the beginning, before the world began. . . . I was there when he set the heavens in place, when he marked out the horizon on the face of the deep . . . when he marked out the foundations of the earth. Then I was the craftsman at his side" (*Proverbs 8:23-30*). Jesus was the Designer of the universe. Compare these with John 1:1-2; Hebrews 1:2; Colossians 1:15-16; 2:3.

When you read the book of Proverbs, put "Christ" in place of "wisdom" in the verse. (See *1 Corinthians 1:30*.) You will see a wonderful power in this book. "We know also that the Son of God has come and has given us understanding, so that we may know him who is true" (*1 John 5:20*).

The purpose of the book of Proverbs is stated clearly at the beginning. See Proverbs 1:2-4. We find that the first of all duties is the fear of God (*Proverbs 1:7*). "Receive the instruction of wisdom, justice, and judgment, and equity" (*Proverbs 1:3, KJV*). This is the true college of spirit education of the self, "for giving prudence to the simple, knowledge and discretion to the young" (*Proverbs 1:4*). Plain common sense is needed in life. Don't be a fool!

God wants to give us of His wisdom—the wisdom that created heavens and earth, that we might use it in all of life (*James 1:5*). This would put an end to all the confusion and evil in this world, wouldn't it? Human wisdom can never solve life's problems. Only God knows the ways of people. "The fear of the Lord is the beginning of wisdom" (*Proverbs 9:10; Psalm 111:10*).

Counsel for Young Men
(Proverbs 1—10)

"Wise Up!"—worship is the first step to wisdom (*1:7*).

"Walk Straight!"—the straight and narrow has the lowest accident rate (*2:20*).

"Directions"—ask God about everything: He knows every road (*3:6*).

"Watch Your Step!"—every step helps mold character; step well (*4:26*).

"God's Black List"—pride, lies, murder, deceit, mischief, betrayal, discord (*6:17-19*).

"A Bad Woman"—read carefully

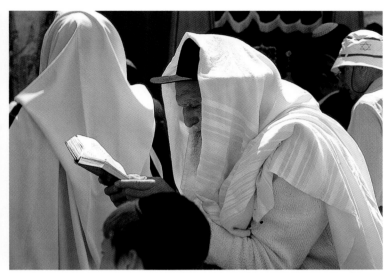

Proverbs 7:15-27.

"Riches"—rubies of wisdom command highest prices on the market of character values (*8:11*).

"More Fun"—nothing you ought not to do is ever more fun. Wait till you see what results (*9:17-18*).

"Wanted! Silence"—wordy men seldom are wise men (*10:19*).

This whole book is extremely practical. It would be well for us all to give it closer study for our guidance in daily life. "In all your ways acknowledge him, and he will make your paths straight" (*Proverbs 3:6*). This is the Lord's rule for our feet. The way of evil—"Avoid it, do not travel on it; turn from it and go on your way" (*Proverbs 4:15*). This is God's "Stop! Look! Listen!"

The fear of the Lord spoken of here is not a fear of fright, but a fear of a son who is afraid he might grieve his father's love. It is the fear coming from love, the fear of displeasing the Lord, that leads to godliness. We shall not begin to be wise until our lives are in right relation with Christ, the fount of all wisdom. "Wisdom is supreme; therefore get wisdom. Though it cost all you have, get understanding" (*Proverbs 4:7*).

God wants to give us instruction "for giving prudence to the simple, knowledge and discretion to the young" (*Proverbs 1:4*). Don't be a fool. God wants you to have plain common sense. The most uncommon thing in the world today is common sense.

In Proverbs 4:23-26, we find that the whole body is included:

"Guard your heart"—verse 23.

"Put away perversity from your mouth"—verse 24.

"Let your eyes look straight ahead"—verse 25.

"Make level paths for your feet"—verse 26.

The duty of parents to chastise their children is enforced and is based upon God's chastening of His children (*Proverbs 3:11,12*). One of the signs of the last wicked days upon the earth is given by Paul as "disobedient to their parents" (*2 Timothy 3:2*). What happened to Eli and his boys because he allowed his sons to sin?

The young are warned against the influence of bad companions, against impurity and intemperance, against anger, strifes and quarrels. (See *Proverbs 1:10-19; 4:14-19; 19;* also *chapters 3; 10; 13; 15; 16; 18.*)

There are many sins of the tongue. We use it too freely. We lie and are deceitful in dealings with others. Much is said about guarding the tongue, for in the tongue is the power of life and death. (See *Proverbs 12:22; 18:21.*)

As we read this book, we find the author pleading with us to shun evil companions, pride, envy, intemperance, sins of the tongue and idleness. This would be impossible to do unless we had Christ, the Wisdom of God, within us.

Read about pride and its consequences in Proverbs 8; 11; 16; 19. See Proverbs 16:18. The Lord wants us always to be humble before Him and not to esteem ourselves better than others. Every truly great person is humble.

Counsel for All Men *(Proverbs 11—20)*
"False Economy"—a gift is never lost; only what is selfishly kept impoverishes *(11:24).*

"Fools"—you cannot convince a fool of his folly; only a wise man will accept a rebuke for foolhardiness *(12:15).*

"Lying"—righteousness and lying are enemies; to a wicked man they are synonymous *(13:5).*

"A gentle answer turns away wrath"—two people ought not to get angry at the same time *(15:1).*

"Clean Sin"—a man deep in wickedness will invent "pretty names for sin" (Charles Haddon Spurgeon, 1834-92, British, Baptist preacher) *(16:2).*

"To Win Friends"—a friendly man will have friends; being a relative does not ensure being a friend *(18:24).*

"Drink Up!"—When you decide for strong drink, don't be surprised when it decides against you *(20:1).*

"People curse the man who hoards grain" *(Proverbs 11:26).* This reveals the sin of the grain speculator. It is a warning to the speculators of our day.

"The righteous man leads a blameless life; blessed are his children after him" *(Proverbs 20:7).* The Douai (Catholic) version of the Bible says: "He leaves behind him blessed children." This is a good man's legacy to the world. Godly parents are a blessing to children *(Proverbs 20:7)* and should instruct them in the right way *(Proverbs 22:6).*

There has never been a time when men did as well as they knew how. However imperfect their instructions, they have never lived up to them. The last thing a man could complain of is a lack of good advice.

Who has heart trouble? Who has woe? Sorrow? Contentions? (Read *Proverbs 20; 23; 31.*) In Scripture drunkenness is roundly condemned with other severe sins: "Do you not know that the wicked will not inherit the kingdom of God? Do not be deceived: Neither the sexually immoral nor idolaters nor adulterers nor male prostitutes nor homosexual offenders nor thieves nor the greedy nor drunkards nor slanderers nor swindlers will inherit the kingdom of God" *(1 Corinthians 6:9-10).* The words in Proverbs are "like apples of gold in settings of silver" *(Proverbs 25:11).* Study the picture, but do not miss the apples of gold depicted here.

Proverbs is an intensely practical book, exposing a series of traps that would ensnare us. "There is no wisdom, no insight, no plan that can succeed against the Lord" *(Proverbs 21:30).* At last we see God's will and God's way! Hasten it, O Lord!

Counsel for Kings and Rulers

(*Proverbs 21—31*)

"Self-Control"—a guarded mouth makes for a serene soul (*21:23*).

"Reputation"—choose a good name rather than great riches. Your name goes on; your wealth stops at death (*22:1*).

"Soberness"—red wine is colorful but calamitous (*23:31*).

"Counsel"—the sober judgment of a sane thinking group is more reliable than your own opinion (*24:6*).

"Women"—better solitude on top of the house than sojourning in the house with a nagging woman (*25:24*).

"Gossip"—fire goes out when fuel gives out; scandal stops when mouths are stopped (*26:20*).

"Tomorrow"—there is never a tomorrow, only today. Get it done now, for now soon becomes then (*27:1*).

"Understanding"—rank does not guarantee an understanding heart (*28:16*).

"Bribes"—seek justice and our land shall stand; accept bribes and it will fall (*29:4*).

"Security"—a trust in God is the only safe soul armor (*30:5*).

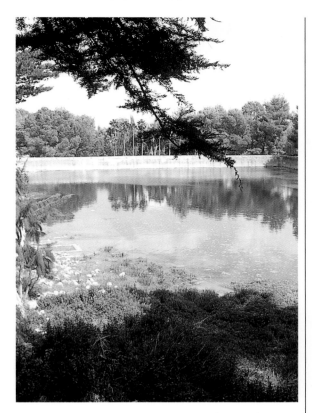

Solomon's Pools, near Jerusalem. In Ecclesiastes, Solomon attends to great works of state. Aqueducts, pools, palaces and other public buildings occupy his thoughts.

Understanding Ecclesiastes

Jesus is the beginning of all in Proverbs.

He is the end of all in Ecclesiastes, the *summum bonum* of life.

Wisdom in Proverbs is piety.

Wisdom in Ecclesiastes is prudence and sagacity.

Ecclesiastes is the soul's autobiography or the book of experience.

"Vanity" *(KJV)* or "meaningless" *(NIV)* is the key word. See Ecclesiastes 2:11.

You do not have to go outside the Bible to find the merely human philosophy of life. God has given us in the book of Ecclesiastes the record of all that human thinking and natural religion has ever been able to discover concerning the meaning and goal of life. The arguments in the book, therefore, are not God's arguments, but God's record of people's arguments. This explains why such passages as 1:15; 2:24; 3:3-4,8,11,19-20; 8:15 are at positive variance with the rest of the Bible.

The writer is Solomon, and the book is a dramatic autobiography of his experience and reflections while he was out of fellowship with God. Solomon may have been wise, but he did not follow his own wisdom. Ecclesiastes has its origin in his tragic sin of forsaking God and seeking satisfaction in philosophy and science "under the sun," that is, based only upon speculation and thought. The inference of the book that "all was vanity and vexation of spirit" *(KJV)*, or "meaningless, a chasing after the wind" *(NIV)* is inevitable. The message of Ecclesiastes is that, apart from God, life is full of weariness and disappointment.

The problem that faced Solomon was how he could find happiness and satisfaction apart from God *(Ecclesiastes 1:1-3)*. He sought satisfaction in science *(1:4-11)*, but could get no answer. He sought it in philosophy *(1:12-18)*, but in vain; he found pleasure *(2:1-11)*, mirth *(v. 1)*, drinking *(v. 3)*, building *(v. 4)*, possession *(vv. 5-7)*, wealth and music *(v. 8)*; but they were all empty.

He tried materialism *(2:12-26)*, fatalism *(3:1-15)* and deism *(3:1—4:16)*, but these likewise were vain. Natural religion *(5:1-8)*, wealth *(5:9—6:12)* and even morality *(7:1—12:12)* proved equally fruitless.

The conclusion is found in Ecclesiastes 12:13 and is the best thing possible to people under the law. It is interesting to notice the place of youth in the argument *(11:9—12:1)*. We must begin young to know God if we are to find life worth living.

Remember, Ecclesiastes only shows us the best that people can do apart from God's gospel of grace.

The name "Ecclesiastes" means "preacher." This is so named because it contains the meditations and sermons of the wise man, Solomon.

Confession *(Ecclesiastes 1—7)*
The great question, "Is life worth living?" is presented. Solomon has tested it to the full. No man could better do it or better tell it—and the answer he gives is not reassuring for the life that now is.

Try wisdom *(Ecclesiastes 1)*! What

better thing is there in all the world? Solomon declared, "I applied myself to the understanding of wisdom." Yet even here he was forced to cry out, "Chasing after the wind. For with much wisdom comes much sorrow; the more knowledge, the more grief" *(vv. 17-18)*. This is always true of mere earthly wisdom. But "The fear of the Lord is the beginning of wisdom" *(Psalm 111:10)*.

Try pleasure *(Ecclesiastes 2)*! "I thought in my heart, 'Come now, I will test you with pleasure to find out what is good.' But that also proved to be meaningless" *(v. 1)*. This is his deliberate conclusion. God made us all to be joyful. He has given us a thousand avenues of enjoyment. Let us not sacrifice true happiness for questionable pleasure. Always make your recreation a re-creation.

Philosophy has failed, says the preacher, so let merriment be tried. Music, dance, wine (not to excess), the funny story, the clever repartee: these are now cultivated. He even goes so far as to say that laughter is foolish *(vv. 1-2)*. Cheerfulness is admirable. A hearty laugh in its place is delightful, but the person who is always giggling is a bore.

Try architecture *(2:4)*! Now he becomes practical. He attends to great works of state. Aqueducts, pools, palaces and other public buildings occupy his thoughts. Now the court fools are frowned upon and great architects are welcomed to the palace. But the excitement incident to building soon fades away.

Try gardening *(2:5-6)*! Vineyards, gardens, orchards, rare flowers, tropical plants are all the rage. Jerusalem and the vicinity bloom like the Garden of Eden. Soon it is like a new toy for a child that pleases for a while but is soon tossed away.

Then the king tries cattle breeding,

art collecting and even becomes an amateur musician (*v. 8, KJV; NIV* says the king acquired a harem). Choruses and orchestras gather in the royal palace. But even though "music hath charms," it is powerless to charm with permanent happiness.

Try just living the weary round of life—with discretion (*Ecclesiastes 3*)! But again, "What benefit or gain is there?" (See *v. 9*; compare with *1:3; 2:11; 5:11,16; 6:11.*) Vanity of vanities!

Try the stoic's philosophy (*Ecclesiastes 4*)! Surely this also is meaningless. He wails, "vanity and vexation of spirit" (*v. 16, KJV*)!

Try ritualism—formal religion (*chap. 5*)! Be sure that "when you make a vow to God, do not delay in fulfilling it" (*v. 4*). This, too, is meaningless.

Try wealth (*chap. 6*)! Solomon had it. He was a man to whom God had given "wealth, possessions and honor . . . But God does not enable him to enjoy them, and a stranger enjoys them instead. This is meaningless, a grievous evil" (*v. 2*). Many agree with Solomon in the emptiness of pleasures, but they think money is the supreme goal in life. Jesus told us to seek first the kingdom of God and His righteousness and all these things would be added (*Matthew 6:33*).

Try reputation (*chap. 7*)! "A good name is better than fine perfume, and the day of death better than the day of birth" (*v. 1*). It doesn't last long in this world. People are soon forgotten when they die. Vanity still!

Admonition (*Ecclesiastes 8—12*)
Now comes a turning point. Ecclesiastes 8:12 says, "I know that it will go better with God-fearing men, who are reverent before God." The full meaning of this is found in the last chapter—"Fear God and keep his commandments, for this is the whole duty of man" (*Ecclesiastes 12:13*).

The "Preacher," as he is called, has been looking out and back and around. Now he looks up and he sees God and is satisfied.

A Jewish boy's Bar mitzvah at the Western Wall, Jerusalem. We must begin young to know God if we are to find life worth living.

The phrase "under the sun" (1:3) is found twenty-eight times in this little book. The "under-the-sun-life" is hardly worth living; but above the sun, and in the heavenlies that Paul describes, it is glorious (*Ephesians* 1).

We find in this book that we can never find satisfaction and happiness in this world. True happiness apart from Christ is impossible.

Ecclesiastes closes with a call to the young! Lay the foundations early. "Remember your Creator in the days of your youth" (*Ecclesiastes* 12:1). This book is given as a danger sign so that we may be spared having to learn the bitterness of life by finding the cisterns we have sought to be empty. The greatest proportion of men and women who are living to serve God have chosen Him in childhood.

Understanding Song of Songs

The Song of Songs has been called the Christian's love song. Key text is Song of Songs 6:3.

This is a song of love in marriage in Middle Eastern language and imagery. The characters in the song are Solomon, the Shulamite maid and the daughters of Jerusalem. The love of Solomon and the maid illustrates the love between Jehovah and His people. This is seen in many passages in the Bible. Moreover, Solomon as a lover was a type of Christ (see *Ephesians 5*). Personal love to Christ is the greatest need of the Church today. The knowledge of sin forgiven and of Christ's redeeming work has drawn us to Him.

Books of the Major Prophets

of the Old Testament

Isaiah • Jeremiah • Lamentations Ezekiel • Daniel

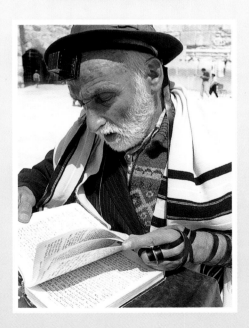

The keynote
of Isaiah is
"SALVATION."
Isaiah's name
means
"JEHOVAH
SAVES."

17. UNDERSTANDING
Isaiah

Isaiah Portrays Jesus Christ, the Messiah

Introduction to the Prophetical Books

The poetical books belong to the golden age of the nation.

The prophetical books belong to the dark ages of God's chosen people.

The prophets were men whom God raised up during the dark days of Israel's history. They were the evangelists of the day, the religious patriots of the hour. Read what God says about them in 2 Kings 17:13: "The Lord warned Israel and Judah through all his prophets and seers: 'Turn from your evil ways. Observe my commands and decrees, in accordance with the entire Law that I commanded your fathers to obey and that I delivered to you through my servants the prophets.'" We read everywhere in the New Testament that God spoke through the prophets. The period of the prophets in Israel covered 500 years from the tenth to the fifth century B.C. Then the voices of the prophets were silenced until John the Baptist. These prophets spoke fearlessly to kings and people alike of their sins and failures.

The office of prophet was instituted in Samuel's time. When the kingdom was divided and Judah and Israel were established as separate monarchies, the great prophets appeared. There were four major and twelve minor prophets.

There are seventeen prophetical books in the Old Testament (including Lamentations). They are subdivided into major and minor prophets. This classification is made not because of their importance, but because of their length.

The captivities of Israel (the Northern Kingdom) and of Judah (the Southern Kingdom) are largely the theme of the Old Testament prophets. The record of these is found in 2 Kings 17:1-23; 24:11—25:21. These are called the Assyrian and Babylonian captivities. Some of the prophets served before the exile, some during and some afterwards. These are called pre-exilic, exilic, and post-exilic prophets.

The prophets before the exile (or pre-exilic prophets) in chronological order of their writings were: Obadiah, Joel, Jonah, Amos, Hosea, Isaiah, Micah, Nahum, Habakkuk, Zephaniah and Jeremiah.

The pre-exilic prophets to Israel were Jonah, Amos and Hosea. The pre-exilic prophets to Judah were Obadiah, Joel, Isaiah, Micah, Nahum, Habakkuk, Zephaniah and Jeremiah.

The prophets during the exile (or captivity in Babylon) were Ezekiel and Daniel. They prophesied to all the Israelites. Jeremiah's lifetime also extended into this period. Those who prophesied after the exile were Haggai, Zechariah and Malachi.

Prophets according to intended hearers:

Three to Israel—Amos, Hosea, Ezekiel

A watchtower in the fields near Samaria. Isaiah wrote that Jerusalem was left as defenseless as a watchman's hut in a vineyard (*Isaiah 1:8*).

Two to Nineveh—Jonah, Nahum
One to Babylon—Daniel
One to Edom—Obadiah
Nine to Judah—Joel, Isaiah, Micah, Jeremiah, Habakkuk, Zephaniah, Haggai, Zechariah, Malachi.

The Prophets—Their Message

The prophet's chief duty was to deal with the moral and religious life of his own people during his day. The prophet was never sent while the nation was walking in obedience to God. All the writings are rebukes because of the bad condition that existed at that very time. Nothing was general about the prophet's denunciations.

The prophet was always an Israelite. He not only spoke of judgment that would come to pass to the people because of their sin, but he was also a foreteller of future events. The events of which he spoke mainly concerned the nation of Israel. Other peoples were mentioned only as they came in contact with Israel.

Let us note some of the prophecies of the future that are recounted. Keep these in mind as you study their writings.

1. The dispersion and captivity of God's chosen people: Everywhere the prophet tells that the Jews are to be scattered among the nations of the world.

2. The coming of the Messiah: Religious Jews were and are still looking for their Messiah.

3. The restoration of the chosen people to their own land under the coming Messiah, David's greater Son: Jewish people are returning from the four corners of the earth to dwell in their own Promised Land. Almost all Jewish people have a longing in their hearts to be a part of Israel as a nation. Now this is possible!

4. The reign of the Messiah over the whole earth: Even though we see the collapse of God's people in the Old Testament—first Israel, then Judah being led into captivity—nevertheless, God revealed that the ending of His nation did not end His plans for His people. There is yet to be a glorious future when the Prince of Peace shall reign over His people and sway His scepter "from sea to sea and from the River to

the ends of the earth" (*Psalm 72:8*).

When you read the Gospels, you constantly find phrases such as, "so was fulfilled what the Lord had said" and "to fulfill what was spoken through the prophet." We find in examining these passages that God fulfills prophecy literally. Learn to interpret the meaning of the words of the prophets in a literal, natural way. Do not force a spiritual interpretation and read out all the real meaning. There are figurative passages, of course. But you will find that as soon as you determine the meaning of the figure that that, too, will have its literal fulfillment. This method makes the study of the prophets a simple one.

The Prophets— Their Character

The prophets were fearless men. They denounced the sins of their day. They called people away from idols back to God. It is true that the prophets were concerned about the moral and political corruption of the nation, but the fact that the people were worshiping idols was their greatest concern. The nation had a wrong attitude toward God. Christ gave us a succinct statement of what our attitude should be: "Love the Lord your God with all your heart and with all your soul and with all your strength and with all your mind" (*Luke 10:27*). God knows that what someone's attitude is toward God will affect that person's whole moral life. Creed always determines conduct. This is true not only of individuals, but also of nations. The adage "it makes no difference what a man believes" is completely refuted in the prophets.

The prophets exposed the cold formalism of their religion. They constantly reminded the people that Jehovah was the only true God. They pointed men to the law. They were statesmen of the highest order. They were prophets in that they came to tell forth what God said. They were not only forth-tellers but also fore-tellers.

So important is prophecy in God's Word that it occupies about one third of the whole Bible. Prophecy is God's revelation of His plans to His children.

G. Campbell Morgan says that there were three elements in the message of the prophets:

1. A message to their own age— directly from God
2. A message of predicted future events
   (a) The failure of God's chosen people and God's judgment upon them and the nations around them
   (b) The coming of the Messiah and His rejection and final glory
   (c) The Messianic Kingdom ultimately to be established on the earth
3. A living message to our own age— eternal principles of right and wrong.

The Spirit of God spoke by the prophets: "as he said through his holy prophets of long ago" (*Luke 1:70*). Read 2 Peter 1:21; Jeremiah 1:9; Ezekiel 2:7 to find how the message was given.

Read what Christ said of the prophets (*Luke 24:25-27*).

The prophecies concerning Christ Himself are so definite that it gives great assurance to us that the Bible is the Word of God.

Understanding Isaiah

God puts a telescope before the eyes of the prophets and lets them look far into the future. Especially do we find this spirit of expectation in Isaiah. We hear the prophet cry, "He is coming!" Isaiah was a man of vision. Read the opening words: "The vision concerning Judah and Jerusalem that Isaiah son of Amoz saw" (*Isaiah 1:1*).

Isaiah was a man who certainly spoke boldly to his own time, but as a prophet he spoke of the future as well; hence he is the prophet for all times. We sit at his feet today, and following his index finger as it points into the future, we hear him say, "Lo, your King!"

This great statesman was the prophet of the Southern Kingdom of Judah. He lived at the time that the Northern Kingdom of Israel was destroyed by Assyria. Isaiah was the one whose voice saved the kingdom of Judah during these trying hours.

It is interesting to note that this is also the time of Romulus and Remus and the founding of Rome. The traditional date of the building of Rome is 753 B.C., just a few years after the birth of the prophet Isaiah. About this time Sparta and Athens in Greece were founded.

The prophets were the most unpopular men in their day, for they dealt with the moral and religious conditions of the hour! Generally conditions were bad. Prophets were sent when the nation was out of step with God—when they were walking in disobedience. The words the prophets used to rebuke or exhort the people were very pointed. They were for the very people to whom they addressed themselves. Truth is seldom popular with the sinner.

Let us find the scriptural definition of a prophet. Look in Deuteronomy 18:18-19.

Although the prophets spoke to their own age, they were ever looking forward to future events. Besides this, we find abiding principles stated for all times. They foretold the failure of the chosen people and the coming of the Messiah. Each showed how God was to bring to pass His purposes through the Messiah. We see today how most religious leaders have failed to recognize Jesus as the promised Messiah.

Isaiah told of the judgment that must fall on Judah because she would not fulfill her mission in the world. But through the whole book we find the ultimate triumph of God's plan through His appointed Servant, the

Lord Jesus Christ, who would bring in final victory through suffering and death (*Isaiah 53*).

Two Emphases

This book of Isaiah is written with two distinct emphases. Because of this, some Bible scholars believe that there was more than one author. This need not be the case. It is the work of one man with two messages. In the first of the book Isaiah pictured Israel. In the last of the book, the prophet beheld Jesus bearing our load of sin, and he told the story; then he beheld Christ exalted and glorified and shouted of his vision from the housetop. It is the same prophet all the time but suiting his language to the theme at hand.

The only way to understand Isaiah is to understand the prophet's Christ. It is far more important that we be familiar with the truths of the book than the theories of its authorship.

The Old Testament opens with God's case against humans because of their sin. Isaiah opens the same way (*Isaiah 1:18*). The first section closes with the prophecy of the coming King of Righteousness and the redemption of Israel (*chaps. 34—35*), just as the prophets close the Old Testament with the prediction of His coming kingdom. The second part of Isaiah (beginning with *chapter 40*) opens with the "voice of him that crieth in the wilderness" (*Isaiah 40:3, KJV*), and is concerned with the person and work of Jesus Christ. The New Testament opens in exact accord with this. John the Baptist, the forerunner of Jesus, is announced as "the voice of one crying in the wilderness" (*John 1:6,23, KJV*). The book of Isaiah ends with the vision of new heavens and a new earth in which righteousness perfectly dwells (*Isaiah 62:1-2; 65:17; 66:22*). The New Testament closes with this same view in Revelation 21. This striking similarity between Isaiah and Revelation is unforgettable when once mastered.

Two Comings of Christ

We see Christ in this book and hear the prophet crying, "He is coming!" and "He is coming again!" He is coming as Savior, pictured in chapter 53, in humiliation as our sin-bearer. He is coming again in power and great glory, pictured in chapter 34.

Isaiah speaks of Christ's death when he says, "Though your sins are like scarlet, they shall be as white as snow; though they are red as crimson, they shall be like wool" (*1:18*). Again, "He was despised and rejected by men" (*53:3*). This speaks of the first time when He came unto His own, and His own received Him not. When He will come again we shall hear, "Arise, shine, for your light has come, and the glory of the Lord rises upon you" (*60:1*). Then he tells us of His coming kingdom. "In the last days . . ." (*2:2-5*).

The life of Christ is portrayed in Isaiah:

Birth—7:14; 9:6
Family—11:1
Anointing—11:2
Character—11:3-4
Simplicity of life—7:15
Gentleness—42:1-4
Death—Chap. 53
Resurrection—25:8
Glorious reign—11:3-16; 32.

Isaiah the Prophet

Isaiah was a man of royal blood. He was a young aristocrat from a princely line. He was brought up in the court and had high standing with the people of Jerusalem. He not only was a prophet, but he also married a prophetess (8:3,18). His training was of the best. After his labor of sixty years, tradition tells us that he died a martyr in the reign of Manasseh at the age of 120.

Isaiah was a special messenger to Judah. Look over 2 Kings 15-20 and note the moral and political rottenness of Judah and Israel, and the danger from the surrounding Gentile nations. Assyria was strong and aggressive, striving for world power. Egypt was on the south, and Palestine was the road between these two enemies. Both Assyria and Egypt aimed at a world empire. Therefore Palestine became the battleground of the ages.

Isaiah did not fail in his ministry. He laid bare the sins of his people and called them to repent and turn to God. "Come back to God," he cried. But his chief theme was the coming One. It was Jesus. He saw Christ's near first coming and His faraway second coming, but in all he saw Christ.

Johannes Kepler (1571-1630, German astronomer, discovered the three laws of planetary motion), in failing to bring the heavenly bodies into satisfactory adjustment with one center, at last conceived of the ellipse with two foci and everything fell into harmony. So when in our reverent study of God's Word we catch the dual center of Christ on the Cross and Christ on the throne, then the Word shines clear and we begin to see what the prophet saw, the world's Redeemer, coming first in humiliation, then again in power and great glory.

Four words to Judah:
Rebellion—"Ah, sinful nation" (1:2-4,10-15,21-23)
Retribution—"You will be devoured" (1:5-8,15,20,28)
Repentance—"If you are willing and obedient" (1:16-19,27)
Restoration—"Zion will be redeemed" (1:9,18,24-31).

Judah thought that in keeping up all outward observances in their religious service all would be well. Isaiah denounced their hypocrisy (1:15). He told them of forgiveness if they would repent, but promised them a sword if they continued in their rebellion against God.

Because of their sin and their forsaking God, Judah was facing judgment (1:1-31; 2:6—3:26). Yet there is a glorious future for Judah when Christ comes again. Jerusalem is to be the capital of the coming Kingdom (*2:1-5; 4*).

God's truths of redemption go beyond our reason, but they do not insult our reason; they rather appeal to it. To worship aright in the presence of God we must be right in the presence of people.

Under Uzziah and Jotham
Isaiah 1—6

Read Isaiah 1:1 and you will discover that Isaiah was prophet during the reigns of Uzziah, Jotham, Ahaz and Hezekiah. During this time, the statesman prophet preached in Jerusalem.

Now turn to Isaiah 6:1-13 and you see that Isaiah received his real commission in the year King Uzziah died. No doubt he had written chapters 1—5 before this time. Uzziah's long reign of fifty-two years was so glorious during the greater part; however, it ended in gloom. For the last four years of his life Uzziah was a leper. He was shut off from all the business of state, and the kingdom was under the regency of his son Jotham. The early chapters of Isaiah fit the situation perfectly.

When Isaiah preached that God was about to abandon Judah, it may have seemed too cruel, but the Lord is infinitely more concerned with the purity of His people than with their prosperity.

Uzziah was a leper and Jotham was regent (*2 Kings 15:5*). "Azariah" is another name for "Uzziah." Uzziah's reign did not directly affect Isaiah's prophecy.

Jotham, Uzziah's successor, is only mentioned twice in the book (*Isaiah 1:1; 7:1*). It does not seem that Isaiah was active during his reign. It is with the reign of the next two kings, Ahaz and Hezekiah, that Isaiah's prophecy deals.

Ahaz reigned sixteen years and Hezekiah reigned twenty-nine years. Ahaz was a wicked king and, more, he was an idolater. Hezekiah was for the most part a good king and he did much to remove idolatry from the people.

Isaiah's Message
Isaiah warned Judah of her folly and rebellion (*1:2-9*). They separated themselves from God by the sins of greed, foreign alliances and idolatry (*2:6-9*). God called them a fruitless vine. God had tried patience, then punishment; now they must be destroyed by foreign kings.

God called Isaiah just as He called Moses, Joshua, Gideon or Paul. Isaiah's commission came at the tragic death of the grand old King Uzziah (*6:1*). His call was a never-to-be-forgotten experience. It taught him his own unworthiness and gave him his real commission to a sinning, needy world calling out for help. It came to him in the form of a "vision." For years Isaiah preached and told of doom and deliverance. Hardship and peril awaited him, but God gave him a victorious strength. He was the man of the hour. Let us look at the steps leading from the opening of the vision to his final commission.

Secret of Isaiah's Life
This experience of Isaiah's should be every disciple's experience. The secret of all Isaiah's power lay in this vision in the Temple: "I saw the Lord!"

Conviction—"Woe to me! . . . I am ruined!" was the cry brought on by the sense of sinfulness before God's holiness (*6:5*).

Confession—"A man of unclean lips." A broken heart and a contrite heart is precious to the Lord (*6:5*).

Cleansing—"Your guilt is taken away

and your sin atoned for." After confession, a flying seraph (an angel) cleansed his lips with a hot coal from off the altar (*6:7*). Consecration—"Here am I. Send me!" (*6:8*). Commission—Go, God's command (see *6:9*).

Under Ahaz *Isaiah 7—14*

"And it came to pass in the days of Ahaz" (*Isaiah 7:1*). Ahaz was utterly bad. He was an open idolater. For this sin God allowed Rezin, king of Syria, and Pekah, king of Israel, to invade his kingdom. Isaiah had been silent under Jotham but this invasion brings him to the front in his ministry. "Then the Lord said to Isaiah, 'Go out . . . to meet Ahaz'" (*7:3*). He appealed to him to put his trust in God for help rather than call in Tiglath-Pileser from Nineveh.

God sent the prophet to encourage Ahaz. Besides predicting the Assyrian invasion in Isaiah 8, the prophet saw an end to all of Israel's troubles through the birth of the Christ child who shall rule over the kingdom of David in righteousness forever and forever. He gave Ahaz a "sign" that Judah was not to perish—the prophecy of Immanuel, the virgin's Son, Jesus Christ. "Therefore the Lord himself will give you a sign: The virgin will be with child and will give birth to a son, and will call him Immanuel" (*7:14*). Read these important words in Isaiah 7:10-16. Ahaz refused the evidence upon which his faith might have been established. He pursued his own plans with Assyria, and that nation on which they now leaned was to become the means of their punishment (*7:17-20*).

Then followed the sentence of doom upon king and land (*8:6-22*). With nations, this is God's policy: doom for idolatry.

Jerusalem from the Mount of Olives. Isaiah delivered a severe judgment on Jerusalem.

Read Isaiah 9:6-7 and find another great prophecy concerning Christ. The Son to be given, the child to be born, was to sit on David's throne. Remember the "throne of David" is as real as the "throne of the Caesars." Yes, Christ will sit on the throne of David. Read the angel's words to Mary in Luke 1:32-33.

We find present woe and future glory strangely mixed in Isaiah 10. But in Isaiah 11 we see the picture of the glory of the future kingdom Christ is coming to establish on this earth. Some day He is coming to Jerusalem to sit upon the throne of David and peace shall cover the earth "as the waters cover the sea" (*11:9*).

In this kingdom, the people will worship the Lord Jehovah. The prophet says, "Sing to the Lord, for he has done glorious things" (*Isaiah 12:5*).

In Isaiah 13 we see great Babylon's doom. She was to carry Judah away captive, but the prophet sees her destruction. God is keeping His promise to Abraham. "I will bless those who bless you, and whoever curses you I will curse; and all peoples on earth will be blessed through you" (*Genesis 12:3*). God always brings a curse on any nation that afflicts Israel. You can follow this truth through history. God often allows nations to punish Israel for her national sins, but retribution is inevitable (*Deuteronomy 30:5-7; Isaiah 14:1-2; Joel 3:1-8*).

Read every word of Isaiah 11 and 12, which gives a picture of this coming King and kingdom.

1. The King Himself (*11:1*)
2. His anointing (*11:2*)
3. His righteous reign (*11:3-5*)
4. His glorious kingdom (*11:6-9*)
5. His gathering together of His people from the four corners of the earth (*11:10-16*)
6. His kingdom worship (*12:1-6.*)

When it was my privilege to drive out old Babylon and look over the ruins of that once magnificent city and see the absolute devastation, I thought of Isaiah's prophecy concerning this city found in Isaiah 13:19-22. Read these verses.

This is true today. Not even the tent of an Arab is pitched there. Only bats and owls make their home in its ruins. Not a shepherd is seen on the plains. There is only desolation. Yes, God's Word is true!

In Isaiah 14:28 we read that King Ahaz died. But Isaiah warns the people that his death must not be hailed as the end of their burdens. Even worse oppressors than Ahaz were yet to come (*14:28-32*).

Under Hezekiah *Isaiah 15—39*

The reign of Hezekiah occupied one of the most important periods in all of Israel's history. Hezekiah was a godly king. The Assyrian armies, like a dark storm cloud, were threatening the northern frontiers. Before Hezekiah had completed his sixth year, Samaria had fallen beneath this invader. This success only whetted the Assyrian appetite for further conquest. Eight years later Judah was invaded. The first invasion was by Sargon and the second by

his son, Sennacherib. Assyrian history tells us this. The critical year in Hezekiah's reign was the fourteenth (*Isaiah 36:1*). It was then we have the Assyrian invasion, the king's mortal sickness and his recovery, and the final withdrawal of Assyrians from the land. (This covered a period of about four years.)

These stony-hearted Assyrian warriors came year after year, blazing with steel and banners. The watchmen on the walls of Jerusalem could see them advance by the smoke of the burning towns and cities.

King Hezekiah stripped the Temple of its treasures and took the gold from its doors and pillars in order that he might send them 300 talents of silver and 30 talents of gold to buy them off (*2 Kings 18:13-16*). In desperation, help from Egypt was sought. But nothing availed in face of the fury of these Assyrians.

Finally the Assyrians built their campfires around the city of Jerusalem and demanded its surrender. Read the intensely dramatic account of the parleyings between the Assyrian general and the chiefs of Jerusalem.

See the account of the swift and terrible disaster that fell upon the Assyrians as they were slain by a mysterious visitation in their camp (*Isaiah 37:36-38*).

Isaiah denounced the alliance with Egypt and said it was relying "on horses" and trusting "in the multitude of their chariots and in the great strength of their horsemen, but do not look to the Holy One of Israel" (*31:1*).

We need to hear the prophet say today, "Woe to those who go down to Egypt for help, who rely on horses, who trust in the multitude of their chariots" (*31:1*).

History reveals a graveyard of the nations that have gone down to death through their own moral rottenness.

Solomon's Temple

Holy of Holies containing
Ark of the Covenant

Holy Place

Altar of Incense

Boaz

Jachin

Bronze Sea

Altar of Sacrifice

Egypt, Babylon and Rome are memorable examples of this.

God wants us to recognize Him in national affairs. He calls His people to "Return to him you have so greatly revolted against" (*Isaiah 31:6*). As a people, we must get right with God before we can get right with other nations.

The kingdoms of Judah and Israel had become so weakened by idolatry and corruption that the enemies swept down upon them from the north like a wolf on the fold. First, Israel rolled in the dust under the tramp of the terrible Assyrian hosts (722 B.C.), and then Judah fell with the Babylonians thundering at her gate and breaking down her walls (586 B.C.). Both kingdoms ended and her people were carried into captivity. Isaiah lived and prophesied in Jerusalem during the Assyrian invasion of the north.

Isaiah spent his life trying to get Judah to become acquainted with God and His Word. He wanted them to trust wholly in God's guidance. Isn't this a worthy aim for any minister today?

Glorious Future— Restoration! *Isaiah 40—66*

This part of the book, chapters 40—66, is called the "Book of Consolation"

because Isaiah tells in glowing terms not only of the restoration of Judah, but also of the coming of Jehovah's "Servant" to be the Messiah King.

The restoration is assured, for they must return to their own land to prepare the way for the coming Messiah, the Servant of Jehovah, who is to redeem His people.

Isaiah 53 gives us a perfect picture of our suffering Redeemer. "Surely he took up our infirmities and carried our sorrows" (*v. 4*). "We all, like sheep, have gone astray . . . and the Lord has laid on him the iniquity of us all" (*v. 6*). He was the substitute for the sinner.

Can you repeat verse 5 and say, "But he was pierced for [my] transgressions, he was crushed for [my] iniquities; the punishment that brought [my] peace was upon him, and by his wounds [I am] healed"? Accepting this great fact makes you a child of God. He was wounded, bruised, pierced—not for His own sins, but for ours. He bore on His own body the sins of the world.

Isaiah 60—66 tells of the coming Kingdom—the future glory of Israel. God's goodness to redeemed Israel is seen in chapters 61 and 62. He promises an era of prosperity in chapters 63—65.

18. UNDERSTANDING
Jeremiah and Lamentations

Jeremiah and Lamentations Portray Jesus Christ, the Righteous Branch

Understanding Jeremiah

Here is the story of a diffident, sensitive lad who was called from the obscurity of his native town to assume, at a critical hour in the nation's life, the overwhelming responsibilities of a prophet. Jeremiah came from the village of Anathoth some three miles from Jerusalem. This gave him the advantages of the Holy City. His father, Hilkiah, was a priest. (Some think that this was "Hilkiah the priest" in *2 Kings 22*, who brought the Book of the Law to the notice of King Josiah, which started the great revival in the kingdom.) He inherited the traditions of an illustrious ancestry. His early life was, no doubt, molded by strong religious influences. God had something better for Jeremiah than to spend his life as a priest serving at the altars. God appointed this young man to be a prophet of the Lord in this most trying hour in the history of the chosen people.

God often chooses unlikely instruments to do His work. He chose the sensitive, shrinking Jeremiah for what seemed a hopeless mission, with the words: "'Do not say, "I am only a child." You must go to everyone I send you to and say whatever I command you. Do not be afraid of them, for I am with you and will rescue you,' declares the Lord" (*Jeremiah 1:7-8*). This is what a prophet is—one that "tells forth" what God says. Although many prophets told of future events, it is not necessary that they do so to be a prophet.

Jeremiah, unlike many of the prophets, has much to say concerning himself. He tells us that he was a priest by birth (*1:1*). He was called by the

Selected Bible Readings

Sunday: Jeremiah Warns Judah
(*Jeremiah 1:1-10; 2:1-13; 3:12,22-23; 4:14-19; 6:1-30*)

Monday: A Rebuke
(*Jeremiah 7:1-15; 9:1-16; 17:5-18*)

Tuesday: The Potter
(*Jeremiah 18:1-17*)

Wednesday: The Faithless Shepherds
(*Jeremiah 23:1-40*)

Thursday: Repentance and Restoration
(*Jeremiah 24–25*)

Friday: Israel's Last Days
(*Jeremiah 30:18—31:40*)

Saturday: The Overthrow of Judah
(*Jeremiah 52:1-34*)

Comfort to the Sorrowing
(*Lamentations 1—5*)

Lord to be a prophet at an early age (*1:6*). He pleaded, first, his youth (only twenty-one), second, inexperience, and third, his lack of eloquence (*1:6*) as reasons for not accepting the call. Are these not just the excuses that youth make today for not obeying Christ?

Jeremiah was assured that Jehovah ordained him to this work before his birth (*1:5*). God tells us in Ephesians 2:10 that we were created unto good works before God even laid the foundation of the world. God has a plan for each one of our lives. (Read *Jeremiah 1:1-8.*) He was not allowed to marry, for God had a special mission for him in life (*16:1-2*). Jeremiah prophesied during the time when Israel had been taken into captivity and Judah was in her declining days.

Soon after Josiah's death, the kingdom of Judah hastened to its end. Judah was reduced to practical vassalage to Egypt at the battle of Carchemish. About twelve years later Nebuchadnezzar, king of Babylon, took Jerusalem and began deporting all the princes and men of station, which ended in the complete captivity of Judah eleven years after. A few of the poorest were left in the land. Jeremiah kept on with his ministry among them until they went into Egypt. He followed them into Egypt and the last we hear of him he was still rebuking his people.

He was called to be a prophet in the thirteenth year of the reign of King Josiah (*1:2*). No doubt his early ministry, and that of the prophet Zephaniah, were among the influences that led to the reforms under the young King Josiah. Jeremiah prophesied for more than forty years. He began his ministry sixty years after the death of Isaiah, the great evangelical prophet.

Jeremiah was contemporary with the prophetess Huldah, and with Habakkuk, Zephaniah, Ezekiel and Daniel, and perhaps even Nahum.

Jeremiah's message was never a popular one. At one time he barely escaped with his life (*26:7-16*). At another time his enemies beat him and put him in prison. Men have always treated God's witnesses thus.

It is almost impossible to outline this book chronologically. Some of the first messages are found later in the book and some of the last messages are first. He wrote on a great roll. No doubt he had given his messages many times to the people and had repeated them often before he began to write. His faithful scribe, Baruch, wrote them down. After he had written one of his discourses, some other message given years before might come to his mind and he would record it, possibly without dating it. He would fill up his parchment as he unrolled it. Later on, when he wished to write down another incident, or record another message, he would have to begin on the roll where he left off, whether it fitted in chronologically or not. This is important to remember.

Analysis of Jeremiah

Because the book of Jeremiah is not arranged chronologically, a division of the book is difficult. The analysis is more moral than structural.

Jeremiah prophesies concerning:
1. Judah—captivity; restoration
2. Cities—Jerusalem; Babylon; Damascus
3. Gentile nations—Egypt; Philistia; Moab; Ammon; Edom; Elam; Babylon
4. Messiah.

Jeremiah uses many symbols given him by Jehovah in teaching the people. On one occasion he wore a rotted girdle; another time he put a yoke on his neck, like an ox; again, he broke a bottle in the presence of the ruler; he bought a field and buried the deed. The interpretation is given in the text.

Christ is pictured in Jeremiah as:
Fountain of Living Waters—2:13
Great Physician—8:22
Good Shepherd—31:10; 23:4
The Righteous Branch—23:5
David the King—30:9
The Redeemer—50:34
Lord our Righteousness—23:6.

Jeremiah was the ninth of the prophets. He prophesied to the Southern Kingdom of Judah, before the exile and during the trying days of the captivity. He saw five kings upon the throne of Judah: Josiah, Jehoahaz, Jehoiakim, Jehoiachin and Zedekiah. He was to Josiah what Isaiah had been to Hezekiah. (Read *2 Kings 21:1-25* to find the history of Jeremiah's time.)

There were three great events in Jeremiah's life:

1. Battle of Megiddo (609 B.C.), between Judah and Pharaoh-Necho of Egypt in which good King Josiah was killed.
2. Battle of Carchemish (605 B.C.) about four years later, during Jehoiakim's reign. He had become a vassal of Egypt. In this battle, the Egyptians were defeated by Babylon under Nebuchadnezzar. The first deportation of Jews followed.
3. Capture of Jerusalem by Nebuchadnezzar (587-6 B.C.), destruction of city and Temple, and exile of greater part of those who were left to Babylon.

There was a great contest for world supremacy in the day of Jeremiah. Assyria had been in the place of leadership for 300 years. Now she was growing weak; Babylon was ascending in power. Egypt, too, was striving for supremacy. In 607 B.C. Assyria was defeated by Babylon. In 605 B.C. Egypt was crushed in the battle of Carchemish, and Babylon became the world's master. In the few years that followed, she invaded Jerusalem and took the Jews captive. False prophets swarmed the city of Jerusalem in these days. They flattered the king and prophesied to him whatever they thought he wanted to hear.

An Eastern shepherd. Christ is pictured in Jeremiah as the Good Shepherd (*Jeremiah 31:10; 23:4*).

Call and Commission of Jeremiah *Jeremiah 1*

This unique tragedy opens in the little village of Anathoth. At twenty-one, Jeremiah was becoming aware that God had ordained him before his birth to be a prophet (*Jeremiah 1:5*). Because he let the Lord have His way, his life affected all of Israel.

We hear Jeremiah speak, "'Ah, Sovereign Lord,' I said, 'I do not know how to speak; I am only a child'" [like a young man] (*1:6*). He protests and shrinks from the task God gave him and begs to be excused. Notice Jeremiah's reluctance to undertake the task.

A prophet is simply God's messenger boy delivering not his own ideas, but conveying to the last detail God's thoughts. (Compare Jeremiah's call with Moses' call, *Exodus 4:10-12*.) God had called Jeremiah to be a prophet and he entered bravely upon the task, but now he is overwhelmed at the thought of hurting anyone. He would rather live at peace with them.

While Jeremiah is pondering, a hand touches his mouth and we hear a voice saying, "Now, I have put my words in your mouth" (*Jeremiah 1:9*). No longer could he complain of inability to speak. God promises to put the message into the mouth of His prophets. (See what Christ said to His disciples in *Matthew 10:20*.) Then Jeremiah heard the voice add, "See, today I appoint you over nations and kingdoms to uproot and tear down, to destroy and overthrow, to build and to plant" (*Jeremiah 1:10*).

Secret of National Power

What God asks us to do He fits us for, and what He fits us for He asks us to do. That was quite a position for just a poor country preacher.

The church and the minister who have answered God's call today are still in a place of power. They need no other weapons than the promise of God, and they really control the building and the breaking, the planting and the plucking of the community.

Jeremiah's commission was worldwide, including not only his own country, but also all nations and kingdoms of Egypt, Ammon, Moab, Tyre and Sidon. His commission was to root out and to pull down, to destroy and to throw down. He must root out the idolatry and pride, but he must finally "build and plant." Jeremiah was to go only to those persons or peoples to whom the Lord sent him. And he was to say only what the Lord commanded him to say. This must be true of us also if we are to be true workers together with God.

Jeremiah's Reluctance

Because Jeremiah was forced into the task that was so distasteful to him, in later years he cried, "Alas, my mother, that you gave me birth, a man with whom the whole land strives and contends!" (*Jeremiah 15:10*). God told Jeremiah, "Do not be afraid of them, for I am with you and will rescue you" (*1:8*). He was not a public speaker, and he shrank from bearing such an unwelcome message to so undisciplined a people. How often he must have thought of that promise of God when he was haled before princes and rulers.

The Touch of God's Hand

"Then the Lord reached out his hand" (*Jeremiah 1:9*). Compare this story of Jeremiah's call with that of Isaiah's (*Isaiah 6:7*). Paul says that prophecy is a spiritual gift (*1 Corinthians 14:1*). The touch of God's hand was a tangible pledge for Jeremiah that God was with him. He could not get away from it.

The Word of the Lord is a power

that carries out His will and accomplishes what He wishes (*Isaiah 55:11; Hebrews 4:12*). Against this power nothing can stand. It is a hammer that breaks rocks into pieces (*Jeremiah 23:29*). God's Word shows its power in two ways—in destruction and in construction. We see this in God's words to Jeremiah. If people accept God's Word it will give life; if they reject it, it will bring condemnation (*John 3:36*).

Before the Fall of Jerusalem
Jeremiah 2—38

The prophecies of Jeremiah before the fall of Jerusalem were made in this order (long silences divide these):

Prophecies in the reign of Josiah (*2:1—12:17*)

Prophecies in the reign of Jehoiakim (*13:1—20:18; 25:1—27:11*)

Prophecies in the reign of Zedekiah (*21:1—24:10; 27:12—39:18.*)

Reign of Josiah

"During the reign of King Josiah, the Lord said to me" (*Jeremiah 3:6*). The first twelve chapters cover the prophecy of this period.

Jeremiah 2—6: These chapters tell of Judah's sin and give God's call to repentance. Judgments are predicted.

Jeremiah 7—9: Again we read of threatenings. We see the prophet's grief.

Jeremiah 10—12: Here we see idolatry and disobedience continued. The Lord's disappointment in His people is shown.

In the early years of his ministry, during the reign of Josiah, Jeremiah's message for the most part was a warning to Judah and a call to her to repent (*Jeremiah 3:6,12-13,22-23*). He spared nothing in exposing the moral rottenness of the people (*7:1-26*). He warned them of coming judgments if they would not return to God. He espe-

A mythical beast in glazed tiles, from an Assyrian gateway in Babylon.

cially told them of the danger from the north (4:6). He said that the avengers would come like a raging lion from the thicket (4:7). They would sweep over the land with chariots like the whirlwind and with horses swifter than eagles, spread terror before them and leave ruin in their train (4:13).

In chapter 26, we see Jeremiah taking a stand on the same spot as in Jeremiah 7. On this occasion he nearly lost his life. The address in chapter 7 was probably given during the reign of Josiah himself.

It is probable that for some time after his call Jeremiah continued to reside in Anathoth, but before long he was compelled to leave the home of his birth and take up his residence in Jerusalem. The men of his hometown had made a conspiracy to put him to death (11:18-23). The disloyalty of his neighbors, and especially his own relatives, came as a painful shock to the unsuspecting prophet. But Jehovah told him that this was only the beginning of his troubles and it was a time of preparation for still greater trials in the days to come (12:5-6). Jeremiah's chief enemies were the priests and the prophets (26:7-8). They had a large following among the people. It is sad to notice that the principal opposition to the message of God came from the professedly religious people. Many people hate God and they will hate His children.

In the death of the good King Josiah, at the battle of Megiddo, Judah suffered a calamity from which she never recovered. In this battle Judah made a noble attempt to withstand the Egyptian army advancing against Assyria under Pharaoh-Necho.

King Josiah was succeeded by his younger brother Jehoahaz whom "the people of the land" placed on the throne instead of the older brother Eliakim. But Jehoahaz was allowed to reign for only three months. He was deposed by Necho and carried off in chains to Egypt, where he died. Necho now virtually was overlord of Judah. He appointed Jehoiakim to be ruler.

Reign of Jehoiakim

It was a sad day for Judah when Jehoiakim ascended to power. It was a bad day for Jeremiah, too. Read what God said to Jeremiah at the beginning of Jehoiakim's reign (Jeremiah 26:1-7). Jehoiakim was a bad ruler. He was proud, selfish, covetous and vindictive. He weighed the land down with taxes to meet the demands of his Egyptian conqueror (2 Kings 23:35). He was indifferent to the suffering of his people. He devoted most of his time to enlarging and adorning his palace and carried out his costly schemes with incredible meanness.

Jehoiakim reigned eleven years, and after his death his son, a youth of eighteen, came to the throne. But Jehoiachin's reign was short (about three months and ten days) because Nebuchadnezzar's army soon appeared at the gates of Jerusalem; and after a three-month siege the city was captured. He took with him many of the princes and the flower of the people to Babylon. Among them were Jehoiachin and the queen-mother. None were left, "only the poorest people of the land" (2 Kings 24:14).

It was then that Jeremiah first mentioned the seventy years' captivity (Jeremiah 25:1-14). God told them just how long they must remain in exile (Daniel 9:2).

Jeremiah did not hesitate to denounce even the king in his shameless wrongdoing. In Jeremiah 22:13-19, we see him verbally putting Jehoiakim in stocks and then releasing the lash of a righteous scorn, predicting that he would die without being mourned and would be buried with the burial of an ass.

The reformation under Josiah only touched the surface. The work was abandoned after his death and the nation, in Jehoiakim's reign, fell back into the worst form of idolatry.

Jeremiah's mission was to endeavor to turn his people back to God. During the reign of Josiah, he began to prophesy the dreadful calamity threatening them from the north (4:6) if they would not return to God. Jeremiah told Judah that her salvation was still possible, but each year her sin grew worse and her doom more certain.

Standing in the Temple, Jeremiah told the people that the Temple would be destroyed and Jerusalem itself would become a desolation. Jeremiah's hearers were shocked (26:7-9). They called his words blasphemy.

They said, "This man should be sentenced to death because he has prophesied against this city" (26:11). The Jewish people always remembered that they were the chosen people of God. God had given them privileges, hence they concluded that God would not proceed to do such things as Jeremiah had said He would do against the people whom He had chosen (Amos 3:2). God had consecrated the Temple as an abode for His name, therefore the people thought He would not let it be destroyed by enemies. This is quite false.

Jeremiah was charged with being unpatriotic. The priests and prophets, aided by the people, laid hold on Jeremiah and threatened him with death. But Jeremiah was delivered from the hand of his enemies (26:15-24).

The fourth year of Jehoiakim was one to be remembered because in this year Jeremiah first put his prophecies in writing on a roll (36:1-2). Baruch, his intimate friend who was such a comfort to him through his trials, took down the prophet's words.

We next see the prophet in a dimly lighted dungeon. What happened? The rulers had bound him so they would no longer be troubled by the word of the Lord. But the Lord told Jeremiah to write the words down. There he was, with his loyal friend Baruch at his side busily writing the words on the roll as the prophet spoke them. Read Jeremiah 36:4-6.

What Baruch was to read were the

words of the Lord. He read them in the Temple (*36:6,8*).

Investigating Committee
The Royal Investigating Committee immediately sent for Baruch and commanded him to read the roll again (*36:14-15*). They decided the roll must be brought to the king. "We must report all these words to the king" (*36:16*). Knowing full well the character of this ruler, they advised Jeremiah and Baruch to go into hiding before the roll was read in the royal presence (*36:19*).

They asked Baruch, "'Tell us, how did you come to write all this? Did Jeremiah dictate it?' 'Yes,' Baruch replied, 'he dictated all these words to me, and I wrote them in ink on the scroll'" (*36:17-18*). Then the princes wanted the king to see it.

The scene changes. We are no longer in the dark dungeon but in the winter palace of Jehoiakim, surrounded by all the luxury of an Eastern court. The king is sitting before his hearth. A fire is burning. Jehudi is reading the roll of Jeremiah. All are listening intently. When three or four columns had been read, Jehoiakim could stand no more. With penknife and angry hands he cut the roll to pieces and threw it into the fire. The very act of Jehoiakim seemed to symbolize the doom of the city, the Temple and all the people of Judah. They had heard God's Word and rejected it (*36:20-26*).

Of course, Jehoiakim gave the order to seize Jeremiah and Baruch but God "had hidden them" (*36:26*).

Now the Lord commanded Jeremiah to take another roll, and to write. "So Jeremiah took another scroll and gave it to the scribe Baruch son of Neriah, and as Jeremiah dictated, Baruch wrote. . . . And many similar words were added to them" (*36:32*).

Jeremiah stood in the Temple gate and spoke boldly for righteousness and God. He uttered a series of accusations against Judah and warnings of God's inevitable judgment of sin. But he always made an appeal to turn back to God and receive forgiveness.

Jeremiah's was a moral battle, and a moral battle is harder to fight and keep fighting.

After the Fall of Jerusalem
Jeremiah 39—52

In the fourth year of Jehoiakim's reign, Nebuchadnezzar invaded Judah (605 B.C.), and it was then that Daniel and his companions were carried away to Babylon and Jehoiakim himself was put into chains.

Nebuchadnezzar placed Zedekiah, Jehoiakim's brother, on the throne in place of Jehoiachin. Only the poor were left in Jerusalem now. Jeremiah likens them to bad, worthless figs, in contrast to those who had gone who were good figs (*chap. 24*). The picked men of the nation were carried away. Remember that Daniel afterward became prime minister of Babylon. The men who were left were so weak and degenerate that the prophet could see nothing but doom for Jerusalem.

Zedekiah was disposed to be friendly to Jeremiah, but he was a weak man and had no courage to make decisions of his own. He was like clay in the hands of the princes who surrounded his throne.

Jeremiah incurred the displeasure of the prophets who had gone to Babylon because, in a letter to the exiles, he directly opposed their prediction of an early return from captivity (*29:1-14*). Neither did the prophets in Jerusalem like it because they thought that soon they could throw off the yoke of Nebuchadnezzar. Zedekiah's advisers were in favor of throwing off the

Babylonian yoke and looking to Egypt for help, but Jeremiah kept insisting that the Chaldeans would certainly capture the city (37:3-10). Finally, Zedekiah broke his covenant with the king of Babylon. Nebuchadnezzar swiftly marched against Jerusalem and the final siege began.

As the siege proceeded, the hostility of Jeremiah's enemies became more intense. They charged him with desertion and thrust him into prison. They even petitioned the king to put him to death (38:4). Weakling that he was, Zedekiah gave Jeremiah over into the hands of the princes. They lowered him with cords into a miry dungeon, and left him to die of starvation and exposure. But God was with him and raised up a friend to deliver him. An Ethiopian, Ebed-melech, heard of Jeremiah's plight and made his way to the king. Gaining permission, he rushed to the dungeon and lowered a quantity of "old rags and worn-out clothes" for the prophet to put under his armpits beneath the cords, for Jeremiah had "sank down into the mud" and the work of getting him out would mean a great strain (38:6-13).

After Jeremiah's deliverance, Zedekiah, driven by fear, visited Jeremiah to find out what was in store for him. Jeremiah could only promise him doom for the city. Jeremiah still insisted that the king should surrender to Nebuchadnezzar, but Zedekiah was afraid of the princes (38:14-28).

After eighteen months of siege, Jerusalem was taken (587 B.C.). Zedekiah's sons were put to death before his eyes, and afterward he himself was blinded and carried in chains to Babylon (39:1-7). Jeremiah was given the choice of going to Babylon where freedom and honor awaited him, but he chose to cast his lot with the remnant left in the land (39:11-12; 40:1-16).

We can see how close Jeremiah was to the affairs of Judah during her captivity. He had seen the condition of Judah's decline after Josiah's good reign till the day of Zedekiah. He saw the people carried away captive and witnessed the destruction of Jerusalem and the Temple.

We find in chapter 24 one of the first discourses of Jeremiah in Zedekiah's reign. Jeremiah urged Judah to submit to Babylon in accordance with God's will, but without effect (21:1-10). Jeremiah never ceased urging this submission to Babylon, so much so that his enemies accused him of being a traitor. King Nebuchadnezzar of Babylon regarded his stand and made him an offer of any honor he would accept, besides saving his life (39:11-12).

At the same time Jeremiah was crying out against Babylon for her heinous crime in destroying God's children, he told them Babylon would be demolished and would be in ruins forever (51:37-43). This is literally true of this wonder city of the ancient world. Read again Isaiah 13:17-22 along with Jeremiah 51:37-43.

By the time of Christ, Babylon's power had gone, and in the first century A.D. it was mostly in ruins.

In 605 B.C. the first deportation of the Jews to Babylon occurred. During this year Jeremiah was ordered to write the predictions he had made and to have them read to the people.

These predictions are scattered throughout chapters 24—49 and concern the future of the Jews, the Babylonian captivity and the coming Messiah.

Predictions

1. Concerning God's future dealings with Judah (*Jeremiah 23; 31*)
2. Conquest of land by Nebuchadnezzar, king of Babylon (*Jeremiah 20:4*)

3. Judah's exile or captivity in Babylon and return after seventy years (*Jeremiah 25 and 26*)
4. Concerning the Messiah (*Jeremiah 23:6; 30:4-11; 33:14-26*)
5. Israel will be scattered among all the kingdoms of the earth (*Jeremiah 24*)
6. Final recovery of Israel (*Jeremiah 23:1-40; 32:37-41; Ezekiel 37:21-22*).

Jeremiah got his messages to the people by speaking to them as they thronged to the feasts. Often he did symbolic things to attract their attention. When he was shut up in prison, he dictated his messages to Baruch, the scribe, who wrote them down and read them to the people. The roll of Jeremiah that Jehoiakim burned no doubt took Jeremiah and Baruch about one and one-half years to prepare. Writing in those days was not like it is now. It was a long and laborious task.

In the days when David's throne was tottering and Judah was going into captivity, the prophet announced the coming Christ, King of the house of David, a righteous Branch. "In his days Judah will be saved and Israel will live in safety. This is the name by which he will be called: the Lord Our Righteousness" (*Jeremiah 23:6*).

Judah's future redemption through Christ is given in chapters 30; 31. The Jews are scattered today, but God is bringing them back (*30:10-11; 31:10*).

Jeremiah 23 is dear to the Jews, God's chosen people, and dear to the heart of God. It tells of the future of Judah, redeemed through the work of their Messiah. Jesus, the Good Shepherd, is promised (*vv. 1,3*). He will gather His sheep from every corner of the earth and they will return to their own country, the Promised Land. This will take place when the King shall come and sit upon the throne of David (*v. 5*).

Judah's History in a Word

"Chosen"—Jeremiah prophesied to God's chosen people Judah before their exile into Babylon.

"Captured"—He warned them of their captivity if they would not listen to Jehovah.

"Carried Away"—They sinned until God allowed them to be carried away by Nebuchadnezzar into Babylon. God tells them they must remain captive seventy years (*Jeremiah 25:1-14; Daniel 9:2*).

"Coming Messiah"—But God will not allow His children to remain scattered through the nations of the world forever. Someday the Jews will be gathered to their own land and the good Shepherd will appear (*Jeremiah 33:14-17*).

Finally those left in Jerusalem all fled to Egypt in spite of God's warning against it (*Jeremiah 43*). They asked Jeremiah to pray for guidance, but when it was given they refused to obey it. The prophet and Baruch were compelled to accompany them. Even in Egypt we find the prophet carrying out his commission. He prophesies the conquest of Egypt by Nebuchadnezzar (*43:8-13*). The Jews who dwelt in the Nile valley were practicing idolatry and Jeremiah warned them against this wickedness. When they refused to listen to his warning, and went on worshiping these other gods, Jeremiah told them the judgment of God would fall (*44:26-28*).

This is the last we hear of Jeremiah. How long he lived in Egypt afterward we know not. Jeremiah's life was one of deepening gloom. He had to watch the people and city he loved fall from sin to sin. And all the time he had no hope that things might change. How deeply he felt all this can be seen in his Lamentations.

Being confined in the court of the

guard attached to the royal palace, Jeremiah had opportunities to talk to the soldiers on duty as well as to the citizens who came along (*37:21*). To every one he declared the Word of the Lord (*37:6-10*). That message was that it was foolish to resist the Chaldeans. It would only result in destruction. This was so galling to national pride that the princes named in Jeremiah 38:1 resolved to kill Jeremiah. Yet King Zedekiah was convinced that Jeremiah was right.

Of course Jeremiah discouraged ("weakened the hands of") the soldiers and people (*38:4, KJV*). The people were convinced that resistance was useless because God had said that Jerusalem would be captured and burned by the Chaldeans. People and soldiers were unwilling to sacrifice their lives any longer in defending the city.

We find, in chapters 40—44, prophecies given by Jeremiah after the fall of Jerusalem.

1. To the remnant in Judah—40:1—43:3
2. To the remnant in Egypt—43:4—44:30.

A bit of history recorded in chapter 52 gives the facts about the captivity of Judah.

Jeremiah and His Times

The prophecy of Jeremiah deals with the certainty of God's judgment because of sin, yet the tenderness and eternity of His boundless love. Judah had forsaken the Lord, and through Jeremiah God sent warnings of impending judgments, beseeching His people to return to His commandments.

Jeremiah was God's prophet, speaking God's words. Read of his marvelous call, Jeremiah 1:4-10. Many times Jeremiah cries, "This is what the Lord, the Lord Almighty says." In Jeremiah 22:29 he adds, "O land, land, land, hear the word of the Lord!" The book abounds in golden passages: 6:16; 9:23-24; 10:10-13; 17:7-8; 18:1-6; 20:9; 22:29; 23:5-6. The golden chapters are 31 and 33.

Christ appears in Jeremiah. He is wonderfully pictured in 23:5-6. His future kingdom is lavishly described in chapters 31 and 33.

Understanding Lamentations

Here is another of the Bible's exquisite books of poetry. It is commonly attributed to Jeremiah. Five beautiful, distinct poems are bound together in the book. It is not all sorrow. Above the clouds of the poet's weeping over the sins of his people, God's sun is shining. In Lamentations 3:22-27, the light breaks through to throw a shining rainbow across the murky sky. God's grace always shines above the clouds of sin (see *Romans 5:20*), and it will always shine in the heart that is trusting in God through faith in the Lord Jesus Christ who gives "to bestow on them a crown of beauty instead of ashes, the oil of gladness instead of mourning, and a garment of praise instead of a spirit of despair" (*Isaiah 61:3*).

19. UNDERSTANDING

Ezekiel

Ezekiel Portrays Jesus Christ, the Son of Man

Ezekiel, the faithful preacher to the exiles in Babylon, is the author of this book.

Jeremiah was the last of the prophets in Jerusalem before the exile. His ministry was still going on when the end came. The young prophet Ezekiel was already at work among the exiles in Babylon. God had prepared a witness to the people in their captivity. God needed a voice to warn the people and to remind them of the reason all these calamities had befallen them. For twenty-two years Ezekiel dealt with the discouraged captives to whom God had sent him.

"The word of the Lord came to me" (*Ezekiel 24:15*). This phrase occurs forty-nine times in Ezekiel. God's greatest communications can only be made by his servants whose own hearts have been broken.

Ezekiel is for the Jewish people today. It tells them that God will fulfill His sure promises. Their land, their city, their Temple will be restored to them. It reveals God's plan for them.

Ezekiel is for the Christian today. It is a book of the times, for God's time is always revealed by His dealing with the Jews. Israel is beginning to return to her land and divine history is being made. The nation now exists officially. When the Jews move we know God is getting ready to act.

You find little of Ezekiel in the Gospels or Epistles. But look in Revelation. Ezekiel and John seem to lock arms across the centuries, and looking into the future they see the unfolding of a new heaven and a new earth. Ezekiel, the prophet, peering forward with rapt gaze, half whispering, says, "Above the expanse over their heads was what looked like a throne of sapphire, and high above on the throne was a figure like that of a man" (*Ezekiel 1:26*). Now read John's words in Revelation 4:2-3.

Like Jeremiah, Ezekiel was not only a prophet, but he was a priest as well. He was a prophet during the captivity. When he was twenty-five years old, he was carried captive to Babylon in 597 B.C. with the upper class of people, eleven years before the destruction of Jerusalem. This means that for eleven

The Muslim Dome of the Rock stands over the original site of the Jewish Temple in Jerusalem.

years 10,000 exiles were living in a concentration camp in Babylon while Jeremiah and the folks at home tried to carry on in Jerusalem. For five years the captives had no preacher. Then Ezekiel began to serve them. He immediately tried to remove their false hopes of an early return to Palestine. He tried to prepare them for the news of the tragic destruction of their beloved Jerusalem. He lived at the same time as Daniel and Jeremiah. Jeremiah remained among the Jews in Jerusalem. Ezekiel lived with the exiles in Babylon, and Daniel lived in the court of the rulers in Babylon.

Ezekiel's Day

The Northern Kingdom of Israel had been taken captive 120 years before by the king of Assyria (722 b.c.). Then God brought judgment upon the Southern Kingdom of Judah. Nebuchadnezzar had come to Jerusalem and carried away ten thousand of the chief men of the Southern Kingdom and some of the royal seed, including Daniel and Ezekiel (*2 Chronicles 36:6-7; Daniel 1:1-3; 2 Kings 24:14-16*). The people of Israel had been living in constant trouble. It took Nebuchadnezzar twenty years to completely destroy Jerusalem. He could have done it sooner, but he wanted tribute money. Then, too, Daniel was his court favorite and he may have been influenced by his young prime minister. He was finally forced to devastate Jerusalem because the city persisted in allying herself with Egypt. It was a tragic hour for Jerusalem when her walls were laid flat, her houses burned, the Temple destroyed and her people dragged away as captives.

God had told of Judah's captivity by Babylon more than 100 years before it happened (*Isaiah 39:6; Micah 4:10*). The seventy years of its duration was foretold by Jeremiah (*Jeremiah 25:11-12*). It is interesting to notice that God told them the exact time of their exile. But the captivity did not bring the people of Judah back to God. This judgment of God only seemed to drive the people into greater wickedness. They worshiped idols and set up shrines in the hills and defiled the sanctuary of Jehovah (*Ezekiel 5:11*). Ezekiel began his prophecies to them.

Ezekiel has a style and method of preaching all his own. He uses symbols, as in the mimic siege of Jerusalem (*chap. 4*), visions (*chap. 8*), parables (*chap. 17*), poems (*chap. 19*), proverbs (*12:22-23; 18:2*) and prophecies (*6; 20; 40—48*).

Ezekiel is an artist. He paints strange pictures for us. They are mystifying and full of terror and sometimes hard to decipher. They glow with life and action. He talks of sin and punishment, of repentance and blessing.

God told Ezekiel to go to the people in captivity. He was a captive ministering to captives. We must get alongside people to help them. This was our Lord's way. God tells Ezekiel to speak "whether they listen or fail to listen" (*3:11*). Ezekiel's responsibility was to deliver God's message. The results were not in his hands.

The Glory of God

The "glory of God" seems to be the key phrase to Ezekiel. It occurs twelve times in the first eleven chapters. Then it does not occur again until chapter 43. The "glory of the Lord" was grieved away from the Temple at Jerusalem by the idolatry of the people. God says, "Because you have defiled my sanctuary with all your vile images and detestable practices, I myself will withdraw my favor; I will not look on you with pity or spare you" (*Ezekiel 5:11*). In Ezekiel 8, we see Ezekiel in a vision transported to Jerusalem and he sees four kinds of idolatry that were practiced in the courts of the Lord's house, even worshiping the sun, with their backs to the sanctuary while their faces were to the East. We see "the glory of the Lord" gradually grieved away from the inner sanctuary by the sin of idolatry, and the brightness filled the court. Then it departed to the threshold and rested over the cherubim. As the cherubim rose from the earth, "the glory of the Lord" abode above their pinions and mounted with them, forsaking the city and removing to the mountains (*chap. 10*).

In the Old Testament, the glory of God refers to the light that shone between the cherubim in the holy of holies as the evidence of the presence of God. Ezekiel opens with this heavenly glory in the vision (*chap. 1*). The book ends with earthly glory (*chaps.

40—48*). Ezekiel's visions given in between tell of the departing of this glory (*9:3*). First it left the cherubim for the threshold of God's house (*10:4*), thence to the east gate (*10:18-19*), and finally clear away from the Temple and city to the Mount of Olives (*11:22-23*). Thus gradually, reluctantly, majestically, the glory of the Lord left the Temple and Holy City. Then captivity came.

This was Ezekiel's message to the nation. Their captivity was a result of their sin, and before they could hope for return to their land they must return to their Lord. This message reaches its climax in the impassioned cry of Ezekiel 18:30-32.

God's judgment on sin is certain and severe. His redemption is equally certain when it is welcomed by the human heart. Ezekiel's message closes with the promise of future glory. Ezekiel 37 is the great classic of Israel's hope. The closing vision of the Temple is equally significant. The glory of the Lord returns (*43:2-6*) and fills the house of the Lord (*44:4*).

Ezekiel's prophecy is intensely practical for nation and Church. As Israel's captivity was the result of sin, so we must remember that sin is a reproach to any people. A nation's troubles are the result of national apostasy from God.

The same is true of the Church of Christ. The glory of the Lord left the house of the Lord because of the sins of God's people. It is also true of individual Christian experience. God's blessing returns to His people when His people return to Him.

Ezekiel and the Captivity

It seems God called Ezekiel that He might explain and justify His action in allowing His children to be taken into captivity. They had been wicked and stiff-necked; they were guilty of unspeakable sin and abomination. When other nations did what Israel had done, God wiped them out. But all of God's dealings with Israel were for correction. They should say, "I know, O Lord, that your laws are righteous, and in faithfulness you have afflicted me" (*Psalm 119:75*). He was punishing His children for their sin and was teaching them great lessons. He said a remnant would survive. "They shall know that I am God" was His purpose. After the captivity, the Jews were cured from polytheistic worshiping of the gods of the surrounding peoples. They had insisted upon it before, in spite of the warnings of God, but after they came out of Babylon, the names of other gods were banished from their lips.

God set Jeremiah to be a tower of strength in the land of Judah. In the same way He set Ezekiel to be a tower among his own captive people by the river Chebar, in the land of the Chaldeans. He told Ezekiel that "I will make your forehead like the hardest stone, harder than flint" (*Ezekiel 3:9*). Strength characterized the ministry of

the prophet whose name means "God will strengthen."

Ezekiel—A Home Missionary

Ezekiel was sent to his own people.

Perhaps God is speaking to us as He spoke to Ezekiel—read Ezekiel 3:5,11. It was difficult to speak to false prophets, elders, shepherds and princes, but God commanded it.

Ezekiel—A Watchman

God told Ezekiel to be a watchman. He told the prophet not to fear the people but give them warning, and that if he did not do it, He would require their blood at his hands (*chaps. 3 and 33*). These chapters state plainly our personal responsibility in giving out the gospel message.

Ezekiel—The Sign

To be God's sign to the people, Ezekiel underwent the loss of all personal interests. He stood ready to do anything God asked of him in order to demonstrate the plan of God for His people, and God asked some extraordinary things of him. He shut himself up in his house (*Ezekiel 3:24*). He was placed in weird positions (*4:4-8*). He ate his food by weight (*4:10*). He sacrificed personal appearance (*5:1*), smote with hand or struck with foot (*6:11*), and even moved personal and domestic goods out of his house to show the removal of Israel into captivity (*12:2-7*).

In Ezekiel 25—32, we hear pronouncements of doom on surrounding nations. We remember Isaiah gave warnings in chapters 13—23. Jeremiah gave warnings in chapters 46—51. Each mentioned different nations. Ezekiel warned Ammon, Moab, Edom, Philistia, Tyre, Sidon and Egypt.

The remarkable thing about these prophecies is that they were given at a time when these cities and nations were strong and powerful. Each one has passed into a state of utter desolation, as Babylon, or has been put into a place of insignificance among world powers. Many of the specific prophecies have already been fulfilled to the most minute detail. "Righteousness exalts a nation, but sin is a disgrace to any people" (*Proverbs 14:34*).

Visions of Ezekiel

Ezekiel is a prophet of visions. The key text of the book shows this: "While I was among the exiles by the Kebar River, the heavens were opened and I saw visions of God" (*Ezekiel 1:1*). It is urgent that you scan all these visions before you enter into further detailed study.

Vision of the Cherubim (*1:1—3:13*)
In this vision, "four living creatures" appear, having unusual faces, but each with the general appearance of a man. The main purpose of the vision is twofold—to commission Ezekiel for service, and to impress upon him the need for assimilating the words God spoke to him and giving them to the people. Note "the scroll" he ate in his vision (*3:1*). The unswerving obedience to God's will of the creatures symbolized the obedience expected of Ezekiel. Their movement as a single unit is the picture of God's will perfectly executed. Ezekiel and Revelation are often alike in symbolism. The "figure like that of a man" upon the throne (*1:26*) is the Son of God. The "appearance of a rainbow in the clouds on a rainy day" spoke of the covenant God made with Noah (*1:28*). The "fire" (*1:4,13,27*) bespoke God's Spirit. In Revelation, all these appear. Christ figures prominently in all the symbolism.

Vision of Glory and Godlessness (*8:1—11:25*)
Before the siege of Jerusalem, Ezekiel is given an extended vision that shows the people's abominations in defiling the sanctuary, and the contrasting glory of God. "Abominations" occur all the way through the section. "Glory" stands in sharp contrast. God was trying to show why Israel was to be led into captivity (*8:17-18*).

Vision of the Burning Vine (*15:1-8*)
The vine becomes a symbol of Judah, and the burning of a useless vine that bears no fruit is the destruction of the people of God. The abominations of Jerusalem are so great as to warrant the most severe punishment. This vision of doom is followed by the parable of the unfaithful wife. Israel was Jehovah's "bride" who had forsaken God to go whoring after other gods. Love of idols, rather than the love of God, caused Israel's downfall (*chap. 16*).

Vision of Dry Bones (*37:1-18*)
In this vision, Ezekiel sees a great valley filled with dry bones, said to be the "whole house of Israel" (*37:11*). The main lesson of the vision is the restora-

tion of God's people. He takes them from among the heathen and gathers them out of all countries through which, as bones without flesh, they have been scattered. It is a picture also of the power of God to raise those who have not only been scattered, but also dead in sins. This "new birth" was explained to Nicodemus. God promises it here to Israel. They are to be brought forth, filled with God's Spirit and brought to their land.

Parables and Signs in Ezekiel

Parables and signs, as well as visions, abound in Ezekiel. The more outstanding ones command great interest. (*1*) The parable of the two eagles (*chap. 17*) reveals the king of Babylon (*v. 12*) and the king of Egypt. The "top" of the cedar (*v. 3*) corresponds to Jehoiachin carried captive to Babylon. The "seed of your land" was Zedekiah (*v. 5*). The "tender sprig" (*v. 22*) Jehovah will plant is the Messiah, the future King of David's line through whom all nations will learn to know God. Jeremiah also tells of the "highest branch" (*23:5-6;* see also *Isaiah 11:1; Zechariah 3:8; Isaiah 53*). For "the mountain of the Lord," see 17:22; 20:40; Micah 4:1-2; Isaiah 2:2-3. (*2*) Chapters 20—23 include several parables, prominent among which is that of the two sisters Aholah and Aholibah. They represent Israel's and Judah's deterioration into idolatry. (*3*) The parable of the boiling caldron (*chap. 24*) symbolizes the holocaust in Jerusalem at the hands of the invading Babylonians. Much fuel, hot fire, boiled flesh and burnt bones show the intensity of the siege (*vv. 5,10*). (*4*) Two sticks—one Judah, the other Israel—are shown as ultimately reunited under the Shepherd King of God's people—Christ (*37:24*). This is one of the important "signs."

Predictions Before the Siege of Jerusalem— Against Judah *Ezekiel 1—24*

As the book opens we see Ezekiel, a young man of about 30, captive, yet being commissioned by God for a great service.

Like the prophets generally, Ezekiel entered upon his ministry only after he had a vision and a call from God. Read of Jeremiah's call in Jeremiah 1:4-10. Turn to Isaiah 6 and review the facts of Isaiah's commission. Ezekiel opens with the description of the experiences of the prophet when he was called.

Burning off useless stubble. In Ezekiel, the vine becomes a symbol of Judah, and the burning of a useless vine that bears no fruit is the destruction of the people of God.

The pivot of the book is the destruction of Jerusalem:

1. Pre-siege *(1—24)*—Ezekiel began six years before the destruction of Jerusalem with his prophecies and kept predicting its certainty until it occurred.

2. Siege *(25—32)*—After that his prophecies deal with Judah's enemies and the overthrow of these heathen nations.

3. Post-siege *(33—48)*—Finally the restoration and reestablishment of Judah is pictured.

Ezekiel gives us a very dramatic picture of his vision and call to service. The Holy Being who appeared to him could go everywhere. He was all powerful, could see everything and could rule the entire universe by His mighty hand.

The vision he saw was unusually complicated and elaborate. Notice how many times Ezekiel uses the words "appearance" and "likeness." He knows he is trying to describe things impossible to picture.

The prophet saw a fiery cloud approaching. From out of the glow were four living creatures, suggested by the cherubim of the Temple. (See *I Kings 6:23-28; Genesis 3:24; Psalm 18:10.*) Each had four wings and four faces: that of a man, a lion, an ox and an eagle, symbolizing intelligence, dignity, strength and speed. They faced east, west, north and south, suggesting that all parts of the universe are open to the gaze of God. The wings showed that no spot was inaccessible to divine power. There were eyes in the wheels—wheels so equipped cannot miss their way. We see a symbol of the omnipotence (all power), omnipresence (all presence) and omniscience (all knowledge) of God.

The mysterious whir of the mighty wings was followed by an equally mysterious silence. The wings dropped.

The chariots stopped. Above the heads of the creatures was a crystal floor on which rested a sapphire throne, and on the throne almighty God Himself, a figure of supernatural brilliance and glory. The terror of divine majesty was softened by the sight of a lovely rainbow around the throne. Little wonder that when Ezekiel saw this vision he fell prostrate. The vision was to destroy all self-confidence the prophet might have.

The Call

Following the vision, the awful silence was broken by the Almighty upon the throne. The prophet was receiving his call. God told the prostrate prophet to rise and accept his commission for service. God wants more than inactive submission. He wants loving service. God called Ezekiel "son of man." One hundred times this phrase is used. Ezekiel was called to declare the message of God—a message of doom to the people. (Read *Ezekiel 2:1-10.*) This doom was justified by their rebellion. Ezekiel had every temptation to "rebel," but he went without flinching to speak the word.

The prophet's authority is suggested by the symbolic swallowing of a scroll. He must make the message his own. He must eat it (*Ezekiel 3:3*). Bitter as its contents were to his mouth, they were sweet as honey, for it is sweet to do the will of God and to be trusted with tasks for Him.

Then Ezekiel heard the whir of the wings and the roar of the wheels when the glory of Jehovah rose from the place and the chariot departed, leaving the prophet in a state of bitterness and heat of spirit. In this mood he found his way to Tel-abib, a colony of his fellow exiles, and remained for a week in a state of utter stupefaction.

The Watchman

At the end of the week he received another message from God. This time it was more explicit. He was called to be a watchman. "I have made you a watchman . . . give them warning from me. . . . [if] you do not warn him . . . I will hold you accountable for his blood. But if you do warn the wicked man . . . but you will have saved yourself" (Ezekiel 3:17-19).

God places a great responsibility on His watchmen. How can we be so careless in the light of such words as these? How can we go to sleep and fail to warn others of their sins? Let us answer this challenge and heed this warning.

Ezekiel 33:7 says, "I have made you a watchman."

As a watchman, Ezekiel must warn individual people of the coming catastrophe he so clearly sees. It is not enough to warn the crowd. He must deal with individuals, good or bad, who compose the crowd and tell them to turn from their evil ways.

God impressed Ezekiel with individual responsibility. Each one must repent. Each one must hear the Word.

Four Symbols of Coming Doom of Jerusalem

1. The siege of Jerusalem—4:1-3. Ezekiel cannot speak, but he is a prophet still and he can preach, if not by word, by symbol (Ezekiel 3:22-27).

2. The exile—its duration—4:4-8. This section is curious. Remember Ezekiel was a sign. He lay upon his side to symbolize the years of punishment the Jews were to suffer in exile—a day for a year.

3. The hardships of the exiles—4:9-17. The horrors of famine due to siege are symbolized here by the prophet's food and drink, carefully measured out—about one-half pound of food a day and a pint of water.

4. The fate of the besieged—5:1-17. This last symbol, the knife and razor, is the most terrible of them all. It suggests the completeness of the destruction.

All of these visions and symbols reveal the method of Ezekiel's prophecy. This is the method used in Daniel and Revelation.

The prophet was shown the way the people profaned the Temple of Jehovah. This justified to the new generation the national punishment (8:1—11:12).

The prophet pled that Jehovah spare a remnant and Jehovah promised to be a "little sanctuary" to them in the land of their exile. He promised to restore them finally (11:13-21).

· The next chapters reveal the past sins of both Samaria and Jerusalem, and the punishment and instructions in righteousness for the elders of Israel (11:22—24:27). God says, "I will give them an undivided heart and put a new spirit in them. . . . They will be my people, and I will be their God" (11:19-20). God wants a religious experience of the heart. God will give His people a new spirit (18:31; 36:26).

Predictions During the Siege of Jerusalem—Judgment Against Judah's Enemies
Ezekiel 25—32

Ezekiel's gloomy predictions are completed (Ezekiel 1—24). With the news of the fall of Jerusalem he immediately begins to prophesy about the future restoration of Israel. God often reveals a bright picture of Israel's future against the backdrop of divine judgment (chaps. 33—48). But before Israel is restored to her land, those who are her enemies must be put out of the way. So at this point we hear of the future doom of these foreign powers. First we hear of her near neighbors who have insulted and harassed her, and then of the more distant and more powerful ones. God pronounces His judgment upon Ammon, Moab, Tyre, Sidon and Egypt for their sins against Israel. All of these powers were ancient enemies of Israel. They dated back before the days of the monarchy. From Israel's petty neighbors with their petty spite, Ezekiel turns to the great empires of Tyre and Egypt. They, too, must go. In a passage of great literary power, Ezekiel describes the brilliance of Tyre, the extent of her commerce, the pity and terror inspired by her fall.

Ezekiel 29—32 tells of the collapse of Egypt. The mighty Nebuchadnezzar with his terrible army will deal a crushing blow and Egypt will be devastated.

Predictions After the Siege of Jerusalem— Judah's Restoration
Ezekiel 33—48

We can now look into the future and see the final restoration and glory of Israel. God will gather together His scattered people. God says over and over, "I will, I will."

Shepherds of Israel had proven faithless to the people, the flock had been scattered; but now Jehovah will set up a Shepherd, "my servant David" (Ezekiel 34:23-24). This, no doubt, refers to the Davidic covenant and to the seed of David, the Messiah. Look up this series of passages: 2 Samuel 7:16; Psalm 89:20-36; Isaiah 7:13-14; 9:6-7; 11:1-12; Jeremiah 23:2-7; Ezekiel 37:21-28; Hosea 3:4-5; Luke 1:30-33; Acts 2:29-31; 15:14-17. All this reveals that the future blessing of Israel will come with the Messiah, David's Son. When the Jews rejected Jesus they did not thwart God's plan or defeat His purpose, for in Acts we read that He was raised from the dead to sit on David's throne, and He will return for that purpose (Acts 2:30).

The restoration Ezekiel tells about does not refer to the feeble remnant that returned to Jerusalem after the seventy years of captivity (see Ezra and Nehemiah), for it is a restoration from all nations (Ezekiel 36:24).

Ezekiel sees a vision of all this. There is a valley of dry bones (37:1-14). The "bones" are the Jews who shall be alive at the restoration of the nation. The "graves" are the nations where they are dwelling but "buried." God first will bring them into their own land. Then they will be converted—a nation shall be born in a day. The Spirit will give them life. The revival of national life is possible! And a nation shall be born in a day (see Zechariah 12:10; John 19:37; Romans 11:26). The resurrection in this chapter is not of the individual Jew, but of the whole nation.

Ezekiel 38 opens with the doom of "Gog, of the land of Magog, the chief prince of Meshech and Tubal." The reference is to the northern (European) powers, perhaps headed up by Russia. (Read these passages in connection with Zechariah 14:1-9; 12:1-4; Matthew 24:14-30; Revelation 14:14-20; 19:17-21.) Before the curtain falls we read the description of the kingdom during the coming millennial age. This is what the thousand-year reign of Christ on earth is called when He shall sit upon the throne of David, in Jerusalem (Revelation 20:6). All the prophets tell us what a glorious day this will be for both Jew and Gentile. We read of the Temple, the worship and the final possession of the land promised to Abraham and to his seed according to the covenant God gave to him (see Genesis 12:1-3; 13:14-15; 15:18; 17:3-8) and of the many

The modern Jewish city of Jerusalem. Ezekiel tells of a restoration of the Jews from all nations (*Ezekiel 36:24*).

nations that will know that God alone is Lord of all (*Ezekiel 38:23*).

Golden Truth About the Golden Age

Back here in the Old Testament, while the Jews were in what seemed hopeless captivity, God declares constantly that He will restore the Jews to their own land, set up the throne and the kingdom of David through David's greater Son. With His reign will come such earthly and spiritual blessings as have not been known since the world began. This is the golden truth about the golden age that is coming to pass here on this earth (*Ezekiel 34:22-31*).

Gabriel's prophecy at Jesus' birth in

Luke 1:30-33 will be literally fulfilled through David's Son, the Lord Jesus Christ. This promise of a Messianic King and kingdom must be carefully distinguished from our Lord's spiritual rule over hearts and lives. The words of Gabriel to Mary still wait complete, literal fulfillment (see *Ezekiel 34:23-24; 37:24; 1 Kings 14:8; Jeremiah 30:9*).

The appearance of the Messiah will usher in a glorious future. God will make a covenant of peace (*Leviticus 26:6; Jeremiah 31:31; Ezekiel 37:26*). Wonderful blessings are promised to His people. They will be assured of absolute protection from idolatrous nations, the evil beasts of Ezekiel 34:25, because they are possessed by none other than God Himself (*34:31*).

20. UNDERSTANDING

Daniel

Daniel Portrays Jesus Christ, the Striking Stone

"Young men without any physical defect, handsome, showing aptitude for every kind of learning, well informed, quick to understand, and qualified to serve in the king's palace" (*Daniel 1:4*)—these are some of the men with whom this book deals. They were skilled in God's wisdom as opposed to human wisdom. They had an understanding of God's revelation that unlocks the mysteries of human science. They had ability in them such as God gives to live the overcoming life!

Chief among these princely young men was the incomparable Daniel. He stands in God's Word as the man who dared to keep a clean heart and body (*1:8*), and the man therefore whom God chose as a channel for His message to the Gentile nations of the world. A large part of this book is concerned with the thrilling personal life of this peerless captive prince of Judah.

Daniel was in the palace at Babylon the same time Ezekiel was toiling in a slave gang. If Daniel's was the easier life in many of its material aspects, it may also be considered by far the more perilous.

Ezekiel's work during these dreary exile years was to proclaim to his people God's truth and to explain the real meaning of the miseries that had befallen them. Daniel's task was to share in the actual government of Babylon.

Daniel has been called the prophet of dreams. God revealed to him His secrets. "During the night the mystery was revealed to Daniel in a vision" (*2:19*). Daniel, like Ezekiel, looks far into the future. He is quoted most in Revelation. One cannot understand the great signs of Revelation without looking at their meaning in Daniel.

Daniel belonged to a family of high rank. He was taken captive to Babylon during the first invasion by Nebuchadnezzar (died 562 B.C., king of Babylonia 605-562 B.C.) at about the age of sixteen. Ezekiel was taken captive eight years later during the second invasion. Daniel lived to be over ninety years of age. He saw the Babylonian kingdom fall (539 B.C.) and the Medo-Persian empire established. He held high positions under kings Nebuchadnezzar, Belshazzar, Darius (550-486 B.C., king of Persia from 522-486 B.C.) and Cyrus (585-529 B.C., called "the Great").

Daniel's whole life from the time of his captivity was spent in the great and glamorous city of Babylon, the ancient Hollywood. He spent sixty-nine years in a vile court. There he lived a life without blame and well favored. Ezekiel 14:14-20; 28:3 refer to him as a model of righteousness.

Although Daniel was a captive, he rose to be prime minister of Babylon. The wonderful thing is that he always remained true to Jehovah God.

Daniel—Book of Devotions

This book is packed with heart-touching devotional passages for the personal Christian life:

The surrendered life (*1:1-21*)
Light amidst darkness (*2:20-22*)
Triumph through trial (*3:17-25*)
The reward of service (*5:17*)
Prayer and confidence in God (*6:10-24*)
Confession of sin (*9:3-19*)

The wisdom of soul winning—12:3. "God honored Daniel in his prayers." Marvelous in power that they were, God sent a special embassy of angels from the throne with the thrilling words, "I have come in response to [your words]" (*Daniel 10:12*). God exhibited His power in a remarkable way in Daniel's life and Daniel never introduced himself or his own actions except as illustrations of that power.

"Daniel was the companion of kings." He was a leader of men. He was a pioneer in reform. He started the first Society of Total Abstinence (*Daniel 1:12*). Daniel was, like Joseph, God's candle shining in pagan darkness. He was chief statesman in the first empire of the world, chief adviser of a great monarch and a great protector of his own people. God gave him favor and love in the sight of the court official, Ashpenaz. Even proud Nebuchadnezzar seemed to have had real affection for Daniel.

The feelings of Darius toward Daniel are revealed when he finds that a trap has been set for him. He was "greatly distressed; he was determined to rescue Daniel and made every ef-

An Assyrian relief of a lion released from its cage in preparation for the hunt. Daniel was sentenced to be put in a lion pit.

fort until sundown to save him" (*6:14*).

No doubt Cyrus was greatly influenced by the aged statesman. Daniel may have shown him the prophecy Isaiah had written concerning him 100 years before he was born. This made Cyrus issue the decree for rebuilding the Temple at Jerusalem (*2 Chronicles 36:22-23; Ezra 1*).

In the book Daniel wrote, we see him preeminently as a prophet of God. He drew back the curtain and unveiled, as no one had ever done before, the hidden things of the future. Indeed, we are seeing more and more that his great prophecies are only history written before it occurred. The book of Daniel is one of the world's great annals in anticipation.

This book reveals the power of God and His universal sovereignty. God's power is contrasted with world power.

God the Keeper—Daniel 1: God's power in keeping Daniel and his companions. They were given understanding and wisdom above all the wise men of Babylon.

God the Revealer of Secrets—Daniel 2: God's power in revealing the dream of Nebuchadnezzar to Daniel. None of the wise men of Babylon could do this.

God the Deliverer—Daniel 3: God's power in delivering Daniel's three companions from the fiery furnace. These young men stood up alone, against a nation, with the calm assurance that God would deliver them, yet adding, "But if he does not, we want you to know, O king, that we will not serve your gods, or worship the image of gold you have set up" (*v. 18*). This occurred after they had been in Babylon about twenty years, and God was demonstrating in this most dramatic way His power over all the gods of this country.

God the Potentate—Daniel 4: God's power in dealing with the mighty

Babylonian monarch, Nebuchadnezzar. God struck him while the proud king was boasting of his power as he was strolling on the roof of his magnificent palace. He was driven from his kingdom to dwell among beasts—victim of a strange form of insanity.

God the Judge—Daniel 5: God's power is shown in the awful judgment revealed to Belshazzar, son of Nabonidus, by the handwriting on the wall. That night the king was slain by the Persian army and his city taken.

God the All Powerful—Daniel 6: God's power revealed in the deliverance of Daniel from the lions' den. Remember, Daniel was an old man. When he was a young man of about twenty he was honored by the highest office in the whole empire. Now at ninety he was thrown into the den of lions. It seems that even the lions honored him.

God used the times of captivity to reveal His power among the nations of the world. When the chosen people were captives in Egypt, He worked miracles and wonders by the hand of Moses and showed, not only to the Israelites, but also to the Egyptians, that the Lord God is Almighty.

Now, during the Babylonian captivity, God uses this as a special occasion to manifest His power. We find these great world monarchs confessing that He is the living God, the Most High, the King of heaven. He visits His children even in exile and shows them again that He is mighty to save.

Unlike the other prophets, Daniel deals more fully with the Gentile nations than with his own Jewish nation.

The book of Daniel is divided into two great sections:

1. historical—narration, chapters 1–6

2. prophetic—revelation, chapters 7–12.

Reign of Nebuchadnezzar
Daniel 1—4

This scene opens upon a little company of four young men, Daniel, Hananiah, Mishael and Azariah (also called Shadrach, Meshach, Abednego). They had been taken captive from Jerusalem by Nebuchadnezzar and carried away to his palace in Babylon. Daniel was only about sixteen years old, Nebuchadnezzar a little older. He came to the throne about the time Daniel was taken captive into Babylon, and was the most powerful and distinguished king of the Babylonian empire. Daniel's career was marked by its extent in time and its greatness in accomplishment.

Daniel was carried to Babylon during the first deportation of the captives. He gained a high position in the kingdom and was influential through the seventy years of his captivity. He saw his captive brothers return to Jerusalem under the decree of Cyrus. He saw world-ruling Babylon pass away and a new empire arise. Even at the age of ninety he received a position of high distinction in the court of Persia.

Daniel and his friends lived in an atmosphere of loose morals and low standards even though they were in a palace. Yet we read that they kept themselves apart from the evil of that court—true to God in a day when everything was against them.

Observe that these brave youths stood with Daniel when they faced their first temptation in the court of the Babylonian king: "Daniel resolved not to defile himself with the royal food and wine, and he asked the chief official for permission not to defile himself this way" (*Daniel 1:8*). To young men like these God could tell His secrets and demonstrate His power. Remember, "The Lord confides in those who fear him" (*Psalm 25:14*).

These youths met every emergency and were victors. We will find them in three difficult positions:

1. In the court of a powerful emperor
2. In the fiery furnace
3. In the den of lions.

In this first scene we find them in the luxurious royal court. The youths were brought very quickly face to face with a serious practical difficulty. As favored ones, they had been put into

Assyrian relief showing the queen feasting with attendants. Daniel and his friends lived in an atmosphere of loose morals and low standards even though they were in a palace.

one of the apartments in the palace and given many of the delicacies of the king's table. It was hard indeed to refuse the king's meat and ask for a simpler fare. The king's meat had probably been offered to idols (see *Exodus 34:15; 1 Corinthians 10:20*), and the flesh food would have been killed with the blood left in the animal, which was unclean (see *Leviticus 3:17; 7:26*).

We are told that God gave these young men knowledge and skill in all learning and wisdom; and Daniel had understanding in all visions and dreams. This was God's reward.

There was a stir in the palace. Nebuchadnezzar had dreamed a dream and not one of the wise men of the kingdom could tell him what it was. A decree had been sent forth that all the wise men should be slain, and Daniel and his friends were sought. But Daniel was not afraid. God would tell him the dream and give him the meaning of it.

Daniel called his prayer partners (*Daniel 2:17*) and they presented their problem before God. "During the night the mystery was revealed to Daniel in a vision" (*Daniel 2:19*). God never disappoints faith.

The Dream of World Empires
Nebuchadnezzar's dream and the interpretation teach us some interesting things about the history of the world from that time till the end of this age. This period the Bible calls "the times of the Gentiles" (*Luke 21:24; Romans 11:25*) because God has put aside His own people, the Jews, for a time and has turned over the government of the world to the Gentiles.

Daniel 2 has been called the ABC of prophecy. It stretches out before us the most complete picture in all the Scriptures of what is to come to pass—the future.

God revealed His plan of the future

to King Nebuchadnezzar in a dream (*2:29*). After Nebuchadnezzar had dreamed, he forgot! But it worried him. No one could tell him his dream but one who knew "the God of heaven." (Master the outline of history given in this second chapter.)

Picture a great image. The head was of gold, its breast and arms of silver, the belly and thighs of brass, and its legs of iron, with its feet and toes of iron and clay. Then a Rock cut out without hands struck the image and broke it to pieces; and the Rock became a great mountain and filled the whole earth. (This Rock was no other than Jesus Christ.)

God first reveals the Gentile powers. Four great empires were to succeed one another in the government of the world from Nebuchadnezzar to the end. God says, "You are that head of gold" (*Daniel 2:38*).

The breast and arms of silver represented the Medo-Persian empire, which overthrew Babylon and became its successor. Its power began with Cyrus under whom the Jews returned to Jerusalem (see *Ezra 1:1-2*).

Then the belly and thighs of brass represented Greece, which overturned the Medo-Persians. It pictures the Grecian rule "over the whole earth" (*Daniel 2:39*) under Alexander the Great (356-323 B.C.). The legs of iron represent Rome.

Daniel's Historical Summary
Daniel tells us what each metal represents. Daniel 2:38 says that the head of gold is Babylon. In Daniel 8:20 we find that the Medo-Persians are to follow. Then in Daniel 8:21 it states that Greece is to follow Persia. Daniel 9:26 indicates a fourth world power. From then on we find an ever-dividing kingdom and a government ever weakened in its power and represented by toes of iron and clay that cannot hold together.

Kingdom of Christ

In the "Rock" cut out without hands we see the Kingdom of Christ, whose Kingdom shall never be destroyed, bringing to an end all the other kingdoms. Christ will come and set up a Kingdom that will last forever (*Daniel 2:44-45*).

Remember, at the time Nebuchadnezzar dreamed his dream the Persian kingdom did not exist. It was merely a Babylonian satrapy. It would have seemed impossible that a strong Grecian empire would rise.

Notice that the metals in the image deteriorate in value—gold, silver, brass and iron. This reveals the weakening in the power of each succeeding empire.

Many ask, "When will this Rock break the iron, the bronze, the clay, the silver and the gold to pieces?" We know not the day nor hour, but the King is coming with power and great glory with all His holy angels to establish His Kingdom.

The great King Nebuchadnezzar fell on his face and worshiped Daniel, and declared that his God was the God of all gods (see *Daniel 2:46-47*). But we find as we go on in the story that this wonderful revelation of God had little real effect upon Nebuchadnezzar.

The Fiery Furnace

As the curtain is pulled back again we face a very tense moment (*Daniel 3*). Nebuchadnezzar had set up a golden image on the plain of Dura and had commanded all peoples to fall down and worship it. If any refused, he should be cast into a fiery furnace.

But three in the throng refused to obey the king. Shadrach, Meshach and Abednego knew what God had said: "You shall not make for yourself an idol . . . You shall not bow down to them or worship them" (*Exodus 20:4-5*).

The story of the fiery furnace is a familiar one. What was the wonderful

The famous Ishtar Gate of the magnificent ancient city of Babylon. The gate led to a processional way to the citadel and temple.

thing about that scene? Yes, the Son of God was with them. What effect did this have on Nebuchadnezzar? He was filled with great admiration for the miraculous power of the God of these men. But still he does not bow to worship God in humility. Erecting an image will be repeated by the beast, the Antichrist, last head of Gentile world dominion (*Revelation 13:11-15; 19:20*).

The King Dreams Again

This time the king has another dream (*Daniel 4:4-27*). See Job 33:14-17.

God has spoken often to men in

dreams to reveal His will when the Bible was not open to them. We find God speaking to Nebuchadnezzar for the third time in the dream of the great tree that was cut down (*Daniel 4:4-27*). This was a warning to Nebuchadnezzar of his coming madness. God was trying to bring this proud king to the end of himself. But a year later we see him a madman, his mind gone. He fancied himself a beast (*4:28-34*). All this because he had set himself up as a rival against almighty God. Hear him say, "Is not this the great Babylon I have built as the royal residence, by my mighty power and for the glory of my majesty?" (*4:30*).

Through his insanity, Nebuchadnezzar's eyes were opened and his conscience was touched. He confessed to the greatness of God and bore his testimony to the goodness of God (*4:34*). He learned that man is not the architect of his own fortune.

Reign of Belshazzar
Daniel 5; 7—8

As chapter 5 opens, we see a great banquet hall with a thousand lords sitting about the tables. It was "ladies' night." All the king's sweethearts were there besides the thousand lords. Belshazzar sent for the sacred golden and silver vessels his grandfather Nebuchadnezzar had stripped from the Temple in Jerusalem. He showed them just how little he regarded the God of Israel. As the people looked, behold, golden and silver vessels adorned the tables! The last prince of Babylon, Belshazzar, drank wine to the idols in these sacred vessels.

God shows His power in the awful handwriting on the wall. Daniel was called in to explain the meaning. The prophet fearlessly condemned this foolish and sensual young king. Read the details of the divine interruption

in Daniel 5.

A bad reign came to a sudden end. "That very night Belshazzar, king of the Babylonians, was slain" (*Daniel 5:30*). Many of the tablets from Babylon tell us that the Persian army took Babylon without a battle.

During the first year of Belshazzar's reign, Daniel had a vision of four wild beasts, which symbolized the four kingdoms pictured in Nebuchadnezzar's dream (*Daniel 7*). Picturing them as beasts gives us a hint about the moral character of these empires, for they are represented by ferocious wild beasts. How history's wars reveal the true heart of nations!

In Nebuchadnezzar's dream-image, we have a human view of the magnificence of these kingdoms. In Daniel's dream we have God's view of the same. See who Daniel says these four beasts are in Daniel 7:17-23. The first—Babylon—was like a lion with eagle's wings. Jeremiah likened Nebuchadnezzar both to the lion and eagle (*Jeremiah 49:19-22*). Persia was the bear, the cruel animal who delights to kill for the sake of killing. The third was a leopard or panther, a beast of prey. His four wings portray swiftness. Here we see the rapid marches of Alexander's army and his insatiable love of conquest. In thirteen short years he had conquered the world. The fourth beast was different from all the rest. He was "terrifying and frightening and very powerful. It had large iron teeth" (*Daniel 7:7*).

This vision of the four beasts covers the same ground as the great image of Daniel 2. Compare them carefully.

The "little horn" coming up among the ten is the Antichrist yet to come. We see him represented in Revelation as the beast coming up out of the sea (see *Revelation 13:1* and *Daniel 7:15-25*). The saints will be oppressed by Antichrist, the last world ruler before

Christ comes. The rule of dictators is beginning to hint at the extent of the power and authority possible to this last great dictator, the Antichrist. This period terminates the great tribulation (see *Revelation 5—18*). This is the period during which the judgments of God are to come upon the earth for the rejection of Jesus Christ.

Two years later, in Daniel 8, we have another vision of the ram and the he-goat. Belshazzar was still on the throne. This vision includes only two of the four kingdoms, Persia and Greece (*Daniel 8:20-21*).

The kingdom of Medo-Persia is overthrown by the king of Greece. It contains the prophecy of the division of the latter kingdom on the death of Alexander between his four generals. Daniel had this vision at Shushan, the capital of Persia, where seventy years later the events recorded in Esther took place.

Reign of Darius *Daniel 6; 9*

One of the most difficult questions in the Old Testament is the identity of Darius the Mede (*Daniel 5:31*). He must have been someone appointed by Cyrus, and the statement that he "took over the kingdom" confirms this.

Twenty-three years after the death of Nebuchadnezzar, his great city, Babylon, fell into the hands of the Medes.

Even under these new rulers Daniel was in a place of power. The jealousy of the other officials was aroused by the preference given to Daniel, and a plot to destroy him was quickly formed. "The administrators and the satraps tried to find grounds for charges against Daniel" (*Daniel 6:4*).

They used his religion to set their trap, with the very same result as always when men are fools enough to try to trip the Lord's faithful children (see *1 Peter 3:12-13; Deuteronomy 9:3*). All unconsciously the king was induced to pass the decree solely for Daniel's destruction.

The envy of these men no doubt was due to Daniel's ability and his Jewish blood. This spirit of anti-

Jerusalem's fabled Golden Gate. God commanded Ezra and Nehemiah to build and restore Jerusalem.

The Cyrus Cylinder tells how Cyrus captured Babylon without a battle.

Semitism is in fulfillment of God's prophecies that the Jewish people would be hated. It continues rampant even in modern times.

Daniel's conduct in face of danger was quite deliberate. He knew he had to deny his religion or be prepared to die for it.

The officials knew that the king would not lift a finger against Daniel, so they had to trap the king. What was their bait? Notice the subtle appeal to the king's pride.

The law of Medes and Persians was unchangeable. (See *Esther 1:19; 8:8.*) The king saw that he had been deceived, and realizing the injustice of putting Daniel to death, did his best to avoid carrying out the law.

Contrast the edict of Darius before and after Daniel's deliverance from the den of lions (*Daniel 6:26-27*). Over the vast realm a proclamation went, declaring the power and greatness of Daniel's God. This scene closes with Daniel's prospering during the reign of Darius, and also on to the reign of Cyrus.

Daniel was thrown into the den of lions, but he fell into the hands of the living God.

Notice that Daniel prayed with thanksgiving (*Daniel 6:10;* see also *Philippians 4:6-7*).

Reign of Cyrus
Daniel 10—12

During the reign of Cyrus the decree was sent out for the captives to return and rebuild the walls of Jerusalem (*Ezra 1:2-4*). Daniel, now nearly ninety years old, was too aged to return.

The Last Days

In Daniel 11 we find the vision that concerns the near future of the kingdom in which Daniel was so great a personage. Three kings were yet to come in the Medo-Persian empire. Then Alexander, the mighty king of Greece, would appear (*11:2-3*). His empire would be divided among his four generals as had already been predicted. The course of affairs is followed down to Antiochus Epiphanes, the "little horn" of Daniel 8. His desecration of the sanctuary is again mentioned (*12:11*).

Beginning with Daniel 11:36, we see the description of the final "little horn" of Daniel 7.

The great tribulation follows. How is it described in Daniel 12:1? This is a time of unparalleled trouble. Our Lord spoke of it in Matthew 24:21. What does He say? Mention is made of two resurrections (*Daniel 12:2*). These two will be 1,000 years apart. (See *Revelation 20:1-6.*) The first is the resurrection of the saints at Christ's coming to life everlasting. This is followed by 1,000 years, called the millennium. Then the resurrection of the wicked to shame everlasting. "Multitudes who sleep in the dust of the earth will awake: some to everlasting life, others to shame and everlasting contempt" (*Daniel 12:2*). Those now that "turn many to righteousness" are given significant rewards, showing us the necessity of diligence in soul winning during our wait for Christ's return (*12:3*).

Daniel's Prophecy of Seventy "Weeks"

Read Daniel 9:24-27.   .

"Seventy sevens" (Hebrew: *shabu'im shibim*) is translated "seventy weeks" in the *KJV*, a poor English equivalent. The term probably means seventy periods of seven years. If there are seventy seven-year periods,

this is 70x7, or 490 years.

Scripture divides these seventy sevens into three divisions (*Daniel 9:24-27*) with a parenthetic time lapse for the present "Gentile rule."

The first "seven weeks"—forty-nine years began at the command to build and restore Jerusalem under Ezra and Nehemiah.

The second "sixty-two weeks"—434 years began at the building of the wall of Jerusalem, and continues to the Crucifixion. Christ is "cut off and will have nothing" (*Daniel 9:25-26*). At this point, after 483 years, the clock of Israel's national life stops.

("Gentile rule"—an unknown number of years, intervenes after the sixty-ninth week. We are in this period now, awaiting the coming of Christ.)

The last, or "seventieth week"— seven years not yet begun, are years during which God deals with Israel exclusively. Beginning after the coming of Christ, Antichrist takes power, makes covenant with the Jews, breaks the covenant after half the week is up. This ushers in the time of trouble of Daniel 12:1—the Great Tribulation of Revelation. When will the seventieth week begin?

Books of the Minor Prophets
of the Old Testament

Hosea • Joel • Amos • Obadiah • Jonah
Micah • Habakkuk • Zephaniah • Haggai
Zechariah • Malachi • Ezra • Nehemiah • Esther

21. UNDERSTANDING

Hosea, Joel, Amos

Jesus Christ, Healer of the Backslider; Restorer; Heavenly Husbandman

Understanding Hosea

With the study of Hosea's prophecy we enter upon twelve books known as the minor prophets. Remember the difference between the major and minor prophets is not a matter of importance, but of the amount of material written.

Hosea was sent to the ten northern tribes called Israel. He prophesied in the reign of Jeroboam II of Israel. He lived in this Northern Kingdom when the splendors of Jeroboam's brilliant reign of forty-one years were beginning to fade into the black midnight of Israel's captivity. He prophesied during the eighth century B.C.

Hosea's contemporaries were Amos, Isaiah and Micah. He has been called the Jeremiah of the Northern Kingdom. Remember, Jeremiah prophesied to Judah. In Hosea, Israel means the ten tribes that formed the Northern Kingdom. Judah means the tribes of Judah and Benjamin that formed the Southern Kingdom. Hosea was not trained in a seminary (school of the prophets), but he was a layman called by God to give the distinct message to Israel that God loved them.

Israel's Unfaithfulness
Hosea 1—3

The hero of this book, Hosea, is one of the greatest lovers in all literature. We find his love so strong that even the worst actions of an unfaithful wife could not kill it. Read Hosea 1:1 for a bit of the personal history of the prophet. We hear God speaking His first words to Hosea himself (*1:2*). The people had given no heed to Amos. Hosea knew that the country was due for a downfall, but they were not disposed to listen to him.

Turn to 2 Kings 15—17 and read the page of history that covers the period of the prophet. About the middle of Hosea's ministry, a large part of the nation was carried away by the Assyrians. At the end of Hosea's life, the kingdom of Israel came to an end with the fall of Samaria. The prophet lived to see his prophecies fulfilled.

We know little about Hosea other than that he had a very sad home life. The book pictures this man as gentle, frank and affectionate. He had a deep

Flowers of the field in Israel. God promises His people new life, blossoming like flowers, when they return to Him.

loving nature that made him attached to his home.

A Strange Love Story

As chapter 1 opens, we see a young man marrying a girl unworthy of him. He loved her truly. God told him to do something that would have been very repulsive to him. What was it (*Hosea 1:2-3*)? It was a severe test. But as in the case of Isaiah, he was to be a sign for Israel.

Hosea is told to marry a harlot. God was using this for a sign to His people of how they remained the object of Jehovah's love in spite of their sinfulness. This all seems very strange to us. But God was making this picture of His redeeming grace.

Hosea obeyed God and married Gomer (*Hosea 1:3*). His name was hers. Home, reputation, God's favor, comfort, were Gomer's. All that he had he gave her. In return, Hosea's name, domestic reputation, love, were all sacrificed on the altar of a shameful and worthless woman.

Gomer ran away from home and left her young husband, Hosea, with two little sons and a daughter to care for. Lured away by the sin about her, she fell into the moral cesspool of the day and finally was carried off a slave. Through it all, Hosea was true to her. Still loving her, he tried everything to win her back to a happy family life. But she would not.

Just as Hosea was married to an unfaithful bride, Gomer, so God was married to unfaithful Israel. This experience of Hosea helped him to understand God's heart of love as He yearned over wayward Israel to come home to Him.

God's Bride

God frequently uses marriage to symbolize His relation to Israel. "As a bridegroom rejoices over his bride, so will your God rejoice over you" (*Isaiah 62:5*). "For I am your husband" (*Jeremiah 3:14*).

There are differing interpretations of this part of the book of Hosea. Some believe that Hosea was told by God to marry a sinful woman, which he did; others, that God told Hosea to marry a woman who did not go into sin until after the marriage; still others, that this experience of Hosea's was only a vision, not an actual experience. In any case, the undefeatable love of a true husband, to whom God likens Himself, is shown; and Israel's strange, sad, persistent backsliding is revealed.

Backsliding a Historical Fact

But why should Israel's backsliding seem strange to us? Isn't it exactly what we all know about by personal experience?

The Word shows us that until the end, people will sin, will break God's heart of love; but a wonderful and patient God has endured this through the centuries.

In Hosea 3:4, the present state of the Jewish people is described. Read it! Read it! Ever since the destruction of Jerusalem by Titus (A.D. 70), the Jewish people have answered the description given here by Hosea. They have been a nation of wanderers over the face of the earth, going from nation to nation, and city to city. They are scattered, despised and often hated people. (See *Deuteronomy 28:63-65*.) But notice what is happening to them today. Hosea 3:5 describes the Jewish people's glorious future. King, prince, sacrifice, image, ephod and teraphim all are then restored in Christ.

Israel's National Sin and Chastisement *Hosea 4—10*

Here we hear a voice from the north where Israel dwelt (*Hosea 4:1*). Two hundred years before, the ten tribes had seceded from Judah and set up an independent kingdom called Israel. They began immediately worshiping idols. God had sent Elijah, then Elisha, to warn them, but in vain. They refused to return to God. Now we hear a new voice. It is Hosea! "Come, let us return to the Lord" (*Hosea 6:1*) is the much-needed cry of the prophet. His message is: Return to God and He will return to you.

Hosea, whose name means "salvation," was poet laureate to the king. But he was more than that. He was God's voice to the people. They did not care to hear his message, for his appeal was to a backslidden nation in behalf of a God grieved by His children's sins. "Hear the word of the Lord, you Israelites, because the Lord has a charge to bring against you who live in the land" (*Hosea 4:1*).

Israel's blacklist of sin:
No faithfulness, no love, no acknowledgment of God (*4:1*)
Prostitution, drunkenness (*4:11*)
Murder (*5:2*)
Deceit, thievery, banditry (*7:1*)
Cheating and defrauding (*12:7*).
God's figures for sin:
An adulterous wife (*3:1*)
A patron of prostitutes and a drunkard (*4:11*)
A stubborn ("backsliding," *KJV*) heifer (*4:16*)
Marauders/robbers (*6:9*)
Adulterers (*7:4*)
Hot as an oven (*7:7*)
A cake not turned (half-baked) (*7:8*)
Like an easily deceived dove (*7:11*)
Like a faulty bow (*7:16*)
Swallowed up (*8:8*)
A worthless thing (*8:8*)
A wild donkey (*8:9*).

Israel's Hope *Hosea 11—14*

Light breaks over these last chapters. They give us a picture of Israel's ultimate blessings in the future kingdom. We get a glimpse into God's heart of love when He, as a father, says, "When Israel was a child, I loved him, and out of Egypt I called my son" (*Hosea 11:1*).

God's Choice

As God looked over the vast and glittering expanse of empire, He did not choose Israel for His people because they were the greatest or richest of the nations of the world (*Deuteronomy 7:6-8*). He rather chose a weak, unattractive slave child to be the object of His love and care and blessings (*Hosea 11:1*).

We can never understand God's choices. He chooses the weak things of the world to confound the things that are mighty. (See *1 Corinthians 1:27*.) Whenever people love God, it is because He loved them first (*1 John 4:19*).

Israel's Sin

But Israel, the child who had been outwardly adopted in history at the time of the Exodus from Egypt, began to grow persistently disobedient and rebellious. The more the prophets warned the people, the farther they went away from God. They showed no gratitude to God for all the blessings of their land. But in their freedom they forgot God and fell into sin and idolatry and were plunging into captivity (*Hosea 11:2*). Israel finished her training in the slave markets of Assyria and Babylon. (Read *Hosea 4:6-7.*)

Nations today are educating themselves away from God. So did Israel. God taught Israel that when people refuse light, the light is withdrawn. (See *Hosea 5:6.*) God reveals to His children through Hosea that knowledge always creates responsibility. See 2 Peter 2:21. It is a dangerous thing to play with God's grace.

The Grace of God

We find grace abounding in the Old Testament as well as in the New.

Jehovah says to Israel here, "I led them with cords of human kindness, with ties of love" (*Hosea 11:4*). Christ drew us with cords of a man when He became man and died for us. See John 12:32.

God has agonized over His rebellious people and will not give them up. His mercy is kindled and He says, "I will heal their waywardness and love them freely" (*Hosea 14:4*).

God has threatened Israel with His wrath, but now God offers her grace. God appeals to Israel to return and repent (*Hosea 14:1-3*). Then He gives her a promised blessing (*14:4-8*).

In Hosea 1:11, God tells Israel that one day Judah and Israel shall be gathered and have one head. They are looking for this Messiah to come who will be their ruler. God again promises

this in Hosea 3. Read Hosea 9:17 to see the condition of the Jewish people today—"wanderers among the nations." God will do more than forgive their backsliding; He will cure them and remove the cause.

Hosea 14 is the best chapter in the Bible for backsliders. Read the wonderful words of the Lord to backsliding Israel in Hosea 14:4. "I will heal their waywardness and love them freely." God's great heart is bursting with love, but our sins keep Him from telling us all that is there. As with Israel, you may know the joy of barriers broken down and love poured out. "I will be like the dew to Israel; he will blossom like a lily" (*14:5*). The dew speaks of the presence of the Holy Spirit. See how God pictures His abiding joy in His people after they are healed.

Understanding Joel

Joel is considered by some to be one of the earliest of all the prophets whose writings have come down to us. He possibly would have known both Elijah and Elisha in his youth.

His personal history is stated in one verse, "The word of the Lord that came to Joel son of Pethuel" (*Joel 1:1*). His name means "Jehovah is my God." His ministry was to Judah. Remember, Hosea prophesied to Israel.

Joel has been called the prophet of "religious revival." He knew that revival must follow repentance.

The land of Israel had just suffered a terrible plague of locusts that had devoured every green thing, leaving only desolation. Joel believed that this had been a judgment sent by God because of the sin of His people. He was the first to prophesy the outpouring of the Holy Spirit upon all flesh (*2:28*). Joel appears just a little before Hosea, only he speaks to the Southern Kingdom of

Judah, while Hosea speaks to the northern tribes. His message is to us all today.

The Plague—The Warning
Joel 1

Appalling famine, caused by an awful plague of locusts, followed by a prolonged drought, devastated the land. People and flocks were dying for lack of food and water.

Using the judgment of a plague of locusts he called his people of Judah to repentance.

Graphically, he described the plague, calling the old men to confirm the fact that there had never been one like it before (*Joel 1:2*). Drunkards felt the effect of it, for the vines had been destroyed (*1:5*). Priests had no meat-offering, nor drink-offering of wine to offer (*1:9*). Cattle and sheep cried in the fields (*1:20*). Joel urged the people to call a fast (*1:13*). Then he continued to describe the plague.

Joel called the people to consider the cause of the calamity. They must mourn with true penitence if they wished to be spared further judgment (*2:12-17*). Desperate, they were ready to listen to anyone who could explain their plight. It was a great hour for the preacher, for now, in their extremity, people would turn to God.

The Fast—The Promise
Joel 2

The blast of the ram's horn calling an assembly for a great fast opens this chapter (*Joel 2:1*). Everyone is there—old and young alike. Even brides and bridegrooms on their wedding day attend (*2:16*). The priests come in black sackcloth, and bow to the ground and cry to God within the sanctuary. "Rend your heart and not your garments. Return to the Lord your God,

for he is gracious and compassionate" (*2:13*). It was an event to bring the people back to God.

The locusts had made an Eden into a desolate wilderness (*2:3*). For one who has not seen it, an army of locusts is an incredible thing. They fill the air and darken the sun like an eclipse (*2:2*). They spread for miles over the land. Armies of "soldiers" with leaders in front advance, destroying everything that is green. In a few minutes every leaf and blade is destroyed. Others following strip the bark from the trees (*1:6-7*). The people dig trenches and kindle fires and beat and burn to death heaps of insects, but the effort is utterly useless. A land that has been devastated by locusts takes years to recover (*1:17-20*). Their flight is heard for miles, much like a roaring fire (*2:5*). The land over which they pass looks as if it had been fire swept (*2:3*). After the country is stripped they go into cities and, like mailed horsemen, they march into houses and consume everything that can be consumed (*2:4,7-9*). God's promise, "I will repay you for the years the locusts have eaten" (*2:25*), becomes more graphic in the mind when one sees the desolation wrought by the consuming insects.

The Promise of Pentecost

The prophet assures the people that God will indeed send both temporal mercies (*Joel 2:18-27*) and spiritual blessings (*2:28-32*). Yes, and God will send deliverance from the sky! Read 2:28-29. Here is the prophecy of Pentecost.

Spiritual deliverance is the great central promise of the book of Joel. To Joel was committed the privilege of telling that He would pour out His Spirit upon all flesh. He tells us that the blessing will flow forth from Jerusalem (*2:32; 3:18*). This prophecy we are definitely told was fulfilled at Pentecost. Peter said, "No, this is what was spoken by the prophet Joel" (*Acts 2:16*). Read all of Acts 2.

The Day of the Lord

"The day of the Lord," spoken of five times in this short book, refers to judgment. It tells of a series of judgments—the present locusts, the armies of invasion that were about to come as a scourge of God upon the land, and the final day of the Lord described in the third chapter of Joel. "The day of the Lord" is the period of time from the return of the Lord in glory until the new heavens and the new earth (See *Isaiah 2:17-20; 3:7-18; 4:1-2; 13:6-9; Jeremiah 46:10; Malachi 4:5; 1 Corinthians 5:5; 1 Thessalonians 5:2; 2 Thessalonians 2:2; 2 Peter 3:10.*) "The day of the Lord" is at least one thousand years in length. (Read *Revelation 20:4.*)

The Blessing—The Future
Joel 3

Enemies—Overthrown—3:1-15
Jerusalem—Delivered—3:16-17
Land—Blessed—3:18
Judah—Restored—3:19-21

Only God could have told Joel of the return of the Jews from captivity. He also tells of the judgment of the nations after the battle of Armageddon (*3:2-7*). (Read *Matthew 25:32* and *Revelation 19:17-21.*) The people's day of decision is over. God's hour of destiny has arrived.

After Israel is restored and the nations of the earth are judged (*Joel 3:1-2*) then will the everlasting kingdom be set up (*3:20*). Once again Palestine, the land of promise, will be the center of power and the gathering place of the nations for judgment. Christ will return to establish His rule as sovereign. God will dwell in Zion (*3:17*).

A locust. Locusts had made an Eden into a desolate wilderness (*2:3*). An army of locusts is an incredible thing. They fill the air and darken the sun like an eclipse.

Understanding Amos

Amos was from Tekoa, a small town about twelve miles south of Jerusalem. He was a sheepherder and dresser of the sycamore trees.

In Amos, we find one of many instances in the Bible of God calling a man when he was occupied in his daily work (*1:1*). God called him, shepherd's crook in hand, and sent him forth to gather his straying people.

On the wild uplands of Judah, beyond Tekoa, Amos received his training as a prophet straight from the hand of God. His beautiful writing abounds with illustrations from his mountain home. Though a native of Judah, he prophesied in and about Israel.

Amos prophesied while Uzziah was on the throne of Judah and Jeroboam II was king of Israel. This was a time of great prosperity. The old boundaries of the kingdom of David were gained back. Money poured in and armies were victorious. Amos and Hosea were prophets to Israel (Northern Kingdom) and Isaiah and Micah to the Southern Kingdom of Judah.

Under these two kings mentioned, the two kingdoms reached the summit

Bethel

of their prosperity (*2 Chronicles 26* and *2 Kings 14:25*). Assyria had not yet risen as a conquering world power. The idea of the approaching doom of their kingdoms seemed utterly improbable to Israel. They were enjoying a period of peace. The surrounding nations were not strong enough to give them trouble. (See *Amos 6:1-13*.) All they thought of was pleasure and having a good time (*2:6-8; 5:11-12; 6:4-6*). God tried to arouse His people to a sense of their danger, hence He sent two witnesses, Hosea and Amos.

Amos was humble—in not hiding his station in life.

Amos was wise—in not preaching over the heads of the people.

Amos was clever—in catching people's fancy by judging their enemies first.

Amos was fearless—in not tickling the ear but telling the truth.

Amos was faithful—"Thus saith the Lord" was his message.

This raw young herdsman, Amos, had a certain rugged frankness about him that was refreshing. He always hit straight from the shoulder (*1:2*). He didn't fail to tell even King Jeroboam II what he should do. God wanted someone to bear His message courageously, and Amos did not fail Him. Israel needed a prophet who would tear the scales from their eyes and let them know the sure consequences of their idolatry, and Amos fearlessly set them forth. God abhors sin. The horrible cruelty of sin must be punished.

Jeroboam had brought Israel to the zenith of her power. The kingdom was flourishing and was at peace with her enemies. About the most unpopular man would be a "calamity howler," and Amos knew that is what they would call him if he delivered God's message. Read Amos 3:12. This sounded like mockery! The idea of powerful

Israel being likened to a poor sheep— or rather the fragments of a poor eaten sheep!

Yet this is what came to pass! In less than fifty years, Israel was utterly destroyed, and the pitiful remnant of her people was not even as the leg of a sheep taken from the jaw of the devourer. Such is the picture of God's abhorrence of sin.

To every question about why great empires have fallen, the answer is sin. The secret of a great person's undoing is sin. Let Amos help you see sin in its true light.

Judgment Against Nations
Amos 1—2

This simple country preacher left his home in Judah and traveled twenty-two miles to Bethel in the Northern Kingdom to preach to the kingdom of Israel. Why did God send him to Bethel? Surely Jerusalem needed his ministry. But God wanted the kingdom of Israel to have a strong word of warning. Bethel was the religious capital of the Northern Kingdom. Idolatry was there. They had substituted calf worship for Jehovah. The people felt no need of preaching. (See *1 Kings 12:25-33*.)

Amos started his preaching to the assembled crowds at Bethel, for it was a sacred feast day, by proclaiming the Lord's judgment upon six neighboring nations—Damascus (Syria), Gaza (Philistia), Tyre (Phoenicia), Edom, Ammon and Moab. Then he came nearer home and pronounced judgment against Judah (*Amos 2:4*), and against Israel itself (*2:6*) and finally the whole nation (*3:12*). Amos's approach was clever. We are always willing to hear of our enemy's doom. Our own is harder to swallow, but we are forced to take it with our enemy.

When the people doubted his authority, Amos gave a series of seven questions to show that the Lord revealed His secret to him. Therefore he must prophesy (3:3-8).

Amos denounced the sin of Israel more graphically than Hosea (chap. 2). He spoke of their careless ease and luxury, their oppression of the poor, the lying and cheating, and worse than all, their hypocrisy in worship. The Lord grieved over His people not heeding His warnings. "'Yet you have not returned to me,' declares the Lord" (4:6). Then the invitation, "Seek me and live" (5:4).

The book opens with judgments on the nations surrounding Israel:

Damascus was threatened because it had invaded Israel (Amos 1:3; 2 Kings 10:32-33)

Gaza and Tyre for conspiracy with Edom in its invasion of Judah (Amos 1:6,9; 2 Chronicles 21:16-17; 28:18)

Edom for continuing hostility (Amos 1:11; compare Obadiah 10-12)

Ammon for attacking Gilead (Amos 1:13)

Moab for pagan practices (Amos 2:1; 2 Kings 3:27)

Judah for neglect of God's law (Amos 2:4; 2 Chronicles 3—19; 2 Kings 25:9)

Israel for her unrighteousness (Amos 2:6; 2 Kings 17:17-23).

The nations of the world, no matter how powerful they may be, cannot withstand the judgments of God. God sets up kingdoms and brings them down.

Judgment Against Israel
Amos 3—6

Amos was called to tell of certain punishment (Amos 3). If people will reject the repeated warning of God, they must be punished (chap. 5).

Amos told the people of Israel they were greedy, unjust, unclean and profane (2:6-12), and that they defended and excused themselves on the ground that they were God's chosen people (3:2). He reminded them that this made their sin the greater. The Israelites looked at their relationship to God differently. They saw it as merely an outward and formal thing. They boasted that they were the chosen nation and no real evil could befall them. We see many professing Christians today in the same danger. They imagine their salvation is secured by their being members of a church. They are conferring a favor upon God and He cannot condemn them. (Read *Amos 5:21,23-24.*)

The first of God's punishments concerns the sins of six of the heathen nations that surround Israel. Then the prophet passes on to Judah and Israel. The sin of Judah had been her contempt of God's law, expressed in her idolatry. Only during the exile was Judah freed of this sin. The punishment of Judah was fulfilled in the destruction of Jerusalem by Nebuchadnezzar (*2:5*).

Amos condemned Israel. Israel was a chosen nation. She knew God's law. Therefore her sin was the greater. Amos told the people about their injustice in the administration of the law. They "sell the righteous for silver, and the needy for a pair of sandals" (*2:6*). He enumerated their evil oppression. They had forgotten righteousness. The rich were cruel and they longed to see the poor oppressed.

Amos called the women of his day "cows of Bashan" because they only cared for luxury and worldly pleasures (*4:1*). This is the prophet's picture of the cruel, heartless, brainless women—a herd of cows, who are heavy, heedless animals treading on all in their way as they seek to gratify their appetites.

Even the religious sacrifices and feasts of the people became an abomination. God said, "I hate . . . your religious feasts" (*5:21*). When they made their pilgrimages from Gilgal to Bethel, they only sinned the more, for it was merely an outward form mixed with idolatry (*5:4-6*). God demands

conduct worthy of Himself, not just empty sacrifices. Amos called attention to how God sent drought, plagues and earthquakes. Still they did not repent.

God always warns before a punishment, yes, and offers a way of escape. God denounces sin, but He offers a remedy for sin. Israel's rejection of repeated warnings should lead her to prepare for God's judgment (*chap. 5*). If Israel had sought the Lord, the "day of the Lord" spoken of in Amos 5:20 would not have overtaken her. She did not seek Him and Assyrian fighters ushered in that day.

Amos tells of Israel's coming judgment in five visions:

1. The devouring locusts—7:1-3 In the first vision the prophet sees locusts stripping the green fields.
2. The consuming fire—7:4-6. In this vision, fire so terrible as to consume the waters and the land is seen. Amos prays: "'Sovereign Lord, I beg you, stop! How can Jacob survive? He is so small!' So the Lord relented. 'This will not happen either,' the Sovereign Lord said."
3. The searching plumb line—7:7-11. In this vision, Amos sees God measuring the city for destruction. The measuring revealed how far out of line Israel was. This time Amos has not the heart even to pray. Israel's judgment was certain—"I will spare them no longer."
4. The basket of ripe fruit—8:1-14. The Lord says, "The time is ripe for my people Israel; I will spare them no longer." The basket revealed the sad truth that Israel, like a basket of overripe fruit, looked fine, outwardly, but was rotting at the heart. The guilty nation was "ripe" for judgment.

5. The Lord at the altar—9:1-10. The last vision shows God standing upon the altar, bidding Amos to break the doorposts and shower the fragments over the people's heads. All the worshipers are to be scattered and slain by the sword. This speaks of final dispersion. The visions end with judgment, but God closes the book with a bright outlook.

Visions Regarding the Future
Amos 7—9

We do not know how long Amos preached in Bethel, but we know that throngs heard his fearless message. When he spoke of the doom of the surrounding nations, the people were drawn to him and they cheered him to the last echo.

Then Amaziah, the priest of Bethel, could not stand up against Amos's preaching. So, backed by the king, the priest rebuked Amos. Read the report he sent to the king in Amos 7:10-11. Amaziah told Amos to go back and mind his own business.

Amos was silenced by the false prophet. He was driven from Israel.

Freedom of speech was not given the true prophet of God. Neither Elijah nor Amos was safe in Israel. When Amos found that Israel would not hear him, he returned to Judah and put his writings in a book so all the people could read and understand it.

Amos, as do most of the prophets, tells us of a bright future for God's chosen people. The whole land will once more be a kingdom under the house of David (*9:11-12*). The Tabernacle of David, now torn down, shall be rebuilt (*Acts 15:16-17*). Israel shall be restored to her land and prosper. A happy people shall dwell in a happy land.

Always keep in mind that the Jewish people who have been scattered over the face of the world are being gathered back to their land of promise. National prosperity will again flourish. Jerusalem shall be the capital of a mighty kingdom. Converted Israel shall be God's witnesses (*9:13-15*).

People need such dealing as Amos gives at times when sin abounds. We get to be too tender and gentle with the common sins of the people. We forget how to denounce; we lose the power of righteous indignation.

22. UNDERSTANDING

Obadiah, Jonah, Micah

Jesus Christ Our Savior; Our Resurrection and Life;
Witness Against Rebellious Nations

Understanding Obadiah

Petra is one of the wonders of the world. It was a city unique of its kind among the works of humans. It perched like an "eagle's nest" (*Obadiah 4*) amid inaccessible mountain fastnesses. Its only approach was through a deep rock cleft more than a mile long with massive cliffs more than 700 feet high rising on either side. The city was able to withstand any invasion. We are told that its temples numbered a thousand. They were cut out of the pink rock on the side of the massive cliffs. The dwellings were mostly caves hewn out of the soft red sandstone (*Obadiah 3,6*) and placed where you can hardly believe it possible for a human foot to climb.

South of the Dead Sea and on the western border of the Arabian plateau lies a range of precipitous red sandstone heights known as Mount Seir. Here Esau settled after he sold his birthright to his brother Jacob. Having driven out the Horites (see *Genesis 14:5-6*), he occupied the whole of the mountain. Read Deuteronomy 2:12. These Horites are first spoken of in the time of Abraham (*Genesis 14:5-6*). Sela, or Petra, "Rock," was their capital. Today it is called "the silent city of the forgotten past."

The descendants of Esau were called Edomites. They would go out on raid-

ing expeditions and then retreat to their impregnable fortress where they kept alive in their hearts a bitter enmity toward the Jews, which began with Jacob and Esau. They never failed in helping any army who attacked the Jews. During the period of the Maccabees, they became bitter enemies of the Jews. And in the time of Christ, through Herod they obtained control of Judea. They disappear from the pages of history after the destruction of Jerusalem by Titus in A.D. 70.

This book includes two important themes—the doom of the proud and rebellious and the deliverance of the meek and humble.

It is directly spoken to Edom and Zion and represents Esau and Jacob, the two sons of Isaac. But it appeals to us all with our two natures—the earthly represented by Esau on one side, so proud and bold, and the spiritual by Jacob, chosen and set apart by God. The story of the bitter family feud that takes us back to the days of the two brothers, Jacob and Esau, unfolds before us.

The Doom of Edom
Obadiah 1—16

Of the prophet who wrote this book we know nothing. His contemporary was Jeremiah. We find the occasion of this prophecy as we read it in Obadiah 11. No doubt, it was the awful day in which Edom took the part of the enemy (*Obadiah 7—14*). Against this people, the prophecy of the unknown prophet Obadiah, "a worshiper of Jehovah," was directed. Edom looked on while Jerusalem was being plundered. They seemed to manifest fiendish delights in the calamity that overtook its inhabitants.

We read the denunciation of the selfish, indifferent and presently hostile spirit of nearby Edom! She, holding the attitude of Esau, remained aloof and allowed Jerusalem to be despoiled. She even became party in the destruction and went in for her part of the spoils.

God had commanded Israel, "Do not abhor an Edomite, for he is your brother" (*Deuteronomy 23:7*). But Edom had shown an implacable hatred to Israel from the time Israel was refused a passage through Edom on the way to Canaan (*Numbers 20:14-21*) to the day of the destruction of Jerusalem by the Chaldeans, when Edom cried, "Tear it down," they cried, "tear it down to its foundations" (*Psalm 137:7*).

Because of the pride and cruel ha-

when Nebuchadnezzar took Jerusalem and reduced it to a desolate heap. The Edomites had helped the marauders by catching the fleeing Israelites, treating them with cruelty and selling them as slaves.

This prophecy was written because of this confederacy against Jerusalem

The mountains near Eilat, on the Red Sea. Moab stretched as far south as the Gulf of Aqaba.

tred of Edom, her utter destruction was decreed (*Obadiah 3—4,10*). Nothing could save the guilty nation. The people were driven from their rocky home five years after the destruction of Jerusalem when Nebuchadnezzar, passing down the valley of Arabah that formed the military road to Egypt, crushed the Edomites. They lost their existence as a nation about 150 B.C., and their name perished with the capture of Jerusalem by the Romans. "As you have done, it will be done to you" (*Obadiah 15*).

Zion's Deliverance
Obadiah 17—21

The book closes with the promise of deliverance for Zion. "But on Mount Zion will be deliverance; it will be holy, and the house of Jacob will possess its inheritance" (*Obadiah 17*). The first step in the future reestablishment of the Jewish nation is the recovery of what was previously their own.

God's chosen people had just been carried into captivity by Nebuchadnezzar; the holy land was deserted; and God had told Edom of her doom. Jeremiah gave this same prophecy in chapter 49. Both Jeremiah and Obadiah had probably said these things many times. Five years later Edom fell before the same Babylon she had helped. She would be as though she had never been, swallowed up forever. This was the prophecy against Edom. But Israel shall rise again from her present fall. She will possess not only her own land, but also Philistia and Edom. She will finally rejoice in the holy reign of the promised Messiah. God's chosen people, the Jews, shall possess their possessions, and among the dearest to them is their Holy Land. Obadiah, as the other prophets, predicts the coming of the day of the Lord and the establishment

of Messiah's kingdom. Remember, a Christian, too, is an heir of promises to be fulfilled when Christ comes. The believer possesses all things in Christ. (Read *2 Corinthians 6:10*.)

God's judgment on Edom as Israel's notable enemy should warn nations today that God has not cast off His people and nations that oppress them will surely bring down His judgments (*Genesis 12:3*).

Understanding Jonah

Jonah was a native of Gath-hepher, a town about an hour's distance from Nazareth. He lived in the reign of Jeroboam II and aided him in making the Northern Kingdom of Israel very powerful and prosperous. (See *2 Kings 14:25*.) Jonah was a famous statesman.

God is in this book. He is taking care of His prophet. God is working. Find the statement four times concerning Him.

God prepared:
A great fish—1:17
A gourd—4:6
A worm—4:7
A vehement east wind—4:8.

Jonah is the test book of the Bible. It challenges our faith. Our attitude toward Jonah reveals our attitude toward God and His Word. Is the story of Jonah mere naturalism or supernaturalism? Right here we stand or fall.

Jesus Christ Himself made the book of Jonah important. When He was asked for a sign to prove His claims, He gave the people only the sign of the prophet Jonah (*Matthew 12:38-40*).

Two events are of great importance in Jonah. One is the great fish swallowing Jonah and the other the possibility of such a large heathen city as Nineveh being converted by an obscure foreign missionary in just a few days. See what Jesus said in Matthew 12:41.

An Obstinate Prophet
Jonah 1—2

As the book opens, God is speaking to Jonah, giving him his commission. "Go to the great city of Nineveh and preach against it, because its wickedness has come up before me" (*Jonah 1:2*).

God is very definite with His orders. He told Jonah to arise and go. "But Jonah ran away from the Lord and headed for Tarshish. He went down to Joppa" (*1:3*). He said no to God. Why did he flee? Read Jonah 4:2. Jonah knew that Assyria was Israel's dreaded enemy. Just at this period in history Assyria seems to have been somewhat weakened in power. It was then that God told him to go to the capital of that hostile country and pronounce judgment against it for its great wickedness. Jonah fears that Nineveh may repent and be spared impending doom. If Assyria falls, Jonah's own beloved Israel may escape judgment at Assyria's hands. Jonah has the spirit of a national hero. He decides to sacrifice himself in order to save his people, but his heroism is sadly misguided.

Nineveh was one of the greatest cities of the world, situated on the east bank of the Tigris, 400 miles from the Mediterranean. It was the capital of Assyria (*Genesis 10:11-12*). The stronghold of the city was about thirty miles long and ten miles wide. It was marvelous in appearance. Five walls and three moats (canals) surrounded it. The walls were 100 feet high and allowed four chariots to be driven abreast.

As soon as Jonah fled, God began to act. Read 1:4. God loved Jonah too much to let him prosper. Failure never relieves us of responsibility to serve.

Read events that took place before Jonah was thrown into the sea (*1:3-15*).

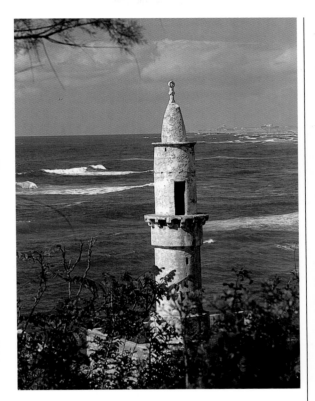

Jonah was cast into the sea, but he was gripped by the hand of God (*1:17*). God's way is best. If we don't accept it, He forces strange things upon us.

The story of Jonah 2 tells us how Jonah came to the end of himself. After much praying, he confessed that he could do nothing by himself. "Salvation comes from the Lord" (*2:9*). Then God could afford to set him at liberty (*2:10*).

An Obedient People
Jonah 3—4

God gave Jonah another chance to be of service. God said again, "Go to the great city of Nineveh and proclaim to it the message I give you" (*Jonah 3:2*).

When God told Jonah to go on a mission to Nineveh, he went to the port of Joppa, modern Jaffa, to take a ship in the opposite direction. Jaffa is today swallowed up in the city of Tel Aviv.

Nineveh

It was not easy for Jonah to go through the streets and cry, "Forty more days and Nineveh will be overturned" (*3:4*). There was no mercy in his message. There was no tear in the prophet's voice. He was obeying God, but his heart was unchanged (*4:1-3*). The common people of Nineveh repented first. Then the nobles followed. This is always true. Revival starts among the people.

Obedient but Perplexed

Look at him sulking as he sits out on the hill on the east side of the city under a gourd that God provided for a shadow over his head, waiting to see what God would do (*Jonah 4:6*).

The book ends abruptly! But we must notice two things in this book. First, Jonah is a type of Christ in His death, burial and resurrection. Read Matthew 12:40. Second, Jonah is also a type of Israel—disobedient to God, swallowed by the nations of the world, who will yet give her up when Christ comes. Then shall Israel be witnesses of God everywhere.

No doubt, two things hindered Jonah when God told him to go to Nineveh—his pride of self and his scorn of the rest of the world. God took this out of him in the fish's belly.

Jonah, Type of Israel

Jonah was called to a world mission. So was Israel.

Jonah refused to fulfill his mission by obeying God. So did Israel.

Jonah was punished by being cast into the sea, Israel by being scattered among the nations.

Jonah was preserved. So was Israel.

Jonah repented and was cast out of the fish and restored to life. Israel shall be cast out by all the nations and restored to her former position.

Jonah, obedient to God, goes on his mission. Israel in obedience shall become a witness to all the earth.

Jonah was blessed in that Nineveh was brought to salvation. Israel shall be blessed in the conversion of the whole world.

Understanding Micah

Micah was a country preacher who lived in the days of Isaiah and Hosea. His home was about twenty miles south of Jerusalem in the town of Moresheth on the Philistine border. He was preaching there the same time Isaiah was preaching in Jerusalem and Hosea in Israel. Micah was a prophet of the common people and country life; Isaiah preached to the court in the city of Jerusalem. Micah knew his fellow country people well. Read what he says his real equipment is in Micah 3:8.

Micah prophesied concerning Samaria, the capital of Israel, and Jerusalem, the capital of Judah, but the burden of his prophecy was for Judah. The times in which he lived were difficult. Oppression was present within the walls and foes were coming from without. The condition was the same both in the kingdom of Judah and in the kingdom of Israel. The kings Jotham, Ahaz and Hezekiah reigned during Micah's day.

The prophet denounced the social sins of his day (*2:2*). Micah felt keenly these social evils. He saw the unfair treatment of the poor by the rich. He felt that these sins cried up to heaven. No class was free from corrupting influences; princes, priests and people alike were all affected (*2:2,8-9,11; 3:1-3,5,11*). Micah makes them all smart under the lash. Micah wanted the people to know that every cruel act to one's fellow citizen was an insult to God. In spite of the state of things, the people tried to carry on their religious observances. Micah shows the uselessness of all this (6:7-8).

The Northern Kingdom of Israel was taken into captivity during Micah's lifetime. Israel would not heed the warning of the prophets. Judah did and was spared for 150 years. Micah knew that national sins would lead to national downfall. "Righteousness exalts a nation, but sin is a disgrace to any people" (*Proverbs 14:34*).

The book of Micah seems to be divided into three parts, each beginning with, "Hear ye" (*Micah 1:2; 3:1; 6:1*). And each closes with a promise.

1. A promise of deliverance (2:12-13)
2. A promise to overthrow the enemies in the land (5:10,15)
3. A fulfillment of promise to Abraham (7:20).

Catalogue of national sins:
Idolatry (1:7; 6:16)
Covetousness (2:2)
Oppression (2:2)
Violence (2:2; 3:10; 6:12; 7:2)
Encouraging false prophets (2:6,11)
Corruption of princes (3:1-3)
Corruption of prophets (3:5-7)
Corruption of priests (3:11)
Bribery (3:9,11; 7:3)
Dishonesty (6:10-11).

Passages concerning Christ:
Birthplace named (5:2)
Christ as King (2:12-13)
Christ reigning in righteousness over the whole earth (4:1,7).
Micah is quoted on three occasions:
1. By the elders of Judah (*Jeremiah 26:18* quoting *Micah 3:12*)
2. By magi coming to Jerusalem (*Matthew 2:5-6* quoting *Micah 5:2*)
3. By Jesus when sending out the Twelve (*Matthew 10:35-36* quoting *Micah 7:6*).

A Message to the People Concerning Israel's Sin
Micah 1—2

As the book opens we hear the cry, "Hear, O peoples, all of you, listen, O earth and all who are in it, that the Sovereign Lord may witness against you" (*Micah 1:2*).

God is not asleep. He knows the sad condition of His people. He will sit in judgment upon His people. Yes, the Lord was coming to call Israel to judgment because of her wrongs. Samaria and Jerusalem were pronounced guilty before the great Judge of the universe.

More and more we are realizing the social value of the gospel of the Lord Jesus Christ. Wherever this gospel goes, we find conditions bettered and a brotherhood that is based on sonship.

A Message to the Rulers Concerning the Coming Christ *Micah 3—5*

"Listen, you leaders of Jacob, you rulers of the house of Israel" (*Micah 3:1*). What does God say of them? Read Micah 3:1-4. God likens their covetousness and self-aggrandizement, even at the price of blood, to cannibalism. The leaders are devouring the poor, defenseless people (*3:2,3*).

The nation was ready to collapse and the princes and priests were responsible for it. God denounces the sin of the rulers (*3:9*), the bribery among the judges (*3:11*), false weights and balances. God describes these men in Micah 3:5. "As for the prophets who lead my people astray, if one feeds them, they proclaim 'peace.'"

Micah, brokenhearted, tells of God's judgment upon Judah for her sins. Jerusalem and its Temple will be destroyed (*3:12; 7:13*). The people of Judah will be taken captive to Babylon (*4:10*). But he seems to hasten over words of judgment, and to linger over the message of God's love and mercy. God will bring His people back from captivity (*4:1-8; 7:11; 14-17*). Micah was a prophet of hope. He always looked beyond doom and punishment to the day of glory when Christ Himself shall reign, when peace shall cover the earth. God gives the promise. The Messiah will come. He will be born in Bethlehem (*4:8; 5:2-4*). Then Israel will be gathered from the nations into which she has been scattered (*4:6*).

Little Bethlehem, smallest among

Captivity and exile were their fate. God rebuked them for social injustice, unfaithfulness, dishonesty and idolatry. What were their sins (*2:1-11; 1:6-9*)?

Micah told them that Samaria, the capital of Israel, would fall (*1:6-7*). A similar judgment would come upon Judah. Judah's sin is described as an incurable wound. Some kinds of disease are cured only by destruction. All Judah's people shall be taken captive, for God finds incurable oppression, violence and injustice. Notice the towns of Judah mentioned in the last verses of chapter 1. Look at a good Bible atlas and you will see that they all surround the prophet's hometown.

The idolatry of Israel spread rapidly to Jerusalem and the strong city of Lachish (*1:13*). This awful spread of idolatry, and all its terrible evils, to Judah under King Ahaz, Micah especially denounced. The oppression of the poor (*2:2*), and women and little children being driven from their homes (*2:9*) were also rebuked by the prophet. The sins of the people are stated in blunt frankness in Micah 2:1-11. God will bring suffering and shame upon them for their unscrupulous use of power.

the towns of Judah, shall be signally honored by the birth of God's Messiah, Jesus Christ, our Lord. His victories shall not be won by might nor by power but by His Spirit. He comes as a little babe to bring salvation to a world so in need of a Redeemer. This 700-year-old prophecy from Micah 5:2-5, together with the star, led the wise men to Jerusalem to seek the new King.

A Message to the Chosen People Concerning God's Argument *Micah 6—7*

In Micah 6:2, God is pictured as one bringing a lawsuit against His people.

They had ignored God. He told them to remember how good He had been to them and how He had kept His covenant with them (*6:3*).

The people, conscience smitten, asked how they could please God. Frantically they asked if burnt offerings would do (*6:6-7*).

God wants righteous conduct and a real personal experience of Him in each life. Because of unrighteous conduct, the people had to suffer unbelievable consequences. God is a righteous Judge (*Micah 1:3,5; 3:12*).

Simple Essentials of Real Religion

The Old Testament gives us a definition of religion. What does God require of you? (Read *Micah 6:8.*)

How does this compare with people's present-day definitions of "religion"?

"Act justly"—good ethics in all of life.

"Love mercy"—consideration for others, when justice has not been done.

"Walk humbly with your God"—personal experience with God.

It is interesting that when Christ summed up the same matter (*Matthew 23:23*), He used the words "justice," "mercy" and "faithfulness." He thus equated "faith with walking humbly with our God," an apt comparison.

23. UNDERSTANDING

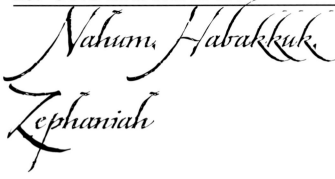

Nahum, Habakkuk, Zephaniah

Jesus Christ, a Stronghold in the Day of Trouble;
the God of My Salvation; a Jealous Lord

Understanding Nahum

Nahum, the writer of this book, was a native of Elkosh. In Assyria, near the ruins of Nineveh, the natives point to a tomb as Nahum's. But most authorities think that this Elkosh was in Galilee. Today Elkosh lies in ruins.

In name and in message, "Nahum" means "comfort" for Judah. "The Lord is good, a refuge in times of trouble. He cares for those who trust in him" (*Nahum 1:7*). Deliverance for Judah, and destruction for her enemy Assyria, was God's great theme for His people. That "Capernaum," where Christ the Comforter wrought so many works, means "village of Nahum" (comfort) is noteworthy. Nearby is the town where he was born, Elkosh.

Nahum was probably a native of Galilee and lived at the time of good King Hezekiah and the great prophet Isaiah. No doubt, when the cruel Assyrians invaded his country and carried away the ten tribes of Israel, he escaped into the Southern Kingdom of Judah. He probably took up his residence in Jerusalem where he later witnessed the siege of that city by Sennacherib, which ended with the miraculous destruction of the Assyrian host. Remember 185,000 perished in one night, as 2 Kings 19:35 records. It may be that Nahum 1:2 refers to this. Shortly after this event, Nahum wrote his book.

Selected Bible Readings

Sunday: The Judge and the
                 Verdict (*Nahum 1*)

Monday: The Execution
                 (*Nahum 2—3*)

Tuesday: Habakkuk's Complaint
                 (*Habakkuk 1*)

Wednesday: God's Reply
               (*Habakkuk 2*)

Thursday: Habakkuk's Song
                 (*Habakkuk 3*)

Friday: Coming Judgments
                 (*Zephaniah 1—2*)

Saturday: The Kingdom Blessings
                 (*Zephaniah 3*)

epoch of three hundred years in which she was a world empire. Ninevah was the capital of this mighty empire. In 722 B.C., she destroyed Israel and threatened Judah, but God was going to see that Assyria's doom was final. The message of Nahum shows what God can do with a wicked and rebellious people. He will utterly destroy them.

The doom of the city was delayed some 150 years after Jonah preached, but it fell at last. Nahum's prophecy was not a call to repentance, but the statement of certain and final doom. Read Nahum 1:9; also 3:18-19. Her name should be utterly cut off (*1:14*). God would dig her grave.

The Judge *Nahum 1:1-7*

In Nahum 1, we see God the holy Judge on the bench of the court of heaven judging the wicked city of Nineveh. The case is presented. This God is a just God, therefore He must avenge all crimes.

There is a two-fold revelation of the character of this Judge of all the world. We find a sublime and powerful statement of those attributes of God that constitute the basis of all His actions toward people. This lesson gives us an excellent opportunity of presenting the attributes of God.

Study the prophet's vision of God in Nahum 1:2-7. Find the words that are used of Him. As Judge, God:

1. Is jealous
2. Is avenging
3. Is filled with wrath at evildoers
4. Maintains wrath against His enemies
5. Is great in power
6. Will not leave the guilty unpunished
7. Is indignant.

As Father, He is:

1. Slow to anger

The theme of this book is the destruction of Nineveh, the city Jonah warned. Nineveh is a culprit and God is sending Nahum to declare His righteous judgment upon her. In the judgment of Nineveh, God is judging a sinning world. Nahum was written about 150 years after the revival of Jonah's day when the city of Nineveh was brought to repentance in "dust and ashes." Mercy unheeded finally brings judgment.

No doubt the Ninevites were sincere then, but it did not last. They were again guilty of the very sins of which they had repented. Nineveh, the glory of the Assyrians, had come to a complete and deliberate defiance of the living God. The people were not just backsliders! They deliberately rejected the God they had accepted (*2 Kings 18:25,30,35; 19:10-13*).

God sent Nahum to predict the final doom and complete overthrow of Nineveh and her empire. Read of her beastlike violence and cruelty (*Nahum 2:11-12*).

Assyria had enjoyed a brilliant

2. Good

3. A stronghold in the day of trouble

4. Knowing them that trust Him.

The first eight words of the vision are awe inspiring, "The Lord is a jealous and avenging God." To think of a God like this makes us examine ourselves. We will find that there is no righteousness in us. How this thought drives us into the loving arms of a Savior who is our "covering for sin" and clothes us with the robes of His righteousness.

Notice God did not bring judgment on Assyria in hot haste. He had been patient for a long time. He is "slow to anger," but God sent ruin. He is a God of absolute justice. He is the Lord, the Lord God, merciful and gracious, long-suffering and forgiving iniquity, yet He will by no means clear the guilty. Jonah dwelt on the first side of God's character, love (*Jonah 4:2*). Nahum brings out the second, the holiness of God that must deal with sin in judgment (*Nahum 1:2,6*).

The Verdict *Nahum 1:8-14*

Nahum 1:8-14 states the battle-and-destruction sentence upon corrupt Nineveh. She has been weighed in the balance and found wanting.

Look at the Verdict of Nineveh:

1. Condemned to utter destruction (*1:8-9*)

2. Captured while defenders were drunk (*1:10*)

3. Name blotted out (*1:14*)

4. God to dig her grave (*1:14*).

We cannot read this without being struck by the solemnity of it all. Nahum told of this destruction as prophecy. We look at it today as history. Yes, the Judge has brought everything to pass. Today the traveler finds this great city Nineveh of the past still lying in ruins.

This book gives us the picture of the wrath of God. Read 1:2 again. This is a picture of God acting in wrath. It is not pleasant to be reminded that God is a God of anger as well as a God of love. But remember both attributes are His. He is a holy God. He hates sin. He will bring judgment upon it.

The Execution *Nahum 2—3*

Read what God says in these short chapters. We find a picture of Nineveh's siege, fall and desolation. All God can do with a rebellious and defiant nation is to destroy it.

The picture of the siege and fall of Nineveh and the desolation that followed are described with graphic eloquence in Nahum 2—3. God would make an end of her with an overrunning flood, her name would be utterly cut off and He would dig her grave. Mustering the armies around Nineveh, and marshaling the forces within the city are pictured in such a way that the prophet makes his hearers see all the horrid sights of the tragic scene.

The cries of the Medes are heard as they shout to one another, "Plunder the silver! Plunder the gold! The supply is endless, the wealth from all its treasures!" (*2:9*). The city is looted while the people stand with their knees smiting together for fear. Nineveh shall no longer terrify the nations because God has made an end of her. This will happen to all wicked nations of the earth.

The Medes and Babylonians completely destroyed Nineveh in 612 B.C. It occurred at the zenith of her power. According to Nahum's prophecy, it came true—a sudden rise of the Tigris, carrying away a great part of the wall, assisted the attacking army of the Medes and Babylonians in its overthrow (*Nahum 2:6*). The city was partly destroyed by fire (*Nahum 3:13,15*).

This city had one denunciation

more, given a few years later by Zephaniah (*Zephaniah 2:13*). In 612 B.C., the whole was fulfilled. So complete was the destruction that all traces of the Assyrian empire disappeared.

Sowing and Reaping

As Nineveh sowed, so must she reap. This is God's law. Nineveh had fortified herself so that nothing could harm her. With walls 100 feet high and wide enough for four chariots to go abreast, a circumference of 80 miles, and adorned by hundreds of towers, she sat complacently. A moat 140 feet wide and 60 feet deep surrounded the vast walls. But Nineveh reckoned without Jehovah. What are bricks and mortar to God! The mighty empire that Shalmaneser, Sargon and Sennacherib had built up, the Lord threw down with a stroke. The inventions of civilization are powerless against heaven's artillery.

Nineveh is a type of all nations that turn their backs on God. In our day, proud civilizations are staking everything upon the strength of people power and machines and there is a terrible disregard of God. We find that Nineveh was overthrown because of

her sin (*Nahum 3:1-7*) and that her great wealth and strength were not sufficient to save her (*3:8-19*). Oftentimes nations depend upon might and power to survive. They forget that it is "'not by might nor by power, but by my Spirit,' says the Lord Almighty" (*Zechariah 4:6*). The person or nation that deliberately and finally rejects God, deliberately and finally and fatally elects doom. Beware of this!

Read Peter's words of warning spoken hundreds of years later—in 2 Peter 3:9-10.

Understanding Habakkuk

Watch and see (*Habakkuk 1*)
Stand and see (*Habakkuk 2*)
Kneel and see (*Habakkuk 3*)

We know little about this prophet of faith except that he asked questions and received answers. He, like many people today, could not reconcile his belief in a good and righteous God with the facts of life as he saw them. He was troubled with an eternal "Why?" Even today, people of faith find themselves bewildered at many things that are going on round about them. We ask, "Why does God allow such awful crimes to go unchecked? Why doesn't God stop people in their mad rush if He is all powerful?"

The question, Why do the wicked prosper? is discussed. It seems to contain a complaint to God that He should destroy His own nation for her wickedness by a nation even much more wicked (*Habakkuk 1:13*). We even see the prophet complaining of the lack of justice in God's management of the world. Why is God silent in times of disaster (*1:13*)?

Habakkuk, in all his difficulties, went to God in prayer and waited patiently for His answer (*2:1*). He went onto the watchtower and listened to God. G. Campbell Morgan says that when Habakkuk looked at his circumstances he was perplexed (*1:3*), but when he waited for God and listened to Him, he sang (*3:18-19*).

Habakkuk was a prophet (*1:1*), but we find something else of interest about him. He was one of the Levitical choristers in the Temple (*3:19*), or helped in arranging the services.

We learn much about him as a thinker and a man of faith from his own words. He was a contemporary with Jeremiah at home and with Daniel in Babylon.

The world empire of Assyria had fallen just as Nahum had prophesied. Egypt and Babylon had then contended for the place of power. At the battle of Carchemish, 605 B.C., in which King Josiah was killed, the Babylonians were conquerors and the great kingdoms of the Babylonians and Chaldeans were united under Nebuchadnezzar. Habakkuk knew only too well that Judah must fall before this great rising power. But one question arose in his mind and troubled him greatly. Why should any nation as wicked as Babylon conquer a

nation like Judah, which was less evil? It seemed to him that it was just a matter of evil triumphing over evil. What good could come of this? God had to show him His ultimate plan. Judah needed punishment. God was using Babylon to correct Judah, but Babylon's turn would come. Babylon would be utterly blotted out. As for God's people, there was yet to be a glorious future and a kingdom where Jehovah Himself would prevail.

This book seems to be a dialogue between Jehovah and the prophet. Two conversations are recorded and the book closes with a hymn and doxology, which reveal that all the questions have been answered and there is a new confidence in God.

Habakkuk's Complaint
Habakkuk 1

This scene opens with the cry of a man who has a problem he cannot solve. "How long, O Lord, must I call for help, but you do not listen? Or cry out to you, 'Violence!' but you do not save" (*Habakkuk 1:2*)!

Habakkuk was confused and bewildered. It seemed to him that God was doing nothing to straighten out the conditions in the world. He had lived during the days of the great reformation under good King Josiah. He had seen Assyria fading in power and Babylon, under Nebuchadnezzar, rising to a place of supremacy. The world about him was in an upheaval. Violence abounded and God was doing nothing about it.

But worse, he saw his own land, Judah, full of lawlessness and tyranny. The righteous were oppressed (*1:4,13*). The people were living in open sin. They were worshiping idols (*2:18-19*). They were oppressing the poor. Habakkuk knew that the day was dark. He knew that this sin was leading to an invasion of Jerusalem by a strong enemy.

Habakkuk asked his question of God. Then God answered—read 1:5. God told Habakkuk that He was not indifferent to His people. He wanted Habakkuk to look beyond the present. He was already working. God called the Chaldeans to the work of punishing Judah. They were a cruel scourge that swept over the land to destroy it (1:5-11).

God's answer horrified Habakkuk. He could not understand how God would allow such awful means to bring about punishing His people, Judah. How could He use such a cruel scourge? How was it possible for God to use such an enemy to punish His own people when He Himself is so pure and holy? Listen to Habakkuk's challenge to God to defend His actions (1:13).

The nations have always been God's object lessons, illustrating His moral laws (1:12).

God's Reply *Habakkuk 2*

As this scene opens, we see Habakkuk facing the great moment of his life. Watch him as he climbs up on the watchtower to wait for God. He expects God to answer him (*Habakkuk 2:1*).

Everything lies in ruins around the prophet. Chaldea is coming up to destroy what is left. There is only One to whom he can turn, so he waits expectantly for God. God gives an answer. Read God's answer in Habakkuk 2:2-20. God admits the wickedness of the Chaldeans, but declares that they will destroy themselves finally by their own evil. Pride and cruelty always bring destruction. It may seem that the Chaldeans are prospering for a time, but they are doomed. "The righteous will live by his faith" (*Habakkuk 2:4*) is the heart of the book.

Five "woes" are mentioned in Habakkuk 2. Find what they are. Remember evil will perish. Only righteousness will remain before God.

Habakkuk's Song
Habakkuk 3

Habakkuk is the prophet who sang in the night. Listen to the magnificent melody with which his prophecy closes—read 3:17-18. This ode was set to music and sung at the public worship by the Jews.

After a sincere prayer (*3:1-16*), God's glory appears. God always responds to the cry for help from His people. Habakkuk realizes that God is in control of this universe and that He is working out His own purpose in His own time. Habakkuk learns that he can trust implicitly in God. He realizes that he can see only a small part of God's plan at one time.

God cannot always give us a satisfactory answer, because our finite minds cannot grasp the thoughts of the infinite. His thoughts are high above our thoughts, and His ways above our ways (*Isaiah 55:9*), but we can trust God, always! "In all things God works for the good of those who love him, who have been called according to his purpose" (*Romans 8:28*).

One of the texts in Habakkuk has great significance in the history of the Reformation. Do you know the story of the young monk Martin Luther (1483-1546, a Catholic priest and leader of the Reformation in Germany) who rose to his feet as he was crawling up the steps of the Scala Sancta in Rome? He remembered these words, "The just shall live by his faith" (*Habakkuk 2:4, KJV*). Not by works! This started him on his great crusade that brought about the Reformation.

Find where Habakkuk 2:4 is quoted

in the New Testament: Romans 1:17; Galatians 3:11; Hebrews 10:38. Mark them.

Understanding Zephaniah

Little is known of Zephaniah, the writer of this book. Two facts of his personal history appear in the first verse of the prophecy. We learn that very likely he was a prince of the royal house of Judah, being a descendant of Hezekiah. He was in a position to denounce the sins of the princes for he himself was an aristocrat. He lived in the reign of good King Josiah. His name means "hidden of Jehovah."

Zephaniah began his ministry as a prophet in the early days of the reign of Josiah (641-610 B.C.). Fifty years had elapsed since the prophecy of Nahum. Three of Hezekiah's descendants had succeeded him (*2 Kings 20—21*). Two wicked and idol-worshiping kings had preceded Josiah on the throne and the land was overrun with evil practices of every kind. Social injustice and moral corruption were rampant on every hand. The rich had amassed great fortunes by grinding the faces of the poor. The condition was as bad as it could be when King Josiah, only sixteen years of age, undertook to promote a religious revival. He became one of the most beloved of the kings of Judah. He took a hatchet and hewed down the altars and images.

Zephaniah depicts God as both loving and severe. Zephaniah 1:2 and 3:17 gives us these two characteristics.

Zephaniah foretold the doom of Nineveh (*2:13*). Who else had prophesied her doom? This came to pass in 612 B.C.

We hear Zephaniah denouncing the various forms of idolatry—Baal and Malcham or Molech all being condemned (*1:1—2:3*). This idol worship was destroyed during Josiah's reign. No doubt Zephaniah was mainly responsible for the revival under Josiah. He was the pioneer in this reform movement. Tradition tells us that Jeremiah was his colleague.

The book begins with sorrow, but ends with singing. The first chapter of the book is full of sadness and gloom, but the last contains one of the sweetest songs of love in the Old Testament.

Zephaniah showed that:
1. A faithful remnant would be delivered from captivity.
2. The Gentile nations shall be converted.
3. One day people could worship God anywhere, not only in Jerusalem (*2:11*; see *John 4:21*).

God is searching out the people. Read Zephaniah 1:12.

Judah Searched *Zephaniah 1*

Jehovah is in the midst of the land for judgment (*Zephaniah 3:5* and *1:17*). He first searches Judah and pronounces doom on all those who are worshiping idols. The land must be freed from idolatry. Jehovah cannot allow such abomination to remain. We see the rulers are denounced, as is every class of sinner (*1:7-13*):

1. The idol worshipers—1:4-5
2. Those who swear by God one time and at another time by Molech—1:5
3. Those who turned back from the Lord—1:6.

Upon all these shall God bring a blast of fire. It shall strike the whole earth, but especially the inhabitants of Jerusalem. The "day of the Lord" is a day of dread. He calls the people to tremble at God's presence. He is "in the midst" of the land to judge her.

The "day of the Lord" is mentioned seven times in the prophecy. Almost without exception, when "day" is used in Scripture it means a period of time. Judah was taught that "the day of the Lord" was coming when there would be a special reckoning.

The Nations Searched
Zephaniah 2

After the prophet calls the people to seek God, hoping that "perhaps you will be sheltered on the day of the Lord's anger" (*Zephaniah 2:1-3*), he declares that nothing can save the nation from doom but real repentance. "Seek the Lord. . . . Seek righteousness, seek humility" is his admonition. Then he turns to the five heathen nations, Philistia, Moab, Ammon, Ethiopia and Assyria. They shall be visited with the wrath of God because of their pride and scorn toward the Lord's people (*2:10*). The desolation of Nineveh is described in wonderfully accurate terms (*2:13-15*). These began to be accomplished in the conquests of Nebuchadnezzar.

The judgment on Israel's local enemies is literally fulfilled (*2:4-15*). The judgment on Israel's enemies over this wide world is yet to be fulfilled. Read God's Word in Zephaniah 3:8; 2:10-11. God says the idols of their enemies shall be broken up, and the Gentiles shall worship God, every one in his own country (*2:11*). Instead of all having to make a pilgrimage to Jerusalem, they may worship God anywhere.

The Jews taught that Jerusalem was the place of worship. The Samaritans declared that Mount Gerizim ought to be the religious center, but Zephaniah taught that spiritual worship did not depend upon a place, but on the Presence of God.

Israel Restored *Zephaniah 3*

The prophet concludes with the most wonderful promises of Israel's future restoration and of the happy state of the purified people of God in the latter days (*Zephaniah 3*). The redeemed remnant will return cleansed, humbled, trusting and rejoicing with their offerings to Zion. They will be established in their land with God "in their midst" (*3:15,17, KJV*). Zion then shall be a delight among nations and a blessing to the whole earth as was foretold in the promise God made originally with Abraham (*Genesis 12:1-3*).

The rejoicing of Zephaniah 3:14-20 must refer to something besides the day when the remnant will return after the captivity of Babylon. Judah's worst judgment followed that return. She has seen little but misery ever since. Neither did anything like this occur at Christ's first coming. It must refer to the day when the Lord Himself shall sit on the throne of David, when His people shall be gathered from the four corners of the earth (*3:19*). This prophecy shall be blessedly fulfilled in the Kingdom age when Christ comes to this earth to reign in power and great glory.

24. UNDERSTANDING

Jesus Christ, the Desire of All Nations; the Righteous Branch; Sun of Righteousness

Note: The greater number of Old Testament prophets spoke before the captivity. During the captivity in Babylon, Ezekiel and Daniel prophesied. After the return from Babylonian exile, Haggai, Zechariah and Malachi prophesied. This makes it easy to remember. Of the sixteen prophets, just two prophesied during the exile, three after, eleven before.

Haggai, Zechariah and Malachi are the last of the prophetic books. They prophesied to the Jews after they returned to Jerusalem. Nebuchadnezzar had captured Jerusalem and completely destroyed the Temple. This, however, did not bring the Jews to national repentance. In reading Ezra, we find that when Cyrus, king of Persia, issued a decree permitting all the captives to return to Jerusalem and to rebuild their Temple, only about 50,000 returned. Most of these were priests and Levites and the poorer among the people. Although the Jews increased in power and in numbers, they never established their political independence. They were a subject people under Gentile rulers from this time on.

Before Haggai's time, the Jews had returned to their own land under Zerubbabel and began to build the Temple (*Nehemiah 12*). But their enthusiasm soon waned. They made no progress beyond laying the foundation. The Samaritans and their enemy neighbors were determined that Jerusalem should not be rebuilt. This meant that the work lay unfinished for fifteen years. During these years, each person became interested in building a private house. It was then that Haggai arose and gave his message. He encouraged the people to build the Temple again. This time it was finished in four years. It seemed incredible that God's people should have waited so long to do the very thing they came back to do.

Understanding Haggai

We know little of Haggai except that he worked with Zechariah during the days following the exile. He prophesied two months before Zechariah. Zechariah prophesied for three years and Haggai prophesied for four months.

Haggai is the first voice to be heard

after the exile. His name means "my feast." His book is a collection of four brief messages written between August and December.

Each message is specifically dated. These dates, rather than places and characters, dominate the scenes. These were given in "the second year of Darius," 520 B.C. Confucius, the Chinese philosopher, was flourishing in China at this time. The book is dominated by one central purpose: Haggai is determined to persuade the people to rebuild the Temple. It is no easy task to move a discouraged nation to rise up and build a temple. But he did it.

A Message of Rebuke
Haggai 1:1-11

A poor handful of people returned to Jerusalem from Babylon where they had lived in captivity. With a colossal task before them of rebuilding the Temple and restoring the worship of Jehovah, the Jews labored under the same old sins—idolatry and intermarrying with idolatrous neighbors. They were few in number, poor, harassed by enemies and worse, they had lost the inner strength that comes from a joy in the Lord. (Read *Nehemiah 8:10*.)

Because of all this, the work dragged and the people lost heart and became selfish. Neglecting the Lord's house, they had become more interested in building homes for themselves than for God (*Haggai 1:4*). God would not allow this to go on and so He sent punishment as a result. Poor crops, droughts, scanty trade, misery and turmoil made their spirits fail (*1:6*). They were working and slaving, but finding no real joy (*1:6, 9-11*).

We see the effect of Haggai's challenge. His stern call to duty proved to be a good tonic. Zerubbabel, the governor of Jerusalem, Joshua, the high priest, and the people arose and began the work of rebuilding the Temple (*1:12-15*). How did God respond to their repentance (*1:13*)?

A Message of Courage
Haggai 2:1-9

Note: How long after the first message was this one given (*Haggai 1:1; 2:1*)? For the history of this period read Ezra 3:8-13.

As the people were building, a new discouragement seized them. The older ones, remembering the splendor of the Temple of Solomon, were greatly disappointed in this new Temple. How inferior in size and costliness of the stones! How limited were their means! And besides, this second Temple would not have the things that made the first one so glorious—the Ark, the Shekinah and all that went with the service of the high priest. These pessimists dampened the enthusiasm of the builders.

But Haggai came with a word of cheer that God was to pour His resources into that new building. The

---

Selected Bible Readings

Sunday:	Haggai's Message (*Haggai 1—2*)
Monday:	Visions (*Zechariah 1—6*)
Tuesday:	Fasts (*Zechariah 7—8*)
Wednesday:	Restoration of Judah and Israel (*Zechariah 9—11*)
Thursday:	The Messiah (*Zechariah 12—14*)
Friday:	Sins of Priests and People (*Malachi 1—2*)
Saturday:	Message of Hope (*Malachi 3—4*)

living God was to be in the midst of this new Temple. Read 2:7-9. What a comfort this must have been to the Jews in their exile.

A Message of Assurance
Haggai 2:10-23

This message of cleansing and blessing was delivered three months after the Temple was started. By the use of questions and answers, Haggai showed the people their impurity. He made them realize their sinfulness. He showed them that the reason their prayers were not answered was that they had put off so long completing the Temple. If they would renew their zeal, they would find God would bless them. Haggai heard their complaints of seeing no visible signs of blessings, although they had been working for three full months. Haggai showed them that the land had been rendered useless by their neglect, but God was working and it would be different now. "From this day on I will bless you" (*2:18-19*). God has begun even before we begin.

Understanding Zechariah

Zechariah is a book of the future. It is a book of revelation of the Old Testament.

The Chosen People and the Temple *Zechariah 1—8*

We now find Judah still a remnant, Jerusalem far from restored, the Gentile nations at ease round about her (*Zechariah 1:14-16*). Zechariah, a young prophet who had stood alongside the aged Haggai, strengthened the children of Israel as they built the Temple and warned them not to disappoint God as their fathers had done.

He pictured God's love and care for His people. He quickened their hopes by painting in glowing colors the time of perpetual blessing that was coming to Israel in the far-off ages.

Zechariah, like Haggai, was a prophet to the remnant of the Jews who returned from Babylon after the seventy years of captivity. The Jews, once a powerful nation as God had planned them to be, were now a pitiful and insignificant remnant, dwelling in their Promised Land only because of the courtesy of a foreign ruler. Both Haggai and Zechariah tried to tell the people that it would not always be so. One day the Messiah would come and God's chosen people would rise into power.

Zechariah was the prophet of restoration and glory. Born in Babylon, he was priest as well as prophet. Zechariah, whose name means "Jehovah remembers," prophesied for three years. The glorious future rather than the sad present was his message. He was a poet; Haggai, on the other hand, was a plain, practical preacher.

Zechariah's keen enthusiasm for rebuilding the Temple kept the people at the task of finishing the work. Serious crop failures and business depression among the Jewish people had made them so discouraged that only Haggai's blunt and consistent hammering kept them at the work. They needed a new voice. Zechariah's was that one. He threw himself into the work of helping his great friend Haggai.

Zechariah does not condemn the people, but presents in glowing pictures the presence of God to strengthen and help. He especially encourages the governor, Zerubbabel, who was conscious of his own weakness. Hear what Zechariah says, "'Not by might nor by power, but by my Spirit,' says the Lord Almighty"

Left: A memorial menorah, or seven-branched candlestand, in Jerusalem. Zechariah saw in his vision a seven-branched lampstand like the one that had stood in the Temple.

(*Zechariah 4:6-10*). He promised that the mountains of difficulty would be removed. How marvelously this truth was fulfilled at Pentecost when God filled people with His power.

Zechariah foretells the Savior more than any other prophet except Isaiah:

Christ the Branch (*3:8*)

Christ my Servant (*3:8*)

Christ's entry in Jerusalem on a colt (*9:9*)

Christ the good Shepherd (*9:16; 11:11*)

Christ the stricken Shepherd (*13:7*)

Christ betrayed for thirty pieces of silver (*11:12-13*)

Christ's hands pierced (*12:10*)

Christ's people saved (*12:10; 13:1*)

Christ wounded in the house of His friends (*13:6*)

Christ's coming on the Mount of Olives (*14:3-8*)

He who ascended from the Mount of Olives shall so come in the same way as He left. Read Acts 1:11

Christ's coming and coronation (*Zechariah 14*).

Two Searchlights

The prophet, looking far into the future, saw the Messiah of the days to come as one Person, but in two aspects. First, he saw Him in humiliation and suffering, and again, in majesty and great glory.

Of the Minor Prophets, Zechariah alone majors in visions (*1:1-6*). "During the night I had a vision" (*v. 8*).

The *angelic horseman* (*1:7-17*): here is a picture of Israel today, outcast but not forgotten by God.

The *horns and craftsmen* (*1:18-21*): the overthrow of Israel by her enemies is foreseen.

The *measuring line* (*2:1-13*): the coming prosperity of Jerusalem is seen. The city, walled in by the presence of God, is great in extent and blessed by His favor.

Joshua, the high priest (*3:1-10*): filthy garments clothing the priest and representing Israel's sin are removed, replaced and the Branch, Christ, introduced.

The *golden lampstand* (*4:1-14*): Israel is shown as God's future light bearer. Olive trees, anointed of God, speak of Zerubbabel the ruler, and Joshua the priest.

The *flying scroll* (*5:1-4*): wicked governments receive God's curse in this unique picture.

The *measuring basket* (*5:5-11*): Borne away on divine wings, wickedness is removed.

The *four chariots* (*6:1-8*): "Administrative forces of righteousness" (G. Campbell Morgan).

The Coronation Scene

The visions are followed by a symbolic act of crowning the high priest (*6:9-11*). Gold and silver brought from Babylon was wrought into a crown and placed on the head of Joshua the high priest. By this act, the two great offices of priest and king are united.

This is a type of Christ the King who will sit on His throne of glory as a priest when He returns to earth to set up His millennial kingdom.

Two years later, we find a committee from Bethel waiting on Zechariah to ask him if the national fasts should be kept (*chaps. 7—8*). The Jews themselves had instituted these fasts. They had been used to fasting on their great anniversary days. Zechariah warned them against cold formalism in their religious observances. He urges them to change their fasts into feasts of joy and be practical in their righteousness. God says, "To obey is better than sacrifice, and to heed is better than the fat of rams" (*1 Samuel 15:22*).

Fasting is only profitable as an outward sign of an inward confession of sin. Merely refraining from eating will never bring a blessing. God wants a humble and contrite heart.

The Messiah and the Kingdom *Zechariah 9—14*

These chapters are full of promises of the coming Messiah and a worldwide kingdom. The prophet no longer pictures a city rebuilt on its old foundations, but a glorious city whose wall is the Lord. It is not armed for war, but is a city filled with peace, for the Prince of Peace reigns. He shall come the first time as the lowly One, riding upon a colt, the foal of a donkey (*Zechariah 9:9*).

But we see this lowly One becoming a mighty Sovereign (*14:8-11*). The Messiah in all His glory and might shall put all the enemies under His feet and He shall establish His kingdom in Jerusalem and sit upon the throne of David. "His rule will extend from sea to sea and from the River to the ends of the earth" (*9:10*).

If we would follow these chapters more closely, we would discover victory over all the enemies of Israel. Chapter 11 reveals the Shepherd who would seek to save Israel, but is rejected. He is sold for thirty pieces of silver, the price of a slave. This all foreshadowed Christ and His betrayal by Judas. Chapter 12 gives us the prophecy of the siege of Jerusalem by the Antichrist and his armies in the last days. Then we see the repentance of the Jews (*v. 12*) when they shall see Him whom they have pierced. The fountain shall be opened to the house of David for sin and uncleanness (*13:1*). Then the return of the Messiah upon the Mount of Olives, which shall cleave asunder by an earthquake (*14:4*), reminds us of the day when He left the earth at that same spot with the promise of His return (*Acts 1:11*). Finally He shall be King over the whole earth and all people shall be holy unto Him (*Zechariah 14:9-20*).

The blessings of the kingdom of Christ:

1. The extent of His kingdom (*14:9*)
2. Abundant rain (*10:1*)
3. Outpouring of the Spirit on Israel (*12:10*)
4. Revelation of the "pierced" Messiah (*12:10*)
5. Changes in Palestine (*14:4-5,10-11*)
6. Kingdom set up on earth (*14:9-15*)
7. Jerusalem center of worship (*14:16-17*).

Understanding Malachi

Malachi is the bridge between the Old and New Testaments. To show this, read Malachi 3:1. Who is "my messenger"? Read John 1:23 and Luke 3:3-4. A silence of 400 years lies between the voice of Malachi and the voice of one crying in the wilderness, "Prepare ye the way of the Lord."

The Old Testament closes with the word "curse." The New Testament

Baptism in the River Jordan. Jesus quoted from Malachi when he referred to John the Baptist.

closes with blessing—"The grace of the Lord Jesus be with God's people. Amen."

By this time, a hundred years or more had passed since the Jews had returned to Jerusalem after the captivity in Babylon. Malachi is the last prophet to speak to Israel in her own land. Israel here means all the remnant of Israel and Judah that returned after the exile. The first enthusiasm after the return from Babylon had spent itself. Following a period of revival (*Nehemiah 10:28-39*), the people had become cold religiously and lax morally.

The prophet Malachi came as a reformer, but he encourages while he rebukes. He dealt with a people perplexed, with spirits failing, whose faith in God seemed to be in danger of collapse. If they had not already become hostile to Jehovah, they were in real danger of becoming skeptical.

"Malachi" means "my messenger" (that is, of the Lord). Like the forerunner John the Baptist, of whom he prophesies, he was but a voice.

The Sins of the Priests
Malachi 1:1—2:9

The skeptical attitude aroused among the people showed itself in religious coldness and social laxity. This is always true. The priests became irreverent and neglectful. Read Malachi 1:6,11-12. God said, "'Where is the honor due me?' . . . 'Where is the respect due me?' says the Lord Almighty. 'It is you, O priests, who show contempt for my name.'" The prophet rebukes these careless priests for offering worthless animals in sacrifice to God that they would not offer to the governor. They stood in marked contrast to God's ideal for the priesthood. They had completely lost sight of their high calling and deserved the ignominy heaped upon them. They refused to work except for money. God's condemnation begins with the leaders (*2:1-9*). As long as the priests were openly unfit, what could be expected from the people at large? This resulted in a carelessness among God's people in keeping themselves separate from the heathen nations. Mixed marriages with women of outside tribes became common. Some men had not hesitated to divorce their Israelitish wives to make this possible (*2:10-16*).

The Sins of the People
Malachi 2:10—3:18

What would you think of a person who deliberately held something before his eyes and then complained that he could see nothing? What would you suggest might quickly solve the difficulty? Well, this is just what Malachi had to do. The people of Israel declared that Jehovah did not love them as He said (*Malachi 1:2*). They could not see that His love had been of any special advantage to them.

Another result of the people's laxity of loyalty to God was in the growing prevalence of social sin (*3:5*). Malachi 3:7 reveals the religious indifference and skepticism of the people.

Sins Malachi rebuked:
Spiritless routine worship (*1:6-8*)
Evil associations (*2:10-12*)
Questioning Jehovah's justice (*2:17—3:6*)
Robbing God (*3:7-12*)
Impatience in waiting (*3:17—4:3*).

The children of Israel could depend on Jehovah to forgive. It was this same picture of the Father Jesus gave when He told of the prodigal's return. The father, seeing the boy while yet a great way off, ran out to meet him. This is ever God's attitude.

The Jewish people had been cured of idolatry, but they had grown careless and indifferent about many things. They had neglected the house of God. The priests had become lax. They were bringing inferior sacrifices to the Temple. They had robbed God of their tithes and offerings. They fell into social sins. They had become so selfish and covetous that Malachi dared

boldly to challenge them with these words, "Will a man rob God?" (*3:8*).

The key that opens God's big blessing windows is your recognition of His ownership by giving back to Him a proper share of the money or the property He permits you to acquire. "Bring the whole tithe into the storehouse" (*Malachi 3:10*). The tenth (or tithe) is the outward recognition that everything belongs to God. We are to bring Him our whole selves—body, soul and spirit. Then He will accept us and open the windows of heaven to pour out His blessings.

Coming Things
Malachi 3—4

Why does God permit such things? This attitude of the people was probably because of the feeling that the glowing promises of Haggai and Zechariah and of the other prophets had not been realized. They said that Jehovah did not seem to distinguish between good and bad people (*Malachi 2:17*). He blesses all alike, and evil people often flourish at the expense of their fellow citizens (*3:14-15*). What's the use of being good? Is this not one of the standing complaints of those who think they are good? They say, "What is God doing that He permits such things?" The answer to such a complaint is that Jehovah does care. He showed this to them by saying that one day He will send His messenger (John the Baptist) to prepare His way, then He will come in person "suddenly" and sit in judgment and separate the evil from the good (*3:1*). His judgment will be searching and effective "like a refiner's fire or a launderer's soap" (*3:2-3*). When God really gets ready to act, what will He do? The action will be final (*3:1-3*).

We find the burden of God's message by Malachi to His people stated in the second verse of the book, "'I have loved you,' says the Lord." What a message to a people who had sinned as Israel had and had spurned the love of Jehovah God. God is always sending His messenger before Him to prepare His way (3:1). He wants all His children to honor and adore Him. He longs to have us obey and worship Him. But who can stand the day of His appearing? And who can endure His purifying fire (3:2)? God's messenger will be a witness revealing our cruelty, our lies, our injustices, our double-dealing. This can be said of us today just as much as of the Jews of old. Jehovah's representative comes and finds us robbing Him of His due (3:2-5). Yet, Jehovah God is unchanging. He never forgets His promises of undying love and everlasting mercy.

Amid all the hypocrisy of the day, there were those in the Jewish community (a remnant) who still feared God and remained faithful. If we turn to Malachi 3:16 we will find this. Malachi longed to develop a strong body of enthusiastic believers who could influence his people's future. It is interesting to note that God bent His ear to hear His people speak about Him (3:16).

Close by reading aloud Malachi's solemn declaration concerning the second advent of Christ for which we wait, Malachi 3:16—4:3. Yes, the Sun of Righteousness will come with healing in His wings.

FOUR HUNDRED YEARS
OF SILENCE

By the time Old Testament history ended, a remnant of the Jewish exiles, chiefly of the tribe of Judah, had returned from Babylonia to Palestine under Zerubbabel, and about eighty years later another company had returned with Ezra. They were living peaceably in their own land with the Temple rebuilt and religious ceremonies set up.

The last three books of history in the Old Testament—Ezra, Nehemiah and Esther—give us the story of this time. They cover 100 years following the decree of Cyrus the king, allowing the Jewish people to return to their land (536-432 B.C.). (Read *Ezra 1:1-4*.)

From Nehemiah to the beginning of New Testament times, 400 years passed by. During this period, no biblical prophet spoke or wrote. In fact, it is called the "period of silence." As we come to the year when Jesus was born, it is important that we know some of the things that happened from the days of Nehemiah and Malachi to that time.

The Jewish People Persecuted

Now the Syrian kingdom arose. In the conflicts between Syria and Egypt, Antiochus Epiphanes, king of Syria, seized Palestine. He began a bitter persecution of the Jewish people. The Jews were forbidden by Antiochus Epiphanes to worship in the Temple and were compelled to eat the flesh of swine, which God through Moses had forbidden (*Leviticus 11:1-8*). Many courageously refused and a

period of martyrdom began.

The cruelties of this terrible king, Antiochus Epiphanes, brought about the revolt of the Maccabees under the leadership of Mattathias. Aroused by the patriotism and religious ardor of Mattathias, a group of patriotic freedom fighters gathered about him and began an insurrection that spread rapidly. When he died, his son Judas took his place. In an attempt to crush this rebellion under the Maccabees, Antiochus was defeated in three deadly conflicts. The cause of Judas had seemed hopeless because his followers were untrained and without equipment, and they were opposed by the trained soldiers of a powerful king. But this band of ragged but loyal Jewish patriots, inspired by an undying faith in God, came out victorious!

The Roman Tribute

In 63 B.C., Rome gained possession of Palestine, preparing the way and the time for Jesus to be born. The Jews had some political liberty, but were required to pay a yearly tax to the Roman government.

Part Two
The New Testament

The Gospels
of the New Testament

Matthew • Mark • Luke • John

25. UNDERSTANDING
The Gospels

The Gospels Portray Jesus Christ, Our Savior and Lord

The word "gospel" is derived from the two Anglo-Saxon words "God," meaning "good," and "spell," meaning "tidings" or "history." The four writers of the Gospels are called "evangelists," from a Greek word meaning "bringer of good tidings." The first three Gospels, Matthew, Mark and Luke, are called the "Synoptic Gospels" because, unlike John, they give a synopsis of Christ's life. The word "synopsis" is derived from the two Greek words meaning "a view together, a collective view." So these three Gospels may be viewed together.

The Synoptic Gospels are striking in their similarities. They are equally striking in their differences. The Synoptics narrate Christ's ministry chiefly in Galilee; but John's Gospel stands in a class by itself. He tells of Christ's ministry in Judea. The Synoptics narrate His miracles, parables and addresses to the multitudes; John presents His deeper and more abstract discourses, His conversations and prayers. The three portray Christ in action; John portrays Him in meditation and communion.

Every prophet in the Old Testament assured God's chosen people again and again that a Messiah should come who would be the King of the Jews. They therefore looked forward with passionate longing and patriotism to the coming of that King in pomp and power.

All that the prophets have said leads us to our Lord's earthly life and work, and all that follows in the Epistles proceeds from them. The Gospels are the source.

The Gospels tell us WHEN and HOW Christ came.

The Epistles tell us WHY and FOR WHAT Christ came.

What Is the Gospel?

"Gospel" means "good news." The good news concerning Jesus, the Son of God, is given to us by four writers— Matthew, Mark, Luke and John—although there is but one gospel, the glad story of salvation through Jesus Christ our Lord. The word "gospel" is never used in the New Testament of a book. It always means "good news." When we speak of the Gospel of Luke, we ought to understand that it means the good news of Jesus Christ as recorded by Luke. Nevertheless, from the earliest times the term "Gospel" has been applied to each of the four narratives that record the life of Christ.

No doubt, originally the good news was oral. Men went from one place to another telling the glad story by word of mouth. After a while, a written record was necessary. More than one attempted this, with no success. See what Luke says in Luke 1:1-4.

There is but one gospel with four

presentations. Four pictures of one Christ are given. The combined gospel records set forth a Personality rather than present a connected story of a life.

Why Four Gospels?

As everyone knows, there are four Gospels, but the question at once arises, Why four? The answer seems plain: Because one or two would not have given us a sufficient portrayal of the life of Christ. There are four distinct offices of Christ portrayed in the Gospels. He is presented as: King in Matthew, Servant in Mark, Son of Man in Luke, Son of God in John. Each of the writers is trying to present a different picture of our one Lord.

Matthew deliberately adds to his account what Mark omits. There is a lack of completeness about His life history in any one of the four Gospels. Hear what John says in 21:25: "Jesus did

View over Lake Galilee. The Synoptics narrate Christ's ministry chiefly in Galilee.

Selected Bible Readings

Sunday: The King Christ Jesus (*Matthew 2:1-12; 21:1-11*)

Monday: The Servant Christ Jesus (*Mark 10:35-45; 2:1-22*)

Tuesday: The Man Christ Jesus (*Luke 4:1-13; John 19:4-13*)

Wednesday: The God-Man (*John 1:1-18; 3:1-16*)

Thursday: Our Redeemer, Jesus Christ (*John 19:16-42*)

Friday: The Master, Jesus Christ (*Matthew 4:18-25*)

Saturday: Our Master, Jesus Christ (*John 21:1-17*)

many other things as well. If every one of them were written down, I suppose that even the whole world would not have room for the books that would be written."

There are deliberate gaps that none of the evangelists professes to fill in. For instance, all omit any account of the eighteen years of Christ's life between the ages of twelve and thirty. Although each Gospel is complete in itself, each is very selective; only a few of His miracles are described and only a portion of His teachings is given. Each evangelist has recorded that which is relevant and pertinent to his particular theme.

Each Gospel presents a different aspect of our Lord's life on earth. Together we have the complete picture. He was a King, but He was the Perfect Servant, too. He was the Son of Man, but we must not forget He was the Son of God.

There are four Gospels with one Christ, four accounts with one purpose, and four sketches of one Person.

Jesus in the Four Gospels

Master this outline and you will be familiar with the contents of the Gospels for life.

King—Matthew presents Jesus as King. It was written primarily for the Jew, for He is the Son of David. His royal genealogy is given in chapter 1. In chapters 5—7, in the Sermon on the Mount, we have the manifesto of the King, containing the laws of His kingdom.

Servant—Mark depicts Jesus as Servant, written to the Romans. More miracles are found here than in any other Gospel. Romans cared little for words; far more for deeds.

Man—Luke sets forth Jesus as the perfect Man. It was written to the Greeks; His genealogy goes back to

Adam, the first man, instead of to Abraham. As a perfect Man, He is seen much in prayer and with angels ministering to Him.

God—John portrays Jesus as the Son of God. Written to all who will believe, with the purpose of leading people to Christ (*John 20:31*), everything in this Gospel illustrates and demonstrates His divine relationship. The opening verse carries us back to "the beginning."

Dr. W. H. Griffith Thomas gives the pictures of the Gospels in this way:

Matthew is concerned with the coming of a *Promised Savior.*

Mark is concerned with the life of a *Powerful Savior.*

Luke is concerned with the grace of a *Perfect Savior.*

John is concerned with the possession of a *Personal Savior.*

All the Gospels are bound up with the promises of the Messiah in the Old Testament. We cannot explain the Gospels apart from the great Messianic prophecies in the Old Testament.

The prophets have portrayed a magnificent picture of the Messiah. They have told of His offices, mission, birth, suffering, death, resurrection and glory. Let us consider the names and titles the prophets have bestowed upon Him.

He is called the King: Psalm 72; Isaiah 9:6-7; 32:1; Jeremiah 23:5; Zechariah 9:9; 14:9. These passages, among many others, tell of the kingly office of the Messiah. The prophets tell much of His kingdom and its extent, and of Christ's ultimate triumph.

He is called the Servant of Jehovah: Isaiah 42:1-7; 52:13-15; 53.

He is called the Man, the Son of Man: Genesis 3:15; 22:18; Isaiah 7:14-16; 9:6.

He is called God: Isaiah 9:6; 40:3-5; 47:4; Jeremiah 23:6. As these four, Jesus is set forth in the Gospels.

Types of People Then and Now

Christ was going to be presented to widely different types of people who made up the world. Each group of people was capable of appreciating one particular kind of presentation more than another.

Jewish people—The four groups of people in Jesus' day represent four types of people today. For example, the Jewish people had special training. They were steeped in the Old Testament Scripture and the prophets. Matthew writes the story of Jesus' life on earth especially for these people. If Jewish people were to be impressed with Jesus, they would need to be taught by one who understood their customs and way of thinking. Jewish people needed to know that this Jesus came to fulfill the prophecies of the Old Testament. Over and over again we read in Matthew, "And so was fulfilled what the Lord had said through the prophet."

We have the same type of people today. They revel in prophecies fulfilled and unfulfilled. They seek to know what the prophets have spoken, and how it is brought to pass.

Romans—Next came the Romans, masters of the world at that time. Mark writes especially for Romans. The Romans knew nothing about Old Testament Scripture. They were not interested in prophecy being fulfilled. But they were vitally concerned about a remarkable Leader who had appeared in Palestine. He had claimed more than ordinary authority and had possessed extraordinary powers. They wanted to hear more about this Jesus—what sort of a person He really was, what He had said and what He had done.

The Romans liked Mark's straightforward message. The word "and" is used in Mark 1,375 times (in the *KJV*). It moves on in a beauty and force all its own. Mark's Gospel is filled with deeds, not words. Clearly it is the Gospel of the Ministry of Christ.

The Romans of Jesus' day were like average business people of today. They are not concerned at first about the genealogy of a king, but with a God "who is able," a God who can meet a person's every need. Mark is the business person's Gospel.

Greeks—Then there is Luke, the Greek doctor, who wrote to his own countrymen, who were lovers of beauty, poetry and culture. The Greeks lived in a world of large ideas. Their tastes were fastidious. The Gospel of Luke tells of the birth and childhood of Jesus. It gives the inspired songs connected with the life of Christ. We find the salutation of Elizabeth when Mary visited her (*Luke 1:42-45*). We hear the song of the virgin mother (*Luke 1:46-55*). Even Zacharias burst into praise when speech was restored to him (*Luke 1:68-79*). At the Savior's birth, a chorus of angel voices rings out (*Luke 2:13-14*), and then the shepherds' song of praise to God in Luke 2:20 is heard.

The Greek of Jesus' day was like the student and idealist today who is seeking after truth, for he or she believes that truth is the means to happiness.

All people—John's Gospel is written to all people everywhere that they might believe that Jesus is the Christ. Christ is portrayed as the Son of God. This Gospel is filled with extraordinary claims that attest His divine character and mission.

The "all people" of John's day were like the masses today who need Christ. They include the "whosoever" who will believe on the Lord Jesus because they have a sense of need and want to receive the gift of eternal life through Jesus Christ the Lord.

Keys to the Gospels

Front-Door Keys

God has hung the key to the Gospel of Matthew right over the entrance. The book opens thus: "A record of the genealogy of Jesus Christ the son of David, the son of Abraham" (*Matthew 1:1*). This shows His covenant position as the Son of Abraham (see *Genesis 12:1-3; Galatians 3:16*), and His royal position as Son of David.

Matthew is presenting Christ as King; he gives the royal genealogy in the first seventeen verses. A king is not chosen by popular ballot, but by birth.

Turn now to Mark. See how this book opens. No genealogy is given. The reason is that Jesus is portrayed as a Servant, and no one is interested in the pedigree of a servant.

Turn to Luke. Is a genealogy given? See Luke 3:23. Matthew traces Christ's line back to Abraham and David to show He was a Jew and of the royal line. Luke traces His line back to Adam. Christ is presented as the ideal Man. He was of the line of Adam.

Turn to John. How does this book open? No genealogy, but "In the beginning was the Word, and the Word was with God, and the Word was God." Christ is portrayed as God in John.

Back-Door Keys

Now let us see how the Gospels close. Hear the King commanding and commissioning His disciples. The Messiah is still on earth, for it is on earth and not in heaven that the Son of David shall reign in glory. Read Matthew 28:18-20.

Now look at the close of Mark. It is very significant and appropriate. Read Mark 16:20. Jesus, the Servant, is pictured as still laboring with His disciples.

Luke ends in a different way. Jesus, the perfect Man, is ascending to the Father. Notice what Luke says in 24:51: "While he was blessing them, he left them and was taken up into heaven."

The closing verse of John is significant: "Jesus did many other things as well. If every one of them were written down, I suppose that even the whole world would not have room for the books that would be written" (*21:25*). Truly, "No one ever spoke the way this man does" (*7:46*)! for He was the very Son of God.

26. UNDERSTANDING
Matthew

Matthew Portrays Jesus Christ, the Promised Messiah

Matthew has a special object in his Gospel: to show the Jews that Jesus is the long-expected Messiah, the Son of David, and that His life fulfilled Old Testament prophecies. The purpose is given in the first verse. Matthew is "A record of the genealogy of Jesus Christ the son of David, the son of Abraham." This statement links Christ with two of the great covenants God made with David and Abraham. God's covenant with David consisted of the promise of a King to sit upon his throne forever (*2 Samuel 7:8-13*). God's covenant with Abraham promised that through him should all families of the earth be blessed (*Genesis 12:3*). David's son was a King. Abraham's son was a Sacrifice. Matthew opens with the birth of a King and closes with the offering of a Sacrifice.

From the beginning, Jesus is associated with the Jewish nation. Matthew used wisdom in not alienating the Jews who might read the story. He is convincing them that this One fulfilled every prophecy spoken concerning their promised Messiah. He quotes freely from the Old Testament more than any of the other evangelists. Twenty-nine such quotations are given. Thirteen times he says that this or that event took place "to fulfill what the Lord had said through the prophet" (*Matthew 1:22*).

Matthew links us up with the Old Testament. On every page he is trying to connect the Gospel with the prophets and show that all of their teaching is being fulfilled in the person and kingdom of Jesus Christ.

It is difficult for us to appreciate how great the transition is from the old to the new. It seemed to the Jews that they must give up their tradition and orthodoxy and accept another creed. Matthew, in his Gospel, and Paul, especially in Galatians, show the Jewish believers in Jesus that they were not giving up their old faith, but rather were only giving up types and shadows for the real substance.

Matthew was well acquainted with Jewish history and customs. He speaks of farming and fishing and the housekeeping of his people in the seven parables in chapter 13. He knew this intimate record would strike responsive chords in the hearts and Luke give his other name, Levi. The only word the author speaks about himself is that he was a "publican" *(KJV)*, which was then a term of reproach, as the term "politician" so often denotes today. The other evangelists tell about the great feast he gave Jesus, and record the significant fact that he left all and followed Him. No doubt he was a man of means.

Matthew breaks the silence of 400 years between Malachi's prophecy and the announcement of the birth of

The town of Bethlehem is built on a hill which is still surrounded by shepherds' fields. Jesus' birth in Bethlehem, the city of David, was according to Micah's prophecy (*Micah 5:2*).

of the Jewish people.

As you read Matthew, get a clear and comprehensive view of the entire Gospel. Keep in mind the Messianic character of this Gospel. Note the balance between Jesus' ministry and teaching. We find the genealogy of the King; His birth in Bethlehem, the city of David, according to Micah's prophecy (*Micah 5:2*); the coming of the forerunner, John the Baptist, as Malachi predicted (*Malachi 3:1*); the ministry of the King; His rejection by Israel; and the promise of His coming again in power and glory.

The author is no doubt a Jewish believer in Jesus (*Matthew 9:9; 10:3*). Matthew, whose name means "gift of the Lord," was a tax collector at Capernaum under the Roman law when Jesus chose him as one of the twelve disciples. His name is found in all the lists of the twelve, though Mark

Jesus. Israel was under the domination of the Roman Empire. No man of "the house of David" had been allowed to sit upon the throne for 600 years.

Herod was not the king of Israel, but a governor of Judea, appointed by the Emperor of Rome. The man who really had the throne-rights of the house of David was Joseph, the carpenter, who became the husband of Mary. See the genealogy of Joseph in Matthew 1, and notice especially one name, Jechonias (Jeconiah), in verse 11. If Joseph had been Jesus' father according to the flesh, He could never have occupied the throne, for God's Word barred the way. There had been a curse on this royal line since the days of Jeconiah. In Jeremiah 22:30 we read, "This is what the Lord says: 'Record this man as if childless . . . for none of his offspring will . . . sit on the throne of David.'" Joseph was in the line of this curse. Hence, if Christ had been Joseph's son, He could not have sat on David's throne.

But we find another genealogy in Luke 3. This is Mary's line back to David through Nathan, not Jeconiah (*Luke 3:31*). There was no curse on this line. To Mary, God said, "Do not be afraid, Mary, you . . . will . . . give birth to a son. . . . The Lord God will give him the throne of his father David, and he will reign over the house of Jacob forever" (*Luke 1:30-33*).

Now the silence is broken and the coming of the Messiah declared.

The book of Matthew follows after the Old Testament and is the beginning of the New. It is the connecting link between the books. It is written for the Jews and it is fittingly placed. It takes for granted that the course of events is known to its readers. The Old Testament had closed with the chosen nation looking for their long-promised King, their Messiah. Matthew's Gospel shows that Jesus was that King. It is the Gospel of fulfillment.

Matthew presents the Lord Jesus in a distinctly Jewish relationship. Only in this one of the four Gospels do we find a record of the Messiah's declaration, "I was sent only to the lost sheep of Israel" (*Matthew 15:24*). What did

His own people do with Him? (See *John 1:11.*)

In the book of Matthew, Israel is in the place of probation and testing by the presence of the Messiah in her midst. Christ is presented as King to the Jews, but most of the religious leaders rejected Him not only as their Messiah, but also as their Savior (*Matthew 16:21*).

Coming of the King
Matthew 1:1—2:23

Jesus would have made it into any book of notables. Matthew is the Gospel of the Messiah, God's anointed One. The main purpose of the Spirit in this book is to show that Jesus of Nazareth is the predicted Messiah, the Deliverer of whom Moses and the prophets wrote, "whose origins are from of old, from ancient times" (*Micah 5:2*). He is the child that was to be born, the Son given, of whom Isaiah speaks who shall be called "Wonderful Counselor, Mighty God, Everlasting Father, Prince of Peace" (*Isaiah 9:6*).

The maps of the world and the calendars of time tell of Christ's birthplace and birthday. Jesus was born in Bethlehem of Judea (*Micah 5:2; Matthew 2:1*), in the days of Herod the king. We know this place and this king. Christianity is a historical religion. The Gospel does not begin with, "Once upon a time," but starts with "Bethlehem in Judea." The town is there, so we can know the very place where Jesus was born.

The time is definite, "in the days of Herod the king." There is nothing mythical about this monster of iniquity.

The Gospel narrative sets its record in the solid foundation of history. We are not building our faith on a myth, but substantial fact. This thing was not

A shepherd minds his flock near Bethlehem. Only in Matthew's Gospel do we find a record of the Messiah's declaration, "I was sent only to the lost sheep of Israel" (*Matthew 15:24*).

Palestine in the Time of Christ, A.D. 6–44

Land given to:

Herod Antipas

Philip

Archelaus

Boundaries

Main route

SYRIA

Mt Hermon

Caesarea Philippi

Phoenicia

Tyre

Gaulanitis

Trachonitis

Batanea

GALILEE

Ptolemais

Cana

Capernaum

Bethsaida

SEA OF GALILEE

Sepphoris

Hippus

Nazareth

Auranitis

Mt. Tabor

Jordan R.

DECAPOLIS

Caesarea

Scythopolis (Bethshan)

SAMARIA

Gerasa (Jerash)

MEDITERRANEAN SEA

Sebaste (Samaria)

Sychar (Shechem)

PEREA

Joppa

Philadelphia (Rabbath Ammon)

Jamnia

Jericho

Emmaus

Jerusalem

Qumran

Bethlehem

hkelon

Herodion

JUDEA

Gaza

Hebron

DEAD SEA

Masada

IDUMEA

NABATEA

| 0 | 10 | 20 | 30 | 40 mi |
| 0 | 20 | 40 | 60 km |

This metal star marks the traditional site of Jesus' birth. His cradle was a manger; he came as a helpless babe. How human was our Lord!

done in a corner, but in the broad daylight.

The story of the birth of Jesus in Matthew differs from the record in Luke. They complement each other. While there is much untold, God has told us all we need to know. Jesus' earthly life began in a stable. His

cradle was a manger. His family and associates were humble folk. He came as a helpless babe. How human was our Lord! But Jesus was heralded by an archangel, welcomed by an angel choir and worshiped by earth's wisest philosophers! How divine was our Lord!

A genealogy is "the history of the descent of an individual or family from an ancestor" (Webster). There are two genealogies of Christ: Matthew 1:1-17 and Luke 3:23-38. They are not alike, and the reason is that each traces the descent of Christ for different purposes.

Matthew traces Jesus' line back to Abraham and David to show that He was a Jew (coming from David). Luke traces Jesus' line back to Adam to show that He belonged to the human race.

Matthew shows Jesus as of royal descent, the King, the Messiah, the Lion of the tribe of Judah, the promised

Go through Matthew and follow this trail of the King

A King's name—"They will call him Immanuel" (*1:23*).

A King's position—"For out of you will come a ruler who will be the shepherd of my people Israel" (*2:6*).

A King's announcement—"Prepare the way for the Lord, make straight paths for him" (*3:3*).

A King's coronation—"This is my Son, whom I love; with him I am well pleased" (*3:17*).

A King's due respect—"Worship the Lord your God, and serve him only" (*4:10*).

A King's proclamation—"and he began to teach them" (*5:2*). "He taught as one who had authority" (*7:29*).

A King's loyalty—"He who is not with me is against me, and he who does not gather with me scatters" (*12:30*).

A King's enemies—"From that time on Jesus began to explain to his disciples that he must go to Jerusalem and suffer many things at the hands of the elders, chief priests and teachers of the law" (*16:21*).

A King's love—"The Son of Man did not come to be served, but to serve, and to give his life as a ransom for many" (*20:28*).

A King's glory—"When the Son of Man comes . . . Then the King will say . . . 'Come, you who are blessed by my Father; take your inheritance'" (*25:31,34*).

A King's sacrifice—"When they had crucified him . . . they placed the written charge against him: THIS IS JESUS, THE KING OF THE JEWS" (*27:35,37*).

A King's victory—"He is not here; he has risen, just as he said" (*28:6*).

Ruler of Israel. Luke shows Jesus as of human lineage, the ideal Man, born of woman.

You will find that these pictures of Jesus are kept all through each Gospel—Matthew portraying Him as Messiah, Luke as Man.

These genealogies give us the key to the whole life of Christ. They show us from the very start that He was not just another man, but that He was descended from a royal family, and there was a king's blood in His veins. If He were not a King, He could not claim the rulership of our lives. If He were not a Man, He could not know "our sorrows" and "be acquainted with our griefs."

Matthew alone tells of the visit of the wise men from the East. These were Persian magi, scholars, students of the stars. They came to worship and honor a King. These wise men did not come inquiring: "Where is He that is born the Savior of the world?" but, "Where is the one who has been born king of the Jews?" (2:2).

Mark, Luke and John are silent about the wise men because they are not recording the birth of a king. The holy, sacred star had halted over a manger in Bethlehem to tell of Christ's birth. The whole world at this time was expecting the advent of some great One. "Where is the one who has been born king of the Jews?" was the question on every lip. With all the prophecies that had been made to Israel, neither the world nor Israel could be criticized for expecting a King who would rule the earth from David's throne (*Jeremiah 23:3-6; 30:8-10; 33:14-16,25-26; Ezekiel 37:21; Isaiah 9:7; Hosea 3:4-5*).

The priests knew where Christ was to be born, but they did not know Christ when He was born.

The wise men were led to a Person, not a creed.

Bethlehem market today. The wise men might have seen similar scenes in their day.

The adoration of the wise men foreshadowed Christ's universal dominion. Some day "every knee should bow . . . and every tongue confess that Jesus Christ is Lord, to the glory of God the Father" (*Philippians 2:10-11*). "He will rule from sea to sea and from the River to the ends of the earth" (*Psalm 72:8*).

The birth of Jesus was followed by twelve years of silence until His visit with the doctors in Jerusalem. Then silence shut Him in again, with only the word "carpenter" (*Matthew 13:55; Mark 6:3*) to throw any light upon the next eighteen years, and let us know what He was doing. Jesus took thirty years of preparation for three years of ministry.

Proclamation of the Kingdom
Matthew 3:1—16:20

John the Baptist had another name. As the prophet Isaiah began to unfold the real message of his book—the coming of the Messiah, Servant of Jehovah—he introduced a character known simply as a "voice." "A voice of one calling: 'In the desert prepare the way for the

Lord; make straight in the wilderness a highway for our God'" (*Isaiah 40:3*). This "voice," although unnamed here, is to be the herald of Jesus Christ. His two functions—that of voice and that of messenger (*Malachi 3:1*)—are all that the Old Testament tells us of John the Baptist.

In Matthew we hear the "voice": "Repent, for the kingdom of heaven is near. This is he who was spoken of through the prophet Isaiah: 'A voice of one calling in the desert, "Prepare the way for the Lord . . ."'" (*Matthew 3:2-3*).

The King must be announced! It was the duty of this herald to go before the King, as a Roman officer before his ruler. John the Baptist did this. He showed that the spiritual roads of the lives of men and women and nations were full of the chuckholes of sin and sharp turns of iniquity, and needed rebuilding and straightening.

We see the King stepping from His personal and private life into His public ministry (*Matthew 4*). He is facing a crisis. Satan met Him. After the benediction the Father had put upon Him at His baptism when He said, "This is my Son, whom I love; with him I am well pleased" (*Matthew 3:17*). Jesus comes forth to carry out the plans for which He came into the world. He was led into the wilderness to face the first major conflict of His public ministry.

Notice that Satan offered Jesus a shortcut to that universal Kingdom He had come to gain through the long and painful way of the cross; but Christ came to be a Savior first, then a King.

The Kingdom Laws

Every kingdom has laws and standards to exercise authority over its subjects. The kingdom of heaven is no exception. Jesus declared that He came not to destroy the law, but to fulfill it. Moses and the prophets were far in advance of their time. Jesus treated this old law as rudimentary and not as perfect and final.

Jesus says any reform that starts on the outside and works in is beginning at the wrong end. The only way of getting a good life is first getting a good heart.

From the lofty pulpit of a mountain, Jesus preached the sermon that contains the laws of His kingdom (*Matthew 5—7*). The teachings of this sermon overtop all human teachings. The world has not yet caught up with its simplest ideals and requirements.

If we let this rule operate in our lives, it will change all our personal relations, heal our social wounds, solve every dispute between nations, yes, set the whole world in order. The root of this law is kindness. It is true, if human society would have its standards as theirs, the world would be set in order. Love would reign instead of lawlessness. Christ shows us that sin lies not just in committing the act, but in the motive behind it as well. (See *Matthew 5:21-22, 27-28.*) No one can expect forgiveness who does not forgive (*6:12,14-15*). Has anyone yet ever fathomed the depth of Matthew 7:12? It is easy to read; it is hard to do.

Jesus preached that the kingdom of heaven is "near" ("at hand," *KJV*). He

Part of this wall around the Temple Mount dates back to the time of Herod the Great. This was probably the site of the "pinnacle of the Temple" where Satan tempted Jesus.

set forth the condition for entrance, its laws, its privileges and rewards. The Sermon on the Mount sets forth the constitution of the Kingdom. Fourteen times the King says, "I tell you." People must not only keep the law outwardly, but in spirit as well. Notice the effect upon the people. (See *Matthew 7:28-29*).

The King's Power

We find the King worked amazing special miracles (*Matthew 8—9*). He met human needs. There are twelve astonishing miracles in these two chapters. After Jesus had performed the miracles in chapter 12, "All the people were astonished and said, 'Could this be the Son of David?'" (*12:23*).

The critical scribes now pass their hostile judgment on the actions of Jesus (*9:3*).

The kingdom was proclaimed "at hand" because the King Himself was there.

The King's Cabinet

Jesus not only preached Himself, but He also gathered others around Him. It was necessary to organize His kingdom, to put it on a wider and more permanent basis. Jesus still has a great message for the world and He needs us to carry it. Spiritual ideas must be clothed with men and women and institutions who will serve as hearts and brains, hands and feet to carry them out. Jesus was calling men and women into His companionship to train them to carry on His work.

Where did Jesus find His helpers? Not in the Temple among the doctors or priests, nor in the colleges of Jerusalem. He found them on the seashore mending their nets. Jesus did not call many mighty or noble, but rather chose the foolish things of the world to confound the wise (*1 Corinthians 1:27*).

A list of the disciples is given in Matthew 10:2-4. These men were given a work to do that would make winning battles and founding empires seem of small consequence. We find their great message was the kingdom of heaven. "As you go, preach this message: 'The kingdom of heaven is near'" (*10:7*).

Note some of the warnings and instructions for the disciples Jesus stated in Matthew 10. If these requirements of discipleship hold true today, could you call yourself a disciple? Consider Christ's words thoughtfully in Matthew 10:32-33.

The Kingdom of Heaven

The word "kingdom" occurs some fifty-five times in Matthew, for this is the

Capernaum

GALILEE

In Matthew 13 Jesus likened the kingdom of heaven to:

- *The sower*
- *Yeast in the dough*
- *The weeds*
- *A hidden treasure*
- *A mustard seed*
- *A pearl of great value*
- *A net*

Gospel of the King. The expression "kingdom of heaven" is found thirty-five times here and nowhere else in the Gospels. Of the fifteen parables recorded in Matthew, all but three begin, "The kingdom of heaven is like . . . "

Jewish people understood the term "kingdom of heaven." Neither Jesus nor John defined it. At Sinai, God said to Israel, "You will be for me a kingdom of priests and a holy nation" (*Exodus 19:6*). Israel at first was a theocracy. God was their King; they formed His kingdom. The prophets had referred to the Messianic kingdom again and again.

These parables, called "the mysteries of the kingdom of heaven" (*13:11*), describe what the result of the presence of the gospel of Christ in the world will be during this present age until the time of His return when He will gather the harvest (*13:40-43*). We see no bright picture of a converted world. Weeds shall be mixed with the wheat, good fish and bad, yeast in the loaf. Then there is an abnormal growth of the mustard seed that admits "birds of the air" to lodge in its branches. This is Christendom. Only Christ can determine what is good and what is bad, and at the harvest He will divide. Some day Christ will come in power and great glory and establish His throne on this earth.

Rejection of the King
Matthew 16:21—20:34

The gospel of the kingdom was first preached to those who should have been most prepared, the children of Israel. As a whole these people rejected their King. From Matthew 12 on we see much controversy among the leaders concerning Jesus.

Jesus announced that the kingdom should be taken away from the Jewish people and given to another nation. "Therefore I tell you that the kingdom of God will be taken away from you and given to a people who will produce its fruit" (*Matthew 21:43*). The announcement offended the rulers, and "they looked for a way to arrest him" (*21:46*).

A millennium of peace and rest is the great desire of diplomats and rulers. But they have no longing for a millennium brought about by the personal return of the Lord Jesus Christ. It was just so with the people in the days of John the Baptist.

The Church Promised

We find Jesus with His disciples up north in Caesarea Philippi, apparently with the object of having a private interview with them in which He would disclose a great truth (*Matthew 16*).

Only in Matthew's Gospel is the Church named. When the kingdom was rejected we find a change in the teachings of Jesus. He began to talk about the Church instead of the Kingdom (*16:18*). "Church" comes from the word *ecclesia*, which means "called out ones." Because all would not believe on Him, Christ said He was calling out anyone, Jew or Gentile, to belong to His Church, which is His body. He began to build a new edifice, a new body of people, which would include both Jews and Gentiles (*Ephesians 2:14-18*).

Life's Most Important Question

When they were far away from the busy scene in which they lived, Jesus asked His disciples the question: "Who do people say the Son of Man is?" (*Matthew 16:13*).

The disciples gave the answers others were giving. All agreed that Jesus was an extraordinary person, at least a prophet or a person who had an element of the supernatural.

Jesus now turned the general question into the sharp personal inquiry. "But whom say ye that I am?" Ask yourself this question. A neutral answer is impossible. He is either God or an impostor.

Life's Most Important Answer

"You are the Christ, the Son of the living God!" exclaimed the impulsive, fervent Peter. It grasps Christ as the Messiah, the fulfillment of the prophecies of the old Hebrew prophets. This confession is great because it exalts Christ as the Son of God and lifts Him above humanity and crowns Him with deity. From now on He reveals to this handful of disciples new truths about His teachings. He said to Peter and the disciples after this answer concerning who He was, "on this rock I will build my church." This is what Christ was going to do—build a Church of which He Himself was to be the chief cornerstone (*Ephesians 2:20*). This Church was born on Pentecost (*Acts 2*).

For the first time, the fateful shadow of the Cross fell across the path of the disciples. From this time on, Jesus began to draw back the curtain that veiled the future and to show His disciples the things that would come to pass. He saw His path running to Jerusalem into the awful hatred of the priests and Pharisees and then on to the terrible cross, but He saw the glory of the resurrection morning (*Matthew 16:21*).

Triumph of the King
Matthew 21:1—28:20

On the morning of Palm Sunday, there was a stir in Bethany and along the road leading to Jerusalem. It was understood that Jesus was to enter the city that day. The people were gathering in crowds. A colt was procured and the disciples, having thrown their robes over it, placed Jesus upon it, and the procession started. Jesus for the first time permitted a public recognition and celebration of His rights as Messiah-King.

In their enthusiasm, the people tore off branches from the palm and olive trees and carpeted the highway, while shouts rang through the air. They believed in Jesus, and with all their warm Middle Eastern enthusiasm were not ashamed of their King. In answer to the crowds who asked, "Who is this?" they boldly answered, "This is the prophet, Jesus, from Nazareth of Galilee." It took courage to say that in Jerusalem. Jesus entered the city and his mission was salvation!

In the evening the crowds dispersed, and Jesus quietly returned to Bethany. Apparently nothing in the way of making Jesus King had been accomplished. His kingdom came not with observation or pageantry. His hour had not yet come. Christ must be Savior first, then come again as King of kings and Lord of lords.

Christ's authority was brought into question as He went into the Temple and ordered the merchants out, overturning their tables and telling them that they had made the house of God a den of thieves. A bitter controversy followed. "Then the Pharisees went out and laid plans to trap him in his words" (*Matthew 22:15*). He bade farewell to Jerusalem until He would come again to sit on David's throne.

The lower slopes of the Mount of Olives, where the Garden of Gethsemane is to be found. When Jesus delivered His Mount Olivet discourse, He foretold the condition of the world after His ascension.

have a witness, though it be only scorn, to the kingly claim.

After hanging on the cruel tree for six hours, the Savior died, not from physical suffering alone but of a broken heart, for He bore the sins of the whole world. We hear His triumphant cry, "It is finished!" He paid the debt of sin and became the world's Redeemer!

Redemption Cost a Great Price!

The mode of the Messiah's death had been foreshadowed by various types and symbols in the Old Testament. The brazen serpent in the wilderness signified that He was to be lifted up; the lamb upon the temple altar that His blood must be shed. But this is not all of the redemption story. Jesus was put in Joseph's tomb, and on the third day He arose, as He had said. This is the supreme test of His kingship. People thought He was dead and His kingdom had failed. By His resurrection, Christ assured His disciples that the King still lived and that one day He will come back to establish His kingdom on earth.

The Future of the Kingdom

When Jesus delivered His Mount Olivet discourse, He foretold the condition of the world after His ascension until He comes back in glory to judge the nations according to their treatment of "His brothers," the Jewish people (*Matthew 25:31-46*).

Much of Jesus' discourse in Matthew 24 and 25 is devoted to Christ's second coming. He exhorts us to be ready in the parables of the faithful servant (*24:45-51*), the ten virgins (*25:1-13*) and of the talents (*25:14-30*).

The Death and Resurrection of the King

We have been passing through some of the highlights in the life of Jesus; now we step into the shadows as we enter Gethsemane. We see the Son of Abraham, the Sacrifice, dying that all the nations of the earth might be blessed by Him. Jesus was slain because He claimed to be the King of Israel. He was raised from the dead because He was the King (*Acts 2:30-36*). On the grounds of blasphemy, and of claiming to be the King of the Jews, thus making Himself the enemy of the Roman emperor, Jesus was delivered up by Pilate to be crucified.

Matthew makes us feel that in the mock array—the crown of thorns, the sceptre, the title over the cross—we

A Worldwide Commission

The climax of Jesus' program is found in His great commission; (see *Matthew 28:18-20*).

On what mission were they sent? To overrun the world with armies and make people submit under the sword? No, but to "make disciples of all nations."

From the mountaintop of His ascension, His disciples started forth on this mission, radiating from that center, and they have gone on until they have everywhere reached the rim of the world. Christian faith is no national or racial religion. It knows no bounds of mountain or sea, but it envelops the globe.

27. UNDERSTANDING

Mark

Mark Portrays Jesus Christ, the Servant of God

John, whose surname was Mark, is the writer of the Gospel of Mark (*Acts 12:12,25*). He was the son of Mary, and cousin of Barnabas (*Colossians 4:10*), and likely a native of Jerusalem. He accompanied Paul and Barnabas to Antioch, and was the cause of a serious disagreement between them (*Acts 12:25; 13:5*). Then he left them, probably on account of hardships (*Acts 13:13*). Finally he became a great help to Paul (*Colossians 4:10-11; 2 Timothy 4:11*). It is believed that the disciples met in the Upper Room of Mark's mother's house in Jerusalem. Peter was the means of Mark's conversion, and affectionately speaks of him as "my son" (*1 Peter 5:13*). We see the influence of the teaching of Peter in this Gospel.

If we turn to Mark 10:45, we can quite easily determine Mark's object in writing his Gospel. "For even the Son of Man did not come to be served, but to serve, and to give his life as a ransom for many." Unlike Matthew, Mark was not trying to prove certain statements and prophecies concerning Jesus. His only object in writing was to tell clearly certain facts about Jesus, His deeds more especially than His words. That Jesus is the Son of God he proves, not by declaring how He came to earth, but by showing what He accomplished during His brief career on this earth, how His coming changed the world.

There is a general agreement that

Mark's Gospel was written for Roman readers. The Roman culture contrasted in many ways with the Jewish. The Romans might have said, "I know nothing of your Scriptures, and care nothing for your peculiar notions; but I should be glad to hear a plain story of the life this man Jesus lived. Tell me what He did. Let me see Him just as He was."

Mark differs widely from Matthew in both character and scope. Mark's Gospel is the shortest of them all.

Matthew has twenty-eight chapters,

Selected Bible Readings

Sunday: The Servant's Coming and Testing (*Mark 1:1-20*)

Monday: The Servant Working (*Mark 2:1—3:25*)

Tuesday: The Servant Speaking (*Mark 4:1—6:13*)

Wednesday: The Servant's Miracles (*Mark 6:32—8:26*)

Thursday: The Servant's Revelation (*Mark 8:27—10:34*)

Friday: The Servant's Rejection (*Mark 11:1—12:44*)

Saturday: The Servant's Death and Triumph (*Mark 14:1—16:20*)

The barren Wilderness of Judea, where John the Baptist proclaimed his message. Of humble birth, little known, dressed like a desert hermit, John the Baptist was approved of God (*Matthew 11:11*).

abounds in parables and portrays Christ as the Son of David with kingly dignity and authority (*Matthew 28:18*).

Mark has sixteen chapters, and gives four parables. Mark portrays Christ as the humble but perfect Servant of Jehovah.

General Characteristics of This Gospel

The skill of an artist may lie in what he or she leaves out. An amateur crowds everything in. In strict harmony with Mark's central purpose of emphasizing Jesus as the Servant are the omissions.

There is nothing about the virgin birth. No reference to His birth is made in the whole Gospel. This is significant. No one is interested in the pedigree of a servant.

There is no visit of wise men. A servant does not receive homage.

No account of Jesus as the boy in the Temple is given. In this practical age, as in the age of Jesus, people demand a Christ who can do things. They are not interested in Jesus the boy, but Christ the man who is able and willing to accomplish today what He did of old.

There is no Sermon on the Mount. Mark presents Christ as a perfect

"Workman"; a servant has no Kingdom and frames no laws.

No quotations from the prophets are imparted. Mark's one direct quotation from the prophets is found in Mark 1:2. Matthew quotes on every page.

No divine titles are used. Jesus is never owned as King in Mark, except in derision. Matthew 8:25 says, "Lord, save us! We're going to drown!" Mark 4:38 says, "Teacher, don't you care if we drown?"

Unlike the other Gospels, there is no introduction in Mark. The opening verse says, "Gospel of Jesus Christ." Mark adds, "Son of God," to guard His divine glory. How different this is from Matthew, where we found the Gospel of the Kingdom.

The word "gospel" is used twelve times in Matthew, Mark, Luke and John together, and eight of those times are in Mark. Yes, the Servant is to bear good news!

Another term is the Greek word *eutheos*, which is translated with terms such as "immediately," "at once," "as soon as," and "without delay." In all, this word is found no less than forty times in Mark's Gospel. This is a servant's word.

In the *KJV*, if you glance at the word that opens twelve out of sixteen chapters, you will see the little word "and." His service was one complete, perfect whole, with no pause or breaks in it.

One of the first things that impresses us as we look at Mark's Gospel is its brevity. It is much shorter than any of the other Gospels. Very little is found here that is not found in the others. It moves off with precision.

Matthew records fourteen parables, Mark only four—the sower, the seed growing secretly (peculiar to Mark), the mustard seed and the wicked husbandmen. Not only do you find omission in number, but also in type.

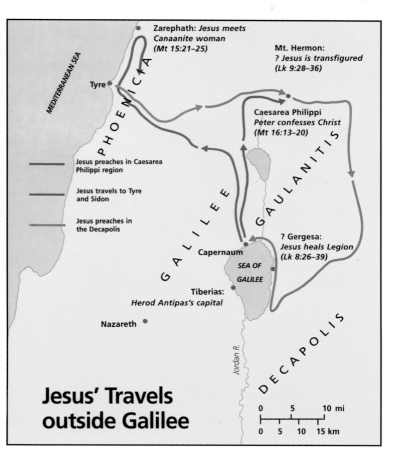

Zarephath: Jesus meets
Canaanite woman
(Mt 15:21–25)

Mt. Hermon:
? Jesus is transfigured
(Lk 9:28–36)

MEDITERRANEAN SEA

Tyre

PHOENICIA

Caesarea Philippi
Peter confesses Christ
(Mt 16:13–20)

Jesus preaches in Caesarea
Philippi region

Jesus travels to Tyre
and Sidon

Jesus preaches in
the Decapolis

GAULANITIS

GALILEE

Capernaum

? Gergesa:
Jesus heals Legion
(Lk 8:26–39)

SEA OF
GALILEE

Tiberias:
Herod Antipas's capital

Jordan R.

Nazareth

DECAPOLIS

Jesus' Travels
outside Galilee

0   5   10 mi

0   5   10   15 km

There is nothing about the house-
holder, or the marriage of the king's
son or talents.

Miracles have a leading place in
Mark, as parables have in Matthew. A
servant works; a king speaks. Mark describes more of Jesus' miracles than he
records Christ's parables. Twenty miracles are given in Mark in detail.

The Servant Prepared
Mark 1:1-13

The book of Mark skips over the first
thirty years of Jesus' life, but these

years were all needful for His human
preparation for His life's work. He
grew in sympathy with daily toil. He
meditated upon the needs of His nation till His heart burned within Him.

Preparation in life is needed. Jesus'
life illustrated this. He spent thirty
years in obscurity in Nazareth before
He appeared for the three years of
public ministry.

Preparation by John the Forerunner
This Gospel begins with John the
Baptist making ready for the coming
of the Messiah. John's coming was in

The River Jordan at the place where, tradition has it, John baptized. Jesus was baptized with John's baptism in obedience to an appointed ordinance.

be repaired and the highway reconstructed. "Prepare the way for the Lord, make straight paths for him." A true revival is always a revival of righteousness.

Preparation by Baptism

John and Jesus met one day. John recognized immediately that this Man was not a subject for the baptism of repentance that he was preaching. John hesitated, and said, "I need to be baptized by you, and do you come to me?" (*Matthew 3:14*).

Jesus was baptized with John's baptism in obedience to an appointed ordinance. "Let it be so now; it is proper for us to do this to fulfill all righteousness" (*Matthew 3:15*). He set a seal of approval on John's message and work, and acknowledged him as the true forerunner of Christ. The baptism by John was ordained of God and therefore was binding on all those who acknowledged God and meant to keep His commandments.

Christ was the standard and example of righteousness. He would fulfill every duty He required of others (*1 Corinthians 10:13*).

Preparation by Receiving the Holy Spirit

"As Jesus was coming up out of the water, he saw heaven being torn open and the Spirit descending on him like a dove" (*Mark 1:10*). This was a symbol. The coming of the Spirit Himself was a reality. Every event in Jesus' life had significance. In any service for God, the Spirit always prepares the life by giving power and equipment.

Jesus came up out of that water a new Man into a new world. His relationship to His Father and His mission were proclaimed.

Preparation by a Divine Call

"A voice came from heaven" (*Mark 1:11*). God endorsed Jesus and His mis-

fulfillment of a Messianic prophecy, "I will send my messenger ahead of you, who will prepare your way" (*Mark 1:2*). This quotation refers to Malachi 3:1 and Isaiah 40:3. Isaiah says the messenger is known simply as "a voice." "A voice of one calling: 'In the desert prepare the way for the Lord; make straight in the wilderness a highway for our God'" (*Isaiah 40:3*). It is this "voice" that is to be the herald of Jesus Christ.

We see this strange man who appears on the scene in an almost sensational way. "John wore clothing made of camel's hair, with a leather belt around his waist, and he ate locusts and wild honey" (*Mark 1:6*).

There is a lesson here for us. God does not always choose the kind of person we would select. He often picks "the foolish things of the world to shame the wise . . . the weak things of the world to shame the strong" (*1 Corinthians 1:27*). Graduated from no outstanding school, of humble birth, little known, dressed like a desert hermit, John the Baptist was approved of God (*Matthew 11:11*).

John's message was as startling as his appearance. He went before his Monarch as any Roman officer would go before his, demanding that the road sion, and showed to the Jewish nation that He was the Messiah. (See *Acts 10:38*). This has been called "Mark's Gospel in a nutshell." Later we hear this same Voice at His transfiguration. "This is my Son, whom I love. Listen to him!" (*Mark 9:7*).

Preparation by Testing

Baptism and temptation are here crowded together. Out of the baptismal benediction of the Father, Jesus stepped into a desperate struggle with the devil.

Mark says, "At once the Spirit sent him out into the desert," which shows how quickly the Spirit moves (*Mark 1:12*). "At once" indicated continuity, showing that temptation was as much a part of the preparation of the Servant for His work as His baptism. Suffering and trial are as much God's plan as thrills and triumphs. Jesus was "led" to be tempted. It was no accident or evil fate, but a divine appointment. Temptation has its place in this world. We could never develop without it. There is nothing wrong in being tempted. The wrong begins when we begin to consent to it. We are not to run into temptation of our own accord. Jesus did not go of Himself, but was led of the Spirit. We will find that the path of duty often takes us through temptations; but see 1 Corinthians 10:13. God always makes a way of escape!

The Servant Working
Mark 1:14—8:30

There is a continuous, unbroken service of the Servant recorded in this Gospel. We read, "And He did this, and He said that." He must teach people; they were in darkness. He must cheer people; they were without hope. He must heal people; they were sick and suffering. He must free people because they were under the power of Satan. He must pardon and cleanse people because they were sinful.

We see Jesus preaching by the seashore and selecting four of the fishermen to become His first disciples to learn under His guidance how to become "fishers of men." Who were they? (See *Mark 1:16-20*.) They were to turn all the practical knowledge and skill they exercised in the art of catching fish into the work of catching men and women. What disciple was called in Mark 2?

How was Christ's call received? "At once they left their nets and followed him" (*Mark 1:18*). Too often there is lost time between our call and our coming.

Jesus is introduced at once as "anointed with power," and as fully engaged in His work. You will find no long discourses in these next chapters, but many mighty deeds. Demons were cast out (*1:21-28*); fever banished (*1:29-31*); different diseases healed (*1:32-34*); lepers made whole (*1:40-45*); paralytic man made to walk (*2:1-12*); withered hand cured (*3:1-5*); multitudes healed (*3:6-12*); storm at sea quelled (*4:35-41*); maniac's mind restored (*5:1-15*); woman's hemorrhage of blood stopped (*5:21-34*); Jairus's daughter brought back to life (*5:35-43*); five thousand fed (*6:32-44*); the sea was

Jesus preached by the seashore and selected four fishermen to become His first disciples to learn how to become "fishers of men."

made His sidewalk (*6:45-51*); all that touched Him were made whole (*6:53-56*); deaf and dumb heard and spoke (*7:31-37*); four thousand fed (*8:1-9*); blind man healed (*8:22-26*).

The action is rapid, and events appear to be happening before our very eyes. His descriptions are abrupt and outspoken, but Mark preserves many things for us that would otherwise have been lost. It is only in the Gospel of Mark that we are told Jesus was a carpenter (*Mark 6:3*).

Mark tells us that He "took one by the hand," and little children "in his arms." Mark tells us that Jesus was "grieved"; that He "sighed," He "wondered," He "loved," He was "angry." He was "touched with the feelings of our infirmities."

Let us spend the Sabbath with Jesus that is recorded in Mark 1:21-34, going with Him to church, listening to His preaching, watching Him when interrupted by a maniac, casting out the unclean spirit and making the healing a powerful aid to His teaching. Then, after service let us go with Him to Peter's house and see Him heal Peter's wife's mother of a severe fever; and then let us spend the Sabbath afternoon in quiet rest and friendly conversation. Toward evening we shall look out in the beautiful twilight and see men and women coming toward the house, bringing great numbers of

people, sick with every kind of disease, and watch them as Jesus lays His tender hands upon them and heals them. The lame jump from their stretchers and leap for joy; the blind open their eyes and see their Healer; lines of suffering are turned to an expression of unbelievable happiness as others are delivered from their painful diseases.

Mark records a wonderful statement concerning the Sabbath. "The Sabbath was made for man, not man for the Sabbath" (*2:27*). This great saying of Jesus is the central principle of Sabbath observance. The Sabbath is not made to annoy humankind, but to enrich and bless them!

Christ answers the question of Sabbath keeping with a practical illustration (*Mark 3:1-5*). His conclusion is that whatever deed is really helpful to people is proper for the Sabbath and is in perfect harmony with God's design of the day. He illustrated this truth with this miracle of healing. Seven of Jesus' recorded miracles were performed on the Sabbath. The Sabbath was "made." It is God's gift to people.

The Servant and His Miracles

The miracles of Jesus were proofs of His mission from God. They showed that He was the promised Redeemer and King, the One we all need. Because Jesus was God, miracles were as natural to Him as acts of will are to us! Through His miracles, Jesus inspired faith in many of those who saw and heard Him.

The Servant at Prayer

The morning following the great Sabbath day of preaching and healing Jesus arose very early and went out of the city to a lonely place and prayed (*Mark 1:35*). His work was growing rapidly, and Jesus needed heavenly communion. The seeming answer was

a larger work, the entrance upon His first Galilean tour of healing and preaching (*Mark 1:37-39*). Only one healing event of this tour, which lasted several days, is recorded—that of a leper whose disease was incurable (*Mark 1:40-45*).

If the Son of God needed to pray before He undertook His work, how much more should we pray.

The Servant Forgives Sin

"A few days later . . . the people heard that he had come home" (*Mark 2:1*). But in another part of the city a paralytic man had heard of this new Prophet and His gospel of healing. His four friends brought him to Jesus and let him down into the presence of the Teacher. We find in this healing the test and proof of Jesus' power not only as a physician of the body, but also as a healer of the soul. "Who can forgive sins but God alone?" (*Mark 2:7*). Sins are against God and, there-

fore, He only can forgive. Jesus said, "'But that you may know that the Son of Man has authority on earth to forgive sins . . . .' He said to the paralytic, 'I tell you, get up, take your mat and go home'" (*Mark 2:10-11*).

God endorsed Jesus' claim to be the Messiah in this miracle. The man arose, took up his bed, and went forth before them all, a living witness to Jesus' power over sin, a visible illustration of the work Jesus came to do. Jesus came to give His life a ransom for many that He might forgive people their sins.

We find the account of choosing the twelve apostles in Mark 3:13-21. Notice the fourteenth verse. It tells why Jesus chose these men, "that they might be with him." This is what Jesus wants of His disciples today—that they will take time to be in His presence and commune with Him.

The parable of the sower sets forth the hindrances to the gospel that dwell in the hearts of the hearers (*4:3-20*).

Everyone should master these parables of the Kingdom in chapter 4. They were a special teaching instrument of Christ. The interpretation of the sower is given in Mark 4:13-20. Jesus used this method of instruction because of the growing hostility to Him and His message. He was surrounded by enemies who tried to catch Him in His words, but no one could object to a simple story. Besides, stories are remembered by the dullest of hearers.

A parable is an analogy. It assumes a likeness between heavenly and earthly things. "Parable" comes from the Greek word meaning "beside" and "to throw." A parable, then, is a form of teaching in which one thing is thrown beside another to make a comparison.

Besides the parable of the sower, our Lord spoke other parables as recorded by Mark:

1. The parable of the lamp (*4:21-25*)
2. The parable of the sprouting seed (*4:26-29*)
3. The parable of the mustard seed (*4:30-33*).

After interpreting the parables, Jesus took a ship to escape the crowd. On the way, as the weary Teacher fell asleep, a violent storm arose on the Sea of Galilee. About to perish, the frantic disciples awoke Jesus. At a word from His lips, the sea became calm. He had power over the elements (*Mark 4:35-41*).

Mark 5 begins again with "And" *(KJV)*. Jesus is still working. What does He do now? Read parallel accounts in Matthew 8:28-34; Luke 8:26-39. Compare this miracle with other recorded cures of demoniacs, in Matthew 9:32-33; Mark 1:23-26; Matthew 17:14-18; Luke 9:38-42.

The miracle recorded in Mark 5, like all others, tested the character of people. It took them off their guard and disclosed their true natures. Notice the contrast in the way people receive the work of Christ.

Some shun the Savior. "Those tending the pigs ran off." Others were afraid (*vv. 14-15*) and "began to plead with Jesus to leave their region" (*v. 17*). Doubtless there were other herds of swine, and they feared the loss of them. What a true picture of the attitude of many toward Christ! There is some gainful business they do not want to give up. There is some sin that lies close to the heart. For these reasons people thrust away Christ.

Some seek the Savior. The healed man begged Him not to depart out of his coast, but "to go with him." It is so with people today. People either ask Jesus to "depart" because they want to keep their sin, or they ask that He might remain "with" them because they want to lose their sin.

"And" starts another episode in Jesus' miracles (*5:21, KJV*). After healing the demoniac, Jesus returned to Capernaum. He heals a woman long sick, and "while Jesus was still speaking" (*5:35*) He was called upon to raise a child already lying in death, Jairus's daughter.

Jesus started out on a third preaching tour of Galilee (*chap. 6*). He sent forth the twelve disciples, two by two, on independent missions (*6:7-13*).

Matthew 10 records the instructions they received. As they preached, Herod heard them and we read of his uneasy conscience, thinking that the man he had murdered was back to haunt him (*Mark 6:14-29*).

After the apostles were trained, Jesus sent them out on an extensive missionary tour among the villages of Galilee (*Mark 6:12-13*). On returning they "gathered around Jesus" (*6:30*), probably at their regular rendezvous, Capernaum. They reported upon their sermons, the number of conversions and the miracles that were wrought. No Christian work can be carried on long without frequent talks with Christ. We need His sympathy, approval, guidance and strength.

We must hasten if we would follow this mighty Servant, this Workman of God. Jesus had gone apart in a desert to rest awhile (*6:31*), but the multitudes followed Him. Feeding the 5,000 follows without an interval (*6:32-44*). It is the only one of the thirty-five miracles that is recorded by all four evangelists.

What miracles are next (*6:45-52* and *53-56*)? Follow Jesus in what He does and says (*7:1-23, 24-30, 31-37; 8:1-9, 22-26*).

Jesus does not tell His disciples who He is. He waits until they tell Him. When He asked, "Who do you say I am?" (*8:29*) the climax of His ministry was reached. He was testing the aim of all His training of the chosen twelve.

The Servant Rejected
Mark 8:31—15:47

Even before Mark sets forth Christ's direct claim to be King of the Kingdom, he reveals the way the King is to be received. His is a pathway of suffering and rejection. Jesus said, "The Son of Man must suffer many things" (*Mark 8:31*). The evangelists write it down in plain language that He was to be rejected by the rulers of Israel, and killed, and was to rise again the third day.

Jesus tells His disciples that He is to be rejected by the elders, chief priests and scribes (*8:31*).

He is to be delivered by treachery (*9:31*).

He is to be put to death by the Romans (*10:32-45*).

He is to rise again the third day (*9:31*).

Jesus, nevertheless, claimed the kingdom by presenting Himself at Jerusalem as the Heir of David, according to the prophecy of Zechariah 9:9 (*Mark 11:1-11*).

How did the people accept this King? At first they welcomed Him because they hoped He might deliver them from the yoke of Rome and free them from the poverty they were enduring. But when He entered the Temple and showed that His mission was a spiritual one, He was hated by the religious leaders with a satanic hatred that led to the plot to put Him to death (*14:1*).

The World's Greatest Sin

The greatest sin of this age, as of every age, is the rejection of Jesus Christ. Yet, remember that everyone who has heard the gospel must either accept the Lord as Savior or trample Him underfoot. The people of Jesus' day made their choice and the people of our day must make theirs.

After Christ's public ministry, described in Mark 10:46—11:26, we read of His last conflict with the Jewish authorities and of His triumph over the leaders (*11:27—12:44*).

Jesus sought to persuade the Jews to receive Him as the Messiah (*11:15—12:44*). It was a busy Tuesday, occupied from morning till night in one great and powerful effort to induce the

Jewish nation to acknowledge Him, and thus become that glorious nation, blessing the world, for which it had been set apart.

In the beautiful Temple courts, the simple Galilean met the religious authorities, arrayed in all the pomp of their official regalia. There is a sharp and prolonged controversy on a puzzling question.

The scribes and chief priests question Him. "'By what authority are you doing these things?' they asked. 'And who gave you authority to do this?'" (*11:28*).

The Pharisees and Herodians try to catch Him in His words, "Is it right to pay taxes to Caesar or not?" (*12:14*).

The Sadducees, who say there is no resurrection, ask Him, "At the resurrection whose wife will she be, since the seven were married to her?" (*12:23*).

The scribes ask Him, "Of all the commandments, which is the most important?" (*12:28*).

After Jesus answered them all, "from then on no one dared ask him any more questions" (*12:34*).

It would seem that He could not escape treason to the Roman government in answering them, but He came out unscathed. Hour by hour Jesus met the attack.

All the way through, the perfect Servant of God was dogged by His enemies. The enemy is not dead! God's servants today are called to tread a similar path. Jesus silenced His enemies, but their hearts would not yield.

Before He goes to the cross, Jesus reveals the future to His troubled disciples in the Olivet discourse (*Mark 13*). He tells them of the end of this age, and of the great tribulation, and climaxes it with the promise of His return in power and glory.

The plotting of the chief priests, how they might take Him by craft and put Him to death, and the anointing of His body in preparation for burial (*v. 8*) opens chapter 14. Then the ever sad story of His betrayal at the hand of His own disciple (*14:10-11*), the celebration of the Passover and the institution of the Lord's Supper all are crowded into twenty-five short verses. Adding insult to injury, we read of

Model of Jerusalem, with the Temple in the foreground. In the beautiful Temple courts, the simple Galilean met the religious authorities.

Peter's denial of his Lord (*Mark 14:26-31, 66-71*).

Isaiah's great message is that the Son of God shall become the Servant of God in order that He might die to redeem the world. Mark records how the sufferings of Jesus in Gethsemane and on Calvary fulfilled the prophecies of Isaiah (*Isaiah 53*).

Jesus was sold for thirty pieces of silver, the price of a slave. He was executed as only slaves were! Yes, Christ was the suffering Servant and died for me! He bore my sins in His own body on the tree.

The Servant Exalted
Mark 16:1-20

After the Servant had given His life a ransom for many, He arose from the dead. We read again the Great Commission (*Mark 16:15*), also recorded in Matthew 28:19-20. Compare the two. In Mark we do not hear a King say, "All authority in heaven and on earth has been given to me," as in Matthew. In Mark we see in Jesus' words that His disciples are to take His place, and He will serve in and through them. He is yet the Worker, though risen (*16:20*). The command rings with urgency of service. Not a corner of the world is to be left unvisited; not a soul to be left out!

Finally He was received into heaven to sit on the right hand of God (*16:19*). He who had taken upon Himself the form of a servant is now highly exalted (*Philippians 2:7-9*). He is in the place of power, ever making intercession for us. He is our Advocate.

But Christ is with us. The Servant is always working in us and through us. We are laborers together with Him (*1 Corinthians 3:9*). He is still "working with [us]" (*Mark 16:20*). Let us, being redeemed, follow our Pattern and go forth to serve also! (See *1 Corinthians 15:58*.)

28. UNDERSTANDING

Luke Portrays Jesus Christ, the Son of Man

The writer of this third Gospel was Dr. Luke, Paul's companion (*Acts 16:10-24; 2 Timothy 4:11; Colossians 4:14*). He was a native of Syria and apparently was not a Jew, for Colossians 4:14 places him with the other Gentile Christians. If this is true, he was the only Gentile writer of the New Testament books.

It is easily seen that Luke was an educated man and a keen observer. We learn from Acts 1:1 that the Acts was written by the author of this third Gospel.

Luke's Gospel was written for the Greeks. Besides the Jews and the Romans, the Greeks were another people who had been preparing for Christ's coming. They differed from the other two in many particulars. They possessed a wider culture, loved beauty, rhetoric and philosophy. Luke, an educated Greek himself, would be well fitted for this task. Luke presents Jesus as the ideal of perfect manliness.

Notice that inspiration does not destroy individuality. In the introduction, verses 1-4, the human element is seen in connection with God's revelation. Luke addressed his Gospel to a man named Theophilus. It is thought he was an influential Christian layman in Greece.

This is the Gospel for the sinner. It brings out Christ's compassionate love in becoming Man to save man.

In Luke, we see God manifest in the flesh. Luke deals with the humanity of our Lord. He reveals the Savior as a Man with all His sympathies, feelings and growing powers—a Savior suited to all. In this Gospel, we see the God of glory coming down to our level, entering into our conditions and being subject to our circumstances.

Luke's Gospel is the Gospel of Christ's manhood. This we must know, however; although He mingles with men, He is in sharp contrast to them. He was the solitary God-Man. There was as great a difference between Christ as the Son of Man and we the sons of men, as Christ as Son of God

---

Selected Bible Readings

Sunday: The Man "Made Like His Brothers"
(*Luke 1:1—3:38*)

Monday: The Man "Tempted . . . Just as We Are"
(*Luke 4:1—8:3*)

Tuesday: The Man "Able to Sympathize"
(*Luke 8:4—12:48*)

Wednesday: The Man "About My Father's Business"
(*Luke 12:49—16:31*)

Thursday: The Man "No one ever spoke the
way this man does"(*Luke 17:1—19:27*)

Friday: The Man, Our Kinsman-Redeemer
(*Luke 19:28—23:56*)

Saturday: The Man in Resurrection Glory
(*Luke 24:1-53*)

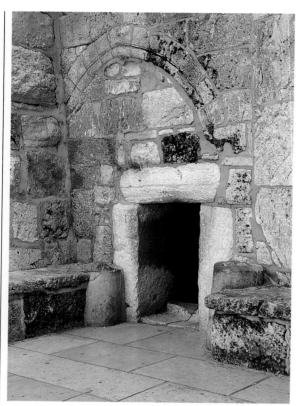

The little doorway into the Church of the Nativity, Bethlehem. The doorway was blocked in to prevent horsemen from riding in.

universe, entered this world like any other person. It is a mystery of mysteries, but enough facts are given to let us see that the predictions are true.

Luke alone tells the story of the visit of the shepherds (*2:8-20*).

We learn from this Gospel that as a boy, Jesus developed naturally (*2:40,52*). As a child, He was subject to Joseph and Mary (*2:51*). There was no record of unhealthy or supernatural growth. Only Luke tells of Jesus' visit to the Temple when He was twelve years old.

As a man He toiled with His hands; wept over the city; "kneeled in prayer," and "knew agony in suffering." All is strikingly human. Five out of six of the miracles were miracles of healing. Luke alone tells of healing Malchus's ear (*Luke 22:51*).

Luke is the Gospel for the outcast on earth. It is Luke who tells of the good Samaritan (*10:33*), the publican (*18:13*), and the prodigal (*15:11-24*), of Zacchaeus (*19:2*) and the thief on the cross (*23:43*). He is the writer who has most to say for womanhood (*chaps. 1 and 2*). Luke records Jesus' compassion for the woman of Nain, and the depths of His mercy to the woman who was a sinner. His regard for women and children is shown in *7:46; 8:3; 8:42; 9:38; 10:38-42; 11:27; 23:27.*

Luke alone tells us: when our Lord beheld the city of Jerusalem He wept over it; of the bloody sweat in Gethsemane; of the Lord showing mercy to the dying thief on the cross. Luke alone mentions the walk with the two to Emmaus. He also tells of Jesus leading His disciples out as far as Bethany, and that as He lifted up His hands and blessed them, He was parted from them.

Luke is a poetic book. It opens with a song, "Glory to God!" It closes with a song, "Praising God." The world has been singing ever since. Thank God

and we the sons of God. The difference is not merely relative, but absolute. Make this fact plain. Read the words of the angel to Mary: "So the holy one to be born" (*Luke 1:35*) refers to our Lord's humanity. It is in contrast to ours. Our human nature is unclean (*Isaiah 64:6*), but the Son of God, when He became incarnate, was "holy." Adam in his unfallen estate was innocent, but Christ was "holy."

In keeping with the theme of his Gospel, Dr. Luke has given us the fullest particulars concerning the miraculous birth of Jesus. We are grateful that our chief testimony concerning this fact should come from a physician. Christ, the Creator of this for such a Gospel! It preserves the precious gems of Christian hymnology: The Magnificat—Mary's hymn of rejoicing (*1:46-55*) Song of Zacharias (*1:68-79*) Song of the angels (*2:8-14*).

Luke speaks more of the prayers of our Lord than any other Gospel writer. Prayer is the expression of human dependence on God. Why is there so much working and activity in the Church and yet so little result in positive conversions to God? Why so much running hither and thither and so few brought to Christ? The answer is simple: There is not enough private prayer. The cause of Christ does not need less working, but more praying.

The hardest thing the Early Church had to learn was that the Gentiles would have full and free admission into the Kingdom and into the Church. Simeon taught this. Read Luke 2:32. Christ sent the seventy disciples not to the lost sheep of the house of Israel alone, as Matthew says, who wrote especially for the Jews, but "to every town and place" (*Luke 10:1*). All of Jesus' ministry over the eastern side of Jordan was to the Gentiles.

The Preparation of the Son of Man *Luke 1:1—4:13*

The opening of this beautiful book is significant. A Man is to be described, and the writer, Luke, will draw his good friend Theophilus into it. He tells him of his own personal knowledge of his subject—"since I myself have carefully investigated everything from the beginning." He seems to bring something warmly human into his task of presenting the Man Christ Jesus.

The opening chapter is characteristic, too. Luke begins like a simple story touching people with, "In the time of Herod king of Judea there was a priest." As the story progresses, we are introduced to human sympathies and relationships that none of the other Gospels tells us. We learn all about the circumstances that accompanied the birth and childhood of the holy Babe, and about the one who was sent as His forerunner. The birth of John the Baptist (*1:57-80*); the angels' song to the shepherds (*2:8-20*); the circumcision (*2:21*); the presentation in the Temple (*2:22-38*); and then the

Hippos, on the eastern side of Galilee, possible site of the healing of Legion. All of Jesus' ministry over the eastern side of Jordan was to the Gentiles.

The marketplace at Nazareth has changed little over the centuries.

Nazareth

poor shepherds in Luke 2:10-12.

Why did the Father allow His blessed Son, now incarnate in the flesh, to be born in this lowly place? Luke is the only one of the four evangelists who touches this point concerning His humanity.

Boyhood Days

"The child grew . . . and the grace of God was upon him" (*Luke 2:40*). When He was twelve years old, He went up with His parents to Jerusalem to the feast, as every Jewish boy did at that age. "The boy Jesus stayed behind in Jerusalem, but they were unaware of it" (*v. 43*). He was found sitting in the midst of the doctors, both hearing them, and asking them questions (*2:46*). We find Jesus' first words here: "Didn't you know I had to be in my Father's house?" (*2:49*) Here we find the first self-witness to His deity.

Again we read, "Then he went down to Nazareth with them and was obedient to them"—these earthly parents (*2:51*). "And Jesus grew in wisdom and stature, and in favor with God and men" (*2:52*). All of these things are peculiar to Jesus as man, and Luke alone records them. It is important that we notice Jesus was a "favorite" in Nazareth. It is not a sign that we are in the grace of God when we are out of favor with others.

Eighteen years of silence followed. We read of John the Baptist, preaching "a baptism of repentance for the forgiveness of sins" (*3:3*). Then Jesus came to be baptized. Only Luke tells us, "When all the people were being baptized, Jesus was baptized too. And as he was praying, heaven was opened" (*3:21*). He is linked with "all the people." He came down to the level of humans. Matthew and Luke record the baptism of Jesus, but John omits it, for Christ is viewed as the only begotten Son of God. Here only do we read of

story of the boy Jesus, twelve years of age (*2:41-52*), are all recorded here.

In chapter 2, Luke notes that "In those days Caesar Augustus issued a decree that a census should be taken of the entire Roman world" (*2:1*). Then comes a fact that we would never find in Matthew, that Joseph and Mary "went to [Joseph's] own town to register" (*2:3*). Luke is not showing here One who has claims to rule, but One who is coming down in humility to be involved fully in human affairs.

God brings to pass what the prophets had spoken. Micah said that Bethlehem was to be the birthplace of Jesus (*Micah 5:2-5*) for He was of the family of David. But Mary lived in Nazareth, a town 100 miles away. God saw to it that Imperial Rome sent forth a decree to compel Mary and Joseph to go to Bethlehem just as the Child was to be born. Isn't it wonderful how God uses the decree of a pagan monarch to bring to pass His prophecies! God still moves the hand of rulers to do His bidding.

Now look on! We hear the message of the angels to the watching shepherds, but we do not find the kings of the East asking for One "who is born King." Read what the angel tells the

the age at which our Lord entered His public ministry (3:23).

Genealogy

The genealogy of Jesus in Luke is given at the time of His baptism, and not at His birth (*Luke 3:23*). There are noticeable differences between the genealogy in Luke and that found in Matthew 1. In Matthew we have the royal genealogy of the Son of David through Joseph. Here it is His strictly personal genealogy through Mary. There it is His legal line of descent through Joseph; here it is His lineal descent through Mary. There His genealogy is traced forward from Abraham; here it is followed backward to Adam. Each is significant! Matthew is showing Jesus' relation to the Jewish people, hence he goes back no further than to Abraham, father of the Jewish nation. But here in Luke is His connection with the human race; hence His genealogy is traced back to Adam, the father of the human family.

In Luke our Lord's line is traced back to Adam, and is, no doubt, His mother's line. Notice in Luke 3:23 it does not say Jesus was the son of

Joseph. What are the words? "So it was thought."

The Davidic genealogy goes through Nathan, not Solomon. This too is important. The Messiah must be David's son and heir, "as to his human nature . . . a descendant of David" (*2 Samuel 7:12-13; Romans 1:3; Acts 2:30-31*). He must be a literal flesh and blood descendant. Hence Mary must be a member of David's house as well as Joseph (*Luke 1:32*).

"Jesus, full of the Holy Spirit, re-

After his baptism in the Jordan river, Jesus went into the desert, where He was tempted.

The so-called "Mount of Temptation," near Jericho.

turned from the Jordan and was led by the Spirit in the desert, where for forty days he was tempted by the devil" (*4:1-2*). Only here do we learn that the Savior was "full of the Holy Spirit" as He returned from His baptism. Then follows the account of His temptation. We may also notice that Luke is the only one to tell us that "Jesus returned to Galilee in the power of the Spirit" (*4:14*), showing that the old Serpent had utterly failed to break the fellowship of the Son of Man on earth with His Father in heaven.

As Jesus came forth from the fire of testing in the unabated "power of the Spirit," so can we. Only as we are filled with His Spirit can we overcome temptation with the power of the Spirit.

The purpose of the temptation was not to discover whether or not Jesus would yield to Satan, but to demonstrate that He could not; to show forth the fact that there was nothing in Him to which Satan could appeal (see *John 14:30*). Christ could be tried and proven.

The Ministry of the Son of Man *Luke 4:14—19:48*

Scan through Luke from chapter 4:14, and find the events in Jesus' life as they are recorded in succession.

His ministry around Galilee is recorded in 4:14 to 9:50:

Ministry in Nazareth, His home-town (*4:16-30*)
Preaching in Capernaum (*4:31-44*)
Call of Peter, James and John (*5:1-11*)
Call of Matthew (*5:27-39*)
The Pharisees (*6:1-11*)
The Twelve Apostles chosen (*6:12-16*)
Disciples taught (*6:17-49*)
Miracles (*7:1-17*)
Discourses of the Teacher (*7:18-50*)
Parables (*8:4-18*)
Real relatives (*8:19-21*)
The sea calmed (*8:22-25*)
The maniac healed (*8:26-40*)
The woman made whole (*8:41-48*)
Jairus's daughter restored (*8:49-56*)
The Twelve commissioned (*9:1-10*)
Five thousand fed (*9:10-17*)
Peter's confession (*9:18-21*)
The Transfiguration (*9:27-36*)
A lunatic healed (*9:37-43*).

Jesus' ministry in Judea is recorded in 9:51—19:27:

The seventy commissioned (*10:1-24*)
The question of the lawyer (*10:25-37*)
Jesus' friends, Martha and Mary (*10:38-42*)
Disciples taught to pray (*11:1-13*)
Seeking signs (*11:14-36*)
The Pharisees denounced (*12:1-12*)
The sin of greed (*12:13-59*)
Repentance (*13:1-9*)
The Kingdom of heaven (*13:18-30*)
Jesus talks on hospitality (*14:1-24*)
Jesus talks on self-denial (*14:25-35*)
The Savior and the lost (*15:1-32*)
The unjust steward (*16:1-30*)
On His way to Jerusalem (*16:31—19:27*).

Jesus' Jerusalem ministry is found in Luke 19:28—24:53:

A donkey tethered in Jerusalem, reminding us of the donkey Jesus borrowed on Palm Sunday.

Triumphal entry (*19:28-38*)
Rulers question Jesus' authority (*20:1—21:4*)
Future things (*21:5-38*)
Jesus' last Passover (*22:1-38*)
Jesus betrayed (*22:39-53*)
Tried before the high priest (*22:54-71*)
Tried before Pilate (*23:1-26*)
Crucifixion (*23:27-49*)
Burial (*23:50-56*)
Resurrection (*24:1-48*)
Ascension (*24:49-53*).

Following the temptation, Jesus "went to Nazareth, where he had been brought up, and on the Sabbath day he went into the synagogue, as was his custom. And he stood up to read" (*Luke 4:16*). He went to the place where He had been "brought up." Bringing up is an important thing in life. We find that Jesus was accustomed to going to the synagogue on the Sabbath day. He had been reared in a godly home.

Jesus here stated that God had anointed Him to preach deliverance to the captives, and bring good tidings to the poor and brokenhearted (*4:18-19*). He selected a text from Isaiah 61:2,

which announced the object of His whole mission on earth. He was commissioned and sent of God, and divinely qualified for His work. He is our Kinsman-Redeemer. He was made like us that He might deliver us. He became man that He might bring man close to God.

At this very early point in Jesus' ministry, we see those of His own hometown determining to kill Him (*Luke 4:28-30*). They said, "Isn't this Joseph's son?" This is the first hint of His coming rejection. He proclaimed Himself to be the Messiah (*4:21*). They were angered that He should hint that their Messiah would also be sent to the Gentiles (*4:24-30*). They believed God's grace was to be confined only to their own kind of people, and so they were ready to kill Him. He refused to work miracles for them because of their unbelief. They attempted to cast Him down the brow of the hill, but He escaped and went to Capernaum (*4:29-31*).

A World Gospel
Luke pictures Jesus as tearing down the barriers between Jew and Gentile, making repentance and faith the only condition of admission to the Kingdom. Read Luke 24:47. The gospel of Jesus Christ is not just one of the religions of the world. It is the living truth of God, adapted to all nations and to all classes. Read Romans 1:16.

As the Son of Man, Christ is looking at the needs of the Gentiles as He is looking at the needs of all people. In Luke 6, which in substance is the same as the Sermon on the Mount in Matthew, we find simple broad moral teachings, suited to the needs and wants of all people. He condenses what Matthew puts into chapters 5 through 7 into a few verses, Luke 6:20-49.

Jesus spoke choice words here to

His disciples. The Beatitudes are a picture of the Christian. "Blessed are" each one of them begins. It is not what you are striving to be, but what you are in Christ that brings you joy. The Beatitudes are a picture of Christ. They are the picture of the face of Jesus Himself, not boastingly, but truly describing the perfect Christian.

Disciples Commissioned

When the Twelve are commissioned, Luke says, "he sent them out to preach the kingdom of God and to heal the sick. . . . So they set out . . . preaching the gospel and healing people everywhere" (*Luke 9:2,6*). He omits, "Do not go among the Gentiles . . ." (See *Matthew 10:5-6*).

Wherever this Man Christ Jesus went, a whole multitude followed Him and "tried to touch him, because power was coming from him and healing them all" (*6:19*). He gave of Himself. Our service must be of this kind.

We find Jesus' power over disease and death (*7:1-17*); we find Him the sinner's friend. He had come "to seek and to save what was lost" (*19:10*). He is called "a friend of tax collectors and 'sinners'" (*7:34*).

Jesus Christ, the Teacher

The scholars—Jesus was a teacher. His disciples were taught and trained to carry on His message (*Luke 6:12-16*).

The school—Matriculation in this school is guarded. Requisites are demanded. Yet, on the other hand, entrance is easy. There is no barrier of age, sex, race or color. (Read *Luke 14:25-33*.)

Entrance requirement—"And anyone who does not carry his cross and follow me cannot be my disciple" (*14:27*). "Any of you who does not give up everything he has cannot be my disciple" (*14:33*).

Examinations—Jesus knows the ability and weakness of each student in His school. His examinations are not the same for everyone. He gives individual tests. It is easy to follow Jesus' tests with Peter. In Luke 5, He is testing Peter on obedience (*5:5*). In Luke 9:18, Jesus sprang an examination upon this impetuous fellow, and Peter gave a startling answer (*9:18-20*).

Rules to be observed—Right relationship with the Teacher must be maintained at all times. Many think that just because they have at one time entered into a relationship with the

Pilgrims in Jerusalem on Good Friday carry a wooden cross through the streets.

great Teacher, this is all that is necessary. But this is false. There must be a constant study of His Word, a laboratory time of prayer (*11:1-4*), a gymnasium of spiritual exercise (*9:59; 5:27*).

A practice school—Jesus not only taught them, but He also made them try out the great facts He presented (*Luke 10:1-12,28,36-37; 11:35; 12:8-9; 14:25-33; 18:18-26*).

The course—The course included a study of the Kingdom and the King (*Luke 7:28; 8:1; 9:2,11,62; 13:20-21; 12:32; 19:12,15; 22:29; 13:28-29; 17:20; 18:29*).

The Suffering of the Son of Man *Luke 20:1—23:56*

Jesus is sitting with His disciples around the table, celebrating the feast of the Passover. At this time, He institutes what we call the Lord's Supper. Listen to His words: "This is my body given for you . . . the new covenant in my blood, which is poured out for you" (*Luke 22:19-20*). This is different from the account in Matthew and Mark. They say, "My blood . . . which is poured out for many" (*Matthew 26:28; Mark 14:24*). His love is ex-

pressed in such a personal way in Luke. The evangelist adds: "Do this in remembrance of me" (*22:19*).

See the sad record of events in connection with His death. We find the disciples arguing over which one of them would be counted greatest in the Kingdom (*Luke 22:24-27*). We follow Peter from that moment and we read a lamentable story—one that ends in denial of his Lord and Master (*22:54-62*).

Look into the Garden of Gethsemane. Jesus is praying, and "as it were" (*KJV*) great drops of blood were on that holy brow (*22:44*). Luke tells us that the angels came to minister to Him, the Son of Man (*22:43*). Matthew and Mark omit the mention of the ministering angels.

In the shadow of the garden, a band of soldiers were approaching; leading them was Judas (*22:47*). He stepped up to kiss Jesus. Why, yes, he was a disciple. But the Scriptures had said that Jesus would be betrayed by a friend and sold for thirty pieces of silver (*Luke 22:47-62; Psalm 41:9; Zechariah 11:12*).

Worst of all, His friends deserted Him. Peter denied Him, and all forsook Him and fled except John the beloved. Luke alone tells us that Jesus looked on Peter, the denier, and broke his heart with that look of love.

We follow Jesus into Pilate's hall; then before Herod (*Luke 23:1-12*). We follow along the Via Dolorosa ("way of suffering") to the Cross (*23:27-38*). Only Luke gives the name "Calvary," which is the Latin name for "Golgotha" ("place of a skull"). Luke omits much that Matthew and Mark record, but he alone gives the prayer (*23:13-46*).

There were three crosses on Calvary's hill. On one of them was a thief, dying for his crimes. Luke tells us this story, too (*23:39-45*). The way this thief was saved is the way every sinner must be saved. He believed on the Lamb of God who died on the cross that day to pay the penalty of sin.

The scene closes with the Son of Man crying with a loud voice, "Father, into your hands I commit my spirit" (*23:46*). The centurion, in keeping with this Gospel, bears this witness, "Surely this was a righteous man" (*23:47*).

The Victory of the Son of Man *Luke 24:1-53*

We turn with great relief from the sorrow and death of the Cross, the darkness and gloom of the tomb, to the brightness and glory of the resurrection morning.

Luke gives us a part of the scene the others leave untold. It is the story of the walk to Emmaus.

He shows these disciples that Jesus, as their resurrected Lord, is just the same loving, understanding friend He had been before His death. After Jesus' walk and conversation with them, these disciples urged Him to come in and spend the night with them. He revealed who He was when He lifted up those hands that had been pierced on the cross and broke the bread. Then they knew Him, but He vanished out of their sight. On returning to Jerusalem, they found abundant proof of His resurrection. He proved to them that He was a real man with flesh and bones. All these details belong to the Gospel of Luke.

No less than eleven appearances of

A Good Friday procession through the streets of Jerusalem.

Jesus are recorded, following His resurrection—not only to individuals, but also to companies and crowds. First, to the women, to Mary, and then to the others (*Mark 16; John 20:14*); then to Peter alone (*Luke 24:34*); then to two men walking to Emmaus (*Luke 24:13*); to ten apostles in Jerusalem (Thomas being absent; *John 20:19*); and subsequently to the eleven remaining disciples (*John 20:26,29*); yet later to seven men at the sea of Tiberias (*John 21:1*). Yet again to the whole number of the apostles on a mountain in Galilee (*Matthew 28:16*); and afterward to 500 brethren at once (*I Corinthians 15:6*). Then to James (*I Corinthians 15:7*); and finally to the little group on the Mount of Olives at His ascension (*Luke 24:51*).

Three times, we are told, His disciples touched Him after He arose (*Matthew 28:9; Luke 24:39; John 20:27*). He ate with them, too (*Luke 24:42; John 21:12-13*).

As Jesus put out His hand to bless them, "he . . . was taken up into heaven" (*Luke 24:51*).

He is no longer a local Christ, confined to Jerusalem, but He is a universal Christ. He could say to His disciples who mourned for Him, thinking when gone He could be no more with them, "And surely I am with you always" (*Matthew 28:20*). How different was the hope and joy of those chosen followers from their despair and shame at the Crucifixion! They return to Jerusalem with great joy.

29. UNDERSTANDING

John

John Portrays Jesus Christ, the Son of God

The author indicates the purpose of this book in the opening eighteen verses, the prologue, and states it very plainly in John 20:31.

John wrote to prove that Jesus was the Christ, the promised Messiah (for the Jews), and the Son of God (for the Gentiles), and to lead believers into a life of divine friendship with Him. The key word is "believe." We find this word ninety-eight times in this book.

The theme of John's Gospel is the deity of Jesus Christ. More here than anywhere else His divine Sonship is set forth. In this Gospel, we are shown that the Babe of Bethlehem was none other than "the One and Only, who came from the Father" (*1:14*). There are abundant evidences and proofs. Although "all things were made" by Him (*1:3*), although "in him was life" (*1:4*), yet He "became flesh and made his dwelling among us" (*1:14*). No person can see God; therefore, Christ came to declare Him.

The author was John, "son of thunder," "the disciple whom Jesus loved." His father was Zebedee, a fisherman in good circumstances; his mother was Salome, a devout follower of the Lord who may have been a sister of Mary, the mother of Jesus (*Mark 15:40; John 19:25*). His brother was James. His position was probably somewhat better than that of the ordinary fisherman.

John had been a follower of John the Baptist. In the reign of the Roman Emperor Domitian, John the Disciple was banished to Patmos, but afterward he returned to Ephesus and became the pastor of that wonderful church. He lived in that city to an extreme old age, the last of the twelve apostles. During this time, he wrote his Gospel concerning the deity of the Christ, co-eternal with the Father.

John wrote nearly a generation after the other evangelists, somewhere between A.D. 80 and 100, at the end of the first century when all the New Testament was complete except for his own writings. The life and work of

Selected Bible Readings

Sunday: Christ Became Flesh
(*John 1:1-51*)

Monday: Christ So Loved
(*John 3:1-36*)

Tuesday: Christ Satisfies
(*John 4:1-54*)

Wednesday: Christ, the Bread of Life
(*John 6:1-59*)

Thursday: Christ, the Light of the World (*John 9:1-41*)

Friday: Christ, Our Shepherd
(*John 10:1-39*)

Saturday: Christ Promises the Comforter
(*John 14:1-31*)

Jesus were well known at this time. The gospel had been preached; Paul and Peter had suffered martyrdom and all the apostles had died; Jerusalem had been destroyed by the Roman legions under Titus, A.D. 70.

All the Synoptic Gospels, Matthew, Mark and Luke, were written before A.D. 70, the fateful year of the overthrow of Jerusalem. Already false teachers had arisen, denying that Jesus Christ was the Son of God, come in the flesh. John, therefore, wrote emphasizing those facts, and gave the witnesses and recorded the words and works of Jesus that reveal His divine power and glory.

John is more elevated in tone and more exalted in view than the other Gospels. In each of the first three Gospels, Christ is viewed in human relationship with an earthly people, but in John we find spiritual relationships with a heavenly people.

As in Luke, divine care was taken to guard our Lord's perfection in His humanity; so in John, His deity is guarded. In these days of widespread departure from the truth, the deity of Christ Jesus must be emphasized.

In John, Jesus is shown dwelling with God before ever a creature was formed (*John 1:1-2*). He is denominated as "the glory of the One and Only" (*1:14*). "This is the Son of God" (*1:34ff.*).

Jesus' Deity Revealed

In every chapter we see Jesus' deity:
  In Nathanael's confession, "You are the Son of God" (*1:49*)
  In the miracle of Cana, He "thus revealed his glory" (*2:11*)
  In His word to Nicodemus, He said He was "his one and only Son" (the "only begotten Son," *KJV*) (*3:16*)
  In His conversation with the

woman of Samaria He stated: "I who speak to you am he" [the Messiah] (*4:26*)
To the impotent man, He disclosed that "the voice of the Son of God" will call the dead to life (*5:25*)
In the bread chapter, He admits that "I am the bread of life" (*6:35*)
In the water of life chapter He proclaims, "If anyone is thirsty, let him come to me and drink" (*7:37*)
To the unbelieving Jews He disclosed, "Before Abraham was born, I am!" (*8:58*)
The blind man was told, "You have now seen [the Son of Man]; in fact, he is the one speaking with you"; Jesus' unique claim to being the Son of God (*9:37*)
Jesus stated, "I and the Father are one" (*10:30*)
Martha's declaration, "You are the Christ, the Son of God" (*11:27*)
To the Greeks, "But I, when I am lifted up from the earth, will draw all men to myself" (*12:32*)
At the supper He said, "You call me 'Teacher' and 'Lord,' and rightly so, for that is what I am" (*13:13*)
In His statement, "Trust in God; trust also in me" (*14:1*)
Likening us to branches on a vine He says, "Apart from me you can do nothing" (*15:5*)
In promising the Holy Spirit He says, "I will send him to you" (*16:7*)
In this prayer chapter He says, "Glorify your Son" (*17:1*)
In His trial He states, "You are right in saying I am a king" (*18:37*)
In His atonement He had the right to say, "It is finished" (*19:30*)
In his confession Thomas the doubter exclaimed, "My Lord and my God!" (*20:28*)
In demanding obedience, "You must follow me" (*21:22*)

Seven Witnesses

The book of John was written that people might believe that Jesus Christ was God. John brings seven witnesses to the stand to prove this fact. Here they are. Turn to the Scripture and hear each one making his or her own statement.

What do you say, John the Baptist? "This is the Son of God" (1:34).

What is your conclusion, Nathanael? "You are the Son of God" (1:49).

What do you know, Peter? "You are the Holy One of God" (6:69).

What do you think, Martha? "You are the Christ, the Son of God" (11:27).

What is your verdict, Thomas? "My Lord and my God" (20:28).

What is your statement, John? "Jesus is the Christ, the Son of God" (20:31).

What do you say of yourself, Christ? "I am God's Son" (10:36).

Seven Miracles

Besides the seven witnesses in John, we find seven signs or miracles that prove He is God. "For no one could perform the miraculous signs you are doing if God were not with him," were Nicodemus's words (John 3:2).

Look over these signs as they occur throughout the book:

Turning water into wine (2:1-11)
Healing the nobleman's son (4:46-54)
Healing the man at Bethesda (5:1-47)
Feeding the 5,000 (6:1-14)
Walking on the water (6:15-21)
Healing the blind man (9:1-41)
Raising of Lazarus (11:1-57).

Seven "I AM's"

There is another proof of His deity running through John. He reveals His God-nature in the "I AM's" of this book. He says:

"I AM the bread of life" (6:35)
"I AM the light of the world" (8:12)
"Before Abraham was born, I AM" (8:58)
"I AM the good shepherd" (10:11)
"I AM the resurrection and the life" (11:25)
"I AM the way and the truth and the life" (14:6)
"I AM the true vine" (15:1).

John, only, records the triumphant shout, "It is finished!" The finished

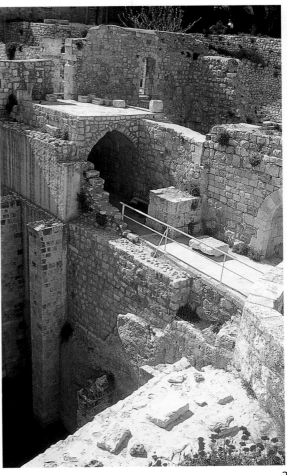

Remains of the ancient pool at Bethesda, Jerusalem, where Jesus demonstrated His power to heal.

work of salvation is accomplished only by the Son of God (*19:30*).

John says that he wrote his Gospel that people might believe that Jesus was the Christ. This part is especially for the Jews, to lead them into a personal belief in the historical Jesus "as the Messiah," who came in fulfillment of all the Old Testament prophecies.

In John, Christ the Messiah is revealed. "Messiah" means "anointed One, who comes as divine King."

To Pilate, Jesus testified that He was King.

The Great Prologue
John 1:1-18

We open the book of John with this question in mind—"What do you think of Christ?" (See *Matthew 22:42*). Is He only the world's greatest teacher or is He actually God? Was He one of the prophets or is He the world's Savior whose coming was foretold by the prophets?

All that John is to discuss in his book he crowds into these first eighteen verses.

Let us study this Gospel with John's purpose clearly in mind. Read it over again, John 20:31. Let us see how the plan is developed and how the purpose is shown as we read the book.

The Son of God

John begins his wonderful record with Jesus the Christ, before His incarnation. God did not send His Son into the world in order that He might become His Son, for He IS the eternal Son.

Our Lord had no beginning. He was in the beginning. He is eternal. Christ was before all things, therefore Jesus is no part of creation—He IS the Creator (*Colossians 1:16; Hebrews 1:2*).

"The Word was with God." He is the Second Person of the Triune God (God

the Father, God the Son, God the Holy Spirit). He is called "The Word." He came to declare God, to tell about God. As words utter thoughts, so Christ utters God. Words reveal the heart and mind; so Christ expresses, manifests and shows God. Jesus said to Philip, "If you really knew me, you would know my Father as well" (*John 14:7*).

Then comes the wonderful announcement that "through him all things were made; without him nothing was made that has been made. In him was life, and that life was the light of men" (*1:3-4*). Yes, "The Word became flesh and made his dwelling among us" (*1:14*). The full claims of Christ are given here: Truly God, Light of Life, Declarer of God the Father, Baptizer with the Holy Spirit.

The Son of Man

John does not open at the manger in Bethlehem, but before all worlds were formed: "In the beginning." Jesus was the Son of God before He became flesh and dwelt among us. "In the beginning was the Word." How like Genesis this book opens!

Christ became what He was not previously—A MAN. But Christ did not cease to be God. He was God-Man. He lived in a tabernacle of flesh here in this world for thirty-three years. Incarnation comes from two Latin words, *in* and *caro* meaning "flesh." So Christ was God in the flesh.

People had sinned and lost the image of God, so Christ "the image of the invisible God" (*Colossians 1:15*) came to dwell in people. No person could see God; therefore the only begotten Son who was "in the bosom of the Father" (*John 1:18, KJV*) came to declare Him to us.

In John, the Baptist is a witness to the Light that all men might believe (*1:7*). He points to "the Lamb of God" (*1:32-36*). These are all characteristics of this Gospel.

The sanctuary of the Temple: a close-up of the model of Jerusalem in Jesus' time.

Jesus is God Himself in human form, coming to earth. Jesus is the Witness of the Father to humans. Jesus knew the Father. He lived with Him from the beginning. He came down to tell what He knew. He wanted humans to know the Father as He knew Him.

He told by His words, His deeds, His character, His love, but most of all by His dying on the cross and His rising the third day. All this was a declaring, a witnessing, a telling.

How was Christ the Word received? Read John 1:11: "He came to that which was his own, but his own did not receive him." He presented Himself as Messiah and King to His people, but He was rejected. All through the book we see Jesus dividing the crowds. As He comes out and speaks the truth, the crowds listen. Some believe and some reject. Tragedy indeed! But not all rejected Him. John presents the results of faith.

The Way of Salvation

What we must do for salvation: (*John 1:12*):

What to do: Believe and receive.
Result: You become a child of God.
What not to count on for salvation:

Sometimes the way to better understand what a thing is, is to find out what it is not. In John 1:13, John tells us what salvation is not: being born "of natural descent . . . of human decision or a husband's will." All of these things are what people are counting on today for eternal life. The "new birth" makes us "children of God."

"Not of natural descent"—heredity; how much we depend on good birth!

"Nor of human decision"—culture and education; it is not what we know but Whom we believe that saves us.

"Nor of the will of man" *(KJV)*—prestige or influence.

"But of God"—by the power of the Holy Spirit of God. God comes down and redeems us, if we will only believe and receive Him as Savior and Lord.

Public Ministry
John 1:19—12:50

A delegation of priests and Levites were sent to ask John the Baptist who he claimed to be. He told them he was not the Messiah; he was not even Elijah or any other prophet Moses spoke of, but merely "the voice of one crying in the wilderness, Make straight the way of the Lord."

The next day, on seeing Jesus, John points to Him and says, "Look, the Lamb of God!"

Then John the Baptist indicates that he knew Jesus was the Messiah because he saw the "Spirit come down from heaven as a dove and remain on him" (1:32). So John adds, "I have seen and I testify that this is the Son of God" (1:34).

Jesus Gives Signs

Jesus' disciples were convinced of His deity by His first miracle, turning water into wine. He spoke and it was so. This was one of the big factors that brought faith into the hearts of the disciples. This was the first "sign" to prove He was the Messiah (2:11).

There was only one place where Jesus could start His ministry—in Jerusalem, the capital city. Just before the Passover, the Lord entered the Temple, and taking a scourge of cords as a badge of His authority, He cleansed the sanctuary, which He declared was His Father's house. By this act, He claimed to be the very Son of God.

When the rulers asked for a sign to prove His authority after Jesus cleansed the Temple and drove out the money changers, Jesus said, "Destroy this temple, and I will raise it again in three days." The rulers were shocked, for it had taken forty-six years to build this edifice. "But the temple he had spoken of was his body," John explains (2:19-22). The supreme proof of Christ's deity is the resurrection.

Jesus gave to Nicodemus the wonderful teachings about eternal life and His love (3:16) and the new birth (3:6). Nicodemus was a moral, upright man; yet Christ said to him, "You must be born again" (3:7). If Jesus had said this to the woman of Samaria, Nicodemus would have agreed with Him. She was not a Jew and could not expect anything on the grounds that she had been born a Samaritan. But Nicodemus was a Jew by birth and he had a right to expect something on this basis. But it was to him Jesus said, "You must be born again" in order to enter the kingdom of heaven. Have you been born again?

Like the Jewish people of his day, Nicodemus knew God's law, but nothing of God's love. He was a moral man. He recognized Jesus as a Teacher, but he did not know Him as a Savior.

Jesus revealed to one woman the truth of His Messiahship. This story gives us Christ's estimate of a single soul. He brought this immoral woman face-to-face with Himself and showed her what kind of a life she was leading. Did the woman believe Christ? What did she do? Her actions spoke louder than any words could have done. She went back and by her simple testimony brought a whole town to Christ (4:1-42).

In healing the son of the nobleman, Jesus gives another sign of His deity. During His interview with the centurion, Jesus brought him to an open confession of Christ as Lord—yes, and his whole household joining with him (4:46-54).

The miracle of feeding 5,000 was an acted parable. Jesus Himself was the Bread from heaven. He wanted to tell them, that to all who put their trust in Him will He give satisfaction and joy (6:35).

The people wanted to make Christ their King because He could feed them. How like people today! They long for someone who can give them food and clothing. But Christ would not be King on their grounds. He dismissed the excited multitude and departed into a mountain. The people were disappointed that He would not be a political leader, and so they "turned back and no longer followed him" (6:66).

The people were divided because of Jesus (7:40-44). We find unbelief was developing into actual hostility, but in His true followers faith was growing. Some people said, "He is a good man." Others said, "Not so." We must say one or the other today, when facing Christ's claims. Either He is God or an impostor. There is no middle ground.

The healing of the blind man led Jesus to reveal to this fellow who He was. When "they cast him out" because of his confession of Christ, Jesus gave a great discourse on the Good Shepherd (chap. 10). See the opposite results produced by His words in 10:19-21. Notice the accusations of blasphemy they made of Christ when He said, "'I and the Father are one.' Again the Jews picked up stones to stone him" (10:30-31). What happened in the face of all this criticism and opposition (10:42)?

The raising of Lazarus is the final "sign" of John's Gospel. The other Gospel records give the raising of Jairus's daughter and the son of the widow of Nain. But in this case Lazarus had been dead four days. In reality, would it be any harder for God to raise one than the other? Nevertheless, it had a profound effect on the leaders (11:47-48). The great claim Jesus made for Himself to Martha is recorded here, "I am the resurrection and the life. He who believes in me will live, even though he dies; and whoever lives and believes in me will never die. Do you believe this?" (11:25-26).

This scene closes with Jesus' triumphant entry into Jerusalem. His public ministry had come to an end. It is recorded that many of the chief Jewish leaders believed on Him, without making an open confession.

The traditional site of Lazarus' tomb in Bethany. The raising of Lazarus is the final "sign" of John's Gospel.

Private Ministry *John 13—17*

Here we leave the multitude behind and follow Jesus as He lived the last week of His life on earth before His crucifixion. We call it Passion Week.

Sunday—the triumphant entry into Jerusalem

Monday—the cleansing of the Temple

Tuesday—the conflicts in the Temple

Evening—the discourse on the Mount of Olives

Thursday—preparation for the Passover

Evening—the Last Supper with His disciples.

The Last Evening Together

Last words are always important. Jesus is leaving His disciples and is giving them His last instructions. This passage, John 13 to 17, is called the holy of holies of the Scriptures. Prayerfully read it all at one sitting.

Jesus divided the Jewish people—some believed Him, others had rejected Him completely. Now He gathered His own around Him in an Upper Room, and told them many secrets before He departed from them. He wanted to comfort His disciples for He knew how hard it would be for them when He was gone. They would be sheep without a shepherd.

It is wonderful that Jesus should have selected and loved men like these. They seem to be a collection of nobodies with the exception of Peter and John. But they were "His own," and He loved them.

What a picture we have in John 13:1-11! Jesus, the Son of God, girded with a towel, a basin of water in His blessed hands, is washing His disciples' feet! He wanted us to serve in the same spirit. He taught us that greatness is always measured by service. There is no loving others without living for others (vv. 16-17).

Jesus foretells His betrayal by Judas (13:18-30), and Judas goes out into the night. It was night in Judas's heart, too. Fellowship brings light. Sin brings darkness. What a pitiable picture Judas is! His opportunities of knowing Jesus were unsurpassed, but he rejected the Lord. This is what unbelief can do. Belief means life; unbelief means death.

After announcing His going, the Lord gives His disciples "a new commandment," that they love one another. Read 13:34-35. Discipleship is tested not by the creed you recite, not by the hymns you sing, not by the ritual you observe, but by the fact that you love one another.

Christ's Answer for a Life Beyond
"I am going there to prepare . . . I will come back and take you to be with me" (14:2,3). This is Jesus' cure for heart trouble—faith in God. We see there is no break between the thirteenth and fourteenth chapters.

Jesus had spoken of His Father, but now He speaks of the other Person of the Godhead, the Holy Spirit. If He

(Christ) is to go away, He will send the Comforter and He will abide with them. This is a wonderful promise for the child of God! Jesus repeats the promise in chapter 15 and again in 16. Look them up (15:26; chap. 16). Few know of this Presence in their lives. It is by His power that we live. Never call the Holy Spirit "it." He is a Person. He is One of three Persons in the Triune God (the Trinity).

"Peace I leave with you; my peace I give you" (14:27). This is Christ's legacy to us. The only peace we can enjoy in this world is His peace.

Jesus reveals the real secret of the Christian life to His disciples in John 15. "Remain ("Abide," *KJV*) in Christ." He is the source of life. Abide in Christ as the branch abides in the vine. The branch cannot sever itself and join itself whenever it will to the trunk. It must abide if it will bear fruit.

After He ended His talk with the eleven disciples, Jesus spoke to the Father. The disciples listened to His loving and solemn words. How thrilled they must have been as He told the Father how much He loved them and how He cared for them! He mentioned everything about Himself that He had taught them. He would keep them (17:11); He would sanctify them (17:17); He would make them one (17:21); and finally, He would let all His children share in His glory some day (17:24).

Let us look at the teaching about the Holy Spirit as given by John:
1. *The Incoming Spirit* (3:5): This is the commencement of the Christian life, the new birth by the Spirit. We are born by the Spirit into the family of God.
2. *The Indwelling Spirit* (4:14): He fills us with His presence and brings us joy.
3. *The Overflowing Spirit* (7:38-39): "Streams of living water will flow

from within him"—not just little streams of blessing, but rivers—Mississippis and Amazons if the Holy Spirit dwells within us.

4. *The Witnessing Spirit (14—16):* He speaks through us. This is the particular task of the Christian through the Holy Spirit—to testify of Christ.

Suffering and Death
John 18—19

Immediately following His prayer, Jesus went into the Garden of Gethsemane, knowing all things that should come upon Him. The change from the scene in the Upper Room (*chaps. 13—17 to chapter 18*) is like going from warmth to cold, from light to darkness. Only two hours had passed since Judas left the supper table. Now we see him betraying his best Friend.

"The hour" had come! The mission of our Lord on earth was ended. The greatest work of Christ remained to be done. He was to die that He might glorify the Father and save the sinful world. Christ came into the world by manger and left it by the door of the cross.

Jesus was now ready to give them the real sign of His authority in answer to the question in chapter 2. Read 2:18-19.

We see Jesus, always poised, always gentle. He knew His hour had come. He was not surprised when He heard the soldiers approach. He stepped forward to meet them. The men retreated and fell before the majesty of His look.

Follow Him, bound as a captive, to the hall of the high priest. Jesus was the One in command of the situation all through this terrible drama. He went forth (*18:4*), a voluntary sacrifice. He deliberately tasted death for every person.

Almost as sad as Judas was Peter, the deserter in the hour of need, denying three times that he had any connection with his best Friend! This is a lesson for us—overconfidence. Poor Peter is to be pitied, for he really loved the Master.

All the disciples but John deserted Jesus in the hour of His greatest need.

Jesus has come to the supreme, crowning act of His life on earth. It was not a crisis, but a climax. He came to earth to "give his life a ransom for many."

Finally the make-believe trials are over. It is morning at last, and yet it seems like night. It is the world's blackest hour. The courtyard is deserted. The fire at which Peter warmed himself is only gray ashes. The soldiers' jeers and Herod's sneers and Pilate's vacillation are over.

The brief interval between Peter's denial and Jesus' climbing the hill to Golgotha was crowded with incidents. The night trial before Caiaphas and the Sanhedrin probably preceded the last denial of Peter. Then came the awful treatment up to the morning session of the Sanhedrin.

Finally Pilate led Him forth and said, "Here is the man!" (*John 19:5*). What a sight! To see the Creator of this universe, the Light and Life of the

A rooftop view of the Old City of Jerusalem.

world, the holy One treated so! But Satan energized the religious rulers, and they cried, "Crucify! Crucify! . . . he claimed to be the Son of God" (*19:6-7*).

At the Cross, we have hate's record at its worst and love's record at its best. People so hated that they put Christ to death. God so loved that He gave people life.

Jesus was crucified on Golgotha, "place of a skull." He is crucified there today—in people's minds. They crucify Him afresh and put Him to an open shame. Salvation is costly. "Christ died for our sins" (*1 Corinthians 15:3*). It cost Him His life.

Victory over Death
John 20—21

We have a Savior who is victorious over death. He "ever liveth."

On the third day, the tomb was empty! The grave clothes were all in order. Jesus had risen from the dead, but not as others had done. When Jesus came forth, His natural body was changed to a spiritual body. The changed body came right out of its linen wrappings and left them, as the butterfly leaves the chrysalis shell. Read what John says in 20:6-8.

Jesus' appearances, eleven in all after His resurrection, helped His disciples to believe that He was God. Read the confession of the sixth witness, Thomas the doubter (*John 20:28*). Jesus wanted every doubt to be removed from each one of His disciples. They must carry out His Great Commission and bear the gospel into all the world (*John 20:21*).

Jesus gave the disciple who denied Him thrice, Peter, an opportunity of confessing Him thrice. He restored him to full privileges of service again. Christ only wants those who love Him to serve Him. If you love Him you must serve Him. No one who loves Christ can help but serve.

What are Jesus' last words in this Gospel? "You must follow me." This is His word to each one of us. May we all follow Him in loving obedience "till He come"!

History

of the New Testament

Acts

30. UNDERSTANDING

Acts Portrays Jesus Christ, the Living Lord

Luke, in his Gospel, shows what Christ began to do on earth; Acts shows what He continued to do by the Holy Spirit.

The ascension of our Lord is the closing scene in Luke. It is the opening fact in Acts (*Luke 24:49-51; Acts 1:10-11*).

Gospels and Acts

The Gospels set forth the Son of Man, who came to die for our sins. Acts shows the coming of the Son of God in the power of the Holy Spirit.

The Gospels set forth what Christ began to do. Acts shows what He continued to do by the Holy Spirit, through His disciples.

The Gospels tell of the crucified and risen Savior. Acts portrays Him as the ascended and exalted Lord and Leader.

In the Gospels we hear Christ's teachings. In Acts we see the effect of His teachings on the acts of the apostles.

Acts is not a record of the acts of the apostles, as no extensive accounts are given of any apostles except Peter and Paul. It records the acts of the Holy Spirit through the apostles. His name is mentioned about seventy times. Look for some work of the Holy Spirit in every chapter of this book.

The word "witness" is used more than thirty times.

"You will be my witnesses" (*1:8*) is the heart of the book of Acts.

Salvation comes to this world through Christ alone (*Acts 4:12*), hence people must know Him. Christ's plan includes us.

Christ told His disciples that He would send the Spirit, and "he will testify about me. And you also must testify, for you have been with me from the beginning" (*John 15:26-27*). This promise of Christ's was fulfilled on the Day of Pentecost when He poured forth the Holy Spirit upon the disciples (*Acts 2:16-17,33*), and from that moment, as they bore witness to the Savior, the Holy Spirit bore witness at the same time in the hearts of their hearers, and multitudes were brought to the Lord.

It is a wonderful thing to know that when the Spirit prompts you to speak to someone about Christ, He has been working in that heart and making it ready to receive your witness. There is a perfect example of this in Acts 8 where Philip was sent to speak to the Ethiopian. Read this ever-thrilling story!

What was the result of the first sermon on the Day of Pentecost (*Acts 2*)?

In each widening circle of influence, we find a marked outpouring of the Holy Spirit. Isn't it amazing that in one generation the apostles had moved out in every direction and had preached in every nation of the then known world (*Colossians 1:23*)?

The infant church was slow to realize what was the extent of their com-

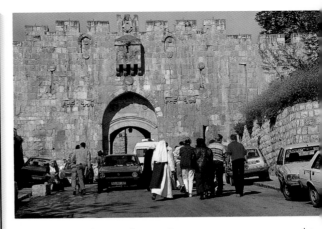

The Lion Gate, Jerusalem. By tradition, it was outside this gate that Stephen was martyred.

mission. They confined their preaching to Jerusalem until persecution drove them out. The blood of Stephen, the first Christian martyr, proved to be the seed of the growing Church.

The book opens with the preaching of the gospel in Jerusalem, the metropolis of the Jewish nation. It closes with the gospel in Rome, the true metropolis of world power.

In Acts 1 through 12, we find Peter witnessing primarily to the Jews. Peter says, "Repent" (*Acts 2:36-38*).

In Acts 13—28, we find Paul witnessing primarily to the Gentiles. He says, "Believe" (*Acts 16:30-31*).

The book tells of the extension of the gospel to the Gentiles. All through the Old Testament we find God dealing with the Jewish people. In the New Testament, we find Him working among all nations.

No doubt Acts is the best guidebook to missions that has ever been written. We find in it the motive for missions. The believers' one aim was to bring people to a saving knowledge of Jesus Christ. He was their one theme, and the Word of God their one weapon.

We find the first church pursuing a definite program in carrying out its plans. They chose some great radiating center of population for a base from which the influence of their work might spread to the surrounding area.

The disciples were simple, straightforward and successful. They depended entirely upon the power of God, through His Spirit. They moved with a zeal that could not be quenched, and a courage that was unflinching.

Power for Witnessing
Acts 1—2

What a wonderful forty days after the resurrection of Jesus the disciples spent with the Lord before His ascension! How anxious they were to hear His last words of instruction! He "spoke about the kingdom of God" (*1:3*). It was then that Jesus "gave this command: 'Do not leave Jerusalem, but wait for the gift my Father promised, which you have heard me speak about'" (*1:4*).

The disciples still were not satisfied regarding the time when Christ would set up His kingdom on earth. They still expected a Kingdom that would give them political independence and establish them in a place of leadership in the world (*1:6*). What was Jesus' answer (*1:7*)?

One day when Jesus "led them out to the vicinity of Bethany, he lifted up his hands and blessed them" (*Luke 24:50*). He told them their power was not to be political but spiritual. Listen to His words (*Acts 1:8*).

At the ascension of Christ, our Lord went "out of sight," but stayed with the people in a far more real way. After He had spoken His last words to His disciples (*1:8*), He was taken up "and a cloud hid him from their sight" (*1:9*). Think of so great an event told in so few words! The Father took His Son back to glory.

Christ Shall Return

"This same Jesus...will come back in the same way you have seen him go into heaven" (*Acts 1:11*). How will His "coming" be, as spoken of here? Will it be merely at death? Is it merely as He comes to dwell in our hearts? No. The promise is that He shall come "in the same way." If this is so, we should examine how He went. Then we shall know how He will come back.

Picture the disciples as they returned from the Mount of Olives to Jerusalem. They went into "an upper room." They "all joined together constantly in prayer" for ten days (*1:13-14*). Jesus had told them to stay in Jerusalem until they should receive power from on high (*Luke 24:49*).

Next in importance to the coming of the Lord Jesus Christ to this earth is the coming of the Holy Spirit. The Church was born on that Day of Pentecost. Become familiar with this account given in Acts 2:1-13. Pentecost was one of the most popular of the feasts, and Jerusalem would be crowded with pilgrims from everywhere. It was fifty days after the Crucifixion. From this time Pentecost was not to be a Jewish feast, but the dawn of a new day, the birthday of the Church of Christ.

The scene opens with the disciples assembled together, with their hearts fixed on Christ, waiting for His promise to be fulfilled. The Holy Spirit Himself descended that day. Luke does not say there was a wind, but sound was a symbol, as were the "tongues of fire" (*2:3*). The violent wind (*2:2*) represented heavenly power. The luminous tongues conveyed the symbol of fire, and tongues expressed power to witness. See the results of this advent in Acts 2:6,12. Fire is a symbol of divine presence. It illumines; it purifies.

The Holy Spirit at Pentecost

The Spirit fell on them (*Acts 2:1-3*). The Spirit came in them (*2:4*). The Spirit worked through them (*2:41-47*).

They were filled with the Holy Spirit and thus endowed for special service. They not only were enabled to preach in power, but also could speak in the different tongues represented that day at Jerusalem (*2:2-4*). Was speaking in new languages a jargon not understood by anyone, or were those present able to understand and benefit (*2:6*)?

The wonderful thing about Pentecost was not the "blowing of a violent wind," or the "tongues of fire," but the disciples being filled with the Holy Spirit that they might be witnesses to all people. If we do not have the desire to tell others of Christ, it is evident that we do not know the fullness of the Holy Spirit.

Do not think that at this Pentecost the Holy Spirit came for the first time to the world. All through the Old Testament we see an account of how He had been guiding people and giving them strength. Now the Spirit was to use a new instrument, the Church, which was born on that very day.

They were "amazed and perplexed" (2:12). People by nature are unbelieving. Is it not a great exhibition of God's grace when people come to believe God truly and really accept His word?

Some mocked. "They have had too much wine" (2:13). People always try to explain away the miracles of God on natural grounds. But rationalism can never give a reasonable explanation of anything that is divine. Also it was only nine in the morning, and no Jew could touch wine till then. Read Peter's defense against this false charge in Acts 2:14-21.

Peter's Sermon

The theme of this first sermon in Acts was that Jesus is the Messiah, as shown by His resurrection.

Peter is the outstanding figure in the first twelve chapters of Acts. The real power of the Holy Spirit was shown when Peter, the humble fisherman, rose to speak and 3,000 souls were saved!

It is a serious thing to charge men with murder; yet Peter did just this (2:36). Will he get away with it? Will he be stoned? The last verses in chapter 2 answer the question (2:37-47).

What a Church was this First Church of Jerusalem, organized with a membership of 3,000 on the Day of Pentecost! What glorious days followed, in "teaching" and "fellowship," and "signs and wonders," and, above all, salvation! "And the Lord added to their number daily those who were being saved" (2:47). This is the real objective of the Church.

Witnessing in Jerusalem
Acts 3:1—8:3

Chapter 3 opens at the Beautiful Gate of the Temple. Peter healed an incurable cripple, lame from birth, who had been carried daily to this place to beg for his living. The miracle attracted the notice of the Jewish leaders and resulted in the first real opposition to the Church.

When a great crowd had gathered around the lame man who had been so miraculously healed, Peter took advantage of the circumstances to preach his second recorded sermon. He did not spare his countrymen. Again he told them that Christ, whom they had crucified, was the long-promised Messiah. So powerful were the words of Peter and John that a total of 5,000 men now turned to this Christ!

The leaders were aroused because the apostles taught the people that this Jesus, whom they had crucified, had risen from the dead, and would appear again (*4:2*). They commanded the apostles not to preach; but opposition made the Church thrive. The work of the Spirit is always a signal for Satan to work. But martyrdom is an aid to the Church, and whenever the truth is faithfully preached, fruit will be brought forth. (See *4:3-4*.)

As soon as Peter and John were released by the rulers, they sought their friends and reported their experiences and united in prayer and praise. The Church must expect opposition, but in all circumstances we can find courage and help in God. See 4:31.

We find that this kind of preaching brought unity in the Church. They were of one heart and of one soul (*4:32*). They went out "to testify to the resurrection of the Lord Jesus" (*v. 33*). Let us tell it out! Dying people need it; the day demands it!

People were not compelled to part with their personal possessions. It was not expected of them. If they brought what they had, it was a purely voluntary act. Sharing property was voluntary, not obligatory; individual, not general; confined to Jerusalem; temporary; limited to believers.

The Church became so unselfish that many sold all they had and gave it to the apostles to distribute "as he had need" (*2:45*). But even this act of love and generosity was open to abuse and deception. Barnabas's liberality was an illustration of the spirit of love. Ananias and Sapphira were an illustration of deception in that they deceived themselves and the apostles as well. But the Holy Spirit revealed the truth about it all. Ananias and Sapphira wanted glory without paying the price. They wanted honor without honesty. They were punished with instant death, for, while claiming to give all to God, they had kept back part (*5:4-5*).

When signs and wonders were wrought among the people, the crowds came to see. When the Holy Spirit was in the midst, the people saw the power of God.

Miracles commonly result in converts. Look in this book of Acts. When the miracle of tongues appeared, the people thronged to the place (*Acts 2*). When Peter healed the man at the Gate Beautiful, "all the people were astonished and came running to them in the place called Solomon's Colonnade" (*3:11*). When the miracle of judgment came upon Ananias and Sapphira, "More and more men and women believed in the Lord and were added to their number" (*5:14*). So we will find instances all through the book.

There will be plenty of service in the church when we give place to the Holy Spirit. The Spirit-filled church will be a serving church.

"Then the high priest and all his associates . . . arrested the apostles and put them in the public jail" (*5:17-18*). Again we see that the wonderful work of the apostles aroused the opposition of the Sanhedrin (a court of seventy religious rulers). A few unlearned fishermen had risen up to teach, and multitudes were listening and following after them; hence the religious leaders were disturbed. Even though the apostles were beaten with rods and prohibited to preach, we find them rejoicing that they were counted worthy to suffer shame for His name! Read Acts 5:42. We find their boldest words in this statement: "We must obey God rather than men!" (5:29). Is this the conviction of your life?

A meeting of the Church was called, and seven members elected as deacons (6:1-7). There were two offices in the Church now. One was to "serve tables," to attend to the benevolence and to care for the needy. The other office was to devote itself to preaching and prayer.

The first two deacons named were Stephen and Philip (6:5). These two men were mighty in their influence over the Church, perhaps more than any besides Peter and Paul.

The opposition was centered around Stephen. Read the experiences as recorded in Acts 6 and 7. Stephen was just a layman, but he was one of the first deacons. He is described as a man "full of God's grace and power" (6:8). We have a record of only one day of his life—the last.

The leaders in the synagogue "could not stand up against his wisdom or the Spirit by whom he spoke" (6:10). Their anger flared into murderous hatred. Stephen was the first martyr of the Christian Church. To Stephen's death we may trace, without doubt, one of the most outstanding impressions made by the followers of Christ on Saul (see Acts 22:20).

Witnessing in Judea and Samaria Acts 8:4—12:25

The disciples had been witnesses in Jerusalem, but Jesus had told them

they must go into Judea and Samaria.

See what kind of a Church this Early Church was. "Those who had been scattered preached the word wherever they went" (8:4). This is the reason the gospel spread at first.

Roman colonnade at Samaria. Philip, one of the seven who had been chosen as a deacon, had settled in Samaria as a result of the persecution.

Philip, the Evangelist

Philip (not the apostle), one of the seven who had been chosen as a deacon (Acts 6:5), was an evangelist. He had settled in Samaria as a result of the persecution. Jesus had said, "You shall be my witnesses . . . in Samaria." Philip preached Christ. Multitudes were following him in his evangelistic campaign. But God called him to leave his successful work and "Go south to the road—the desert road—that goes down from Jerusalem to Gaza" (8:26). Philip obeyed and left, and on the way he met an Ethiopian. "By chance," you say? When you are in the will of God, things do not just happen.

Philip's convert no doubt preached the gospel in Africa. There is nothing to show that Africa previously had any knowledge of the Son of God. The gospel was on its way to the "uttermost part of the earth."

Samaria

Saul

At Stephen's death, we have the first mention of Saul. Stephen's martyrdom seemed to have inflamed this persecutor of the Church. The story of Saul's conversion is one of the most thrilling accounts in history. He was a man "breathing out murderous threats against the Lord's disciples" (*9:1*). Then we find him preaching "in the synagogues that Jesus is the Son of God" (*9:20*).

At every step of his three great missionary journeys, Paul made known Christ's will with unmistakable clarity. There is no doubt that Paul holds the most important place of any man in the New Testament. He was converted and made an apostle by Christ Himself. It was to him that Christ gave first-hand revelations of truth, and to him Christ committed the doctrine of the Church. To what people was Paul especially sent? He was the apostle to the Gentiles, as Peter had been to the Jews.

Peter

What had Peter done since Pentecost? Christ had told Peter that he was to be a witness. Peter helped start the first Church, worked miracles and baptized thousands. His work had been among the Jewish people.

We find Peter now in the house of Simon the tanner (*10:5-6*). God was going to show Peter that the gospel was for the Gentiles as well as the Jews (*Acts 10:9-16*). The high wall of religious difference between Jew and Gentile must be broken down.

At Pentecost, Peter had used the "keys of the kingdom" (see *Matthew 16:18-19*) entrusted to him to open the door of the gospel to the Jews. While Paul was in Tarsus, Peter in the house of Cornelius put the key into the lock of the door that had barred the Gentiles, and opened it (*Acts 10:1-48*).

Witnessing in Earth's Uttermost Parts *Acts 13—28*

The death of Stephen was only the beginning of great persecution of the believers in Jesus, most of whom were Jewish. How did they ever get to Antioch? (*Acts 11:19-21*). Someone has called the Church in the early days "A Tale of Two Cities"—Jerusalem and Antioch.

Up through Acts 12, we have seen the beginning of the Church, with Peter as its leader, in Jerusalem. From Acts 13 through 28, we are going to see Paul and the Church at Antioch. Antioch is the new base of operations. All the wonderful missionary journeys of Paul started from here, not from Jerusalem. It became the new center of the Church for carrying out Jesus' commission.

The Jewish believers in Jesus who had been compelled to leave Jerusalem because of persecution were naturally thrown in with all the Gentiles. They could not help but talk about that which interested them most. The power of the Lord was so manifest that a great crowd joined the Church (*11:21*).

It was here in this church that a new name was given to Christ's disciples. They were first called "Christians" at Antioch (*11:26*).

It is interesting to note here that the Church had lost track of Paul. They did not care what had become of him, but Barnabas looked him up (*11:25*). If it had not been for Barnabas, Paul might have remained in obscurity all his life!

Beginning of Foreign Missions

We see Paul and Barnabas, the first foreign missionaries, starting westward from Antioch (*Acts 13:2-3*). The greatest enterprise in the world is foreign missions, and this is the very start of this great movement. The whole idea began just the way it should, at a prayer meeting.

While Paul and Barnabas were preaching the gospel and suffering all kinds of persecution and hardship, many at home in Jerusalem were stirring up the most troublesome question the Church had ever faced. It was this: "Must a Gentile become a Jew, accepting Jewish laws and ceremonies, in order to be saved?" (*15:1*). Paul and Barnabas had said nothing about the law of Moses. They had stated: "Believe in the Lord Jesus, and you will be saved" (*16:31*). The law doesn't save anyone.

Luke now joined the missionary party (*16:10*). The first convert in Europe was not a famous scholar or some mighty ruler, but a businesswoman, Lydia, a seller of purple dyed garments.

In Philippi, we find Paul and Silas in prison. Why do we find men like

The Areopagus, "Mars Hill", Athens, where Paul preached his immortal sermon.

these locked behind iron bars? Read Acts 16:16-24. The second Christian in Europe was very different from the first. Lydia was converted in a prayer meeting, but it took an earthquake to arouse the next convert—a jailer. The jailer's question is one of the most important questions in all the world (*16:30*).

Paul's First Missionary Journey

Paul's Second Missionary Journey

MACEDONIA
Philippi
Berea
Neapolis
Thessalonica
Amphipolis
Apollonia
Troas
GALATIA
AEGEAN SEA
ASIA
Corinth
Athens
Ephesus
Iconium
Cenchreae
Lystra
ACHAIA
Derbe
Tarsus
Antioch
RHODES
SYRIA
MEDITERRANEAN SEA
0   50   100 mi
0   50   100 km
Caesarea
Jerusalem

Paul's experiences in the greatest cities of his day are crowded with interest. He founded a church at Thessalonica (*17:4*).

In famous Athens, Paul preached his immortal sermon on Mars Hill. This is one of the great scenes in history. What effect did it have on those listeners (*Acts 17:32*)?

Paul left Athens and arrived at Corinth, very much discouraged. We do not know whether he was successful in starting a church in Athens, but in Corinth, one of the most wicked cities of the ancient world, he founded a church and remained there eighteen months to establish the people in the faith (*18:8*). Here Paul found Aquila and his wife, Priscilla, who afterward became his loyal friends.

After an absence of three or four years, Paul returned to Antioch by way

of Ephesus. In Antioch he reported his entrance into Europe.

Paul's Third Missionary Tour

Now we find Paul spending three years in one of the greatest cities of his day. Next to Rome, Ephesus was perhaps the world's largest and most cosmopolitan city. Multitudes of Jews and Gentiles of Asia heard the gospel preached. Ephesus was notorious for its luxury and licentiousness, and for the worship of the goddess Diana. The years Paul spent here are so crowded with interesting details that it is hard to choose the most important. Enthusiastic converts burned their books on "the black art," magic, and threw away their silver idols. There was a great bonfire in Ephesus.

Such blessings as these could not last long without opposition. If we read on to the end of the chapter, we will see the results of Paul's work. The silversmiths stirred up a riot, and the apostles were rescued from danger only by the help of the city officials.

As Paul traveled, he kept writing his wonderful letters. We read them today with great profit and interest. From Ephesus, Paul sent his First Epistle to the Corinthians (*1 Corinthians 16:8*). During this third journey, Paul wrote 2 Corinthians, Galatians and Romans.

Paul's Farewell

Paul's last missionary journey must have been a heartbreaking experience. He had to say farewell at every place. He knew it was a final farewell. Read Acts 20:37-38. They all wept and "embraced him and kissed him," the Middle Eastern expression of sorrow, knowing they would never see him again.

Remains of the Temple of Apollo, Corinth, one of the most wicked cities of the ancient world.

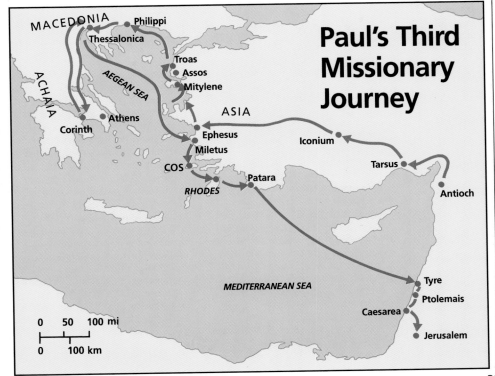

Paul's Third Missionary Journey

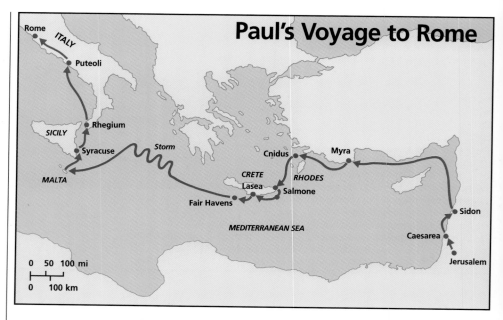

Paul's Voyage to Rome

Rome
ITALY
Puteoli
SICILY
Rhegium
Syracuse
Storm
MALTA
Cnidus
Myra
CRETE
RHODES
Lasea
Salmone
Fair Havens
Sidon
MEDITERRANEAN SEA
Caesarea
Jerusalem

0 50 100 mi

0   100 km

Sailing out of the harbor of Ephesus, Paul bids his friends a last farewell. He is headed for Jerusalem, and from now on he is seen as "the prisoner of the Lord." Paul makes his last visit to Jerusalem, and here one of those swiftly formed mobs that gather so quickly in the excitable East rushes against the apostle and binds him, declaring he is teaching the Jewish people to forsake Moses. Finding that Paul is a Roman citizen, the chief captain promises to give him a fair trial. Paul makes his defense before the Roman governor Felix at Caesarea. After two years' imprisonment, Paul is tried a second time before the new governor, Festus, and appeals from him to Caesar himself, the emperor (*21:27—26:32*).

After a most exciting voyage, in which his ship was wrecked in a terrific storm off the coast of Malta, Paul arrived in Rome. Here he was kept a prisoner in his own hired house for two years. Even in prison the great preacher and evangelist led the servants in Nero's own palace to Christ. Service for the Master can brighten life's darkest hours. When we seek to lift others' burdens, we lighten our own (*27:1—28:24*).

During his imprisonment, Paul wrote many of his Epistles—Philemon, Colossians, Ephesians and Philippians. It was probably during a second imprisonment in a dungeon in Rome, expecting at any hour to be beheaded, that he wrote his second Epistle to Timothy.

Paul changed the Early Church from a sect within Judaism to a worldwide influence. He tried to break down the barriers between Jew and Gentile and between slave and free.

Letters of Paul
of the New Testament

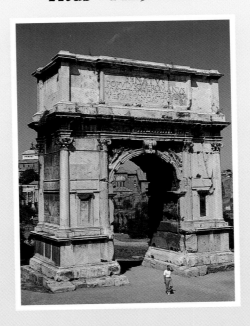

31. UNDERSTANDING

Romans

Romans Portrays Jesus Christ, Our Righteousness

We now begin a study of the Epistles (letters) in the New Testament. Thirteen of the twenty-one were written by Paul, hence they are called the Pauline Epistles. He wrote his letters to the churches at Thessalonica, Galatia, Corinth and Rome during his missionary journeys. While he was a prisoner in Rome he wrote his letters to the church at Ephesus, one to the Colossians, one to Philemon and one to the Philippians. After his imprisonment, he wrote two letters to Timothy and one to Titus.

Paul was born at Tarsus, "circumcised on the eighth day, of the people of Israel, of the tribe of Benjamin, a Hebrew of Hebrews; in regard to the law, a Pharisee" (*Philippians 3:5*). His teacher was Gamaliel, the great teacher of the Pharisees. Like all Hebrew boys, he learned a trade—he was a tentmaker. At Jerusalem, he was present at the stoning of Stephen, the first Christian martyr. No doubt this scene made a tremendous impression upon the young Saul. On the way to Damascus, on a mission of persecution of the Christians, the young Pharisee had a head-on collision with Jesus Christ! After his miraculous conversion, he was baptized and received his commission to preach the gospel. He spent three years in Arabia in study and preparation.

After laboring for three years in Tarsus and one year in Antioch, directed by the Holy Spirit, Paul became the great missionary to the Gentiles. On his three missionary journeys, he founded many churches and wrote his Epistles. The combination of Roman

Part of the ancient forum, Rome.

Selected Bible Readings

Sunday:	What We Are by Nature (*Romans 1:1—3:20*)
Monday:	How to Become a Christian (*Romans 3:21—5:21*)
Tuesday:	How to Live a Christian Life (*Romans 6:1-23*)
Wednesday:	A Struggle (*Romans 7:1-25*)
Thursday:	The Life of Victory (*Romans 8:1-39*)
Friday:	The Jews Set Aside (*Romans 9:30—11:12*)
Saturday:	The Christian's Service (*Romans 12:1-21*)

citizenship, Greek education and Hebrew religion wonderfully qualified him for his great work, but you will find that he trusted alone in the grace and apostleship he received directly from Jesus Christ (*Romans 1:5*).

The Church at Rome

Paul was eager to visit the church at Rome, and sent them this letter from Corinth, from the home of Gaius, a wealthy Corinthian Christian, while he was on his third missionary journey. It was written in the fourth year of Nero, then Emperor of Rome. In this Epistle, he sets forth his gospel (*Romans 1:16-17*).

Paul the servant (*1:1*), writes to the saints at Rome (*1:7*), concerning the Savior (*1:3-4*).

After Paul's greeting to the church, he thanks God for their faith (*v. 8*). Notice Paul's expression of obligation to this church (*vv. 14-15*):

"I am debtor" (*KJV 1:14*)

"I am eager" to fulfill my obligation (*1:15*)

"I am not ashamed" of the message (*1:16*).

Why was Paul not ashamed of the gospel of Christ? Because it reveals what the sinner needs and what he may have on the ground of simple faith. "A righteousness of God"—the righteousness of Jesus Christ.

The gospel has dynamic power. It is the power of God unto salvation. Do you realize that nothing short of the power of God could make one Christian?

Paul was not ashamed of the gospel of Christ even in Rome. The terrible sinfulness of humans, as pictured in 1:18-32, had reached its climax in Rome.

After Paul states the subject of the book of Romans, in 1:16-17, he then reveals people's need of this righteousness. *For all have sinned, and all the world may become guilty before God.* From his elevated pulpit, Paul looks around and sees zealous Jews, proud Greeks, boastful Romans and a multitude of ordinary, common sinners like ourselves. What a terrible picture he presents in 1:18-32! First the unrighteousness of the Gentiles is portrayed; then that of the Jews.

The book of Romans tells us of God's method of making guilty people

Tombs along the ancient Appian Way, outside Rome. Paul was probably executed in Rome.

Rome

good. The key of this great thesis is found in Romans 1:16-17.

The Person of the gospel—Christ

The Power of the gospel—"power of God"

The Purpose of the gospel—"for salvation"

The People to whom sent—"to everyone"

The Plan of acceptance—"to everyone who believes"

The Particular result—"the righteous will live by faith."

Paul was proud of the gospel because he had proved its power in his own life and in the lives of all who would believe.

The first three chapters describe the hell of sin. The last five chapters describe the heaven of holiness. Intervening chapters describe Christ, the Way.

In Romans, Paul shows us God's method of making a guilty person good. He reveals a sinner's needs and then presents what the person may have by faith: a righteousness from God—Christ, our righteousness. The righteousness of God is a Person. The righteousness God demands is in a Person, Jesus Christ. No one will ever get into heaven with any less righteousness than Christ's righteousness. When you look at Jesus, you see the righteousness God requires.

What We Are by Nature
Romans 1:1—3:20

Why do we need salvation? Because we are sinners. The book of Romans presents a courtroom scene. God, the Judge of all the earth, summons Jew and Gentile before the bar of justice. Prisoner after prisoner is brought up.

The general charge is stated—"all under sin" (*Romans 3:9*). Both the Gentile (*2:1-16*) and Jew (*2:17—3:8*) are given the opportunity for a hearing.

Their special pleas of "not guilty" are carefully considered and answered, clearing the way for the final verdict from the Judge.

Finally the Judge pronounces the verdict: the "whole world held accountable to God" (*3:19*). If this were today, newspapers everywhere would blaze this headline. All the television reporters would be announcing it. Can't you hear them? "ALL – THE – WORLD – FOUND – GUILTY!"

The condemnation of the world is settled. The next step in order will be to reveal the plan of God to save a lost world. Remember, the book of Romans tells us God's method of making people good.

Do not say, "God is love. He will not condemn me." Listen to God's words here: "The wrath of God is being revealed from heaven against all the godlessness" (*1:18*). He has already passed sentence on everyone. "All . . . guilty." There is no chance of appeal. It is the decision of the Supreme Court of the universe. Sin is universal—"All have sinned!" Hence we need a world's Savior. Because God is a God of love, He has provided just this One! Repeat aloud John 3:16. The Judge on the bench says, "Is there anyone to appear for the prisoners?" Then the Son of God says, "Yes, I am here to represent these. It is true that they committed these sins. It is true that they are guilty, but I bore their guilt on the cross. I died in their place that they might go free. I am their righteousness." And the Judge sets them free.

We get an awful picture of sin in these first three chapters of Romans. Remember, "sin" is a marksman's word. It means "missing the mark"—the standard God has set for us. God's Word says, "For all have sinned and fall short of the glory of God" (*3:23*). Fall short in our good deeds? No—of the glory of God. Do not measure your life by any other standard but this. Do not compare yourselves among yourselves. Of course you may not have fallen as short as some others you know, but you are "short" as far as God is concerned. We are all sinners because we were born into a sinful race.

Christ not only saves us from the penalty of sin, but He is also able to free us from the consciousness of guilt and the power of sin. The result of sin is a sense of guilt. The first thing that is necessary for the freedom of a sinner is that the dreadful consequences of the person's guilt be taken away. The sinner needs more than pardon, for that would leave the person with his or her guilt. Any president or governor or king can pardon a criminal, but not one has the power to remove the guilt. Proper punishment for the deed must be given. This is what Christ has done. "The wages of sin is death" (6:23) and because all of us "have sinned," Christ came to die and bear the penalty for the sins committed against a holy God.

How to Become a Christian
Romans 3:21—5:21

Question: How does God save sinners? Answer: "Through the redemption that came by Christ Jesus" (*Romans 3:24*). When God looks at us, He sees no righteousness (*3:10*). When God looks at us "in Christ," He sees not only an improvement, but also perfection, for God sees only His own Righteousness, Jesus Christ.

You have become acquainted with one great word of Scripture, "salvation." Here is another—"justification," "just-as-if-I'd. . . ." Everything Christ has done has been credited to my account. His righteousness is mine!

When Christ's righteousness is reckoned as ours, this is called "justification"—we are counted just (righteous) before God. "The just shall live by faith." No one is counted just because of works, but rather by believing on Christ (*3:28*). Not only are we saved by faith, but we must also live by faith, trusting in Christ.

Paul gives us illustrations of justifi-

The Colosseum, Rome. Many believers faced martyrdom in this great arena.

cation by faith from the Old Testament. Especially does he tell us of how Abraham's faith was counted for righteousness (*chap. 4*). Abraham received three things by faith: righteousness, inheritance and posterity (*4:3,13,17*).

We, too, have great benefits when we are justified by His grace. Grace is unmerited favor. In this life, we find that faith is followed by peace, pardon and promise (*5:1-5*) and more than all, an assurance of salvation (*5:6-11*). How can a person be justified by God? Read Romans 3:24-28.

Salvation

You will find the stream of sin and the river of salvation running along together from Romans 1 through 16. "Where sin increased, grace increased all the more" (*Romans 5:20*). Paul shows sin in all its squalor and salvation in all its splendor. Some simple steps in these next paragraphs will show you how to become a Christian!

One does not have to be a sinner in the sight of people to be lost. Of course there is a difference in the degree of sin, but not in the fact of sin and its results, "for the wages of sin is death." We may be drowned in seven feet of water and be as dead as if we had been submerged in seventy feet of water. In our inability to save ourselves, we are all on the same level— "There is no difference" (*Romans 3:22*).

We are saved by Christ's righteousness. He has made it available for us by His death. We are "justified freely by his grace through the redemption that came by Christ Jesus. God presented him as a sacrifice of atonement, through faith in his blood" (*3:24-25*).

I am a person condemned to die because of my sin, "for the wages of sin is death." But I can look on the cross and see that Christ has already died for

me. I believe that He died for my sin. And so in exchange for my poor, sinful, condemned life, I can accept His righteousness and His life (*1 Peter 2:24*).

"Whoever believes in the Son has eternal life" (*John 3:36*). "But now a righteousness from God, apart from law, has been made known, . . . This righteousness from God comes through faith in Jesus Christ to all who believe" (*Romans 3:21-22*). Apart from a person's effort to be good, God has provided His righteousness, the Lord Jesus Christ. Our righteousness is as filthy rags (*Isaiah 64:6*).

Your sin is on Christ. He has borne it for you. Have you accepted Him as your Savior and passed from death unto life (*John 5:24*)? If you have decided to let Christ be your sin bearer, you now have His salvation (*Romans 3:24*).

Justified by Faith

A murderer may stand at the bottom of a mine and you on the highest peak of the highest mountain, but you are as little able to touch the stars as he. You cannot attain unto the righteousness that God demands, no matter how far you climb.

Forgiveness is the removal of our unrighteousness, an unclothing or putting away of sin.

Justification is the act of being clothed with the righteousness of God's own providing. It is perfect.

The person who put faith in Christ an hour ago is just as much justified as the oldest Christian living. We never become any more justified than the minute we received Christ.

Justification depends upon something done outside of us, something done on the cross of Calvary.

Justification takes care of all the sin and guilt upon us, buries all this sin and guilt in the grave of Jesus Christ, and then sets us in heavenly places with Christ our Savior.

None of us likes the idea of being called a "sinner," but we must face what we are. Listen to what Paul says in Romans 5:12-21. We were born sinners. When I was born in this body, I was born a descendant of Adam. I have his nature, which is sinful. When I am born into the family of God, by Christ Jesus, I have Christ's nature, which is holy. In the words of Scripture, "For as in Adam all die, so in Christ all will be made alive" (*1 Corinthians 15:22*). I did not choose to be a descendant of Adam. I may choose to be a child of God. If one man's sin made it possible for all the race to die, one Man's righteousness made it possible for all the race to get out of this condition (*Romans 5:15*).

How to Live a Christian Life
Romans 6—8

We have learned how to become a Christian. Now we must find out how to live like a Christian.

In Romans 6, there are three important words.

1. "Know" that Christ died for you (*6:3-5,10*); know that you died with Christ (*6:8*).
2. "Reckon" (*KJV*) on this! "In the same way, count yourselves dead to sin but alive to God in Christ Jesus" (*6:11*). Reckoning makes things real! Because we are dead to sin and alive unto God, how shall we live? (See *6:13*.)
3. "Yield" (*KJV*)—Read 6:13. This means "let go" of your life and "let God" live through you. This is the surrendered life.

Romans 6 reveals the secret of a life of victory. I am living in Christ! Dead to sin but alive to God! It tells me how I can lead a Christian life. Self, we have learned, was a condemned thing, un-

able to be good, never righteous (*chap. 3*). Now when self becomes a Christian and tries to live a Christian life, it finds this to be impossible. We are saved by faith, and we cannot live by our own efforts.

This sad truth is revealed in Romans 7. It tells us why we cannot live a victorious life. Mark the little *I* and you will find it is used thirty-eight times in the twenty-five verses of this chapter (in the *KJV*). The Holy Spirit is never mentioned. Although *I* tries, it finds only defeat.

Read the words of the man who tries to live by his own effort in Romans 7:24-25.

Finally, *I* finds that there is One who is sufficient. Struggling yields to power, defeat is changed to victory, misery is transformed into joy. When *I* goes out, Christ comes in.

The life "in Christ" is a wonderful thing. Paul says, "Because through Jesus Christ the law of the Spirit of life set me free from the law of sin and death" (*8:2*). This is what happens. When I am in an airplane I am free from the law of gravity. The higher law operates in the plane to lift it above the clouds, although the law of gravity a few minutes before held me fast to the earth. The law of gravity is not destroyed, but rendered inoperative.

This is what happens in my life when I am "in Christ." The law that operates by the Spirit in my life lifts me above the world and sin, and sin no longer has dominion over me. I am free. I am without condemnation.

This glorious chapter opens with "no condemnation," and ends with "no separation." This is a picture of our life "in Christ." Christians are safe: Christ is around them; the Spirit is within them; and God is for them.

Why Israel Is Set Aside
Romans 9—11

The story of the Jewish people being set aside and scattered throughout the world without a homeland, without a king is a warning for us (*Romans 9—11*). God is a sovereign God, and He will do what He will. He has a perfect right to turn to the Gentiles, because most Jewish people would not seek the righteousness of God, which is by faith (*9:32*). They tried to set up their own righteousness. But people do not build up righteousness. They only receive it. If God will put aside His chosen people, will He not put us aside if we are disobedient? The Old Testament story of the Hebrew people is a solemn lesson to us. Read the wonderful description of God's mercy in Romans 11:32-36.

How to Serve God
Romans 12—16

Read Romans 12:1. It may surprise you to find out that up to this point we have not had to do a thing but believe on Christ and yield ourselves to Him to use as He will. Now we are to serve!

The first part of Romans is what God did for us. The last part of Romans is what we may do for God.

We find our Christian service in:
Church (*12:3-8*)
Government (*13:1-14*)
Disputed things (*14:1—15:3*)
The whole world (*15:4-13*).

32. UNDERSTANDING
First Corinthians

First Corinthians Portrays Jesus Christ, Our Lord

The name "Lord" is very prominent in this book (*1 Corinthians 1:31; 2:8,16; 3:20; 4:4; 5:4-5; 6:13*, etc.). This is full of meaning because much of the confusion that had crept into the church at Corinth had come because the believers failed to recognize Jesus Christ as Lord.

Corinth was the most important city of all Greece in Paul's day. Its wealth was fabulous. Men spent their days in tournaments and speeches. Luxury, dissipation and public immorality were rampant among this great industrial and seafaring population. Corinth attracted great crowds of foreigners from the East and West. Their gods were gods of pleasure and lust. There was, besides, much culture and art. The city abounded in studios of language and schools of philosophy.

As in most cities, there was a large colony of Jews who had kept a strong moral standard and held to their religious beliefs. But the city itself was the center of a debased form of the worship of Venus.

If we read Acts 18, we find how the gospel reached this wicked city. The apostle Paul, then a man about fifty years of age, in the garb of a working man, entered the busy metropolis and went through its streets in search of a workshop where he might earn his own living. This tradesman came into town and began his tentmaking. This was a leading industry in that day, as building is today. He went into business with the well-to-do tentmakers Aquila and Priscilla. He was always able to support himself, making enough to carry on his missionary work. A wonderful work was done in Corinth during the year and a half Paul was there. He began by speaking in the synagogues to mixed congregations of Jews and Greeks.

First Corinthians is a difficult book to outline, for it takes up many wonderful subjects. It deals with Christian conduct.

Selected Bible Readings

Sunday: Division in the Church (*1 Corinthians 1:10-31*)

Monday: Human Wisdom (*1 Corinthians 2:1-16*)

Tuesday: Worldliness in the Church (*1 Corinthians 3:1-23*)

Wednesday: Immorality in the Church (*1 Corinthians 5:1-13*)

Thursday: The Lord's Supper (*1 Corinthians 11:1-34*)

Friday: Hymn of Love (*1 Corinthians 13:1-13*)

Saturday: The Resurrection (*1 Corinthians 15:1-58*)

Corinth

Corrections in Christian Conduct
1 Corinthians 1—11

The wonderful church at Corinth, the brilliant jewel in the crown of Paul's labor, was failing. The worldliness (carnality) of the city had infected the fellowship of believers.

Practices common to this wicked city soon crept into the church. There were divisions among them; Christians were going to law with Christians before heathen judges; behavior at the communion table was disgraceful; the women of the church no longer observed standards of modesty; the church membership was arguing over marriage and even spiritual gifts. Finally, the church wrote Paul about these things and asked his advice on the matter. These two letters to the Corinthians were written in answer to their requests.

After the usual greeting (*1 Corinthians 1:1-3*), Paul refers to the coming again of our Lord Jesus Christ (*1:7-8*). Then he plunges right into the question of the failure of the church about which he had been told. The source of his information he gives us in 1 Corinthians 1:11.

People had lost sight of God. Three kinds of selfishness had blinded them:
Self-admiration, their intellect had been perverted.
Self-will, their conscience had been darkened.
Self-indulgence, their passions had been given full rein.

The greatest danger to the Corinthian church was from within.

Paul speaks first of the divisions and cliques about which he had learned from friends and travelers. Nothing eats out the heart and life of the Church like party politics.

The Greek spirit of party politics had entered into the church, dividing it into four parties, each trying to get the mastery. Their names are given in 1 Corinthians 1:12. Paul, Apollos and Peter (Cephas) were parties named for their favorite teachers. The Christ Party held to that name as if it did not belong to everyone in the church.

This dissension about religious leaders meant that the Christians at Corinth had slipped off center. There is only one Leader in every church. That Leader and center is Christ. If the Church gets off center here, it goes off all down the line.

Jesus Christ is the only cure for division (*1 Corinthians 1:13*). Every eye, every heart, every spirit must be turned to one object—Jesus Christ, our personal Savior. Paul said, in effect, "Your factional spirit is a sin. Can you follow a mere man, hoping that he can give you life? Was that man crucified for you? Trusting in what people have to say is foolish. People see nothing in the cross of Christ. Christ alone has all the power and wisdom of God."

The Cross

"A stumbling block to Jews," an obstacle they could not get over (*1:23*). The Jews could not understand how such a display of weakness could be a source of power. A man dying on a cross did not look much like a world Savior to them. The scribes and Pharisees scornfully turned from the Cross. To them, the Cross meant failure. The Jews needed signs of power. They demanded something they could see and grasp. The Messiah must be a world prince, a miracle worker.

"And foolishness to Gentiles." The Greek-influenced Gentiles regarded with contempt the unscientific religion first taught in an unschooled corner of the world like Nazareth, by the son of a carpenter who never studied in Athens or Rome. The Greeks idolized brains. But God has never despised the humble things.

Either the Cross is the "power of God" or it is "foolishness." If "foolishness," then you think it is unfit to do any good in your life.

Paul did not preach Christ the conqueror or Christ the philosopher, but Christ crucified, Christ the humble. Read his words in 1 Corinthians 2:2. Paul remembers that his words will be tried by fire (*3:13*). To know Christ crucified is the maximum of knowledge.

The Minister

One objection to Paul was that his preaching was too simple. He answered that he could not preach any differently because they were mere babes in Christ. They could not stand anything but a milk diet. The proof of their childish state (carnality) was in this division among them (*3:1-4*).

Paul points out that the Christian minister is not the head of a school or a rival sect, as the Greek philosophers. He is the servant of God, not a master of people. Paul always called himself a servant of the Lord Jesus Christ. Christian service is only acceptable to God when done in the spirit of Christ, for His glory.

Everyone has four faces—one the world knows, one our friends know, one we know ourselves, one God knows. Paul describes this in 1 Corinthians 4. Do not depend on human judgment. The world judges our character upon a single act. The voices of criticism may be loud, but if you go high up on the hilltop with God, you will see the bustle of the crowd, but you won't hear it.

Beware of your friends' judgment because they may be too favorable in their opinion of you. We like to believe all the good things said about us and resent unfavorable criticism.

Paul says, "I do not even judge myself" (*1 Corinthians 4:3*). Beware when you stand at the bar of your own conscience. When your conscience says to you, "You may do it," it is always well to go to Jesus Christ and say, "May I?" It is hard to be fair with ourselves. No one, no matter how honest, is permitted to judge in his or her own cause.

Paul says there is one judgment to which he will submit—one that is always right. "It is the Lord who judges me" (*4:4*). I am Christ's steward and to Him am I ultimately responsible. From His judgment there is no escape. His calm eyes are upon me. Seek praise from Him, which is praise indeed.

Vice in the Church

The Corinthians, living in the Hollywood of their day, needed admonition just as we do. Righteousness is from Christ and for Christ. "What would Jesus do?" should be the query to every questionable thing of life. Christ in you is the secret and the way of life.

In the church at Corinth, a member actually was having an incestuous affair with his own stepmother, which was socially immoral among the pagans to say nothing of Christians. Paul reproves them for being puffed up with pride while this scandal existed in the church. He urges them not to

A quiet corner of Nazareth. The Greek-influenced Gentiles regarded with contempt the religion first taught in an unschooled corner of the world such as Nazareth, by the son of a carpenter who never studied in Athens or Rome.

tolerate evil among them while calling themselves Christians. Just as leaven spreads through all the dough, so a bad person's spirit spreads through all the Church. The Church should exclude the wrongdoer so as to prove that it does not condone sin (5:13). Discipline in the Church should always commence with mourning and sympathy, not anger or pride or revenge (5:2).

Paul then makes a personal application, useful in our own lives. "Therefore let us keep the Festival . . . with bread without yeast, the bread of sincerity and truth" (5:8). Self-examination is often the most difficult thing we do, but it is one of the most important.

"Do you not know" ("Know ye," KJV) is one of Paul's expressions. His faith was built on facts. He wanted to know things. Underline the "know ye's" in chapter 6. What are we supposed to know?

First, Paul makes the statement that, although it might be necessary at times for Christians to go to law, Christians never should quarrel with each other and then drag this quarrel before a worldly court. What a terrible impression of Christianity this gives to the world! We say when we do it, "We, as Christians, are just as bad as other folk. We want our way. We are covetous and just as ambitious for our own rights as you are." Paul says, "Dare you do such a thing?"

Paul then gives us a picture of the Corinthians as he found them, in 6:9. When we finish verse 11, we find what grace has done!

Christ has paid a great price to purchase us, and it is His purpose to make us like Himself (6:19-20).

If our bodies have been redeemed by the Lord Jesus Christ, then they no longer belong to us, but to the One who purchased us with His precious blood. "You were bought at a price."

God used to have a temple for His people; now He has a people for a temple, see Ephesians 4:30.

Liberty Not Recklessness

The Scripture does not lay down little rules for our conduct, and tell us just the things we ought to do or not do, but rather states principles that should guide the Christian's actions. Someone has well said that Christian liberty does not mean the right to do as we like, but rather to do as we ought. Paul puts it, "'Everything is permissible for me'—but not everything is beneficial. 'Everything is permissible for me'— but I will not be mastered by anything" (1 Corinthians 6:12). If your liberty harms another, then your liberty has gone too far.

Yes, I can do anything I want to, but I must be sure my desires are to please Christ. What I do is an example to others and may harm or bless them. I should not only answer the question, "Does my action harm weaker Christians?" but also, "Does it glorify God?"

Marriage

Paul discusses the subject of marriage for the Christian. Controversy had arisen between the Jewish and Greek philosophers about the importance of marriage. Paul would keep the church from scandal, hence his words in 1 Corinthians 7:2. Society is pure and virtuous in proportion as marriage is deemed honorable. Some of the church had tried to discourage marriage, and others thought that when one becomes a Christian one should divorce a heathen mate. But Paul was wise. He knew the evil condition in Corinth and advised every man to have his own wife and every woman to have her own husband. He did not believe in a Christian divorcing a pagan partner. He told them that perhaps the

Christian would lead an unbelieving mate to Christ *(7:16)*.

Mark 1 Corinthians *7:9,13* in your Bible. Think over these verses. They will tell us much of our Christian responsibility to those who are not Christians.

The Lord's Supper

Paul gives a careful account of the beginning of the Lord's Supper and then tells of its value.

It was established on the night in which Christ was betrayed.

It is celebrated in remembrance of His undying love for His followers.

It was a symbol of His body, which was broken for them *(10:16)*.

It was a new covenant in His blood.

It was a pledge of His coming again *(11:26)*.

We should be careful not to eat or drink in an unworthy manner. "A man ought to examine himself" *(11:28)* and never eat without self-critique and thankful love.

And "For whenever you eat," do it "in remembrance of me" *(see 11:26)*. Christ wants us to remember Him! Think on Christ when you go to His table. He longs for your love!

It was the custom of the Corinthian church to eat a meal in connection with the Lord's Supper. They all brought food for themselves. Often this led to excesses among the rich, while the poor had nothing. What an unworthy observance of the supper itself this led to! Paul reminds them of the deep spiritual significance of this supper, and of the scandal of their behavior.

Paul closes this scene with these words: "And when I come I will give further directions" *(11:34)*. Other things needed to be straightened out, but he would leave his corrections and go on with his instructions.

Instructions in Christian Conduct
1 Corinthians 12—16

In 1 Corinthians 12, we see the gifts the Spirit gives to believers. In verses 1-3, he tells of the change that had come into the lives of these Corinthian Christians when they turned from worshiping dead idols to the living Christ. So they might develop in their

Christian lives, Christ gave them the gifts of the Spirit (*12:4-7*). The Holy Spirit is the Giver of spiritual gifts (*12:8-11*). One cannot teach the Scriptures unless the Spirit gives wisdom. One must pray "in the Spirit" and to sing acceptably to God "in the Spirit." Sometimes we say when we look at a successful Christian man, "My, he is a man of natural abilities," when really he has received many gifts from the Spirit.

Many people in Paul's day were making much of the spiritual gifts Paul mentions. They were coveting the more showy gifts, such as speaking with tongues.

The Corinthian Christians were using these gifts as ends in themselves. Many people today, like the Corinthians of old, pray constantly for the power of the Spirit. They forget that all the gifts God gives were given that Christ might be exalted and others blessed. If God gives me any little gift at all, He gives it not that I may gather people about myself, but that it may through me be a blessing for others. God gave these nine gifts mentioned in 1 Corinthians 12 to assist in the founding of the new church, but they were being used by people to gratify their pride. Paul shows that the purpose of the gifts is for building the church (*chap. 12*); that they should be used in love (*chap. 13*); and that their value was to be measured by their usefulness to the church.

God gave gifts such as healing, miracles and tongues, we believe, for "sign" gifts (*12:12*), to prove to the world that Jesus was the true Messiah and that the apostles were divinely appointed. These miracles, tongues, visions and signs were given to put the stamp of authority upon the apostles and their preaching. Today we are also to believe and walk by faith. If it is God's will for us to have any of these

gifts, He will give them to us; otherwise He will not. The Holy Spirit "gives them to each one, just as he determines" (*12:11*).

The way to use these gifts the Spirit gives is beautifully told in 1 Corinthians 13. This chapter is called the Hymn of Love. Gifts without love are poor things. People talk of love, but they do not live it. Until the love of Christ is in a heart, it is impossible for people to love one another with any degree of permanency. People seem to worship force. But history shows us that the victories of force do not last.

The Pillars of the Gospel

No doubt there was a group in the Corinthian church who did not believe in the resurrection of the dead. Paul in answering this starts out by giving a wonderful statement in 1 Corinthians 15:1-11 of what the gospel is. Paul did not give a new gospel. It was the old gospel, given in Genesis, Exodus and Leviticus.

1. Christ died for our sins according to the Scriptures (*15:3*).
2. He was buried (*15:4*).
3. He rose again the third day according to the Scriptures (*15:4*).
4. He was seen by many witnesses (*15:5-6*).

If we deny the Resurrection, we deny one of the greatest of all truths of the gospel. Preaching is vain; faith and hope are all vain. But more than all that, no resurrection would mean no gospel at all, for we would be worshiping a dead Christ. There would be no "good news," for there would be no proof that God had accepted Christ's death as an atonement for our sins. If a sailor on jumping overboard to rescue a drowning man were drowned himself, then we would know that he did not save the man after whom he went. If Christ did not come out from the grave, then He could not bring anyone with Him from the grave. Christ's body died, and it was His body that was raised again. His soul was committed into the hands of the Father.

Because Christ lives, we shall live also. "Where, O death, is your victory? Where, O death, is your sting?" (*15:55*).

Paul gives the many proofs of Christ's resurrection in 1 Corinthians 15:

1. Christ's resurrection
2. His coming again
3. Resurrection of believers
4. Overthrow of Christ's enemies
5. His glorious reign
6. Our mortal bodies shall be changed to immortal.

33. UNDERSTANDING
Second Corinthians

Second Corinthians Portrays Jesus Christ, Our Sufficiency

Paul was somewhat worried about how the church at Corinth would receive his first letter. He wondered how they had accepted his rebukes, so he sent Titus, and perhaps Timothy, to Corinth to find out the effect of his Epistle. During Paul's third missionary journey, while he was in Philippi, Titus reported that the majority of the church had received the letter in the proper spirit. But there were those who doubted his motives and even denied his apostleship, saying that he did not have the proper credentials for an apostle. Perhaps they questioned this because he was not one of the original Twelve.

Under these circumstances he wrote his second Epistle, to express his joy over the encouraging news of how his first Epistle had been received, and to defend his apostleship.

Paul gives more of his personal history in this letter than in any of his other Epistles. He reveals his courage and his self-sacrificing love. He speaks of glorying or boasting thirty-one times because he was compelled to. Read 2 Corinthians 12:11.

Paul tells us of some things that happened in his life that are revealed only in this letter.

His escape from Damascus in a basket (*11:32,33*)

His experience of being caught up to the third heaven (*12:1-4*)

His thorn in the flesh (*12:7*)

His unusual suffering (*11:23-27*).

The Temple of Apollo, Corinth, the only building from Paul's time to survive the Roman development of the city.

An Orthodox Jew at Jerusalem's Western Wall. The teachers of Jewish law of Paul's day were among his chief trouble-makers

He begins by telling of the great trouble through which he had been passing. Through all of his trials he had learned to know God better. God is always made more real to us in times of sorrow. We find that God never fails.

Paul's sufferings in Asia were of a very serious nature. Very likely he went through a dangerous sickness in which they despaired of his life (*1:4-11*). He appreciated their prayers and now he was appealing to their love and sympathy. He wanted them to be ready for much that he was to write about concerning the defense of his apostleship.

Paul had a clear conscience about his sincerity and faithfulness while he labored among them. He explained that he sent his first letter instead of coming himself, that when he did come he might be able to praise and not scold them (*1:23—2:4*). To this statement he calls God to witness.

The teachers of Jewish law of Paul's day carried letters of introduction with them. They were Paul's chief troublemakers. They tried in every way to fight him. We hear them asking, "Who is this Paul?" "What letters of recommendation from Jerusalem does he have?" How foolish this question was to Paul! Did he need a letter of recommendation to a church he himself had established? He answers, "You yourselves are our letter, written

He told none of these until he was compelled to, to prove that if we wanted to boast, he had good reason.

The epistle begins with "Comfort": "Praise be to the God and Father of our Lord Jesus Christ, the Father of compassion and the God of all comfort" (*1:3*).

It closes with "Comfort": "Finally, brothers, good-by. Aim for perfection, listen to my appeal, be of one mind, live in peace. And the God of love and peace will be with you" (*13:11*).

In the middle we find the reason for comfort: read 9:8.

The source of this comfort is: "'My grace is sufficient for you'" (*12:9*).

Paul's Ministry
2 Corinthians 1—7

Paul opens this second Epistle with his usual greeting and thanksgiving (*2 Corinthians 1:1-3*). Everyone loves a true story. Paul tells so many personal experiences of his life in this letter that it makes everyone love to read it.

on our hearts, known and read by everybody" (3:2).

The lives of true Christians at Corinth served as letters to recommend both Paul the servant and Christ the Lord. Living epistles are read when Bible Epistles are not. Remember your life is an open letter. Christian lives are about the only religious books the world reads. They do not study God's Word, but they do study God's people. This gives us a great opportunity for good, for we may lead people to Christ.

Paul's gospel was a triumphant and transforming gospel (3:18).

Paul's ministry was a triumphant one, but it was filled with suffering. Warfare always is full of illustrations of triumph through suffering. Victory costs! Paul tells us much about his tribulations (chaps. 4; 6; 11). When Paul was so gloriously converted, the Lord said, "I will show him how much he must suffer for my name" (Acts 9:16). It seems as though the trials began immediately and followed his pathway for thirty years. But Paul was always optimistic because he knew that afflictions here would increase glory beyond (2 Corinthians 4:17-18).

Paul could sing as he suffered for he knew the wonderful grace of God. He was always conscious of the presence of the Lord Jesus Christ. He knew that the greater the suffering in this present world, the greater the glory of eternity (4:8-18). Paul lived with his eye on the future!

Paul finds his comfort through all his troubles in the fact of the resurrection that Christ promised. He lived under the inspiration of the fact that one day he was to have a changed, glorified body. Our suffering bodies will soon be exchanged for painless glorified bodies. Whether we live or die, we must keep this reward in view (2 Corinthians 5:10).

The aim of Paul's ministry is that people may be reconciled to God (5:20). People are God's greatest concern. As Christ's ambassador, he makes his appeal to people of the world.

He follows this with an appeal to holy living (6:11—7:16). Holy living means wholly unto God. Read these verses, every one! He appeals to his fellow workers not to receive God's loving kindness in vain, but to open their hearts to Him. God demands a clean and separated life. He wants Christians to separate themselves from unbelievers.

Liberal Giving
2 Corinthians 8—9

Paul tells the church at Corinth of the generosity of the churches of Macedonia to the Palestine Famine Fund. Although poor themselves, they begged for an opportunity to give, and they gave liberally because first they gave themselves to the Lord. The fund was gathered from all the churches of Asia Minor and Greece. It had been started a year before (1 Corinthians 8:10). Paul was in Macedonia at the time he wrote this. He had accepted no pay for his work from any of the churches except Philippi. Christ was the example for these early Christians (8:9). The Lord knows that if He gets us, He will get our gifts and our service.

How should we give?
Give out of your poverty (8:2)
Give generously (8:3)
Give willingly (9:7)
Give proportionately (8:12-14)
Give cheerfully (9:7)
Give bountifully (9:6).

God has ever promised to reward the generous giver (9:6). He enriches us with spiritual graces as well as with material things. These gifts strengthened the ties of brotherhood between

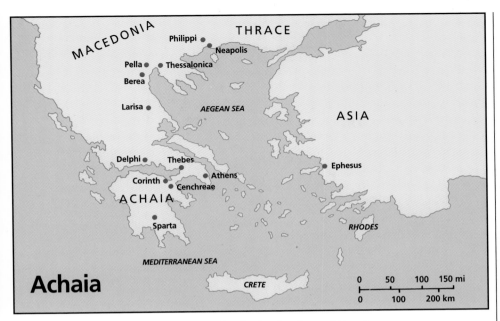

Achaia

the Jewish and Gentile Christians. "Thanks be to God for his indescribable gift!" (*9:15*).

Paul's Apostleship
2 Corinthians 10—13

The charge against Paul by some in the church was that he was a coward. He was bold in his writings, but was weak in personality.

His enemies said that no apostle would work with his own hands and support himself; they pointed to the other apostles. But Paul explained that he had the right to receive pay, yet refused it lest his example be abused by these false teachers who would commercialize the ministry. He declared that at least he founded his own churches and did not go around troubling churches founded by others, as they were doing.

Paul stated also that if these false teachers could boast of their power

and authority, then he would boast, too. In a dramatic manner, he challenged these critics to compare themselves with him in every way. He was a loyal Hebrew; he had worked more than all the rest of them put together; as a martyr he had suffered more than they all, on land and sea. He realized the poor taste of boasting about oneself, and he disliked to do it, but they had forced him to it. When Paul boasted, it was for the glory of God.

"When they measure themselves by themselves and compare themselves with themselves, they are not wise" (*2 Corinthians 10:12*). We all have a tendency to take a wrong standard for measuring character. We compare ourselves among ourselves. We conclude we are as good as the average. But average Christians are not what the Bible requires. Let us pray Wesley's (John Wesley, 1703-1791, British, founder of the Methodists) prayer, "Lord, make me an extraordinary Christian."

Paul was caught up into "paradise," even to the third heaven. Recall that Jesus went into paradise at His death (*Luke 23:43*). There Paul had been given marvelous visions and revelations, and heard things that could not be put into speech (*2 Corinthians 12:4*). No doubt no human language could describe the glory. It would have been like trying to picture a sunset to a person born blind. Paul had nothing to compare it with that we could understand.

It seemed as though because of these heavenly experiences, God allowed Paul to suffer "a thorn in [his] flesh." The Lord knows the danger of pride of heart after such an experience, and so He permitted a "a messenger of Satan, to torment [him]." Paul himself called his affliction "a thorn in my flesh" (*12:7*). There have been many speculations about what this "thorn" really was. It would appear that God has not told us what it was so that all might know that the grace that was sufficient for Paul in his trouble would be enough for any thorn given to any of us.

Purpose of Testing

Many wonder why God does not remove "thorns" from the flesh when we pray to Him. We must learn that God always answers prayer, but some-

times the answer is no. He knows it will be better for us to bear the thorn than be without it. "Thorns" in the flesh have made many to lean on Christ. Paul says, "For when I am weak, then I am strong" (*12:10*). There is strength and courage in the heart in which Christ is dwelling.

The Duty of Self-Testing

"Examine yourselves to see whether you are in the faith; test yourselves" (*2 Corinthians 13:5*). In this second letter, Paul emphasizes that the Corinthians might know themselves— test themselves to make sure of their faith. He was anxious that none of them should be deceived. Use every means to know where you really stand spiritually.

Examine yourself about the motives that move your life. Is it to please God or people? What do you love? The adversary always tells us we are "good enough," but Christ says we must be perfect. Here are some tests to use:

Do I love to think of Christ?

Do I love to pray?

Do I love to study God's Word?

Do I love Christian friends?

Do I love the Church?

Do I love to serve Christ?

Second Corinthians closes with the benediction that today brings to a close many a church service (*13:14*).

34. UNDERSTANDING

Galatians

Galatians Portrays Jesus Christ, Our Liberty

Galatians shows that the believer is no longer under the law but is saved by faith alone. "It is for freedom that Christ has set us free. Stand firm, then" (*Galatians 5:1*). The "law" is that portion of God's Word found in the first five books of Moses (*Genesis—Deuteronomy*) by which every phase of Israel's life was to be guided.

During Paul's second missionary journey (*Acts 16:6*), he was delayed in Galatia by sickness (*4:13*). Though ill, this tireless servant of the Lord could not remain silent, but kept on preaching the gospel. The theme of his sermon was "Christ crucified" (*3:1*). It was at this time that he succeeded in founding the Christian churches in Galatia (*1:6*). They were scattered over a rural district and the people were country folk. Teachers of the law had followed Paul, teaching salvation by works, claiming that even if Christianity were true, Christians should be circumcised and do all the works of the law. These teachers explained that the reason Paul had not taught the Galatians this was that he was not a true apostle and had learned his doctrines from others. This had upset the new converts.

Circumcision was the initial rite of the Jewish religion. If people born Gentile wished to become Jewish, they had to observe this ceremonial law. It was much like foreigners in our country taking out citizenship papers.

If they actually take out papers, although born on foreign soil, they are just as much a citizen as those born here.

False teachers had begun to "bewitch" the people by telling them they must keep all kinds of ceremonies. Paul wanted them to know that nothing, no fetishes or works or ceremonies could bring them to Christ. Salvation comes by believing on Christ—nothing else.

Being very fickle and loving something new and a change, the Galatians were on the verge of accepting the views of these false teachers. When

Selected Bible Readings

Sunday: Only One Gospel
(*Galatians 1:1-24*)

Monday: Justified by Faith
(*Galatians 2:1-21*)

Tuesday: The Law Points to Christ
(*Galatians 3:1-29*)

Wednesday: Law and Grace
(*Galatians 4:1-31*)

Thursday: Stand Fast in Christian Liberty (*Galatians 5:1-16*)

Friday: Sinful Nature Versus Spirit (*Galatians 5:17-26*)

Saturday: Sowing and Reaping
(*Galatians 6:1-18*)

Paul heard it, so urgent did the matter seem that, because no one was with him to write it, he wrote the letter himself (*6:11*).

It has been said that Judaism was the cradle of Christianity and very nearly its grave. God raised up Paul as the Moses of the Christian Church to deliver it from this bondage. This Epistle has done more than any other book in the New Testament to free our Christian faith from Judaism, and from the burden of salvation by works, taught by so many false cults, which has threatened the simple gospel of the Lord Jesus Christ. Many people want to do something to be saved. The question of the Philippian jailer, "What must I do to be saved?" is the question multitudes ask. The answer is always the same. "Believe in the Lord Jesus, and you will be saved" (*Acts 16:31*).

A religion without the cross is not Christ's religion. Christ did not come merely to blaze a trail through a tangled forest or to set us an example of true living. He came to be a Savior. The power of the Cross is:

To deliver from sin (*1:4; 2:21; 3:22*)
To deliver from the curse of the law (*3:13*)
To deliver from the self-life (*2:20; 5:24*)
To deliver from the world (*6:14*)
In the new birth (*4:4-7*)
In receiving the Holy Spirit (*3:14*)
In bringing forth the Spirit's fruit (*5:22-25*).

This Epistle of Galatians is the Christian's Declaration of Independence. Liberty is not freedom from law—that is recklessness. Liberty is freedom from the Mosaic law system, but subjection to "Christ's law" (*1 Corinthians 9:20-21*). Paul speaks of the liberty we have "in Christ" (*2:4*). "Where the Spirit of the Lord is, there is freedom" (*2 Corinthians 3:17*). This is the one great secret of liberty.

This is the liberty that is told of in this book, so get hold of Galatians and let Galatians get hold of you. In Galatians we are not servants working for a living, but sons working in our living. Learn what it is to be free in Christ! Christ said, "I no longer call you servants, . . . Instead, I have called you friends" (*John 15:15*).

Galatians contrasts Law and Grace:
In Romans we find our *standing*.
In Galatians we take our *stand*.

Introduction *Galatians 1:1-11*

This is the only time in all of Paul's writings in which he does not express his thankfulness. Rather he says, "I am astonished" (*1:6*). This is the only church of whom he does not ask prayers. How could he, seeing they were bringing dishonor upon the Lord (*Galatians 1:6-9*)?

Paul marvels that these new Christians could give up the gospel of liberty so quickly and accept a legalistic message that was no gospel at all. Twice he pronounced a curse upon those causing the trouble. He says if an angel from heaven were to preach any other gospel than the one he preached "let him be eternally condemned ("accursed," *KJV*)!" (*1:8-9*).

What was this gospel Paul preached? Paul's gospel shuts out all works. "Know that a man is not justified by observing the law, but by faith in Jesus Christ . . . because by observing the law no one will be justified" (*2:16*). The difficulty about salvation is not that we should be good enough to be saved, but that we should see that we are bad enough to need salvation. Christ can save only sinners. Grace cannot begin until the law has proven that we are guilty, as the book of Romans shows each of us to be. Then Christ offers us His righteousness.

A gospel of mixed law and grace has no power. The false teachers of this kind of gospel were "accursed" because they pervert (not deny) the gospel. They admitted that Christ must die upon the cross, but denied that faith alone in His sacrifice was sufficient for salvation. They taught that to be saved one must keep some part of the law at least. They thought that simple faith according to the gospel Paul preached was not sufficient for salvation. People still like this kind of preaching because they believe they can do something to obtain merit before God.

Paul shows us the seriousness of our condition outside Christ. When a medical specialist says, "Your only hope is this or that," you know you must be in a critical and serious condition. Here are the words of a great gospel expert. Paul declares that our position is so serious that the gospel of the grace of God is our only hope. There is no other.

Paul introduced the atonement (*1:4*), a truth once so dear to them, but now practically rejected. Christ gave himself for our sins.

Paul Defends His Apostleship
Galatians 1:12—2:21

Paul's teaching was authorized by God Himself (*Galatians 1:11-24*). He proves that he received his gospel directly from the Lord. Only God could have changed him from a murderer to a preacher.

We can learn many things by experience, but that is not so with the things of God. To know them they must be revealed to us. "I did not receive it from any man, nor was I taught it; rather, I received it by revelation from Jesus Christ" (*1:12*).

Paul did not consult with anyone about what he should preach, but retired to the wilds of Arabia for three years and there listened to God. He was taught by the Spirit. He had been with Peter and James only fifteen days after the three years in Arabia so he couldn't have learned much from them.

The authority behind Paul's gospel is shown by his rebuke of Peter (*2:11-21*). To prove that Peter was not a greater apostle than he, he points out in Galatians 2:11-21 how he had openly rebuked Peter for being two-faced about Jewish customs when he was in Antioch. He made no secret attempt to undermine Peter's authority. Paul was not dominated by this strong apostle to the Jewish people. Verse 11 is an unanswerable argument against the supremacy of Peter. "I want you to know, brothers, that the gospel I preached is not something that man made up" (*1:11*). It is good to know that the friendship between Peter and Paul was so real that it stood this severe test. (See *2 Peter 3:15*.)

What does "justified" mean? God credits to my account what Christ has done—just-as-if-I'd done it. A criminal is pardoned though the person cannot be regarded as righteous. But justification is that act of God whereby He not only forgives us, but also puts Christ's righteousness to our account. God justifies sinners without justifying our sin. He gives us a righteousness not our own, but Christ's.

How are we justified? "Not by works" (*Galatians 2:16-17, KJV*). Works are excluded! We are not justified by the works of the law, but by the faith of Jesus Christ.

There are no degrees of justification. The moment we believe on Christ we are made just. Justification is:

By God (*Romans 3:26; 8:33*)
By grace (*3:24*)
By blood (*3:25; 5:9*)
By faith (*3:21-28*).

Paul ended his great apology by a personal word of testimony, which gives us a complete picture of the Christian life both positively and negatively. "I have been crucified with Christ and I no longer live, but Christ lives in me. The life I live in the body, I live by faith in the Son of God, who loved me and gave himself for me" (*Galatians 2:20*). It is a paradox.

This verse is true of every believer.

We do not need to be crucified with Christ. We have been crucified with Him. He died in our place. Now we live not by law but by faith. Christ was our sacrifice for sin and now is our sufficiency for the new life. The Christian life is a dying life—dying daily to self and sin. The crucified Savior lives in those who have shared His crucifixion.

Paul Defends the Gospel
Galatians 3:1—4:31

Religion is the best people can do. Christianity is the best God can do. See the results of people's best: "by observing the law no one will be justified" (*Galatians 2:16*). How can a person be made just? "By faith in Christ and not by observing the law" (*2:16*). Christianity is God's best. Christ is no sheriff. He is "the Lamb of God, who takes away the sin of the world" (*John 1:29*). We are pronounced righteous not by works of the law, but by faith in Him.

Paul is defending the gospel of Christ. He describes his own preaching as having so fully set forth the cross that it was as if they had seen Christ crucified in their midst (*Galatians 3:1*). He shows what the law could not do, but what grace had done.

Paul puts a challenging question to these "foolish Galatians." He cries, "O foolish Galatians, I have brought you the true gospel, and you received it with eagerness and gratitude. Now suddenly you drop the gospel. What has got into you?

"Come on now, my smart Galatians, you who all of a sudden have become professors while I seem to be your pupil, did you receive the Holy Spirit by the works of the law or by the preaching of the gospel?" (author's paraphrase). This question was a challenge to them because their own experience proved the truth of Paul's preaching to them.

"You cannot say you received the Holy Spirit because you kept the law. Nobody ever heard of such a thing. But as soon as the gospel came, you receive the Holy Spirit by the simple hearing of faith," Paul adds (author's paraphrase).

It is hard for us to believe that the priceless gift of forgiveness of sins and the gift of the Holy Spirit are not gained by real effort, but God offers them to us free of charge.

"Consider Abraham: 'He believed God, and it was credited to him as righteousness'" (3:6). Abraham may have had a good standing with others for his upright life, but not with God. In God's sight, Abraham was a condemned sinner. You see righteousness had been given to Abraham on the ground of his faith, not his works. If faith without works was sufficient for Abraham, why should we turn from faith to law? "Abraham believed." That is faith. Faith says to God, "I believe what you say."

It must have startled the proud and troublesome legalists when Paul told them that not those born of Abraham's flesh and blood, but those who believe in Christ Jesus are the true children of Abraham (3:26-29). Though born in obscurity, through the new birth, all can sit down with Abraham as a child of the father of the faithful (3:14,29). Abraham believed God and it was accounted to him for righteousness (3:6-7).

The Curse of the Law

The curse of God is like a flood that swallows everything that is not of faith. Remember, the law Paul is talking about is not civil law. Civil law has its place, but civil righteousness will never deliver a person from the condemnation of God's Law. Just because I am a law-abiding citizen does not mean I am a Christian. Governmental laws are blessings for this life only, but not for the life hereafter. Otherwise many unbelievers would be nearer heaven than some Christians are, for unbelievers often excel in civil righteousness. The civil courts require that you keep the law. The court of heaven

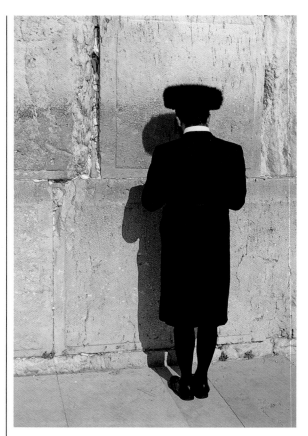

An Orthodox Jew at the Western Wall. "Christ redeemed us from the curse of the law by becoming a curse for us" (3:13).

us. O foolish Galatians, who hath bewitched you, that ye should turn from the blessing of faith to the curse of law?" (author's paraphrase of several verses).

The law deals with what we are and do, while grace deals with what Christ is and does. What good is the law? We find the answer in Galatians 3:19-20. Everything has its purpose. Let us see the purpose of the law. The law is given to restrain the wicked by giving punishment for crime, just as civil laws keep people from murder and theft because of the fear of jail or the electric chair. These restraints do not make people righteous, but they do restrain them from crime.

Another purpose of the law is spiritual. The law reveals to us our sin, and blindness and contempt of God. As long as we are not murderers or thieves, we would swear we are righteous. How does God show us what we really are? By the hammer of the law. As long as we think we are right, we are proud and despise God's grace. This monster of self-righteousness needs a big ax, and the law is just that. When people see by the law that they are under God's wrath, they begin to rebel and complain against God. The law inspires hatred of God. What does this beating by the hand of the law accomplish? It helps us to find the way of grace. When the conscience has been thoroughly frightened by the law, it welcomes the gospel.

Law reveals sin, but does not remove it. The law proves that we are all sinners by nature and directs us to Christ! We so often think that we become sinners when we commit some sinful acts. But it is because we are already sinners that we commit the act. We lie because we are liars. We steal because we are thieves. We do not become liars when we utter the lie. The law only proves we are liars.

requires that you have faith in Jesus Christ.

The law cannot give righteousness but it does bring death upon all those who do not keep it (*Galatians 3:10*). Law demands perfect obedience. The Bible tells us that a curse (a sentence) is upon all who break the law, while a blessing is upon all those who live by faith.

"Christ redeemed us from the curse of the law by becoming a curse for us" (*3:13*). As all had broken the law, all had come under its curse. But Christ has redeemed us. "Don't turn back to the law from which Christ redeemed

The law too was given to drive us to Christ by showing us our need. The gospel tells us that Christ is the only One who can meet that need (*3:23—4:11*). Paul says the law was our "schoolmaster" *(KJV)* to shock us into a sense of our need of Christ that we might be justified by faith in Him (*3:24*). God's law is not like the cruel schoolmaster of former times, a regular tyrant. His law is not to torment us always. God's law is like the good schoolmaster who trains children to find pleasure in doing the things they formerly detested. The law really has a place in leading us into a Christian experience.

Sons of God

Paul tells us that all are not the children of God. We find that it is faith in Christ, not works of the law or the Fatherhood of God or the brotherhood of people, that makes us children of God. "You are all sons of God through faith in Christ Jesus" (*Galatians 3:26*). Faith, not works, puts us into the family of God.

As long as an heir is underage there is no difference between that person and a slave, for the heir is under the control of a guardian. So Paul shows us in Galatians 4:5-6 that all believers are children of God, yet all children are not "sons"—grown-up ones. "Adoption" is a Roman legal word and means "the placing of a son" in a son's legal position. It might be receiving into a family one who does not belong to it by birth or the legal act of acknowledging the person coming of age. Christ came to ransom us so that we would be no longer slaves under the law, but possess all the privileges of full-grown sons and daughters and heirs.

As another illustration of their state of freedom in Christ, Paul reminds them that Abraham had two sons—

Contrasts in the Book of Galatians

Grace and Law
The one thing that distinguishes our Christian faith from all others is the grace of God. Grace is unmerited favor of God to us when we are undeserving.

Law shows us our need.
Grace shows God's provision to meet that need.
Law says we must work for our salvation—"Do."
Grace says salvation is free, a gift—"Done."

Faith and Works
Faith makes us receive salvation by believing.
Works keep us striving to earn it.

Fruit of the Spirit and Works of the Flesh
The Spirit gives us daily victory over sin.
The flesh makes us prone to sin.

Cross and the World
The Cross means love and sacrifice.
The world suggests force and selfishness.

Ishmael, the child of Hagar the bondwoman, and Isaac, the child of Sarai the free woman. Ishmael did not enjoy the blessings of a son in Abraham's house, but was left out in the cold, although he was the firstborn; Isaac was called. This is what happens to those who seek to be saved by keeping the law. But Isaac, the child of promise and faith, was the heir of all things. So we are heirs of a spiritual promise.

Paul Desires the Gospel Be Applied *Galatians 5—6*

The first application of the gospel pertains to one's own personal freedom from the law. Paul wants the Galatians to hold fast to their personal liberty. The gospel of God's grace gives true liberty (*Galatians 5:1-12*). "It is for freedom that Christ has set us free. Stand firm, then, and do not let yourselves

Harvesting with the sickle in the traditional way. If we sow to the Spirit, we shall reap a spiritual harvest.

be burdened again by a yoke of slavery" (*5:1*). If the Galatians seek to be saved by keeping the law, they are bound by the law. Their liberty should be prized because it cost so much, the blood of Christ.

The gospel of grace guards against recklessness (*Galatians 5:13-15*). Many people are afraid to live under grace instead of law for fear it will lead others to "live as they please and do as they like." Grace will always lead a person to live as God pleases and like what He likes.

We abuse our liberty:

By lack of love (*Galatians 5:13-14*). "Serve one another in love. The entire law is summed up in a single command: 'Love your neighbour as yourself.'" Use love!

By unclean living (*Galatians 5:16-26*). See how the flesh "acts up." Read this list of its seventeen evil works, 5:19-21. These are sins of the mind as well as the body. This is what we are by nature and these are the things we do. Christ has given the Holy Spirit to make us free from these. "Live by the Spirit, and you will not gratify the desires of the sinful nature" (*v. 16*). Let the Holy Spirit rule your life.

Children begin to walk by someone holding on to their hand. We begin our walk by the Spirit holding on to us. But He is not only a help outside as in the case of a child, but He helps within. Think of walking arm in arm with the Holy Spirit! This means no running ahead or lagging behind (*5:16*).

The nine graces are:
1. Toward God (a) love (b) joy (c) peace.
2. Toward others: (d) patience (e) kindness (f) goodness.
3. Toward myself: (g) faithfulness (h) gentleness (i) self-control.

In contrast to the work of the sinful nature, we see the ninefold fruit of the Spirit (*5:22-23*). If we abide in Christ (*John 15*) we shall be free to bear fruit with God. Are we showing this cluster of fruit in our lives?

Sowing and Reaping
Galatians 6:7-9

"A man reaps what he sows" (*Galatians 6:7*).

If we sow to the Spirit, we shall reap a spiritual harvest. If we sow to the flesh (the lower appetites), we will reap moral weakness (*6:7-8*).

The harvest will not be according to how much we know, but how much we sow. We may have a large supply of seed in the barn of the mind, but unless it is planted in suitable soil it will bear no harvest. Sow the seed of thoughts in word and deeds. God's Word always brings forth seed after its kind.

Sow the seeds of your life in the soil of the Spirit, not the soil of the flesh. In the Spirit it will honor God, but in the flesh the seed will rot and bring forth corruption. The Spirit brings forth only good fruit, the flesh only evil.

The Christian worker is not likened to a salesman or mechanic, but to a farmer. We are not just to fix over "run-down" lives, but we are to plant the living Word.

In Christ we are free to know the boundless life that is in Him. In Him we are "a new creation" (*Galatians 6:15*). We are a new creation; we have a new life in Christ. No wonder Paul cries out, "May I never boast except in the cross of our Lord Jesus Christ, through which the world has been crucified to me, and I to the world" (*6:14*). "Let the world go by! I have Christ, and having Him, I have all things," Paul is saying. Oh, the joy of a free, full life in Christ Jesus.

35. UNDERSTANDING

Ephesians

Ephesians Portrays Jesus Christ, Our All in All

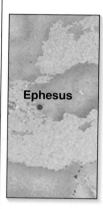

Ephesus

In this Epistle, we enter the holy of holies in Paul's writings. Paul speaks in 2 Corinthians 12:2 of being "caught up to the third heaven." Here, as it were, he gives his report. He seems to be carried away as he tells of it. It is the greatest revelation of truth that God has given to us. It is the mystery that has been hidden from before the foundation of the world.

This book shows us the great mystery of the Church. The real Church is the Body of Christ, and believers are members of that sacred Body of which Christ is the Head. The Father not only prepared a body in which Jesus Christ would suffer, but He also prepared a Body for Him in which He should be glorified. The Greek word for church is *ecclesia*, which means an assembly

of called-out ones. Christ is taking out a people for His name (*Acts 15:14*). The Church is an organism. It is the Body of Christ. Every believer is a member of Christ's Body, and He is the Head of the Church.

Imagine for a moment that the Body is like a great building. The "stones" are redeemed human beings. Christ, the Head, occupies the great throne room. All the parts are like "rooms" in the building. With this picture in mind, it is easy to see the whole story of the mystery of the Church. The suffering of Christ in an earthly body now to be made up for by erecting a spiritual body or "building." Come with Paul through this glorious structure as he outlines it in Ephesians:

The believer's position—chapters

The famous theater at ancient Ephesus, site of the silversmiths' riot.

Relief from a Roman temple at Ephesus.

1—3: (*1*) in Christ, and (*2*) in "heavenly places."

The believer's walk—chapters 4—6: (*1*) ecclesiastically, chapter 4; (*2*) morally, chapter 5; (*3*) socially, 5:21—6:9; (*4*) martially, 6:10-24.

Paul seems to present a picture of "Christ's Temple of Ephesus," which the Christian may enter. It is "a holy temple in the Lord" (*2:21*). We approach in these chapters, one after another, six magnificent rooms in this great temple. They are all "in Christ." Let the scenes of this book be laid in each of these rooms successively.

The Anteroom *Ephesians 1*

Let us enter this sacred temple with hushed voices and bared heads. Christ is going to allow us to go into His holy presence. The door opens into the spacious anteroom, where we read upon the walls our standing with God through Jesus Christ. "Blessed . . . with all spiritual blessings. Chosen . . . in him before the foundation of the world . . . holy and without blame be-

fore him in love. . . . Accepted in the beloved" (*Ephesians 1:3-6, KJV*). These are some great wall mottoes for Christians. It will tax every spiritual energy to live up to them.

Our Blessings
The blessings of the Christian are not only "heavenly," but also "in the heavenly realms." Go through this first chapter and mark all you find "in Christ."

We are saints in Christ Jesus (*1:1*)
Blessed in Christ (*1:3*)
Chosen in Him (*1:4*)
Adopted by Christ (*1:5*)
Lavished with love in Christ, the One God loves (*1:6*)
Redeemed and forgiven in Christ (*1:7*)
Revealed His will in Himself (*1:9*)
Everything centered in Christ (*1:10*)
Participants in God's good plan in Christ (*1:11*)
Glorified in Christ, sealed with the Holy Spirit (*1:12-13*)
Inheritance in Christ (*1:14*)
Faith in Christ (*1:15*)
Wisdom in Him (*1:17*)
Hope in Christ (*1:18*)
Power in Christ (*1:19-20*)
Made alive in Christ (*2:5-6*)
Created in Christ (*2:10*)
Brought near to God in Christ (*2:13*)
Growing in Christ (*2:21*)
Built in Christ (*2:22*)

Sharers in His promise in Christ
(*3:6*)

Wisdom of God manifested in
Christ (*3:10-11*)

Freedom and confidence through
Christ (*3:12*).

Was this always our position? (*2:11-13*). We learn on entering this temple that our calling and position have been planned and worked out by God the Father, the Son and the Holy Spirit before the foundation of the world (*1:4*). All Christians should know their calling above everything else (*1:18*). The true knowledge of it will govern their lives.

Our Redemption

The Father planned it (*1:4-6*)
The Son paid for it (*1:7-12*)
The Spirit applied it (*1:13-14*).

Read Ephesians 1:7.

Redemption is the most glorious work of God. It is greater far than His work of creation. He spoke a word and worlds were formed, but it cost Him the life of His beloved Son to redeem the world. Paul delighted to dwell on this theme. The reason was that he had experienced Christ's redeeming love. He had been redeemed from sin, from the curse and bondage of the law. He had been washed clean

in the blood of Christ, and anointed by the Holy Spirit. Well might he glory in his Redeemer.

To redeem means to buy back, to pay the ransom price. This is what Christ did for us when we were captive under sin.

The captive is in a miserable state and needs to be redeemed.

The provision for our redemption is: Christ is our Redeemer! "In whom we have redemption."

The means of redemption—"In whom we have redemption through his blood . . ." "Not with perishable things such as silver or gold . . . but with the precious blood of Christ" (*1 Peter 1:18-19*). Christ voluntarily took our place. He stood charged with our sins and paid the penalty with His blood.

The fruits of redemption—Even "the forgiveness of sins" is the result of redeeming love and this is "according to the riches of his grace." Grace is unmerited favor. His forgiveness is according to His abounding favor, without limiting it by our demerit.

He casts our sins behind His back. He blots them out of His book of remembrance. He sinks them into the depths of the sea. He removes them as far as the east is from the west. Yes, He forgives "according to the riches of his grace."

We hear a great prayer in this anteroom. Think of hearing Paul pray (*Ephesians 1:15-23*)! Paul wants every one of us who are believers to realize fully our privileges in Christ. He wants the eyes of our understanding to be enlightened that we might behold the glory of Christ. There is no use of showing a gorgeous sunset to a blind person. So we cannot understand the greatness of God until the Great Physician has healed our spiritual eyes.

Each believer should know the three "whats" in this prayer. Do you

The reconstructed Library of Celsus, ancient Ephesus.

know the answers?
What is the hope of His calling?
What are the riches of the glory of
His inheritance in the saints?
Think of Christ's inheritance in
us. He has suns and stars, but He
wants sons and saints.
What is the exceeding greatness of
His power? What the Church
needs today is power. She is
shorn of her real strength.

The Odeon amphitheater, ancient Ephesus.

The Audience Chamber of the King *Ephesians 2*

Next we are conducted into the glorious audience chamber of the King, into the divine Presence. We "have access to the Father by one Spirit" (*Ephesians 2:18*). We would tremble as we entered if we did not hear the gracious words sound out, "You were dead in your transgressions and sins, . . . But because of his great love for us . . . made us alive with Christ . . . and seated us with him in the heavenly realms" (*2:1-6*). But best of all, there is a sweet Voice sounding through the corridors, Welcome here! "Consequently, you are no longer foreigners and aliens, but fellow citizens with God's people and members of God's household" (*2:19*). All of this is in sharpest contrast to what we were "formerly" (*2:11-13*). We once were "far off." Now we are "near."

In this audience chamber, we find that God has made both believing Jews and Gentiles "one" in Christ. Christ makes each one of us a new person and gives us access and approach into the very audience chamber of the King.

This new person has access to God through the blood of His Son (*2:13*). He is our Mediator, and He says, "No one comes to the Father except through me" (*John 14:6*). Then when we have been redeemed, the Holy Spirit intro-

duces the new person at the court of heaven. He does not ask Peter for the privilege, nor does He consult the saints, nor does He invoke the "Mother of Jesus." There is only one Mediator and that is the Lord Jesus Christ. The Father rejoices in the new person and welcomes us into His very presence.

The Masterpiece Planned

God is producing a masterpiece, His Church. Paul says, "For we are God's workmanship" (*2:10*). This comes from the Greek word *poiema*—poem or masterpiece.

In Ephesians 1, we find how God planned and worked in the production of this masterpiece. We were "chosen in Christ" to be holy and blameless (*1:4*). In the ages of past eternity, God was thinking about us, loving us and planning to bless us. Know this, before Satan ever appeared to spoil the happiness of people upon this earth, God made plans to make all who would believe on Him to be blameless.

Then in Ephesians 2:1-10 we find how it was produced. Look at the material He used. Read these verses. How does God take us up and produce a masterpiece out of such material? We see:

What the nature of a person is (*2:1-3*)

What the walk of a natural person is (*2:2*).

"But God"—see God act! He changes all by His touch! This "But God" is the bridge that leads us out of our dark and hopeless condition (*2:4*). When all human strength is at an end—"But God." Remember Christ comes to give life to the dead.

The greatest proof of Christianity is that it has produced a new person who is approved unto God. Only God could make a Paul out of Saul.

Destiny of the Masterpiece

What a destiny it is (*2:7*)! What is a little suffering with a few trials here in comparison to the glory in the "ages to come" *(KJV)*. He will show the "exceeding riches of His grace" *(KJV)*. He will tell the universe what He has accomplished.

Salvation is the gift of God. "For it is by grace you have been saved, through faith—and this not from yourselves, it is the gift of God" (*2:8*). Faith is a gift, too. "Faith comes from hearing the message" (*Romans 10:17*). Faith is the channel of salvation. It is the hand that receives the gift. It connects us with God.

The Throne Room
Ephesians 3

Standing at the doors of the throne room are the stalwart guards of Law. They demand: "Who goes there? Why do you come? What are your credentials?"

I answer feebly, "A sinner; I come to see the Lamb. I have nothing to recommend me for admittance."

Then I hear the voice of the Lamb from within, the call of the Son of Grace. "It is one of my sheep. Invite her in. My blood covers all. She needs

no credentials." And Grace brings me past the stern guards of Law unto the throne of His mercy.

"In him and through faith in him we may approach God with freedom and confidence" (*Ephesians 3:12*). What a piling up of words to persuade us of our privilege and position as Christian believers! We are "accepted in the beloved" (*1:6, KJV*).

Here we behold the King! With Paul we bow our knee "before the Father, from whom his whole family in heaven and on earth derives its name" (*3:14-15*). Is posture a small thing? Kneeling is the attitude of humility, confession and entreaty. Remember the holiest men in the Bible have approached God this way. David, Solomon and Daniel knelt upon their knees. These men stooped to conquer, knelt to prevail.

Paul tells how God had held back from the Gentiles the secret that they should be heirs and shareholders of the gospel and have admission into the Church (His Body) on the same terms as the Jewish people (*3:8-10*). To "bring all things in heaven and on earth together under one head, even Christ" (*1:10*) was God's plan.

The word "mystery," which occurs three times here, does not mean something mysterious. It merely means it is hidden until the appropriate time comes for God to reveal it.

The mystery of the Church is that the Gentiles are to be equal partakers with the Jewish people of God's promises (*Ephesians 3:6*). All this was "by faith" (*Romans 15:9-10; Galatians 3:8-9*). This is a radical thing that God would make the Gentiles with the Jews coheirs of Christ and comembers of His Church.

Paul prays again and his prayer is recorded in Ephesians 3:13-21. The first prayer recorded in chapter 1 gave us three "whats." This prayer gives us

The site of the ancient harbor for Ephesus can be seen in this view from the top terraces of the great amphitheater.

four "thats" and is steeped in the love of Christ.

That they should be strengthened by His Spirit.

That they might have Christ dwelling in their hearts.

That they might understand what is the breadth, length, depth and height of the love of Christ.

That they might be filled with the fullness of God.

Paul enjoys the "riches" of the gospel. It is bountiful in its gifts and inexhaustible in its resources.

If we are to enjoy this life in the Temple of God, we must be yielded in obedience to Him. If we yield to His plan for our lives as willing subjects, we will find that in His hand our lives will be filled with joy and beauty.

The Jewel Room
Ephesians 4

Here amid the flash of the jewel room we will get our decorations and our garments of holiness—"Be completely humble and gentle; be patient, bearing with one another in love" (*4:2*). Here are our banners and emblems—"one Lord, one faith, one baptism" (*4:5*). Here are the brilliant gems of the

graces as we will take them—"But to each one of us grace has been given as Christ apportioned it" (*Ephesians 4:7*). We must "put off," or lay aside, the old life as we would lay aside a garment, and "put on" the new life as a new garment (*4:22-25*).

We must be different, but how? In what respect? What are the things we should be very careful about? We must put away lying. Our speech

The world famous temple of Artemis once stood on this boggy site at Ephesus.

shows our spirit. We must put away all bitterness and anger and harsh words. Be kind to each other. We must not have anything to do with deeds of darkness for we are children of light. Read all of Ephesians 4:31-32.

We must go into God's robing room not to make the garments, but to put them on. God is the Tailor and He makes our dress to conform to our position and purpose in life. God wants His sons and daughters to wear suitable garments.

We have discovered as we have come into this temple what our riches are in the heavenlies (1:18-21). Now we must "live a life worthy of the calling you have received" (4:1). The way we live must correspond to our creed. A heavenly calling demands a heavenly conduct.

What is a "walk"? It is not a path or a way of moving about over the earth or even a sphere of work. A Christian's walk includes conduct, attitudes and consecration; it is, in short, "a way of living before men."

We are to walk (Ephesians 4:1-3):
Humbly—"Be completely humble and gentle"
Lovingly—"Be patient, bearing with one another in love"
Peacefully—"Make every effort to keep the unity of the Spirit through the bond of peace."

We know that our spiritual lives affect our social lives. But many turn it around and attempt to create a social life that will create a spiritual life. This cannot be. When we are in right relation to God, we will be in proper relation to people.

When God puts upon us His jewels of grace, He seals us by His Spirit (4:30). It is like a young man putting a diamond upon the engagement finger of one whom he has promised to marry. The Lord knows them that are His and we are sealed unto the day of redemption. The seal is the mark of ownership. "They are mine." A seal is set for security. We are sealed unto the day of redemption. Have you the seal? Show it then!

The Choir and Oratory Room
Ephesians 5

In the jewel room, we were bedecked as children of God and enjoined to walk worthy of our calling. We were sealed with the seal of ownership. Now we are to go out and be followers of God as dear children. A Christian is *I* following Christ—Christ-*I*-an. The walk of a Christian:

Walk in love—Ephesians 5:1-2
Walk in light—5:8
Walk carefully—5:15-16.

"Do not get drunk on wine, which leads to debauchery. Instead, be filled

Relief of a Roman soldier, Ephesus. We are able to stand in the victory Christ wrought on Calvary.

with the Spirit" (5:18). The body, mind and spirit cannot function without outside stimulants. No one will think clearly or feel deeply unless something without excites him or her. But this is where the tragedy comes. The world has plenty of powerful stimulants that give quick and joyous reactions. But the results are devastating. Our bodies and minds are not made for such ruinous flames and are destroyed. Our bodies are for God's altars. "Therefore, I urge you, brothers . . . to offer your bodies as living sacrifices, holy and pleasing to God—this is your spiritual act of worship" (Romans 12:1) is God's plea. The Holy Spirit fires our bodies and spirits and sets them aglow, but never destroys. Therefore God commands, "Be not drunk with wine . . . but be filled [set aflame] with the Spirit" (KJV). We can burn and never be consumed. We may live dangerously for God and never be in danger.

It is just as great a sin not to be filled with the Spirit of God as it is to be drunk with wine. Don't think that only ministers and missionaries need to be filled with His blessed Presence, but all! God's Spirit is waiting that He might fill His temples (5:19-20).

"Speak to one another with psalms, hymns and spiritual songs. Sing and make music in your heart to the Lord" (5:19). Sing, Christian, sing! Christ wants it so. A singing heart guarantees a transformed life. When the Spirit fills the heart, the lips overflow with praise. We will walk the Christian life as we sing and talk about Christ. This joyful praise of Christian meetings is in contrast to the noisy drunken revelings of Ephesus.

Christ is the key to a life of victory in the Son of God. He teaches that a child of God can and must, under all circumstances, be a living witness to the power of Christ in his or her life.

The Armory Ephesians 6

Now we stand in a room hung with the whole armor of God. The armor is His, not ours! But He tells us to put it on. We must put on the whole of it if we will be safe.

Paul says, "Finally, be strong in the Lord and in his mighty power" (Ephesians 6:10). You can be strong! You must be strong! But remember this! "Be strong in the Lord, and in the power of his might!" As soon as we are brought into communion with God, we need to be fitted for the fight of faith. All who belong to the kingdom of God's dear Son have the forces of the kingdom of Satan against them, so they need to be covered with the whole armor of God.

The Christian's walk includes a warfare. Let us know the wiles of the forces marshaled against us! We have been raised to the heavenly places of fellowship with Christ. Let us maintain the honor of our calling and the wealth of our high estate. As good soldiers, let us stand and defend our interests. The crying need of our day is for strong people. In Ephesians 5, we were asked to put on clothing suited to the new person moving in society. Here we are to put on armor necessary to the soldier.

You must come to Calvary for each piece of this wonderful armor. When we come and take it for ourselves, we can see that our whole body is covered. We are to "be able to stand against" the enemy. Stand, Christian, in the victory Christ wrought on Calvary. But you notice there is no armor for the back. The Christian is never supposed to run from enemies, but fight the good fight of faith, praying always!

"The full armor of God":
Girdle of truth
Breastplate of righteousness
Shoes of readiness to bear the gospel
Shield of faith
Helmet of salvation
Sword of the Word
Prayer.

36. UNDERSTANDING

Philippians

Philippians Portrays Jesus Christ, Our Joy

The Epistle to the Philippians was written to the first church founded in Europe. Paul was called there by the vision and the cry, "Come over to Macedonia and help us" (*Acts 16:9*).

Paul urges the church to have Christian unity and joy. This letter shows how unity among Christians can be broken. Christ is the secret of joy. "Finally, my brothers, rejoice in the Lord!" (*Philippians 3:1*). Then there is a pause. Paul is trying to think of some better last word to speak, but he can't find it. Presently he cried out, "Rejoice in the Lord always. I will say it again: Rejoice!" (*4:4*). This is joy in the midst of trouble and problems.

Paul and Silas, you remember, sang in the jail there at Philippi at midnight when their backs were bleeding and sore! He is rejoicing now as he writes this letter, chained to a Roman soldier, for he knows that his very chains are helping him to spread the gospel. He could reach some in Caesar's household that he never otherwise could have brought to Christ. He urged his Philippian converts to rejoice because they were allowed to suffer for Christ (*1:29*).

"The joy of the Lord is your strength" (*Nehemiah 8:10*). The word "joy," or "rejoice," occurs in this Epistle sixteen times. Paul seems to laugh out loud for sheer joy in this letter. He is the rejoicing apostle.

"Joy" and "rejoice" and "all" are the words to underline. "Be glad" is Paul's exhortation. We are commanded to rejoice. We break a commandment if we rejoice not, for joy drives out discord. It helps in the midst of trials. "Joy is a bird; let it fly in the open heavens, and let its music be heard of all men." Sinners, like Augustine, are attracted to Jesus by the joy of Christians.

It hardly seems possible that Paul is writing from prison with chains holding him. His words seem to come from a light heart. It is evident that the soul of this great apostle is free! There

Selected Bible Readings

Sunday: Joy Triumphs over Suffering (*Philippians 1:1-30*)

Monday: Joy in Christ (*Philippians 2:1-11*)

Tuesday: Joy in Salvation (*Philippians 2:12-30*)

Wednesday: Joy in Christ's Righteousness (*Philippians 3:1-9*)

Thursday: Joy in Christ's Will (*Philippians 3:10-21*)

Friday: Joy in Christ's Strength (*Philippians 4:1-7*)

Saturday: Joy in Christ's Provision (*Philippians 4:8-23*)

Philippi

is an atmosphere of joy even from prison.

This letter has no definite plan, but it is the sweetest of all Paul's letters. There is no scolding. It is more of a love letter.

Paul mentions the Savior's name forty times in this short Epistle. Some of the most wonderful things concerning Christ and the Christian life are here. So that your life may be purified, dangers avoided and progress made, Christ must be your joy, your trust and your aim in life. Paul tells us of his joyful triumph over trying circumstances because of his trust in Christ.

Joy in Living *Philippians 1*

Paul loved to call himself the servant (really "bond servant") of Jesus Christ. He had been made free by Christ and now he wants to serve Him as long as he should live. He starts his Epistle, "Paul, a slave of Jesus Christ." That is the reason he says, "For to me to live is Christ" (*1:21*).

Notice when Paul writes his letters he puts his name first. How sensible this is, for the first thing you do in opening a letter is to turn to the end and find out who wrote it.

Although in prison, Paul could pray for his friends. "I thank my God every time I remember you. In all my prayers for all of you, I always pray with joy" (*Philippians 1:3-4*).

Paul lived to intercede for others. So should every true Sunday School teacher, Christian friend, father, mother, brother or sister remember others in their prayers without ceasing.

Although Paul was in prison, chained to a soldier, people came to hear him preach. The Roman guards were so interested in the gospel that they spread it around. This encouraged others to be bold in preaching, and

many found Paul's Christ.

There is great power in the witness of a consistent life. You may be bound to unsympathetic companions, but by your life you may win them for God. Your obstacle may become your pulpit. Christians who work for Christ when everything is against them stir up others.

"For to me, to live is Christ" (*1:21*). Can you say this? Is Christ everything to you? Do you live for Him? Is your one aim and purpose to glorify Him?

Christ is the *giver of life*—"I have come that they may have life, and have it to the full" (*John 10:10*).

Christ is *life itself*—"I no longer live, but Christ lives in me" (*Galatians 2:20*).

Christ is the *model of my life*—"Be perfect, therefore, as your heavenly Father is perfect" (*Matthew 5:48*).

Christ is the *aim of my life*—I desire to make known "the power and coming of our Lord Jesus Christ" (*2 Peter 1:16*).

Christ is the *reward of my life*— "Thanks be to God for his indescribable gift!" (*2 Corinthians 9:15*).

Paul says:

When I travel, it is on Christ's errands.

When I suffer, it is in Christ's service.

When I speak, the theme is Christ.

When I write, Christ fills my letters.

Joy in Service *Philippians 2*

Paul gives us the wonderful Example of the Christian life that we may follow in His steps. We must imitate Christ for although He is Lord of all, He became servant to all! Paul urges the Church to complete his happiness by living together in love and unity. Is there anything more Christlike for Christians to do? "Make my joy complete by being like-minded"

(*Philippians 2:2*). This is not an easy thing to do. It means love without compromise.

"In humility consider others better than yourselves" (*2:3*) is an astonishing phrase; in other words, "I am willing to be third."

We must always bear in our thoughts the example of Jesus Christ (*2:5-11*). Paul says, "Your attitude should be the same as that of Christ Jesus," which is self-forgetting love. Although He was God, He humbled Himself. Not only did Christ take on Himself the form of man, but also the form of a servant. Then He humbled Himself more. He who was Author of life became obedient unto death. But even more than this, He faced an ignominious death, "even the death of a cross." This must be our spirit. (See *Matthew 16:25*.)

Paul is practical as well as profound. He never leaves us in the clouds. He never separates knowledge from action. Christianity is both life and creed. The creed without the life amounts to little. After Paul has scaled the heights in Christ's exaltation, he has no idea of leaving us there. "Therefore, my dear friends...continue to work out your salvation with fear and trembling" (*Philippians 2:12*). "Work out" means live out—not working for salvation, but showing the works of salvation. God has a plan for each of our lives as He had for Jesus. We must live it out. It is an absolutely personal matter. No one can do it for you. God plants in our hearts salvation in Christ, great, divine and wonderful to be lived out. Can you go about it without "fear and trembling"? Happy is the person who finds God's plan for life and falls in with it.

Christian experience is not something that is going on around you, but in you. "Christ liveth in me"!

"Do everything without complaining or arguing" (*2:14*). Paul is saying, "Don't be grouchy! You can't glow if you are!"

If Christ is our Example, then we see that there is no cross without a crown. If we suffer with Him, we shall also reign with Him. We are God's luminaries in a dark age. No flame can shine brightly when it is filthy. The

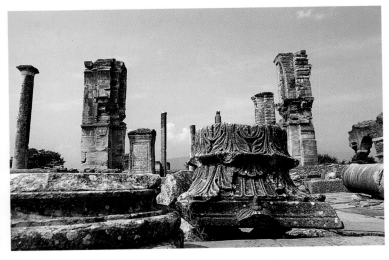

Remains of the market area of Roman Philippi, in Macedonia.

Christian who brings honor to the Lord must be faultless, innocent and unblamable.

Joy in Fellowship
Philippians 3

Paul tells the Philippians that the duty of all Christians is that they be joyful. A long-faced Christian is the worst advertisement against Christianity. The world doesn't want a greater burden; it wants a light heart. How can a Christian be joyful in a world so full of sorrow? Paul tells us in the first verse—"Rejoice in the Lord"!

Saul of Tarsus, a man rich in religious background, seeking for the best, had gone from one religion to another. He was an earnest searcher after truth and blameless as far as the law was concerned, but he had found nothing that satisfied him. One day Christ found him, and in this marvelous paragraph we see he gladly sacrificed everything and counted the treasures of this world as nothing in comparison with Christ. He set a new standard of values. He had a new reason for life. Christ had stepped in between Paul and his old ideals and made him change the headings at the top of his ledger. He erased "gains" (credits) and wrote "loss" (debits). This was his choice in life.

Paul weighed both the world and Christ and remembered the words of the Lord Jesus, "What good will it be for a man if he gains the whole world, yet forfeits his soul?" (*Matthew 16:26*).

In Philippians 3:12-14, Paul tells us that every person's life is a plan of God! The one thing I do should be to carry out this plan. Neither the successes nor failures of the past must keep me from "pressing on" today. "I am ready for anything and equal to anything through Him Who infuses inner strength into me; I am self-suffi-

cient in Christ's sufficiency" (*4:13, AMP*).

When Paul met the Lord on the way to Damascus (*Acts 9*), his whole being was changed. His eyes were opened. He discovered in Christ a store of spiritual wealth that made him count all that he had as trash (*Philippians 3:7*). He had boasted of lineage and pedigree; he was blameless in the law; he had every honor and privilege, but now he was willing to lose everything to gain Christ.

Here are some of the ambitions of Paul's heart. Mark these in your Bible.

"That I may gain Christ" (*3:8*). Christ had won him. Now he wished to win Him as a daily prize.

"I want to know Christ" (*3:10*). There are degrees of knowing Him.

"And be found in him" (*3:9*). To be found in Christ means we are blameless and complete.

"I want to know Christ and the power of his resurrection" (*3:10*). The power of the gospel is in a risen Christ.

"I want to know . . . the fellowship of sharing in his sufferings" (*3:10*). This means a life consecrated to Him, conformable unto His death.

"I press on to take hold of that for which Christ Jesus took hold of me" (*3:12*). He wanted to know Christ's purpose for seizing him on that road to Damascus.

"I press on toward the goal to win the prize" (*3:14*). The higher the calling, the greater the prize.

Do you know that your citizenship is in heaven, that you have been born from above? (*3:20-21*). Therefore we should live as citizens of a better country, a heavenly Kingdom. Love not the world nor the things of this world, but be loyal to Him who rules in the "heavenly Jerusalem." When Christ comes, He will change these bodies of ours into bodies like unto

His own fit for His heavenly kingdom.

Christ's residence was for thirty-three years here on earth, but it did not naturalize Him as a citizen of earth. Let us not forget where our citizenship is. Remember Paul's advice in Romans 12:2: "Do not conform any longer to the pattern of this world, but be transformed by the renewing of your mind."

Joy in Rewards *Philippians 4*

"Rejoice in the Lord always. I will say it again: Rejoice! Let your gentleness be evident to all. The Lord is near" (*Philippians 4:4-5*). This blessed hope of Christ's coming again casts its gracious influence over all of life. Paul prays that the Christian may have joy at all times and not be worried by cares.

The way to be anxious about nothing is to be prayerful about everything. The prayer of faith must be a prayer of thanksgiving because faith knows how much it owes to God. Put your prayers into God's hands and go off and leave them there. Do not worry about them. Give them completely as the farmer gives the wheat to the soil after the soil has been properly plowed. If you do this, then the peace of God will stand guard over your heart and mind.

Guard your thoughts! Paul tells us what to think about and remember. "As [a man] thinketh in his heart, so is he" (*Proverbs 23:7, KJV*). Thoughts determine your life! Therefore whatsoever things are true, honest, just, pure, lovely, of good report, virtuous, praiseworthy, think on these things!

Paul expressed his gratitude for the loving thought that had promoted the church at Philippi to send him gifts. He was especially happy about their gifts, not because he was in want, for he had learned to be content in any circumstance with Christ (*Philippians 4:11*). He could do all things through Christ who strengthened him. But their gifts meant "fruit that may abound to your account" (*4:17, KJV*). He opened God's bank account to them. "And my God will meet all your needs according to his glorious riches in Christ Jesus" (*4:19*).

37. UNDERSTANDING

Colossians

Colossians Portrays Jesus Christ, Our Life

Ephesians and Colossians were written about the same time, while Paul was a prisoner in Rome. They both contain great doctrines of the gospel, and were to be read aloud in the churches. They are very similar in style, yet very different in emphasis.

Ephesians talks about all believers, calling them the "body of Christ." Colossians talks about the Head of the Body, Jesus Christ.

In Ephesians, the Church of Christ is the important item. In Colossians, the Christ of the Church is emphasized.

Both are needed. There cannot be a body without a head, nor a head without a body. Notice this all the way through Colossians—"Christ," "Christ," "Christ."

Heresy had broken out in the church at Colosse, misleading the young believers, calling for the worship of angels (*Colossians 2:18*) and a strict observance of Jewish ceremonies (*2:16,21*). This heresy was a mixture of Jewish, Greek and Oriental religions, and all this called forth this statement of the truth of the Supreme Lordship of Christ. This Epistle draws a faithful portrait of Christ in all His glory and dignity.

Christ Our Head

Christ is all in all. The failure of the Colossians was at this very point, not holding fast to the Lord. The place Christ holds in any religious teaching

determines whether it is true or false. Some thought in Paul's day, as now, that Jesus was but a man, and Christ was the divine Spirit that came at His baptism and left Him at the cross. This meant that Christ did not die, but simply that Jesus died. You can see that this is the root error of many cults today. Every modern cult is based on just the same old heresy and misrepresents the truth in regard to Christ and His Person and work. It is good for us, in reading the Colossian letter, to examine our own belief and see that we

Selected Bible Readings

Sunday: Paul's Greeting and Prayer (*Colossians 1:1-14*)

Monday: Seven Superiorities of Christ (*Colossians 1:15-29*)

Tuesday: Christ Exalted (*Philippians 2:1-11*)

Wednesday: Complete in Christ (*Colossians 2:1-19*)

Thursday: Old and New Nature (*Colossians 2:20—3:11*)

Friday: Christian Living (*Colossians 3:12-25*)

Saturday: Christian Graces (*Colossians 4:1-18*)

the church. These false teachings took Christ off the throne and denied His headship of the Church. To help answer them, Paul sent this letter back by Epaphras. He writes especially on the preeminence and deity of Christ, for Christ is very God.

The gospel, by this time, had been brought to "all over the world" (*1:6*) and "has been proclaimed to every creature" (*1:23*). Thirty-two years after Christ's death, the gospel had reached the whole Roman world. It needed only one generation to establish the Church as a worldwide fact.

The Church's position "in Christ":
United in Christ—Colossians 2:2
Complete in Christ—2:10
Dead in Christ—2:20
Buried with Christ—Romans 6:4
Risen with Christ—Colossians 3:1.

Christ Our Life
"And your life is now hidden with Christ in God" (*Colossians 3:3*). This Epistle tells us that Christ is our life and we are complete in Him (*2:10*).

The Christian life is not a creed or a system of doctrine or a certain kind of worship, but a life that is Christ's very own within you. Christ is all in all:

In His deity—The image of the invisible God (*1:15*)

In creation—Sovereign Creator of the universe (*1:15-16*)

In preeminence—Before all things (*1:18*)

In redemption—Reconciling the universe through His blood (*1:20-22*)

In headship—Over all principalities and powers (*1:18; 2:14*)

In His Church—The Head of the Body (*1:18; 2:19*)

In His indwelling presence—The Christian's hope (*1:27*).

God has given Christ preeminence in all things (*1:18*). We dare not give Him a lower place!

Classical relief of an angel-like figure. Heretics in Colosse were calling for the worship of angels.

always put the Head, Christ Jesus, in His rightful place in our thinking and glorify this wonderful One.

Have you noticed that many of the Epistles were used to answer the heresies that crept into the early churches everywhere?

This letter begins, like twelve others, with the name of Paul, and is addressed to Gentile believers.

The church was likely founded by Epaphras (*1:7*) in the town of Colosse, about 100 miles east of Ephesus. It consisted of Gentile Christians. Philemon was a member. Paul kept in close touch with the people and was greatly beloved.

Epaphras went to Rome to tell Paul of the heresies that were creeping into

In Romans we are justified in Christ
In 1 Corinthians we are enriched in Christ
In 2 Corinthians we are comforted in Christ
In Galatians we are free in Christ
In Ephesians we are made alive in Christ
In Philippians we are joyful in Christ
In Colossians we are complete in Christ.

Colossians presents the glorious culmination of it all. We are "complete in him." We are "rooted and built up"; we are "grounded and settled." We discover the facts of this building process in the four chapters of this book.

Building "downward," rooted in Jesus, *established and firm* (*1:23*)
Building "upward," *built up in him* (*2:7*)
Building "inward," *hidden with Christ* (*3:3*)
Building "outward," *be wise in the way you act towards outsiders* (*4:5*).

"The deeper life" is rooted in eternity. It begins in Him Who was "in the beginning with God." God gives eternal life.

The "higher life" is the life Jesus is living for us at the right hand of God, and living in us, for "I have been crucified with Christ and I no longer live, but Christ lives in me" (*Galatians 2:20*).

The "inner life" is all the life we have as Christians. It is the life "hid with Christ" in God. It is life real and sufficient, for we are "complete in him" (*Colossians 3:3; 2:10*).

The "outer life" is that expression of life that makes Christ known to others. "What you are speaks so loudly, people cannot hear what you say."

The Deeper Life *Colossians 1*

Paul opens this letter as he opens so many: "We always thank God" (*Colossians 1:3*). He rejoices in the good news from the brethren scattered abroad in the various churches he founded.

Notice Paul's favorite words, "faith," "love" and "hope" (*vv. 4-5*), which he so often uses. He wants everyone to have faith in Christ, love toward oth-

The ancient forum, Rome. Colossians was written while Paul was a prisoner in Rome.

Colosse

ers and hope of heaven.

Paul tells us the secret of the deeper life that we as Christians should have in Christ. Dig downward first and become "established and firm" ("grounded and settled," *KJV*) in Christ (*1:23*).

Next Paul presents a glowing description of the mighty Christ, the Superior One. He is "all in all."

We find in this first scene that not only are we in Christ, but also that Christ is in us. "Christ in you, the hope of glory" (*1:27*). This is what it is to be a Christian: living in Him—this glorious, wonderful Person, the Creator of this universe, in whom we have redemption through His blood—and having Him live in us.

In closing this scene, notice Paul's beautiful prayer for the Church in Colossians 1:9-14. He expresses his desire for all Christian believers:

That they might be filled with a knowledge of Christ's will. He wants us to know how to live a Christlike life, for the fullness of Christ's wisdom will keep us from error.

That they might walk worthy of the Lord, fruitful in work, increasing in knowledge.

That they might be strengthened with might so as to be able to withstand all temptations.

That they might be thankful.

The Higher Life *Colossians 2*

"So then, just as you received Christ Jesus as Lord, continue to live in him, rooted and built up in him" (*Colossians 2:6-7*). Paul is always practical. Again he says, "Act out what you believe. You commenced well. Go on as you have begun! We have received Christ, and have been grounded and settled in Him. Let us therefore walk in Him" (see *1:23*). Paul always wants our walk and life to correspond with

our belief. It is sad when a Christian believes in Christ and acts like the devil. No one will accept our profession as sincere. If we have received Christ, let us walk as He would have us. If we have been rooted in Him, let us grow up in Him. If we have been founded on Him, let us be builded up on Him. All of these are outward evidences of a changed heart. "Walking" expresses life. "Growing" exhibits an inner power. "Building up" shows progress of character until the structure is complete.

We have to do a great deal more than just believe "truths about Christ." We must "receive Christ" if we are to have life. We cannot earn it or purchase it. It is a free gift (*2:6*). We are rooted in Christ. That means we draw our nourishment from Him. A plant cannot grow unless it is in touch with the life-giving soil. We are built up in Him. We have our foundation in Him. Every structure needs a foundation. All this must be our experience if we would be built up. The Christian life is starting in Christ and then growing in His grace and gifts. We must be as dependent on Christ for steadfastness of walk as we were for our assurance of salvation.

All the life we have as Christians is the life "in Him."

Walking in Him (*2:6*)
Rooted in Him (*2:7*)
Built up in Him (*2:7*)
Brought to perfection in Him (*2:10*)
Dead with Him (*2:20*)
Risen with Him (*3:1*)
Hidden with Him (*3:3*).

This is the life—real and satisfying eternal life. We find in this chapter that Christ is all-sufficient, "For in Christ all the fullness of the Deity lives in bodily form" (*2:9*). This is a tremendous truth for us to grasp. In this Jesus, who walked on the earth, dwelt the whole Godhead. But more than this—in Him was the fulness of the Godhead.

Let us look again. "For in Christ all the fullness of the Deity lives in bodily form." This Jesus was very God in all of His fullness. Neither angels, nor prophets, nor saints rank with Him—for He is the very embodiment of the divine fullness!

Our lives must first be built downward, "rooted in Christ." Next we must build upward, "rooted and built up in him, strengthened in the faith" (*2:7*), rearing a stately structure to His praise, and of course, wholly by His grace. This is the higher life.

The higher you go with the Lord, the steadier is your disposition, the less disturbing are temptations and the smoother is your everyday life.

We see Paul's personal concern for the Church at Colosse. He longs for the Christians to be established and kept firm in their convictions so that the shrewd philosophers and legalists of their day would not deceive them. The best way to be protected from the snares of the world and its philosophy is an understanding of the perfection of Christ, for He is all and in all. Be rooted and grounded in the Word lest you be swept away by false teachers.

Some of the popular street-corner philosophers of the day were teaching that people are unworthy to approach Christ directly. They needed to approach Him by means of angels (*2:18*). Some in our day teach that we need to approach God through the virgin Mary or through some other person. Christ says He is the only Mediator between God and people. He adds, "I am the way . . . No one comes to the Father except through me" (*John 14:6*). Paul rebukes the Colossians for their failure to recognize the supreme Headship of Christ and the only Mediator between God and people.

Paul reminds the Christian that when Jesus died on the cross, He freed us from the law. Therefore we need not let others judge us regarding food or drink or severe treatment of the body (see *Colossians 2:16-23*). The sac-

View of the site of ancient Colosse: the green mound in the middle distance marks the center of the ancient town.

rifice God asks is a broken spirit, not a beaten body. A sinful heart can dwell in a fasting body. Self-imposed hardships are of no value in offsetting the thoughts of a sinful heart. We like to think that when we have done something bad we can erase our record by doing something we think is good. But we must remember that only what Christ does is good, for "there is no one who does good, not even one" (*Romans 3:12*). If *God* is taken out of *good*, nothing—*0*—is left.

The Inner Life *Colossians 3*

Building our life cannot be only downward, "rooted in Christ," but upward, "built up in him," but our building must also be inward. Let us know that Christ is the believer's life. Many believe that Christ gave us life as one would put a living seed into a flower pot. The pot would hold a detached thing—life. But Christ is more than that. He Himself is in the believer. The life that is in Christ is in the believer.

The illustration He gives, "I am the vine; you are the branches" (*John 15:5*).

We find that our new life in Christ makes us less interested in the things the world offers. We become "dead to the world." We find ourselves "hid with Christ," and as we know Him we discover, one by one, the beauties of the Lord Jesus. "Compassion, kindness, humility, gentleness and patience" (*Colossians 3:12*). "Let the word of Christ dwell in you richly" (*3:16*). It will make a difference.

Because we are rooted in Christ and our life is in Him, we are not only identified with Him in His death, but we are also in union with Him in His resurrection. In Christ's death we died to sin, and in His resurrection we rose to walk in a new life. Because we are "risen with Christ," we should seek those things that are above, and show to the best of our ability the goal of our lives.

We live in the world, but we must set our minds (affections) on things above, for we are citizens of a heavenly country. Look upon Christ and He will draw you upward.

The Christian's Wardrobe

First we must "put off" the old nature. Paul tells us to put it to death (*3:5-9*). After we receive our new life in Christ Jesus, then we must "put to death, therefore, whatever belongs to your earthly nature." It should not be necessary to tell Christians they must put off things that are more like the devil than the Savior!

Paul admonishes us to destroy our old nature and "put off" all its vices. Read over Paul's black catalogue. There is immorality, impurity, passion and greed. Then there are passionate anger and wrath and the many sins of speech. Let us forever give up these sins. It is possible in Christ.

Can you imagine how ridiculous

you would look if when you went to buy a new suit you refused to take off the one you had on, but rather insisted that the new one should be tried on without "putting off" the old one! This is what many Christians do. They try to put the garment of a new life on over their old nature. It just doesn't fit. We must lay aside sin first, then "put on the new man."

A Christian's conduct is what people see you do. As clothes indicate what kind of a person you are—they tell whether you are careful or careless; they tell whether you are a soldier or civilian, a king or a commoner —so outward expression will show

Classical relief of a couple in Roman dress, from Galatia. As clothes indicate what kind of a person you are—so outward expression will show "whose [you are] and whom [you] serve" (*Acts 27:23*).

"whose [you are] and whom [you] serve" (*Acts 27:23*).

Now Paul thinks of our new nature in Christ. "Put on the new self" (*3:10*). This new nature we receive from Christ is ever being renewed as we grow in the knowledge of our Lord and Savior. But we must not become so absorbed in our great privileges in Christ that we neglect our duty to our fellow humans. Our knowing Christ should make us much more thoughtful of others. The new Christian not only puts away, but also puts on or adds to his or her life. Let us "put on" the excellences of this new life, such as tenderness, kindness, humility, patience, forgiveness and love (*Colossians 3:12-14*). Yes, these are the things with which we are to adorn ourselves. If we lived like this we would find perfection on earth. Paul says all these virtues are like pieces of clothing, all held in place by a belt of love. This fills our lives with the peace of God. As long as we live, there is something new for us to learn. We should never stop growing.

Set down all the commands given to you in this chapter.

Christ Is Our All or Nothing

Yes, "Christ is all, and is in all" (*3:11*). If Christ is not all in your life, He is nothing. No surer test can be given to any false teaching of today than this: Where does it put Jesus Christ? The Bible says: "Every spirit that acknowledges that Jesus Christ has come in the flesh is from God" (*1 John 4:2*). This is the test of every creed. Does it proclaim that "we have redemption, the forgiveness of sins" (*1:14*)? If so, it is true; if not, it is false (*1 John 4:1-3*).

A Christian heart is a singing heart (*Colossians 3:16*). Christ wants us to be taught in His Word, and then He wants us to express our joy in Him by singing hymns.

The Outward Life
Colossians 4

This chapter introduces another phase of our life in Christ, the outward life. We found we must build within, cultivating the virtues of the new life in Christ. But there is something more.

We want our new life to be seen and felt among others (*Colossians 4:5*). This is the way we present Christ to the world. Remember, "Christians" mean "little Christs." Christ is living in us. His life is told today in living epistles that are known and read by all people.

38. UNDERSTANDING

First Thessalonians

First Thessalonians Portrays Jesus Christ, the Coming One

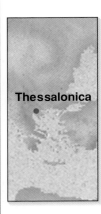

Thessalonica

The second coming of the Lord Jesus Christ is the truth Paul is presenting in these two letters to the Thessalonians, and it would be missing the mark not to recognize it. The two Epistles contain twenty different references to the coming of the Lord. This is the hope of the Church. It is mentioned in the closing of every chapter of 1 Thessalonians: "To wait for his Son from heaven" (*1:10*); "in the presence of our Lord Jesus Christ when he comes" (*2:19*); "in the presence of our God and Father when our Lord Jesus comes with all his holy ones" (*3:13*); "caught up together with them in the clouds to meet the Lord in the air" (*4:17*); and in the last chapter, "May your whole spirit, soul and body be kept blameless at the coming of our Lord Jesus Christ" (*5:23*). In view of all this, should anyone raise the question: Will Christ come again?

Christ's first coming was sudden and a surprise to the philosophers of His time. We learn that His second coming will be no less surprising.

Paul, accompanied by Timothy and Silas, had spent only three Sundays at Thessalonica on his second missionary journey, but during that time he not only founded a church, but he also grounded it firmly in the faith. In the short time he was there, Paul created a great stir. His enemies accused him of having "turned the world upside down" (*Acts 17:6, KJV*). On account of this great stir, the brethren sent the

apostle away. He went on to Berea and Athens and Corinth. It was from here he wrote this first letter to the Thessalonians and sent it by Timothy. We know he had only been gone a short time, for he said he was "torn away from you for a short time" (*1 Thessalonians 2:17*).

It is an unprecedented thing even in the ministry of Paul, this establishment of a flourishing church in less than a month. He preached to them for three Sabbath days, although no doubt he continued his meetings during these weeks.

During this short stay in Thessalonica, a great number of Greeks and women believed (*Acts 17:4*). Paul began at once to feed this church with the meat of the Word. He talked of the Holy Spirit (*1 Thessalonians 1:6*), of the Trinity (*1:6*) and of the second coming of Christ (*1:10*). The church was composed mostly of Gentiles rather than Jewish believers.

Being greatly concerned about the young converts, Paul sent Timothy from Athens to strengthen their faith and to bring him news of how they were getting along. Timothy brought back a favorable report that was a great comfort to the apostle-founder of the church. However, Timothy had discovered that there were some faults to be corrected. The church held some false views concerning the Lord's coming. They were worried about some who had died, fearing that they would not have any part in the rapture and glory of the Lord's return. Others were so overwhelmed by the truth of Christ's return that they were neglecting their daily tasks (*4:10-12*). Wishing to correct these wrong views and to inspire and comfort these new converts, Paul wrote this Epistle.

This is an intimate Epistle. The letter is a heart-to-heart talk. Paul gets very close to his "brothers" (i.e., brothers and sisters in the church). This word occurs fourteen times. It is a message of comfort and instruction to those who are in the midst of persecution.

There should be nothing doubtful or divisive about this "blessed hope" of our Lord's return. No one can read the Word without finding the teaching. Let us not quarrel with one another about so sweet a message as our Lord's "I will come again." This is the Christian's hope. Let us rather be watchful, for we know not the day nor the hour when the Son of man comes.

Selected Bible Readings

Sunday: Christ's Coming an Inspiration to Young Christians (*1 Thessalonians 1*)

Monday: Christ's Coming an Encouragement to the Faithful Servant (*1 Thessalonians 2*)

Tuesday: Christ's Coming an Incentive to Love Among Christians (*1 Thessalonians 3:1— 4:12*)

Wednesday: Christ's Coming a Comfort to the Bereaved (*1 Thessalonians 4:13-18*)

Thursday: Christ's Coming a Challenge to Holy Living (*1 Thessalonians 5*)

Friday: Christ's Sudden Coming (*Matthew 24:1-27*)

Saturday: Tribulation Days (*Matthew 24:29-51*)

Christ's Coming
1 Thessalonians 1

In Paul's greeting he includes his fellow-workers, Silas and Timothy. Silas had been with him when he founded the church at Thessalonica, and Timothy had been his special messenger

Kavalla, the ancient port of Neapolis, Macedonia.

to them, carrying the good news of their progress and reporting their needs back at Corinth. We can learn much from Paul. He knew the secret of friendship so many would like to possess. He loved people. The Bible tells us how to have friends. "There is a friend who sticks closer than a brother" (*Proverbs 18:24*). This is just what Paul did. He always acknowledged others in his service and expressed appreciation for their part in every work done.

Praying as Paul Prayed

"We always thank God for all of you, mentioning you in our prayers" (*1:2*). Do we follow up our new converts as Paul did? Teacher, do you? Paul's converts were in more than a score of different cities, yet he carried them "all" in his heart and kept in touch with them.

Are we realizing as Christians why we are in the world? How seriously are we taking our task? Have we any evidence that we have been "approved by God" (*1 Thessalonians 2:4*) to be entrusted with the gospel? Paul sets forth in this letter the intensity of his ministry; his willingness to die for his new converts; and his dealing with each one.

Paul thanks God for this church. The beauty of this church did not consist of a gorgeous building of mortar and stone, but a people who are in God the Father and in the Lord Jesus Christ (*1:1*). He is very pleased about the wonderful growth these young converts have made. He holds them up as an example everywhere he goes (*1:7*). Already their zeal has made a profound impression all over Macedonia and Achaia (Greece), and everyone is talking about the wonderful way God is working in this young, vigorous church at Thessalonica.

"You became a model to all the believers in Macedonia and Achaia" (*1:7*). This is what everyone in the world is looking for—Christians who live the Christian life, who act what they believe. This is just what the Thessalonians did. Nothing was mentioned of the financial condition of their "annual budget." But their faith in God was known everywhere (*1:8*). Their missionary enthusiasm in sounding forth the Word of God had been felt all through Greece. They were what every church should be.

Life in Three Tenses

(*1 Thessalonians 1:9-10*)

Past tense—"turned to God": The believers at Thessalonica "turned to God from idols." There must be a personal turning to God from sin and unbelief if one is to become a child of God. The idols of our lives are numerous and varied. To turn to God is to forsake everything that would divide our affections or hinder us in following Him with our whole heart.

Present tense—"to serve the living God": They "turned to God from idols to serve the living and true God" (*1:9*). What a change! Serving a living God instead of going through a dead ritual that only mocked their needs by a dead silence!

Future tense—"to wait for His Son from heaven": They were serving and waiting! These early Christians believed that Christ would come again, as He had promised. This was called "that blessed hope." The prophets of old waited for the coming of the Messiah long ages before He came, but "in the fullness of time" Christ did come. The Church may have to wait long for His promised coming again the

second time. Many have lost the vision and hope. But in the fullness of time He will come as He said. Mark in your Bible these blessed promises: John 14:3; Acts 1:11; 1 Thessalonians 4:16; Revelation 1:7.

Paul believes that his one reward for all his toil and pain and suffering will consist in presenting to Christ these converts of his ministry when He comes again.

Christ's Coming
1 Thessalonians 2

Paul gives us these descriptions of his services at Thessalonica:

"Not a failure" (2:1)

"We dared to tell you his gospel" in spite of contention (2:2)

Not from "error" or "impure motives," nor trickery (2:3)

"Not trying to please men but God" (2:4)

"Never used flattery" (2:5)

For God's glory, not "for praise from men" (2:6)

"Gentle" (2:7)

Affectionate (2:8)

"Worked night and day" (2:9)

Backed by holy living (2:10-12)

Successful in its results (2:13-18).

Paul urged the Thessalonians "to live lives worthy of God" (2:12). A Christian's walk is a Christian's life. An Indian pastor who was worried about the inconsistent lives among some of his flock said to a missionary, "There is much crooked walk by those who make good talk." Our walk and our talk should be twins going along on the same trail.

Paul's letter to the Thessalonians abounds in plenty to do right now while we wait for that day of Christ's appearing. All the way through, Paul enjoins us to "work" and "labor" while we "hope."

Paul looked forward during these trying days to the "Lord Jesus Christ at his coming." His greatest reward, after he has seen his wonderful Savior's face, will be to present to Christ the young converts of his ministry, letting them share in the glory of His advent. They will be his "crown of rejoicing" (2:19-20, KJV).

Christ's Coming
1 Thessalonians 3:1—4:12

This scene describes Paul's "labor of love" among the brethren. Paul was aware of the strain under which the members of the church at Thessalonica were living. He sent Timothy from Athens to encourage them under their bitter persecution.

Timothy had brought back the good news of their "faith" and "love." This report filled Paul with unbounded joy. How glad Paul was to hear of their firm stand in the faith and to know that they thought kindly of him and his fellow workers and longed to see them! In the midst of their persecution and suffering, Paul flashed the light of that wonderful day when they would be made "blameless and holy," when they shall be changed in a moment at the return of Christ and His holy ones (1 Thessalonians 3:13).

The test of any hope a person holds is what it does for him *now*. Paul told them that the coming of the Lord should be an incentive to:

Right living (3:13)

Consistent walk (4:1)

Purity (4:3-7)

Love (4:9-10).

Paul urges personal purity and a life that is consistent with their testimony (4:1). This is the place where most Christians fail. Let us strive to have our ideals beyond reproach. Our attitude toward each other should be one of love. Remember the two commandments

Jesus gave. First, "You shall love the Lord your God," and second, "your neighbor as yourself." Paul charges us to "make your love increase and overflow for each other" (*3:12;* see also *4:9-10*).

We discover that looking for His glorious appearing does not mean living a life of idleness (*4:11-12*). Looking for Christ never makes idle hands. If we were expecting a loved one to return home after a long absence, we would not just sit down as the day of his return approached. Rather, we would be busy getting everything ready, doing the things the loved one wanted done.

Christ's Coming
1 Thessalonians 4:13-18

A little band of Indian converts in Canada came to a missionary with a strange request. "We are always hearing what God has done," they said. "Now tell us what He is going to do."

Where would you find an answer to that wise request? We have it in our Bibles. He shall come again (*1 Thessalonians 4:16*)! If one of your best friends said he was coming to see you,

you would not rest until you found out when he was coming and how. But our wonderful Lord and Savior says He is coming and He will transform the whole world and glorify all humanity. Can it be possible that we would be less curious about His coming than we would be about the fleeting visit of an earthly friend?

There is so much in these few verses that end with, "Therefore encourage each other with these words" (*4:18*). There is comfort because of His sure return.

The Christians at Thessalonica were disturbed because of their mistaken ideas about Christ's coming. They were under the impression that Christ's coming was soon and they were worried about what would happen to those who had died. What part would they have in His glorious coming and kingdom?

When Christ returns to earth, He will not come alone. Our loved ones who have fallen asleep in Christ "will God bring with him." What a meeting that will be! Death does not end all. Parents and children, husbands and wives, loved ones and friends will be united. How anxious we are to know

341

that "ours" will be in that happy throng.

"The Lord himself will come down from heaven" (*4:16*). Christ does not say He is going to send the messenger of death to bring His bride (the Church) home. He is coming Himself for her! "This same Jesus . . . will come back in the same way you have seen him go into heaven" (*Acts 1:11*). And "they will see the Son of Man coming on the clouds of the sky, with power and great glory" (*Matthew 24:30*). What a marvelous hope this is!

The Dead Shall Rise

Those who have Christian loved ones who have died should not give way to undue sorrow when they lay them in the grave, for they have a double assurance from Christ's Word. There is the hope that one day all the dead in Christ shall rise and the additional assurance that He may come again at any time. When Christ comes, He will greet the believers who are dead first and bring them with Him (see *1 Thessalonians 4:13-14*). When the archangel shall sound the trumpet call of God, announcing the Lord's coming, then "the dead in Christ will rise first" to meet Him (*4:16*). Then those that are alive and remain shall be caught up in the clouds to share with them the glory of His coming, and to be forever with the Lord (*4:17-18*).

The Living Shall Meet Him

Read 4:17. Paul assures us that all shall not die before He comes; see 1 Corinthians 15:51-52.

"And so we will be with the Lord forever" (*1 Thessalonians 4:17*). Made like Him, we shall ever be with Him. He has gone to prepare a place for you. "I will come back and take you to be with me that you also may be where I am" (*John 14:3*). Heaven is where Christ is now. There we will be.

This is heaven's greatest honor conferred on mortals.

This is the order of these great events:

The Lord's descent from heaven
The dead in Christ raised
The living believers changed
The whole company caught up to meet the Lord in the air.

Christ's Coming
1 Thessalonians 5

Christ's second coming will be like the coming of a thief in the night or like the flood in Noah's time. The world will know nothing of His return. They scoff at the idea. But Jesus said there would be "signs" before His coming so that watchful believers may know when the time is drawing near. Over and over again Jesus told them that His coming would be as a thief in the night (*Matthew 24:36,42; 25:13; Mark 13:32-37; Luke 12:40; 21:25-35*). He warned His disciples to be ever on the watch. This should be their duty and their attitude. Christians need have no fear of that glorious day.

Don't fix dates! We should live watchful lives. We should not live lives of sleepy indulgence, but "be alert and self-controlled" (*1 Thessalonians 5:6*). The hope of Christ's coming does not mean a life of idleness. Activity should be the theme of our lives, as we find it in this chapter.

While you wait, Paul gives you a grand octave upon which to play great melodies of hope. Strike every note on this wonderful octave. If you do, your life will be rich.

"Be joyful always" (*5:16*)
"Pray continually" (*5:17*)
"Give thanks in all circumstances" (*5:18*)
"Do not put out the Spirit's fire" (*5:19*)

"Do not treat prophecies with contempt" (*5:20*)

"Test everything" (*5:21*)

"Hold on to the good" (*5:21*)

"Avoid every kind of evil" (*5:22*).

"You also must be ready, because the Son of Man will come at an hour when you do not expect him" (*Luke 12:40*). Every morning when we rise we should say to ourselves, "Be ready for your Lord's return for He may come today." Every night our closing question should be, "Would I be ready for my Lord if He should come before I wake?" (*1 Thessalonians 3:12-13*). Don't live to be ready to die, but live that you may be ready for Christ's coming (*5:4-8*)!

39. UNDERSTANDING
Second Thessalonians

Second Thessalonians Portrays Jesus Christ, Our Returning Lord

This is the second Epistle about the "blessed hope," or the coming again of our Lord Jesus Christ. These Thessalonians were forward-looking people. Paul talks to them about what is uppermost in their minds and thoughts. The first Epistle says, "He is surely coming again." The second Epistle says, "But work and wait till He comes."

The second coming of Christ is mentioned 318 times in 260 chapters of the New Testament. From this, we see how important this subject is. We read the prophecies of the Old Testament with deepest interest to find out about our Lord's first advent upon this earth. We should be just as interested to discover what the New Testament teaches regarding His second coming "in power and great glory." He said He was coming again. Here are His words: "And if I go and prepare a place for you, I will come back" (*John 14:3*). He intended that His disciples should understand that His second coming would be in as literal a sense as His going away.

First Thessalonians tells about Christ coming for His Church. The coming of Christ should be cleared up a bit in our minds. One day Christ will come to take away His bride, the Church. He will not be seen of the world at that time, but those who are His, including the dead in Christ, shall be "caught up" to meet Him. This is the teaching of 1 Thessalonians. After a period of seven years of tribulation for those left on the earth, Christ will appear to the world with His Church to establish His throne upon the earth. Then He will be seen by all people. His "coming," then, includes both of these two events, seven years apart. We as Christians are looking for the first event. The world will not see Him until the end of the seven years (*2 Thessalonians*).

Second Thessalonians tells about Christ coming with His mighty angels. The two events, Christ coming for His Church and His coming with His mighty angels, are really two aspects of but one occurrence. Between these two aspects, the Jewish people reoccupy their own land of Palestine; the gathering of the Gentile nations against them takes place; the Antichrist becomes the world ruler; he makes a covenant with the Jewish people and breaks it. Following this is the great tribulation. (See *Matthew 24:21-22.*) Then Christ will come with His saints and set up His kingdom on this earth with Jerusalem as the center. Christ will come first and receive His own unto Himself before that great and terrible day "of His revelation" in judgment upon His enemies.

This second letter was written almost immediately after 1 Thessalonians. In addition to their trials and persecutions, the Thessalonian Christians were "unsettled" and "alarmed" (*2 Thessalonians 2:2*) by deceivers who made some believe that they were already passing through the great tribulation and that "the day of the Lord was already here." Paul tries to clear up the difficulty. Always, when war is threatening and sorrow seems to cover the earth, people wonder if they are in the end "tribulation" time. This second epistle to the Thessalonians is good for all to read so that these errors in our thinking shall be cleared up.

The church at Thessalonica was carried away with the expectation of Christ's glorious return. Who can help but be thrilled when thinking about His triumphant coming? But we must keep our feet on the ground. We must work while we wait, and pray as we watch, for there is much to do while Christ tarries.

The message here is something like our Lord's word to His disciples in Acts 1:6. You remember their eager question, "Lord, are you at this time going to restore the kingdom?"

"Leave that with the Father," Jesus in effect replied. "Do your day's work and wait. The kingdom is coming."

Christ's Coming
2 Thessalonians 1

We find that Silas and Timothy are mentioned again in the salutation of this letter. From this we judge that this letter followed the first rather quickly. These two aides were still with Paul. Paul commends the young Christians at Thessalonica warmly before he rebukes them. Let us always look and see if we can find something to commend in those we would criticize. Paul did this so often. He noticed that the promise of the Lord's coming again had inspired them to a growth in faith (*2 Thessalonians 1:3*) and "perseverance" (*1:4*). They knew that when

Selected Bible Readings

Sunday: Paul's Salutations (*Ephesians 1:1-2; Philippians 1:1-4; Colossians 1:1-3; 1 Thessalonians 1:1-3; 2 Thessalonians 1:1-4*)

Monday: Christ's Coming Our Comfort (*2 Thessalonians 1:5-12*)

Tuesday: Events Preceding Christ's Coming (*2 Thessalonians 2:1-12*)

Wednesday: An Appeal to Sound Doctrine (*2 Thessalonians 2:13-17*)

Thursday: The Close of the Age (*Matthew 24:13-31*)

Friday: Warnings to the Wicked Concerning His Coming (*Matthew 24:30-31; Mark 8:38; 2 Thessalonians 1:7-8; Jude 14-15; Revelation 1:7*)

Saturday: Consistent Christian Conduct (*2 Thessalonians 3:1-18*)

Christ came, wrongs would be righted and the Lord would deal with those who had oppressed them, for this was a much persecuted church (*1:5-7*).

How does Paul describe this event of the coming of Christ? It is sudden and startling. "This will happen when the Lord Jesus is revealed from heaven in blazing fire with his powerful angels." This is no mild appearing for "those who do not know God." It will be very different for His own. We read that unbelievers "will be punished with everlasting destruction and shut out from the presence of the Lord and from the majesty of his power on the day he comes" but that Jesus will "be glorified in his holy people and to be marveled at among all those who have believed" (*1:7-10*). What a wonderful day this will be for them! Yes, He is coming. Remember the promise of the two as Jesus went into heaven. Read Acts 1:11. What a sharp contrast is shown between the glorious destiny of believers when Christ comes and the punishment of the wicked (*2 Thessalonians 1:7-12*)!

Many believe that Christ will not come to set up His kingdom till all the world is converted, but verses 7-12 of this first chapter seem to destroy this view. Read them carefully and you will find that the thing emphasized is that the coming of the Lord will be a terror for the disobedient, and Christ says, "When the Son of Man comes, will he find faith on the earth?" (*Luke 18:8*).

The world has never seen our Lord Jesus since it crucified Him. He has been hidden from its view. But one day He will appear to the whole world. In 1 Thessalonians 4, Paul says that at first Christ will descend from heaven and, with the shout of the archangel, the Church will be caught away to be forever with the Lord. At that time He will be seen only by His own. He is coming for His Church. Read 1 Thessalonians 4:16-17.

Here in 2 Thessalonians Paul says He will appear to the world with the angels of His power "in blazing fire with his powerful angels. He will punish those who do not know God" (*1:7-8*). First He comes to take His own out of this world. They will be caught up to meet Him in the air (*1 Thessalonians 4:17*). Then He appears for judgment (*Jude 15*).

Christ's Coming
2 Thessalonians 2

The Thessalonian Christians were suffering great persecution, and some of them had begun to think they were passing through the great tribulation of which Christ spoke as the terrible time that should precede His coming, and that the day of the Lord was already present. They were disturbed about the time of the Lord's coming and were entertaining wrong views about the nearness of His return. The reason for this was that a forged letter and report, both supposed to have come from the apostle Paul, had confused the church and added fuel to the fire (*2 Thessalonians 2:2*). Jesus had told the disciples, "See to it that no one misleads you" (*Matthew 24:4, NASB*).

The coming again of Christ to the earth is the "blessed hope" of the Church. His coming is "at hand" because it is the greatest future event, but it may not be immediate because God must finish His plan before Christ comes. Do not be anxious. God will take care of His own program of the ages. But know this—the "man of lawlessness" (*2 Thessalonians 2:3*) must be revealed first, and the "secret power of lawlessness" (*v. 7*) work itself out.

The "man of lawlessness" ("man of sin" in the *KJV*) is the same as the Antichrist spoken of by Daniel the prophet, and by the Lord in Matthew 24:23-24. In Revelation 13:1-8, John tells about him.

The Antichrist is a counterfeit Christ. Satan in a last desperate effort will try to imitate Christ. The world would not have God's Man; now they must have Satan's man.

Before the Day of the Lord's Judgment

The Lord's coming will be "sudden," but sudden does not necessarily mean "immediate." They were to wait expectantly for this time when the Lord would gather His children to Himself. Christ tells us always to be ready. The "day of the Lord" is "at hand" but it will not come until certain things take place. God always follows a program. Paul warns the people against confusing the hope of Christ's coming for His Church with the day of the Lord's judgment. Before this "day of the Lord's judgment," the following things must happen:

A great "falling away" from the faith

(*2 Thessalonians 2:3, KJV*). How true this is, in the day in which we are living! People are leaving "the faith that was once for all entrusted to the saints" (*Jude 3*), and "denying the sovereign Lord who bought them" with His own precious blood (*2 Peter 2:1*), and "crucifying the Son of God all over again and subjecting him to public disgrace" (*Hebrews 6:6*). The world acknowledges Christ to be a teacher, but not the Savior. "Because of the increase of wickedness, the love of most will grow cold" (*Matthew 24:12*). These are perilous times. Scoffers will arise and ridicule the idea of Christ's coming.

The "lawless one" must be revealed. He will be revealed before Christ appears to the world. But not until the Lord has caught up His own will the lawless one come into public view (*2 Thessalonians 2:8*). This "lawless one" is described in 2:4. He will oppose God; he has the title "Antichrist."

The "man of lawlessness" will open his awful campaign against the Lord.

When Christ comes, He will find the Antichrist ruling with all power and signs and lying wonders. It will be a time marked with strong delusions. This is Paul's prediction of the Antichrist. "The sin of man has its final outcome in the man of sin." Read Matthew 24:24. He will be destroyed by Christ.

The Antichrist—"Christ's counterfeit":

Will establish himself in Jerusalem (*Matthew 24:15*)
Will make war with the saints (*Revelation 13:7*)
Will be worshiped as God (*2 Thessalonians 2:4*)
Will do signs and lying wonders (*2 Thessalonians 2:9*)
Will work for only three and a half years (*Revelation 13:5-6*)
Will be cast into the lake of fire at Christ's coming (*Revelation 19:20*).

Is the World Getting Better?

Does Paul teach that the world is

The Hinnom Valley, Jerusalem, where fires of garbage burned continually, giving us the name "Gehenna" for the place of "blazing fire."

getting better? Is it true that the preaching of the gospel is going to win the whole world for Christ? If so, has the gospel failed? What is God's plan for this present age?

The gospel has not failed. It is accomplishing just what Christ intended it should accomplish—the gathering out from the world of a people for His name, the Church. On the other hand, there is this "mystery of lawlessness" working (*2:7, NASB*), a development of anarchy among all classes of society. Don't be disheartened. Paul gives us a picture of the state of the world at the close of this age when Christ shall come again. There will be a great departure from the faith. In fact, Christ asks, "When the Son of Man comes, will he find faith on the earth?" (*Luke 18:8*). This is the picture of the Church preceding Christ's return—a falling away, a great apostasy. Does Christ really mean this? We should judge so from His description of the end days in Matthew 24:1-14,36-42.

When Christ returns, He will find Antichrist (the man of lawlessness) carrying out his satanic plans. From the description of the man of lawlessness in the Scriptures and his diabolical role of "counterfeit miracles, signs and wonders" (*2 Thessalonians 2:9*), we do not see how that and the millennial glory could exist together. It is just as God said it would be. Indeed, the darkest clouds that are gathering are but harbingers of the golden day that is surely coming when our Lord Himself shall return to take up the reins of government.

Christ's Coming
2 Thessalonians 3

The time of this glorious event is to be left with God. The delay in the Lord's coming gives us real opportunities for service. We might have two wrong views of the Lord's coming. Either we become restless and troubled because of having to wait so long, or grow idle because we know that when He comes He will right every wrong and overthrow iniquity. But both of these attitudes are wrong. We are not just to stand and wait, but rather have "our loins girded" for service, making ready for the glorious day when He shall come. Let us not abandon the work Christ has given us to do.

Paul gives some instructions to the Thessalonians:

Stand firm—don't be influenced by false teaching (*2:15*).

Hold to the teachings we passed on to you—don't lose any of your foundation truth (*2:15*).

Encourage your hearts (*2:17*).

Strengthen you in every good deed and word (*2:17*).

Then Paul asks for their prayers (*2 Thessalonians 3:1*). His heart was burdened and he needed their fellowship. He had great confidence in their faith.

The hope of Christ's coming stimulates without exciting; sobers without depressing. It is a balancing doctrine. We find in this Epistle that our Lord's delay gives us opportunities to:

Be loyal to Him (*2:15*)
Evangelize the world (*3:1*)
Pray for His servants (*3:1-2*)
Patiently wait for Him (*3:5*)
Live a holy life (*3:6-14*).

Some thought that because Christ was coming they would just withdraw from business and not work, claiming the right to be supported by the brethren who had money. Paul was very drastic in his dealing with these lazy fellows. The attitude on the part of these men was absolutely wrong, and he asked them to look to him for an example. He never ceased to labor while he was preaching to them. He laid down a great principle of life that "if a man will not work, he shall not eat" (*2 Thessalonians 3:10*).

40. UNDERSTANDING
First Timothy

First Timothy Portrays Jesus Christ, Our Teacher

The key verse to 1 Timothy is 3:15, that "you will know how people ought to conduct themselves in God's household, which is the church of the living God." Realizing that behavior is based upon belief, Paul stresses sound doctrine.

First and 2 Timothy and Titus are the three pastoral Epistles, written to ministers in charge of important churches instead of to the churches themselves. Both Timothy and Titus were given explicit directions for shepherding the sheep, for guarding the churches after Paul should be called "home," as he knew he soon would be (*2 Timothy 4:7-8*). Timothy had been entrusted with the government and supervision of Ephesus, and Titus of the church at Crete. How inadequate both of these young men felt!

Because Timothy was a young man, we may expect to find in Paul's writings to him valuable suggestions for other young men who are living the Christian life, and we are not disappointed in this expectation; but we also find helpful suggestions for those who are older in years. It would be interesting for your class to select from the two letters to Timothy the admonitions that are up to date. It would be helpful for those who think the Bible is out of date.

In this day of modern education, it is well to offer to young people a commendation of the faith of their fathers, and to warn them against what is falsely called "knowledge" (*6:20*). It is well to enjoin them to "fight the good fight, holding on to faith and a good conscience" (*1:18-19*). And when athletic contests threaten to consume the major portion of interest and time in scholastic circles, it is good for young Christians to remind themselves that "physical training is of some value, but godliness has value for all things, holding promise for both the present life and the life to come" (*4:8*). And who can hear Paul's words to his young associate without hearing him say across the years to our own young people: Whatever it costs, "keep yourself pure" (*5:22*).

It was a real honor for the young Timothy to enjoy the friendship of the apostle Paul. He was one of Paul's own converts, and Paul calls him "my son whom I love, who is faithful in the Lord" (*1 Corinthians 4:17*). During the impressionable days of Timothy's boyhood, while Paul was visiting Lystra, the people first tried to worship the apostle, then sought to take his life. How Timothy had listened to the gospel preached by Paul! He saw him heal the cripple, heard him as he appealed to the multitude and then saw him stoned and left for dead. But the next day Paul rose and came again into the city. Among the most enthusiastic converts of that city were Eunice and her son Timothy.

When Paul came back to Lystra on his second missionary journey, he took Timothy along as his companion. What a wonderful thing for so young a man! After long years of training under this mighty man of God, Timothy was left in charge of the important church at Ephesus. This brought the timid young man face-to-face with serious problems. Think of this inexperienced young fellow being left in that big church to take the place of a man like its founder Paul! How unworthy he must have felt! How he leaned on the apostle for advice and direction!

While Timothy was acting as pastor in Ephesus Paul wrote his two letters to Timothy, as letters of instruction and guidance indeed to Timothy, but also as a handbook for Christian pastors through the centuries. Paul instructed Timothy to deal severely with false teachers, to direct public worship, choose church officers and to work with all classes found in the church. But most important of all, he must lead a life that would be an example to all. Timothy had a hard task.

Paul had won a vast multitude to Christ during his stay in Ephesus. In the succeeding years, the number of converts increased tremendously. Within the next fifty years, so many of the non-Christians turned to Christ that their idolatrous temples were almost forsaken.

One of the things to remember about this time of the Early Church is that there were no church buildings. Groups of Christians met in homes. No churches were built until about 200 years after Paul's day, and not until Constantine (Constantine the Great, d. 337, Roman emperor) put an end to the persecution of Christians. This meant that there would be hundreds of small congregations, each with its own pastor. These pastors were called "elders" (*Acts 20:17*). In these letters to Timothy they are called "overseers" (*1 Timothy 3:1*; "bishops" in the *KJV*). Timothy's work was with these various pastors.

Warning Against False Teaching *1 Timothy 1*

Paul calls Timothy his "true son in the faith" (*1:2*). It is clear that the boy was led to Christ by Paul. He was an example of one accepting Christ as a child because he had been brought up in a home in which the Scriptures were taught. This is the kind of Christian experience we need to emphasize today as not only possible, but also as that which should be the normal experience.

There has never been a day when the Church has been free from false teachers who present new and strange doctrines. They are hard to combat because they base their teachings on parts of God's Word, and do not "correctly handle the word of truth"

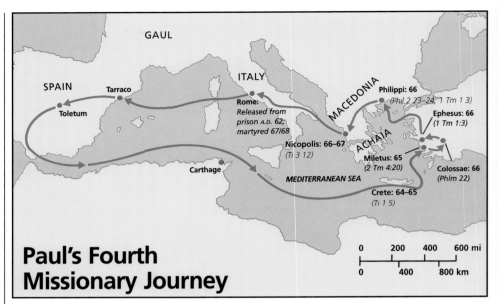

Paul's Fourth Missionary Journey

GAUL

SPAIN
Tarraco
Toletum

ITALY
Rome:
Released from
prison A.D. 62;
martyred 67/68

MACEDONIA
Philippi: 66
(Phil 2 23–24; 1 Tm 1 3)

Ephesus: 66
(1 Tm 1:3)

Nicopolis: 66–67
(Ti 3 12)

ACHAIA

Miletus: 65
(2 Tm 4:20)

Colossae: 66
(Phlm 22)

Carthage

MEDITERRANEAN SEA

Crete: 64–65
(Ti 1 5)

| 0 | 200 | 400 | 600 mi |
| 0 | 400 | | 800 km |

Paul may have embarked on a fourth missionary journey, during which he wrote 1 Timothy and Titus.

(*2 Timothy 2:15*) and interpret it as a whole. What the Church needs today is instruction in the vital truths. In contrast with the teaching of the Law and "myths and endless genealogies" (*1 Timothy 1:4*), Paul puts "the glorious gospel of the blessed God" (*1:11*). Therefore Timothy must safeguard against any other doctrine. Don't mix fables and legends with the gospel!

Paul warns Timothy to hold "faith and a good conscience" (*1:19*) because these save people from spiritual shipwreck.

Paul wants Timothy to live a life that will vindicate the truth he preaches. He challenges him to be a good soldier of Jesus Christ. Let us remember that we will not fight very hard for a truth we do not live. As with Timothy, so with us. "What Timothy will preach will be empowered and made mighty by what Timothy is." Timothy is charged to fight the good warfare (*1 Timothy 1:18*). This presents the thought of a cam-

paign and all the responsibilities of the officer in command.

Paul humbly declares: "Here is a trustworthy saying that deserves full acceptance: Christ Jesus came into the world to save sinners—of whom I am the worst" (*1:15*).

Here we catch a glimpse of the man, who probably did more for Christ than any other throughout the ages since the world began, bowed to his knees with the feeling of his own unworthiness. Although Paul was once a blasphemer, now God in His grace had appointed him an apostle; and although he had persecuted Him, now he could proclaim His love. The closer we get to the heart of Christ, the more we realize our own unworthiness.

Directions for the Church
1 Timothy 2—3

The Church has a great calling. We are not only called upon to plead with people to turn to God, but also to plead with God the cause of people. Read what Paul says: "I urge, then, first of all, that requests, prayers, intercession and thanksgiving be made for everyone—for kings and all those in authority" (*1 Timothy 2:1-2*). Yes, he tells us to pray for rulers. It is well to remember that Nero was the emperor of Rome at this time! Under this wicked despot, Paul was imprisoned and soon would be beheaded. This proves to us that we must pray for bad rulers as well as good, "that we may live peaceful and quiet lives in all godliness and holiness" (*2:2*).

Remember when we pray that God "wants all men to be saved and to come to a knowledge of the truth. For there is one God and one mediator between God and men, the man Christ Jesus" (*2:4-5*). Paul makes it clear that when we pray for someone we can go straight to God for that person. We need no saint or virgin to approach near to God, only the One who gave Himself a ransom for all. Our blessed Lord Himself stands in God's presence pleading for us.

Finally, let all who pray be clean in conduct and pure in character (*2:8-10*). Let us lift up "holy hands" when we pray. That means that we should not fill our lives with worthless pleasures or needless things that absorb, but come to the Lord with a heart that is cleansed (*1 John 1:9*).

Church Leadership
Two officers are described who shall direct the church: bishops and deacons. Paul outlines the requirement for both groups.

We find as we look at this that the pastor must be a man of blameless character, "husband of but one wife, not quarrelsome, not greedy for money. He must be a skillful teacher, and one who makes his own children obey. He must not be a new convert lest his head be turned with pride. He must have a good reputation in his community (*3:2-7*). It is important that the Church have the right leadership. Good pastors lead a church forward. How we need good and faithful shepherds today!

Deacons must have the same moral qualifications as elders or pastors. This office is not inferior, but different. The two offices were to be complementary to each other. A deacon must be as carefully chosen. Sometimes it may be necessary to appoint women to this office.

Paul shows us the need of Christian conduct. Church manners are a lost art in most places today. It makes a great deal of difference how we behave, for behavior reveals character. It is not "do-havior" but "be-havior" that counts. What we are speaks so loudly that people cannot hear what we say.

The Church
Paul gives us a beautiful description of the Church and states her purpose. He tells you how Christians "ought to conduct themselves in God's household, which is the church of the living God, the pillar and foundation of the truth" (*3:15*). The Church upholds all truth in the sight of people. She is the only earthly institution to which Christ committed the preaching of the gospel.

Directions for the Pastor
1 Timothy 4—6

Picture the young pastor Timothy awed by his instructor, the fifty-year-old apostle Paul, as he says, "in later times some will abandon the faith" giving themselves up to spiritualism and all of its teachings. They will tell you if you would be holy, you must not marry, neither should you eat certain kinds of food. But let us not put a ban on that which God has given for our good. Turn a deaf ear to foolish "isms" filled with "do this" and "don't do that." People are always trying to find what they can "do" to inherit eternal life (see *4:2-5*). But Paul goes on to say, "If you point these things out to the brothers, you will be a good minister of Christ Jesus" (*4:6*).

Lead a godly life. "Godliness has value" (*4:8*). True religion is an appeal to common sense. God says it pays. In one way, Christianity is a business. It asks us to get out our account books, to study the current prices, to consider the possibilities of profit and loss, and decide, "What good is it for a man to gain the whole world, yet forfeit his soul?" (*Mark 8:36*). Paul, after taking account, found that what he had counted as "gain" was "loss."

Paul says to the young minister and to those of you who may be ministers, "Don't think entirely in terms of the physical, how you can please your body." Everyone is thinking in terms of "having fun," of "doing things." The body must be fed, clothed, entertained and pleased! "Physical training is of some value," says Paul, "but godliness has value for all things, holding promise for both the present life and the life to come" (*1 Timothy 4:8*). Start living for eternity!

"Set an example for the believers in speech, in life, in love, in faith and in purity" (*4:12*). Carry conviction and command respect. In order to do this, give much attention to your reading and preaching and teaching. The best way to combat any error is by reiterating the simple gospel truth. The Bible itself will do the job, if only you give it a chance. "Give yourself wholly to" the Scriptures (*1 Timothy 4:15*).

The way a minister treats his flock is of vital importance. He must deal wisely and fairly with each one. The widows must be cared for. Elders must be honored and supported, but they must also be reproved, even in public, if they are found guilty, that others may be warned. In other words, sin can never get by in the Church, no matter who is guilty of that sin.

Paul even remembers the Christian slaves. They must be taught. Those who serve unbelieving masters are to let their service be a testimony to these unbelievers. Those who serve Christians should not take advantage because of their spiritual relation. Love should make us serve the better.

"Fight the good fight of the faith" (*6:12*). Christ makes His appeal to the heroic in a man or woman. The Christian life is not a thing to be entered into lightly. We will not be carried into heaven on flowery beds of ease. We must fight if we would be conquerors. But it is a "good fight."

41. UNDERSTANDING
Second Timothy

Second Timothy Portrays Jesus Christ, Our Example

"Endure hardship with us like a good soldier of Christ Jesus" (*2 Timothy 2:3*). Be loyal to Christ and His Word! In 1 Timothy, Paul enjoins a straight gospel; in 2 Timothy, a straight life.

In 1 Timothy, Paul is saying, "Guard the doctrine which is our message from God." In 2 Timothy, Paul is saying, "Guard the testimony which is our life from God."

After writing his first Epistle to Timothy, Paul was arrested again, in Greece or Asia Minor, and hurried back to Rome, this time as a criminal (*2:9*). While waiting in the Roman dungeon for "the time for his departure" (*4:6*) he wrote this last letter to his beloved son in the gospel, Timothy. His arrest had been so sudden and unexpected that he had had no time to collect his valuable books and parchments, or even to take his warm cloak with him (*4:13*).

This second imprisonment was very different from the first. Then he had his own rented house; now he was kept in close confinement. Before, he was the center of a large circle of friends, accessible to all, but now he was alone (*4:10-12*). Before, he had hoped for freedom; now he was expecting to die (*4:6*). Paul had already appeared before the wicked Nero, but his case had been postponed (*4:16-17*). He expected to appear again in the winter and wrote urging Timothy to

come immediately and bring Mark with him. He asked him to bring the things that were left (*4:9,11,13,21*). Being uncertain whether Timothy could get there before his death (and he did not, for his trial probably took place in June rather than the next winter), he wanted to give him his

Selected Bible Readings

Sunday: Fan to Flame the Gift of God
(*2 Timothy 1:1-9*)

Monday: Guard the Good Deposit
(*2 Timothy 1:10-18*)

Tuesday: Endure Hardship Like a Good Soldier
(*2 Timothy 2:1-15*)

Wednesday: Follow Righteousness
(*2 Timothy 2:16-26*)

Thursday: Know the Scriptures
(*2 Timothy 3:1-17*)

Friday: Be Faithful to the End
(*2 Timothy 4:1-22*)

Saturday: Receive a Crown
(*1 Corinthians 9:25;*
2 Timothy 4:8;
James 1:12;
1 Peter 5:4;
Revelation 2:10; 3:11)

last words of warning and encouragement.

It is well to remember that this is Paul's last writing. This Epistle is very personal. He mentions twenty-three individuals. Although alone and facing death, yet he forgot himself in thinking of others.

Endure in the Camp— The Home 2 *Timothy 1*

Timothy had been reared in a Christian home with his mother, Eunice, and his grandmother Lois. Paul mentions these wonderful Christian women and commends Timothy for having had early training at a consecrated hearth (*2 Timothy 3:15*).

Paul remembers Timothy's pure faith that "first lived in your grandmother Lois and in your mother Eunice and, I am persuaded, now lives in you also" (*1:5*). Someone said, "When you want to make a great person, start with his grandmother." Whatever may be the value of that observation, one thing is sure—when you want to build a Timothy, you must begin in the Primary department.

Paul calls Timothy "my true son" (*1 Timothy 1:2*). It seems clear that the youth was led to confess Christ by Paul during his first missionary journey. He was a Christian from childhood. It is no surprise that Paul saw in Timothy a lad of promise as a minister in the Early Church. He became Paul's understudy, and at the end of the apostle's life, he was the best man to whom Paul could turn over his work.

Timothy possessed fine qualities, but he had excellent training as well. He was a thoroughly Christian young man. He had a splendid reputation in his own church. He was the constant companion of the great apostle Paul. He knew the Word of God and made use of it in his life and teachings (*3:14-*

16). He demonstrated a splendid spirit of unselfishness in his service. He was given great responsibilities by Paul. All this was instrumental in a large degree in his training (*1:3; 3:15; 4:6-12*).

Man of God

Timothy is addressed as "man of God" (*1 Timothy 6:11*). What does that mean? Godliness comes from the Word and prayer, God speaking to us and our speaking to God.

The key verse is 2 Timothy 1:13: "What you heard from me, keep as the pattern of sound teaching, with faith and love in Christ Jesus." Paul's life was characterized by an unceasing effort to guard in its purity the priceless treasure of the Christian faith. He wanted it kept untarnished. We live in a day when it is being said that it is deeds not doctrine that count, but Paul's teaching was that conduct must be based on creed. "As a man thinketh . . . so is he" (*Proverbs 23:7, KJV*). Wrong thinking makes for wrong acting. World War II was brought about by men possessed with wrong creeds. These creeds soon became conduct, and millions died to correct it.

Stir the Gift

How easy it is for us not to make use of our gifts and natural endowments! How many lose all initiative! How few people think! Timothy had one of the gifts of the Spirit (*1 Corinthians 12*). He seems to have been neglecting to use it. In the first letter (*4:14*) Paul says, "Do not neglect your gift" and in the second letter (*1:6*), Paul writes, "Fan into flame the gift of God." How about our gift? Have we ever let God tell us what it is? Cultivate whatever God has given.

We find in this first chapter one of the apostle's "I know's." It is a verse that gives us great assurance. "I know whom I have believed, and am con-

Timothy was sent to Ephesus by Paul, and is believed to have become bishop of the church in that city.

vinced that he is able to guard what I have entrusted to him for that day" (*1:12*).

Endure in the Field
2 Timothy 2

We must "endure hardship . . . like a good soldier" (*2 Timothy 2:3*) away from home, in the school, in the office and in the place of business. This is our field of service and discipline. Here we are to stand the test as one who "needeth not to be ashamed."

Paul says, as a faithful steward "entrust to reliable men who will also be qualified to teach others" (*2:2*). As a brave soldier, endure hardships. A soldier does not become entangled with ordinary affairs, but is under the authority of a superior officer. He leaves his business and friends to serve in the army. Let that be our attitude. The athlete, too, must observe this to gain the wreath of victory. Just as the farmer is the first to enjoy the fruit of the harvest, so will it be with you. Avoid business entanglements that will keep

you from rendering the best service. Watch, too, lest the comforts of life and the common enjoyments make us love ease too well (*2:3-7*).

Endure your hardships courageously and with the spirit of a hero. Don't just endure!

For one who was a good man, Paul was enduring the cruelest of suffering. He was charged as a criminal and was being put in chains. But he was glad to suffer anything, just so the gospel would not be chained. He reminds Timothy that he is worshiping a living Christ. "Remember Jesus Christ, raised from the dead, descended from David. This is my gospel," he said (*2:8*). Even though his body was bound, his mind was on "eternal glory."

Paul urged the people to keep away from foolish discussion, for these only breed quarrels and a Christian should not quarrel (*2:24*). Do not argue about the Christian life. Live it! Outlive the world—live better than they do—and they will soon listen to what you have to say. The best argument for Christ is a victorious life.

God gives us a sure foundation upon which to build our lives—the foundation laid by God (2:19). It "stands firm," for that Rock is Christ. All who build on it are sealed for Him. This is the inscription: "The Lord knows those who are his." It is wonderful to know that we are known personally by Him. This is not true of any other religion under heaven. In Christianity we are God's children and He knows every one of us. "And even the very hairs of your head are all numbered" (Matthew 10:30). He calls us by name.

God's work needs real gentility. It was said of the Messiah, "You stoop down to make me great" (Psalm 18:35). Gentleness and conviction in the ministry will break down hatred for the Church and give the Church its rightful place. Study to be gentle.

Endure in the Fight
2 Timothy 3

When the battle is on and our faith is assailed, stand firm and strong. Fight effectively with a life that is lived "godly in Christ Jesus" (3:12). During every engagement, let us wield the Word that is the sword of the Spirit. Let us be soldiers "thoroughly equipped for every good work" (3:17).

There is but one way to be strengthened against all these vices today. We find it in verses 14 through 17. The Scriptures will make us wise unto salvation (3:15). Jesus met His temptations by the Word of God. We can do no better.

Paul's catalog of first-century vices sounds like a list of twentieth-century vices (3:1-5):

Lovers of themselves more than lovers of God.

Lovers of money—those who will do anything to gain possession of what they want.

Proud and boastful—pride fills the natural heart.

Blasphemers (KJV)—taking God's name in vain.

Disobedient to parents—there seems to be no respect today in the home.

Unthankful—no gratitude, taking everything for granted.

Unholy—those who care for neither God nor people.

Without natural affection (KJV)—mothers taking the lives of their own children; divorce courts full; pornography and homosexuality rampant.

"Truce-breakers" (KJV)—promises mean nothing.

Lovers of pleasure—this age has gone pleasure-mad.

Having a form of godliness but denying its power—there is only one source of power and that is the gospel of Christ Jesus.

Endure to the Death
2 Timothy 4

To endure to the end and look back over a hard and bitter fight and say, "I have won!"—that is enduring as a good soldier. Life's last hours for Paul were full of glory. He forgot that the lions in the arena or the flames at the stake or a cruel cross might end his earthly life at any moment. His good fight was ended, his long hard race was run, and now only the memories of a noble life gave him great peace.

He closes this letter with a solemn farewell charge to Timothy before God and Christ who will judge him and who soon will appear to spread the gospel everywhere. "Preach the Word; be prepared in season and out of season . . . For the time will come when men will not put up with sound doctrine" (vv. 2-3).

Paul's Valedictory

This is the grandest utterance of the grandest mortal who ever lived. Where can we match Paul's words that he wrote from his dungeon to Timothy, his own true son in the faith? Let us picture the old battle-scarred hero of the Cross, standing in the gloomy dungeon, bound with chains and looking up through the one opening in the roof of his cell through which only a tiny shaft of light could enter, but which reveals his countenance with the expression of perfect peace. Read 2 Timothy 4:7-8.

Ever since Jesus had laid His hand upon him, Paul seemed to have been contending in the arena and running in the stadium. There had been scarcely a moment of rest. It was an intense training and a strenuous wrestling all the way through. But within, peace reigned. His questions were answered. His sins were forgiven. His wants were supplied. Peace within but the athlete's contest without. This is the true Christian life.

Coming with Crowns

The crown is for Paul but it is also for us—"to all who have longed for his appearing." You and I, whose achievements are so much less than Paul's, may yet be partakers of Paul's heaven.

Surely the "crown" that gleams before us should spur us on to a new diligence in service. Do we love His appearing?

The last verses of this letter give us a glimpse of the loneliness of this great wrestler and runner. Many were leaving him under the stress of persecution. "But the Lord stood at my side and gave me strength, so that through me the message might be fully proclaimed" (*4:17*). This is the secret of Paul's success. This is why he could fight a good fight and finish the course. His greatest opportunity seemed to be reserved for the end. He stood in Nero's courthouse, face-to-face with the "lion," as he designated him. He was alone as far as human help was concerned. The great basilica was crowded and every eye was fastened on the forsaken old man at the bar. Did he lose heart? Was he afraid? No, indeed! He leaped to the height of the momentous occasion. He was not content in defending himself. That he did, but much more. To the multitude, curious and hostile, he told clearly the gospel of Christ, and all the Gentiles heard.

42. UNDERSTANDING
Titus and Philemon

**Titus and Philemon Portray Jesus Christ,
Our Pattern; Our Lord and Master**

Understanding Titus

The importance of good works is stressed in this Epistle. Not that we are saved by good works, but we are saved for good works. God presents His ideal for the Church and its officers and members.

The Epistle to Titus was written by Paul. Titus was bishop of Crete, a hard post (*1:12-13*). Paul had given Titus the difficult task before of settling the differences at Corinth and tactfully persuading the Church to do the right thing in the matter of divisions. Paul's second letter to the Corinthians shows how successful Titus was in this mission. Titus was a Gentile. No doubt he was one of Paul's converts during the early years of the apostle's ministry. He accompanied Paul and Barnabas to Jerusalem seventeen years after Paul's conversion.

When Paul heard that Apollos was about to go to Crete, he took the opportunity to send this letter to Titus (*3:13*). It is full of practical advice to the young pastor and directed him in his administration, and warned him against the heretics of his day. He asks Titus to come to him and to report about the condition of the church in the island. Although this is a personal letter, it undoubtedly was to be read to the church also.

The letter is very much like Paul's first letter to Timothy, being written about the same time, and dealing with the same subjects.

Works for Church Officers
Titus 1

Paul presents himself in this scene as the "servant" of the Lord Jesus Christ, then as His apostle. Paul loves to call himself a bondslave of Christ. Another time he says of Christ, "whose I am and whom I serve." It is terrible to be a slave to most anyone or anything, but to be a slave of Jesus Christ—to be bought by Him, that is wonderful! It is a slavery of love.

"In grace," Charles H. Spurgeon once said, "you can be under bonds yet not in bondage. I am in bonds of wedlock but I feel no bondage. On the contrary it is joy to be so bound."

Paul kept his eyes steadfastly on heaven as he neared the end of his earthly life. Read what he says of his apostleship: "for the faith of God's elect and the knowledge of the truth . . . resting on the hope of eternal life" (*1:1-2*).

Paul left Titus in Crete to superintend the work of the church organization there. It was a hard situation, but Paul had given him a difficult task before at Corinth and he had worked out the problem. In Crete he was to set things in order and ordain elders in every city (*1:5*).

The Corinthian Temple of Apollo at dusk. Paul had given Titus the difficult task of settling the differences at Corinth and persuading the Church to do the right thing in the matter of divisions.

What kind of officers the church should have was well described. These qualifications are stated carefully. Only a man of character should even be considered. He must be blameless in his home life (*1:6*), blameless in his personal life (*1:7-8*) and true to the Word (*1:9*).

How do you act at home? What kind of a Christian are you there? This is so often the test of your Christianity. It is the home life that counts. The Christian household is the main evangelizing agency everywhere. When the home is Christian, the community is Christian. For this reason, the "bishop" ("overseer" or "elder") and pastor are enjoined to set a good example before the people. He must have but one living wife, but he is not compelled to be married. On the other hand, he is not to be prohibited from marriage, as the Roman Catholic Church normally decrees. Because a minister is judged by his family life, he must rule his own children well, for he who cannot rule his own household well cannot rule the church of God (*1 Timothy 3:5*). He must be a man of moral courage and sympathy. He must be a good teacher and encourage others by his teaching.

The Cretan churches were being upset by outside teachers who, for the sake of making money, were working havoc in "whole households" (*Titus 1:11*). This probably meant whole congregations, for the Early Church met in private homes. Paul calls these fellows "detestable, disobedient and unfit" (*1:16*) and said they must be stopped in their teaching. He demands severity in dealing with them.

As all is being shaken in confusion about us, and "there are many rebellious people, mere talkers and deceivers, . . . They must be silenced, because they are ruining whole households by teaching things they ought not to teach—and that for the sake of dishonest gain" (*1:10-11*), who "claim to know God, but by their actions they deny him" (*1:16*), so let us, I say, rest our faith not on the reasonings and opinions of people, but on the infallible Word of God. By this Word alone judge new and strange doctrines, and stop the mouths of those who handle the Word of God deceitfully (*1:9-11*).

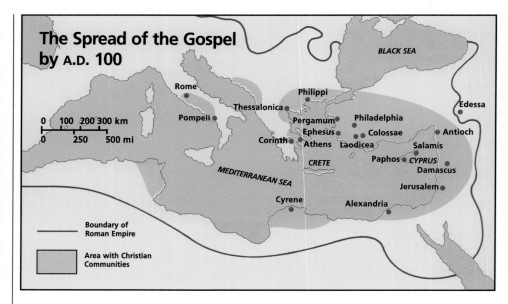

The Spread of the Gospel by A.D. 100

BLACK SEA

Rome

Philippi

Thessalonica

Pergamum

Philadelphia

Edessa

Pompeii

Ephesus

Colossae

Antioch

Corinth

Athens

Laodicea

Salamis

CRETE

Paphos

CYPRUS

Damascus

MEDITERRANEAN SEA

Jerusalem

Cyrene

Alexandria

0   100   200 300 km
0   250   500 mi

—— Boundary of Roman Empire

▨ Area with Christian Communities

Works for Church Members
Titus 2—3

Paul believed that doctrine must be expressed in life, and so he had a word to Titus about the aged (*Titus 2:2-3*), the youth (*2:4-6*) and the slaves (*2:9-10*).

The Aged:

Older Men—"temperate, worthy of respect, self-controlled, and sound in faith, in love and in endurance."

Older Women—"be reverent in the way they live" and "not to be slanderers or addicted to much wine, but to teach what is good" (*2:3*); and to train younger women to become good wives and mothers.

Youth:

Exercise self-control, be examples of a noble life.

Servants:

Obey masters, be diligent and faithful, give satisfaction; don't contradict, don't steal.

Life with a Capital L

Leave the old life.

Live the new life.

Look for that blessed hope and glorious appearing of Christ (*2:11-13*).

How essential that this be our foundation! Then we can "make the teaching about God our Savior attractive" (*2:10*). To think that we in any way can adorn the wonderful gospel by our lives! Just as we put a frame on a beautiful picture to enhance its beauty and make it more conspicuous, so we must adorn and make more beautiful the gospel of Christ. A king in his royal robes is more easily recognized as such than one in ordinary clothing. How we can either make or mar the gospel! What is the "gospel according to you"? In all things show thyself a pattern of good works (*2:7*). The test of fellowship is not warmth of devotion, but holiness of life. One cannot live on strong "feelings." Some mistake religious feeling for holiness and good thoughts for good conduct. There is use and abuse in religious emotion.

Be so faithful in your attitudes and obligations of life that critics of your religion will be silenced (2:8). Make others say, "If this is what Christ can do for you, there must be something to your religion."

Not that we are saved by good works, but we are saved unto good works. Paul says we are saved by His mercy (3:5), and justified by His grace (3:7). But because we have been saved at such a cost, we should show it by "good works."

Good Works

"God our Savior" did not save us as a result of our good works, but through His kindness and according to His mercy. He cleansed us by His blood and gave us a new life by His Holy Spirit. But we are to show forth good works:

"An example by doing what is good" (2:7)

"Eager to do what is good" (2:14)

"Ready to do whatever is good" (3:1)

"Careful to devote themselves to doing what is good" (3:8)

"Doing what is good . . . for daily necessities" (3:14).

Paul urges citizens of the heavenly kingdom to be good citizens of the country under whose flag they live. Every Christian should be submissive to rulers and authority (3:1-2; Romans 13:1-7; 1 Peter 2:13-17).

Don't say anything of a person if you can't say something good, is a wonderful admonition to follow. Paul said it long ago. "Slander no one" (3:2). Don't be quarrelsome. Show a gentle spirit in your dealing with others. It is well for us to remember that "we too were foolish, disobedient, deceived and enslaved" (3:3). Yes, we had all the faults we hate in others. It is well to remember that the things we criticize in others are very apt to be our own weaknesses. We like to call attention to these faults in others to take eyes off ourselves. Try this test on yourself.

Avoid controversies and foolish discussions. They are always useless and futile. Often an argument only strengthens a person in what was believed before. Do all you can to correct someone, but if the person persists in causing divisions among you, after being warned once or twice, have nothing more to say to that person. Reject the person (3:10). Devote your time in doing good.

Understanding Philemon

Christian love and forgiveness are given prominence in this book. It shows the power of the gospel in winning a runaway thief and slave, and in changing a master's mind. This is a book in applied Christianity, a textbook of social service.

Notice the courtesy and tactfulness of Paul's letter. Our letter writing can be a ministry for God, if we make it so. Some who find it hard to speak to anyone about Christ can write about Him. Then, too, a letter is good for the one who receives it, for the person has a chance to read and reread and think it over. Use the pen in witnessing to your friends. Remember all that has been preserved to us of Paul's ministry has come mainly through his Epistles. What a heritage his letters are for all Christians today! In order to appreciate what God thought of correspondence, see how many letters He kept for us in Holy Scripture.

In this letter, Paul intercedes with Philemon (who was an outstanding member of the church at Colosse) for a runaway slave by the name of Onesimus who had stolen from his master and made his way to Rome. There he had been providentially brought face-to-face with Paul and had found Christ as his Savior. He became endeared to the apostle by his devoted service. But Paul knew he was Philemon's lawful slave and so he could not think of keeping him permanently. So Paul sends him home and pleads with Philemon to take him back. He makes himself personally responsible for the debts that Onesimus owes, asking that they be charged to his (Paul's) account. He wished to save the runaway slave from the severe and cruel punishment he deserved according to Roman law. Paul believes the slave must not encounter his outraged master alone.

This letter deals with the question of slavery. Paul does not demand the abolition of slavery, but he shows that slavery can never be the fruit of Christianity. This beautiful letter from God's aged servant, in bonds for the gospel, foreshadows the time when the bonds of Christ's love should break the bands of slavery.

Onesimus was merely one of a world of slaves belonging to a handful of masters. In 300 B.C., 21,000 citizens of Athens owned 400,000 slaves. It was not so different proportionally in the days of the Roman Empire, at the time of the writing of this Epistle. Roman masters owned from ten to two hundred, even a thousand or more slaves, who had no rights of life or liberty!

Paul's Plea for Onesimus
Philemon 1-25

Here is a letter from Paul, the aged (*Philemon 9*). It is not always the passing of years that brings old age. The apostle had become prematurely old through work, anxiety and eagerness of spirit. He was only about sixty, but

he was a prisoner, and as such he appealed to his friend Philemon.

Paul speaks of himself as a prisoner, not, as in the letter to the Colossians, with the authority of an apostle. He writes as a friend to a friend. He says of Philemon that he is "our dear friend and fellow worker" (*v. 1*). He does not say these kind things just to flatter his friend, but because he always looked for the good in others.

This letter is addressed to a man and his wife, and presumably a son, in Colosse. A little meeting of Christians was held at their home. Paul gives us a beautiful picture of a Christian home in the time of the Early Church. This family was the nucleus of that home-church and doubtless other believers in Colosse gathered there for worship. One of the causes for the spiritual decline today is the lack of "the church in thy house." Is there one in your house? It begins around the family altar.

Paul always begins his letters with commendations unless there is a reason for not doing it, as in Galatians. He speaks of love and faith, and tells of the joy he finds in fellowship. Even though he was separated by a great distance from his friend Philemon, nevertheless this man's loving helpfulness to others had done Paul good in that far-off prison in Rome. He prays that Philemon's faith may ever grow.

Paul was a wonderful student of human nature. The picture he portrays of himself as the bent and battered "prisoner of Christ Jesus" (*v. 9*) opens a well of sympathy in the heart of Philemon as he reads his friend's letter. Onesimus, whose name means "profitable," had robbed his master and run away to the big city of Rome. In some way, he fell in with the little band of Christians surrounding Paul and was converted. Paul sends the boy back to his master with this friendly

The Acropolis, Athens. Onesimus was merely one of a world of slaves belonging to a handful of masters. In 300 B.C., 21,000 citizens of Athens owned 400,000 slaves.

personal note. He takes pleasure in playing with the fellow's name. The "unprofitable" servant now will be "profitable." Christ makes a person profitable to others.

In approaching the main purpose of the letter, Paul does not blurt it out at once. He anticipates anger, and so he uses the finest tact. He admits that Onesimus had been good for nothing in the past, but playfully alludes to his name, hoping to put the reader into a favorable mood.

While Philemon's voice trembles, Mother Apphia is wiping her eyes on her apron, and son Archippus is clearing his throat. All three read on into the letter. Paul has his little joke and pun, and the faces of the trio break into smiles. Onesimus, meanwhile, nervously fumbles with his cap in back of the door, then breaks into a broad grin, and the tension is over.

Social Management

The secret of the solution of the capital-labor problem lies in the love of Christ, such as undoubtedly existed between Philemon and Onesimus after the slave returned home.

This Epistle gives a clear idea of the attitude of Christianity to the social organization of the world. The subject of the Epistle is slavery, which was widespread in that day. If slavery is wrong, why did not Paul say so instead of apparently condoning it in this letter to the owner of a runaway slave? If Paul had made slavery an issue, he would have torn society to shreds. Instead he presents principles that would surely undermine slavery and in time actually did so. Brotherhood in Christ is more than emancipation. Christianity does not merely free the slaves, but teaches them that they and their masters are one in Christ.

Has Christianity yet driven slavery from the world? Here in this Epistle began the abolition of slavery. This terrible menace has been vanquished wherever brotherly love of Christ has been shed abroad. But there are still portions of the world in which slavery is practiced. Sometimes it is disguised by other names, but wherever human life is sold, wherever forced labor is carried on, it exists. It takes changes in people's thinking to destroy slavery. Christ came to change people; He frees us from sin's slavery and sends us forth to abolish slavery of every kind.

If Timothy or Tychicus took Paul's dictation of this letter, Paul took the stylus or quill and wrote in his big, nearsighted scrawl: "I, Paul, write it with my own hand, I promise to repay it [in full]—and that is to say nothing [of the fact] that you owe me your very self" (*v. 19, AMP*).

General Letters
of the New Testament

Hebrews • James
1 Peter • 2 Peter
1, 2 and 3 John • Jude

43. UNDERSTANDING
Hebrews

Hebrews Portrays Jesus Christ, Our Intercessor at the Throne

We as Christians have that which is better—better in every way. The key word to the book of Hebrews is "better." It occurs thirteen times (in the *KJV*).

Some words in this book help us in understanding it. Trace the words "eternal," "perfect," "once," "blood" (mark this in red), "without," "better (superior, greater)," and the expression "we have . . . therefore let us," "sat down" and "heavenly."

The author of this Epistle is unknown. Many have speculated, but there is no certainty. Hebrews is attributed to Paul, and although many question his authorship, there is abundance of evidence in his favor.

This book has been called the fifth Gospel. The four describe Christ's ministry on earth; this one describes His ministry in heaven at God's right hand.

The glories of our Savior are exhibited in this Epistle. Our eye is fixed upon Jesus, the "the author and perfecter of our faith" (*Hebrews 12:2*). He is set before us "crowned with glory and honor" in the heavens (*2:9*).

This book was written, first of all, to Jewish believers in Jesus, probably of Jerusalem, who were wavering in their faith. Because of the taunts and jeers of their persecutors, the Jewish believers in Jesus were beginning to think they had lost everything—altar, priests, sacrifices—by accepting Christ. The apostle proves that they had only lost the shadow to be given the substance (Jesus Christ). They were undervaluing their privileges in Christ and were engaged in self-pity and discouragement. They were in danger of even giving up their faith (*5:11-12*). They had started well (*6:10*), but had not made progress (*6:11*). The Christian life is like riding a bicycle—if you do not go on, you go off. The writer is trying to lead them from an elementary knowledge to a mature grasp. He exhorts them to be loyal to Christ. He shows them the superiority of Christ over all previous revelation. The writer wanted to keep them from drifting back into their traditional rites and ceremonies. They were urged to let go of everything else in order to hold fast the faith and hope of the gospel.

The book is also a timely warning

An Orthodox Jew in Jerusalem. Hebrews was written, first of all, to Jewish believers in Jesus, probably of Jerusalem, who were wavering in their faith.

and a word of comfort to all, especially in this day when many have little instruction in the things of Christ and are inclined to be led astray by many fads and cults.

Hebrews shows skill in dealing with the discouraged Jewish believers in Jesus. The writer tells all that we have in Christ.

How often when you take a trip for the first time over a new road, you drive straight along anticipating where it will lead, and what difficulties you may encounter. It seems to be the thing to do. Coming back over the same road, you look around and notice things. Do this in studying the book of Hebrews. Read it through, and do not be overanxious about the things you cannot understand. Then you can go back over the road in your reading and take notice of the many things along the way. You could spend months in Hebrews. It presents so

many wonderful truths. At the first reading, you will be impressed by one fact above all others: that Jesus Christ is prominent on every page. This is not true in all the other books of the New Testament. In Acts, the apostles, disciples, Jews and pagans are predominant. In Romans, a great doctrine attracts our attention. In the other letters, the Church and its problems are considered, but here it is our Lord Himself. He is:

Greater than prophets (*1:1-3*)
Greater than angelsm (*1:4—2:18*)
Greater than Moses (*3:1-19*)
Greater than Joshua (*4:1-16*)
Greater than Aaron (*5:1—10:18*).

The reason the writer uses these comparisons stated above is that each of these held a place of great importance in rabbinical Judaism. They were the framework of Jewish worship, and it must be proved that something or some One "better" had come to take their place if their followers are to transfer allegiance.

This book was written to strengthen the faith of wavering believers. Paul's great argument is the superiority of Christ over all others.

Do we know the real difference between having Christ as a Savior and as a Priest? Well, this book answers the question.

The book of Hebrews proves that we can never understand the Old Testament without the New, or the New without the Old.

The Superiority of the Person of Christ *Hebrews 1:1—4:13*

Nowhere is our Lord's deity and humanity so emphasized as in Hebrews 1 and 2. As our great High Priest, Christ is able to understand all our need because He is perfect Man. He is able "to sympathize with our weaknesses" because He "has been tempted in every way, just as we are—yet was without sin" (4:15). He is able to meet all our needs because He is perfect God. He is able.

The opening sentence of the book of Hebrews (1:1-4) is one of the grandest in the Bible. It ranks with the opening words of Genesis and of John. We find Jesus there: His deity, His glory, a Creator, Heir of all things, superior to all things and Savior.

Write down all you find about Christ in Hebrews 1 and 2. If you knew nothing more about Him than you found in these two chapters, you would know much.

Two great truths are taken for granted—the existence of God, and that He reveals Himself to us. He revealed Himself before, "in the past . . . to our forefathers through the prophets . . . but in these last days he has spoken to us by his Son." The Bible records a series of stories of how God speaks to people and reveals His will and His plan to them. How marvelous to hear His only begotten Son speak!

Remember, this letter is written to correct the erroneous idea that the Jewish believers in Jesus had lost some things because they had taken up Christianity. The letter is written to remove this misconception. Christianity is not "giving up," but "receiving," receiving the greatest gifts of life, in fact Life itself, for Christ is Life.

Superiority of the Person of Christ

The Lord Jesus Christ is greater than any human leader (prophets) (1:1-3):

He is God's Son.
He is Heir of all things.
He created the universe.
He is Himself very God.
He sustains all things by His word.
He cleansed us from sin.
He sat down at the right hand of God.

The Lord Jesus Christ is greater than angels (1:4-2:18):

He has the more excellent name of Son (1:4-5).
Angels worship Him (1:6).
He is the eternal God (1:7-12).
His throne is forever (1:8).
He is the ruler of the coming age (1:11-13).

The Lord Jesus Christ is greater than Moses (3:1-19):

Moses was a faithful servant.
Christ is the Son over His own house.

The Lord Jesus Christ is greater than Joshua (4:1-16):

Joshua was a great leader. He led the Hebrews into the Promised Land, but he did not lead the people into rest. What he failed to do, the Son accomplished. Jesus is greater, for He alone gives real rest.

It is well to notice that angels and human spirits (of those who die) are not the same. Human life is a different order of creation than angels. We do not become angels when we die. Angels are a separate creation of God. They are now and will be in heaven, our servants (1:14). Angels worship Christ just as we do.

When God wanted to save us from our sin, He did not send an angel, but His Son. God came not in the form of an angel, but in the form of a man. He became Man to redeem man. He suffered as a man and died as a man that He might be our Redeemer (2:10). Jesus tasted the bitterness of death for us, in order that He might render the devil powerless who has the power of death. He came up from the grave with the keys of hell and of death; no longer can the devil lock any of us in death.

Consider Jesus

This is our weakness. We look at our-

"Consider Jesus." An artist's impression of Jesus' arrest and taunting. Cease from self-effort and yield yourself to Christ (*2 Timothy 4:10*).

selves and our own weakness. Consider Him (*3:1*). This is the astronomer's word. Set your telescope to the heavens and gaze upon Him.

Many Jewish believers in Jesus were confused about Christ's ministry on earth. They thought He came to enforce the laws Moses had given. Moses was the lawgiver and Christ must enforce them. This was their interpretation. But Christ is His own Lawgiver. The old Mosaic system was imperfect and weak (*7:11,18*). It had served its purpose. Now Christ has a "better way." Christ is over Moses. Moses was only a servant; Christ is a Son, the Master in His own house. He is the Heir (*3:6*).

Canaan, the land that flowed with milk and honey, was the Promised Land into which Joshua led the children of Israel. But this is only a picture of the rest of faith in God Himself that every Christian should enjoy. Saint Augustine said that no soul found rest until it found its rest in God. Joshua could not lead the children of Israel into this perfect rest and trust in God, but Jesus did. Cease from self-effort and yield yourself to Christ (*4:10*). Trust Jesus as your Joshua and "enter in" to His land of promise. Cease struggling and place all in His hand. (Read *Psalm 37:5.*)

Two Great Warnings

Warning 1: Give heed not to neglect so great salvation as is offered to us not by angels, but by the Lord Himself. Take heed to what the Son speaks (*2:1-4*).

Warning 2: Take heed not to depart from the living God (*3:12*).

Hebrews 4:12 shows the power of God's Word. Let the Word search and try you! Let God's Word have its proper place in your life. It searches out every motive and desire and purpose of your life, and helps you in evaluating them. Christ is the living Word of God. He is alive (quick) and powerful and all wise and all knowing.

The Superiority of the Priesthood of Christ
Hebrews 4:14—10:18

Here begins the main theme. "Now the main point of what we have to say is this: We have such a High Priest" (*Hebrews 8:1, AMP*). Christ has been compared with all others, the prophets, angels, Moses and Joshua, but the most important comparison is with Aaron, the high priest. The writer shows that the priesthood of Christ is greater than the priesthood of the Levitical law.

The central point in the book is Christ's eternal priesthood and His sacrifice that availed for the sin of the world. The Epistle dwells upon the supreme importance and power of the blood of Christ in obtaining redemption for us. He has purged us from our sins and opened the way into the heavenly sanctuary and to the very throne of God.

Christ is Himself a priest. Listen to the Word: "Therefore, since we have a great high priest who has gone through the heavens, Jesus the Son of God, let us hold firmly to the faith we profess. For we do not have a high priest who is unable to sympathize with our weaknesses, but we have one who has been tempted in every way, just as we are—yet was without sin. Let us then approach the throne of grace with confidence, so that we may receive mercy and find grace to help us in our time of need" (*4:14-16*).

Jesus Christ not only had the qualifications of a priest like Aaron, the earthly high priest, but He also is a High Priest forever after the order of the eternal Melchizedek priesthood because this priesthood is continuous and will never end. The Aaronic priests could not make people perfect because they themselves were sinful, but Christ is eternal and sinless.

Christ's Priesthood Is Like Melchizedek (*Genesis 14*)

A royal priesthood—Both were kings of peace and righteousness.
Was universal—Not only for Jewish people.
Had no human ancestry—"Without father or mother."
Had no successor—When Melchizedek passed away, no one stepped into his place. So Christ is a priest forever.

Let us find an important fact here. Christian ministers are nowhere called "priests" in the New Testament except as all Christians are called "priests" (*1 Peter 2:9*). We have learned from Paul's letters that Christian ministers are called "teachers" and "pastors."

The glories of our Savior are exhibited in this Epistle. Three great "betters" are connected with our High Priest.

Christ—A Better Priest

Of a better covenant (Hebrews 8:13): A better covenant because it is based on better promises. These promises are written on the heart, not on tablets of stone (*8:10*).
Of a better tabernacle (9:1-12): Christ officiates in heaven. The Tabernacle was of this world. The high priest entered into the holy of holies once a year, but Christ has entered into the heavenly sanctuary "once for all."
Of a better sacrifice (10:18): He Himself is the sacrifice. He offered Himself as a lamb without blemish to cleanse us. The sacrifices of the Old Testament were calves and goats. They could not take away sin. They were but the shadow. This Sacrifice needed to be offered only once.

Christ is called our High Priest. What

does that mean? We are taught very plainly in the Word that sin has cut people off from God. No sinner can approach God. The way has been closed. In the Old Testament, a representative, the high priest whom God appointed, could come into God's presence only once a year after sacrifice for the sins of the people had been made. He must offer the blood of calves and goats not only for the sins of the people, but also for his own sins, for he, too, was a sinner. He then would go into the holy place, then on beyond the veil into the holy of holies where the Ark of the Covenant rested. Here was the mercy seat, and here God met people through the mediator, the high priest.

How can we approach God today? Christ has made that possible. He is our High Priest, our representative before the Father. He entered into the heavenly sanctuary, God's presence, bearing the blood of His own sacrifice to cleanse us from our sins and to give to us eternal salvation. His blood had to be shed, for "without the shedding of blood there is no forgiveness" (9:22). "But when this priest had offered for all time one sacrifice for sins, he sat down at the right hand of God" (10:12). "It is finished," He said on the cross (John 19:30). All His work of redemption had been completed, hence we see Him sitting. We find this picture of Christ often in Hebrews.

Our High Priest is at the right hand of the Father at this minute, making intercession for you and for me (7:25; 8:1; 10:12). He has gone "now to appear for us in God's presence" (9:24). This is why we can have boldness to enter into the holiest by the blood of Jesus, by a new and living way (10:19-20). Avail yourself of this glorious privilege.

In Hebrews 9, our Lord's three great appearings stand out:

This man is dressed in authentic copies of the High Priest's garments. Christ is our High Priest, our representative before the Father, having entered the heavenly sanctuary.

Past—On the cross—"But now he has appeared once for all at the end of the ages to do away with sin by the sacrifice of himself" (9:26).

Present—At the right hand of the throne—"now to appear for us in God's presence" (9:24).

Future—In the clouds of glory— "and he will appear a second time, not to bear sin, but to bring salvation to those who are waiting for him" (9:28).

Christ, a Better Sacrifice

Christ offered Himself as the sacrifice, a Lamb without blemish or spot. The priest offered the lives of calves and goats, but these sacrifices could not take away sin. This better Sacrifice had only to be offered once and for all (10:10-18).

As Christ has made a new and living way into the presence of the Father, let us come boldly to the throne of grace.

mal and gloomy. Others live on the ground floor. They leave the first foundations and go on. Some sunlight enters, but their outlook is upon the circumstances about them. They live very close to the world. Still others live up higher. Sunlight and warmth flood the rooms. The noise and attractions of the worldly street do not disturb them. The air is pure. The outlook is toward the blue skies and distant mountains. These live above the world, hid with Christ in God. God wishes us all to live continuously in this high realm.

Let us study a few men and women of God whose names are given in Hebrews 11 who were living a high life. The Holy Spirit tells us the secret of each life is faith, yet it is not so much his or her faith as their reliance upon our faithful God.

A Working Faith

The secret of Christian living is simply allowing Christ to meet our needs. Some say, "I have no faith; I can't believe." Yet we constantly place faith in our fellow humans. You want to go to New York from San Francisco. You buy your ticket and get on the airplane. In the course of your journey, a pilot will guide your plane. Without seeing him or knowing a thing about his ability, you trust your life to him. Faith is just trusting God, believing Him. There is nothing mysterious about faith. It is a simple act of the will. Either we will believe God or we won't. We decide. It is as simple as turning on an electric light switch. This is not a difficult or baffling or mysterious thing to do. But the result? Light and power. When we decide to believe God absolutely, then supernatural life and power enter our lives. A miracle is wrought within us. One of the practical results of faith is that it makes weak people strong (*11:34*).

Because Christ has made this new and living way into the presence of the Father, let us come boldly to the throne of grace. The sin question is settled forever.

Let us not only approach the throne of grace, but let us also not neglect "meeting together, as some are in the habit of doing" (*10:25*). There is nothing like Christian fellowship to make us grow.

The Superiority of the Life in Christ
Hebrews 10:19—13:25

From now on, the writer tells us the kind of life we should live because of Christ's work as High Priest for us. We know He is at the right hand of God and that He ever liveth to make intercession for us.

After one has accepted Christ, there are levels of Christian living. Some Christians live in the basement of Christian experience, merely inside the building, but where it is dark, dis-

To live in the Hall of Faith forever we need to do two things. First, like anyone entering a race, "let us throw off everything that hinders" (12:1). Yield everything to Christ. Second, we are really to believe that Jesus is trustworthy. When we do, we have given up the sin that so easily besets us—for that is the sin of unbelief. We give up that sin when we "fix our eyes on Jesus" (12:2).

Only one kind of human being in the world can please God. Who is it? (11:6). It is not what we do for God, but what God does for us that makes a life of power and strength.

Because of the great company of witnesses on the bleachers watching from heaven, let us run the race of life God has set before us. As any athlete does when preparing for a race, let us lay aside every sinful habit and anything that would hinder us (12:1-2).

Let us have patience (12:1)
Endure chastening (12:11)
Follow peace and purity of heart (12:14)
Always looking to Jesus, the author and finisher of our faith.

A life well pleasing in His sight will be made possible by the Lord Himself. Read Hebrews 13:20-21.

44. UNDERSTANDING

James

James Portrays Jesus Christ, Our Pattern

The law of Christ for daily life is found in the word "doers." "But be ye doers of the word, and not hearers only" (*James 1:22, KJV*).

The author of the book is no doubt James, the brother of our Lord. He may well be called the practical apostle. He stands for efficiency and consistency in life and conduct.

Three men by the name of James are mentioned in the New Testament—the son of Zebedee, the son of Alphaeus, and James the Great, our Lord's brother. Although James refers to his own brother Jesus only twice, he does it in a most reverent manner. Though he knew Him so well, there was no familiarity, for he called Him Lord and Christ. He associates his brother with God so as to imply an equality with the Almighty. If Jesus were not deity, this would be blasphemous.

Guidebook for Everyday Religion

The book of James is the most practical of all the Epistles, and has been called "A Practical Guide to Christian Life and Conduct." This book is the Proverbs of the New Testament. It is filled with moral precepts. It states the ethics of Christian faith. It is full of figures and metaphors. It is often quite dramatic in style. It compels real thought. Hebrews presents doctrine; James presents deeds. They go to-

gether in vital Christian faith.

Neither is there conflict between Paul and James. Only superficial reading of both would bring that indictment. Paul says, "Take the gospel in." James says, "Take it out." Paul saw Christ in the heavens establishing our righteousness. James saw Him on the earth telling us to be perfect even as His Father in heaven is perfect.

Paul dwells on the source of our faith. James tells of the fruit of our faith. One lays the foundations in Christ; the other builds the superstructure. Christ is both "author and finisher" (*Hebrews 12:2*) of our faith. Not only believe it, but live it! Although Paul lays great stress upon justification by faith, we have noticed in his Epistles, especially in Titus, that he lays great stress on good works. It is an astounding fact that while Paul uses the expression "rich in good deeds" (*1 Timothy 6:18*), James uses "rich in faith" (*2:5*). It is well to notice, too, that when James seems to speak in a slighting way of faith, he means a mere intellectual belief and not a "saving faith" that is so essential. James exalts faith. He says its trial worketh patience. His Epistle opens and closes with a strong encouragement to pray (*1:6; 5:14-18*). He only denounces the spurious faith that does not produce works.

James calls himself a "servant of Jesus Christ." He proudly accepts this title as a description of what his relationship was to Jesus. This speaks of real humility because James nowhere refers to the fact of his earthly relationship to the Lord Jesus Christ, a brother.

James mentions the name of God seventeen times, but he repeats the name of Jesus only twice. James was bitterly opposed to Jesus and His claims up to the time of His death, but after the Resurrection he was converted by a special private interview with the risen Lord (*1 Corinthians 15:7*). This adds value to James's testimony about the deity of our Lord. Immediately he became a man of prayer and was made bishop of the church at Jerusalem (*Acts 15:13-21*). His life work was to win the Jewish people and to help them believe in Jesus their Messiah. At the end, he was slain by the religious leaders in A.D. 62. Tradition says he was probably forced to the roof of the Temple by the high priest and rulers and commanded to blaspheme the name of Christ. He,

rather, boldly proclaimed the fact that Jesus is the Son of God. James was hurled from the roof to instant death.

James says his Epistle is written "to the twelve tribes scattered among the nations" (*1:1*), to those who lived outside the holy land. Then there were no lost tribes for he addressed his letter to the twelve whose location was well known at the time. Like Hebrews, it is addressed to the Jewish believers in Jesus. The Jewish people to whom he wrote had not ceased to practice their religion, although they had embraced Jesus as Messiah. Many of them had believed on the Day of Pentecost, and had carried home only a partial understanding of the gospel. In their enthusiasm at having found the true Messiah, they neglected the graces and virtues that should accompany faith in Christ. They taught that all that was necessary to have salvation was to believe that Jesus was the true Messiah and Savior. They were in great danger of being discouraged in their faith by the persecution of their own unbelieving country people.

Faith Victor over Temptation
James 1:1-21

After the briefest of greetings, James plunges straight into his subject. Realizing that these Jewish believers scattered everywhere outside of Palestine were undergoing severe testing of their faith, he begins by telling them how they must meet temptation and tries to encourage and comfort them.

"Count it all joy when ye fall into divers temptations" (*1:2, KJV*). Use your trials. What is the purpose of testing? God makes our trials the instrument of blessing (*1:3*). Too often our trials work impatience, but God will give grace that His real purpose may be accomplished. Patience is more necessary than anything else in our faith life. We forget that time is nothing with God, for with Him a thousand years is as one day, and one day as a thousand years. Christ's purpose in our lives is that we shall be perfect and entire, wanting nothing.

Let us be careful where we lay the blame of temptation. Read James 1:14 carefully. Testings of character come from God (*Genesis 22:1*), but temptations to evil never come from Him, but from the adversary through our own corrupt nature (*James 1:13*), and the appeal is made to meet a proper desire in an improper way (*1:14*). Instead of wrong things coming from God, we find that only good and perfect gifts come from above, from the Father of lights, who never changes (*1:17*). Our God is a God who loves to give.

It is hard to behave wisely, but God's wisdom will help you to do it. Put together the teaching on wisdom in this short letter. Pray for wisdom to behave wisely in time of trial. When you are wronged and insulted, ask God how you shall act. "If any of you lacks wisdom, he should ask God, who gives generously to all without finding fault, and it will be given to him" (*1:5*). What a sad lack! What a mess such a lack can lead us into. Does James say, "If you lack wisdom, sit down and think or study"? No, he says the wisdom we need is from above.

Did it ever occur to you to thank God for temptations? Do you think of your temptations as blessings? Yet James says, "Consider it pure joy, my brothers, whenever you face trials of many kinds" (*1:2*). Do you count it so? Then he adds, "Blessed is the man who perseveres under trial" (*1:12*). How spineless and weak you would become without temptation. Valueless is the character that knows no testing. There is a joy of overcoming. There is no greater satisfaction than to know we have resisted temptation victoriously.

James begins and ends with prayer (*1:5-8; 5:13-18*). Prayer is one of the easiest subjects to talk upon, but one of the hardest to practice. Find all you can about this subject in this Epistle. What about his practice? Tradition tells us that on his death they discovered that his knees were worn hard as a camel's through constant habit of prayer.

Faith Shows in Our Actions
James 1:22—2:26

Don't be merely listeners to God's Word, but put the gospel into practice. What is the good of people saying they have faith if they do not prove it by actions? We must not be satisfied with only "hearing." We must go on "doing" (*James 1:22*). People who are hearers and not doers are like those looking at themselves in a mirror and then going away and forgetting how they looked (*1:24*).

James says we must keep looking into the mirror of God's Word to remember how we look, to find out the sin in our lives. Those who look carefully into the Scriptures and practice them will be blessed in what they do. Those who think they are religious and don't control their tongues, these people's religion is vain. The religion that does not influence the tongue is not a true or vital one. An uncontrolled tongue in a Christian is a terrible thing—guard it. Control your temper. It is dangerous. Under trial, be slow to speak. Keep the draft closed and the fire will go out (*1:26*).

What shall we do with the Word?
Receive it (*1:21*)
Hear it (*1:23*)
Do it (*1:22*)
Examine it (*1:25*).

Works Are Results

Works do not save us, but they are a pretty good evidence that we are saved. "Whatever you did for one of the least of these brothers of mine, you did for me" (*Matthew 25:40*) is not a "saving" text, but a "sign" text. What He has done is our salvation; what "you have done" is the proof of it. Keep faith and works in their proper place.

Because of all this, James says in effect, "The faith you have is the faith you show." "Religion that God our Father accepts as pure and faultless is this: to look after orphans and widows in their distress and to keep oneself from being polluted by the world" (*1:27*).

Christianity is a brotherhood that has no "respect of persons" (*2:1-4, KJV*).

How the world today ignores James's command not to show favoritism! The world worships the successful, strong and wealthy, and despises the person who is poor. A Christian must not show partiality to the person of wealth and position, James tells us, but it seems that money and honor are the only things that people worship today. Showing favoritism is not only a breach of good manners and discourtesy to the poor, but it also is a sin to worship rank and insult the poor. By doing this, we break the law of God. "Love your neighbor as yourself" (*Leviticus 19:18*). This law of love is a royal law (*2:8*). It comes from heaven's Royalty. We are not only to admire and respect others, but also to love them as we do our own selves (*2:1-13*).

What Is Sin?

To disobey God's law is sin. It is human to gloss over sin. A little girl said when excusing herself for something she had done, "I haven't broken the commandment, I only cracked it." James says that whosoever obeys the whole law and only makes a single slip is guilty of everything (*2:10-11*). That person is a lawbreaker. If brought into court for violating a traffic ordinance, he or she does not plead that all the other laws have been kept. The judge is interested only in the fact of whether this person has broken this particular law. If so, this person is

Don't be merely listeners to God's Word, but put the gospel into practice. What is the good of saying we have faith if we do not prove it by our actions?

classified as a lawbreaker. We may have a fine chain, but of what use is it if all the links are good except one? That broken link renders the entire chain useless.

It is clear that the one sin thought of here is mentioned in 2:9—showing favoritism to the wealthy.

Faith that does not express itself in works is of no value. Faith is revealed by what we do. What is the use of us saying we have faith if we do not prove it by our actions? Just as a body without a spirit is dead, so faith is dead without actions (*2:17*).

Has the phrase "friend of God" ever gripped you? God evidently needed a friend, and He found in Abraham the friendship He desired. What is essential to become a friend of God (see *2:23*)?

Faith Shown in Our Words
James 3:1-18

Our speech reveals what and whose we are. It expresses our personality more than anything else. Anyone who controls his or her tongue, James says, is a perfect person (*3:2*). If a person has mastery over that difficult member, the tongue, the rest is easy. A person is able to curb the whole nature. Just as we control a spirited horse by a firm hand on the bridle, so the hand of the Man, Christ Jesus, can grip and firmly use the bit and bridle on our tongues. Just as a great ship is controlled by a very small rudder and turned in any direction the captain determines, so the pierced hands of Jesus can firmly control and wisely use the helm of our lives—our tongue. The tongue, though small, is very powerful. It can determine the course of human life.

Remember, this same tongue can be used to testify for Christ and praise His holy name. It is the instrument the Holy Spirit uses to magnify the Lord (*3:9-10*). We should not praise God and curse people who are made in His likeness!

Faith Shown in Our Purity of Character *James 4:1-17*

The devil has organized this world system upon principles opposed to God in every way. They are principles of force, greed, ambition, selfishness and pleasure. The believer should be crucified to this world (*Galatians 6:14*). We should count its passing pleasures, its honors, its treasures as of little value, and remain unmoved by its attractions. The world is that system of things about us or that spirit within us that is blind and deaf to the value of spiritual things and cares nothing about doing the will of God. Because we live in the world, surrounded by all its attractions and the things needful to our daily living, we must be very watchful to keep our affections above the border line of the world (*James 4:4*).

People keep asking, "How can we end war?" But James goes back farther and tells us what causes war. A cause of most of the wars that have devastated the earth has been some nation's desire to get what does not belong to it. This has always been the cause of quarrels between individuals. Selfishness is the root of it all. Next, people fail to pray, or if they do it is with a wrong motive, to spend what they get upon themselves instead of having their lives glorify God (*4:1-3*). God promises to answer prayer, but He will not give to those who would consume it on their own pleasures.

Four times the word "lust" is found in the first five verses of James 4 (in the *KJV*). Dr. Jowett (Benjamin Jowett, 1817-1893, British educator and theologian) defines it as "anything that steams the windows of the soul and

A narrow street in the Old City of Jerusalem. Evidently, many of the humble folk among the Jewish believers were being oppressed by the rich.

blurs our vision." This word "lust" can be translated "pleasures." This helps give meaning to these verses and furnishes the clue to the teaching they contain.

Overindulgence in pleasure is sinful:

First, there are "fights and quarrels among you" (*4:1*). The newspapers are filled with horrible pictures of this every day.

Second, your desires "battle within you" (*4:2*). If pleasure is allowed to have its own way in us, a war is on and we are mastered by it.

Third, "When you ask, you do not receive, because you ask with wrong motives, that you may spend what you get on your pleasures" (*4:3*). Overindulgence in pleasure always affects the prayer life. We stagnate in our Christian life.

Fourth, "You adulterous people"— how a pleasure lover degenerates in the Christian walk! He or she becomes a friend of the world, an enemy of God (*4:4*).

What is the cure for all this?

Examine 4:6-10.

Submit to God (*4:7*). We have made a mess of our lives because of a lack of surrender to God.

"Come near to God and he will come near to you" (*4:8*). Come with clean hands and a pure heart.

"Humble yourselves before the Lord" (*4:10*). Remember yourself as a sinner and take the lowly place. Then God will lift you up.

To be friends with the world means to be at enmity with God (*4:4*). Jesus said, "You cannot serve both God and Money" (*Matthew 6:24*). Therefore surrender yourself to God and be not subject to the devil.

How easy it is for us to plan without God, yet how futile! Let us submit all our plans to the Lord and see what His will is in the matter. "If it is the Lord's will" (*James 4:15*).

Faith Shown by Our Prayer Lives *James 5:1-20*

Evidently, many of the humble folk among the Jewish believers were being oppressed by the rich and their hard earnings were being "kept back by fraud" (*James 5:4, KJV*). James warns the rich! "You have hoarded wealth in the last days" (*5:3*).

Here again the tongue is brought in. It is amazing how many Christians take the name of the Lord in vain in ordinary conversation (*5:12*). God says, "The Lord will not hold anyone guiltless who misuses his name" (*Exodus 20:7; Deuteronomy 5:11*). This is a serious indictment.

Prayer is a golden key that, kept bright by constant use, will unlock the treasures of earth and heaven.

James gives us a series of short phrases of advice. If anyone is in trouble, he should pray. If anyone is merry, he should sing. If anyone is sick, he should send for the elders of the church and let them anoint him with oil and pray for him (*5:13-14*). The Bible says, "And the prayer offered in faith will make the sick person well; the Lord will raise him up. If he has sinned, he will be forgiven" (*5:15*). If anyone has wronged another, he should confess his fault to that one (*5:16*). The prayer of faith demands confession of sin, and a will surrendered to God. Elijah's mighty prayer that opened and closed the heavens is an example to us, for "the prayer of a righteous man is powerful and effective" (*5:16*).

This Epistle closes abruptly on a high plane. It is with the gracious act of a Christian who finds someone erring from the truth and converts that person. Although only God can save a soul, He uses human instruments to accomplish it. "Whoever turns a sinner from the error of his way will save him from death and cover over a multitude of sins."

45. UNDERSTANDING

First Peter

First Peter Portrays Jesus Christ, Precious Cornerstone of Our Faith

Jesus lived the kind of life described in this letter of Peter's and 1 John: "Whoever claims to live in him must walk as Jesus did" (*1 John 2:6*). To "abide in Christ" is to rest quietly where we are. We who have received Christ as Savior are "in him" (*Colossians 3:3*). The secret of walking "in newness of life" (*Romans 6:4, KJV*) or victorious Christian living is simply to "remember Jesus Christ" (*2 Timothy 2:8*) and to rest on the blessed eternal fact of His sufficiency.

"Now to you who believe, this stone is precious" (*1 Peter 2:7*). Peter talks about seven precious things. Mark these in your Bible:

Precious trial of faith (*1:7*)
Precious blood (*1:19*)
Precious Cornerstone (*2:4-6*)
Precious Christ (*2:7*)
Precious spirit (*3:4*)
Precious faith (*2 Peter 1:1*)
Precious promises (*2 Peter 1:4*).

Peter has been called the "apostle of hope," as John was the "apostle of love" and Paul the "apostle of faith." The word "hope" is found in 1 Peter 1:3,13,21; 3:15.

Another word (or its equivalent) is used fourteen times in this short Epistle (in the *KJV*), and that is "suffering," the suffering of Christ and of Christians in following Him.

Try a complete reading at one sitting of this short four-page letter, preferably in *Phillips* or *New International Version* or another modern translation. Mark in two colors each mention of *joy* and *grace* and *glory* (in red perhaps), and of *suffering* (in black). At least twenty-six times Peter dwells on the joy and glory that are ours who have received God's grace against the fourteen times he mentions the suffering of Christ and the Christian following Him.

Try to see that Peter was enlarging on the statement, "Let us fix our eyes on Jesus, the author and perfecter of our faith, who for the joy set before him endured the cross, scorning its shame, and sat down at the right hand of the throne of God" (*Hebrews 12:2*). He knew the connection between suffering and joy and glory.

This book was written by Peter toward the close of his busy life (around A.D. 67) and was delivered by Silas (*5:12*), one of Paul's companions. Peter had become a leader of the apostles. He was the spokesman. He belonged to the inner circle of the three friends of Christ. He was the preacher at Pentecost. The first twelve chapters of Acts are centered around this apostle and his ministry. He went about preaching to the Jewish people. At last he died a martyr's death, being crucified under the Roman emperor Nero. According to tradition, at his own request, he was crucified with his head downward, considering himself unworthy to even resemble his Master in death.

The Christians to whom Peter is

writing were suffering "fiery trials" from people who did not believe in Jesus. This letter was evidently written at a time when general dislike of Christians was threatening to pass into active persecution (*2:15; 3:13-17; 4:12*). It was about the time of Nero's persecutions. Peter himself suffered under this cruel emperor not later than A.D. 67. Read 1:1-3,6-9; 2:13-17; 4:12-19.

A subject repeatedly mentioned is the "reappearing" of our Lord and Savior. Mark this as the letter is read. The influence of this "blessed hope" on the Christian's way of life cannot be escaped. This short Epistle is full of golden nuggets of truth, which can be marked and memorized. Try it!

This book gives us good plain advice from Peter about how we ought to live. Read it and take heed! We find here how Peter has been growing in his experience. This letter shows him some twelve or more years after the last record of him in Acts 15. He wishes to encourage the believers and so he gives his own personal testimony. He adds assurance because he could prove from his own experience all he was saying. There is power in personal testimony. This personal note sounds through all the letter. The Christians were experiencing a time of trial (*1:6*). They needed encouragement from one who knew what trial meant. Peter points away from the trials to the future glory that awaited them (*1:7*), to the example of Christ (*2:21*) and the reward that would follow (*4:13*).

Privileges of the Christian
1 Peter 1:1—2:10

Peter, who is an apostle of jubilant hope, addresses this Epistle to the "strangers" scattered everywhere. It is a letter to homesick Christians. He tells these persecuted and discouraged ones of a near and precious Savior. Let

---

it lift you up and fill you with joy! This is the purpose of the book.

What are our privileges as Christians? First, we are redeemed by the precious blood of Christ. This is our position in Christ (*1:18-19*). Because of this relationship to Christ, we have everything in Him that God desires us to possess. If God has given us His Son, will He not freely with Him give us all things? (*Romans 8:32.*)

The life of faith is described at the beginning. We are born of God (be-

The Sea of Galilee from Tabgha, where the multiplication of the fish is commemorated.

gotten) (*1:3*). At the end there is an inheritance for us (*1:4*), and to assure us of it we are "kept" by the power of God (*1:5*). What a life this is!

We have been begotten by Jesus Christ into a lively hope (*1:3*)

We have in reserve an imperishable inheritance (*1:4,5,10*)

We are kept by the power of God (*1:5*)

We are being purified to fit us to stand with Christ (*1:7*)

We have salvation for our souls (*1:9*)

We have a gospel that angels desire to look into (*1:12*)

We have a great hope (*1:13*)

We have redemption through His blood (*1:18-19*)

We shall not be put to shame (*2:6*)

We are born again by His Word (*1:23*)

We are built up a spiritual house (*2:5*)

We are a chosen people (*2:9*)

We shall have a crown of glory (*5:4*).

Peter gives good plain advice about how we ought to live (*1:13-16*). Here he says, "Therefore, prepare your minds for action; be self-controlled; set your hope fully on the grace to be given you when Jesus Christ is revealed" (*1:13*). Fashion your life after the Lord Jesus Christ. Don't live your life after the old pattern. "Be holy, because I am holy" (*1:16*). "Love one another" (*1:22*). Seeing you are "born again" (*1:23*), live like it. You are a new creature in Christ Jesus.

How can anyone put away all wickedness as Peter commands (*chap. 2*)? Not by effort! Not by trying! Not by practice! Not by setting our willpower against sin! But by trusting that God by His grace can do it. The only people who can "put away" sin are the ones who, having received Christ as Savior, know that Christ has "put away" their sin.

First, we must "rid ourselves." Peter summons us to abandon some ugly things—wickedness, guile, hypocrisy, envies and evil speaking (*2:1*). From the root of wickedness all these noxious weeds spring. These must go from our hearts if we would grow.

Christian Infants

We are called "newborn babies" (*2:2*). As new Christians, we have a new longing in our hearts, a new hunger. Peter describes the attitude as desiring the spiritual milk, "the sincere milk of the word" (*KJV*). Spiritual milk makes us grow unto salvation. The Word as "milk" suggests that it is a perfect food for children, containing all the elements for building up the body. So the Word is perfect for building up the soul.

"Word" in 2:2 could very well mean Christ as well as His Word, for in the third verse we read that if you have once tasted of the Lord you will find He is gracious. He is the nourishment of our souls.

Peter says that when we become "children of God" (*John 1:12*), we are like newborn babies (*1 Peter 2:2,3*). We need food to make us grow. This is just what God has provided in His Word. Desire the Word as newborn babes, and eating it, grow thereby. You will find that it tastes good (*Jeremiah 15:16; Ezekiel 3:1-3*). Christ will become real and gracious to you (*1 Peter 1:23; 2:2-3*).

A Study in Stones

Right here Peter turned to another figure and called Christ a "stone," rejected by men, but precious in God's sight (*2:4*). Everyone in this world has to do something with this "Stone," Christ Jesus. He is in every person's path. We can lift Him up and put Him in as the chief Cornerstone of our lives, which is God's will. But if we do not, we must stumble headlong over

Him, tragically, to our death. To many people in the first century, He was a stumbling block and a rock of offense. To many today, He is just that. What have you done with this precious "Cornerstone"? Is He in His rightful place in your life?

And we are stones, too, laid up on Christ as the foundation and cornerstone to make a spiritual temple to God. This makes it very important for each one of us to find our right place in God's plan and stay in it. The "spiritual house" (2:5), built up of believers, is the corporate temple of the Holy Spirit, as the individual Christian is the individual temple of the Holy Spirit (1 Corinthians 6:19).

We are not only "living stones" in a spiritual temple, but each of us is also a priest in this temple. Priests represent God to people, and people to God. Christians are a "holy priesthood" (1 Peter 2:5). Are you representing God to others by your life, and others to God by your intercessory prayer? As priests, we cannot offer lambs and goats today, but Paul tells us to offer ourselves a living sacrifice (Romans 12:1).

Duties of the Christian
1 Peter 2:11—4:11

Peter is giving us wise counsel by telling us how to behave in the game of life. Up to this point, he has been exhorting the Christians to walk worthy of their new calling. Now he urges them to glorify God before an ungodly and persecuting world. A greenhouse religion is of very little value to others. It is good for us to be compelled to justify our faith before our fellow humans.

Peter offers a simple program. Anyone can follow it. Any earnest seeker can find the way Peter commends. His first suggestion is that we remember we are "pilgrims" (KJV). We are not settled here, but we are on our way to an eternal city. It is important that we keep this in mind, otherwise we will be tying our lives to stakes that will be shaken loose some day.

But for Christians who have followed Peter's plan, all is different. They have invested time and thought and money in the pursuit of Christ's plan for their lives. Christians find life "sweeter as the years go by," and the end is the best of all!

Christians are not at home in this world. They are away from home, "as aliens and strangers in the world" (1 Peter 2:11; "as strangers and pilgrims," KJV), for "our citizenship is in heaven" (Philippians 3:20). We are in the world, but not of it (John 17:11,14).

Peter makes an earnest appeal in this scene. First there is a call to purity of life. Christians are warned against all fleshly appetites, for they are like an infection in our blood. If we once let them have a place in your lives, they will contaminate our souls and pollute our characters worse than any disease harms our bodies. There is no health, strength or personhood left in us and all on account of sin. The soul may be dragged down to hell or lifted up to heaven. The body is the main channel through which debasing influences affect the soul. A Christian's life is to be true in the presence of those who are not yet Christian. This will disarm opposition and glorify God. Peter says, "I urge you . . . to abstain from sinful desires" (2:11).

The Power of Influence

We are to influence others by what we say and do. "Keep your behavior excellent among the Gentiles" (1 Peter 2:12, NASB). This subject of the way a Christian lives is discussed from 2:12—4:11. It was the all-important topic in Peter's mind for those Christians who were the only "Bible" known or read of the world in their day.

"Though [the pagans] accuse you of doing wrong" (*2:12*). The Christians were accused of horrible crimes. They were called atheists because they denied the Roman gods. They were regarded as unpatriotic because emperor worship was the official religion. To reject the state religion was considered an outrage against the state itself. The Christians would often be obliged to depart from social customs and often bore the stigma of evildoers. The answer to all this must be in the superior moral life of every Christian. They must live beyond reproach.

Freedom Defined

"Live as free men, but do not use your freedom as a cover-up for evil" (*2:16*).

Peter tells his readers how to live their lives (*2:17, KJV*).

"Honour all men!" Show respect for others.

"Love the brotherhood." Every social problem could be solved.

"Fear God." The fear of the Lord is the beginning of wisdom.

"Honour the king." Show respect for your government.

One of the most convincing and powerful demonstrations Christians can give that they have a newborn life is the enduring of wrong and injustice patiently (*2:19-20*). That is when we show forth the grace of God. That is what Christ did while He was on earth and in submitting to His crucifixion and death. This is what His followers are to do as we "follow in his steps" (*2:21*). Patience in undeserved punishment is one way of testifying for Christ. Patience is noble because it is Christlike (*1 Peter 3:17-18; 4:12-16*). Peter points to the example of his Master. The secret of patience is always found in divine grace (*James 1:3-4*).

The Man Who Suffered for Me

"Christ suffered for you" (*2:21*). A lady was visiting in a hospital. She went up to a bed on which lay a wounded soldier and said gently, "Thank you for being wounded for me." The young man's face brightened. That was a new thought to him. It made the pain more bearable to look upon it in that light. Do you realize that many years ago

One was wounded for you? And that One was the Son of God Himself? Yes, He was wounded for my transgressions, by His stripes I am healed (2:24).

We find in chapters 2 and 3 some instructions for the various relationships of our lives. First, there are some personal instructions (2:1-12). Next we find our social relationships. Servants should obey their masters with respect, not only those masters who are good and considerate, but also those who are arbitrary. In 3:1-7, our home relationships are mentioned. Naturally the home begins with the marriage relationship. "Wives, in the same way be submissive to your husbands." This means unselfish devotion so as to win his love and admiration. This might sound unreasonable if we did not hear the injunction to husbands (3:7) that they "be considerate as [they] live with [their] wives, and treat them with respect." This makes a wife subject to love that acts in knowledge and not according to selfish desires. It is manly for a husband to be tender toward his wife. God's plan is that the love of husband and wife should be a mutual thing. Each one shall consider the other. The result of all this will be a marriage relationship in which prayers are not hindered (3:7). Prayer is the surest secret of success in any married life.

Peter says that the Christian is a:
"Baby" (2:2), desiring the milk of the Word.
"Living stone" (2:5), built into the temple of life.
"Priest"—offering spiritual sacrifices.
"Stranger"—to keep himself unspotted from the world.
"Alien" ("Pilgrim," KJV)—good deeds along the way.
"Citizen"—render obedience to rulers.
"Man"—honor all people in the fear

of God.
"Servant"—subject unto Christ.
"Sufferer"—to be patient, committing all to Christ.
"Steward" (4:10).
"One speaking the very words of God" (4:11).

Peter gives the way to be happy in a world that is wretched. "For, 'Whoever would love life and see good days must keep his tongue from evil and his lips from deceitful speech. He must turn from evil and do good; he must seek peace and pursue it. For the eyes of the Lord are on the righteous and his ears are attentive to their prayer, but the face of the Lord is against those who do evil'" (3:10-12). He quotes Psalm 34:12-14. This is a remedy that works today as well as it worked in David's time. The best way of making this life happy and prosperous is to keep from speaking evil and from slander and to be always ready to overcome evil with good.

A Ready Answer

Another important command is given in 1 Peter 3:15. This is for every one of us. "Always be prepared to give an answer to everyone who asks you to give the reason for the hope that you have." Have you an intelligent answer to give to others of your trust in Christ? If not, stop right here and get one ready. What does Christ mean to you?

Christ's sufferings in the flesh were physical and literal. "He himself bore our sins in his body on the tree" (2:24). Christians' sufferings, spoken of in 4:1, are spiritual. Christ suffered when He was put to death on the cross. "For Christ died for sins once for all, the righteous for the unrighteous, to bring you to God" (3:18). Christians take up their cross and follow Christ, denying themselves (Matthew 16:24). The phrase "Arm

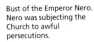
Bust of the Emperor Nero. Nero was subjecting the Church to awful persecutions.

yourselves also with the same attitude" (*1 Peter 4:1*) means the same as the words, "If anyone would come after me, he must deny himself and take up his cross and follow me" (*Matthew 16:24*). Such a high resolve will involve a measure of actual suffering, for God's will may cut across our desire to gratify some bodily craving. Very few in this world escape suffering, either mental, physical or spiritual. We cannot choose the way we shall suffer.

Often God allows us to go through life denied the one thing we wish more than anything else. But we should be comforted in this that whom God loves, He chastens. If He grinds down the surface of our lives, it is that the stone may shine the more brilliantly. The many facets of the diamond are what make it dazzling. Know that the greater the suffering in this world, the greater the glory in heaven. This is what Peter means in 4:2.

Be careful not to follow the world, "doing what pagans choose to do" (*1 Peter 4:3*). What the heathen world wanted the Jewish believers in Jesus to do Peter names here. "Debauchery" is mentioned. The Greek word means "that which disgusts"; the English word,

"anything which excites impure desire."

Trials of the Christian
1 Peter 4:12—5:14

Nero was subjecting the Church to awful persecutions. Christians were burned every night in Nero's gardens. It looked as if the devil were about to devour the Church (*1 Peter 5:8*). It was a "fiery trial," but God would use its very heat to burn out the dross and leave the pure gold (*1:7*). History is replete with the record of the many persecutions of Christians. Some have been even more brutal than Nero's. Millions of Christians through the centuries have been subjected to every conceivable kind of torture. These words have been for them, too. How ashamed we should be even to mention our little troubles in light of these!

Don't be surprised when you are tried in the fire, as if some strange thing were happening to you (*4:12*). Don't think that Christ has promised that we, as Christians, shall be spared from pain or misfortunes or death. In fact Christ says, "In this world ye shall suffer persecution." This means no doubt that people will persecute the real Christian, because the world hates Christ and anything called by His name.

Peter exhorts the leaders of the Church to care for the flock, "not lording it over those entrusted to you" (5:3), but to serve them. Jesus had told Peter to "feed my sheep" (John 21). Undershepherds are to receive their rewards from the Chief Shepherd when He shall appear (1 Peter 5:4). His crown of glory shall be fadeless.

The Christian life is like a jungle battle. Peter tells us who our enemy is. He is the devil. His work is opposed to all that is good in this world. He is pictured as a roaring lion, seeking his prey (5:8). This adversary is cagey, appearing sometimes as an angel of light, at another time as a serpent, coiled for the strike. He always "prowls around like a roaring lion looking for someone to devour." He is watching for the vulnerable spot, for the unguarded door to our hearts. Paul tells us what armor we should wear in Ephesians 6. But we need not be afraid, for "the God of all grace, who called you to his eternal glory in Christ, after you have suffered a little while, will himself restore you and make you strong, firm and steadfast" (5:10).

46. UNDERSTANDING
Second Peter

Second Peter Portrays Jesus Christ, Our Strength

The first letter was to console; the second to warn.

In his first letter, Peter was trying to encourage Christians who were suffering terrible persecutions from without. In his second letter, he is warning them of danger within the Church.

Peter, in warning against the dangers from within, urges them to grow strong in "the grace and knowledge" of Christ (*2 Peter 3:18*). Christian knowledge is the best way to overcome the false teaching that was creeping within the walls. We obtain knowledge of Christ through His Word. Don't neglect the Word of God! It is indeed "a lamp to our feet, and a light to our path" (*Psalm 119:105*). In 1 Peter, we hear much about suffering. In 2 Peter, we hear much about knowledge. Shallow knowledge makes superficial Christians. Peter knew that heresy often leads to immoral living. Leaders in the church were permitting wrongdoing of every sort. The false teachers were laughing at the Lord's coming, and the Church could easily cease from looking for that "blessed hope."

Simon Peter, a servant and an apostle of Jesus Christ, is the writer. The first name, Simon, suggests his old, unstable nature. The name Peter (meaning a "rock") suggests the new nature Christ had given him, strong and true. He calls himself a bondslave (servant). Slavery is the happiest life in the world when the slave has the right master. There is only one right Master, and He is Jesus Christ. His slaves know the only true meaning of freedom.

Peter, the apostle of hope, speaks again to the younger Christians in the faith. He urges them to look toward heaven while dwelling for only a season in a very bad world. He stirs up their pure minds "as reminders to stimulate you to wholesome thinking" (*3:1*). He talks about the readers as those who have obtained "a faith as precious as ours" (*1:1*). We remember how Peter's faith was kept through Christ's prayer for him. "But I have prayed for you, Simon, that your faith

Selected Bible Readings

Sunday:	Christian Virtues (*2 Peter 1:1-14*)
Monday:	Christ's Word Exalted (*2 Peter 1:15-21*)
Tuesday:	Christless Teachers (*2 Peter 2:1-14*)
Wednesday:	Christ Against the Backslider (*2 Peter 2:15-22*)
Thursday:	Christ's Coming Scoffed (*2 Peter 3:1-9*)
Friday:	Christ's Coming Assured (*2 Peter 3:10-18*)
Saturday:	Christ Our Hope (*2 Peter 1:1—3:18*)

may not fail. And when you have turned back, strengthen your brothers" (*Luke 22:32*). This is how our faith can be preserved also.

Christian Virtues
2 Peter 1:1-21

Do the days seem dark to you and does sin seem to abound everywhere? That is the way the world looked to the young Christians of Peter's day. So they would not be discouraged by this outlook, he showed them how to escape "the corruption in the world caused by evil desires" (*2 Peter 1:4*). Here it is. God has "given us everything we need for life and godliness" (*1:3*).

The way I can escape the awful sins in this world every day and all the day is by partaking of God's nature and letting Him live through me. Lay hold of the "very great and precious promises, so that through them you may participate in the divine nature" (*1:4*). I am a sharer in the very nature of God. Everyone does not have the nature of God. The divine is not within human hearts. His image remains in us, though marred (*1 Corinthians 11:7*), but not an atom of His life. We are dead and lifeless apart from Christ. The "divine nature" of God becomes ours only when the divine Savior becomes ours. This is a wonderful truth. We ought to take courage when we remember that with Christ in us, "the divine nature" also is within us. The "very great and precious promises" are before us. We ought to go straight ahead, fearing nothing (*2 Peter 1:4*).

The "divine nature" God has given us should be shown in the everyday practices of the Christian life. That is all Christian character is. It is no more or less than the practice of Christian virtues. If we turn to Galatians 5, we will find that Christian virtues are only the fruit of the Spirit.

Although God gives us a changed, divine nature, He wants us to do our part in developing this priceless gift (*1:5-11*). We are sharers in the very life of God, therefore we should press on to possess more. God says, "Add one grace to another."

Multiplication—"Grace and peace be yours in abundance" (*1:2*)
Addition—"Add to your faith" (*1:5*)
Subtraction—"Cleansed from his past sins" (*1:9*).

Steps to Heaven
Seven steps go up from faith, and the last one is love. These steps are the Christian virtues every Christian should have. Let's climb slowly and thoughtfully up this flight of stairs and see how far we have gone. To your faith add goodness, knowledge, self-control, perseverance, godliness, brotherly kindness and love. This is the result of our precious faith.

The fuller the measure of these virtues, the greater will be our knowledge of Jesus Christ our Lord. Know Christ, for to know Him is life eternal, and in none other is there salvation. (See *Acts 4:12*.)

Peter, like Paul, warns Christians from standing still. Don't remain babes in Christ, tripping over every teaching, but grow strong.

"But if anyone does not have them, he is nearsighted and blind" (*2 Peter 1:9*). Nearsighted Christians we will be, unfit for enlistment in God's army, if we do not have these virtues. Be sure of your position in Christ. Don't ever doubt your calling in Him. Spare no effort to put God's call and choice beyond all doubt. Spare no effort in prayer, in study and in talking with older Christians. Life is full of so much uncertainty, but you do not have to be uncertain in spiritual things. A spiritual certainty produces a stability in life, and "you will never fall" (*1:10*).

A Christian's ambition should be to have a full life. Peter wants you to have an abundant entrance into the haven of rest, Christ's eternal kingdom (*1:11*).

Folding Our Tents

Peter, like Paul, was conscious of his approaching death. He has a beautiful name for death, "I will soon put [this tent of my body] aside" (*1:13,14*). *Moffatt* says, "The folding up of my tent." Because he knew he was about to leave them, he wanted to stir them up by putting them in remembrance of what he so well knew. His memory pictured before him the great transfiguration scene. There he had witnessed the glory of Christ. Any doubt about His reality or of His coming again in power was forever banished from his mind. God Himself had borne testimony of His glory and honor, and a voice said, "This is my Son, whom I love; with him I am well pleased" (*1:17*). He heard the voice from above. This is the testimony of deity. Now Peter knew. He was sure. He wanted them to know that he was not telling them fairy stories when he told them of the power and coming of the Lord Jesus Christ, but he was an eyewitness of His majesty.

Remember, Peter suffered and died for this truth he was telling. At one time he said, "We cannot help speaking about what we have seen and heard" (*Acts 4:20*).

Added to the evidence of the transfiguration is the "word of the prophets made more certain" (*1:19*), rather, prophecy made sure. This does not put Christian experience (the vision on the mount) over against prophecy, but it says the word of prophecy is confirmed by experience. They go together. Peter throws much light on the inspiration of the Scriptures. See

1 Peter 1:10-12; 2 Peter 1:4,16-21; 3:15. Remember the divine origin of the Scriptures.

Peter was present at Jesus' transfiguration, which probably took place on Mount Hermon.

Christless Teachers
2 Peter 2:1-22

Are the times in which we live hard, temptations strong and opposition powerful? Expect it and rise above it. We are warned that it shall be so. The world always has been and always will be full of antagonism to the truth and to those who speak it. But God will bring it to naught. In the meantime, "the Lord knows how to rescue godly men from trials" (*2 Peter 2:9*).

Peter tells of the coming, the influence and the doom of the false teachers in this dark and appalling chapter. We need not be surprised at their coming, for Christ warned us of that in Matthew 7:15; 24:11,24, and we have listened to Paul's words about them to Timothy (*1 Timothy 4:1-3; 2 Timothy 3:1-9*).

What a terrible list is this account in Peter's second Epistle of the false teachers' deeds!

"Secretly introduce destructive heresies" (*2:1*)

"Denying the sovereign Lord who bought them" (*2:1*)

"Bring the way of truth into disrepute" (*2:2*)

"Exploit you with stories they have made up" (*2:3*)

"Follow the corrupt desire of the sinful nature" (*2:10*)

"Despise authority" (*2:10*)

"Bold and arrogant" (*2:10*)

"Not afraid to slander celestial beings" (*2:10*)

"Like brute beasts" (*2:12*)

"Blaspheme in matters they do not understand" (*2:12*)

"Pleasure is to carouse in broad daylight" (*2:13*)

"Blots and blemishes" in society (*2:13*)

Revel in "their pleasures while they feast with you" (*2:13*)

"Eyes full of adultery, they never stop sinning" (*2:14*)

"Seduce the unstable" (*2:14*)

"Experts in greed" (*2:14*)

"An accursed brood" (*2:14*)

"Left the straight way and wandered off" (*2:15*)

"Springs without water" (*2:17*)

"Mists driven by a storm" (*2:17*)

"Mouth empty, boastful words" (*2:18*)

"Appealing to the lustful desires of sinful human nature" (*2:18*)

"Slaves of depravity" (*2:19*).

The false teachers of today do just what is told here. First, they "secretly introduce destructive heresies" (*2:1*). They do it subtly. They don't believe in the deity of Christ—that Jesus, who was born of a virgin, was actually God. Peter describes the "damnable heresy" *(KJV)* they bring in. This is it—"denying the sovereign Lord who bought them." It does not say that they deny the Lord that "taught" them. Practically every false religion acknowledges Christ as a great teacher, but will not accept Him as Savior, the One who "bought" us with His own precious blood. They deny the blood atonement.

God can only do one thing with false teachers, and that is to destroy them. "Light that is trifled with becomes lightning." Peter declares with no uncertain sound that that shall be the end of false teachers who cover themselves with the cloak of the Church (*2:3-9*). They shall certainly be punished. God did not even spare the angels who sinned! He sent a flood upon a godless world in Noah's day. Sodom and Gomorrah were reduced to ashes. All these were as a warning to the godless of every generation of what God has in store for them. One thing we can be sure of, no matter how severe the judgment for the false teacher may be, the deliverance of God's people is promised. Leave the punishment of the wicked with God.

As we read on, we find much else that these wicked teachers will do. They will malign Christ's apostles; they will ensnare weak people, promising them freedom, while as a matter of fact they are enslaving them in corrupt habits (*2:2-22*).

Christ's Coming
2 Peter 3:1-18

False teaching about Christ that denies His deity and power results in false thinking. The first question it raises is about the coming of Christ. To help the Church in this, Peter reminds them of the things Jesus had said. People misunderstood Him and thought His return might be in that generation. Peter tells them that time is nothing with God—"With the Lord a day is like a thousand years, and a thousand years are like a day" (*2 Peter 3:8*). He will keep this promise as He has kept all His promises, but according to His own time.

"The Lord is not slow in keeping his promise. . . . He is patient with you, not wanting anyone to perish, but everyone to come to repentance" (*3:9*). The last days are to be sad days, for scoffers shall make fun and say, "Ha, ha, where is the promise of Christ's coming? As far as we can see, everything is going on just as it has from the beginning of creation. Nature goes along in the even tenor of her way. There have been no signs of any radical change. The promise of His coming has failed." These scoffers were evil, but the sad truth today is that good people scoff at the promise of His coming. They make sport of the great hope of the Church. How illogical was their reasoning about Christ's not coming! Here they are! He had not come, hence He was not coming. Nothing different had happened, hence nothing unusual was going to happen. Because our Lord has not come as yet, shall we give up hope? No, indeed. Rather, rejoice in the fact that His return comes nearer every day.

Floods and Fires

Peter reminds these skeptics that a mighty flood did drown the world once, and Christ likened His coming to the flood in Matthew 24:37-38. No doubt Peter heard Him say it. But next time God will destroy the earth by fire.

We know that when God's clock strikes the hour, the earth will melt with a fervent heat. The earth shall be burned up and in the great explosion the heavens will pass away. Then "new heavens and a new earth" will emerge (*3:13*).

Today people are heady and high-minded. They think they know everything. But all this is to be expected. Satan will not give up his hold on this earth without protest. But his days of liberty are numbered and Jesus shall reign. "First of all, you must understand that in the last days scoffers will come, scoffing and following their own evil desires. They will say, 'Where is this "coming" he promised?

A view of the Dead Sea. Sodom and Gomorrah, which once stood nearby, were reduced to ashes.

Ever since our fathers died, everything goes on as it has since the beginning of creation.' But the day of the Lord will come like a thief" (*2 Peter 3:3,4,10*). It will not be entirely a destruction, but a new earth will be constructed. Look toward the East, for the "Sun of righteousness will rise with healing in its wings" (*Malachi 4:2*).

What effect should all this have on our lives? Peter answers in verse 14. We will be diligent in our service, striving always to be peaceable, spotless and blameless in character. Don't grow careless because He is delaying, for one day the Lord will come suddenly. Be patient while He delays, knowing that He does it because He is longsuffering and would give the last man, woman and child a chance to accept Him.

What lives we ought to live while we wait for His coming! We may hasten it by our holy living. Faith in the return of our Lord must lead to this. Then we may hasten it by a holy conversation. Watch your speech. Don't forget to look forward with an eager gaze. Then be diligent that you

be "found spotless, blameless and at peace with him" (*3:14*). Are you looking forward to His coming? What effect has this hope had upon your life and conversation?

Peter's last word of warning is "Beware!" This is a note of caution. "Be on your guard so that you may not be carried away by the error of lawless men and fall from your secure position" (*3:17*).

Know and Grow

The remedy against falling back is to "grow"—make progress. "Grow in grace and in the knowledge of our Lord and Savior Jesus Christ." Are you growing in your knowledge? Christian knowledge is an effective weapon against heresy. Christianity without a creed cannot stand against the attacks of the critics. If you are not growing, beware lest you fall by the way, for we are living in a wicked world where people are enemies of God and His truth. A living thing ought to grow. When there is no growth, there is no life. The foundation of growth is the knowledge of Christ. As we grow in this, we grow in likeness to Him.

47. UNDERSTANDING

First, Second, Third John and Jude

Jesus Christ, Our Life; the Truth; the Way; Our Keeper

Understanding First John

First John was written by the aged apostle John in the year A.D. 90, probably in Ephesus. Unlike the other apostles, he does not address his letter to any church or any particular person. He writes to all Christians, old and young (*2:12-14*). He calls Christians by a tender word *teknia*—which means "born ones" or "bairns." God is dealing with His very own born-again children.

John told us why he wrote his Gospel—that "you may believe that Jesus is the Christ, the Son of God, and that by believing you may have life in his name" (*John 20:31*).

He wrote his Epistle that those who believe in Christ might KNOW that they have eternal life (*5:13*).

Turn to the Gospel of John 20:31 and read it along with 1 John 5:13. The Gospel was written to show us how we might receive eternal life. The Epistle of 1 John was written to assure those who have believed that they have eternal life by believing "that Jesus is the Christ." The Epistle of 1 John appears to have been intended as

a companion to the Gospel of John. Thus we find the word "believe" running all through the Gospel of John, and the word "know" running through the Epistle. The word "know" is used more than thirty times in this short letter. Underline it each time you discover it.

Selected Bible Readings

Sunday:	Walking in Fellowship (*1 John 1:1—2:14*)
Monday:	Walking as Children of God (*1 John 2:15—3:24*)
Tuesday:	Walking in Love (*1 John 4:1-21*)
Wednesday:	Walking in Knowledge (*1 John 5:1-21*)
Thursday:	Walking in Truth (*2 John 1-13*)
Friday:	Walking in the Way (*3 John 1-14*)
Saturday:	Walking Without Falling (*Jude 1-25*)

John wrote for four reasons:

1. That they might be happy (1:4)
2. That they might not sin (2:1)
3. That they might be on guard against error (2:26)
4. That they might KNOW (5:13).

John was the disciple whom Jesus loved. He stood close to Him on the cross at Calvary. He looked into the empty tomb on that morning of the Resurrection. On Patmos, he was lifted up by the Spirit and saw a door opened into heaven. This one gives us his witness of these facts. "We know," he says, "There is no possibility of doubt about it." "That which was from the beginning, which we have heard, which we have seen with our eyes, which we have looked at and our hands have touched—this we proclaim concerning the Word of life"—JESUS (1 John 1:1)! John gives us evidence for his knowledge. He has heard and seen and handled the Word of life. He longs to bring his hearers into intimate fellowship with the Father and His Son, that their joy might be full (1 John 1:3-4,7; 2:13-14).

Christ, who was God, took on flesh and dwelt with people so they could hear His voice, see His face and feel the touch of His loving hand. This brought God down to people that we "may have fellowship." To walk in fellowship is to live in agreement.

God wants us to have fellowship with Him, and in Him to have fellowship with one another (1:3).

John says we not only must believe like Christians, but we also must act like Christians. In chapters 1-3, we find out whether we are living like Christians. In chapters 4 and 5, we discover whether we are believing like Christians. Striking lightning is accompanied by thunder. So "striking" faith is accompanied by life and testimony (2:3). Some people say they believe

God, but act more like the devil. This cannot be. We must be as orthodox in our behavior as we are in our belief. Do the truth and believe the truth. "If we claim to have fellowship with him yet walk in the darkness, we lie and do not live by the truth" (1:6).

John exalts God in his Epistles:
God is Light (1:5)
God is Love (4:8,16)
God is Righteous (2:29)
God is Life (5:11-12)
God is Truth (2 John)
God is Good (3 John).

Right Behavior
1 John 1:1—3:24

John gives us seven tests of Christian behavior. Read these and find what your rating is as a Christian. They are easy to find because each of these tests is introduced by "if we say" or "the one who says." The test is this— "if we say" one thing and do another, we are not living as Christ would want us to, in full fellowship with Himself. How much easier it is to talk than it is to do! As Dwight Moody said, "We talk cream and live skim milk." For "our fellowship is with the Father and with his Son, Jesus Christ" (1 John 1:3). We are to walk together, talk together and live together. We are to eat at the same table (Revelation 3:20). We are one family (Ephesians 3:15). God is my Father because Jesus Christ my elder Brother has made me a child of the King. Therefore I must behave that way. Fellowship brings joy (1:4). There is no joy greater than fellowship with a friend.

I walk with a God of light. "God is light; in him there is no darkness at all" (1:5). If my walk is with Him, I will walk in the light of His love and grace. There are seven tests of our walk with God.

First Test—Walk in the Light

"If we claim to have fellowship with him [the God of light] yet walk in darkness, we lie and do not live by the truth" (*1:6*).

Is there known sin in your life? If there is, you are not walking with Christ. His presence throws light on your conscience and heart and shows the presence of sin in your life (*Ephesians 5:13*). A Christian who is walking in fellowship with God will enjoy fellowship with other Christians (*1 John 1:7*). Light reveals sin. Known sin will keep you from fellowship with Christ, but fellowship with Christ will keep you from sin. Do you ask Him to throw His searchlight upon your heart?

Second Test—Admit You Are a Sinner

"If we claim to be without sin, we deceive ourselves and the truth is not in us" (*1:8*). You cannot walk with God and practice sin in your life at the same time. God keeps showing us the sin in our lives. On the cross He redeemed us from the penalty of sin once and for all. But let us know, too, that if we confess our sins, He keeps cleansing us from the sins that creep into our lives by our contact with this world.

When a farmer plows his field, he throws out every stone he finds. But the next year as the plow goes deep into the furrow, he finds other stones that had remained hidden the year before. He throws these aside as they turn up. Then the next year the same thing occurs. So in our lives! God will reveal by the plow of His Spirit the sins that are hidden in our lives we did not know were there. Don't be discouraged, but use His remedy.

"If we confess our sins, he is faithful and just and will forgive us our sins and purify us from all unrighteousness" (*1:9*). Don't pray in an indefinite way. Name it before God. Is it pride, lack of trust, anger, love of pleasure more than God? Well, whatever it is, lay it out before God and tell Him what it is. Call it by name. Then claim God's promise. "He is faithful and just" not only to "forgive us our sins," but also to "purify us from all unrighteousness." A human parent can forgive our misbehavings, but only God can cleanse us from sin.

Third Test—Obey God's Will

"The man who says, 'I know him,' but does not do what he commands is a liar, and the truth is not in him" (*2:4*). Obedience is a real test. God makes a very strong statement. If you say you are a Christian and do not obey Him, you are a liar. The one who is a Christian keeps God's commandments.

What are Christ's commandments? "Love the Lord your God with all your heart and with all your soul and with all your mind and with all your strength" (*Mark 12:30; Luke 10:27*). Do you love God that way? Put yourself to a few tests. Do you spend more time watching television than you do with God? Then you don't love Him with all your heart. Are you obedient to His Word? His still small voice? Many times we do not want to let God talk to us. We will not listen to Him because we are afraid of His will for us.

Fourth Test—Imitate Christ

"Whoever claims to live in him must walk as Jesus did" (*1 John 2:6*).

We should be Christlike in all our life. Christ says, "You are the salt of the earth" (*Matthew 5:13*). Salt preserves food from spoiling. Are you the preservative of your crowd? Do you keep the language clean? Do you refrain from using God's name in vain? Does your presence keep them from doing questionable things?

People are too lazy to look up. Few

When a farmer plows his field, he throws out every stone he finds. But the next year as the plow goes deep into the furrow, he finds other stones. So in our lives God will reveal by the plow of His Spirit the sins that are hidden in our lives.

try to find Christ. So Christ wants others to see Him reflected in us. In the famous Sistine Chapel in Rome, the beauty of the art is in the ceiling. As you enter, you are given a mirror. It seems strange to see people walking around looking down when the paintings are above. But they see all the glory reflected in the mirrors before them, without breaking their necks. Be a reflector. Let the beauty of Jesus be seen in you.

Fifth Test—Love Others

"Anyone who claims to be in the light but hates his brother is still in the darkness" (*2:9*).

Another acid test of the Christian life is love (*2:7-11*). Love changes a person. Love makes us have a concern for the welfare of others.

God speaks of love to others, personal attitudes. There are three chief attitudes toward others: hatred, which is murder (*3:15*); indifference—a feeling akin to hate—no concern (*4:20-21*); love. Love shows itself in different ways (*2:9-11; 3:14*); physically—concern for welfare (*3:16-18*); spiritually—concern for another's soul.

Sixth Test—Relationship to the World

"If anyone loves the world, the love of the Father is not in him" (*2:15*).

We live in a present evil world (*Galatians 1:4*). The scheme of things as they exist today is not the standard for the Christian. Whenever you find Christians obeying them, they are walking on forbidden ground.

All sins may be put into three categories: (1) lust of the flesh (2) lust of the eyes; (3) pride of life (see *2:16-17, KJV*).

1. *Lust of the flesh.* Temptations come through the body and its appetites and passions, what the *NIV* calls the "cravings of sinful man." The devil tempted Jesus in this way first. Jesus had been fasting forty days, and every atom of His being cried for bread. How plausible was Satan's temptation! It was the same appeal to appetite Satan made to Eve. In all those thousands of years, the devil has invented no new weapons of attack.

"Tell this stone to become bread" (*Luke 4:3*). The temptation for self-gratification is one of the strongest that can assail us. Appetite is still one of the most vulnerable points when Satan attacks us. The necessity for bread and pleasure is supposed by some to justify any means to get them. It is not necessary that we should live at all! There is only one moral necessity—to trust God and keep His commandments.

2. *Lust of the eyes.* Foiled with one weapon, Satan quickly drops it and tries another. Taking Jesus into a high mountain, he showed Him (lust of the eyes) all the kingdoms of the world in a moment of time. "So if you worship me, it will all be yours" (*Luke 4:7*). Satan was working his second trick.

How people worship at the altar of riches and honor because they long for what their eyes see of this world!

Your eyes can blacken your soul! Be careful what you see. If you throw a white tennis ball against a sooty wall, a black mark will be left upon it. If your eye is thrown against impure objects, be sure a mark will be left upon your mind and heart. Be careful what you see!

3. *Pride of life.* Everyone wants spectacular success, and to be able to boast "of what he has and does." The devil took Jesus to the pinnacle of the Temple and told Him to cast Himself down, and if He was the Son of God, He would be kept by angels. It was a proposal to leap from the pinnacle of the Temple into immediate popularity. It is a temptation for any person to be popular. We all have human ambitions. How many people of genius have been led astray because the glittering prize of ambition has been held up before them! We want to win it at a single stroke. How strong is the temptation to take a shortcut to our ambition, whether of education or wealth

or position and power! We are in danger of selling our very souls to gain our end! Even Jesus saw the world spread before Him and saw how short and alluring was the step that was promised Him, but to become the subject of the prince of this world would have ended His mission as the Savior of the world.

Seventh Test—Prove Christ Is Righteous by Your Life

Do we acknowledge Christ by our life (*2:22*)? Read 2:29. Others watch us to see if we "do righteousness." Those who abide in Christ will bear the same fruit in their lives that Christ bears and that is righteousness.

A few verses in chapter 3:1-10 are difficult to understand unless we know what the original text means.

"Everyone who commits (practices) sin is guilty of lawlessness; for [that is what] sin is, lawlessness." This is *The Amplified Bible* translation of 3:4. If we know Christ as God dwelling in our lives, we will not "practice sin." "No one who continues to sin has either seen him or known him" (*3:6*), and in verse 9, "No one who is born of God will continue to sin, because God's seed remains in him; he cannot go on sinning, because he has been born of God." It is possible for Christians under strong temptation to fall into sin for the time, but they will not keep practicing it. If people continually practice sin, they may well doubt their conversion! We should consider sin as God does. Sin cost God His Son!

Right Belief *1 John 4:1—5:11*

We need a creed by which to live. The word "creed" comes from the Latin word *credo*—"I believe." There are sins of the body that we all commit, but there are sins of the heart and disposition as well. God is as interested in what you believe as in how you act.

You cannot believe things that are not true about Christ and at the same time have fellowship with Him.

The unsound teachers of John's day were denying the fact that Christ truly suffered and truly rose again. They said He was only a mystery man who appeared and vanished, but He was not God.

You cannot deny the death of Christ on the cross and find a pardon for your sin. You cannot deny the resurrection of Christ and enjoy the privileges of Christianity that are found in a living Christ. You cannot deny that Christ is God and find any access to the Father.

Your sin can start in your intellect. What do you believe? Christ wants to be our only Teacher. What we believe determines how we act.

Is a creed necessary? Read John 3:16 and see if you think it is. It says, "Whoever believes in him shall not perish but have eternal life." Christianity is Christ-centered. Christ out of Christianity leaves nothing. This means death. If we believe not, we shall die, but if we believe, we shall live (Romans 10:9-10).

Many Christians are spiritual babes in Christ. They are led astray with every new "wind of doctrine." They are susceptible to all about them. When doubt fills their minds, they sink in despair. Hence, everyone ought to be given a way whereby to test every religion to see if it be true. Especially is this true in this day of so many religious beliefs. John states the test very clearly in 4:1-3; read these verses.

What Shall We Believe?

John makes some plain statements in 1 John 4:1-3:

1. We must believe "that Jesus Christ has come in the flesh"—in *carnis* (4:1-2; 5:20-21). He is the incarnate Lord. This is the first thing we must be sure of. We must believe that when Jesus walked this earth He was God clothed in human flesh. "Veiled in flesh the Godhead see; Hail th'incarnate Deity," wrote Charles Wesley (1707-1788, hymn writer and brother of John Wesley). He took upon Himself the form of a man that He might die in our place, and bare our sins in His own body on the tree.

John records, "The Word became flesh and made his dwelling among us. We have seen his glory, the glory of the One and Only, who came from the Father, full of grace and truth" (*John 1:14*). Christ's earthly life was thirty-three years, but that is not His whole existence. Christ was with the Father from the beginning. More than 1,900 years ago, this Man of the ages came to this earth at His first advent. He did not begin life at the manger. He merely took upon Himself the form of a man. Then He remained on this earth thirty-three years. He died and was buried and rose again. Then He went back to where He came from.

Think how Christ was received on the earth the first time He came! "He came to that which was his own, but his own did not receive him" (*John 1:11*). They did not think that this One "in the flesh" before their eyes was God. They called Him a blasphemer when He claimed to be equal with God, "I and the Father are one" (*John 10:30*). For this they put Him to death. They would not believe that Jesus Christ was God come in the flesh!

2. We must believe in the deity of Christ (4:15; 5:5), that He is the Son of God, the only begotten Son. The liar is the one who denies that Jesus is the Christ, the promised Messiah (2:22). The Old Testament prophets told us the Messiah was coming. The angel

chorus said that the Babe born in Bethlehem was this Messiah who was prophesied. Simeon saw Christ in the Babe (*Luke 2:25-35*).

3. We must believe that "God is love" (*4:8*). There is no force in the world to compare with Christian love. Its power is seen in the great fact that "God is love." All through this chapter, it isn't our love that is the definition of love at its best, but God's love that is the measure. Listen! "Love comes from God. . . . God is love. . . . This is love: not that we loved God, but that he loved us and sent his Son as an atoning sacrifice for our sins. Dear friends, since God so loved us, we also ought to love one another" (*4:7-11*). Love turns our hearts away from ourselves. We cannot really love God without loving others. So we become channels of blessing to others around us because of what God is in us.

Nothing could influence our lives as much as the love of God, for "God lives in us" (*4:12*).

God's love was shown in the gift of His Son to be a sacrifice for our sins (*John 3:16; 1 John 4:9-10*). When we look at the cross, we catch a glimpse into God's heart of love. The cross was the only way God had of showing us His heart. It is a picture of infinite love poured out in all its fullness. Christ did not die *to make* God love people. He died *because* God had loved people always with an everlasting love. "For God so loved..." Our salvation does not depend upon what we are, but upon what God is, and God is love!

God's love is first directed toward the individual. Then the individual must affect society. God is unseen and there are many who need God's love. So we will show it to others when we love. And when we love, we are like God. We ought also to love one another.

4. We must believe that Christ is our Savior (*5:10-12*). Christ was sent to be "the atoning sacrifice [or, propitiation] for our sins" (*2:2; 4:10; Romans 3:25*) because sin barred people from God's love, for "the wages of sin is death" (*Romans 6:23*). So Christ took the judgment of sin upon His own body on the cross and made it possible for God to show mercy righteously. Propitiation is the satisfaction by Christ's death of the whole demand of the law upon the sinner. Propitiation is the cause of life, for through the sacrifice of Christ we have everlasting life (*4:10*).

Read 1 John 5:10-12.

God and Love

Love is the supreme test of our Christian faith. "We know that we have passed from death to life, because we love our brothers. Anyone who does not love remains in death" (*3:14*). The word "love" occurs forty-eight times in this first Epistle of John (in the *KJV*). We find out how love acts in 1 Corinthians 13.

"Whoever does not love does not know God, because God is love" (*4:8*). Love is the first instinct of the renewed heart. Where do we get our love? From within? No, from above. "We love because he first loved us" (*4:19*). What if we do not love? God says, we "do not know God."

We should show our love to Him by loving one another (*1 John 4:7*). Those who have love in their hearts have fellowship with God (*4:16*). But where there is no love, there is no fellowship (*4:19-21*).

Rich Rewards *1 John 5:12-21*

The rewards of life in Christ are stated in the last verses:

Assurance of eternal life (*5:13*)
Power of prayer (*5:14-15*)

Power of intercession (5:16)
Victory (5:18 and 5:4-5).

Underline the word "know" in verses 12-20. We can have confidence when we know Christ. John uses the word "know" more than forty times in his Epistles. True Christianity is more than a creed—it is something that can be known and felt. We *know* that Christ was manifested to take away our sins. We *know* that we have passed from death unto life. We *know* that whatsoever we ask we shall receive. John assures us of these truths.

Understanding Second John

Second John is a good example of John's private correspondence to an individual. This letter was addressed to an unknown Christian woman. This is the only book in the Bible addressed to a woman.

The word "truth" is found five times in this short letter of thirteen verses. It is the key word. "Love" also occurs five times. Truth and love are inseparable.

We must test all the teachings in the world by the Scriptures "for the truth's sake" (v. 2, *KJV*). This is the final test. Test your experience by the Word of God, but never test the Word of God by your experience!

The truth John speaks of is from above, the truth as it is in Christ Jesus. We are to walk in the truth, not just admire it. Then we will love one another (v. 5). This love is genuine and not subject to change. "Christ's love compels us" (*2 Corinthians 5:14*). The proof of our love is in our walk. "And this is love: that we walk in obedience to his commands" (*2 John 6*).

John speaks of the teaching, or doctrine of Christ; see verse. 9. This is the test of the gospel. Not what I think or what someone else has thought or said or done, but what has Christ said?

What is He to you? Is He the Son of God?

Many false teachers were traveling among the churches (*vv. 7-11*) who would not confess that Jesus Christ was here in the flesh. This is "the deceiver and the antichrist" (*v. 7*). See also 1 John 4:1-2. They did not believe in the humanity of Christ. They denied His incarnation. If you call Him "Lord" and deny His deity, you are a liar and an antichrist. John says this.

Apply this test to some of the popular religious movements of our day—Christian Science, Spiritualism, Unity, Jehovah's Witnesses, the Unification Church, Scientology, Transcendental Meditation and other similar movements. They deny the "Christ doctrine" mentioned here.

Don't be friendly with these false teachers, John commands, or entertain them, for thus you share in their wicked work.

Understanding Third John

Third John was written to John's generous and warmhearted friend called Gaius. This man was the type of the true Christian layman who has dedicated his wealth and talent to the Lord. All he has belongs to Christ. Such people, scattered here and there, have through the years kept not only the Church alive in an unfriendly world, but have also kept Christ's love burning brightly in the midst of God's people when all seemed dark.

Gaius was noted for his loving hospitality. John urges him to continue entertaining the traveling preachers in spite of bitter opposition of an autocratic and blustering church official named Diotrephes. Hospitality is a manifestation of Christian love.

You can be either a Gaius, helping in the kingdom, or a Diotrephes, hindering the cause.

What a splendid thing to be rich and powerful and to choose to lay all your gifts and talents at Jesus' feet, like Gaius and Demetrius!

Understanding Jude

Jude was a brother of the Lord. He knew Peter. They walked with the Master and no doubt talked together after His departure. They evidently thought much alike about the great issues of the day. Second Peter and Jude are very similar in thought and language. Both men were dealing with the dangers confronting the doctrines of the Church.

No doubt certain persons who denied "the only Lord God, and our Lord Jesus Christ" had joined the church. They were not outside, but inside the church. They had crept in unawares.

Alas! What church is without them today? They are with us, but not of us. Christ will judge these evil people as He did the fallen angels.

These intruders had begun to teach error in the church (vv. 3-4,8,16,19). A leaven of evil was at work among the readers. These intruders were:

"Godless men"—worldly

"Change the grace of our God into a license for immorality"—carnal

"Deny Jesus Christ our only Sovereign and Lord"—skeptical

"Reject authority and slander celestial beings"—lawless

"Grumblers and faultfinders"—critical

"Flatter others for their own advantage"—flatterers

"Follow mere natural instincts and do not have the Spirit"—immoral.

In contrast to these evil fellows we find the true followers of the faith, lifting high the cross of Christ (vv. 20-23). They were building on the foundation of Christ:

"Praying in the Holy Spirit" (v. 20)

"Keeping" in God's love (v. 21)

"Waiting" for God's mercy (v. 21)

"Winning" souls for Him (vv. 22-23)

"Resting" on His keeping power (v. 24).

Thank God for this noble army of faithful ones! Of these God says that their reward shall be that there He will "keep you from falling and . . . present you before his glorious presence without fault and with great joy" (v. 24).

Prophecy
of the New Testament
Revelation

48. UNDERSTANDING

Revelation

Revelation Portrays Jesus Christ, Our Triumphant King

Revelation is the only book of prophecy in the New Testament. It is the only book in the divine library that especially promises a blessing to those who read and hear. "Blessed" is a strong word. "Blessed is the one who reads the words of this prophecy" is what the book of Revelation says of itself (*Revelation 1:3*), but after reading the first chapters about the churches, and the last chapters describing heaven, not many of us read much in this book.

Revelation presents a glorious, reigning Christ. It tells of Christ's complete and eternal victory over Satan. It describes Satan's defeat and punishment, first for a thousand years, then eternally. It tells more about Satan's final doom than any other book. No wonder Satan doesn't want people to read it!

Does "revelation" mean a riddle? Most people, when speaking of this book, seem to think it does. No, it means just the opposite—"unveiling." It is written in symbols. It was sent and signified by the angel to John. The hard of hearing have a sign language. Each gesture is filled with meaning. So is every sign in Revelation. There are 300 symbols in this book and each has a definite meaning. Symbols are wonderful and speak great truths.

The content of the book seems to indicate that most of its events are yet to be fulfilled.

This book is the Revelation of Jesus Christ, not the revelation of John. It is not the revelation of the growth of the Church and the gradual conversion of the world, but it is the Revelation of Jesus Christ! It was given by Christ Himself to John (*Revelation 1:1-2*). The book deals with the return of the Lord to this earth. It describes the readiness or unreadiness of the Church for this great happening (*3:20*). There are descriptions of the tremendous events on earth and in heaven just before, during and after His coming.

What is meant by "the time is near" (*1:3*)? Almost 2,000 years have passed since these words were spoken, but the idea is "the next on the program." No matter how much time may intervene, the next thing after the day of grace is the kingdom age to be ushered in by our Lord's coming.

Few people who have any imagination have not sat down and thought, *I wonder how it would feel to be a king*. But Christ says when He comes He will make us reign as kings (*1:6*)!

Then "those who pierced him" shall see Him (*1:7*). Although that refers especially to the Jewish people, who at Christ's coming will turn to Him as a united people and be saved (*Romans 11:25-26*), at the same time it means many others who have pierced Christ will see Him. Have YOU pierced Him?

Christ is the theme of this wonderful book. It gives an authentic portrait

0

of the Lord Jesus as the triumphant One. No less than twenty-six times do we find in it Christ's sacrificial title "Lamb" (*Revelation 5:6*). In addition, we see a vision of the future of the Church and the world in relation to Him.

It has been said that the saving blood of Christ runs through the entire Bible like a red cord. It has also been said that the second coming of Christ runs through the Bible like a golden cord. We are saved and washed clean in His blood in order that we may be ready and eager for His return.

Revelation is a wonderful way to finish the story that began in Genesis. All that was begun in the book of beginnings (*Genesis*) is consummated in Revelation. In Genesis the heaven and earth were created. In Revelation we see a new heaven and a new earth. In Genesis the sun and moon appear; in Revelation we read that there is no

Selected Bible Readings

Sunday: Christ and the Churches (*Revelation 1:1–3:22*)

Monday: Christ's Throne and the Seven Sealed Book (*Revelation 4:1—6:17*)

Tuesday: Christ's Trumpets Sounded (*Revelation 7:1—9:21*)

Wednesday: Christ and the Woes (*Revelation 10:1—12:17*)

Thursday: Christ and Antichrist (*Revelation 13:1—15:8*)

Friday: Christ's Final Triumph (*Revelation 16:1—18:24*)

Saturday: Christ the Lord of All (*Revelation 19:1—22:21*)

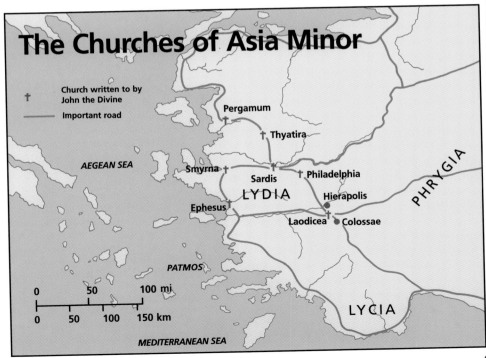

The Churches of Asia Minor

† Church written to by John the Divine

—— Important road

Pergamum

† Thyatira

AEGEAN SEA

Smyrna †

Sardis † Philadelphia

LYDIA

Hierapolis

Ephesus †

Laodicea † ● Colossae

PHRYGIA

PATMOS

| 0 | 50 | 100 mi |
| 0 | 50 | 100 | 150 km |

LYCIA

MEDITERRANEAN SEA

need of the sun or moon, for Christ is the light of the new heaven. In Genesis there is a garden; in Revelation there is a holy city. In Genesis there is the marriage of the first Adam; in Revelation the marriage supper of the second Adam, Jesus Christ. In Genesis we see the beginning of sin; in Revelation sin is done away. So we can follow the appearance of the great adversary, Satan, and sorrow and pain and tears in Genesis, and see their doom and destruction in Revelation.

Things are very dismal in the world today. No one living has ever known such uncertainty about the future of human events. But things were dismal when the apostle John, an old, old man, was exiled to the Isle of Patmos. He had been banished for his testimony of Jesus (1:9). While on the island, John was forced to labor hard in the mines and quarries. But His Commander-in-Chief appeared to him and delivered a ringing message and ultimate glory.

God had determined from the beginning that His Son would be the Ruler of this universe (Isaiah 9:6-7).

Revelation is the greatest drama of all time. The plot is tense throughout; the final scene is glorious, for Christ comes unto His own. The Hero is our Lord Himself; the villain is the devil. The actors are the seven churches. The characters unloosed by the seals of chapters 6 and 7 are introduced by the "four horsemen." Then those summoned by the trumpets in turn leave the center of the scene of action, and we see the Antichrist, the world ruler, stalking across the stage (chap. 13). This incarnation of the devil himself is determined to set up his own kingdom and be worshiped by people. But Christ brings all to naught. This majestic Actor, bringing His hosts with Him, comes forth—the long-looked-for

King of kings and Lord of lords. He drives His enemies from the stage in utter defeat (chap. 19).

After all the struggle has ended and the beasts have been destroyed and the devil bound and "the old order of things has passed away. He who was seated on the throne said, 'I am making everything new'" (Revelation 21: 4-5). This book brings to a climax the great story commenced in Genesis, and as all good stories should, it ends "And they lived happily ever after."

Notice the sevens in this book:
• Seven churches
• Seven signs
• Seven seals
• Seven last plagues
• Seven trumpets
• Seven dooms
• Seven new things.

Past—What You Have Seen
Revelation 1:1-20

Here is the last picture of Jesus Christ given in the New Testament. Many artists have tried to portray Him, but they have failed. Here is an authentic portrait (1:13-16). He is standing in the midst of the seven golden lampstands, representing the churches (v. 20). Lampstands prove that the Church is to be a light bearer. "You are the light of the world" (Matthew 5:14). How many churches today—electronic or otherwise—are for entertainment, bazaars and to promote money-making schemes, instead of lights to shine in a dark place!

Christ is likened to a "son of man," but it is clear from the vision that the One whom John saw was more than human. He was the Son of Man. Everything symbolizes majesty and judgment, and this thought of judgment strikes the keynote of the book. Christ is presented to the whole world as Judge:

"Dressed in a robe reaching down

to his feet"—flowing robes a token of dignity and honor

"Head and hair were white like wool"—He is the Ancient of Days

"Eyes were like blazing fire"—intelligence; bringing hidden things to light

"Feet were like bronze glowing in a furnace"—brass symbolizes judgment

"Voice was like the sound of rushing waters"—power and majesty

"Right hand"—in these are kept the seven stars

"Mouth"—out of it came sharp double-edged sword of judgment

"His face was like the sun shining in all its brilliance" (*1:12-18*).

John's vision was not of this age in which we are living, but of a future day when people shall appear before Christ to be judged (*John 5:27-29*). Now, we may have all of God's grace, mercy and forgiveness for the taking. Now, Christ is before us to be judged. We can reject Him if we choose. In Revelation, John is picturing Christ in judgment. The day of mercy is past, now we stand before the Judge.

When John saw this glorious One, he fell at His feet as dead, so overpowering was the vision (*Revelation 1:17*). But Christ's words were reassuring. He said He was the living One, and though He had been dead, He was alive forevermore, and held the keys of death and Hades. Then follows the command to write what is found in this book (*1:19*). We do not have the usual picture of Christ starting in Bethlehem and ending at the Mount of Olives, but here we have His life in heaven, as the crown and culmination of all.

Have you ever seen the Lord? When Moses saw Him, his face shone. Job abhorred himself and repented in ashes. Isaiah saw himself unclean. Thomas said, "My Lord and my God."

Remains of the great Temple of Artemis, Sardis.

Saul (Paul) fell down and worshiped Him as Savior. What would happen to us if we really saw the Lord?

Present—The Things Which Are *Revelation 2:1—3:22*

In the second and third chapters, we find Christ's love letters to His churches. These letters are alike in pattern. Christ dictated them to the angels of the seven churches to whom He addressed these letters. In each, look for the speaker, praise, reproof, exhortation and promise.

The churches named were churches that actually existed in John's day. In dealing with them, He seems to give us a brief church history from the first-century Church to the Church of today, in seven periods:

Ephesus—the Church of the first love, the apostolic Church (*2:1-7*)

Smyrna—the persecuted Church—Diocletian to Constantine (*2:8-11*)

Pergamos—The Church under imperial favor—under Constantine (*2:12-17*)

Thyatira—the papal Church—the Dark Ages (*2:18-29*)

Sardis—the Reformation Church—Protestantism, sixteenth and

seventeenth centuries (3:1-6)
Philadelphia—the missionary
Church-period ushered in by the
Puritan movement (3:7-13)
Laodicea—the rejected Church—
Church of the final apostasy
(3:14-19).

Discover where you find Christ at
the end of this Church age. Read 3:20.
He is outside, knocking to get in. The
Church will not let Him in, but He
pleads with the individual: "If anyone
. . . opens the door, I will come in."
Have you opened your heart's door to
Christ?

Let us take heed to words such as
those found in this letter: "Yet I hold
this against you. . . . Nevertheless, I
have a few things against you. . . .
Nevertheless, I have this against you"
(2:4,14,20). These are the warnings of a
faithful Savior.

Discover how Christ is set forth in
these two chapters. Remember, this
book is the Revelation of Jesus Christ.
What are the promises to the over-
comers? See if you can find seven.

Future—The Things
Which Shall Be
Revelation 4:1—22:21

The great revelation proper unfolds
with the sound of trumpets and "a
door standing open in heaven. And the
voice . . . said, 'Come up here, and I
will show you what must take place
after this.'"

First the throne of God comes into
view (4:1-3). Revelation becomes the
"book of the throne." This is the great
central fact that pervades the book.
This throne speaks of judgment. The
throne of grace is no longer seen. The
scene is a courtroom. The Judge of all
the earth is on the bench; the twenty-
four elders, representing the twelve
patriarchs of the Old Testament and
the twelve apostles of the New, are the

jury (4:4). The seven spirits of God
(4:5; 5:6) are the prosecutor, and the
four living creatures are court attendants, ready to carry out the will of
the Judge.

Next in importance to the Lamb
Himself is the sealed book (5:1). Who
can possibly open the book? None,
save One. He "has triumphed. He is
able to open the scroll and its seven
seals" (v. 5). Christ prevailed in the
wilderness after forty days. He prevailed in Gethsemane. On Calvary He
prevailed when He dropped His divine
head on His pulseless breast and said,
"It is finished" (John 19:30). On the
third day He arose from the dead and
conquered death, sin, hell and Satan.
This same Christ now claims the kingdom of the world by right of conquest.

The day of tribulation begins with
the opening of the seven seals (chap.
6). This describes the Great
Tribulation period spoken of by the
prophet Jeremiah in Jeremiah 30 as the
"time of Israel's sorrow." Christ also
referred to it as a great tribulation
such as has never happened upon the
earth (Matthew 24:21). During the
Great Tribulation, God will allow sin
to work out its tragic results. God's
hand will be lifted from humans and
beasts. The earth will be filled with
war, hunger, famine and pestilence.
Judgment must come on those who
have rejected the Son of God and put
Him to an open shame. We as
Christians can look for Christ, not for
calamity, because our Savior is coming
to receive us to Himself and free us
from this day.

Four Horsemen

In the sixth chapter we see the famous
"four horsemen" (Revelation 6:1-8).
Restraint is removed as the seals are
broken. The forces of evil have been
held in check. When the seals are torn

away, war and destruction are set loose. People will reap what they have sown. The anguish and horror of the period will be the result of human ambition, hatred and cruelty.

First, we see the white horse of religious witness come before the final catastrophe upon the earth. Then comes the red horse, and universal war breaks upon the world when peace will be taken from the earth. The black horse of famine and scarcity follows upon universal war. Lastly, the pale horse of pestilence and death comes forth with merciless tread.

The sixth seal (6:12-17) brings social chaos, the complete breaking up of society and a boasted civilization. Darkness, falling stars, heavens rolled up as a scroll, islands moving, is the picture presented. Then the most tragic prayer meeting on earth with kings and priests, rich and poor, fleeing from God in a general stampede, praying for death, for "For the great day of their wrath has come, and who can stand?"

There is a momentary pause (chap. 7) while the saved of the tribulation period are presented. These are "a great multitude" (7:9) with their garments washed and made white in the blood of the Lamb. The "sealed" are all Israelites—whom God will gather unto Himself (Hosea 1:9-10; Romans 11:25-26). The "great multitude" is from all nations. This proves that the gospel preached in the tribulation period will be most effective.

The Seven Trumpets

Silence in heaven for thirty minutes! This is the calm before the storm (chap. 8). War, famine and pestilence have devastated the earth. Now His judgments have come upon the earth and Satan, knowing his time is short, is exceedingly wrathful. We find unprecedented activity of demons, 200 million demons sweeping across the earth. Hell is let loose! Sin is allowed its full sway, and death is preferable to life (9:1-21). Satan does his last work upon the earth.

Finally we see Satan incarnating himself in the Antichrist. His portrait is given in Revelation 13. See also Daniel 12:11; Matthew 24:15; 2 Thessalonians 2:3. This Antichrist will be a world ruler. He demands the honors due to Christ Himself. He will be the political ruler of this world. He is the embodiment of wickedness. He will be shrewd and clever and a real leader of people. The Antichrist will be a Caesar, an Alexander, a Nero, a Hitler, a Stalin, a Mao Tse-tung all in one. A person can neither "buy or sell unless he had the mark." The "mark of the beast" is like the brand mark of ownership or the token of allegiance such as the swastika. It will be impossible for people to buy or sell without permission. The number 666 is "the number of a man." Six is the number of evil, so three sixes express a trinity of wickedness.

The final doom of the Antichrist will be the lake of fire at Christ's coming (Revelation 19:20). There will be plagues such as those of Egypt—blood, hail, fire, locusts, darkness, famine, sores, earthquakes, war and death. In these plagues is summed up the wrath of God upon a Christ-rejecting world.

The Seven Golden Bowls

In the trumpets, Satan is releasing his power to accomplish his objectives. The bowls are God's power released against Satan. The bowls are God's answer to the devil. The bowls blast the dominion of Satan. Satan has dared to challenge God's power. God is now answering the challenge. Satan is forced into action. His kingdom is shaken to its foundations and he is undone. This event ends in the battle of

Armageddon (*16:13-16*). This battle is described in chapter 19. In the closing scene of the war, Christ takes the leadership of His armies and brings His foes to their doom.

The Dooms
The seventh bowl announced the "dooms" that were to follow. Civilization has come to utter collapse. Even though God has revealed its utter evil, nevertheless people blaspheme God and do not repent (*16:9,11*). Today, amid the luxuries of invention, people are dissatisfied and far from God. Hatred has turned into wars of colossal dimension. God pronounces seven "dooms" (*chaps. 17-20*). First the doom of great systems—ecclesiastical (*chap. 17*), commercial (*chap. 18*), political (*19:11-19*); then the beast and the false prophet (*19:20-21*), followed by the nations (*20:7-9*), and the devil (*20:10*), and finally, the doom of the lost is pronounced (*20:11-15*).

The Marriage of the Lamb
The "Hallelujah Chorus" (by George Frideric Handel, 1685-1759) announces the coming of the long-promised King, our Lord Jesus Christ, the heir of David's throne, to catch away His bride (*1 Thessalonians 4:17*). Hell has been let loose on earth. Satan and his cohorts have done their worst and Christ has finally triumphed. Righteousness, long on the scaffold, is now to mount the throne. The marriage of the Lamb is come (*Revelation 19:7*). The marriage supper of Christ will take place in the air. The saints will be rewarded in the air according to their works. This time of rejoicing will continue until Christ returns to the earth with His bride, to set up His millennial kingdom.

After the Battle of Armageddon (*19:17-19*), Christ, having subdued all His enemies, will take alive Antichrist (*19:20*) and the false prophet and cast them with a strong arm into the lake of fire. This is a name for Gehenna, the place where torment never ceases and from which none return. Christ will make an end of Satan's entire system.

The Millennium
This is the time when Christ, the Prince of Peace, will establish His kingdom upon the earth for a thousand years. The devil is to be bound for a thousand years (*20:3*); the saints Christ brings with Him will reign with Him for a thousand years (*20:4,6*); the wicked dead will not rise until the end of the thousand years (*20:5*).

There will be a thousand years of peace and joy upon the earth, when "the earth will be filled with the knowledge of the glory of the Lord, as the waters cover the sea" (*Habakkuk 2:14*). It will be a glorious time to live. No wars, no weeds, no wild animals, no taxes, no heartache of death! When this period has come to an end, then the devil will be released again. He will come to test the nations (*Revelation 20:7-9*). We discover their real attitude and learn that they prefer Satan to Christ. We can hardly believe it, but read 20:7-8: "When the thousand years are over, Satan will be released from his prison and will go out to deceive the nations in the four corners of the earth—Gog and Magog—to gather them for battle. In number they are like the sand on the seashore."

Satan is the author and instigator of war. After a thousand years of peace, Satan gathers them to "the war." Not a few gather, but a countless number, like "the sand on the seashore." But "fire came down from heaven and devoured them" (*20:9*). Human rebellion against God seems almost unbelievable, but "The heart is deceitful above all things and beyond cure. Who can understand it?" (*Jeremiah 17:9*).

Satan's Doom

Satan is treated too lightly by the average person. He is mighty! He is the deceiver of the whole world. He fell from the highest place, next to God Himself, to the lowest depths—"the lake of fire." Christ described it as "the eternal fire prepared for the devil and his angels" (*Matthew 25:41*). The devil is given a life sentence (*Revelation 20:10*).

The blazing white throne of the final judgment is set. The One sitting upon it shall judge all people. Read Revelation 20:11-15. The "dead" are brought before Him. The sea gives up its dead. The grave gives up its dead. Hades gives up the dead. The dead are judged according to their works (*20:12-13*). Final doom is pronounced. The Savior is now the Judge. "If anyone's name was not found written in the book of life, he was thrown into the lake of fire" (*20:15*). Judgment must come before the golden age of glory can be ushered in. Someone has called hell the penitentiary of the universe, and the universal cemetery of the spiritually dead.

John names seven new things:
A new heaven and earth (*21:1*)
A new people (*21:2-8*)
A new bride (*21:9*)
A new home (*21:10-21*)
A new temple (*21:22*)
A new light (*21:23-27*)
A new Paradise (*22:1-5*).

Happily Ever After

Yes, God's story ends "and they lived happily ever after." Read the triumph of God in Revelation 21 and 22. Satan has not been victorious in his attempt to separate people from fellowship with God by sin ever since his meeting with the first man and woman in the garden of Eden. He has utterly failed and we will be with Christ forever and ever!

Don't try to analyze or interpret these chapters. Rather, meditate upon them. This is heaven! How limited words are in explaining its glory! The fellowship between God and people is restored. God "dwells with his people." Every purpose is realized and every promise is fulfilled. Heaven is the opposite of what we experience here. All is beautiful!

The last words of Christ in His Revelation are, "Yes, I am coming soon." Our response should ever be, "Amen. Come, Lord Jesus" (*22:20*).

Appendices

A Glossary of Bible Words
Becoming a Member of God's Family
Index

A GLOSSARY OF BIBLE WORDS

Abba (Ab-uh)
An Aramaic word that means "Daddy." Aramaic was the language spoken by Jesus and other Jews living in Palestine.

admonition
Teaching, instruction, usually with the idea of a warning.

adultery
Sexual union between a man and a woman when either or both of them are married to someone else. Adultery is a sin.

adversary
An enemy or someone who is against you. Can refer directly to Satan (*1 Peter 5:8*).

advocate
Someone who supports, comforts, gives help to or speaks up for another person. Jesus and the Holy Spirit are *advocates* for members of God's family (*John 14:16,26; 1 John 2:1*).

affliction
Great trouble or pain.

alien
A person from another country; a foreigner.

altar
A place where sacrifices were made to worship God. An *altar* could be a pile of dirt or stones, a raised platform of wood, marble, metal or other materials. The *bronze* or *brazen altar* was used for burnt offerings in the Tabernacle's courtyard. It was a large box, eight feet square and four-and-a-half feet high, made of wood covered with bronze. A much larger altar replaced it when Solomon built the Temple. The *altar of incense* (also called the *golden altar*) was smaller, covered with gold, and placed just in front of the veil to the holy of holies. Every day, both morning and evening, incense was burned here, symbolizing the prayers of the people.

Amalekites (uh-MAL-uh-kites)
Nomadic, warlike people inhabiting the region southwest of the Dead Sea. Because of their vicious attack against the Israelites after the Exodus from Egypt, God pronounced judgment on them.

amen
"Let it be so!" or "This is the truth!" *Amen* is often said after a prayer to show that people agree with what has been said and believe that it will happen.

Ammonites
Descendants of Ben-Ammi, grandson of Abraham's nephew, Lot. They lived east of the Dead Sea, and were nomadic, idolatrous and vicious. The Ammonites often opposed Israel.

Amorites
Descendants of Canaan, a son of Ham, and grandson of Noah. Because of their wickedness, God told Abraham of future destruction He would bring. This punishment occurred under Moses and Joshua, and their land was given to the tribe of Reuben.

Ancient of Days
A name for God that describes Him as the everlasting Ruler of heaven and earth (*Daniel 7:13-14*).

angels
Heavenly beings created by God before He created Adam and Eve. *Angels* act as God's messengers to men and women. They also worship God.

anoint
To pour oil on a person or thing. A person was *anointed* to show that God had chosen him or her to do a special job. Samuel *anointed* David to show God had chosen him to be king.

antediluvian (ANT-ay-da-LOO-vee-un)
Before the Flood. The term is from the Latin, and is used in reference to the period and people before Genesis 7—9.

Antichrist (AN-tih-christ)
A great enemy of Christ Jesus who pretends to be the

Messiah. The Bible tells us that before the second coming of Christ, an *antichrist* will rule over the world.

Antioch (AN-tee-ock)
1. The capital of Syria, site of the first Gentile church, which sent Paul and Barnabas on their first missionary journey. 2. A town in Asia Minor that Paul visited on his travels.

apostle
A person chosen and sent out as a messenger. In the New Testament, *apostle* usually refers to one of the twelve men Jesus chose to be His special disciples. Paul and some other leaders in the Early Church were also called *apostles*.

appeal to Caesar (SEE-zer)
If a Roman citizen accused of a crime thought that the trial or verdict was unfair, he could request that the emperor hear the case. Paul, a Roman citizen, once did this.

Arabia
The large area between the Persian Gulf to the east, the Indian Ocean to the south, the Red Sea to the west, and Palestine, Syria, and Mesopotamia to the north.

Aram (AIR-um)
A son of Shem, grandson of Noah. The name is sometimes applied to all the land and people of the Fertile Crescent, but usually is focused on the region that became known as Syria. The Aramaens were a Semitic people, and their history often intersects that of the Hebrews.

Aramaic (air-uh-MAY-ik)
The main language spoken by Jesus and other people who lived in Palestine when Jesus was alive. At least some parts of the books of Daniel and Ezra were written in Aramaic.

Ararat (AIR-uh-rat)
A mountainous region of Armenia, between the Black Sea and the Caspian Sea where Noah's ark ran aground.

archangel
Chief angel. The term in the New Testament refers to Michael.

Ark of God, Ark of the Covenant
A special wooden chest that was covered with gold. On top, two golden figures of angels faced each other. The two tables of stone on which the Ten Commandments were written, a pot of manna and Aaron's rod that budded were kept inside the *Ark*. The *Ark* was placed in the most holy place in the Tabernacle.

Armenia (arr-MEEN-ee-uh)
The area north of Assyria, containing the Ararat mountain region.

armor bearer
A person who carried the large shield and necessary weapons for a king or army officer.

Artemis (AR-tuh-mis)
A Greek goddess whose Roman name was Diana. Her most beautiful and influential temple was built in Ephesus.

ascend
To go up. Jesus *ascended* to heaven to return to God the Father.

Assyria (uh-SEER-ee-uh)
Powerful and aggressive nation, the most powerful middle eastern empire from the tenth century B.C. through most of the seventh century. Nineveh was the capital city. *Assyria* conquered Israel and took its inhabitants captive.

Athens
A major Greek city, center of its art, science and learning. *Athens* was visited by Paul on his second missionary journey.

atonement
To make up for a wrong act; to become friends again. In the Bible, *atonement* usually means to become friends with God after sin has separated us from Him. The New Testament teaches that Jesus Christ made *atonement* for our sins when He died on the cross.

Baal (bale), **Baalim** (BALE-um)
The name *Baal* means "master." *Baal* (plural, *Baalim*) was the name of many false gods worshiped by the people of Canaan. They thought the *Baalim* ruled their land, crops and animals.

Babel (BAB-ul)
The name popularly given to the tower built in a vain attempt by people to reach "the heavens" (*Genesis* 11:1-9). God blocked their effort by confusing their languages.

Babylon (BAB-u-lun)**, Babylonia**
Babylon refers to both the capital city and country, among the major political and cultural centers of the ancient world. The city of *Babylon* was located at the

junction of the Euphrates river and major east-west caravan routes. For nearly a thousand years, until the rise of Assyria in the ninth century B.C., *Babylon* dominated much of the Middle East.

balm
A sticky, sweet-smelling sap that was used as a medicine to heal sores or relieve pain. The plant or tree from which the sap was taken is unknown today.

balsam trees
Trees that grow in the Jericho Plain. The sweet-smelling sap of the trees and the oil from their fruit were used as medicine.

baptize
In the Old Testament, to *baptize* meant to wash with water. But in the New Testament, when John the Baptist called the people to be *baptized,* he was using water to show that people were truly sorry for the wrong things they had done and that they were asking God to forgive their sins. Today, a person is *baptized* to show that he or she is a member of God's family.

barren
A woman who could not have children was called *barren.* Fields that did not produce crops or fruit trees that did not grow fruit were also called *barren.*

Beelzebub (bee-EL-zee-bub)
A god the Philistines worshiped. In the New Testament, *Beelzebub* (or Beelzebul) is another name for Satan—the prince of the demons.

believe
To have faith or to trust that something is true. The Bible tells us that we can *believe* that Jesus Christ is God's Son and trust Him to keep His promise to forgive sins. We show that we *believe* that God loves us and wants what is best for us by obeying His commands.

Bethel
A site, a few miles directly north of Jerusalem, where God confirmed to Jacob the covenant He had made with Abraham. Jacob named the place *Bethel,* meaning "House of God."

Bible
The word *Bible* comes from the Greek word *biblos,* meaning book.

birthright
The special rights the oldest son in a Hebrew family enjoyed. When his father died, the oldest son received a double share of all that his father owned. He also received the right to make decisions for the entire family. Esau sold his *birthright* to Jacob for a bowl of soup.

bishop
Overseer, a leader in the Early Church.

bitter herbs (urbs)
A bitter green salad eaten at Passover to remind the Israelites of the sorrow, pain and bitter hardships they suffered as slaves in Egypt.

blaspheme
To say bad things against God, to swear using God's name, or to do actions that show disrespect to God. The Bible says that *blasphemy* is a sin. The

Jews punished *blasphemers* by stoning them to death. Jesus and Stephen were falsely accused of *blasphemy.*

blemish
A spot or mark that makes something not perfect.

bless
The word *bless* is used in different ways in the Bible: 1. When God blesses, He brings salvation and prosperity and shows mercy and kindness to people. 2. When people bless, they (a) bring salvation and prosperity to other persons or groups; (b) they praise and worship and thank God; (c) they give good things or show kindness to others.

breastpiece
A square of colored linen cloth worn by the high priest when he entered the Holy Place. The *breastpiece* was decorated with twelve precious stones. Each stone represented one of the twelve tribes of Israel. The *breastpiece* reminded the priest to pray for each of the tribes of Israel.

breastplate
A piece of metal armor that protected a soldier's throat and chest.

burnt offering
A sacrifice, or gift, to God that was burned upon an altar. The offering was a perfect animal, such as a goat, sheep, lamb or ram. *Burnt offerings* were always given for cleansing, or atonement, for sin.

Caesar (SEE-zer)
The family name of Julius *Caesar,* a famous Roman leader. Later the name *Caesar*

was added to the name of each Roman ruler, so it became a title that meant the same as "emperor" or "king."

Calvary
A rugged bluff outside ancient Jerusalem. *Calvary* is from the Latin word for "skull," either because the hill resembled a skull, and/or because it was the site of executions.

Canaan (KAY-nun), **Canaanites**
Canaan was a son of Ham and a grandson of Noah. His descendants settled in and gave his name to the areas God promised to Abraham and which were later known as Palestine and Israel.

canon of Scripture (KAN-un)
Measuring rod or standard. For Protestants, the sixty-six books of the Old and New Testaments have been widely and historically accepted because they have met the standard of being true and authoritative. (Catholics and Orthodox Christians also revere the Apocrypha.)

capstone
The stone that holds two walls together; the final most important stone that finishes a wall. When the Bible calls Jesus a *capstone*, it reminds us that He is the Head of the Church and that He holds all Christians together.

captivity
The seventy-year period when Jews were in exile in Babylon.

Carmel (KAR-mel)
A high ridge that juts into the Mediterranean Sea. *Mount Carmel* was the site of Elijah's contest with the prophets of Baal.

centurion (sen-TOUR-ee-un)
An officer in the Roman army who was the leader of 100 men.

chaff
The worthless husks removed from grain. Farmers in Bible times got rid of *chaff* by throwing grain in the air on windy days. The light *chaff* blew away on the wind; the heavier grain fell to the ground. In the Bible, the word *chaff* often means something bad or worthless.

Chaldea (kal-DEE-uh)
The country of Babylon. The term is also used of the southern region of Babylonia. The *Chaldeans* overthrew the Assyrians in the late seventh century B.C. and established the regime that brought Babylon to its greatest power.

chief priest
See *high priest.*

cherub, cherubim
Heavenly beings, described as having multiple wings and both human and animal form. They are presented in Scripture as directly serving God. Carved representations of *cherubim* were placed on the Ark of the Covenant, and they were embroidered on the Tabernacle's curtains. Solomon's Temple contained huge figures of *cherubim.*

chosen people
The Jews, as descendants of Abraham, were selected by God to be "a great and mighty nation, and all the nations of the earth shall be blessed in him" (*Genesis 18:18-19*). The New Testament declares that the Church has become the spiritual recipi-

ent of this blessing and responsibility (*1 Peter 2:9*).

Christ
The Greek word that means God's Chosen One. Messiah is the Hebrew word meaning the same thing. Jesus was the *Christ.*

Christian (KRIS-chun)
In the Bible, the word meant "little Christ." Today people who believe Jesus Christ is God's Son and follow His teachings are called *Christians.*

church
An assembly or gathering. The word *church* is used to refer to both local groups of believers in Christ as well as all believers.

circumcise
To cut an unneeded flap of skin, called the foreskin, from the penis. For the Israelites, *circumcision* was a sign of the special agreement (or covenant) they had with God: If they worshiped and obeyed Him, He would be their God and they would be His people. Abraham was the first Hebrew to be *circumcised.*

cistern
A hole dug in the earth or a rock to collect and store water.

City of David
City of David has three meanings: 1. It is another name for the town of Bethlehem where David was born; 2. Part of the city of Jerusalem was known as the *City of David;* 3. The entire walled city of Jerusalem was sometimes called the *City of David.*

city of refuge

One of six cities set aside by Moses where a person who had accidentally killed someone could stay until a fair trial could be held. While the person was in a *city of refuge,* he would be safe from family or friends of the dead person who might want to kill him.

commandment

A rule or teaching people are to follow. Moses received the Ten Commandments from God. The Bible gives *commandments* for Christians to follow because they love Him and want to obey His Word.

concubine

A slave woman in Bible times who lived with an Israelite family and had children by the father of the family. She was considered an extra or second-class wife.

confess

To *confess* means to tell or agree about what is true. *Confess* sometimes means telling God your sins. *Confess* can also mean to say in front of other people that you believe that Jesus is God's Son and that He died and rose again to forgive you of your sins.

conscience

A feeling about what is right and what is wrong; a sense of knowing what is good and what is bad.

consecrate

To set apart something or someone to serve God in a special way.

convert

A person who has changed from one belief or way of thinking to another. A person who decides to follow God's way instead of his or her own way has become a *convert.*

Corinth

A city in Greece. Always a commercial center, the Roman conquerors made *Corinth* the capital city of the province. Paul taught in *Corinth* for a year and a half.

cornerstone

A large stone in the foundation of a building at the corner of two walls. It holds the two walls together. The *cornerstone* is the first and most important stone laid when a building is started. Jesus is called the *cornerstone* of our faith in God because He is the most important part of our knowing who God is.

counselor

One who gives advice or help. Sometimes the Bible uses the word *Counselor* as another name for Jesus. In the New Testament, the Holy Spirit is also called the *Counselor* of Christians.

covenant

An agreement. In the ancient Near East, sometimes covenants were made between two people or groups of people. Both sides decided what the agreement would be. However, in the Bible, the word usually refers to agreements between God and people. In a *covenant* between God and people, God decides what shall be done and the people agree to live by the *covenant.* The *Old Covenant* of law set standards of behavior in order to please God. The *New Covenant* of grace presents God's forgiveness based on faith in Jesus' death and resurrection.

covenant fathers

Abraham, Isaac and Jacob, (father, son and grandson) often mentioned together in Scripture in reference to God's promises to His people.

covet (KUV-et)

Wanting very much to have something that belongs to someone else.

crucify

To nail or tie a person to a cross until he or she is dead. *Crucifixion* was a slow, painful punishment the Romans used for their enemies and the worst criminals.

cuneiform

Wedge-shaped form of writing used in ancient Sumeria, Babylon and Persia.

curse

In the Bible, to *curse* does not mean to swear or to use bad language. When a person *cursed* something, he or she wished evil or harm to come to it. When God *cursed* something, He declared judgment on something.

Dan

One of the twelve tribes of Israel, whose territory was directly north of Judah and west of Benjamin and Ephraim. Also the northernmost city in Israel.

deacon

Helpers or servants in the church. In the New Testament, men and women *deacons* were chosen to take care of the needs of people in the church.

dedicate

To set apart for a special purpose. In the Bible, the word usually means that a person or thing is given to God to serve Him in a special way.

demon

An evil spirit working for Satan (the devil). People can be tempted, harassed or "possessed" (controlled) by *demons*. Jesus has authority over all *demons* and in his earthly ministry ordered evil spirits to come out of many people.

denarius (duh-NAIR-ee-us)

Roman money. A *denarius*, which was a small silver coin, was the payment for about one day's work.

devote

To set apart for a special purpose or reason.

disciple

Someone who follows the teachings and example of another. In the New Testament, *disciple* usually refers to a person who believed that Jesus is God's Son and loved and obeyed Him. Sometimes *disciples* means the twelve men Jesus chose to be His special friends and helpers.

dispersion

Refers to the deportation of and emigration of Jews from Palestine. The term usually focuses on the Assyrians' forced relocation of people from the Northern Kingdom of Israel to distant locations throughout the Assyrian Empire.

doctrine

Teaching, instruction, usually referring to the content of what is taught.

Eden

The perfect garden God created, between the Tigris and Euphrates rivers, in which Adam and Eve lived before they sinned.

elder

In the Bible, the word *elder* has several meanings: 1. In the Old Testament, an older man in a family, tribe or town was called an *elder*. 2. Also in the Old Testament, each town had a group of older men known as *elders*. They made major decisions for the town. 3. The first four books of the New Testament usually refer to the Sanhedrin—the group of men who governed the Jewish people in Jesus' time—as *elders*. 4. In the Early Church, the church leaders were often called *elders*.

Ephesus (EFF-uh-suss)

A city on the eastern coast of the Aegean Sea. *Ephesus* at one time was a commercial center, but had fallen into decline by the first century A.D. The city was the site of a large temple to the goddess Diana. Paul visited Ephesus on his missionary travels.

Epistles

Letters sent to individuals or groups. Twenty-one New Testament books were letters, most of which were sent to specific churches or church leaders.

eternal

Lasting forever; without end. God is *eternal* and members of God's family have *eternal* life.

eunuch (YOU-nuk)

1. Men who could not have children because their sex organs were damaged, altered or defective were called *eunuchs*. 2. The title *eunuch* was sometimes given to the man who was the most important helper or advisor to a king or queen.

evangelism

Evangelism is the act of telling the good news of the gospel of Jesus Christ to others.

evangelist

Someone who tells the good news about Christ. The term is from the Greek work meaning "a messenger of good."

everlasting

Never ending; forever.

faith

Faith has two meanings in the Bible: 1. To be certain about the things we cannot see or to trust someone because of who he or she is. For example, a Christian has *faith* that Jesus is God's Son. 2. "The *faith*" means the whole message about Jesus Christ—that He is God's Son and that He came to take the punishment for our sin so that we may become members of God's family.

faithful

Always loyal and trustworthy. God is *faithful*. We can always trust Him to do whatever He has promised. We are also to be *faithful* in doing what is right.

Fall

The original sin of Adam and Eve that broke the perfect relationship between people and God.

famine (FAM-in)

A time when there is not

enough food to keep people and animals alive. *Famines* can be caused by lack of rain, wars, insects that eat crops and bad storms.

fear

Today, *fear* most often means being afraid of something or someone. However, the Bible often uses the word *fear* to describe the sense of respect or awe that sinful people (and we are all sinful, according to *Romans 3:23*) should have for God because of His perfection, sovereignty and holiness.

feasts

1. Dinners, celebrations and banquets are often called feasts in the Bible. 2. Jewish religious holidays and celebrations are also called feasts.

fellowship

A time when friends who are interested in the same things come together. In the Bible, *fellowship* often means the friendship Christians share because they love God and His Son, Jesus.

firstborn

The first child born into a family. A *firstborn* son received special rights and power. He became head of the family after his father died and he received twice as much money and property as his brothers.

firstfruits

An offering to God of the first vegetables, fruits and grains the Israelites picked from their fields. The people offered their *firstfruits* to God to thank Him for supplying their food.

flint

A very hard stone that can be sharpened to a fine cutting edge.

forefather

A person from whom one is descended—an ancestor. Your father, your grandfather, your great-grandfather and your great-great-grandfather are some of your *forefathers*.

forgive

A decision of the will to stop feeling angry and to stop blaming a person for something wrong he or she has done; to be friends again. God *forgives* everyone who repents of sin and believes that Jesus died to take the punishment for his or her sins. When God *forgives* a person, God forgets the person's sins forever.

forsake

To leave, to go away from, to leave completely alone.

frankincense (FRANK-in-sense)

A very expensive, hard gum made from the sap of a terebinth tree. *Frankincense* was used to make sweet-smelling perfume. The Israelites used *frankincense* in religious ceremonies. One of the special gifts the wise men brought to Jesus was *frankincense*.

fruit

Evidence, outcomes, results. Although *fruit* is sometimes used in Scripture to refer to foods, it is commonly used to refer to the actions produced by good or evil in people's lives. The *fruit* of the Spirit (*Galatians 5*) refers to virtues produced in a Christian's life by the Holy Spirit.

Galilee (GAL-uh-lee)

The northern part of Palestine in Jesus' day. Jesus grew up, preached and did most of His miracles in *Galilee*. *Galilee* is also the name of a large lake in this area.

gall (gawl)

A bitter poisonous plant. The juice from the plant may have been used to make a painkiller. Jesus refused a drink of *gall* mixed with wine when He was dying on the cross.

Gaza (GAH-zuh)

A major Philistine city. From the time of the judges until its destruction by Alexander the Great, Gaza was at times under the control of Israel or Egypt.

generation

The length of time from birth till procreation. Grandparents, parents and children are three different *generations*.

Gentiles

All people who are not Jewish.

Gibeon (GIB-ee-un)

The only Canaanite city to make peace with Joshua, although done deceptively. The town, located a few miles northwest of Jerusalem, became an important place of worship, and Solomon had come to offer sacrifices at Gibeon when God spoke to him in a dream.

gifts

Abilities provided by God to believers that allow the accomplishment of good works.

Gilead (GILL-ee-ad)

The region of Israel west of the Jordan river.

Gilboa (gill-BO-uh)

A mountainous area south of Lake Galilee, was the site of

King Saul's final battle against the Philistines. Both Saul and his son Jonathan died in this battle.

Gilgal (GILL-gal)
A town near Jericho, site of the Israelites' first camp after crossing the Jordan river. *Gilgal* was the site of Saul's confirmation as king, and the place where he disobeyed Samuel's instructions, resulting in his being rejected by God as king.

glean
To pick fruits or grain that the harvesters missed. The Bible told farmers to leave some crops in the field for hungry people to *glean*.

genealogy
A listing of ancestors. Various such lists are included in Scripture to show lines of family descent.

glorification, glorify
The act of being made perfect, as God is perfect. Also to honor, praise and magnify God for His perfection.

glory
Great beauty, splendor, honor or magnificence that can be seen or sensed. The Israelites saw the *glory* of the Lord in the cloud that filled the Tabernacle. The shepherds saw the *glory* of the Lord when the angels told them Jesus had been born. *Glory* can also mean to praise; to be proud or happy; to boast.

Golgotha (GAHL-gah-thah)
The place outside Jerusalem where Jesus was hung on a cross. In Aramaic, *Golgotha* means "the place of the skull."

Gomorrah (gah-MORE-uh)
A city near the Dead Sea in the time of Abraham. Gomorrah and its neighbor Sodom were destroyed by fire from heaven because of the great wickedness of the people.

Goshen
The area of the Nile River delta where Jacob and his family settled under the protection of Joseph, Egypt's prime minister.

gospel
Gospel means "good news." The good news of the Bible is that God sent His son Jesus to take the punishment for sin and then raised Him from the dead so that any person who believes may have new life. The story of the life, death and resurrection of Jesus Christ told in the first four books of the New Testament is also called the *gospel*. The books are also called the four *Gospels*.

grace
Love and kindness shown to someone who does not deserve it—especially the forgiveness God shows to us. We don't deserve God's *grace* because we sin against Him. God showed *grace* to all people by sending His Son, Jesus, to be our Savior. God's *grace* allows us to become members of His family (see *Ephesians 2:8*). God's *grace* also keeps on helping us live as God wants us to (see *Acts 20:32*). A person cannot earn God's *grace* by trying to be good; it is God's free gift.

Greece
A leading cultural, political and commercial center of the an-cient world. In the fourth century b.c., under Alexander the Great, Greece conquered much of the Mediterranean and Middle East, resulting in the spread of Greek culture throughout the region, even after Alexander's successors were defeated by the Romans.

Greek
The international language of the Mediterranean world in the time of Jesus. Most of the New Testament was originally written in "common" Greek, not in the classical language of ancient Greece.

Hades (HAY-dees)
A Greek word that means "the place of the dead." Another word used in the Bible that means the same as *Hades* is "Sheol." *Hades* was thought to be a dark, shadowy place. Hell, or Gehenna, was a much more fearful place—it is not the same as *Hades*.

Hallelujah
A Hebrew word that means "praise the Lord!"

harlot
A prostitute; a woman who gets paid for having sexual relations with another person. Sometimes the Bible uses the word *harlot* to describe people who turn away from God to worship idols.

heaven
1. The sky or universe beyond earth. 2. The dwelling of God, the angels and those granted salvation.

Hebrew
A name derived from Eber, a descendant of Noah's son Shem, and used to refer to the nation God chose to be

His special people—the Israelites, later in history known as the Jewish people. *Hebrew* is also the name of any member of that nation, as well as the language they speak. Most of the Old Testament was originally written in the *Hebrew* language.

Hebron (HEE-brun)
An ancient city less than twenty miles southwest of Jerusalem. Abraham lived there for a time, and David made it his capital during the seven and a half years he was king of Judah, before moving the capital to Jerusalem when he had been accepted also as king of Israel.

heir
Someone who has the right to receive the property or position of another person when that person dies. In Bible times, the *heir* was usually a son. The Bible says that anyone who is a member of God's family is His *heir*. God will never die, but because we are His children, God keeps on giving us great love, care and kindness.

Herod (HAIR-ud)
The family name of five kings appointed by the Roman Emperor to rule Palestine in New Testament times. Jesus was born during the rule of *Herod* the Great. The names of the other four kings are *Herod* Archelaus, *Herod* Antipas, *Herod* Agrippa I and *Herod* Agrippa II.

high place
Altars and places of worship built on the tops of hills or mountains. Sometimes altars to God were built at *high places*. However, the *high places* were usually for the worship of idols. The Israelites were told to destroy the *high places* in their land where idols were worshiped.

high priest
The most important priest of all the priests who served God in the Tabernacle and later in the Temple. In the Old Testament, he offered the most important sacrifices to God for the people. In New Testament times, he was also a powerful political leader. He was the head of the Sanhedrin—the group of men who governed the Jewish people. He even had a small army. The *high priest* wore special clothing described in Exodus 28:1-39. Aaron was the first *high priest*. All other *high priests* were his descendants.

Hivites (HIGH-vights)
One of the Canaanite tribes defeated by Joshua.

holy
Pure; set apart; belonging to God. God is *holy*. He is perfect and without sin. Jesus is *holy*, too. He is without sin and dedicated to doing what God wants. Because Jesus died to take the punishment for sin and then rose again, people who believe in Him have the power to be *holy*, too.

holy place, holy of holies
The Tabernacle and the Temple were divided into two main areas. The larger area, known as the *holy place*, could only be entered by the priests who were carrying out their sacred duties. The smaller area, known as the *holy of holies*, was separated by a large curtain (veil), and could only be entered once a year by the High Priest on the Day of Atonement.

Holy Spirit
The personal but unseen power and presence of God in the world. The book of Acts tells us that the *Holy Spirit* came to followers of Jesus in a special way after Jesus had gone back to heaven. The *Holy Spirit* lives within each one whose sins have been forgiven. Jesus said that the *Holy Spirit* is our helper and comforter. The *Holy Spirit* teaches us truth about God. He helps us understand the Bible and helps us pray in the right way. He gives us the power and strength to do what Jesus wants.

Hosanna
A Hebrew word that means "Save now!" The Hebrews shouted the word to praise someone important.

hypocrite
A person who pretends to be something different from what he or she really is. Jesus called the Pharisees *hypocrites* because they did many things to make themselves very religious, but they would not listen to God.

idol
A statue or other image of a god that is made by people and then worshiped as if it had the power of God. Idols are often made of wood, stone or metal.

Immanuel

A name for Jesus that means "God with us."

incense

A mixture of spices held together with thick, sticky juice that comes from trees and plants. *Incense* is burned to make a sweet smell. In the Tabernacle and Temple, *incense* was burned on a small golden altar to worship God.

inheritance

Money, property or traditions received from another person. Often a person receives an *inheritance* after another person's death. The Bible tells us that everything that is God's belongs to Jesus Christ. By His death on the cross, Jesus made it possible for us to share His *inheritance* with Him.

inspiration

The process by which God communicated His word to the human writers of Scripture. *Inspiration* is from the Hebrew and Greek words meaning "breathed", conveying a vivid image of God imparting His truth to His people.

Israel

In the Bible, the word *Israel* has several meanings: 1. It is the special name God gave Jacob (meaning "Prince with God"). 2. It is another name for the Hebrew nation—God's chosen people. 3. It is the name of the nation ruled by the judges and the first three Hebrew kings—Saul, David and Solomon. 4. It is the name given to the Northern Kingdom after Jeroboam led ten tribes to separate from Rehoboam and the two southern tribes. (The Southern Kingdom was called Judah.) 5. After the Northern Kingdom of *Israel* was captured by the Assyrians, the word *Israel* was sometimes used to mean the Southern Kingdom. 6. It is also a name used for the people of God. The Bible often uses the term "children of *Israel*," meaning they were descendants of Jacob.

Israelite

A citizen of the country of Israel; a descendant of Jacob (Israel).

jealous

Jealous has several different meanings: 1. It can mean being careful to guard or keep what one has. This is the kind of *jealousy* the Bible is talking about when it says that God is a *jealous* God. He loves His people and wants them to turn away from sin and to love and worship Him. 2. Another kind of *jealousy* is to be angry and unhappy when someone else has something you want. The Bible calls this kind of *jealousy* a sin. 3. Another kind of *jealousy* is being afraid of losing someone's love or affection.

Jebusites (JEB-yoo-sights)

A Canaanite tribe that controlled the hilly terrain of Jerusalem until defeated by David.

Jehovah

This is an English translation of one of the Hebrew names for God. A more accurate translation is Yahweh. This name was considered to be very holy, and religious Jews would not take this name on their lips.

Jericho (JERR-ih-koh)

A city several miles north of where the Jordan River enters the Dead Sea. *Jericho* was the first city conquered by the Israelites under Joshua's leadership.

Jerusalem

The most important city of Bible times. It was the capital of the united kingdom of Israel and the kingdom of Judah. The Temple was built in *Jerusalem*, so many people traveled to the city to worship God. In 587 B.C., *Jerusalem* was captured and mostly destroyed by Babylonian armies. The city was rebuilt when the Jews returned after seventy years of exile in Babylon. Jesus taught in the city of *Jerusalem*, was crucified outside the city wall, was buried near the city and then rose again. The first Christian church began in *Jerusalem* after the Holy Spirit came to the believers there.

Jews

At first, *Jew* referred to anyone who was a member of the tribe of Judah. By the return from exile in Babylon, it meant anyone who was a descendant of Abraham or who was a follower of the Jewish religion.

Jordan river

The main part of the *Jordan river* from the Sea of Galilee, winding southward into the Dead Sea. Numerous biblical events involved this famous waterway, including Jesus' baptism.

Josephus (joh-SEE-fuss)

A Jewish historian. Written near the end of the first century A.D., his *Antiquities* contains the first non-Christian reference to Jesus.

Judah

1. One of the sons of Jacob and Leah. 2. The descendants of *Judah*, who became the tribe of *Judah*. 3. The Southern Kingdom when the Israelites divided into two separate countries after the death of King Solomon. (The Northern Kingdom was called Israel.)

Judaism (JOO-day-izm)

The faith, laws, traditions and teachings of the Jewish religion. Judaism is based on worshiping the one true God, circumcision as a sign of being one of God's chosen people, worship on the Sabbath (Saturday), obeying God's laws and following the traditions given from one generation to another.

Judaizers (JOO-day-ize-urs)

People who claimed that a person must keep the Jewish laws in order to become a true believer in Jesus.

judge

In the time of Moses, a *judge* helped people settle their disagreements. When the Israelites were settling the Promised Land after the death of Joshua, God chose leaders called *judges* to rule the people. Often these *judges* led the people in battle against their enemies. Some of the *judges* were Deborah, Gideon and Samuel. After kings began to rule Israel, *judges* once again settled disagreement and took

care of official business.

judgment

1. In the Old Testament, *judgment* can mean God's laws of instructions. 2. *Judgment* can also mean God's punishment of a person or nation for disobeying Him. 3. In the New Testament, *judgment* can mean to criticize or disapprove of someone. The Bible says Christians are not to *judge* each other. 4. *Judgment* can also mean the end of the world as we know it when God will *judge* sin, and reward those people who have lived for Him.

justice

That which is right and fair. Most of the prophets in the Bible emphasized that God is *just*, and that He wants His people to act *justly*. Many of the warnings given by the prophets were done so because the leaders and people were guilty of *injustice*, cheating others, especially the poor.

justification, justify

God's action of declaring that sinners are made righteous by faith in Jesus Christ. God forgives their sin and becomes their friend. God also gives them the power to live right. *Justification* is possible because Jesus Christ died to take the punishment for sin.

Kadesh (KAY-desh)

A location between the Sinai desert and the southern boundary of Canaan. From here, Moses sent twelve spies into Canaan, but the people rebelled, resulting in the Israelites spending an entire generation in the desert.

kingdom of heaven

The *kingdom of heaven* is also called the "*kingdom* of God." It means God's rule in the lives of His chosen people and His creation. In the Old Testament, the people in God's *kingdom* were the Israelites. In the New Testament and now, the people in God's *kingdom* are those who believe in and follow the Lord Jesus Christ. When Jesus comes again, then God's *kingdom* will become visible to all people.

kinsman

A relative.

Lamb of God

A name for Jesus that tells us that He died to take away our sins. When a Jewish person had sinned, he or she offered a lamb as a sacrifice to God. Jesus became like one of those lambs when He gave Himself as a sacrifice to die so that our sins can be forgiven.

law

The word has several meanings in the Bible: 1. It can mean all the rules God gave to help people to know and love Him and to live happily with each other. The Ten Commandments are part of God's *law*. 2. The first five books of the Bible are called the *Law*. 3. The entire Old Testament is sometimes called the *Law*. 4. Any rule that must be obeyed, whether it was decided by God or by people, is a *law*. 5. God's rules in the Old Testament plus other rules added by Jewish religious leaders are sometimes called the *Law*. 6. In Romans 2:14-16, the conscience of an unbeliever who knows he or she has not followed his or her own moral code.

leprosy (LEP-ruh-see)
A name used for several serious skin diseases. People with *leprosy* were called *lepers*. The Jewish law said that *lepers* had to stay away from people who did not have the disease. *Lepers* lived outside their cities and towns, either by themselves or with other *lepers,* until the disease showed signs of healing.

Levites (LEE-vites)
Descendants of Levi, one of the sons of Jacob and Leah. Some of the *Levites* were religious teachers. Others took care of the Tabernacle, and later, the Temple. Only *Levites* who were descendants of Moses' brother Aaron could become priests.

Lord's Supper
The Passover meal Jesus celebrated with his disciples the night of his arrest. Also the continuing observance in which Christ's followers gather to eat and drink in order to "proclaim the Lord's death until he comes" (*1 Corinthians* 11:26).

locust
A large insect like a grasshopper. Sometimes *locusts* travel in huge swarms, eating all the plants they can find.

lute
A stringed musical instrument. It has a pear-shaped body and a neck. It is played by plucking the strings.

lyre (lier)
A small harp with three to twelve strings. A *lyre* was held on the lap when it was played.

Magi (MAY-ji)
Men who lived in the countries of Arabia and Persia and who studied the stars. People thought the *Magi* had the power to tell the meaning of dreams. Several of the *Magi* followed a star to Bethlehem and brought Jesus expensive gifts. The *Magi* honored Him as a newborn king.

manger
A box in a stable where food was placed for cattle, donkeys or other animals. When Jesus was born, His first bed was a *manger.*

manna
The special food God gave the Israelites for the forty years they traveled in the desert. The Bible says that *manna* looked like white seeds or flakes and tasted sweet.

mantle
A loose fitting outer robe or coat.

master
1. A name for Jesus. It means "teacher." 2. An overseer, boss or owner of a slave.

mediator
A person who settles differences or arguments between two or more people. Jonathan was a *mediator* between David and Saul. Moses was a *mediator* between God and Israel. By paying the punishment for sin, Jesus became the *mediator* who makes it possible for us to have peace with God.

mercy
Showing more love or kindness to a person than he or she expects or deserves.

Mesopotamia (MESS-oh-poh-TAME-ee-uh)
The region between the Tigris and Euphrates rivers. The term derives from two Greek words meaning "middle" and "river." The Assyrian nation developed in northern Mesopotamia, Babylon in the central region, and Sumer (including Ur) was in the south.

Messiah
The Savior whom God promised to send. Jesus is the *Messiah.* In Hebrew, *Messiah* means "the Anointed One." In Greek, the word for "the Anointed One" is "Christos." Christ is the name used in the New Testament to show Jesus is the Savior.

millennium
Thousand years. The term is used in reference to Revelation 20:1-15, which mentions a thousand-year period in which Satan is bound and Christ rules.

millstone
One of a pair of large stones used to grind grain into flour.

miracle
Some event or wonderful happening done by the power of God.

Moabite (MOE-uh-bite)
A person from the country of Moab, located just east of the Dead Sea. Moab often fought against Israel and at times was under the control of Israel's kings. Ruth, an ancestor of David and of Jesus, was a Moabite.

Moriah (MO-rye-uh)
The hill in Jerusalem on which Solomon built the Temple.

Jewish tradition claims this is the same Mount Moriah on which Abraham began to sacrifice Isaac.

Mount of Olives, Mount Olivet
A hill just outside Jerusalem, the site of many biblical events.

myrrh
The sap of the *myrrh* bush. *Myrrh* was used to make anointing oil smell good, as a perfume, as a pain killer and to prepare a body for burial. The Magi brought Jesus a gift of *myrrh*.

mystery
A truth that is understood because of God's revelation. The term appears only in the New Testament, mostly in the letters of Paul, and refers to God's plan to redeem the world through Christ.

nard
A pleasant-smelling oil made from the roots and stems of spikenard plant. This plant grew in India. Because the oil had to be brought from India to Palestine, it was very expensive. Mary poured *nard* over Jesus' feet.

Nazarene (NAZ-uh-reen)
A person who lived in the town of Nazareth. Because Jesus lived in Nazareth for almost 30 years, He was often called a *Nazarene*. Later, Christians were sometimes called *Nazarenes* because they were followers of Jesus.

Nazirite (NAZ-uh-rite)
A Hebrew person who promised to serve God in a special way for a certain length of time. The time could be anywhere from 30 days to a lifetime. To show dedication to God, a *Nazirite* would not cut his or her hair, eat or drink anything made from grapes, or touch a dead body. At the end of the time, the person lived like other people. Samuel and Samson were *Nazirites* all their lives. Some scholars believe John the Baptist was also a *Nazirite*.

Nebo
A mountain, adjacent to Mount Pisgah, overlooking the Dead Sea. Moses viewed the Promised Land from these peaks.

New Covenant See Covenant.
New Testament See Testament.
Northern Kingdom
Refers to Israel, formed when Jereboam led the northern tribes in rebellion against Rehoboam. From the beginning, Israel's kings led the people in idolatrous practices, resulting in God's judgment in the form of Assyrian conquest. A series of massive relocations dispersed the Israelites throughout the Assyrian Empire, and replaced them with people who became known as Samaritans.

oath
A serious promise that what a person says is true. In Bible times, people often made an *oath* by saying, "God is my witness."

offering
A gift of money, time or other possessions a person gives to God because he or she loves Him. In Old Testament times, people brought food and animals to the Tabernacle or Temple as *offerings* to God.

The *offerings* were often burned on the altar. Animal *offerings* were always killed. Their blood symbolized sins being forgiven by death. Christians believe that we no longer need to offer sacrifices for the forgiveness of sins because Jesus' death is the once-for-all sacrifice through which our sins can be forgiven. (See Sacrifice)

offspring
For humans, *offspring* are sons and daughters. For animals, *offspring* are their young.

oil
In the Bible, *oil* almost always means olive *oil*. Olive *oil* was used to anoint priests and kings.

ordain
The word *ordain* has several meanings in the Bible: 1. It can mean to cause to happen. Psalm 65:9 says that the streams are filled with water to provide people with food because God has *ordained*— or caused—it. 2. To appoint or set apart a person to do special work. Paul was *ordained* to be a missionary to the Gentiles. 3. *Ordain* can also mean to decide or command.

overseer
A person who watches over and takes care of others. In the New Testament, leaders in the Early Church were sometimes called *overseers*.

pagan
A person who does not worship the true God, especially a person who worships idols.

Palestine
The name refers to the Philistines, a nation who oc-

cupied territory along the southeastern coast of the Mediterranean Sea. The term was originally used just for that coastal area, but gradually came to refer to all of the land between Egypt and Syria.

parable
A story that teaches a special lesson or truth.

paradise
Heaven.

paralytic (PAIR-uh-lih-tic)
A person who has lost the ability to move one or more arms and/or legs.

Passover
One of the Jews' most important feasts. The Jews celebrate *Passover* every spring as a reminder that God freed them from slavery in Egypt.

The word *Passover* comes from the way the angel of death "passed over" the homes of Israelites on whose doorposts the blood of a lamb was sprinkled. In Egyptian homes, where there was no blood on the door posts, all the firstborn sons died. This terrible disaster convinced the Egyptian Pharaoh to let the Israelites leave Egypt. The *Passover* feast was the last meal Jesus ate with His disciples before He was crucified.

Passover Lamb
The lamb killed at Passover as a sacrifice. The Bible says that Jesus is our *Passover Lamb*. He was sacrificed to deliver us from sin, just as the first *Passover Lamb* was sacrificed to deliver the firstborn sons of the Israelites from death and to provide them with es-

cape from Egypt. (*See* Passover)

patriarch
A father, either of a family or a nation. The word usually refers to either Abraham, Isaac or Jacob—the founders of the Hebrew nation. Jacob's sons and David are also called *patriarchs.*

patriarchal period
The term refers to the time before Moses when the oldest male in a family or clan was the undisputed head in both temporal and spiritual matters.

penitence
Repentance, expression of remorse for sins.

Pentateuch (PEN-ta-tuke)
The first five books of the Old Testament. The term is from the Greek word meaning "five scrolls." These five books are also referred to as the Books of the Law, the Books of Moses and the Torah (Hebrew).

Pentecost
A Jewish feast celebrated 50 days after Passover. Today the Christian Church remembers *Pentecost* because on the first *Pentecost* after Jesus' resurrection, the Lord sent the Holy Spirit to His followers as He had promised (see *Acts 2*).

Perizzites (PEAR-ih-zite)
One of the Canaanite tribes defeated by Joshua.

Persia
The territory between the Persian Gulf and the Caspian Sea, and the last of the Middle Eastern powers before the conquest by Alexander the Great.

Pisgah (PIZZ-guh)
A mountain, adjacent to Mount Nebo, at the northeastern end of the Dead Sea, which Moses climbed to view the Promised Land.

Pharaoh
A title of the rulers of ancient Egypt, just as "president" or "king" or "prime minister" are titles of top officials in countries today.

Pharisee
A Jew in the time of Jesus who tried very hard to obey every part of the Jewish law. Many sincerely tried to please God and to be holy. Some of the *Pharisees* worried more about keeping every little rule than about caring for people. Jesus commended the *Pharisees* for what they taught, but often scolded them because of what they did.

Philippi
A city in Macedonia (northern Greece). The first European city visited by Paul on his missionary journeys.

Philistines
The people of Philistia, a region along the southeastern coast of the Mediterranean Sea. During most of Old Testament history, the Philistines were major competitors with Israel for territory and power. The Philistines, whose origins may be traced to Crete or Greece, were far ahead of the Hebrews in technology, having mastered skills in working with metal. They adopted at least some of the Canaanite gods and often controlled much of Palestine

until a series of decisive defeats at the hands of David. Still, battles with Judah and Israel continued for centuries.

plague

1. A very serious disease that spreads quickly among people in an area. It often causes death. 2. Anything that causes great harm or suffering. For example, sometimes crops were destroyed by a *plague* of locusts. 3. The ten great disasters God sent to the Egyptians to convince their king to free the Israelites. Read about these *plagues* in Exodus 4—12.

pomegranate (PAHM-uh-GRAN-ut)

A fruit about the size of an apple.

precepts

Commands, rules or laws.

predestined

Decided or chosen beforehand. In the Bible, the term refers to God's choice.

priest

Among the Jews, a *priest* was a man who offered prayers and sacrifices to God for the people. They led the public worship services at the Tabernacle, and later at the Temple. Often the *priests* also taught the Law of God to the people. The *priests* of Israel were all descendants of Aaron's family. The New Testament says that Jesus Christ is now our High *Priest*, the One who offered Himself as the perfect sacrifice for our sins (see *Hebrews 8—9*). All Christians are also *priests* (see *1 Peter 2:9*). We are to help others learn about and worship God.

proconsul (PRO-kon-sul)

A ruler in the Roman government. The Roman Empire was divided into provinces or states. The highest Roman official in each province was called the *proconsul*.

prophecy

The message from God that a prophet spoke or wrote to people. Some *prophecies* told about what God would do in the future.

prophets

Men and women in the Old and New Testaments chosen by God to tell His messages to people. Also refers to the 17 Old Testament books written by *prophets*.

proverb

A short, wise saying. The Bible book of *Proverbs* is made up of many wise sayings.

psalm

A Hebrew song or poem. A *psalm* usually praises God or tells the deep feelings of God's people. The Bible book of *Psalms* is made up of many Hebrew poems and songs.

publican

A tax collector. In the New Testament, the tax collectors secured revenue for the Romans, earning bitter condemnation as traitors.

purge

To make clean and pure.

Purim (POOR-im)

A Jewish holiday to celebrate the victory of Queen Esther and the Jews over wicked Haman.

rams

Mature male sheep. *Rams* were used for sacrifices and food. Their horns were sometimes used to make trumpets.

ransom

The price paid to buy the freedom of a captive or slave. The New Testament says that all people are held captives to sin and death. When Jesus died on the cross, He paid the price—the *ransom*—to rescue us from the powers of sin and death. (See redeem)

reap

To gather ripe grain and fruit. The Bible also uses the word *reap* to describe the reward or punishment people receive for their actions (see *Galatians 6:9*).

reconcile

To help people who have been enemies become friends. In the New Testament, the word usually refers to bringing God and people together again through Jesus' life, death and resurrection. Sin separates people from God, but by dying, Jesus took the punishment for sin. When a person comes to know and love Jesus, he or she learns to love God instead of being His enemy. When this happens, the person is *reconciled* to God.

Red Sea

The Hebrew name for the body of water crossed by Moses and the Israelites when escaping from Egypt means literally "Sea of Reeds."

redeem, redemption

To buy freedom. In Bible times, a person could buy a slave and then set the slave free. The slave had been *redeemed* by the person who had paid the price and then given freedom. The New Testament tells us that by dying, Jesus paid the price to "buy us back" and set us free from our slavery to sin. (See ransom)

redeemer

A person who redeems someone else. The term is used in the Old Testament to refer to God and to the Messiah who was promised to come.

remnant

A small part that is left over. In the Old Testament, *remnant* usually refers to the few Israelite people who remained faithful worshipers of God after their exile in Babylon.

repent

Repent means to turn around and go in the opposite direction. In the Bible, to *repent* means sorrow for wrongdoing, but must include that you stop doing wrong action and start doing what God says is right. *Repentance* always involves making a change away from sin and toward God.

restore, restoration

1. To bring back; to establish again. 2. To bring back to a former or original condition. 3. To return something lost, stolen or taken. The return of the Jews from being captives in Babylon is referred to as their *restoration*.

resurrection

1. To come back to life after being dead. Jesus died, and was buried. After three days He rose from the dead. That event is called the *Resurrection*. It shows Jesus' power over sin and death. 2. A future time when everyone who has ever lived will live

again in new, spiritual bodies that will never die. Those who do not love God will be separated from Him forever.

retribution (re-truh-BYOU-shun)

A payment that is deserved, revenge. The punishment that comes to a person because he or she has broken God's law is called *retribution*.

revelation

To make known something that was hidden or unknown. In Old Testament times, God *revealed* Himself through His mighty acts and through His words to the prophets and to other people such as Abraham, Moses and David. In the New Testament, God made Himself known by sending Jesus Christ. As Jesus lived on earth, He *revealed* God's love, His holiness and His power, helping us know what God is like. One of the ways God *reveals* Himself to us is through His Word, the Bible. The last book of the Bible is called the *Revelation* of Jesus Christ because it shows how Jesus will triumph over evil.

righteous

Thinking and doing what is *right* and holy. The word is used in three ways in the Bible: 1. To tell what God is like: He does only what is *right* and holy. 2. A person who has accepted Jesus as Savior is looked at by God as being free from the guilt of sin. God sees the person as being *righteous*. 3. People who are members of God's family show their love for Him by living in *righteous*

ways. They do what is *right* and holy.

Roman

1. A person who lived in the city of *Rome*. 2. A person who was a citizen of the *Roman* Empire. A *Roman* citizen enjoyed special rights and protection. For example, he or she could not be punished without a fair trial, nor could a citizen be crucified.

Rome

A city in Italy, capital of the Roman Republic and Empire. The Romans defeated the remnants of Alexander the Great's Empire and established control over most of the Mediterranean world, including Palestine, in the first century B.C. The spread of Christianity in the first centuries A.D. in spite of widespread, official persecution, was certainly aided by the ability to travel freely through the Empire.

Sabbath

The weekly day of rest and worship God set apart for all people. In the Old Testament, it is the seventh day of the week (Saturday). For the Jew, *Sabbath* starts at sundown on Friday and lasts until sunset on Saturday. Many Jews and some Christians observe the *Sabbath* on Saturday.

Because Jesus rose from the dead on a Sunday, most Christians set aside Sunday as the day of rest and worship (see *Acts 20:7*).

sackcloth

A rough, dark cloth usually woven from goats' hair. When someone died, the person's friends and family wore clothes made of *sackcloth* to show that they were very sad. A person would also wear *sackcloth* to show that he or she was sorry for sinning.

sacred
Holy; belonging to God; set apart for God.

sacrifice
A gift or offering given to God. A *sacrifice* usually involved killing an animal to pay for sin. The New Testament tells us that Jesus died as the once-for-all *sacrifice* for sinners and that no further *sacrifices* for sin are necessary.

Sadducees (SAD-you-seez)
A sect of Jewish religious leaders in New Testament times, to be distinguished from the Pharisees (see Pharisees). They said that only the laws in the first five books of the Old Testament had to be obeyed. They did not believe in the Resurrection or in angels or spirits. When the New Testament speaks of the "chief priests," it is referring to the *Sadducees*.

saints
The word means "God's people." The New Testament says that all Christians are *saints*. Paul often addressed his letters "to the *saints*."

salvation
Sometimes *salvation* (or deliverance) means to be rescued from evil. Sometimes it means to be kept from danger or death. In the New Testament, *salvation* usually means to be rescued from the guilt and power of sin. By His death and resurrection, Jesus brings *salvation* to people

who believe in Him.

Samaritan (suh-MARE-uh-tun)
A person who lived in or came from the area in Palestine known as Samaria. The *Samaritans* were only partly Jewish. They worshiped God differently than the other Jews did. The Jews and *Samaritans* hated each other.

sanctification, sanctify
To be set apart for God's use. A Christian's *sanctification* is an ongoing process. When a person becomes a Christian, he or she is *sanctified*. The Holy Spirit continues helping him or her become more and more like Jesus, which is the process of *sanctification*.

sanctuary
A holy place; a place where God is worshiped. In the Bible, *sanctuary* usually refers to the Tabernacle or to the Temple.

Sanhedrin (san-HEE-drun)
The highest Jewish political and religious court. In New Testament times, the *Sanhedrin* was made up of 71 men who were experts in Jewish laws. The *Sanhedrin* included the high priest, members of wealthy or prominent Jewish families and members of the Pharisee and Sadducee religious groups.

Satan
The most powerful enemy of God and all people. Other names for *Satan* include the devil, the evil one, the prince of this world, the father of lies, the enemy, the adversary, Lucifer. *Satan* is the ruler of a kingdom made up of demons. He hates God and

tries to destroy God's work. The Bible tells us that in the end, God will destroy *Satan* and the demons.

Savior
A word that means "he who saves." The Old Testament almost always speaks of God as the *Savior* of His people. Sometimes God sent someone to help His people, and that person was called a *savior*. In the New Testament, *Savior* refers to Jesus. He died and rose again to rescue or save us from our sin.

scepter (SEP-tur)
A short rod held by a king or queen to show that he or she was the person who had the most authority and power.

scribe
1. An expert in understanding the Jewish law. Scribes taught the people God's laws. They also copied the Old Testament writings onto scrolls. Ezra was a *scribe*. By New Testament times, the *scribes* often served as judges in Jewish courts because they knew so much about the law. 2. A writer or secretary who earned his living writing letters or important papers for other people.

Scripture
The Bible. Before the New Testament was written down, *Scripture* meant the Old Testament. After the New Testament was written down, Christians began calling both the Old and New Testaments *Scripture*. The word *Scripture* means "writing."

scroll
A long strip of papyrus or parchment that has writing

on it. A stick was attached to
each end of the strip so that
it could be rolled up to make
it easier to read, store and
carry.

seal

A small tool or ring that had a
design cut into one side. The
owner of each seal had his or
her own special design.
When the owner wanted to
put his or her own special
mark or brand on something,
the person would press the
seal into hot wax or soft clay.
As the wax or clay hardened,
it kept the design in it. Also
called a signet.

Second Coming

The promised return of Jesus
Christ to rule the earth at the
end of this present age.

seer (SEE-uhr)

A prophet; a person who, with
God's help, could see what
would happen in the future.
(See prophet)

Semite

Descendants of Shem, one of
Noah's three sons. The term
also refers to people who
know languages belonging to
the "Semitic Family" of lan-
guages. In ancient times the
Semites included the
Canaanites, Hebrews, Arabs,
Assyrians, Babylonians,
Arameans (Syrians) and
Ethiopians.

sensual (SEN-shoo-uhl)

1. Appealing to the body's
senses. 2. Caring too much
for physical pleasures.

seraph, seraphim

Heavenly beings, mentioned
only in Isaiah's vision of God
(*Isaiah 6*). *Seraphim* are evidently similar to, or possibly
the same as, the cherubim

mentioned elsewhere in the
Bible.

sexual immorality

To use *sex* in ways that God
says are wrong; *sexual* union
between two people who are
not married to each other is a
sin.

sheaf, sheaves

A bundle or bundles of cut
grain stalks.

Shechem (SHEEK-um)

An area and a city, west of the
Jordan river, near Samaria. It
is mentioned frequently in
the Old Testament, and
Jereboam made it the first
capital of Israel when the
Northern Kingdom split from
Judah in the south.

sheep pen, sheepfold

A protected place for sheep to
stay.

shekel (SHEK-uhl)

A small weight of silver or gold
that was used as money.

Shiloh

A town in the hill country west
of the Jordan river, between
Bethel and Shechem. For
about 400 years, from the
time of Joshua until the
building of Solomon's
Temple, Shiloh was home to
the Tabernacle. However,
when the Ark of the
Covenant was captured by the
Philistines in the days of
Samuel, Shiloh gradually
faded in importance.

sickle

A tool having a sharp curved
blade that is attached to a
short handle. A *sickle* is used
to cut stalks of grain.

signet *See* seal.

sin

Any act or thought that is
against the way God wants us

to act or think. The Bible says
that all people have *sinned*.
Sin separates us from God.
God sent Jesus to die to take
the punishment for *sin*.
Because Jesus died, our *sins*
can be forgiven and the separation between God and us
can be removed.

Sinai (SIE-nie)

A desert peninsula between
Palestine and Egypt at the
northern tip of the Red Sea;
also a mountain on the
peninsula where Moses re-
ceived the Ten Command-
ments. Thus, *Sinai* is also
used in reference to the Old
Testament's covenant of law.

slander

To say untrue things about a
person in order to hurt his or
her reputation. The Bible says
that *slander* is sin.

slave

A servant who is owned by his
or her master and could be
bought or sold like property.
People became *slaves* if they
were defeated in battle by an
enemy or if they were unable
to pay their debts.

Sodom (SOD-um)

A city near the Dead Sea in the
time of Abraham. Fire from
heaven destroyed *Sodom*
along with its neighbor,
Gomorrah, because of its
great wickedness.

Son of Man

A name for Jesus. Jesus called
Himself the *Son of Man* many
times. The name means that
Jesus is a real man and that
He is the One God promised
to send in Daniel 7:13. *Son of
Man* is also the title by which
God called the prophet
Ezekiel.

soothsayer (SOOTH-say-er)

A person who said he or she could tell what would happen in the future—a fortune-teller. Both the Old and New Testaments say that *soothsaying* is wrong.

sorcerer (SORE-sir-er)

A person who claimed to be able to make spirits work for him or her. The Bible says that *sorcery* is a sin.

soul

In the Bible, the word *soul* usually refers to the part of a person that cannot be seen, but controls what a person thinks, feels and does. Sometimes *soul* means the whole living person. The words *soul* and "spirit" can mean about the same thing, but sometimes are distinguished from one another.

Southern Kingdom

Refers to the kingdom of Judah after Jereboam led the northern tribes to rebel against Rehoboam and form the Northern Kingdom of Israel. For more than two centuries, until the destruction of Israel by the Assyrians, the two kingdoms were contentious neighbors. The longer existence of Judah is attributed to the occasional godly kings who led the people in spiritual reforms.

spirit

The unseen part of a person that controls what he or she thinks, feels and does; soul. The Bible says that God is a spirit, showing that He does not have a physical body. (See soul)

staff

1. A strong stick used for support when walking or climbing. 2. A strong wooden rod that has a hook on the end used by a shepherd as he cared for sheep.

statute

A law or command. In the Bible, *statutes* usually refers to God's laws.

stiff-necked

Stubborn, rebellious and unwilling to learn.

stone

To throw large stones and rocks at a person until he or she is dead. *Stoning* was the way people were punished for disobeying certain parts of the Jewish law. Stephen was *stoned* for teaching that Jesus is God's Son (see *Acts 7*).

Sumer (SOO-mur), **Sumerians**

The region and people of southern Mesopotamia, one of the oldest cultural centers in the ancient Middle East. Ur, one of the major cities of Sumer, was the original home of Abraham.

synagogue

A place where Jews meet together to read and study the Old Testament and to worship God.

Syria

The region directly north of Palestine, called Aram in the Hebrew Bible and some modern English translations. The name *Syria* was not widely used until after Alexander the Great.

Tabernacle

The portable tent where the Israelites worshiped God. They used it while they wandered in the desert after they left Egypt and for many years after they entered the Promised Land. Moses and the people built the *Tabernacle* by following God's instructions. The *Tabernacle* was used until it was replaced by a permanent place of worship called the Temple. The *Tabernacle* is described in detail in Exodus 26.

table

The Tabernacle and Temple were furnished with a golden *table* on which twelve loaves of bread, one for each tribe of Israel, were placed each week, symbolizing the presence of God among His people.

talent

A large amount of silver or gold worth a huge amount of money. One *talent* was considered to be the amount of money a working man would earn in about ten years.

Temple

The permanent place in Jerusalem where the Jews worshiped God. The first *Temple* was built by King Solomon and the people by following the instructions God had given Solomon's father, King David. The *Temple* was a very beautiful place. It was destroyed and rebuilt twice. In A.D. 70, the *Temple* was destroyed again. It has not been rebuilt.

tempt

In the Bible, the word *tempt* has two meanings: 1. To test a person to improve his or her spiritual strength. 2. To try to get someone to do something wrong.

testament

An agreement, covenant. The 39 books of the Hebrew Bible are called the Old *Testament*, referring to God's original covenant of law. The 27 books of the New *Testament* present the covenant of grace that came through Jesus Christ.

testimony

In the Bible, *testimony* has more than one meaning: 1. In the Old Testament, it often refers to the Law of God. 2. In the New Testament, *testimony* usually means giving proof that something is true.

tetrarch (TET-rarck)

When a country in the Roman Empire was divided into sections, the head of each part was called a *tetrarch*. In the New Testament, Herod Antipas is sometimes called a *tetrarch* and sometimes a king. He was the ruler of Galilee in the time of Jesus.

threshing floor

The place where grain was trampled by oxen or beaten with a stick to separate the heads of grain from the stalk. A *threshing floor* was usually a large, flat rack or a large area of clay that was packed hard. *Threshing floors* were usually built where wind would blow away the chaff and leave the heavier grain. (See winnow)

Tishbite

A person, such as Elijah, from Tishbe, a town somewhere in Gilead, the West Bank region, between the Jordan river and the desert.

tithe

To give God one-tenth of what you earn. For example, if you had ten dimes, you would *tithe* by giving one dime to God.

tomb

A place where dead people were buried. In Bible times, *tombs* were often natural caves or caves dug into stone cliffs.

tongues

Languages. The New Testament records miraculous speaking in *tongues*, indicating the Holy Spirit enabling believers to speak in languages they had never learned.

trance

In the Bible, a *trance* is the deep, dreamlike state in which a person received a message from God. Peter was in a *trance* when God showed him the vision of the animals in a sheet (see *Acts 10:10*).

transfigured

To have been changed in appearance or form. The Bible tells us that Jesus' physical appearance was changed— *transfigured*—as three of His disciples watched. His face glowed and his clothes became shining white. Moses and Elijah appeared and Jesus talked with them about His coming death.

transgression

A sin; disobeying the law of God.

trespass

To go against the rights of someone else. We *trespass* against people when we do something unfair to them or when we break laws made to protect people. We *trespass* against God when we break His laws. In the Bible, another word for *trespass* is "sin."

tribe

The twelve *tribes* (clans, families) of Israel. Each of the *tribes* was descended from one of the twelve sons of Jacob. The descendants of Levi were assigned the honor of caring for the Tabernacle and were not given a territory as were the other eleven *tribes*. (They were given 48 townsites in which to live.) The descendants of Joseph were divided into two "half *tribes*," Manasseh and Ephraim, Joseph's two sons.

tribulation

Trouble, affliction, sometimes as punishment for wrongdoing. The *Great Tribulation* refers to a period of extraordinary, worldwide suffering when the Antichrist is allowed temporary control of human affairs.

tribute

In the Bible, *tribute* usually means money or services a weaker nation was made to pay to a stronger nation.

trumpet

A straight tube that was bell shaped at one end. *Trumpets* were played at every Temple service. (Also see trumpet of rams' horns)

trumpet of rams' horn

A curved ram's horn, blown as a signal. *Trumpets of rams' horns* were used in religious ceremonies and in battle.

tunic

A loose shirt reaching to the knees. A *tunic* was usually worn as an undergarment.

unclean

Unclean does not mean dirty. It means any action, thought, food, person or place God had said is displeasing to Him. One of the ways a Jewish person could become *unclean* was by eating food God had said not to eat. Other ways a person could become *unclean* were by touching a dead body or by getting a skin disease called leprosy. A person could become clean again by going through certain ceremonies.

unleavened bread
Bread made without yeast. *Unleavened bread* is usually flat, like a pancake or cracker.

Ur of the Chaldees
A major cultural and commercial city in ancient Mesopotamia. *Ur* was the original home of Abraham.

vengeance
Punishment for wrongdoing. In the Old Testament, a person was told exactly how much he or she could do to punish someone for a wrong he or she had done. But the New Testament tells people not to punish those who have wronged them. Instead, they are told to trust God to take care of the punishment because He is the only one who is completely fair and just.

violate
1. To break the law. 2. To force someone to have sex; to rape. 3. To make something unholy.

viper
A poisonous snake.

virgin
A person who has never had sexual intercourse.

vision
A *vision* was a way God showed someone a truth that would otherwise not be known. God used *visions* to show a message of truth in pictures. Sometimes people were asleep when God gave them *visions* (see *Ezekiel 8:1-4* and *Acts 10:9-29*).

vow
A promise made to God.

wail
A long, loud cry to show sorrow.

wilderness
A large area of land where few people lived. Depending on the amount of rainfall, the land might be a barren desert or it might grow grass and other vegetation on which sheep and other herds of animals could graze.

will
Purpose, intention, plan.

wineskin
A bag made from an animal skin. Wine, milk, water and grape juice were stored in *wineskins.*

winnow
To separate the kernels of grain from the worthless husks removed from the grain. This was done by tossing the grain into the air during a strong breeze. The breeze would blow away the light husks and the heavier kernels of grain would fall to the ground.

wisdom
Knowledge, understanding, applying knowledge and insights to life situations. *Wisdom* in the Bible usually refers to a God-given ability, rather than human common sense.

witness
1. In the Bible, a *witness* was a person who told what he or she had seen. 2. To tell others what you have seen. Jesus told His followers to be *witnesses.* We are to tell what we have seen Jesus Christ do in our own lives.

woe
Misery, sorrow or great suffering.

wonder
A miracle. A thing or event that causes surprise and awe. God did many *wonders* to convince Pharaoh to let the Israelites leave Egypt.

works
Actions, deeds. Although the Bible encourages us to do good *works,* it clearly teaches that no *works* can earn enough merit to secure salvation.

world
1. The planet Earth. 2. People who follow Satan. 3. Anything that belongs to life on earth instead of eternal life with God.

worldly
Attached and attracted to values and commitments that go against God rather than being attracted to the values and commitments of the eternal kingdom of God.

worship
Anything a person does to show love and respect. Some people *worship* idols. Some people *worship* the one true God.

wrath
Very great anger.

Yahweh
An English equivalent of the Hebrew word for God; also translated "Jehovah."

yoke
1. A wooden bar that goes over the necks of two animals,

usually oxen. The *yoke* holds the animals together when they are pulling something such as a cart or plow. 2. Two oxen *yoked* together. 3. The word *yoke* is sometimes used as a word picture for any burden or demand. Slavery, imprisonment, taxes or unfair laws were called *yokes*. 4. A partnership.

Zealot (Zel-ut)
A member of a Jewish group in the time of Jesus who wanted to fight against and overthrow the Roman rulers in Palestine. Jesus' disciple Simon (not Peter) was a Zealot.

Zion (Zie-un)
Zion has several meanings: 1. One of the hills upon which the city of Jerusalem was built was called Mount *Zion*. 2. The entire city of Jerusalem was sometimes called *Zion*. 3. *Zion* is another name for the nation of Israel. 4. *Zion* is another name for heaven.

BECOMING A MEMBER OF GOD'S FAMILY

This appendix has a threefold purpose. First, it can be used by a teen to read about becoming a member of God's family. Second, it can be used by parents, in the home, to help their children become members of God's family. Third, it can be used by a teacher to help a student become a member of God's family. Any person who wishes to lead another person to Christ should become familiar with the explanation given in this appendix.

In the Old Testament, God promised to send a Messiah or Savior to His people. The Messiah would save God's people from their sin, from the wrong things everyone has done. The people in the Old Testament times knew about the promise of a Savior and looked for Him.

In the New Testament, God's promise came true! The Savior was born in Bethlehem, just where God promised! (see *Micah 5:2*). Jesus Christ was born, grew up and died for our sins.

God's Word always comes true. You can trust God's faithfulness, for He made it possible for you to become a member of His family. Here's how:

Step One: God Loves You

The Bible says in 1 John 4:8 that "God is love." He loves you very much. He loves you because He made you and

He is concerned about you and your life today.

Step Two: You Have Sinned

The Bible also says that you and all other people have sinned. In Romans 3:23 we read, "For all have sinned and fall short of the glory of God."

We have all done wrong and our sins keep us from being friends with God. As you read in the books of the Old Testament, sin always leads to trouble. Because you are a sinner, your sin will cause much trouble in your life. Romans 6:23 tells us how bad this trouble will ultimately be. "For the wages of sin is death."

God does not want people to ruin their lives with sin. It makes Him sad when you sin and spoil your happiness and the happiness of other people. Because of sin, people cannot enjoy God's loving presence in their lives, nor can they live with God in heaven. Not one of us is able to remove sin from our lives or to earn God's forgiveness by even our very best efforts.

In the beginning of the Bible is the story of Adam and Eve, the first two people. Adam and Eve lived happily with God until they disobeyed Him. That was the first sin. One of the results of the sin was that Adam and Eve were separated from God, thereby robbing life of its greatest joy and ultimately bringing the penalty of death upon themselves. All of us sin, so someday each of us will die, too.

However, the Bible is clear that there is another life after we die. The Bible is also clear that sin will continue to separate people from God's love forever. Because everybody has sinned, how does anybody get to go to heaven?

Step Three: God Paid the Price

The Bible says in Romans 6:23, "For the wages of sin is death, but the gift of God is eternal life in Christ Jesus our Lord." We have seen that the result of sin is death. However, because God loves you so much, He offers eternal life as a free gift. You cannot work hard enough to earn eternal life. All you can do is accept it as a gift.

God gave His only Son to die for you on the cross. The Bible says in 1 Corinthians 15:3, "Christ died for our sins according to the Scriptures." Because Jesus was the perfect Man— without sin—He accepted the results

of sin—death—in your place. The Bible says in 1 John 4:14, "The Father has sent his Son to be the Savior of the world."

Step Four: Ask God for His Forgiveness

If you admit that you have sinned and believe that God gave His only Son to die in your place, God will forgive you and make you clean from all sin.

Tell God that you know you are a sinner.

Tell God you believe Jesus Christ is your only way to have your sins forgiven.

Tell God you want to learn to love and follow Christ in every area of your life.

Tell Him that He is great and wonderful.

It is easy to talk to God. Jesus taught us to talk to Him as we would to a loving Father. He is ready to listen. What you are going to tell Him is something He has been waiting to hear.

If you believe and have told God you believe, you are now a child of God! God has forgiven all your sin. You are a

Christian. And that makes you a member of His family.

God has made everything right between you and Him. He has forgiven you and He looks upon you as if you had never sinned!

Step Five: Live as God's Child

The Bible says in John 1:12, "Yet to all who received him, to those who believed in his name, he gave the right to become children of God." As a child of God, you receive God's gift of everlasting life. God is with you now and forever.

Now that you are a member of God's family, God wants you to live as His child.

You Can Talk to God

Because God is your heavenly Father, He wants you to talk to Him in prayer. You can tell God how you feel, thank Him for His gifts to you and ask Him to help you obey and follow Him.

You can also talk to God when you sin. Ask God to forgive you and He will. The Bible says in 1 John 1:9, "If we confess our sins, he is faithful and just and will forgive us our sins and purify us from all unrighteousness." God will forgive you and help you do what He says.

You Can Read God's Word

God gave His Word so that everyone can read about Him and His great love. Find out more about God by reading about Him in your Bible. The Bible says, "I have hidden your word in my heart that I might not sin against you" (*Psalm 119:11*). As you read God's Word, you will stay close to Him. It's just like reading a letter again and again. You can do the same thing with your Bible.

You Can Obey God

Your heavenly Father wants you to obey Him. He tells you in His Word how you should live. Jesus summed up God's law with two commandments (see *Matthew 22:37-40*):

1. Love God with all that you are.

2. Love your neighbor as yourself.

God wants you to be an expression of His love in the world.

You Can Tell Others About Jesus

Jesus said in Acts 1:8, "you will be my witnesses." Jesus was talking to His disciples before He went back to His Father. Even though Jesus was talking to His disciples, He was saying these words to you, too. You can be a witness when you tell others about Jesus and how His love has helped you. Ask God to give you opportunities each day to tell about—and to show—God's love.

INDEX

Continue Your Adventure in God's Word

What the Bible Is All About®
KJV Edition
Henrietta C. Mears
This classic is fully updated and revised to include new articles, maps, Bible reading plans and a complete glossary.
Hardcover • ISBN 08307.18931
Paperback • ISBN 08307.18966

What the Bible Is All About®
NIV Edition
Henrietta C. Mears
All-time classic has been fully updated and revised for easier study of the popular *NIV* Bible.
Hardcover • ISBN 08307.18303
Paperback • ISBN 08307.18974

What the Bible Is All About®
for Young Explorers
Henrietta C. Mears
The best-selling Bible handbook for kids. More kid-friendly and visually appealing than ever!
Hardcover • ISBN 08307.23641
Paperback • ISBN 08307.23633

What the Bible Is All About®
Reference Library CD-ROM
Henrietta C. Mears
Search quickly and easily for key words and topics in more than a dozen Bible reference titles.
CD-ROM • UPC 607135.003984

What the Bible Is All About®
Elmer L. Towns
This inspirational video seminar presents an outline of God's plan for the ages. Includes a reproducible syllabus and a copy of Henrietta Mear's classic book.
Video • ISBN 85116.00906

What the Bible Is All About®
Quick-Reference Edition
Henrietta C. Mears
Provides a brief overview of the people, events and meaning of every book of the Bible.
Hardcover • ISBN 08307.13905
Paperback • ISBN 08307.18486

Available at your local Christian bookstore.

Regal
FROM GOSPEL LIGHT